Moral Rights

Principles, Practice and New Technology

Mira T. Sundara Rajan

OXFORD
UNIVERSITY PRESS

OXFORD
UNIVERSITY PRESS

Oxford University Press, Inc., publishes works that further Oxford University's objective of excellence in research, scholarship, and education.

Oxford   New York
Auckland   Cape Town   Dar es Salaam   Hong Kong   Karachi   Kuala Lumpur   Madrid   Melbourne
Mexico City   Nairobi   New Delhi   Shanghai   Taipei   Toronto

With offices in
Argentina   Austria   Brazil   Chile   Czech Republic   France   Greece   Guatemala   Hungary   Italy
Japan   Poland   Portugal   Singapore   South Korea   Switzerland   Thailand   Turkey   Ukraine
Vietnam

Published by Oxford University Press, Inc.
198 Madison Avenue, New York, New York 10016

Oxford is a registered trademark of Oxford University Press
Oxford University Press is a registered trademark of Oxford University Press, Inc.

Library of Congress Cataloging-in-Publication Data

Sundara Rajan, Mira T. (Mira Teresa), 1971-
  Moral rights : principles, practice and new technology / Mira T. Sundara Rajan.
    p. cm.
  Includes bibliographical references and index.
  ISBN 978-0-19-539031-5 ((pbk.) : alk. paper)
1. Copyright—Moral rights.   I. Title.
  K1430.S864 2010
  346.04'82—dc22   2010024426

1 2 3 4 5 6 7 8 9

Printed in the United States of America on acid-free paper

Note to Readers
This publication is designed to provide accurate and authoritative information in regard to the subject matter covered. It is based upon sources believed to be accurate and reliable and is intended to be current as of the time it was written. It is sold with the understanding that the publisher is not engaged in rendering legal, accounting, or other professional services. If legal advice or other expert assistance is required, the services of a competent professional person should be sought. Also, to confirm that the information has not been affected or changed by recent developments, traditional legal research techniques should be used, including checking primary sources where appropriate.

(Based on the Declaration of Principles jointly adopted by a Committee of the
American Bar Association and a Committee of Publishers and Associations.)

You may order this or any other Oxford University Press publication by
visiting the Oxford University Press website at www.oup.com

This book is dedicated to Professor Colin Tapper:

Guru sakshat para brahma.

Contents

Acknowledgments

Ernest Hemingway once wrote that "work can cure almost anything." I do not know how interested Hemingway was in the law. But work is work, and the writing of this book may be the closest I will ever come to testing his theory.

No words can express the loss I experienced in the loss of my father, P.K. Sundara Rajan, shortly before I began to work on this book. He was a brilliant person who believed in the power of the Word. When it came to copyright law, he may have been one of the most knowledgeable non-lawyers in the world. He was the first person to realize that the problems surrounding the works of Indian National Poet, C. Subramania Bharati (1882–1921) were, to some extent, copyright problems. The historic importance of this insight may not be immediately apparent to readers outside India; but it took boundless imagination and courage, as well as legal intelligence, to reach it.

When I picked up my own courage to start writing, I benefited from a great deal of help and support. Colleagues from all over the world have contributed their knowledge to my study of moral rights. There is no doubt in my mind that our relationships are the very foundation of this work. They have contributed their richness and authenticity to this book.

I would like to extend my heartfelt thanks to them in this note. Professor Hector MacQueen of Edinburgh University; Professor Toshiko Takenaka of the University of Washington Law School; Akiko Ogawa and the research team of Professor Ryu Takabayashi at Waseda University in Japan; Mr. Pravin Anand, India's pre-eminent intellectual property lawyer, and Gowri Trimurti of the Chennai office of Anand & Anand; Mr. Jagdish Sagar, a distinguished drafter of India's copyright amendments in the 1990s, Marina Drel, head of the litigation and enforcement practice at Gowlings International office in Moscow; Hungarian expert on geographical indications, Dr. Agnes Szabo Kokai-Kuun and copyright expert, Peter Munkácsi; Rihoko Inoue, Visiting Scholar, George Washington University Law School and Assistant Professor, National Institute of Informatics in Tokyo; film and Russian law expert, Elena Muravina; Edson Beas, a scholar based in Sao Paolo, Brazil; and Professor Shigenori Matsui of the Faculty of Law at the University of British Columbia.

I am permanently indebted to Professor Clare Harris, Dr. Chris Morton, and Dr. Laura Piers of the Pitt Rivers Museum at Oxford University. Our association during my stay at Magdalen College in the Spring of 2009 opened my imagination onto the world of the museum in a new technological environment.

Magdalen College of the University of Oxford generously hosted me as a Visiting Fellow during Trinity term 2009, and the College continues to welcome me as an Honorary Member until 2015. My stay at Magdalen, and the support of the librarians of both Magdalen College and the Bodleian Law Library, greatly facilitated the European research in this book. The beauty and interest of my time at Magdalen cannot be summarized in a few words; my thanks to the members of its extraordinary Senior Common Room for giving me the opportunity to be part of Magdalen's intellectual life.

I immensely enjoyed the opportunity to be at New York University School of Law, as a Global Engelberg Research Fellow, in the Spring of 2010. I am particularly grateful for the insightful comments of Professor Rochelle Dreyfuss, who generously shared her expertise on sections of this book dealing with moral rights in the American context. This work has benefited from my participation in the Global Fellows Forum at NYU, and from the availability of NYU research resources during the final preparation of the manuscript.

It was in every way a privilege to work with Matt Gallaway at Oxford University Press, New York, who allowed me the luxury of perfect freedom. I am also grateful to Ellie Bru of OUP New York for her exceptional support with work on the *Intellectual Property: Eastern Europe* series during the writing of this book.

I acknowledge with special gratitude the outstanding research assistance of Tom Horacek, LLB, in the final preparation of this manuscript, who brought extraordinary devotion and patience to a difficult task; and Elvira Akhunova, LLB, of Smeets Law Corporation in Vancouver, who has become one of the most dedicated intellectual property lawyers I know. I benefited substantially from the expert assistance of Lutz Riede, LLM, an associate lawyer at Freshfields in Vienna, Austria. Thanks are also due to Katja Ischenko, who is currently completing her legal studies at Moscow University, for her excellent research assistance; and to Dave Peltier (LLB, Class of 2010) at the University of British Columbia Faculty of Law.

The invaluable assistance of Megan Coyle at UBC's Law Faculty, always given with good cheer and efficiency, lifted a burden from my shoulders!

This work would not have been possible without the support of the Social Sciences and Humanities Research Council of Canada (SSHRC), which awarded me a generous Standard Research Grant for this project. SSHRC support is an extraordinary honor that makes it possible to carry out independent and truly global research. It is a resource to be treasured, and deserves to be a source of national pride for Canadian scholars.

Finally—this book is dedicated to Professor Colin Tapper of Magdalen College, who is, to me, the living embodiment of Oxford's 700-year old tradition of legal thought. *Guru sakshat para brahma*—the teacher himself is reality. The ancient Indians believed that the mere presence of an extraordinary teacher is enough to bring enlightenment to the student!

Any errors are entirely my own responsibility. I hope that readers will bring them to my attention in order to correct and improve the picture of moral rights drawn in this book.

Above all, I hope that readers will find this work engaging. Moral rights have something important to offer to the worldwide community interested in authorship, creativity, and culture. This is just the beginning.

Mira T. Sundara Rajan
New York, April 27, 2010

Foreword

At first sight in the British context moral rights seem to form a rather small and insignificant part of copyright law. First recognised explicitly in statute only just over twenty years ago, it is still possible to find, even amongst those not raised in the traditions of Austinian positivism, the notion that a merely moral right cannot possibly be a legal one. While the assertion of an author's attribution right is standard in books published in the United Kingdom, judicial decisions have not encouraged a wide view of integrity rights, suspicions of which also remain high in the cultural sector. When our attention turns to the international scene, we seem to find confirmation of the general unimportance of moral rights. While it is true that performers outside the audiovisual sector (i.e. outside the film and broadcasting industries) have gained moral rights under the WIPO Performances and Phonograms Treaty of 1996, the TRIPs Agreement of 1994 carefully excluded moral rights from its ambit and the European Union's harmonisation of the copyright laws of its member states has deliberately not extended to this subject either.

Mira Sundara Rajan's study successfully combats such blinkered perspectives. Using the widest of comparative lenses, she perceives and documents an expansion of moral rights doctrine around the world. Particularly significant in her analysis is the deployment of moral rights in developing and post-socialist economies of, respectively, India and Russia. The latter is a jurisdiction of which Dr. Sundara Rajan's previously published work has given her a deep knowledge and understanding. She further argues that moral rights are crucial in the digital environment, where they contribute to the authentication of both origin and quality in a world where works can be speedily and endlessly transmitted and retransmitted, readily modified and re-shaped, and integrated, in whole or in part, in other works. Moral rights also contribute to the protection of cultural heritage: in India, a country and a culture for which Dr. Sundara Rajan also has a special affinity, they have provided a remedy against what the courts took to be unjustified destruction of an artistic work in the care of the government.

Dr. Sundara Rajan further challenges the common belief that moral rights are a uniquely Civil Law construct, somehow alien to and incompatible with Common Law approaches to copyright. Most striking is her demonstration that what we would now call moral right ideas are prominent in the arguments of Lord Mansfield for the existence of a common law right antecedent to the rights provided by the Statute of Anne, and which also survived the demise of the statutory term of protection. Perhaps a Scottish lawyer may be allowed to suggest, in the light of the 1773 decision in Hinton v Donaldson and subsequent Scottish case law, that a crucial element in the development of "common law copyright" after Donaldson v Beckett in 1774 was the position of the unpublished work and recognition of the author's right to decide when if at all it might be disclosed to the public. The link between this and the author's personality rather than any property rights was long maintained in Scotland before dissolving in the great case of Caird v Sime in 1885-7. Today, as the concept of personality rights to identity, reputation and dignity gains footholds in Common Law thinking (helped along by the impetus provided by human rights), it may become possible to see moral rights more as part of that picture than as something necessarily to be linked to and contrasted with the economic rights conferred by copyright. Dr. Sundara Rajan's contribution should help substantially with that process of conceptual development.

A final target of this book is the "Death of the Author" school in literary and copyright criticism. Dr. Sundara Rajan shows clearly how deep and widespread (across very different cultures) is the idea of an intimate connection between author and work justifying a privileged position for that person, if not necessarily one having to be reflected in economic advantage. With digitization enabling so many would-be authors to lay their wares before any audience that it may be able to command, the case for legal reinforcement for rights of attribution and integrity is not necessarily undermined by the parallel increase in possibilities for collaboration with others and the re-working and re-use of existing material. Nor are moral rights inconsistent with ideas of open access licensing. What may still remain to be fully tested is how far the law may go in allowing moral rights to be given up or waived in relation to all comers. The British rule allowing waivers is, as Dr. Sundara Rajan demonstrates, not a unique departure from moral right norms.

Anglophone studies of moral rights have for too long proceeded on the basis of difference and consequential difficulties. It is more than time to accept that the rights form an important part of the modern law rather than being an isolated beachhead of no particular significance. Mira Sundara Rajan makes this case with style and formidable breadth of learning in both law and general culture, and her work deserves, and will reward, a widespread readership.

Hector MacQueen
Edinburgh, July 2010

Preface

Once upon a time, in a far-away country, lived a poet.

One evening, the poet went out for a walk. As he passed the local blacksmith's shop, he heard the sound of singing. He suddenly stopped, and stood as if riveted to the spot.

The blacksmith was singing a song that he recognized. In fact, it was the poet's own song—but not as he had written it. Strange words took the place of the words he had written. The rhythm was distorted.

After listening for a few moments, the poet entered the shop. Inside, the blacksmith had kept good order. The tools and implements of his trade were neatly organized on the shelves. The poet promptly began to move around the shop, removing items from their place, rearranging things at random.

The blacksmith jumped up and approached the poet. "Crazy man! What do you think you are doing?" he cried. "These tools are my property—my livelihood."

The poet replied, "I am doing to your property what you were doing to mine. I am the poet who wrote the song you were singing. Poetry is, to me, what your property is to you—it is my livelihood."

This story was written by Indian National Poet, C. Subramania Bharati, who lived from 1882 to 1921 in South India, and whose writings gave birth to the Tamil Renaissance of the early twentieth century.

CHAPTER
1

Introduction

Moral Rights in the Virtual Age

"Born in the heart of the poet, [aesthetic experience]
flowers as it were in the actor and bears fruit in the
spectator. All three in the serene contemplation
of the work, form in reality a single knowing
object fused together."

—Bharata, *Natya Shastra*

Why moral rights?

New technology is like a river that has burst its banks. The rush of words, music, and images flows everywhere; the Internet provides unlimited access. Technology seems impossible to resist. Entire industries are overwhelmed, facing the ultimate choice to adapt or die. Copyright, with its insistence on authorization and control, its emphasis on the rights and privileges of owner-ship, seems hopelessly old-fashioned. What is the relevance of ownership in an environment where the digital transformation of a work renders it irrevo-cably into the hands of the public? When most individuals can easily repro-duce and communicate a work from the convenience of their own homes, how can copyright represent an effective restriction on use?

Digital technology has led to a struggle for rights—a struggle for control. But the attempt to re-establish control in a digital environment masks a more troubling reality. Fundamental questions are largely ignored, yet new tech-nology generates fundamental social change. In fact, technology alters human relationships with knowledge—an individual's relationship with his or her own mind. Its impact on the intangible products of the mind affects creative expression in all its forms—knowledge, information, culture, folklore, oral traditions, myths. Few aspects of our mental life, as individuals or as groups, truly remain untouched.

What is the fate of the products so transformed?—The intangible, perhaps ineffable, essence that is exchanged by the digital community?

At least three issues should be considered.

First, let us turn to the facts. What exactly is the intangible substance, matter, work, or product that is subject to transformation and communica-tion in the Digital Age? In fact, the digital world is a playground for the entire spectrum of human creative activity. It involves information, knowl-edge, and culture; it brings together phenomena from around the world, and draws upon the entire time frame of civilized history.[1] It would be no exag-geration to say that the entire wealth of human knowledge and culture, as it currently exists and is still being discovered, provides the substance of digital exchange. From the digital perspective, all of this is known simply as "con-tent." It has been called the "raw material" that feeds the digital circuit.[2]

It is worth noting that the digital transformation of knowledge has another consequence. Whether knowledge originates with individuals, groups, or countries, digitization imposes new degrees of separation between

---

1. For example, Google is now digitizing classic works of Italian literature that are hundreds of years old. *See Google to digitize ancient Italian books* BBC News (Mar. 10, 2010), *available at* http://news.bbc.co.uk/2/hi/technology/8561245.stm (last visited June 15, 2010). The books, all published before 1868, represent Italian cultural treasures; the Italian government has arranged the project with Google in order to promote conservation in a cost-effective and reliable way.

2. Jack Ralite, *Vers un droit d'auteur sans auteurs*, 528 Le Monde diplomatique 5 (1998).

a work and its original creator. The transformation of a work into digital format distances it from the human being behind its creation. Indeed, each subsequent transformation into new media—performance to recorded album, album to Internet-based music files—has the potential to place a further step between a work and its author. Each new exposure makes it more difficult for the person receiving the work to recognize it as a human creation, or to identify with the human author who made it.

A second issue then becomes, what happens to this intangible substance when it is digitally transformed? The transformation must meet the technical requirements of digital media; it must also respond to the needs, real or perceived, of marketing a work successfully to a digital audience. Youth, limited attention span, "cult" appeal—these are some of the apparent qualities of the new marketplace. Digital media can imply the separation of integral works into different parts, such as the splitting of a musical recording into separate songs or pieces for download;[3] it can involve the combining of different elements in new ways, such as the mixing of music from different genres to create a new album; and it can lead to new uses of data, such as the "Genius" function which allows Apple's iTunes software to recommend music that is likely to interest a listener based on his or her pre-existing library. Indeed, from a technological perspective, there is virtually no limit to what can be done with the manipulation of a work once it is digitized.

As a counterpart to this freedom, whenever a given product is transformed into digital format, the possibility of error arises. Something may be eliminated or added, whether intentionally or accidentally. The technical format in which the work is presented may deteriorate due to carelessness or forgetfulness, as well as obsolescence. The perfection of technology is limited by human error.

Finally, what are the consequences of these phenomena for society? It seems almost impossible to overstate them. We live in a world that is increasingly driven by the digital medium; it represents the one "thing" of universal value in a post-industrial universe. At the same time, twenty-first century society experiences a new and acute need for knowledge. From climate change to religious extremism, the abuse of knowledge may represent the single most dangerous problem of our time. It allows unprincipled leaders to exploit entire populations; it is the secret power behind fanaticism. Improving the conditions of human life depends, as never before, on education, in the broadest sense of the term; and education depends on access to knowledge.

---

3. This common form of packaging led to a suit for the infringement of the musicians' moral right of integrity. *See Pink Floyd Wins Court Battle With EMI Over Downloads*, NEW YORK TIMES (Mar. 11, 2010), *available at* http://www.nytimes.com/2010/03/12/business/media/12pink.html?emc=eta1 (last visited June 15, 2010). The potential for suits like this one is discussed in Chapter 6, *infra*, dealing with moral rights in music.

The digital world offers the very exciting prospect of democratizing knowledge, and of being able to do so on a grand scale. However, technology simultaneously creates a danger that knowledge as we know it will disintegrate. Knowledge may be degraded beyond recognition by alteration and manipulation. This dark side of the digital reality is likely to be favored by a global economy that hungers for technology as an engine of growth.[4]

Copyright rules play into both sides of this equation. They represent a method of generating economic value from knowledge by imposing legal restrictions on its circulation where few limitations exist in practice. By restricting the unauthorized dissemination of works, copyright may also help, indirectly, to promote the integrity of knowledge. But this should not be considered a strong argument for the expansion of economic rights in knowledge. On the contrary, copyright happens to support integrity largely as a side effect of its commercial function. In its current form, copyright law largely controls knowledge at the discretion of corporations. Conserving knowledge is not an objective of modern copyright policy. Where knowledge is concerned, copyright law cannot, by any means, claim to accommodate a breadth of social needs or interests.

The concept of moral rights responds directly to the changing status of knowledge in a digital environment. Moral rights originally developed in the nineteenth century, as French judges sought to address the practical problems of authors and artists in an era of rapidly expanding mass-market publication. The doctrine was systematically explored by German-speaking legal theorists, who analyzed the concept from every imaginable angle, and it came to feature universally in the legal systems of Continental Europe. The English term "moral rights" is a translation, both imperfect and ambivalent, from the French *droit moral.*

Moral rights are based on the idea that an author is personally invested in his or her work. In view of this special relationship, an author's interest in the work transcends the motive of financial gain. Moral rights offer legal recognition to an author's special relationship with his or her own work.

---

4. But Colin Tapper notes that technology "also has potential to prevent manipulation of knowledge, since such copying may take place at different points of time and at different locations in the chain of distribution, so potentially creating exposable inconsistency between different versions, and thus revealing change" (personal communication with the author, Apr. 12, 2010). The point is an important one; among other things, it raises interesting questions about the development of technologies for data comparison, not only in relation to copyright, but specifically in relation to moral rights. Examples that come to mind are anti- plagiarism technologies used by universities, or Audio fingerprinting technology. *See, e.g.,* Michael Brown, *Audio Fingerprinting,* Maximum PC, Apr. 3, 2009, *available at* http://www.maximumpc.com/article/features/white_paper_audio_fingerprinting (last visited Aug. 18, 2010) and Bill Rosenblatt, *New Applications for Music Fingerprinting,* July 16, 2008, *available at* http://www.drmwatch.com/watermarking/article.php/3759456 (last visited Aug. 18, 2010).

Since moral rights developed as a practical doctrine, they include a great variety of possible interests. In each country where moral rights are protected, the nuances of interpretation reflect the unique qualities of its culture. At the same time, two basic moral rights are generally recognized. These are an author's right to have his own work attributed to him by name, usually called the right of "attribution," and his right to protect the work from harm, known as the right of "integrity." Since 1928, the moral rights of attribution and integrity have been included in the most important international agreement on copyright matters, the *Berne Convention for the Protection of Literary and Artistic Works.*[5] The United States and Russia were the last major powers to accede to this Convention—in 1989 and 1995, respectively—and virtually every country in the world is now required to protect moral rights to the minimum standard defined by Berne.[6]

Although moral rights "belong" to an author, their implications extend far beyond the individual author. The interests that moral rights protect are for the general benefit of society as a whole. The right of integrity has an obvious connection with culture; its objective is to protect cultural heritage, whether material or intangible, from damage. Where the right of integrity extends to works in the public domain, it can become a means of protecting cultural heritage throughout the lifetime of a work. The social benefit of the right of attribution is a subtler issue, but it, too, protects society by preserving historical truth where issues of identity and authenticity are concerned. Moral rights are

---

5. The Convention dates from 1886; the moral rights were implemented in 1928 at the revision conference held in Rome. The implementation of the Agreement on Trade-Related Aspects of Intellectual Property Rights (TRIPs) at the World Trade Organization in 1994 did not really supplant Berne, as virtually all of the substantive provisions on copyright in TRIPs are drawn from the Berne Convention. In fact, members of TRIPs are required, by Article 9.1 of the Agreement, to join the Berne Convention and adhere to its substantive articles. Notable exceptions to this norm are the TRIPs provisions on computer programs and databases, which make specific provision for their recognition as "literary works"; Berne implies this without stating it explicitly. *See* Chapter 4, *infra*, on international copyright agreements.

    Berne Convention for the Protection of Literary and Artistic Works (adopted Sept. 9, 1886) 1161 U.N.T.S. 3, *available at* http://www.wipo.int/treaties/en/ip/berne/trtdocs_wo001.html (last visited June 15, 2010); also available in a useful format at the Legal Information Institute, Cornell University Law School, http://www.law.cornell.edu/treaties/berne/overview.html (last visited June 15, 2010) [Berne Convention]. *See also* Agreement on Trade-Related Aspects of Intellectual Property Rights (opened for signature Apr. 15, 1994, entered into force Jan. 1, 1995), Annex 1C to Marrakesh Agreement Establishing the World Trade Organization, 1869 U.N.T.S. 299; 33 I.L.M. 1197 (1994), *available at* http://www.wto.org/english/docs_e/legal_e/27-trips_01_e.htm [TRIPs Agreement].

6. *See* WIPO accession documents: Berne Notification No. 121, Nov. 21, 17, 1988, for U.S. accession, *available at* WIPO website, http://www.wipo.int/treaties/en/html.jsp?file=/redocs/notdocs/en/berne/treaty_berne_121.html; Berne Notification No. 162, Dec. 13, 1994, for Russian accession, *available at* WIPO website, http://www.wipo.int/treaties/en/html.jsp?file=/redocs/notdocs/en/berne/treaty_berne_162.html.

something more than a "personal" right of the author, although the author will often be the best person to watch over the status of his own work.

Moral rights should be viewed comprehensively. They represent vital social interests; they are vested in authors, at least for a period, because authors are personally linked to their work, enjoy human rights as the person who created the work, and are well placed to champion the protection of the work. The characterization of moral rights as "personal" rights is both correct and useful, but it provides only a partial picture of the rights. Other terms that arise in the literature—personality rights, intellectual rights, or spiritual rights—may help to capture their larger significance.

With these factors in mind, it is apparent that moral rights offer one possible solution to the problems of knowledge in the Digital Age. But, as with copyright law as a whole, a critical question remains. In an environment where technology has delivered control over knowledge into the hands of the public, how can moral rights be enforced?

The enforcement of any right in the digital context is fraught with difficulties, and moral rights are no exception. However, the fact that rights are difficult to enforce does not necessarily mean that they should be dispensed with. Moral rights involve fundamental social issues; there is every likelihood that moral interests will be important for the future of human culture. The difficulty of enforcement should not be a reason to forego what is, essentially, a form of protection for human rights in the digital context.

The problems of enforcement need to be addressed effectively. In the case of moral rights, coercion, alone, will not be adequate to enforce them. Where copyright or moral rights are concerned, enforcement depends, to an important degree, on persuasion. Moral rights can be enforced, as can copyright, provided that the public wants the law and can be convinced of its value. As J.A.L. Sterling observes:

> At the end of the day, copyright will only survive because the public wants it, and knows it wants it, and knows its value. The challenge to the copyright lawyer is therefore not only to forge solutions to the philosophical and legal problems [confronting copyright]…, but to contribute to public education in every possible way.[7]

There can be no doubt that the enforcement of moral rights depends on educating the public. Indeed, it is essential to secure public support for moral rights. The rights support the public interest in many ways; but the public needs to understand how they do so, and to be prepared to uphold moral rights by their own behavior. When it comes to moral rights, a law without credibility in the public mind would be profoundly disappointing.

---

7. J.A.L. Sterling, *Philosophical and Legal Challenges in the Context of Copyright and Digital Technology*, 31(5) Int'l Rev. Indus. Prop. & Copyright L. 508, 525 (2000).

Attempts to expand the reach of copyright law beyond public support should be resisted for a more general reason. They contribute to a widening chasm between the letter of the law and its practical reality in a digital environment. In these circumstances, modern copyright law risks playing a part in undermining the worldwide credibility of the rule of law.[8] For a fragile branch of the law that has led a sheltered existence among specialists for most of its life, it is an awesome responsibility to share.

A. Moral Rights: Theory and Purpose

The doctrine of moral rights is based on a number of philosophical notions about the author, the work, and the nature of the relationship between the two. Ultimately, it assumes that harm to the work is, in fact, a form of damage to the author himself. The purpose of moral rights is to protect the author from suffering the consequences of moral, intellectual, or spiritual harm inflicted on him through the mistreatment of his work.

1. The Doctrine of Moral Rights

a. The Author

Influential research on the history of moral rights identifies them closely with the rise of Romanticism in Western Europe.[9] The Romantics saw the creative author as a being with unique gifts: he was an original and independent genius who produced great works out of his talent. Crucially, this picture of the author as an independent creator represented a dramatic break with the past, including the traditional belief, well established in medieval Europe, that creativity was divinely inspired and therefore required little recognition of the individual artist. Even lawyers were not immune to the intoxicating ideals of Romanticism, and nineteenth-century jurists came to support the principle that the extraordinary personality of the author was entitled to a special status in law. The informal recognition of moral rights in

---

8. The enforcement of copyright norms is especially difficult in countries that have a poor record of respect for the rule of law. Post-socialist countries are an example. *See* Mira T. Sundara Rajan, Copyright and Creative Freedom (Routledge 2006), especially Chapter III, "Copyright Law in Transition." An updated version of this chapter is available as Mira T. Sundara Rajan, *Introduction, in* Intellectual Property: Eastern Europe and the CIS (Mira T. Sundara Rajan, ed., Oxford Univ. Press 2008) [*IP Series*].
9. *See* Martha Woodmansee, *The Genius and the Copyright: Economic and Legal Conditions of the Emergence of the "Author,"* 17 Eighteenth-Century Studies 425 (1984).

the courts of European countries was codified in European laws over the course of the twentieth century.

This history offers insight into the development of moral rights, but it is not a comprehensive picture of the past. The idea of moral rights was already well-known in the ancient world, and well beyond the confines of Continental Europe.[10] The European origins of the doctrine are not its most important feature. Rather, what is specifically important about the moral rights concept is its ability to link a work with the personality of its author. Indeed, whether in ancient Rome, seventh-century India, or post-Revolutionary France, the appearance of moral rights is invariably associated with the flowering of artistic personality at the individual level.

In the Romantic context, moral rights reflected a new and practical emphasis on the rights of individuals, and on secular thought. Indeed, in British law, the moral rights idea emerged a number of decades before its appearance on the French scene, as part of a broader drive towards freedom of expression.[11] The creation of individual rights of authorship was seen as a way to remove the control of publication from the hands of the Sovereign, and it was in this context that an author's rights in his work were first recognized in the Statute of Anne of 1709/10.[12] Support for moral rights in Britain was short-lived, not out of congenital distaste, but because of broader concerns that moral rights could be used to circumvent the very goals that the Statute of Anne was designed to support. Ironically, freedom of the press, which led to the first legal recognition of authors, would eventually become the altar on which the British concept of moral rights would be sacrificed.[13]

b. The Work

The work was, above all, "original." It was a product of the unique abilities of the author, and a true reflection of his personality. As a result, it enjoyed a special status flowing from the unique position of the author himself. In particular, the work was considered to be generally independent of other works of knowledge—an essential quality distinguishing it from other, lesser varieties of creative expression. For example, a composer of music created an original work; but the status of a performer who interpreted his compositions

---

10. *See, e.g.,* T.S. Krishnamurti, *Copyright—Another View,* 15(3) Bull. of Copyright Soc'y of U.S.A. 217, 218 (1968), commenting on the ancient Indian belief that ideas should be protected.
11. The concept was articulated by Lord Mansfield in the seminal case of *Millar v. Taylor* (1769) 4 Burr. 2303, 98 Eng. Rep. 201. The case was overruled five years later by *Donaldson v. Beckett* (1774) 2 Brown's Parl. Cases 129, 1 Eng. Rep. 837, which rejected the concept of a common law copyright, and, with it, the moral rights of the author.
12. Statute of Anne (1710) 8 Ann., c. 19.
13. *See* discussion of British copyright history, Chapter 3, *infra.*

was inferior to that of the composer. A performer's role was to disseminate the original work of the author-composer through his or her performance, and the performance could not be considered an original work in the same sense as a composition. A performer could hardly be considered an author in his or her own right.[14]

c. A Special Relationship

The work could only have been produced by its author, and was considered to be a reflection of his unique personality. Accordingly, the work was practically an extension of the author himself—his "spiritual child." Any harm done to the work would effectively be inflicted on the author, as well. The damage might not be physical, but it could affect the author, in a multitude of other ways. At the same time, the author might continue to have certain needs in relation to the work even after he had sold it. For example, an artist who created a work of visual art might want to continue to have access to it for personal or creative purposes even after it was purchased—and, indeed, an artist's right of continued access to his own work is a recognized moral right in some jurisdictions.[15]

2. Legal Implications

a. The Protection of "Moral" Interests

The nature of the creative process implies an intimate relationship between an author and his work. The author becomes vulnerable to harm through the mistreatment of his work. From a legal point of view, the focus is on possible damage to the author and on just redress for the harm suffered. Accordingly, the legal interpretation of moral rights leads to a focus on protecting the relationship between an author and his work, as it is this aspect of the creative process that exposes the author to the danger of personal harm.

Ideally, moral harm to the author would be prevented by the possibility of legal sanctions, which would create an environment of greater safety for the

---

14. The French word for performer, "*interprète*," perfectly captures this distinction.
15. The purpose of the access right is often to allow the artist to make reproductions of his work. A similar situation may arise in relation to recordings of traditional music: see the fascinating discussion of his experiences as an anthropologist documenting the traditional music of the Suyá of Brazil, in Anthony Seeger, *Ethnomusicology and Music Law, in* Borrowed Power: Essays on Cultural Appropriation 52, 57–65 (Bruce Ziff & Pratima V. Rao eds., Rutgers University Press 1997). When deposited in research libraries, research recordings of this kind may become inaccessible to the original creators. Nevertheless, they may desire access for a number of practical purposes, including the ability to preserve their own knowledge and cultural heritage.

pursuit of creative work. The deterrent effect of moral rights is well worth noting—the ideal of moral rights law is not only to compensate for damage after it has happened, but also, to create a context in which damage is less likely to occur. This is important; compensating the author for the harm may not be sufficient to restore him to his rightful situation. For example, where visual art is concerned, damage to a single piece may be irreparable in every sense of the word: the work might not be recoverable, and the artist's life could be permanently affected by the loss.[16] It is perhaps for this reason that countries such as the United States and Canada have chosen to extend extra protection to moral rights in the visual arts, despite their generally cautious attitude to moral rights.[17]

The legal approach to moral rights also attempts to forestall moral harm in another sense: it grants privileges aimed at preserving the sanctity of the relationship between artist and work. For example, an artist who creates a work of visual art is sometimes granted a right of access to his work even after it has been sold. The right is usually confined to the practical objective of allowing an artist to have access to his work for the purpose of making reproductions.[18] However, there is no obvious reason why it could not also

---

16. This scenario arose in the Indian case of *Amar Nath Sehgal v. Union of India* 2005 (30) PTC 253 (Delhi High Court), where the sculpture in question was irrevocably damaged by mishandling. *See* Mira T. Sundara Rajan, *Moral Rights and the Protection of Cultural Heritage: Amar Nath Sehgal v. Union of India*, 10(1) INT'L J. OF CULTURAL PROPERTY 79 (2001) [Sundara Rajan, *Moral Rights and the Protection of Cultural Heritage*]; the note informs the decision of the Delhi High Court, and is quoted in paragraph 41 of the final judgment.

17. *See* Canadian Copyright Act, R.S.C. 1985, c. C-42, http://laws.justice.gc.ca/en/C-42/index. html (last visited May 2, 2010) [Canadian Copyright Act], sec. 28.2 (2) and (3); Visual Artists Rights Act of 1990, Pub. L. No. 101-650, 104 Stat. 5128, 17 U.S.C. § 106A, http://www. copyright.gov/title17/92chap1.html#106a (last visited May 2, 2010) [*Visual Artists Rights Act*, VARA].

18. *See, e.g.*, art. 25 of the German Copyright Law: Urheberrechtsgesetz, 9.9.1965, Bundesgesetz-blatt, Teil I [BGBl.I] at 1273, last amended by Gesetz, 10.8.2004, BGBl. I at 1774, § 13, *available at* http://www.iuscomp.org/gla/statutes/UrhG.htm; the Russian Copyright Act of 1993, art. 17.1, was an exactly similar provision. The 1993 Russian law has since been overruled by Part IV of the Russian Civil Code, completed in 2006, and in effect since January 1, 2008. *See* Russian Federation Law on Copyright and Neighboring Rights (No. 5351-I of July 9, 1993) [Russian Copyright Act 1993]; Grazhdanski Kodeks Rossiiskoi Federatsi, Chast' Chetvërtaya [Civil Code of the Russian Federation, Part IV], Federal Law No. 230-FZ of December 18, 2006, *Rossijskaja Gazeta* No. 289 (4255) of December 22, 2006 = Sobranie zakonodatel'stva RF (SZ RF) No. 52 (Part I) of Dec. 25, 2006, Item 5496, at 14803 [2008 Civil Code]. The new Part IV is not yet available in English; it may be found in the original Russian on the website of Rospatent, the federal agency of the Russian Federation responsible for intellectual property matters, *available at* http://www1.fips.ru/wps/wcm/connect/content_ru/ru/documents/ russian_laws/codeks_rf/gkrf_ch4. The 1993 Act is still *available at* http://en.wikisource.org/ wiki Russian_Federation_Law_on_Copyright_and_Neighboring_Rights.

protect, quite simply, the artist's right to see his own work, which would fit well with the idea of the work as the artist's "spiritual child."

Once a work has sustained damage, the hope arises that it may be at least partially corrected. Specific remedies for violations of moral rights aim to address these situations from a practical point of view. The withdrawal of works from circulation, the correction of errors in labeling or marketing, and the payment of damages, are all possible remedies for the infringement of moral rights.

b. Attribution and Integrity

Given the breadth of the doctrine, which potentially includes a vast array of different interests, it is hardly surprising that legal interpretations of moral rights vary tremendously across different legal cultures. The civil law countries of Continental Europe, where the modern doctrine originated, have traditionally favored strong protection for moral rights. Moral rights in France focus almost entirely on the individual rights of the author, with little overt attempt to weigh the interests of the public against the author's desire.[19] French law includes explicit protection for moral rights well beyond the confines of attribution and integrity, such as the right to withdraw one's work from circulation for personal reasons.[20]

Common law countries, whose copyright law is said to be rooted in strong commercial traditions, have preferred to grant more limited recognition to moral rights. In these jurisdictions, moral rights are often protected through common law actions, such as tort, which are more limited in scope than copyright laws.

In contrast, developing countries—even those with a common law heritage—and the post-socialist countries of Central and Eastern Europe have routinely provided rigorous legislative protection for moral rights.[21] For these countries, moral rights undoubtedly represent a means of prioritizing culture, creativity, and innovation in circumstances where they are desperately needed.

---

19. Henri Desbois, Le Droit d'auteur en France (3d ed. Dalloz 1978).
20. *See* art. L121-4 of the French *Code de la Propriété Intellectuelle* [Intellectual Property Code]. *See Loi N° 92-597 du 1er juillet 1992 relative au code de la propriété intellectuelle (partie législative)*, Journal officiel de la République française, 8 février 1994; *Légifrance: Le service public de la diffusion du droit*, http://www.legifrance.gouv.fr/affichCode.do?cidTexte=LEGITEXT000 006069414&dateTexte=20100412 (last visited May 2, 2010) [CPI, Intellectual Property Code, *Code de la Propriété Intellectuelle*].
21. *See, for example,* Copyright & Creative Freedom, *supra* note 8, at Chapter III; an updated version of this chapter appears as Introduction to the *IP Series, supra* note 8.

c. International Protection

An archetype of moral rights protection may be found in the *Berne Convention for the Protection of Literary and Artistic Works*, the world's first, and still most important, international copyright agreement.[22] The Berne Convention was concluded in 1886, and it sets minimum standards of copyright protection to be implemented in the domestic laws of all member states. Its provisions on moral rights were adopted in the 1928 revisions to the Convention, as a new Article 6*bis*.[23] Article 6*bis* originally represented an uneven compromise between civilian and common law views that clearly favored the European position on moral rights.[24] The Article was subsequently amended to reflect a growing concern that common law systems could not accommodate moral rights in their copyright laws, maintaining, instead, a definite preference for the more limited protection offered by the law of tort.[25]

The current version of Article 6*bis* retains the original focus of the law on the two moral rights of attribution and integrity. The right of attribution allows an author to ensure that his work is consistently attributed to him by name. The right of integrity prohibits the "distortion, modification, or mutilation of the work." However, according to the language of the Berne Convention, the author must be able to show that the treatment of his work has a negative impact on his "honor or reputation" before he can claim that his right of integrity has been violated.

Article 6*bis* has remained unchanged since 1967, and continues to set the international standard for the protection of moral rights. Although the Berne Convention has now been supplanted by the *Agreement on Trade-Related Aspects of Intellectual Property Rights* (TRIPs) at the WTO as the world's primary instrument of international copyright law, Berne remains essential.[26]

In fact, the TRIPs Agreement deals with copyright largely by requiring member states to adhere to the substantive provisions of the Berne Convention

---

22. Berne Convention, *supra* note 5.
23. Rome Act of the Berne Convention for the Protection of Literary and Artistic Works, 123 L.N.T.S. 233 (revised June 2, 1928).
24. Indeed, it is possible that the common law countries agreed because they believed that the enactment of Article 6*bis* would not require any changes to their legislation.
25. Berne Convention for the Protection of Literary and Artistic Works, 33 U.N.T.S. 217 (revised June 26, 1948) [Berlin Act]; Berne Convention for the Protection of Literary and Artistic Works 828 U.N.T.S. 221 (revised July 14, 1967) [Stockholm Act]. *See* SAM RICKETSON & JANE GINSBURG, INTERNATIONAL COPYRIGHT AND NEIGHBORING RIGHTS: THE BERNE CONVENTION AND BEYOND (2d ed. Oxford University Press 2006), paragraph 10.12 .
26. TRIPs Agreement, *supra* note 5.

including, at first glance, Article 6*bis* on moral rights.[27] However, the TRIPs Agreement also specifies that moral rights are excluded from the dispute-settlement and enforcement mechanisms at the WTO.[28] Unique among all aspects of copyright law, the enforcement of moral rights remains excluded from the TRIPs regime.

An important new treaty, adopted by the World Intellectual Property Organization (WIPO) of the United Nations in 1996 and entering into force in 2002, initiated the first innovation in the international protection of moral rights since 1928. The WIPO Performances and Phonograms Treaty (WPPT) established a moral right for performers.[29] Article 5 of the WPPT creates rights of attribution and integrity for performers that closely resemble authors' moral rights under the Berne Convention. One notable difference is the elimination of the word "honor" from the definition of the performer's right of integrity—an omission that international copyright expert Mihály Ficsor considers significant.[30] But it is difficult to say. In current usage, reputation may encompass both dimensions of how an author appears in the eyes of the world.

The WPPT was adopted alongside the WIPO Copyright Treaty (WCT).[31] The Internet Treaties, as they are collectively known, were developed by WIPO to address the changing landscape of copyright in the Digital Age. While the WCT does not address authors' moral rights explicitly, the creation of a performer's moral right by the WPPT represents a major innovation. The WPPT elevates the performer from the status of a person who merely

---

27. *Id., supra* note 5, art. 9.1. The first part of this article states that member countries "shall comply with Articles 1 through 21 of the Berne Convention (1971) and the Appendix thereto."

28. This amounts to a crucial omission: Dreyfuss & Lowenfeld identify the linking of dispute-settlement with intellectual property as one of the two most important achievements of the WTO. Rochelle Cooper Dreyfuss and Andreas F. Lowenfeld, *Two Achievements of the Uruguay Round: Putting TRIPs and Dispute Settlement Together*, 37 VA. J. INT'L L. 275 (1997).

29. WIPO Performances and Phonograms Treaty (adopted Dec. 20, 1996, entered into force May 20, 2002), S. Treaty Doc. No. 105-17, 36 I.L.M. 76 (1997), art. 5, *available at* http://www.wipo.int/treaties/en/ip/wppt/trtdocs_wo034.html (last visited Apr. 26, 2010) [WPPT]. Although the Internet Treaties were adopted in 1996, their entry into force was made conditional on a certain minimum number of signatories. In the case of both the WIPO Copyright Treaty and the WIPO Performance and Phonograms Treaty, this requirement was met in March and May 2002, respectively. See the summary and discussion of the Treaties in J. Reinbothe and S. von Lewinski, *The WIPO Treaties 1996: Ready to Come into Force*, 24(4) E.I.P.R. 199 (2002).

30. *See* MIHÁLY FICSOR, THE LAW OF COPYRIGHT AND THE INTERNET: THE 1996 WIPO TREATIES, THEIR INTERPRETATION AND IMPLEMENTATION 617–18 (Oxford University Press 2002).

31. WIPO Copyright Treaty (adopted Dec. 20, 1996, entered into force Mar. 6, 2002), 36 I.L.M. 65 (1997), http://www.wipo.int/treaties/en/ip/wct/trtdocs_wo033.html (last visited Apr. 26, 2010).

disseminates the work of an original author to that of an author in his own right.

d. Characteristics of Moral Rights

i. Independence of Moral and Economic Rights

The transformation of moral rights doctrine into legal rules was initiated by judicial decision-making, which subsequently led to the codification of moral rights in law. Although the general approach was to incorporate moral rights into copyright laws, the philosophical basis of moral rights was exceptionally broad. Many strands of thought played into the doctrine, including theories of creativity, culture, and human rights.[32]

It is interesting that human rights instruments, including such fundamental documents as the *Universal Declaration of Human Rights* and the *International Covenant on Economic, Social and Cultural Rights*, make commitments to both the "moral and material" interests of authors in their work.[33] Interestingly, neither convention recognizes property as a human right, so the basis for including authors' economic interests in this formulation must be something else—a labor-based justification, perhaps, or the protection of freedom of speech. Where economic copyright is concerned, the material benefits that an author should enjoy are generally determined by market conditions.[34] But moral rights are different; they reach beyond commercial interests, and most countries that recognize them impose restrictions on market dealings with moral rights, such as waivers.

In practice, this translates into a crucial distinction between moral and economic rights. Moral rights continue to be held by the author *whether or*

---

32. *See* the discussion in Chapter 2, *infra*, notes 138–84 and accompanying text, including a discussion about German theorists of moral rights and the diversity of their thinking about the idea.

33. *See* Copyright and Creative Freedom, *supra note* 8, Chapter IX, "Copyright and Human Rights: The Post-Soviet Experience and a New International Model." The economic rights of creators could also be seen as human rights, and are noted as such in both the United Nations Declaration of Human Rights and the International Covenant on Civil and Political Rights. Article 27(2) of the Declaration states: "Everyone has the right to the protection of the moral and material interests resulting from any scientific, literary or artistic production of which he is the author"; section 15(c) of the I.C.E.S.C.R. mirrors this language: "(c) To benefit from the protection of the moral and material interests resulting from any scientific, literary or artistic production of which he is the author." Both instruments are available online, http://www.un.org/en/documents/udhr/; http://www2.ohchr.org/english/law/cescr.htm.

34. But some countries also pay a state-determined stipend to recognized artists. *See, for example,* Hans Abbing, Why Are Artists Poor? The Exceptional Economy of the Arts 40 (Amsterdam Univ. Press 2002).

not he retains the economic rights in his work. The author may sell his work, and thereby, part with all his rights to exploit it. Nevertheless, he retains his moral rights in the work.[35] Moral rights are said to exist "independently" of the status of economic rights in a work.

ii. Perpetual Protection

Different legal systems take different approaches to the relationship between moral and economic rights. Some countries extend the principle of independence to its greatest reach, while others attempt to limit it.

The French tradition is an example of extreme independence. Known as "dualism," French legal theory draws a clear distinction between an author's moral rights and his economic rights. Not only are an author's moral rights immune to his dealings with the economic rights in a work, but they are also protected without any limitation in time. Under dualist theory, an author's moral rights last forever.[36] The author's relationship with his work, as its creator, remains permanently intact.[37]

In contrast, the German treatment of moral rights is known as "monism." In German jurisprudence, the author's right is perceived as a *sui generis* right; the author's economic and moral rights share a common origin in the principle of an author's right. The basic idea of independence is maintained, in the sense that the status of moral rights remains independent of the economic rights. Moral rights will still subsist in a work even after the economic rights have been sold. However, German moral rights last only for the duration of the economic rights in a work.

Despite this important difference, both schools of thought share one fundamental principle: moral rights are protected for a significant time after the author's death. Although the rights are personal to the author, he leaves behind a memory and a reputation that continue to command respect. Indeed, it is largely in the context of protection after the author's death that

---

35. Of course, in countries where it is possible for authors to waive their moral rights, moral rights could be excluded by contractual agreement between the artist and the buyer of the work. But Continental European jurisdictions generally restrict or prohibit waivers. See the detailed discussion in Chapter 2, *infra.*

36. But consider the example of Canada, which distinguishes between economic and moral rights, but creates a regime of lesser protection for moral rights. See the decision of the Supreme Court of Canada in *Théberge v. Galerie d'Art du Petit Champlain Inc.* [2002] 2 S.C.R. 336, 2002 SCC 34 (Can.), and the discussion of Canadian moral rights in Chapter 3, *infra.*

37. The recent case of *Pierre Hugo v. Editions Plon*, Court of Appeals [CA] Paris, Mar. 31, 2004, 202 RIDA (Oct. 2004), *reversed,* 04-15.543 Decision 125 of Jan. 30, 2007, *Cour de Cassation–* First civil chamber [*Hugo*], was brought by a great-great-grandson of Victor Hugo against the publishers of a sequel to *Les Misérables* in 2001, 125 years after the author's death, in 1885.

moral rights are transformed into an instrument of cultural policy. After the author's death, moral interests do not cease to be important. Rather, they become different in nature: the public continues to have an interest in maintaining the quality and integrity of its own cultural heritage.[38]

Where duration is concerned, the approach of Continental countries presents a striking contrast to the common law world. In common law systems, the protection of moral rights is often entrusted to tort law, with the implication that the protection of personal interests ceases with the death of the author.

iii. Inalienability and the Possibility of Waiving Moral Rights

The moral right of the author is considered to be a personal right: it originates with the person, or personality, of the author himself. Regardless of what happens to the economic rights in his work, the author's moral rights persist. Even after a work of art is sold and the author has parted with his economic rights, he retains his moral rights.

The doctrine of moral rights implies that an author cannot alienate his moral rights, whether by transfer, sale, or an attempt to relinquish them altogether. Interestingly, at least one French commentator sees this aspect of the doctrine as "patronizing," and a demeaning treatment of the author by the state.[39] Nevertheless, it is a logical consequence of the doctrine. The inherent quality of the relationship between the author and his work is not altered by the external circumstances of mere ownership or possession of the work.[40]

The power of moral rights can create a sense of uneasiness. It leads to the question of whether mechanisms exist to limit the possibility of negative effects on industry or, indeed, culture. One approach is to allow the author to waive his moral rights, in whole or in part, by contractual agreement.

In an ideal world, where pure freedom of contract might reign, waivers might present a perfect solution. But the world as we know it is one of great inequality. The bargaining power of parties to a contract is rarely equal, and contracts are shaped by the dynamics of relationships that are far

---

38. The importance of moral rights from the point of view of protecting a public interest in culture is considered in Sundara Rajan, *Moral Rights and the Protection of Cultural Heritage, supra* note 16, at 89–91.

39. *See* Pierre Recht, Le Droit d'Auteur, une nouvelle forme de propriété: histoire et théorie 278 (1969).

40. Indeed, the term *"droits innés,"* or *angeborene Rechte,* was used by German theorists of the nineteenth century, to discuss moral rights. *See* Chapter 2, *infra,* note 144 and accompanying text.

from balanced.[41] When it comes to moral rights in publication contracts, it is no surprise that waivers generate both practical and conceptual problems.

Practically speaking, countries like Canada and the United Kingdom have seen the development of standard-form contracts in which complete waivers of moral rights are required before any publication activity will be undertaken. In this situation, the author is in a position of great bargaining inequality. He is practically required to surrender his moral rights in order to realize the publication of his work. But standard-form waivers may effectively nullify moral rights, making a mockery of statutory protections for them.

At the doctrinal level, allowing moral rights to be waived creates certain inconsistencies. The general implication of moral rights doctrine is that the relationship between an author and his own creation is permanent and unbreakable, at least as long as the work continues to exist, making moral rights inalienable in law. However, the severity of this doctrinal conclusion may be softened by allowing authors to waive their moral rights in limited circumstances. This approach is adopted by Germany, where waivers are sometimes permitted.[42] However, Germany has taken strong measures to support greater equality of bargaining power between authors and publishers, including, most recently, the introduction of a special law to improve the conditions of authors.[43]

3. Practical Implications

The legal protection of an author's personal rights has a number of practical consequences, not only for authors, but also, for those who receive, enjoy, and use their work. The practical implications of moral rights are sometimes minimized by commentators, who tend to become absorbed in doctrinal issues—they are, after all, exceptionally interesting. However, the practical implications of the doctrine are at the heart of the controversy that it generates, and there can be little doubt that practical concerns exert an overwhelming influence on the international evolution of moral rights.

---

41. JOHN D. MCCAMUS, THE LAW OF CONTRACTS (Irwin Law 2005), Chapter 11, "Duress, Undue Influence and Unconscionability."

42. The issue of waivers and their significance for moral rights receives a detailed treatment in Gerald Dworkin, *The Moral Right of the Author: Moral Rights and the Common Law Countries*, 19 COLUM.-VLA J.L. & ARTS 229, 244–66 (1995).

43. Jens Schovsbo, *Integrating Consumer Rights into Copyright Law: From a European Perspective*, 31(4) J. CONSUMER POL'Y 393 (2008). *See also* Chapter 2, *infra*, notes 154–59 and accompanying text.

a. Economic Consequences of Moral Rights

Moral rights are personal in nature and attempt to address the noncommercial interests and issues arising out of human creativity. Nevertheless, moral rights have two, potentially major, economic consequences. First, the mere presence of moral rights in copyright statutes may inhibit the exploitation of creative works, whether it is for purely commercial purposes or for new creative projects. It can do so by bringing uncertainty to the process of using, editing, modifying, or interpreting works, discouraging the growth of both industry and art around the existing wealth of human culture.

Secondly, a legal claim for moral rights could entail high costs, whether in the form of legal defense costs or the payment of damages. Losses can also result from a decision to withdraw a work from circulation. The decision to withdraw may be enforced because the work has been produced and marketed in reliance on a pre-existing work in such a way that it violates the moral rights of the original author; or, as can happen, the author may no longer be satisfied with his own work. Considerations like these have exercised a strong influence on the Hollywood film industry. The potentially large number of moral interests involved has led the industry to lobby successfully against the adoption of extensive legal protections for moral rights in films, both in the United States and internationally.[44]

b. Public Policy: The Dissemination of Knowledge

Concerns about moral rights may arise on grounds of public policy. From the perspective of society, the argument goes, knowledge should circulate as widely as possible. The presence of moral rights in legislation may inhibit the publication of creative works, while moral rights claims could penalize those who undertake to disseminate them.

In fact, copyright law, as a whole, restricts the circulation of knowledge by reserving the ability to control the dissemination of works to the author. It is for this reason that copyright is known as a monopoly right, and is granted to the author for a limited term only. However, moral rights can act as an additional restriction imposed on the circulation of knowledge. If they are protected in perpetuity, they may limit the dissemination of works indefinitely.

---

44. Many countries protect moral rights in film, such as France, India, and Russia; but international agreements on moral rights explicitly exclude "audiovisual works." *See, e.g.,* the WPPT, art. 5, which restricts the moral rights of a performer to "his live aural performances or performances fixed in phonograms." The role of the American film industry in inhibiting the international development of moral rights is discussed by Stephen Fraser, *Berne, CFTA, NAFTA and GATT: The Implications of Copyright Droit Moral and Cultural Exemptions in International Trade Law,* 18 Hastings Comm. and Ent. L.J. 287, 305–20 (1996).

Moral rights could have an especially strong impact on those areas of human knowledge that build directly on pre-existing works.

B. Moral Rights in the Digital Context

In the Digital Age, the doctrine of moral rights faces three kinds of challenges. First, copyright law has become the primary form of legal regulation governing new technologies. Notably, computer programs and databases, two major types of new creation, enjoy copyright protection as "literary works." The logic of extending copyright to these new forms of intellectual creation follows a long tradition of bringing diverse kinds of intellectual work into the ambit of copyright law. Copyright began as a right in literary property; it was later extended to the protection of musical and artistic works as being analogous to literary property.[45] Copyright law has generally proven to be a flexible and adaptable instrument of social policy, able to accommodate many of these new aspects of knowledge.

However, the extension of copyright concepts to technological works may stretch the literary analogy beyond its natural limits. In jurisdictions where moral rights are recognized, they are automatically included within the bundle of rights enjoyed by creative authors under copyright rules. Accordingly, the question of whether creators of new technologies should enjoy moral rights is important, but it remains largely unresolved. Indeed, the applicability of moral rights to the products of new technology is an issue that has received little attention. Nevertheless, the availability of moral rights could have a variety of implications for both technology and culture.

A second series of concerns arises out of the new creative possibilities generated by technology. Technology provides novel ways of creating traditional artworks; it also raises the possibility of new kinds of creation, artistic or otherwise, such as multimedia or computer-generated works. In a sense, the composite work is the archetypal creative work of the Digital Age. From a legal point of view, it leads to endless permutations of simultaneous, and possibly conflicting, rights and interests. There is also a possibility that new technologies and artistic creation will overlap—for example, where a computer program, itself protected by copyright law as a literary work, is additionally designed to generate a work of art. All of these issues involve new and unfamiliar types of works, which may or may not fall easily into copyright categories, and conflicts over rights and interests that may prove to be intractable.

---

45. Copyright Act 1842, 5 & 6 Vic., c. 45 (Eng.).

Finally, it should be noted that new technologies have made it possible for members of the public to intervene in creative works in a new way, making seamless and imperceptible changes. It is most appropriate that they have come to be known as "users" of copyright works. In effect, new technologies have initiated a breakdown in the traditional hierarchy between creators and their public. The terms of this new relationship will affect the legitimacy and enforceability of moral rights—as, indeed, it has generally influenced the environment for copyright law. These new phenomena present fundamental challenges to the concept and practice of moral rights.

1. Conceptual Challenges

In the digital environment, the concepts underlying moral rights doctrine have become fluid. Long-established ways of understanding authorship, work, and reputation, on which the edifice of moral rights rests, are being transformed by the all-pervasive influence of technology. No definitive solution is in sight, but in the meantime, wherever creative work is concerned, multiple possibilities present themselves.

a. Authorship: Human or Machine?

In a technological environment, the concept of authorship has new connotations. Two issues are likely to arise with ever-greater frequency. First, human authorship may be increasingly intertwined with technological methods of creation. Accordingly, the "creator" of a work—and, thereby, the person whose moral rights should be protected—may be a human being, a machine, or, what is most likely, a combination of the two. It may be preferable to express the same thought in less sensational terms, by pointing out that the intervention of technology often has the effect of distancing an author from his own creation. In this case, is it still true that an author's work is a reflection of his personality? Does the author's moral right still deserve to be protected as such?

The second issue involves the fact that digital creation tends to make extensive use of pre-existing material. Much of this matter is, itself, an earlier product of creative authorship. Within this framework, two conflicts can arise. First, and most obvious, is the problem of shared authorship. How are the moral rights of collaborators in a work to coexist? When does one author's moral right take precedence over another's? If the work of an author is used without his consent—even accidentally, or in passing—when does that author have a right to claim his moral rights?

The second conflict is, in a way, even more interesting. If the new work makes use of earlier works that are now in the public domain, there is clearly no need to respect copyright rules. Copyright in the work has expired.

This may also hold true where moral rights are concerned. If the term of protection for moral rights is the same as the duration of economic rights, there is no need to recognize moral rights; they, too, would have expired. Nevertheless, the factual reality remains: the material used in the making of the new work originates, not with its author, but with another author. At what point will this problem become so important that the connection between the new author and his composite work is deemed to be too fragile for moral rights to subsist in the new work? If the strength of the relationship between a work and its author is the criterion for moral rights protection, anything that dilutes the author's creative presence in the work can raise an argument against moral rights. In the digital context, the nature of authorship is changing, and the complexity of authorship should certainly be reflected in new subtleties where the protection of moral rights is concerned.[46]

The relationship of author and audience is also fundamentally different in a digital environment. For example, in a technological context, the performance of an author's original work may acquire a new importance in its own right. The "performer" may be executing the instructions in a computer program. Without his role in translating the instructions of the author into action, the work might be incomprehensible to the audience or even, in an extreme case, incapable of being perceived by it.[47] The nature of the performer's role creates a new dynamic among the three groups involved in the aesthetic experience—author, performer, and audience.

The new role of the public deserves close scrutiny. The public has a new potential for involvement in the creative work. In particular, once a work has been transformed into a digital format, any member of the public can intervene and make changes that would be imperceptible to a subsequent "user." The audience has an opportunity to become a more active participant in the creative process. Of course, to be actively involved in an aesthetic experience requires something beyond mere physical manipulation of the work. The ultimate goal is nothing less than the re-creation and development of the mind-set of the artist within the person who receives the work.

The idea of the audience as aesthetic participant may be somewhat unfamiliar to Western "high" culture. However, it is an ancient and well-established

---

46. Colin Tapper notes that the "copyright test for protection of [an] adaptation" may be useful in this regard (personal communication with the author, Apr. 12, 2010). Accordingly, if a new work is not sufficiently transformative to qualify as an adaptation, then moral rights should rest with the original author.

47. It is interesting to note the parallel that the situation of technological creation presents with the traditional situation of music performance: the average person is most often unable to read the musical score, itself a form of "code" notation.

principle in cultures of the East.[48] The Sanskrit term, *"rasa,"* describes the ecstatic essence of the creative moment, and it is made possible by the shared experience of artist and audience.[49] The idea is beautifully explained by Bharata, the fabled author of the Sanskrit treatise on classical performance known as the *Natya Shastra*:

> Born in the heart of the poet, [aesthetic experience] flowers as it were in the actor and bears fruit in the spectator. All three in the serene contemplation of the work, form in reality a single knowing object fused together.[50]

By enabling a physical *rapprochement* between author and audience, through engagement with the work, digital technology supports the possibility of a new and closer relationship between them. But technological interaction is no guarantee of human closeness. Whether or not technology will lead to spiritual connection depends, more than ever, on the terms of the underlying relationship between human beings. At a minimum, any author's participation in the world of technology should be decided on a voluntary basis, and not against his or her own will. Freedom is the necessary foundation for a meaningful relationship.

b. The Disintegration of the Work

Questions about the nature of the work raise another series of issues. In various ways, a technological work, or a work featuring technological elements, may be different from traditional forms of creative expression. This consideration leads to the question of whether mistreatment will affect the author in the same way that a creative artist would be harmed by the abuse of his work. Resolving this problem depends on how we eventually come to understand the place of technology in creative works. At present, it is still early in the history of the Digital Age. Our enthusiasm ignites for the possibilities of technology, rather than the ends that technology can achieve. But a distinction should be drawn between the role of technology as an end-product and its function as a means to an end in the creative process. When technology serves

---

48. *See, e. g.*, the detailed study of Indian art and aesthetics in Sneh Pandit, An Approach to the Indian Theory of Art and Aesthetics 88–89 (Sterling 1977). The intersection of traditional culture with digital technology is explored by James Tunney, *E.U., I.P., Indigenous People and the Digital Age: Intersecting Circles?*, 20(9) Eur. Intell. Prop. Rev. 335, 335 (1998).

49. *See* C. Subramania Bharati's essay, *Rasa—The Key-Word of Indian Culture, in* C. Subramania Bharati, Agni and Other Poems and Translations & Essays and Other Prose Fragments 69 (1980).

50. Bharata's identity is disputed; but the text itself lays the foundation for Indian classical dance, drama, and music as it has developed over the past 2000-odd years.

to realize the creative vision of the author, it cannot be accused of distancing the work from the personality of its creator.

The creative entanglement of collaborators in a work also raises questions about moral rights. Once again, two scenarios present themselves. First, when coauthors are involved in the creation of a work, how can we establish the identity of the final work? This question can be asked in another way: who should make the final decision about which version of the work is the ultimate result of the creative process? A perfect example of this problem is illustrated by film, a collaborative work made out of the work of many contributors—writers and composers, as well as actors and performers—overseen by a producer who finances the work, but also, by a director, whose role, throughout the twentieth century, has moved towards increasing creative leadership. A major competing claim exists between the producer and the director as to who has the authority to decide on the identity of the final work. But, to varying degrees, all of the creative contributors to a film have claims, potentially over the final form in which the work is realized, and, in a more immediate sense, over the use of their individual contributions in the final product. On this issue, French law takes the stance that a film cannot be said to be complete until all of the structural contributors—writer, composer, director, and producer—have agreed upon the final version.[51]

The second example takes this problem and throws the doors open to the public. When "users" become involved in the manipulation or modification of a work, how does their input affect its status? Could situations arise where the involvement of a "user" is somehow so significant that he or she effectively alters the work, and bears the responsibility for a new "final" version? And if so, is this situation to be seen in a positive light? Does it represent the destruction of cultural heritage, cultural renewal—or, in some sense, both?

c. Fame: A Relic of the Past?

Moral rights doctrine is fundamentally preoccupied with the problems of artistic reputation. In some countries, a moral right to one's reputation is recognized. Others follow the formula of the Berne Convention, and make reputation an essential component of the right of integrity. In these jurisdictions, modifying the work will not be enough to invoke the integrity right. Rather, the author must also be able to show that the modification has damaged his reputation.[52]

Reputation, also known as fame, is the essence of artistic existence. Without it, an artist cannot expect to sell his work; without it, there is no measure of

---

51. CPI, *supra* note 20, art. L121-5.
52. Article 6*bis* of the Berne Convention, *supra* note 5, provides that the alteration must be "prejudicial to hishonour or reputation," leaving questions open about the extent and nature of the proof required.

recognition. Even an artist who disdains celebrity is in some sense dependent upon it for his survival.[53] An artist cannot live without fame.[54]

In many ways, fame has always been an unhappy master. The work of truly great thinkers tends to be far ahead of its time—sometimes by decades, or even centuries—and fame does not arrive in time to improve their lives. Vincent van Gogh is a tragic example: the painter struggled for basic physical and psychological sustenance, and sold only one painting, to his beloved brother Theo, during his lifetime. Now, van Gogh's paintings routinely set records on the art market for the most expensive works of art ever sold.[55] Other examples can be found in the lives of no lesser geniuses than William Shakespeare and J. S. Bach—artists whose work was valued by their contemporaries, but which, after the death of the artist, fell into neglect for decades before its true stature was realized.[56] In such cases, fame is for the benefit of an artist's name, or perhaps, for the vindication of his descendants.[57] It offers little benefit to the artist himself.

---

53. An interesting example is J.D. Salinger: the writer apparently spent his youth obsessed with achieving fame only to discover, when he did become famous, his intense distaste for celebrity. *See* the fascinating article by Charles McGrath, *J. D. Salinger, Literary Recluse, Dies at 91*, NEW YORK TIMES (Jan. 28, 2010), *available at* http://www.nytimes.com/2010/01/29/books/29salinger.html (last visited Apr. 26, 2010).

54. The ideal is well-known in the poetry of the Sangam age in South Indian literature, some 2000 years ago. *See* K. A. NILAKANTA SASTRI (THE LATE), R. C. CHAMPAKALAKSHMI, & P. M. RAJAN GURUKKAL, ILLUSTRATED HISTORY OF SOUTH INDIA, adapted from K. A. NILAKANTA SASTRI, A HISTORY OF SOUTH INDIA (Oxford Univ. Press 2009) (1955).

55. Van Gogh's "Sunflowers," "Irises," and his "Portrait of Dr Gachet" have all set records for their sale prices. *See On this Day*, BBC NEWS (Nov. 11, 1987), *available at* http://news.bbc.co.uk/onthisday/hi/dates/stories/november/11/newsid_2539000/2539613.stm (last visited Apr. 26, 2010). In 1990, the "Portrait of Dr Gachet" was purchased by a Japanese businessman, Ryoei Saito, for $82.5 million. He claimed that he wanted to have the painting cremated with him—either to avoid inheritance taxes imposed on his heirs, or out of love for the work! And indeed, since his death in 1996, the work has disappeared. The painting held the record for most expensive painting ever sold until 2004, when it appears to have been broken by Picasso's "Garcon a la Pipe." Currently, the record for most expensive painting sold at auction is held by Gustav Klimt's "Portrait of Adele Bloch-Bauer," purchased for $135 million in June of 2006. works. *See The Art Gems that Broke the Bank*, BBC NEWS (June 19, 2006), *available at* http://news.bbc.co.uk/2/hi/entertainment/4883296.stm (last visited Apr. 26, 2010). The ordering of paintings on lists of the most expensive works depends on a number of factors, including the sale venue and the adjustment of price for inflation, and varies across different sources. Nevertheless, van Gogh and Picasso are both consistently well represented in this group.

56. The Romantics were responsible for re-discovering both Bach and Shakespeare.

57. The fame of Boris Pasternak, Russian poet and novelist, comes to mind. Awarded the Nobel Prize in 1958, Pasternak was vilified by the Soviet government and by the Soviet community of writers—a situation that may have precipitated his death. *See* Peter Flinn, *The Plot Thickens: A New Book Promises an Intriguing Twist to the Epic Tale of "Doctor Zhivago,"* WASHINGTON POST (Jan. 27, 2007), *available at* http://www.washingtonpost.com/wp-dyn/content/

Fame, of even the most ordinary variety, takes time to develop. What is its place in a digital world?

A characteristic quality of digital space is its curious relation to time. Digital technology involves the speeding-up of everything—perhaps quite natural, since digital communication is defined by the movement of photons, particles of light that move faster than anything else in the universe. But there is also another dimension to digital time, which can perhaps be best expressed as an inverse relationship between the volume of information available and the attention span of any given individual. In the digital environment, information is produced and consumed at tremendous speed. Journalists used to speak of "yesterday's news," but the old news of the digital era could be news that is only hours old. Rare indeed are the personalities that can command more than a few minutes or hours of fame in the age of the Internet.

At the same time, the range of digital technology is such that reputation, such as it is, can be communicated across a much larger population than ever before. If fame in the digital context is limited in terms of its depth, it covers a vast surface area during its brief existence. It can generate both publicity and wealth on a scale not previously known, as illustrated by numerous examples of artists and personalities who have made a sensation through Internet phenomena such as YouTube, the near-ubiquitous free video-streaming site.[58]

The nature of fame may have changed, but it has not, by any means, become outmoded. If anything, fame has acquired a renewed importance in the digital context. Copyright rules have become difficult to enforce; since copyright has long served as the primary means of securing money from creative work in a modern society, it has now become essential to find new ways of earning wealth that can compensate for the fragility of copyright. At least in the popular genres, artists are increasingly bypassing the traditional formulae for public recognition—in music, recording with a label, releasing singles and albums—in favor of offering their work directly to the public. The intervention of a middleman is no longer necessary. YouTube, again, has proven to be revolutionary. Aspiring bands post their videos online and hope to be noticed. In the Digital Age, fame, in its new incarnation, translates into new kinds of earnings—advertising revenues, dates for live performances, media attention. No doubt, reaching out to the world through technology also satisfies a more fundamental human urge for connection that

article/2007/01/26/AR2007012601758.html (last visited Apr. 26, 2010). Pasternak's son finally accepted the Nobel Prize on behalf of his father in 1989.

58. Singing sensation Susan Boyle is a case in point. *See* Sarah Lyall, *Unlikely Singer Is YouTube Sensation*, NEW YORK TIMES (Apr. 17, 2009), *available at* http://www.nytimes.com/2009/04/18/arts/television/18boyle.html (last visited Apr. 26, 2010).

has never really gone away. Fame still matters. Technology changes, but human nature remains the same.

2. Enforcement Difficulties

In a technological environment, the enforcement of moral rights presents many of the same general problems confronted by copyright. The rights of attribution and integrity become as complicated to implement in the digital context as copyright royalties are difficult to collect. But the connotations of these two failures are different.

The very conditions that favor greater audience involvement in the creative process can lead to difficulties in the enforcement of moral rights. The nature of new technology is such that the appearance of a work in digitized form allows it to be altered in such a way that a person who subsequently sees the work will be unaware that any changes have been made. Information such as the identity of the author may be suppressed quite easily, without anyone's knowledge. Reproductions of the work can also be made without any significant loss of quality, regardless of the number of new copies. Finally, the Internet provides a means of worldwide distribution at minimal cost, and access to the work may be acquired on an individual basis—through file-sharing, e-mail, or websites—all of which are difficult to monitor. In these circumstances, there is a likelihood that the moral rights of the author will suffer.

The copyright response to this problem has been to try to fight fire with fire—to wield technology as a weapon against itself. Indeed, technology has been preferred over law as a solution to copyright problems because, so the argument goes, technology has the power to address problems at a practical level, in a way that no law enforcement initiative can match. In particular, technological protection measures can limit the uses of a work on an individual basis, and they act instantaneously to prevent the potentially infringing activity from being carried out. In contrast, copyright rules really become functional where large-scale infringement is concerned.[59] The rules, themselves, are also rigid and unresponsive—slow to change—while technology moves ahead and changes rapidly.

In an attempt to prevent copyright infringement, a variety of technological protection measures (TPMs), also known as "anti-circumvention" measures, have been developed.[60] These include encryption technology, which "locks"

---

59. *See, for example,* the discussion of scale of infringement, and the resulting harm to the interests of the copyright owner, in *MGM Studios, Inc. v. Grokster, Ltd.*, 545 U.S. 913 (2005).

60. This awkward term refers to technological measures that are implemented in order to discourage interference with copyright works: they are against—"anti"—the "circumvention" of copyright rules.

the work to prevent someone from gaining unauthorized access to it; water-marking, which allows copying of the work to be traced, though not pre-vented; and digital rights management, which identifies the origin of a work. From a moral rights perspective, encryption and watermarking are credible approaches to the integrity right; as for attribution, it is supported by digital rights management. Digital rights management also lends indirect support to the integrity principle, by offering a measure of the authenticity of the source. Attempts to circumvent these safeguards have become criminal offenses in some countries, including the United States.[61] However, the caveat that applies to security technologies is that technology never stands still. Every attempt to restrict access to a work through technological measures has its own, technological antidote. Technological protection measures, however sophisticated, seem doomed to obsolescence.[62]

Circumvention also involves a psychological dimension. For some users, circumventing copy protection is a technological challenge to be met; for others, it is a form of political activism against unfair restrictions on media. The fact that there is little attempt to provide policy justifications for the criminalization of circumvention can lead to anger. In the process—ironically—talent and human potential are wasted. Condemning circumven-tion makes a certain type of innovative activity illegal, but there may not be anything inherently nefarious about it. Context is everything. A code-breaker during World War II was a hero; in the Digital Age he is, apparently, a criminal.

In view of these considerations about enforcement, have moral rights become irrelevant to the creation and dissemination of creative works in the Digital Age? This question deserves something more than a curt "yes," on the basis that moral rights have become difficult to enforce in practice. More than ever, a principled approach should come first. Without principles, it is certain that moral rights, copyright, or any other rule governing digi-tal media will become difficult to enforce. Based on sound principles, how-ever, a society can hope to educate its members and command respect for these rules by offering credible justifications for them. Social censure is the first step in penalizing any wrongdoing. Without it, the penalty becomes meaningless.

---

61. Digital Millennium Copyright Act, Pub. L. No. 105-304, 112 Stat. 2860 (codified as amended in scattered sections of 17 U.S.C. (1998)), *available at* http://www.copyright.gov/title17/ (last visited May 2, 2010) [DMCA].

62. The relevant United States provisions are sections 1201 (a)(1) and 1201 (a)(2) of the DMCA. The American approach to circumvention technologies is discussed by David Balaban, *The Battle of the Music Industry: The Distribution of Audio and Video Works via the Internet, Music and More*, 12 FORDHAM INTELL. PROP. MEDIA & ENT. L.J. 235, 259–65 (2001). The relevance of anti-circumvention technology to the moral right of integrity is considered briefly by Thomas P. Heide, *The Moral Right of Integrity and the Global Information Infra-structure: Time for a New Approach?*, 2 U.C. DAVIS J. INT'L L. & POL'Y 211, 263–66 (1996).

To what extent, then, do the moral rights of authors continue to be relevant in the environment of digital technology? The answer to this question lies in the fact that moral rights are closely connected to culture. What is happening to culture in the Digital Age? It is subject to endless transformation and manipulation, leading to confusion about its identity and uncertainty over its significance. Authenticity and integrity are constantly at issue. At the same time, the creative human personality, which generates culture in all its forms, seems curiously removed from the virtual world where culture is experienced and shared. In a society that is increasingly driven by the needs and characteristics of machines, the creativity of human beings should be a matter of concern. Moral rights, it would appear, are indeed relevant to the Digital Age. Their new role is compelling.

As a matter of principle, these considerations can help us to answer the question of whether moral rights are relevant. They should also lead us towards new and better ideas on how to encourage compliance with moral rights, and enforcement of the principle. Above all, there can be little doubt that the viability of moral rights in a digital environment will depend on the awareness of the public, and on its willingness to support the status of creative expression. Authors and artists should take a moment to reflect. They will need to explore the implications of a more democratic relationship with their public, keeping in mind that the public has an essential role to play in protecting their interests.[63]

C. Scope and Structure of this Study

Moral rights in the Virtual Age present a vast question—a field of study that is, as yet, largely unexplored. The greatest challenge of this work has been to explore the basic features of this universe within the covers of a single book.

The book is essentially divided into two parts. The first considers the origins of modern moral rights in nineteenth-century Europe, and explores their subsequent development as they came to be disseminated across different parts of the world throughout the twentieth century. The objective is to establish what is meant by moral rights doctrine, not so much as it

---

63. *See* Mira T. Sundara Rajan, *Moral Rights in the Digital Age: New Possibilities for the Democratization of Culture*, 16 (2) Int'l Rev L. Computers & Tech. 187 (2002). The importance of the cooperative element in the development of digital copyright is emphasized by Sterling, *supra* note 7, at 525.

existed in Continental Europe of two centuries ago, but in its current form, as a worldwide phenomenon. These chapters examine moral rights as they are found in countries that represent the world's major legal systems, including civil law and common law regimes, developing countries, and post-socialist states. The group of developing countries is the most difficult to examine, as it is tremendously heterogeneous. The world's poorest countries, perhaps among the richest in terms of culture, deserve a special treatment in their own right, as do countries emerging from a state of war, such as Iraq and Afghanistan.

The informal and practical nature of moral rights has also led to the difficulty of deciding which aspects of the doctrine should be examined. Rights such as *droit de suite*—a visual artist's right to a royalty on the sale of his work by subsequent owners—are arguably hybrid rights, and not true moral rights at all. They are referred to, but not discussed in depth. However, rights that appear to be "new" moral rights, expanding the doctrine, are dealt with in detail. Proposals for Aboriginal cultural rights, and the reinstatement of copyright terms for persecuted authors in post-socialist countries, are among the most fascinating examples of an evolving theory. It is also important to note the interconnected and overlapping nature of the technologies involved—as a cursory example, downloading from the Internet affects both music and film—leading to a degree of necessary overlap in the issues discussed across different chapters that is, hopefully, illuminating rather than repetitive.

The first part of the book aims to draw a precise and, as far as possible, comprehensive picture of what is meant by moral rights on the global scale. Based on this analysis, the second part examines moral rights issues in relation to new technological phenomena. Here, too, certain choices have been made about the areas of technology to be considered. Chapters deal with music and film, relatively more conventional categories of "copyright work" that are subject to change in a digital environment; and computer programs and open access movements, purely technological phenomena. Many more areas could have been explored, but had to be left out for the sake of reasonableness. Open access movements involving books are discussed; but the general transformation of literature in the Digital Age has largely been left for a future occasion, as has the vast and developing area of performers and their moral rights.

By the conclusion of this book, readers should have an understanding of the moral rights principle, where it comes from and why it developed, how it is interpreted and applied in many of the world's major jurisdictions, and the challenges that arise from new technological phenomena. Above all, the book attempts to make a case for moral rights as an essential weapon in the fight to preserve human creativity in the Digital Age. Moral rights protect material culture; they also support history and truth in a context where knowledge is vulnerable. As a distinguished colleague once assured me, "Intellectual property lawyers are different from other lawyers; they are also human beings." Moral rights represent the human side of copyright, and they can help us to see, faintly behind the dazzling brilliance of technology, the human face of the author.

CHAPTER

2

Moral Rights

History of an Idea

*[I]n English society as an author I was not of much
account, but . . . in France, where an author just
because he is an author has prestige, I was.*
—W. Somerset Maugham, *The Razor's Edge*[1]

---

1. W. SOMERSET MAUGHAM, THE RAZOR'S EDGE 9 (Vintage 2003) (1943).

Moral rights are based on a simple idea. The author of a work develops a special bond with his creation. The relationship between them is permanent. An author is, and always will be, the author of his own work.

Writers describe this relationship in a number of ways. Words such as "intellectual," "personal," and "spiritual" often appear; one venerable scholar of copyright refers to the theory that a work is the "spiritual child" of the author.[2] The terminology, with its impractical overtones, is not universally approved. Yet it serves to describe something that may not be less real because of its incorporeal quality. It should stir the sympathy of copyright lawyers, whose work involves a routine struggle with equally abstract concepts such as originality, authorship, and creativity.

Out of this high-minded and abstract doctrine, a number of very practical rights emerge. The two most widely recognized moral rights are *attribution* and *integrity*. An author's right to have his own work attributed to him by name was once known as the right of "paternity"; the scope of the *attribution* right is frequently considered to be broad enough to accommodate an author's right to write under a pseudonym, or anonymously.[3] The broadest approach to attribution would recognize that attributing the works of one person to another may violate the rights, not only of the true author, whose name is *not*

---

2. *See* Stig Strömholm, *Droit Moral—The International and Comparative Scene from a Scandinavian Viewpoint*, 14(1) Int'l Rev. Indus. Prop. & Copyright L. 217 (1983) [Strömholm IIC], who calls the author the "spiritual father" of the work and cites the Swedish Royal Commission on Copyright Law for the term "spiritual children." Strömholm IIC, at 228. *See also* Sam Ricketson, The Berne Convention for the Protection of Literary and Artistic Works: 1886–1986, para. 8.93 (Centre for Commercial Law Studies, Queen Mary College, Kluwer 1987), pointing out that "[t]he adjective 'moral' has no precise English equivalent, although 'spiritual,' 'non-economic' and 'personal' convey something of the intended meaning."

3. *See* Georges Michaélidès-Nouraos, Le Droit moral de l'auteur: Etude de droit français, de droit comparé et de droit international 12, para. 120 (Publications de l'Institut de droit comparé de l'Université de Paris (1ière Série), Collection d'études théoriques et Pratiques de Droit Etranger, de Droit Comparé et de Droit International sous la Direction de H Lévy-Ullman, Librairie Arthur Rousseau, Paris 1935). The French names for this right include *droit à la paternité (de l'oeuvre)*, or *droit de paternité sur l'oeuvre*; *droit d'attribution;* and *droit au nom*. Article L121-1 of the French Intellectual Property Code provides that the author enjoys the right to respect for his name, his quality as author, and his work "L'auteur jouit du droit au respect de son nom, de sa qualité et de son oeuvre." *See Loi N° 92-597 du 1er juillet 1992 relative au code de la propriété intellectuelle (partie législative)*, Journal officiel de la République française, 8 février 1994; *Légifrance: Le service public de la diffusion du droit*, *available at* http://www.legifrance.gouv.fr/affichCode.do?cidTexte=LEGITEXT000006069414 &dateTexte=20100412 (last visited Apr. 29, 2010) [*Code de la Propriété Intellectuelle*, CPI]. This extremely useful website includes a history of each provision of the CPI, including the dates of adoption and amendment. Another online source for French copyright law is CELOG, which provides an annotated code that features a selection of court rulings relevant to each provision, *available at* http://www.celog.fr/cpi/ (last visited May 2, 2010). The site claims to provide more than 1000 judgments throughout the body of the Code.

recognized, but also of the person who is falsely named.[4] This is the case of false attribution, or forgery. An example may serve to clarify: attributing works by an unknown author to a famous poet may violate the poet's right of attribution.[5]

Additionally, a right to the *integrity* of one's work is generally acknowledged. The circumstances in which an author may assert this right, however, vary widely across jurisdictions. In France, for example, an author's claim that the integrity of the work has been affected will be accepted at face value; it is the defendant who bears the burden of proving that his dealings with the work have not damaged it.[6] In most other countries, the situation differs from French law, and an author must be able to prove that mistreatment of the work has resulted in damage to his reputation. For this reason, the right of integrity is also known in some countries as a right of *reputation*.[7] The acceptable forms of evidence, and the standard of proof to be satisfied, can present

---

4. See the comments in J.M. PONTIER, J.C. RICCI, & J. BOURDON, DROIT DE LA CULTURE para. 345 (2d ed. Dalloz 1996): they refer to the "positive" and "negative" aspects of the attribution right. The "negative" aspect is "the impossibility of attributing a work to a person who is not the author." Interestingly, not all legal commentators agree with this interpretation of attribution—at least, as it is drafted in Article 6*bis* of the Berne Convention. *See* SILKE VON LEWINSKI, INTERNATIONAL COPYRIGHT LAW AND POLICY, para. 5.99 (Oxford Univ. Press 2008) [von Lewinski, *International Copyright Law and Policy*]. Von Lewinski suggests, instead, that a violation of the attribution right only occurs where the author's name is *not* used. This approach to the interpretation of moral rights is controversial, as discussed below: *see* note 35 and accompanying text.

5. The example is drawn from the case of Indian National Poet, C. Subramania Bharati. *See* Mira T. Sundara Rajan, *Moral Rights in the Public Domain: Copyright Matters in the Works of Indian National Poet C. Subramania Bharati*, SINGAPORE J. LEGAL STUD. 161 (2001) [Sundara Rajan, *Moral Rights in the Public Domain*].

6. The language of Art. L121-1 of the CPI (*supra* note 3) makes this clear: it protects the right of integrity in extremely open-ended terms, providing simply that the author shall enjoy a right of "respect for his name, quality of authorship, and work"—"L'auteur jouit du droit au respect de son nom, de sa qualité et de son oeuvre."

7. Until 2006, the Russian Copyright Act of 1993 protected integrity as an author's right to the protection of his reputation. *See* Russian Federation Law on Copyright and Neighboring Rights sec. 15 (No. 5351-I of July 9, 1993) [Russian Copyright Act 1993]; as of January 1, 2008, the law has been overruled by Part IV of the Russian Civil Code on intellectual property. *See* Grazhdanski Kodeks Rossiiskoi Federatsi, Chast' Chetvërtaya [Civil Code of the Russian Federation, Part IV], Federal Law No. 230-FZ of Dec. 18, 2006, *Rossijskaja Gazeta* No. 289 (4255) of Dec. 22, 2006 = *Sobranie zakonodatel'stva RF* (SZ RF) No. 52 (Part I) of Dec. 25, 2006, Item 5496, at 14803 [2008 Civil Code], *available at* http://www1.fips.ru/wps/wcm/connect/content_ru/ru/documents/russian_laws/codeks_rf/gkrf_ch4 (last visited May 2, 2010). An accurate version of the provisions can still be seen, in English translation, on WikiSource, a public domain source for legislative documents, *available at* http://en.wikisource.org/wiki/Russian_Federation._Law_on_Copyright_and_Neighboring_Rights#Article_15_Moral_Rights. Moral rights in the 1993 Act are discussed in detail in MIRA T. SUNDARA RAJAN, COPYRIGHT AND CREATIVE FREEDOM 173–83 (Routledge 2006) [Sundara Rajan, *Copyright and Creative Freedom*].

the author with difficult, and perhaps insurmountable, challenges. In common law countries, courts may ask authors to provide proof that they have suffered financial loss or economic damage in order to show damage to reputation—a potentially absurd interpretation of the integrity right. The case of an author whose artistic integrity is damaged, but whose work actually sells better because of intervention—for example, the addition of erotic scenes to bring excitement to a film adaptation of a novel—might have little hope of success.[8]

The presence of moral rights in the international copyright arena was established with the codification of attribution and integrity in the *Berne Convention for the Protection of Literary and Artistic Works*, finalized in 1928, in the course of a major revision conference in Rome.[9] However, the theory of moral rights is not by any means limited to the rights of attribution and integrity. In countries where moral rights are well-developed, a number of other rights have emerged—a right to protest malicious criticism of your work; a right to withdraw your work from circulation if your ideas, or your assessment of the quality of the work, has changed; and a right of continued access to your work, in certain circumstances, even after it is sold.[10]

Indeed, the doctrine could clearly lead to the practical recognition of a number of legal rights. New moral rights would reflect the society of their era

---

8. The question of evidence in moral rights cases does not receive adequate treatment in the literature of common law countries. The brief Canadian case of *Snow v. The Eaton Centre* (1982) 70 C.P.R. (2d) 105 [*Snow*] makes the helpful but cryptic point that expert evidence will be valued in moral rights claims in that country.

9. Berne Convention for the Protection of Literary and Artistic Works (adopted Sept. 9, 1886) 1161 U.N.T.S. 3, *available at* http://www.wipo.int/treaties/en/ip/berne/trtdocs_wo001.html (last visited Apr. 29, 2010); also available in a useful format at the Legal Information Institute, Cornell University Law School, http://www.law.cornell.edu/treaties/berne/overview.html (last visited Apr. 29, 2010) [Berne Convention]. The Convention itself dates from 1886 and is the first international copyright agreement. It is the founding document of what is now considered international copyright law, and it remains the primary source of international copyright rules. Since 1928, moral rights have been amended twice. The Brussels revision conference of 1948 introduced a provision that the minimum duration of protection for moral rights should be "at least until the expiry of the copyright." Further clarification in 1967 made special provision for countries to limit "some" of those rights to the lifetime of the author. The amendment was designed to accommodate common law countries, who have traditionally protected moral rights interests through personal torts, which can only occur during the lifetime of the person affected. The adoption of moral rights in the Berne Convention is described in Ricketson's authoritative work. THE BERNE CONVENTION *supra* note 2, paras. 8.92–8.115.

10. On the *droit d'accès*, see Strömholm IIC, *supra* note 2, at 238–40. He points out that the main purpose of the right is usually considered to be the maintenance of the author's right to make reproductions of his work, and that it can also serve the purpose of allowing the author access to the work in order to gather evidence for use in disputes. In the German law of 1965, the right was not classified as either moral or economic, but belonged in a special category of other rights of the author.

in much the same way that the moral rights of 1928 reflected the prevailing beliefs of the Romantic generation about human creativity. In fact, to be precise, the moral right is inevitably framed according to the values of the preceding generation, for invariably, law is the last institution to be touched by social change. This time lag is one of the great difficulties of law in the Digital Age. Moral rights exist in an environment of constant metamorphosis, initiated by digital technology. Among other things, digital technology ensures that international agreements on copyright tend to be out-of-date from the very moment of their adoption, leading to great difficulties in harmonizing international copyright rules.[11]

For all its apparent simplicity, the idea of an author's moral right leads to an amazing array of consequences. The implications are philosophical, cultural, and economic, as well as legal. And, however innocuous they may appear at first glance, moral rights are intensely controversial—the first clue to the power, dangers, and opportunities which they entail.

The reasons for the controversy can be readily distilled into three issues. First, lawyers often fail to distinguish between the theory of moral rights and the law. Yet, in order to avoid confusion and misinterpretation, it is essential to separate the two. The doctrine and the law are two different kinds of animal. Of course, doctrine and law have a common origin; but the eventual separation of the two flows logically from the contrast between the informal character of the doctrine, which emerged out of the case-specific pronouncements of judges in the course of the eighteenth and nineteenth centuries, and its later crystallization into a lattice of legal rules. The doctrine grew out of judge-made law; it was a theory of authorship. It came to reflect the larger process by which the "natural rights of man and the citizen" were recognized in Revolutionary France, inaugurating a new era in the history of Continental

---

11. The Agreement on Trade-Related Aspects of Intellectual Property Rights (TRIPs) of the WTO is a perfect example. This mammoth and ground-breaking agreement, negotiated over a decade, came into effect on January 1, 1995. By that date, digital technology had entered a new phase, and the rules in TRIPs could not accommodate the new reality. Officials at the World Intellectual Property Organization (WIPO) quickly grasped this situation, leading to the WIPO Internet Treaties of 1996—innovative new agreements whose provisions were specifically aimed at capturing the changes brought by digital technology to the copyright arena. *See* Agreement on Trade-Related Aspects of Intellectual Property Rights, Apr. 15, 1994, Annex 1C to the Marrakesh Agreement Establishing the World Trade Organization, 1869 U.N.T.S. 299; 33 I.L.M. 1197 (1994), *available at* http://www.wto.org/english/docs_e/legal_e/27-trips_01_e.htm (last visited Apr. 29, 2010) [TRIPs Agreement]. A contrast is provided by the WIPO Internet Treaties of 1996, specifically designed to shape copyright rules in a new technological environment. *See* WIPO Copyright Treaty (adopted Dec. 20, 1996, entered into force Mar. 6, 2002) (1997), 36 I.L.M. 65 [WCT], *available at* http://www.wipo. int/treaties/en/ip/wct/trtdocs_wo033.html (last visited Apr. 29, 2010); WIPO Performances and Phonograms Treaty (adopted Dec. 20, 1996, entered into force May 20, 2002) (1997), 36 I.L.M. 76, *available at* http://www.wipo.int/treaties/en/ip/berne/trtdocs_wo001.html (last visited Apr. 29, 2010) [WPPT].

Europe and beyond.[12] The law is something different—the expression of the doctrine in the precise language of national copyright legislation.[13]

In the sophisticated example of codification offered by France, the doctrine loses its breadth and generality, but it is translated into well-defined principles of great pragmatism. The shift is elegantly described by French professor Pierre Sirinelli and his coauthors in terms of a movement from *droit moral*—the term "moral right" in singular form, which grew out of judicial

---

12. For an illuminating discussion of French copyright and its development during the Revolutionary period, see Gregory S. Brown, Literary Sociability and Literary Property in France, 1775–1793 116–42 (Studies in European Cultural Transition Vol. 33) (Aldershot 2006). A seminal article by Martha Woodmansee explores the origins of moral rights in Western European Romanticism. *See* Martha Woodmansee, *The Genius and the Copyright: Economic and Legal Conditions of the Emergence of the "Author,"* 17 Eighteenth-Century Stud. 425 (1984). But this approach should be treated with caution; as William Patry remarks:

    > Another, more recent trope is the idea of copyright arising out of a Romantic view of authorship. The scholarship on this is highly selective, and is limited to a few authors in a few countries. It ignores vast amounts of contrary evidence, and in any event suffers fatally from historical determinism: copyright developed as it did allegedly because authors, legislatures, and society evolved to the point of finally recognizing that no work is as much a man's or woman's as the fruits of his or her own mind. A variant on this, much beloved by some law professors, is a Lockean view of property, in which copyright came to be analogically with its real property cousin. At least one academic career was made on this theory, a theory which UK scholars have effectively debunked on many grounds, not the least of which is that when it came to intellectual property, Locke was not a Lockean.

    See The Patry Copyright Blog, Why UK Scholars Eat Our Lunch (Nov. 14, 2006), *available at* http://williampatry.blogspot.com/2006/11/why-uk-scholars-eat-our-lunch.html (last visited Apr. 29, 2010). In many ways, the birth of the human rights concept can be situated in the French Revolution. The Revolutionists' motto—"liberté, égalité; fraternité"—resonated as far away as twentieth-century South India, where a pioneer of the Freedom movement took it as the motto of his nationalist, anti-British magazine. *See generally* S. Vijaya Bharati, Subramania Bharati (New Delhi: Government of India 1974); statement by Dr. S. Vijaya Bharati (personal communication with the author, Apr. 27, 2010).

13. To some extent, national copyright norms originate with the language of international treaties. These treaties are not necessarily "law" in the usual sense: in the case of the Berne Convention, its terms represent minimum standards, not law *per se*, and must be enacted in national legislation in order to become law. In this sense, the Berne system is similar to other forms of supra-national law-making, from the Directives of the European Union to the *osnovy* of the former Soviet Union. A possible exception to this rule would be apparent in relation to countries whose implementation of international treaties is "automatic" and does not need to be separately implemented in national law. The Russian Federation is an example of such a country. *See ITAR-Tass Russian News Agency v. Russian Kurier, Inc.*, 153 F.3d 82 (2d Cir. 1998). This difference means that a Russian plaintiff could invoke the Berne Convention provisions directly in court, but an American or Canadian plaintiff could not in the courts of his own country. This difference could create some ambiguity about the cross-border experience of copyright: for example, an American plaintiff in Russia could rely on the Berne Convention directly, but could not do so in the United States. This point is significant in relation to moral rights, since an American could thereby enjoy moral rights in Russia through Article *6bis* of the Berne Convention, without deriving a similar benefit from Berne in his own country.

decision-making—to *droits moraux*, the plural "moral rights," in the *Code de la propriété* intellectuelle, France's initial 1957 codification of moral rights.[14] The digital revolution may lead to a situation where the separation of doctrine and law is effectively undone, and, satisfying the rhythms of a cyclical return to the past, the two converge again into a single entity, defined by broad principles applied on a case-by-case basis. For the moment, however, the analytical distinction between doctrine and law is a defining characteristic of the moral rights landscape.

The intuitive, or common-sense, aspect borne by the doctrine leads to related difficulties, and in this sense it is perhaps fair to say that the intuitive appeal of the idea is as much a shortcoming as a strength. To say that moral rights are intuitive is to link them with theories of natural law. But the relationship between natural law and legal instruments is complex, particularly in the common law tradition. The claims of natural law exceed written laws. Principles of natural law are often reflected in legal instruments, but they do not depend on legal language for their existence.[15] Law may reflect natural rights, but natural law exists before, beyond, and after the law. It is a result of "nature," whereas formal law, human law, is *artificial* in the true sense of the word—a construction.[16] The difficulty of understanding natural law, articulating its

---

14. CPI, *supra* note 3.
15. John Locke is perhaps the philosopher most closely associated with reliance on theories of natural rights in the intellectual property field. See the commentaries by William W. Fisher III, *The Growth of Intellectual Property: A History of the Ownership of Ideas in the United States*, German version available as *Geistiges Eigentum–ein ausufernder Rechtsbereich: Die Geschichte des Ideenschutzes in den Vereinigten Staaten, in* EIGENTUM IM INTERNATIONALEN VERGLEICH 265–91 (Vandenhoeck & Ruprecht 1999), *available at* http://cyber.law.harvard. edu/people/tfisher/iphistory.pdf (last visited May 2, 2010); and Adam D. Moore, *Toward a Lockean Theory of Intellectual Property, in* INTELLECTUAL PROPERTY: MORAL, LEGAL, AND INTERNATIONAL DILEMMAS 81 (A.D. Moore, ed., Rowman and Littlefield 1997). For Locke's original arguments, see J. LOCKE, TWO TREATISES OF GOVERNMENT, Book II, Chapter V, "Property" (Project Gutenberg e-book), *available at* http://www.gutenberg.org/dirs/etext05/ trgov10h.htm (last visited Apr. 29, 2010). In particular, in section 27 of this chapter, Locke notes how property develops out of the mixture of human labor with the environment:

    Though the earth, and all inferior creatures, be common to all men, yet every man has a *property* in his own *person*: this no body has any right to but himself. The *labour* of his body, and the *work* of his hands, we may say, are properly his. Whatsoever then he removes out of the state that nature hath provided, and left it in, he hath mixed his *labour* with, and joined to it something that is his own, and thereby makes it his *property*. It being by him removed from the common state nature hath placed it in, it hath by this *labour* something annexed to it, that excludes the common right of other men: for this *labour* being the unquestionable property of the labourer, no man but he can have a right to what that is once joined to, at least where there is enough, and as good, left in common for others.

16. *See* the entry for "artificial," emphasizing the sense of "workmanship," *in* OXFORD ETYMO-LOGICAL DICTIONARY, with the assistance of G.W. S. Friedrichsen and R. W. Burchfield (C.T. Onions, ed., Oxford Univ. Press 1966). The online etymological dictionary says: "Late 14c., 'made by man' (opposite of *natural*), from O.Fr. *artificial*, from L. *artificialis* 'of or belonging to art,' from *artificium* (see *artifice*). Another early use was in the phrase *artificial day* 'part of

principles, and defining its relationship with *laws* is one of the fundamental dynamics animating twentieth-century legal thought. The issue was
famously debated by Hart and Dworkin in the post-World War II era.[17] In the
wake of a Holocaust that was, in many respects, "legal," these questions seem
inevitable.

Moral rights represent traditions of natural rights, but their embodiment
in the different legislations of the world must still be distinguished from the
philosophy of natural law. The failure to do so, as an American judge observed
in the *Shostakovich* case of 1948,[18] would throw legal situations into chaos.
Clarity and precision, which allow us to know the extent of our legal rights
and obligations, would be lost. As in the *Shostakovich* case, the result is to
inhibit the recognition of moral rights, despite their initial appeal.

A second reason for the controversy over moral rights relates closely to
their complex and various origins, and has to do with the ways in which their
story is told. The diversity of origins means that, correspondingly, there are a
variety of approaches to narrating the history of moral rights. As historians
and lawyers can both affirm, albeit with different reasons in mind, the method
by which a tale is told can lead to very different perceptions of the truth.[19]
Depending on one's perspective, moral rights might truly be French in origin,
or truly, German; they might be inimical to English law, unfairly suppressed
by its development, or latent within it. One thing, at least, is certain: at the
point in copyright's history where we have now arrived, it is important to
build the most complete picture possible of where moral rights come from,
for a better understanding of their current status and potential evolution.

Thirdly, and finally, moral rights are something more than a strictly legal
idea: they express an aesthetic reality. Moral rights transcend the law. Indeed,
as reflected through the prism of complex social movements underlying art,
moral rights are but one color. The breadth of the rights, and the quality

---

the day from sunrise to sunset' (late 14c.). *Artificial insemination* dates from 1897. *Artificial
intelligence* 'the science and engineering of making intelligent machines' was coined in 1956."
See http://www.etymonline.com/index.php?term=artificial (last visited May 2, 2010).

17. *See* Hart's seminal work, H.L.A. HART, THE CONCEPT OF LAW, with Postscript edited by
    Penelope A. Bulloch & Joseph Raz, 2d ed., Clarendon Law Series (Peter Cane, Tony Honoré,
    and Jane Stapleton, eds., Oxford University Press 1994) (1961) (paperback 1997). Dworkin's
    reply was initially developed in R. DWORKIN, TAKING RIGHTS SERIOUSLY (Harvard Univ.
    Press 1977).

18. *Shostakovich v. Twentieth Century-Fox Film Corp.*, 80 N.Y.S.2d 575 (N.Y. Sup. Ct. 1948), *aff'd*,
    87 N.Y.S.2d 430 (N.Y. App. Div. 1949) [*Shostakovich*].

19. *See, for example*, the comments of a distinguished historian of India, Romila Thapar,
    discussing perspectives on history in a post-colonial context. ROMILA THAPAR, A HISTORY
    OF INDIA, VOL. 1, "Introduction" xvii–xxx, and Chapter I, "Perceptions of the Past," 1–36
    (Penguin Books 1966). In the copyright context, see Roberta Rosenthal Kwall, *Copyright and
    the Moral Right: Is an American Marriage Possible?*, 38 (1) VAND L. REV. 1 (1985).

which would lead scholars to call them "interdisciplinary," are noted by Swedish scholar, Stig Strömholm:

> The development leading to *droit moral* as we know it today was anything but silent. It took place to an intensive verbal accompaniment, since what was involved were attitudes, interests and disputes concerning people whose business was words, a *genus irritabile* which could be relied on to make sure that nobody got hanged in silence. The prehistory and history of *droit moral* reflect, above all, the different conceptions successively prevailing in the Western world as to the true nature of literary and artistic creativity. The development of evaluations of that activity is a subject of considerable interest for the general history of ideas, reaching far beyond the normal limits of legal history.[20]

Moral rights rest on the foundation of a special relationship between author and work, a creative reality that has little to do with the law *per se*. In this sense, it must be acknowledged that the presence of moral rights in formal law is something of an anomaly. It is worth noting that the recognition of the moral right in at least one ancient culture saw it develop as an accepted branch of aesthetic theory, while law codes remained silent on the issue.[21] Indeed, concepts of fame and integrity were widely familiar in the ancient world, but the idea of payment for an author's work seems to have been quite radical. In some cultures, including those of Western Europe and India, the connotations of money were frankly negative. Payment for one's work was considered fundamentally incompatible with creativity.[22] Money was associated with the rise of the print industry in Western Europe, and the

---

20. Strömholm IIC, *supra* note 2, at 221.
21. The example is India, and the same could be said of copyright as a whole. The notion of "literary theft" is recognized by a famous writer on aesthetic theory, Anandavardhana. *See* T.S. Krishnamurti, *Copyright—Another View*, 15(3) BULL. COPYRIGHT SOC'Y OF THE U.S.A. 217, 218 (1968) for a description of Anandavardhana's approach. A discussion of Anandavardhana's role in the development of aesthetic philosophy in India can be found in S. PANDIT, AN APPROACH TO THE INDIAN THEORY OF ART AND AESTHETICS 10–11 (Sterling 1977). Pandit identifies his main contribution as the recognition of the special and distinct quality of aesthetic experience. Anandavardhana's famous DHVANYALOKA has been translated by D.H.H. INGALLS, J. M. MASSON & M. V. PATWARDHAN, with an Introduction by D.H.H. INGALLS, THE DHVANYĀLOKA OF ĀNANDAVARDHANA (Harvard Univ. Press 1990).
22. *See* Woodmansee, *supra* note 12. In the society of ancient India, Brahmins were the keepers of knowledge and the teachers charged with its dissemination. Members of other social castes were responsible for bestowing wealth, and even life's necessities, on Brahmins for the service. But this was done out of their own obligation to respect social codes of conduct, and the principle of *dharma*, which can be very roughly translated as "duty." It was not a payment for services rendered, *per se*. The culture persists today, and is doubtless among the reasons copyright piracy is so widely tolerated in India.

onset of an era when the professionalization of the arts gradually replaced the older systems of patronage by which they had previously survived.[23]

As an interesting consequence of their association with aesthetic theories, moral rights suffer from the same kinds of preconceived notions that afflict the arts themselves. In much the same way that characters in fiction can be confused with the writer who created them, or the emotions generated by music focused on the performer, the qualities of the artist are associated with moral rights.[24] Like society's vision of artists, moral rights, too, are infused with stereotypes. They are otherworldly in nature, esoteric, and utterly removed from the crass realities of money— a fatal idea that has made misery of the lives of countless artists! Moral rights certainly represent interests beyond commercial gain—their very purpose is to recognize those interests— but there can be no doubt that the exercise of moral rights has far-reaching economic consequences. The cost of exercising an author's moral rights can be extraordinary for the person who pays it. Although it often remains unspoken, the risk of economic loss is built into the idea. It is surely part of the explanation for the hostility that moral rights can arouse.[25]

Above all, to meet the challenges of moral rights in a digital future, it is essential to paint an accurate picture of their past. This is true of moral rights more than any other aspect of copyright law. Common misconceptions dominate international perspectives on moral rights, and they inhibit a logical and purposive approach to the rights. As one commentator observes, the doctrine of moral rights is

> still relatively new. . . . [M]oral rights were long known in the European continental legal systems but were accepted in the common law countries only recently and grudgingly with the adoption of the Berne Convention. To many, moral rights are in inherent tension with common law concepts of property ownership. As a result, the doctrine has often been misunderstood and adopted

---

23. *See* Woodmansee, *supra* note 12.

24. Ernest Hemingway seemed to live this dream, or nightmare! He is perhaps the most well-known victim, or beneficiary, of this confusion, as much of the reading public identifies him directly with the glamour of characters and situations in his fiction. The assumption that all writing is biographical is not true, unless in the subtle sense that a writer must use whatever raw materials he has, most of which are drawn from experience of one kind or another. For an interesting analysis of Hemingway's case, see Jackson J. Benson, *Ernest Hemingway: The Life as Fiction and the Fiction as Life*, 61(3) Am. Literature 345 (Oct. 1989); this approach, among other things, leads to what Benson calls, "the biographical fallacy." Benson, at 348.

25. Economic considerations are undoubtedly at the heart of Hollywood's objections to moral rights. For a detailed discussion of this issue, see Chapter 7, *infra*, "Twenty-First Century Classics: Film and the Complexities of the Collaborative Work." *See also* the insightful discussion by Stephen Fraser, *Berne, CFTA, NAFTA and GATT: The Implications of Copyright Droit Moral and Cultural Exemptions in International Trade Law*, 18 Hastings Comm. and Ent. L.J. 287 (1996).

in minimalist form in those countries with more developed legal systems, particularly for copyright protection.[26]

History is an invaluable lens through which to view moral rights. A historical perspective can make two important contributions. The first has to do with myth-making. In the legal context, moral rights present an example of a constructed myth. Moral rights are often treated as mythical legal constructions, in both positive and negative senses of the expression. The language of certain modern French commentators falls into mythical rhythms when describing the rationale for moral rights. For example, in his illuminating study, Henri Desbois states:

> The French Law of March 11, 1957 presents, at least, among the flowering of foreign laws which have multiplied over the course of the last ten years, a notable particularity: it has raised to a place of honour "moral rights," by which is expressed the relationship that exists between the author and the work, mirror of his personality.[27]

Jean Escarra affirms, in what Desbois himself describes as a "profession of faith":

> [T]he protection of works of the mind and of the genius of their creators remains the dominant preoccupation of the idealistic country that we wish to remain.[28]

In contrast, English law is informed by its own myth, equally monumental in its own way—the idea that moral rights are incompatible with English notions of copyright and, indeed, that they have always been so. However, a look at English copyright history in the period following the Statute of Anne shows that English judges were well aware of the idea of personal rights of authorship. The rejection of a personal rights approach signified something else—a much-needed solution to a social problem of infinitely greater gravity—censorship. English courts struggled with the prospect of renewed restrictions on freedom of the press coming into being through what were, effectively,

---

26. Anonymous peer review, Oxford University Press, New York (personal communication from Matt Gallaway to the author, Aug. 21, 2008).

27. Henri Desbois, Le Droit d'auteur en France vii (3rd ed. Dalloz 1978). "La loi française du 11 mars 1957 présente, du moins, parmi la floraison des lois étrangères qui se sont multipliées au cours des dix dernières années, une notable particularité: elle a élevé à la place d'honneur le "droit moral", par lequel s'exprime la relation qui existe entre l'auteur et l'oeuvre, miroir de sa personnalité."

28. Quoted in Desbois, *supra* note 27; the original statement may be found in Jean Escarra, *Le projet de loi sur la propriété littéraire et artistique*, RIDA Revue Internationale du Droit d'Auteur) 53 (1954). "[L]a défense des oeuvres de l'esprit et du génie et de leurs créateurs demeure la préoccupation dominante de la nation idéaliste que nous voulons rester . . . ."

powers of censorship exercised by a powerful printers' monopoly, and took appropriate measures to resist that trend.[29] By revealing the ambiguities within these monolithic attitudes, history can help us to understand our own legal traditions in a new way and, perhaps, stimulate our capacity to imagine new kinds of law.

A second reason for considering copyright's history has to do with the recurrence of historical cycles. Our present age—like the ages of all generations past?—is fundamentally characterized by a lack of historical perspective.[30] We believe in the uniqueness of our problems, and the unprecedented qualities of our technology probably serve to increase our egocentrism. However, a closer examination of our circumstances suggests that there is a striking element of continuity in human civilization. Indeed, continuity prevails even in relation to those aspects of society which are directly influenced by technology. Human beings, and human "nature," it would appear, remain remarkably consistent through time.[31]

In the sphere of copyright, the problems of the eighteenth century bear close resemblance to the current scenario. By changing the names of the players, we could as easily be describing the present as the past. When Carla Hesse speaks of the government's "interest in encouraging and empowering both the individual author and the public at large at the expense of [a] . . . corporate monopoly," she could as well be talking about twenty-first century North America or Europe as about the Paris Publishers' and Printers' Guild in 1777.[32] The problems of copyright appear in different forms, but their essence remains the same. Solutions to the problems of the present may lie, deeply buried and waiting to be discovered, within the experiences of the past.

---

29. The seminal cases involved in exploration of the idea of moral rights as part of the British common law tradition—and its eventual rejection are *Millar v. Taylor* (1769) 4 Burr. 2303, 98 Eng. Rep. 201 [*Millar*], and *Donaldson v. Beckett* (1774) 2 Brown's Parl. Cases 129, 1 Eng. Rep. 837 [*Donaldson*]. This history is told in detail by Lyman Ray Patterson in his pioneering work, Lyman Ray Patterson, Copyright in Historical Perspective (Vanderbilt Univ. Press 1968). This moment in copyright history also receives a detailed reconsideration in Ronan Deazley, *Re-Reading Donaldson (1774) in the Twenty-First Century and Why It Matters*, 25(6) Eur. Intell. Prop. Rev. 270 (2003).

30. *But see* Mark Bauerlein, The Dumbest Generation: How the Digital Age Stupefies Young Americans and Jeopardizes Our Future (Or, Don't Trust Anyone Under 30) (Jeremy P. Tarcher/Penguin 2008). Drawing from Mark Bauerlein's analysis, there may be something special about lack of historical perspective in the Digital Age! Bauerlein argues that this occurs through the destruction of reading as a habit, pastime, or source of knowledge.

31. The idea of art as biological necessity is explored in fascinating research by Ellen Dissanayake, Homo Aestheticus: Where Art Comes From and Why (Free Press 1992) (reprinted in paperback, University of Washington Press 1995).

32. Carla Hesse, *Enlightenment Epistemology and the Law of Authorship in Revolutionary France, 1777–1793*, 30 Representations 109–113 (1990).

Building upon an exploration of the past, this chapter seeks to establish a guide to the modern interpretation of moral rights. In particular, the goal is to determine which aspects of moral rights have become standard, either in their countries of origin or at the international level. Based on this analysis, approaches to the protection of moral rights in the digital context will be considered.

The comprehensive definition of moral rights developed in this chapter will specifically confront controversial aspects of the rights. In particular, the nature of moral rights doctrine has led to conventions of interpretation that often seem to emphasize the nicety of legal points at the expense of common sense. This work will argue for clarity and accessibility in the interpretation of the rights, without which, their future life seems highly uncertain. Moral rights share the overall problems of copyright in a digital environment. However sophisticated the legal theory behind them may seem, moral rights must ultimately stand or fall on the practical ability of the public to grasp the idea, and to want it. To some extent, as in the case of copyright more generally, the public must be willing participants in both the recognition and the enforcement of moral rights. The alternative is coercion—through the language of the law, through police intervention, and through technological measures.[33] It is an approach that sits uncomfortably with democratic rhetoric.

A. Principles of Interpretation: Legal Virtuosity and its Limits

Moral rights should maintain a connection to well-defined objectives of policy. The right of attribution provides a simple example. The scope of the attribution right should be determined by our interest in maintaining a connection between a work and the name of its author. If our goal is fundamentally to maintain this connection, it is clear that separating an author's name from his work will be, at least *prima facie*, a violation of the right. This will be the case, regardless of how the separation occurs—whether it involves the attribution of the author's work to someone else, or the attribution of someone else's work to him. The legal nicety of arguing that the attribution right arises when we credit the author's work to someone else's name, but not when we attribute his name to another person's work—on the grounds that the author's relationship

---

33. For an interesting discussion of technological protection measures (TPMs) from the perspective of consumer experience, see Pamela Samuelson & Jason Schultz, *Should Copyright Owners Have to Give Notice of Their Technological Protection Measures?*, 6 J. TELECOMM. & HIGH TECH. L. 42 (2007).

with his own work is not affected by the second transaction—would be a poor fit with this policy. The attribution right seems naturally to extend to the second case, which could also be described as forgery.[34]

In relation to the right of integrity, the question of whether, and to what extent, the destruction of an artwork amounts to a violation of the author's moral rights has been argued on both sides.[35] Once again, a reevaluation based on policy considerations may be worth the attempt. If we consider the purpose of the right of integrity, we can see that it has two distinct objectives: the preservation of cultural heritage, and the protection of an author's reputation. The relationship between the reputation and integrity interests is clear, but, rather like a marriage between equals, the relationship does not define either party completely. Indeed, each could exist independently of the other. A bridge between them is built by the language of the Berne Convention.

The plain meaning of the term "integrity" indicates a focus on the condition of the work; the language of "reputation" points to the author. It therefore seems clear that the interpretation of the integrity principle probably should extend to the prohibition of destruction. To argue, instead, that destruction would not qualify as a violation of the right of integrity on the grounds that there is no modification of the work *per se*, does not support the policy of maintaining the integrity of a cultural work. If we follow the language of the Berne Convention, which states that damage to a work must affect the author's reputation negatively before it can be considered a violation of the integrity right, we are led into a further difficulty. The mistreatment of a work must be shown to have a negative impact on the author's reputation. In the case of destruction, however, the work itself ceases to exist. Therefore—so the argument goes—the state of the work can no longer affect the author's reputation at all.[36] It is a subtle point of legal interpretation. However, two alternatives should be considered.

---

34. Von Lewinski, *supra* note 4.
35. In fact, as Ricketson notes, a proposal to prohibit destruction explicitly was proposed by the Hungarian delegation to the Brussels revision conference of the Berne Convention. Ricketson notes that it "was not adopted because some delegates thought that this did not relate to the author's moral interests. But the conference also stated its moral support for the principle, which has never since been pursued. *See* Ricketson, *supra* note 2, at para. 8.109.
36. The arguments are given a helpful overview by Irini Stamatoudi, *Moral Rights of Authors in England: The Missing Emphasis on the Role of Creators*, 8(4) Intell. Prop. Q. 478, 482–83 (1997) [Stamatoudi, *Moral Rights of Authors in England*]. Surprisingly, there is even a French precedent to the effect that unauthorized modification of a work will damage its integrity, but destruction will not. *See* Stamatoudi at 483; *see also L'affaire des fresques de Juvisy*, Tribunal Civ. Versailles (1932) D. 487; Cour d'Appel de Paris (1934) D. 385. Interestingly, Stamatoudi notes, citing the scholarship of Adolf Dietz, that "the opinion which seems to be gaining ground today is that which considers destruction the ultimate form of distortion." As Dietz points out, "[destruction] depriv[es] the author of the authentic means of proof for his artistic and professional skills and self conscience." In other words, the destruction of a work may diminish the professional image and standing of the author by eliminating one of his

First, the argument that destroying a work does not damage an author's reputation is questionable. Destruction of a work may very well affect the author's reputation, because it affects his body of work as a whole.[37] As this author has observed, in a phrase adopted by the High Court of Delhi:

> Of course, destruction of a work can prejudice an author's reputation by reducing the volume or quality of his creative corpus, . . . [although] this argument does not appear to be strongly persuasive in international copyright circles.[38]

Secondly, regardless of the impact of destruction on an author's reputation, it is clear that the integrity principle seeks to protect the work. At the very least, this leads to the consideration that countries which do not employ the Berne link between reputation and integrity in their legislative formulae, and prefer to define the integrity right as a form of protection against the abuse of a work, should definitely prohibit destruction. Current French law, and early Indian law, are two cases in point.[39]

This analysis of the integrity principle leaves unanswered the important practical issue of how to define damage to a work. Should subjective or objective standards be applied, or some combination of both? Henri Desbois' assessment brings out the fundamental characteristics of French law:

> An individualist conception animates the law in its entirety, and particularly, fundamental provisions of a general kind, such as Article 1, which specifies that an

---

creations. Especially in cases where the reputation of an author depends on a limited number of creations, the destruction of even one of them, may substantially affect his status." Stamatoudi at 483 (footnotes omitted). For more recent support for the position that destruction does not violate an artist's integrity, see von Lewinski, *supra* note 4.

37. For a summary of the positions on this issue, see Mira T. Sundara Rajan, *Moral Rights and the Protection of Cultural Heritage:* Amar Nath Sehgal v. Union of India, 10(1) Int'l J. Cultural Prop. 79 (2001) [Sundara Rajan, *Amar Nath Sehgal*]. This article informs the decision of the Delhi High Court and is quoted in paragraph 41 of the case: *Amar Nath Sehgal v. Union of India*, (30)PTC 253 (Delhi High Court 2005) [*Sehgal*].

38. Sundara Rajan, *Amar Nath Sehgal, supra* note 37, at 83. *See Sehgal* para. 56: "There would therefore be urgent need to interpret Section 57 of the Copyright Act, 1957 in its wider amplitude to include destruction of a work of art, being the extreme form of mutilation, since by reducing the volume of the authors creative corpus it affects his reputation prejudicially as being actionable under said section. Further, in relation to the work of an author, subject to the work attaining the status of a modern national treasure, the right would include an action to protect the integrity of the work in relation to the cultural heritage of the nation."

39. CPI, *supra* note 3, art. L121-1; Indian Copyright Act 1957, Act 14 of 1957, sec. 57; the Act is published by the Government of India, *available at* http://copyright.gov.in/Documents/CopyrightRules1957.pdf (last visited May 2, 2010) [Indian Copyright Act]. The Act is available in many online versions, some of which are out of date; for example, the pre-1994 section 57 provisions can still be found on the website of the Commonwealth Legal Information Institute, http://www.commonlii.org/in/legis/num_act/ca1957133/ (last visited May 2, 2010).

author enjoys a right in [his] intangible property, exclusive and opposable against the world, *from the sole fact of its creation*. . . . An explanation like this would have immediate repercussions for the structure and function of the integrity right: if the economics of authors' rights were arranged for the collective interest, from the perspective of society, not every alteration would be condemned, because more than one attempt at improvement, to which the author claims to be opposed, has, for an impartial judge, a beneficial effect and improves the quality of the work.

The formula of Article 1 cuts these errors short: it is enough that the author has impressed the stamp of his personality on the work, that, in other words, he has created it, for him to be entitled to protection. His work demands to be respected as it is, such as he has wanted it to be, because, through the creative act, it is the personality of the creator which receives help and protection.[40]

If the fundamental objective of French law is, as described by Desbois, the protection of the author's individual rights, the approach to the integrity right is informed by a "subjective" standard of proof as to what constitutes damage to a work, based on the author's personal experience. The author's own judgment is the preferred standard. This approach to the integrity right is essentially a human rights approach. It is not, by any means, the only possible approach to the integrity right—"objective" standards of proof could be applied to an open-ended integrity right, as well, requiring that objective proof of damage to reputation be offered. But the legal culture that gives pre-eminence to an author's rights as rights of an individual creator is also disposed to recognize his or her own right to judge damage to the work. Experience shows that legislative treatments which restrict the integrity right to cases of damage to reputation are accompanied by requirements for "objective" proof of that damage. In these cases, the approach is not fundamentally driven by a focus on the author as a creative individual, but it takes into account what Desbois would call "l'intérêt de la collectivité"—the collective interest, or, in American translation, the public interest.

---

40. Desbois, *supra* note 27, at 538–39, para. 449:

"la conception individualiste anime la loi tout entière et singulièrement les dispositions fondamentales, d'ordre général, telles que l'article 1er qui précise que l'auteur jouit d'un droit de propriété incorporelle, exclusif et opposable à tous, *du seul fait de sa création*. . . . Une telle explication exercerait une répercussion immédiate sur la structure et la fonction du droit au respect: si l'économie des droits d'auteur était aménagéé dans l'intérêt de la collectivité, dans une perspective sociale, toute altération ne serait pas condamnable, car plus d'une retouche, à laquelle l'auteur prétend s'opposer, a pour un esprit impartial un effet bienfaisant et améliore la qualité de l'oeuvre.

la formule de l'article 1er coupe court à ces errements: il suffit que l'auteur ait imprimé le cachet de sa personnalité à l'oeuvre, *qu'en d'autres termes il l'ait crée,* pour que protection lui soit due. Son oeuvre appelle le respect telle qu'elle est, telle qu'il a voulu qu'elle soit, car, à travers la création, c'est la personnalité du créateur qui reçoit aide et protection."

The Berne approach, which undertakes an implicit balancing act between the principles of integrity and reputation, involves a kind of "doublespeak."[41] Desbois does not hesitate to point out that the Berne formula is not so much a guarantee of authors' rights as "a means of satisfying the aspirations of the group, whether good or bad."[42] It is a valid policy choice. But if reputation outweighs integrity, the right should be called a right of reputation; it should not pretend to accomplish anything more than the protection of an author's reputation from harm, a kind of quasi-defamation principle. Interestingly, this approach was taken in the Russian legislation of 1993: the Copyright Act recognized "the right to the protection of the work, including the title thereof, against any distortion or other derogatory act liable to prejudice [the author's] honor or dignity (right to the protection of the author's reputation)."[43] The irony, however, is that this right of reputation represented a lower level of legislative recognition for the integrity right than at any time in the Russian past. While reputation had powerful connotations in the post-Soviet context, the term still represented a move away from very strong recognition of the integrity principle, framed simply as the "inviolability" of the work, in early incarnations of Russian law.[44]

These reflections suggest that the time may have come for a less legalistic interpretation of moral rights. Moral rights are fundamentally concerned with social issues beyond the ordinary bounds of copyright relations. For this reason, at least, it may be appropriate to focus, not on the subtleties of legislative language, but on the policies that the language seeks to express. Above all, no interpretation of moral rights can afford to ignore the sensitive issues exposed by new technologies. In establishing a guide to interpretation, this analysis will be informed by the reality of digital technology, their ultimate testing ground.

This line of argument leaves us with one awkward question: does an author have the right to destroy his own work? The individualist theory of French

---

41. This term is invoked in an Orwellian sense; Orwell himself focused on the yet more frightening "doublethink," which means simultaneously holding two conflicting beliefs. *See* George Orwell, Nineteen Eighty-Four, (Secker & Warburg 1949).

42. Desbois, *supra* note 27.

43. The 1993 Act is still available online, http://en.wikisource.org/wiki/Russian_Federation._Law_on_Copyright_and_Neighboring_Rights (last visited May 2, 2010). *See* Sundara Rajan, *Copyright and Creative Freedom*, *supra* note 7, at 173–83.

44. Interestingly, the principle of "inviolability" was well-established in Soviet law. Given the framework of Soviet publishing, where the appearance of works was effectively controlled by government, the right of inviolability had bittersweet overtones; see Sundara Rajan, *Copyright and Creative Freedom*, *supra* note 7, at 97–100. In the post-socialist period, restoring the reputations of those maligned by the Soviet government was a preoccupation; but Russian legislators could have found ways of recognizing reputation without undermining the principle of inviolability of a work. In the post-Soviet environment, Russia perhaps needed both rights; it chose to uphold only one.

law, characterized by Desbois as near-absolute, suggests that he would. This result maintains the purity of the subjective theory underlying French law; it is the ultimate form of acceptance for the author's verdict on his own work. But from the perspectives of both reputation and integrity, this result creates a sense of dismay. And the destruction of works that could be valuable or important represents a tremendous loss to society. An author may or may not be in the best position to judge his own work—for reasons from perfectionism to privacy, an author might destroy work of excellent quality. This case is not as unusual as it might seem at first glance: composer Johannes Brahms is known to have done both.

B. Origins of the Doctrine

It is widely acknowledged that moral rights originated in Continental Europe. The development of the doctrine saw it divide into two major streams, emanating from France and Germany. Strömholm refers to moral rights as a product of

> the strange interaction which takes place between, on the one hand, *French practical solutions*—with a weak or non-existent theoretical basis—and, on the other hand, German theorizing, which develops, for a long time, with no or hardly any support in legislation and case law.[45]

What is perhaps less well-known, and more interesting, is the fact that the idea of an author's moral right received early recognition in English law. Within the space of five years and two historic decisions in the mid-eighteenth century, the concept was raised and rejected out of political and practical concerns.[46] Contrary to the popular belief among English lawyers, there is nothing inherently inimical about the English law attitude to moral rights—except that, when the rights eventually found their way back into English law, it was as a French import that was viewed with no small degree of concern for cultural incompatibility.

France and Germany—the German-speaking principalities of the nineteenth century, and Prussia in particular[47]—are usually considered the heartland of the doctrine. In fact, there can be no doubt that the idea of moral rights was widely dispersed throughout both Western and Eastern Europe in the course of the nineteenth century, if not before. Italy's copyright law is generally based on

---

45. Strömholm IIC, *supra* note 2, at 225.
46. *Millar* and *Donaldson, supra* note 29.
47. Prussian Law of 1794. *See* Hesse, *supra* note 32, at 110; *see also* Woodmansee, *supra* note 12.

personality rights, and classic French copyright scholar, Georges Michaélidès-Nouaros observes that, "Roman law recognized and developed respect for the personality of the individual [author] in all its expansiveness."[48] Copyright in Russia was based on early recognition of the author as a legal personality, first described in a statute of 1828, and moral rights were explicitly included in the landmark revision of copyright law that occurred in 1911.[49] Elena Muravina does not hesitate to call moral rights, "the fundamental principle of Russian copyright protection."[50]

Notwithstanding their importance in European law, it should be recognized that moral rights also have a significant place in the histories of the world's legal systems beyond Europe. This is an essential part of the richness of the doctrine. Indeed, one of the keys to understanding the subsequent development of moral rights in modern times lies in a consideration of why the doctrine has been successfully absorbed into legal cultures and traditions that are profoundly different from those where it is said to "originate." Informed by this analysis, an assessment of the "modern" doctrine of moral

---

48. *See* Georges Michaélidès-Nouaros, Le droit moral de l'auteur: Étude de droit français, de droit comparé et de droit international, para. 3 (Librairie Arthur Rousseau 1935): "Le Droit romain a reconnu et développé le respect de la personnalité de l'individu dans toute son ampleur." He continues: "La protection de la personnalité a eu lieu par l'extension de l'injuria. Les Pandectes lui consacrent un titre spécial–Dig. 47.10: De injuriis et de famosis libellis; il en est de même des Institutes de Justinien . . . ." The quotation is also valuable in indicating the common origin of moral rights and torts such as "injurious falsehood," slander, or libel, which effectively serve to protect moral rights in the United States and, to some extent, in other common law jurisdictions. In her recent work, Elizabeth Adeney quotes the interesting comment of an Italian lawyer—"Roman law knew nothing of that law that is called copyright. But it fully recognized the droit moral." *See* Elizabeth Adeney, The Moral Rights of Authors and Performers An International and Comparative Analysis: New Edition, para. 1.01 (Oxford Univ. Press 2006); she cites the statement from the Actes de la conference reunie a Rome 316, 7 mai au 2 juin 1928 (Bureau Internationale pour la Protection des Oeuvres Littéraires et Artistiques 1929). The 1928 revision conference of the *Berne Convention for the Protection of Literary and Artistic Works* was a moment of unsurpassed significance in the history of moral rights: it introduced the text of moral rights provisions into the world's first, and most important, international treaty on copyright law. *See* Strömholm IIC, *supra* note 2, at 221: Strömholm seems right to point out the absurdity of trying to find an ancient antecedent to moral rights.

49. *See* Sundara Rajan, *Copyright and Creative Freedom, supra* note 7, at 82–85. *See also* the Russian Copyright Act 1911, Art 2: by an interesting irony, the 1828 law was a censorship statute. *See* Vladimir Gsovski, Soviet Civil Law: Private Rights and Their Background under the Soviet Regime 606 (H.E. Yntema, ed., Michigan Legal Studies Series, Univ. of Michigan Law School 1948); Gsovski comments that copyright "was conceived [in the provisions of 1828] as the exclusive right of the author or translator to publication and sale of his work during his lifetime. . . . This principle of copyright as the right of the author (droit d'auteur, Urheberrecht) was maintained by the imperial laws and taken over by the [S]oviet legislation when protection of copyright was restored under the Soviet regime."

50. *See* Elena Muravina, *Copyright Transactions in Russia, Part II, "Post-Glasnost Days,"* 18 New Matter 25, 26 (1993).

rights suggests that it has moved away from its origins in interesting ways, and may move yet further under the pressure of cultural trends. In particular, it is worth exploring the transformational potential of authors' moral rights in a digital world.

Nevertheless, the special place claimed by France and Germany in the history of moral rights is important. While they are both supportive of the moral rights concept, the two countries also represent two, somewhat distinct, systems of thought. In particular, each situates moral rights differently in relation to the broader framework protecting the economic rights of the author. The "dualist" system of France theorizes that moral rights and economic rights are two distinct types of rights, leading to different practical consequences. In contrast, German "monism" suggests that the two rights are two sides of a single coin, the links between an author's economic and moral interests being inseparable in theory and practice. These two ways of thinking about the relationship between moral and economic rights not only affect the current interpretation of the law in these countries; they also have implications for copyright and moral rights reform, particularly in countries where the rights represent an innovation in local law. The choice of monist or dualist approaches to moral rights has legal and practical implications far beyond the courtliness of a Franco-Prussian exchange.

C. Moral Rights at Home: France

Moral rights are a French notion. The idea that they originated in French law is widely accepted by legal historians, with the existence of a legal principle of attribution being affirmed in a French court of law as early as 1813.[51] This legal history is, of necessity, incomplete. Robert Merges identifies the earliest modern copyright statutes as originating in fifteenth-century Venice.[52] Is it relevant that the moral rights idea makes an appearance in the Indian aesthetic theory of Anandavardhana, going as far back as the ninth century?[53] Strömholm affirms that moral rights principles were familiar to the ancients,

---

51. Citing the legal treatise of Pardessus, and a landmark French decision, Strömholm argues, "If we want to fix a definite date for the earliest manifestations of the legal view which rejects the most far-reaching consequences of the doctrine of intellectual property and recognizes that despite any transfer of his economic rights the author retains a moral right to his work, the year 1814 would probably be the strongest candidate." Strömholm IIC, *supra* note 2, at 217.

52. *See* Thomas Paris, Le droit d'auteur: l'idéologie et le système 105. Préface de Jean-Daniel Reynaud, Sciences sociales et sociétés, collection dirigée par D. Desjeux (Presses universitaires de France 2002). The point is noted by Michaélidès-Nouaros in his useful overview of moral rights history, Georges Michaélidès-Nouaros, Le droit moral de l'auteur: Étude de droit français, de droit comparé et de droit international 13, para. 4 (Paris: Librairie Arthur Rousseau 1935).

53. *See* note 21.

whereas the Middle Ages, for reasons having to do with the decline of authorship itself, were a time of stagnation.[54] Art flourished, but in a context dominated by religion, and anonymity was the prize of the artist.[55]

Even within Europe, it is evident that the rights were known in what is now Central and Eastern Europe throughout the history of this region. There was strong and consistent recognition for moral rights even in a society like Russia's, whose absolutist government fiercely resisted concessions to individual rights.[56] The recognition of moral rights is undoubtedly linked with the importance of authorship in Russian culture.[57]

Happily, research reveals significant traces of this kaleidoscopic past to the outside observer, but the details remain inevitably shrouded by time and distance.

Strömholm observes:

> Those legal scholars who have written about *droit moral* have . . . consciously or unconsciously [been] dominated by the ancient juristic notion that law, likewise, improves with age: *prior tempore, potior jure* . . . .[58]

The difficult area of moral rights is further obscured by the absurdity of the twin propositions, "it has always existed," and "we discovered it first." As this very brief survey of the world's legal traditions shows, the claims of any one to be the "first" to discover moral rights may represent a meaningless contest. The nature of their past, characterized by informality and even imprecision, provides an important clue towards a more realistic appreciation of moral rights. The concept emerged through a process of evolution, and its present form reflects those beginnings. As Thomas Paris observes:

> The origin of copyright is uncertain, because it is diluted. In the first place, the system was not conceived as a law fulfilling a precise objective. On the

54. STIG STRÖMHOLM, Le droit moral de l'auteur en droit allemand, français et scandinave avec un aperçu de l'évolution internationale–Etude de droit comparé, t. 1, PREMIÈRE PARTIE: L'EVOLUTION HISTORIQUE ET LE MOUVEMENT INTERNATIONAL (P.A. Norstedt & Söners Förlag 1967) [Strömholm 1967, vol. 1].

55. *See* SNEH PANDIT, AN APPROACH TO THE INDIAN THEORY OF ART AND AESTHETICS 134 (Sterling Publishers 1977); he quotes from the pioneering writer on Indian art and aesthetics, Ananda Coomaraswamy.

56. *See generally* Sundara Rajan, *Copyright and Creative Freedom, supra* note 7.

57. *See, e.g.,* Sundara Rajan, *Copyright and Creative Freedom, supra* note 7, at 150–86; *see also* Mira T. Sundara Rajan, *Copyright and Free Speech in Transition: A New International Perspective, in* COPYRIGHT AND FREE SPEECH: COMPARATIVE AND INTERNATIONAL ANALYSES 315 (J. Griffiths & U. Suthersanen eds., Oxford Univ. Press 2005), and Susan Eva Heuman, *Perspectives on Legal Culture in Prerevolutionary Russia, in* REVOLUTION IN LAW: CONTRIBUTIONS TO THE DEVELOPMENT OF SOVIET LEGAL THEORY, 1917–1938, 3 (Piers Beirne, ed., M.E. Sharpe 1990).

58. Strömholm IIC, *supra* note 2, at 221.

contrary, it was forged out of timely decisions made in response to particular problems. Accordingly, it emerged locally. Moreover, it did not appear from the beginning in its current form but acquired its different components bit by bit.[59]

There are many reasons why French tradition is important to moral rights, the antiquity of the law being but one. There are at least two other reasons for referring to French law, particularly in a study of moral rights that is offered in the unfriendly "foreign tongue" of English. First, the intricacy of moral rights in modern French law makes them one of the most comprehensive sets of provisions on moral rights in the world. In this sense, they are model pro-visions—worthy of study and critique by every jurisdiction in the world interested in the moral rights concept. Secondly, the moral rights doctrine found its way into English law, like so much else, via France—a fact that is of crucial significance to the common law world.

The translation of France's *droit moral* into the English "moral right" is not fortuitous. In English, morality and law stand in a relationship of inevitable tension.[60] In French, the sense of a *droit moral* is much simpler, invoking rights of a personal, intellectual, or even spiritual nature. The use of the word "spiritual" is sadly ambiguous in the twenty-first century, but it still conveys the sense of a relationship beyond the purely, or merely, commercial.

1. An Unresolved Past: Moral Rights and Revolutionary Ideals

In France, the idea that authors enjoyed individual rights in their work emerged in a period of flux surrounding the cultural shock wave of the French Revolution. The twin concepts of moral rights and literary property, the term by which economic rights were then known, emerged from different legisla-tive directions, and on either side of the Revolution.

Moral rights can be traced to a series of Book Trade Regulations in 1777, which introduced the concept of an author's right in his works for the first

---

59. Paris, *supra* note 52, at 105. "L'origine du droit d'auteur est flue, car diluée. D'une part, le système n'a pas été conçu comme une loi répondant à un but précis. Au contraire, il s'est forgé à partir de décisions ponctuelles prises en réponse à des problèmes singuliers. Il a donc émergé localement. D'autre part, il n'est pas apparu dès l'origine sous sa forme actuelle mais a acquis ses différentes composantes petit à petit."

60. This point is illustrated by the great legal theory debate of the twentieth century between H.L.A. Hart and Ronald Dworkin; *see supra* note 17.

time.[61] The regulations were an attempt to break the publishing monopoly consolidated by the Paris Publishers' and Printers' Guild, which covered not only the printing of individual texts, but also extended to "whole areas of knowledge."[62] By recognizing the author, Hesse concludes that the French administration hoped to "encourag[e] . . . and empower [. . .] both the individual author and the public at large at the expense of . . . corporate monopoly."[63]

But, in contrast to the English experience surrounding the Statute of Anne, the goal was not to liberate publishing from Sovereign control. On the contrary, the author would now become directly responsible to the State for the substance of his writings. As Hesse points out:

> The creation of the author by the absolutist state was the product of a political initiative within the royal administration rather than a result of commercial protest, and it had the explicit purpose of consolidating state control over the form, content, and means of disseminating knowledge by removing the publisher as intermediary between the state and the author. Now the author would be directly accountable to the Crown and its laws for the publication of knowledge.[64]

The ease of censoring publication through a printers' monopoly might be greater; but the advantages of making authors personally responsible are also apparent. It is rare for individual authors to have power enough to confront the state—even international "celebrities" such as Soviet writers, Boris Pasternak and Alexander Solzhenitsyn, could not succeed—and the threat of violence holds sway over individuals as it cannot work against groups.

Despite the political logic of the move, recognition for individual authors was also a reflection of the intellectual currents of the time, and laid the foundation for a copyright principle based on the author's rights as a creative individual. Recognition of individual rights of authorship is a prerequisite to the recognition of moral rights; it would also be fair to say that, once authors' rights are recognized as individual rights rather than property-based interests alone, moral rights are implicit in the concept. Individual rights are a sort of proto-concept underlying moral rights.

---

61. Hesse, *supra* note 32, at 111. The six royal decrees on the book trade were issued on August 30, 1777; see *infra* note 65. Hesse observes that "The first legal recognition of the author in France can be dated quite precisely to the six royal decrees on the book trade of August 30, 1777. Prior to this date there was no formal legal recognition of the author or his relation to his text" (footnotes omitted).
62. Hesse, *supra* note 32, at 112.
63. Hesse, *supra* note 32, at 113.
64. Hesse, *supra* note 32, at 114.

Interestingly, the last of the 1777 Regulations defines a right that may represent the first codification of moral rights in France. The right is a right of first publication, or disclosure, which later came to be known in French law as the *droit de divulgation*. The concept of disclosure serves to recognize that the author has a right to determine the circumstances in which his own work will first appear before the public, and it relates particularly to unpublished works.[65] The related provision in the Decree allows an author to enjoy a permanent right, or "*privilége*," to sell his own work "*chez lui*," in his own home. As is characteristic of moral rights, this right is permanent—it continues to exist "*à perpétuité*"—but the decision to cede this privilege to a bookseller will remove its perpetual character, and make it a right that lasts only for the lifetime of the author. Article V of the Decree states:

> Every author who obtains the privilege of his work in his own name shall have the right to sell it on his own premises, without being allowed, for any reason, to sell or to negotiate the sale of other books; and shall retain this privilege, for himself and his heirs, in perpetuity, provided that he does not cede it to any bookseller; in which case, the term of the privilege shall, by the sole reason of its transfer, be reduced to the lifetime of the author.[66]

The recognition of the individual author served a political purpose; but the question of an acceptable logic for the new measures in fluctuating historical times remained. The debate gained in intensity during the years following the Decrees, and Hesse traces the development of two clear positions on literature—the rights of individual genius, as described and defended by Diderot, and the importance of the public domain, championed by de Condorcet.[67] The circulation of these ideas was interrupted by the onset of the Revolution. This brutal rupture with the past also involved a break with the pre-existing

---

65. See Claude Colombet, *Grands principes du droit d'auteur et des droits voisins dans le monde: Approche de droit comparé* 39–40 (2d ed. UNESCO–Libraire de la *Cour de cassation* 1992). He notes the distinction between *divulgation* and *publication* clarified in Spanish law; in the digital environment, the two concepts tend to merge, and are generally treated in this work under the single term, "disclosure." Colombet also emphasises the role of "secrecy"— potentially "trade secrets"—in the United States.

66. Tout auteur qui obtiendra en son nom le privilége de son ouvrage, aura le droit de le vendre chez lui, sans qu'il puisse, sous aucun prétexte, vendre ou négocier d'autres livres; et jouira de son privilége, pour lui et ses hoirs, à perpétuité, pourvu qu'il ne le rétrocède à aucun libraire; au quel cas, la durée du privilége sera, par le seul fait de la cession, réduite à celle de la vie de l'auteur. The ancient spelling of "privilége," rather than the modern "privilège," is transcribed from the text of the Decree itself. French Decree of August 30, 1777, on the duration of privileges, Paris (1777), Citation: French Decree of August 30, 1777, on the duration of privileges (1777) (Source: Bibliothèque nationale de France: Mss. Fr. 22073 no. 146), Primary Sources on Copyright (1450–1900), L. Bently & M. Kretschmer (eds.), *available at* http://www.copyrighthistory.org.

67. Hesse, *supra* note 32, at 114–17.

culture of publication. When the Revolution sought a new model on which to build a modern publishing regime, all of these ideas were at the disposal of reformers. The choice was a compromise solution that embraced aspects of both of these views, superficially contradictory though they might seem.[68]

Le Chapelier's law of 1791 represented the first attempt to consolidate the cultural transition into a new regime. The solution to the problem of cultural chaos, experienced by authors as a descent into "piracy," was literary property.[69] However, the recognition of economic rights of authorship in the law of 1791 served a specific purpose. This conceptual tour-de-force meant to bring about the resolution of a decades-long debate over the use of dramatic texts in France. In particular, the goal was to break the monopoly of the *Comédie française*, France's national theater, on the production of classic French plays.[70] Recognition of an individual right of authorship was a means to this end.

Le Chapelier's law of 1791 codified the notion of literary property for the first time. Although it did so in the specific context of dramatic works, the principle on which it was based was subsequently extended to other areas of intellectual and creative work. As such, the law provided the basic model for the regulation of publishing in the post-Revolutionary era. Le Chapelier's law was generalized in a new statute, the Decree on the Property Rights of Authors of July 19, 1793.[71] The 1793 legislation created a general right of literary property, to be exercised by authors in all genres as an exclusive right over their work, for a limited time: the lifetime of the author and ten years after his death.[72]

By an interesting irony, the new laws, while bringing legal substance to the concept of literary property, actually reduced the practical extent of authors' rights. As Gregory S. Brown points out:

> The limited dimension of the authors' victory has been little appreciated due to La Harpe's and Le Chapelier's broad rhetorical framing of the authors' objectives as the "liberty" of "all men of letters" and the abolition of "exclusive privilege" on behalf of "the public." These claims, politically effective in 1790–91,

---

68. In fact, copyright policy should aim at a natural reconciliation between these two important, social interests. *See* Sundara Rajan, *Moral Rights in the Public Domain, supra* note 5.

69. *See* Hesse, *supra* note 32, at 127–28.

70. *See* Jane C. Ginsburg, *A Tale of Two Copyrights*, 64(5) Tulane L. Rev. 991, 1005–09 (1990).

71. *Décret relatif aux droits de propriété des auteurs d'écrits en tout genre, compositeurs de musique, peintres et dessinateurs* (L. 15, 139; B. 32, 147; Mon. de 20 juill. 1793. Rapp. Lakanal), 19 au 24 juillet 1793; *see* Brown, *supra* note 12, at 138.

72. *But see* Hesse, *supra* note 32, at 128: she mentions that the ten-year term *post-mortem auctoris* is for the benefit of both heirs and publishers, suggesting that the author, in keeping with pre-Revolutionary practice, would normally assign his work to a publisher on a permanent basis. She goes on to comment that, with the new law, "the cultural capital of the Old Regime was definitively remanded from the private hands of heirs and publishers into the public domain," because the classic authors had all been dead for more than ten years.

have confused the issue for historians, many of whom have not recognized that the law did not grant the primary concern of authors . . . These writers had not sought *droits d'auteur* in the sense of "human rights" but instead wanted to redefine their own literary sociability as the pursuit of the public good.[73]

The point is an important one, because it shows how the authors' perceptions of their own interests were, in a sense, co-opted by the rhetoric of the French Revolution. But Brown's analysis would also benefit from a consideration of its immediate context. The law of 1791 followed upon a period of regulatory chaos, and, measured against this, the extent of the rights it conferred upon authors, as well as the novelty of those rights, was significant. The post-Revolutionary scheme for authors offered less practical protection than the pre-Revolutionary Book Decrees. But the rights that were offered worked on a new conceptual footing—a human rights basis for individual rights of authorship—and did not come accompanied by the shadow of retribution by the state.

The history of moral rights in France is noteworthy in two ways. First, the doctrine emerged informally, through judges' pronouncements, and continued to develop in the same way for centuries. As such, it is an ancient doctrine; but the first mention of authors' rights *per se* in French legislation occurs at the relatively late date, vis-à-vis English law, of 1777.[74] By this time, English law had already considered and rejected the concept of moral rights, and it did so by analyzing and testing the relatively ancient Statute of Anne of 1709/10.[75]

The complexity of the French concept in the Revolutionary environment is striking. Carla Hesse discusses the opposing ideological forces that shaped the emerging concept of authorship and the law that was to contain it. In doing so, she arrives at a key insight: there is a fundamental tension at the heart of copyright between the natural rights rationale for authors' rights and corresponding copyright notions of property, ownership, and public interest—what she calls "an epistemologically impure and unstable legal synthesis."[76] From the very beginning, the French view of copyright was

---

73. Ironically, the adoption of the new law actually signified a scaling back of authors' rights in the practical sense of a reduced term of protection, and the consequent loss of benefits to the authors' heirs. *See* Brown, *supra* note 12, at 138–39, and, in particular, his discussion of Carla Hesse's analysis of the 1777 Book Trade regulations, at 138.

74. See Hesse, *supra* note 32, at 111–14.

75. See the *Millar* and *Donaldson* cases, *supra* note 29.

76. Hesse points out:

    Contrary to Foucault's Diderotist interpretation, the revolutionary legislation actually reflected not one but both sides of the Enlightenment debate, effecting an epistemologically impure and unstable legal synthesis that combined an instrumentalist notion of the public good with a theory of authorship based upon natural rights. Precisely because of this legal instability, the regime by which the public exchange of ideas was regulated would be challenged and renegotiated repeatedly over the course of the revolutionary

driven by competing policy rationales—a fact that is apparent in most copyright systems.[77] In particular, according to Hesse, the concept of authors' rights that emerged in eighteenth-century France "combined an instrumentalist notion of the public good with a theory of authorship based upon natural rights." Reconciling these two interests—balancing the public interest against the prerogatives of authors—remains a key policy issue in copyright law. The modern version of this debate is a conflict between the rights of copyright *owners* and the public interest, although the language it adopts is, crucially, the language of authorship.[78]

Interestingly, Brown comments that the dynamics surrounding French Revolutionary copyright have colored our appreciation of the public domain, by distorting the authors' vision of their own relationship to the public:

> In the longer term, this rhetoric has led to a misunderstanding of public domain as it was conceived in 1790. Intended as a claim made by authors about their own position as advocates for a shared cultural heritage, public domain became instead a value-neutral category to which commercial intermediaries—in this case, theater managers—would lay claim and thereby situate themselves as arbiters between the authors and the public.[79]

In other words, the Romantics, too, cared about public access to knowledge as well as the recognition of authors. The simultaneous recognition of both principles led to conceptual instability in the law, but it was also an inevitable result of practical concerns about knowledge and its place in society. In early French law, the fundamental concern was to liberate copyright from the restrictions of corporate control, or sovereign censorship. The same conflict had been played out in England, nearly a century earlier, but with different results. The French solution was to exalt authorship; the English, to exalt law, and, in particular, to affirm the integrity, and impregnability, of the Statute of Anne.

But these solutions were never definitive. At best, one stream of theory or policy can dominate others for a time. The nature of copyright is such that it involves diverse interests; it is an area of law that is deeply intertwined with

---

period. The legal history of French authorship thus suggests that Foucault's essay requires a historical revision: the central mechanism of the modern regime of knowledge, as it emerged from the epistemology of the French Enlightenment, was unstable from its very beginnings.

See Hesse, *supra* note 32, at 130.

77. *See* the discussion of English copyright history, *infra* section E.: the same was clearly true of English copyright law.

78. *See* the discussion of *Millar v. Taylor* and *Donaldson v. Beckett*, *supra* note 29. The strategy of using "authorship" to promote the prerogatives of ownership is as old as the 1700s.

79. Brown, *supra* note 12, at 139.

social phenomena, which are constantly changing. While Hesse draws attention to the dark side of this reality—"impur[ity]" and "[in]stab[ility]" at the level of concepts—there is also a bright side. Copyright, despite the monolithic term, is built upon many interconnected concepts; it may therefore have the potential to adapt to a great variety of social circumstance.

First codification marks an important point of recognition, transforming the rights from purely customary to formalized interests. In the case of French authors' rights, the moment of initial codification was one of powerful coincidence. Authors' rights were defined as the French Revolution ignited, and the concept of individual rights of authorship was part of a much larger movement in which the idea of human rights was first articulated in the Western world, embodied in the epoch-making "Declaration of the Rights of Man."[80] Moral rights were not identified as such in the Revolutionary document, but the recognition of individual authorship laid the foundation for moral rights to emerge. The recognition of a right to disclose one's unpublished work is framed in terms that outline the shape of moral rights. It is ironic, but encouraging, to think that human rights emerged from a context of violence and decay—that moral rights, similarly, were born out of oppression and represented a reaction to it.

The timing is also crucial from another point of view: although France was a pioneer in recognizing moral rights, the country was a relative latecomer to formal codification of them. Moral rights were not brought into French legislation until 1957, and they are now subject to detailed explanation in the current *Code de la propriete intellectuelle*.[81]

2. The Modern Doctrine: A Controversial Model Law

The French provisions on moral rights are framed with great elegance. A formal preface provides a clear description of the rights.[82] They protect the author's "name, quality of authorship, and work." The rights are inalienable, but they are also permanent, and may be inherited or assigned to a third party by an author's will.

Each right is balanced by definite limits on its exercise. These are described alongside the statement of the right itself, in each paragraph of the law. While these structural features easily make the French Code a model of legislative clarity and precision, the substance of the rights, judged by international norms, is controversial. In some respects, French law includes provisions that

---

80. Declaration of the Rights of Man and of the Citizen (adopted August 26 or 27, 1789, by the National Constituent Assembly).
81. CPI, *supra* note 2; the French Code was adopted in 1992, and replaced the previous copyright law of 1957.
82. CPI, *supra* note 3, art. L121-1.

are unusually extensive, and in others, its terms imply practical limits on the acquisition and use of copyright works. The provisions seem to fit well with French priorities. Would a moral rights framework of such breadth be appropriate for other countries? The following analysis will attempt to shed light on the applicability of a French model of moral rights reform to the international copyright community at large.

a. The Pre-Eminence of Moral Rights

Historical and cultural forces have combined to shape a powerful law of moral rights in France. The clarity and comprehensiveness of French moral rights language almost certainly reflects judicial elaboration of the relevant principles, whose character is practical and informal, and on whose foundation the legislation is built.[83]

In the French Code, moral rights precede the economic rights of the author,[84] a structural choice that infuses them with a sense of priority. Indeed, current commentators note the "*prééminence*" of moral rights, leading, among other things, to consequences for the interpretation of artists' contracts according to the requirements of moral rights—their provisions, adjusted accordingly.[85] In common law jurisdictions, too, contracts can, of course, be modified according to doctrines of fairness and equity, such as the unconscionability of contract terms, or the unfair influence of duress in bringing about an agreement. However, in the French scheme, the possibility of reading the terms of contracts into conformity with moral rights provisions is built into the Code.

The pre-eminence of moral rights is not universally agreed upon by French authors. In his 1969 study, Pierre Recht takes issue with this view, arguing that the importance of moral rights in French law is greatly exaggerated by commentators.[86] Indeed, Recht argues that moral rights are "unreal." Instead, authors' rights include both economic and moral interests that are inseparable. Recht comments:

> [M]y research seeks to show that the property right of the author, in particular, includes monetary and moral prerogatives that are indissolubly united and cannot be separated. The so-called moral right is an unreal creation, which, for a century, we have attempted in vain to define in a manner that is petty and perfectly superfluous.

---

83. CPI, *supra* note 3.
84. The economic rights are known as *droits patrimoniaux* in French law.
85. Pierre Sirinelli, Sylviane Durrande, & Antoine Latreille, eds., CODE DE LA PROPRIÉTÉ INTEL-LECTUELLE COMMENTÉ, EDITION 2009, Codes Dalloz, ed. Jeanne Daleau (Dalloz 2009) [Sirinelli et al.], Titre Deuxième Droits des Auteurs, Commentaire 92.
86. PIERRE RECHT, LE DROIT D'AUTEUR, UNE NOUVELLE FORME DE PROPRIÉTÉ: HISTOIRE ET THÉORIE 274–75 (1969).

. . . The truth is that copyright should be considered a new kind of unitary property right made up of multiple prerogatives, monetary and moral, different from property in the usual sense, which, during the first half of the nineteenth century, was called upon to resolve every problem.[87]

In this light, it is worth considering the most recent decision of the *Cour de cassation* on moral rights, involving a claim by a great-great-grandson of Victor Hugo, and confirming the principle that, on French soil, moral rights may be asserted without any limitation in time.[88] The court found that a sequel to Victor Hugo's *Les Miserables* which imagines the subsequent life of the characters after the close of Hugo's novel, would not violate the author's moral right of integrity. The case has drawn sharp criticism from some French commentators, who argue that the ruling signifies a reduced status for moral rights in the French copyright hierarchy, and a corresponding reorientation of French law towards the commercial model favored in the international community.[89] Evidence that Hugo himself disliked the idea of a sequel to his

---

87. Recht, *supra* note 86, at 274–75. "[M]on étude tend à montrer que le droit de propriété de l'auteur, notamment, comporte des prérogatives pécuiniaires et morales indissolublement unies et qu'on ne peut séparer. Le droit dit moral est une création irréelle, que depuis un siècle on a essayé vainement de définir d'une façon congrue et parfaitement superflue. . . . La vérité c'est qu'il faudrait concevoir le droit d'auteur comme une forme nouvelle de propriéte uni- taire comprenant des prérogatives multiples, pécuniaires et morales, différente de la pro- priété ordinaire à laquelle on a vainement, pendant la première moitié du XIXè siècle, demandé de résoudre tous les problèmes." Interestingly, Recht cites Canadian commentator Fox, who succinctly expresses his critique of moral rights in the Berne Convention as "vague, poorly drafted, sententiously expressed and without practical use": Recht at 273.

88. *Hugo c. Societe Plon*, Arrêt n° 125 du 30 janvier 2007, Cass. Civ. lre, *available at* http://www. courdecassation.fr/jurisprudence_2/premiere_chambre_civile_568/arret_no_9850.html (last visited May 2, 2010). The *Cour de cassation* of Paris is France's main court of appeal; *see* the excellent website of the court, *available at* http://www.courdecassation.fr/institution_1/ (last visited May 2, 2010). When a case is appealed to the *Cour de cassation*, the appeal may be rejected, accepted with the court sending the case back to a lower court for re- examination, or accepted with the *Cour de cassation* itself deciding on final measures in the litigation.

89. *See* the interesting Internet article by Xavier Skowron-Galvez, who comments: "Thus, in the name of freedom of creativity, the moral right should bow down before every sequel to a work that is (as desired by its author) finished. Provided that, of course, that the second work respects the "spirit" of the first: we have seen with what rigor the Court of Paris has com- pelled respect for the spirit of *Les Misérables*. Moreover—let us repeat—it is not clear why the moral right must be considered the enemy of free speech, since the undertaking of inserting oneself in the wake of the author in order to take advantage of a story and characters created successfully by him, and thereby snatching a profit from this success oneself, is not the first example of what comes to mind when we speak of creation. How much longer until the legitimation of economic parasitism in the name of liberty, commerce, and industry?" [Ainsi, au nom de la liberté de création, le droit moral devrait s'incliner devant toute suite d'une œuvre se voulant (car voulue par son auteur) finie. Sous réserve, bien entendu, du respect par l'œuvre seconde de "l'esprit" de l'œuvre première: on a vu avec quelle sévérité la Cour de Paris s'est employée à faire respecter l'esprit des Misérables. Outre que–répétons-le—on ne

work was offered in the case.[90] In choosing to reject its significance, the court certainly moved away from the traditionally "subjective" approach that would accept the author's own view—in this case, represented both by evidence of Hugo's own opinion and the representations of his descendant—as correct and sufficient evidence of a violation of the right of integrity, a hallmark of French practice.[91] The movement towards "objective" proof of damage to an author's reputation mirrors standards that are favored in common law countries, in relation to reputation-based claims.[92]

---

voit pas pourquoi le droit moral devrait être considéré comme l'ennemi de la liberté de créa-tion, la démarche qui consiste à s'insérer dans le sillage d'un auteur pour s'emparer d'une histoire et des personnages créés par lui avec succès, et ainsi venir tirer profit de bribes de ce succès pour soi-même n'est pas la première illustration qui vient à l'esprit lorsque l'on parle de création. A quand la légitimation du parasitisme économique au nom de la liberté du com-merce et de l'industrie?"

Xavier Skworon-Galvez, *Un (mauvais) coup porté au droit moral de l'auteur—L'affaire "Les Misérables,"* available at http://www.village-justice.com/articles/mauvais-porte-droit-moral-auteur, 5433.html (last visited May 2, 2010).

90. "The case demonstrates that if the latter never formally admitted and, even less, opposed, dramatic adaptations of his books, leave alone the adoption by other authors of certain of his characters, *it was on the other hand established that the writer would not have accepted that another writer could create a sequel to Les Misérables,* that accordingly, it mattered little that the characters, resuscitated for some and revived for others, remain in the books under examination which are wrongfully presented as an adaptation of the first work because Plon claimed, beyond the judicial terrain, that they were the continuation, faithful or not, of those brought into the world for literary eternity by Victor Hugo, that to prohibit every sequel to *Les Misérables* could not constitute, as it was wrongly asserted, an attack on the principle of creative freedom because, in this case, this work, a veritable monument of world literature, was not, in the first place, a simple novel, in the sense that it is also a philosophical and politi-cal undertaking, as Victor Hugo explained, and moreover, it follows that no sequel could be made for a work like *Les Misérables* without violating Victor Hugo's moral right . . ."

"[L]'arrêt énonce que si ce dernier ne s'était jamais formalisé et encore moins opposé aux adaptations scéniques de ses livres, voire à l'adoption par d'autres auteurs de tel ou tel de ses personnages, *il était en revanche établi que l'écrivain n'aurait pas accepté qu'un tiers auteur puisse donner une suite aux Misérables,* que dès lors peu importait que les personnages, res-suscité pour l'un d'entre eux et ranimés pour les autres, soient demeurés dans les livres présentés à tort comme une adaptation de l'oeuvre première puisque la société Plon revendi-quait, hors du terrain judiciaire, en être la continuation, fidèle ou non, à ceux mis au monde pour l'éternité littéraire par Victor Hugo, qu'interdire toute suite aux Misérables ne pouvait constituer, ainsi qu'il était soutenu à tort, une atteinte au principe de la libre création puisque, en l'espèce, cette oeuvre, véritable monument de la littérature mondiale, d'une part, n'était pas un simple roman en ce qu'elle procédait d'une démarche philosophique et politique, ainsi que l'avait explicité Victor Hugo et, d'autre part, était achevée, qu'il s'ensuivait qu'aucune suite ne pouvait être donnée à une oeuvre telle que "Les Misérables" sans porter atteinte au droit moral de Victor Hugo . . . ." (emphasis added).

91. Desbois, *supra* note 27, at 538–39, para. 449.

92. *See, for example,* the Canadian case of *Snow* (*supra* note 8): expert evidence was considered to be "objective" proof of damage to the author's reputation. The principle has been applied in *Prise de Parole Inc. v. Guérin éditeur Ltée* [1996] F.C.J. No. 1427.

It is worth noting that the French ruling also lends legal support to the increasingly popular phenomenon of fan creativity, which has developed via the Internet, in genres as diverse as fiction and film. If fan fiction remains noncommercial in nature, however widespread it may become, its authors should be shielded from charges of copyright infringement.[93] If we accept the *Hugo* ruling as decisive, it now appears that the authors of fan fiction cannot be held liable for violating the original author's moral right of integrity, either. In this sense, the caveats introduced by the French court are also useful: if the new works can somehow be shown to imply an alteration of the original, or if they would give rise to confusion about authorship, a violation of moral rights could still be found.[94] These standards of proof are demanding ones, and the court clearly affirmed its intention to support "freedom of creativity" in preference to authorial control.[95]

However, as a claim on the integrity right, the facts were far from convincing. No direct treatment of the work at all was at issue in this case; yet, it is widely accepted that a violation of the integrity right can only follow from actual intervention in a work.[96] Special cases do exist—for example, the tradition in some countries that inappropriate conditions for displaying an artistic work violate the author's moral rights.[97] The *Cour de cassation* itself has

---

93. In copyright, the crucial distinction has always been that between commercial and noncommercial use, with commercial exploitation attracting copyright sanctions. The ruling of the U.S. Supreme Court in *MGM Studios, Inc. v. Grokster, Ltd.* 545 U.S. 913 (2005), indicated a fundamental shift in this principle, with the court arguing that the volume of infringement apparent in music file-sharing is so great that even private and noncommercial use has effectively become a violation of copyright principles. Whatever its practicality from an industry perspective, the idea is difficult to accept. *See* detailed discussion, Chapter 6, *infra*, "More than Musicians."

94. The *Cour de cassation* criticized the earlier ruling, arguing that, "sans avoir examiné les oeuvres litigieuses ni constaté que celles-ci auraient altéré l'oeuvre de Victor Hugo ou qu'une confusion serait née de leur paternité, la cour d'appel . . . n'a pas caracterisé l'atteinte au droit moral et s'est déterminée en méconnaissance de la liberté de creation." Quoted in Hervé Hugueny, "Les héritiers de Victor Hugo déboutés en cassation" (Jan. 30, 2007), *available at* http://www.livreshebdo.fr/actualites/DetailsActuRub.aspx?id=537 (last visited Aug. 25, 2010).

95. The *Cour de cassation* disapproves the earlier ruling in favor of Hugo as "une atteinte au principe de la libre creation," and goes on to comment: "Qu' en statuant ainsi, par des motifs inopérants tirés du genre et du mérite de l'oeuvre ou de son caractère achevé, et sans avoir examiné les oeuvres litigieuses ni constaté que celles-*ci auraient altéré l'oeuvre de Victor Hugo ou qu'une confusion serait née sur leur paternité*, la cour d'appel, qui n'a pas ainsi caractérisé l'atteinte au droit moral et s'est déterminée *en méconnaissance de la liberté de création*, a violé les textes susvisés . . . ." (emphasis added). The judgment is available online at http://www.courdecassation.fr/jurisprudence_2/premiere_chambre_civile_568/arret_no_9850.html (last visited May 2, 2010).

96. An American court affirmed this idea in *Shostakovich*, *supra* note 18.

97. This was formerly the case in India; the possibility is now explicitly excluded by section 57 of the Indian Copyright Act.

found that including a song in a compilation flanked by music from other groups with shadowy political associations would be a violation of the author's right of reputation.[98] But the facts of the *Hugo* case do not quite fall into the category of a work placed in an improper context. The *Cour de cassation* saw the making of a sequel as analogous to making an "adaptation," a right that would become freely available to all once the term of copyright expires, and the work falls into the public domain. Yet, when Victor Hugo affirmed that, "An author's sole literary heir is the public domain," it seems doubtful whether he wanted the public to exploit his literary creation in quite this way. Indeed, the use of works in the public domain to generate a new work that enjoys a new term of copyright protection may itself be damaging to the public interest—if a theatre director now wanted to stage a play imagining the future life of Hugo's characters, would the person need the permission of François Cérésa? What about the case of a person using the characters who were the subject of the sequel for an interactive website?

A sequel is something more than an adaptation, involving creative engagement with a work in a way that an adaptation usually would not, but it is hard to qualify it as an actual intervention in the work. Given the existing shape of the integrity right in France, it falls through the cracks. The case might have succeeded on a classic interpretation of the integrity right, which would trace it to the principle, fundamental in French law, that the author's individual rights should be protected as such.[99] But the *Cour de cassation* might have gone against the winds of public opinion with such a finding, which increasingly sees access to works as under threat. In these circumstances, the Court's appeal to "freedom of creativity" represents a new approach to the interpretation of French copyright law.

b. *Les droits moraux*: The Rights Defined

Regardless of differences of opinion about the place of moral rights within the French copyright framework, there can be little doubt that the French law represents the most comprehensive and developed set of provisions on moral rights in the world.[100] When moral rights were first recognized by French judges, they referred to the author's *droit moral*, a term that communicates the unity of the doctrine underlying the different types of moral rights.

---

98. *See also M. jean X . . . dit Jean Y . . . c société Universal Music SA, venant aux droits de la société anonyme Polygram et autres,* Arrêt no 401 du 8 février 2006 (modifié par arrêt en rectification d'erreur matérielle no 773 du 21 février 2006), *Cour de cassation*—Chambre sociale, *available at* http://www.courdecassation.fr/jurisprudence_2/chambre_sociale_576/arret_no_962.html (last visited Apr. 29, 2010).

99. Noted by Henri Desbois, *supra* note 27.

100. A conviction also noted by Sirinelli et al., *supra* note 85: Chapitre premier Droits moraux, Commentaire at 92.

The legislation, however, converts the term into its plural form, *droits moraux*. Pierre Sirinelli and his colleagues comment:

> Before codification, it was a matter, in the law, of the "moral right." Since then, the legislation deals with "moral rights." This passage into the plural causes us to lose sight of the fundamental unity of the moral right and the importance of common rules, but it can be explained by little differences in the regime which can arise according to the prerogatives. Thus, the fate *post mortem* of the latter is quite different.[101]

The Code protects five moral rights: attribution,[102] integrity,[103] disclosure, or first publication,[104] withdrawal,[105] and a right against abusive criticism. With the exception of the right of disclosure, none of these rights is absolute; each must be weighed against the defense offered by the alleged offender. The French law has carefully framed exceptions to moral rights, including the special cases of parody and pastiche, elaborated below.

i. Disclosure

The French Code makes explicit provision for the author to determine the circumstances in which his work is first published. Article L121–2 creates an exclusive right to decide on publication, and to negotiate the circumstances in which publication will occur. The right is as near to absolute as any right could be, but its impact is slightly softened by the subsequent Article L121–3, which makes provision for a court to intervene in the case of a deceased author whose heirs or descendants present unreasonable obstacles to the publication of the author's work. The exception applies only to the case of an author who is deceased, and represents the case, extremely rare in French law, of interference with the author's right of disclosure. Where the author remains alive, he alone controls disclosure of his work. No measure of reasonableness can be applied to the decision to refrain from publication.[106]

---

101. Avant la codification, il était question, dans la loi, du "droit moral." Depuis cette dernière, la législation traite des "droits moraux." Ce passage au pluriel fait perdre de vue l'unité de fondement du droit moral et l'importance des règles communes mais s'explique par les petites différences de régime qui peuvent se rencontrer suivant les prérogatives. Ainsi, le sort post mortem de ces dernières est assez différent. Sirinelli et al., *supra* note 85: Code, Chapitre premier Droits moraux, Commentaire at 92–93.

102. *Attribution, paternité.* Paternity, of course, is no longer favored.

103. *Droit au respect de l'oeuvre.* The French terminology, "the right of respect for the work," emphasizes the cultural aspect of the right, focusing on the work rather than the author. *See* discussion of the French integrity right *infra*.

104. *Divulgation.*

105. *Droit de repentir ou retrait.*

106. Presumably, evidence of the author's own objections to the publication of a given work would be enough to allow the heirs to continue to refuse publication. Historical

ii. Withdrawal

The right of withdrawal allows an author to remove from circulation a work that he has already published; it is also known as a right of recall. The reasons for withdrawing a work may be diverse—a change of mind or belief, as the idea of "repentance" is built into the French terminology for the right; new circumstances after the publication of a work; or any other factor that leads to what Michaélidès-Nouaros refers to as "profound discord between the new state of the author's mind and his work."[107]

The objective of the right is to remove a work from circulation, but this generally cannot be achieved without significant costs to the publisher. Accordingly, the right is balanced in Article L121–4 by a requirement that the author must reimburse those who expect to suffer a commercial loss as a result of his decision. Interestingly, should the author decide to publish the work again, the original publisher will have the first right of refusal on the work and will be entitled to publish it on the very terms of the original agreement.[108] The clause provides careful protection against the possibility of an author using the right of withdrawal to escape from the terms of a publication contract which he might later find undesirable—or, indeed, to alter those terms through the exercise of the right, by seeking to re-publish the work on new terms, with a new publisher.

The right of withdrawal was codified only in 1992, but a consideration of French treatises such as Michaélidès-Nouaros' 1935 work shows it to be an established part of French moral rights tradition.

iii. Integrity vs. Reputation: Proof

French law frames the right of integrity in broad and simple terms: Article L121–1 tells us that the author has a right to "respect for his work." By implication, any modification of the work is to be considered a violation of the right of integrity. In contrast to the Berne Convention, there is no requirement that an author needs to show damage to his reputation or honor. In this respect, the French right of integrity is framed in the strongest possible terms.

A practical implication of this right is to place the burden of proof in such cases upon the person defending the claim. The author need only show modification of his work. His or her personal objection is sufficient grounds for a legal action. Under the terms of French law, any modification of the

---

circumstance could see the author's will being overridden, but this would violate the integrity of the author's individual prerogative to disclose, or withhold, his own work.

107. Michaélidès-Nouaros, *supra* note 52, at para. 163 ("un désaccord profond entre le nouvel état d'esprit de l'auteur et son oeuvre").

108. CPI, *supra* note 3. The work must be offered to the original publisher "par priorité."

work against the author's will is, *prima facie,* a violation of the integrity right. The person who has made the modification bears the burden of showing that it does not violate the integrity of the work.

The requirement is onerous, and artistic integrity is notoriously difficult to judge. The result is to lead effectively to case-by-case determinations on integrity claims. The recent case of *Hugo* illustrates the point: the suit proceeded all the way to the *Cour de cassation* before any limiting principle appeared. At the *Cour de cassation*, the idea that a work must be directly modified before an integrity violation can be claimed, finally found a voice.[109]

iv. Criticism

A right to protect one's work from abusive criticism is recognized in French law, but it is subject to strict limitations. The criticism must be unfair, excessive, or "vexatious"—and if the critic can show that he is truly engaged in the creation of a parody or pastiche of the original work, he will be exempt from liability.[110]

c. *Le dualisme*: The Theory of Protection and Its Practical Effects

The French Code is based on the theory of an unbreakable relationship between author and work. In the French case, this ideal translates into a theory that is known as dualism, meaning that economic and moral rights are two distinct and independent types of rights.[111] In practice, dualism means that limitations on economic rights need not apply to moral rights, and indeed, moral rights are expansive in startling ways. Article L121–1 identifies two fundamental characteristics of moral rights: inalienability and perpetual protection. This second feature of moral rights stands in dramatic contrast to the principle that the protection of an author's economic rights is always for a limited time only.[112] Both conceptual features lead to practical effects which are worthy of note.

---

109. This occurred in the *Hugo* case, *supra* note 88.
110. Parody and pastiche are defined elsewhere in the Code and offer important defenses in an integrity dispute. *See* CPI, *supra* note 3, art. L122-5(4). Somewhat awkwardly, the provisions appear in the section of the Code dealing with economic rights *(droits patrimoniaux)*, but the language provides clearly that the author cannot object to these re-uses of his work once it is disclosed—"Lorsque l'oeuvre a été divulguée, l'auteur ne peut interdire [Once the work has been disclosed, the author cannot prohibit]"—presumably for neither economic nor moral reasons.
111. The contrast with German monism, which sees the two as varieties of the same right, is discussed below.
112. According to the U.S. Constitution, the idea of rights "prescribed for limited times" seems to be the very essence of copyright protection, an issue that defined the debate on extending

i. Inalienability and the Prohibition of Waivers

In French law, inalienability translates into a general prohibition on the waiver of moral rights. Waivers are officially forbidden—the rights are "perpétuel, inaliénable et imprescriptible." An author or artist cannot make a contract to divest himself completely of moral rights, even if he should want to do so. Pierre Recht finds this approach intolerable, and argues that it is inexcusably patronizing to refuse this choice to authors.[113]

In fact, limiting an author's right to choose is probably a concession to a tough bargaining environment, in which the right to waive one's rights is separated by just a hair's breadth from the expectation that one will do so. In practice, making comprehensive waivers unavailable means that French copyright industries must work with moral rights as a fact of doing business in France. There is no question of using copyright contracts to soften the French legislative regime on moral rights, a usual occurrence in common law jurisdictions.[114]

And yet, the practice of "ghostwriting" is common in France. An author writes a text to be published under someone else's name—the biography of a celebrity, for example. How can this phenomenon be reconciled with the idea that the author is not allowed to waive his or her right of attribution?

To get around this problem, a small trick of legal sleight-of-hand may help. The ghostwriter does not waive his right of attribution; rather, he asserts his right to remain anonymous, or to write under a pseudonym, both of which are implicitly protected as part of the moral right of attribution in France.[115] Numerous commentators, including Michel Vivant and Jean-Michel

---

copyright term in the *Eldred* case. It does not necessarily follow that the U.S. constitutional framework is incompatible with moral rights, but the recognition of those rights in the United States would clearly require an approach different from the French. *Eldred v. Ashcroft*, 239 F.3d 372 (2001), *aff'd*, 537 U.S. 186 (2003).

113. Pierre Recht, Le Droit d'Auteur, une nouvelle forme de propriété: histoire et théorie (Editions Gembloux, 1969).

114. Canada is perhaps the most extreme example, as it is standard to waive moral rights in that country. Accordingly, Canadian law, despite its statutory provisions on moral rights, arguably fails to provide a legal environment conducive to their practical enforcement. Based on Canada's weak record of case law involving moral rights, Vaver argues that Canadian "exceptional[ism]" in relation to common law moral rights is "folklore." *See* David Vaver, *Moral Rights Yesterday, Today and Tomorrow*, 7(3) Int'l J. Tech & L. 270, 275–76 (1999). Vaver discusses the 1989 UK provisions on moral rights and comments that the "widespread use of written waivers" is a serious obstacle to moral rights where great inequality of bargaining power between authors and publishers is the norm. Vaver at 274–75.

115. Canadian law offers explicit protection to these aspects of attribution. *See* Canadian Copyright Act, R.S., 1985, c. C-42, sec. 14.1 (1), http://laws.justice.gc.ca/eng/C-42/page-2.html#anchorbo-ga:l_II (last visited Aug. 21, 2010).

Bruguière, recognize this possibility;[116] but Vivant and Bruguière prefer to interpret French jurisprudence as indicating that the right of attribution may be temporarily "suspended," with the possibility that the author can choose to come forward and claim it at any time. At the same time, the agreement for "ghostwriting" must be entered into in good faith, and an attempt to claim attribution in these circumstances should not have been pre-meditated as the contract was under negotiation. These points of legal principle are extraordinarily subtle, and they involve the interpretation of what Vivant and Bruguière call a *"jurisprudence tourmentée."*[117] It may be best to say, as Vivant and Bruguière admit, that the practice of ghostwriting simply amounts to "usages *contra legem."*[118]

ii. Permanent Protection

The ultimate result of honoring dualist theory is to offer perpetual protection to moral rights. Economic rights are limited in time, but moral rights last forever. The relationship between an author and his work is permanent. He will always be its author. No work created in France can ever be exempt from moral rights, even after it has fallen into the public domain. The *Hugo* case, brought 122 years after the author's death, is but one illustration of the limitless potential of this rule.

The key practical issue becomes who will exercise the author's moral rights after his death. The French Code provides clearly that the rights can be exercised by the author's heirs or by a third party whom the author has designated in his will.[119]

d. Technological Features

French law makes special provision for moral rights in the context of film, from 1992,[120] and, based on a 1994 amendment, for computer programs as well.[121]

---

116. Michel Vivant & Jean-Michel Bruiguière, Le Droit d'Auteur, paras. 464–66 (Dalloz 2009); they also cite A. and H.J. Lucas, who point out that it is difficult to distinguish between the abdication of the right and the assertion of anonymity (para. 465).

117. *Id.*, para. 465.

118. *Id.*, para. 465.

119. CPI, *supra* note 3, art. L121-1.

120. *Id.*, arts. L121-5 & L121-6.

121. *Id.*, art. L121-7. India, with France, represented the vanguard of countries to consider moral rights in computer programs, although it chose to address the issue in an indirect manner. *See* Indian Copyright Act 1957, *supra* note 39, secs. 57 and 52(1)(aa). Interestingly, in its law of 1985, France adopted an initially restrictive stance towards moral rights in programs, maintained in the 1992 codification; but its position was subsequently changed in a 1994 codification amendment. This history can be traced on the website of Légifrance, *supra* note 3.

i. Audiovisual Works

The French regime on films is worth close consideration. Objections to moral rights in film are one of the stumbling blocks to establishing moral rights protection internationally.[122] Yet France has created a regime for recognizing the moral rights of those involved in the making of a film.[123]

France fundamentally approaches film as a collaborative work. It is a product of the creative efforts of the director, a number of "coauthors," and the producer. Coauthorship extends to the author of the screenplay, adaptation, or dialogue, and to the composer of original music for the film.[124] It considers the problem of choice that is involved in the final production of a feature film—which takes, cuts, images, and performances to use, and how—and specifies that the final product, as agreed upon by the director, coauthors, and producer, is the audiovisual work for the purposes of copyright law.

Any modification of the final work requires the consent of all parties, and any conversion of the work to a new format must be "preceded by consultation with the director." The language of Art L121-5 does not go so far as to say that the agreement of the director is required, but the article should probably be interpreted to mean that only unreasonable objections by the director may be overruled. All moral rights apply only to the final work.[125]

This last point provides an important clue about the issue of potential conflicts over moral rights between coauthors, and their resolution. Prior to the establishment of the final version of a film, any coauthor should be able to signal his objections to the use of his contribution by refusing to consent to the final film. Unless and until moral rights conflicts are resolved, the final version of a film cannot be settled, as the agreement of *all* coauthors *and* the producer is required. Once the final version is established, however, a coauthor can no longer object to the manner in which his contribution is used. What each coauthor can do is to object to the use of the film as a whole, or of his component contribution, by a third party. The section provides a neat, though indirect, solution to the problem of internal conflict among the makers of a film.

---

122. *See, for example,* the illuminating discussion in Fraser, *supra* note 25. It is noteworthy that the WIPO Performance and Phonograms Treaty, which introduces moral rights for performers, nevertheless excludes moral rights in performances recorded in audiovisual works. WIPO Performances and Phonograms Treaty, adopted by the WIPO Diplomatic Conference on Certain Copyright and Neighbouring Rights Questions in Geneva, Dec. 20, 1996, *available at* http://www.wipo.int/treaties/en/ip/berne/trtdocs_wo001.html [WPPT].
123. CPI, *supra* note 3, art. L121-5, introduced in 1992.
124. *See* CPI, *supra* note 3, art. L113-7, created by the Loi 92-597 1992-07-01 annexe JORF 3 juillet 1992.
125. The CPI, *supra* note 3, states: "Les droits propres des auteurs, tels qu'ils sont définis à l'article L121-1, ne peuvent être exercés par eux que sur l'oeuvre audiovisuelle achevée."

Should any one of the contributors be unable or unwilling to complete his part in the project, he will nevertheless be required to allow the others to use the work that he completed before the rupture. Art L121-6 concludes with the remark—"He will have, for this contribution, the quality of authorship, and will enjoy the rights that flow therefrom." This should probably be interpreted to mean two things. First, based on his limited contribution, the contributor continues to retain his rights of authorship. Secondly, however, he can only exercise those rights in relation to the use of the final work. He can have no right to intervene in the overall realization of the work, which has since fallen to other hands than his own.

ii. Computer Programs

In relation to computer programs, the French Code specifies that dealings with a computer program by the rightholder (*cessionnaire*) can lead to a violation of the author's right of integrity only if they are prejudicial to his honor or reputation. From the French perspective, this represents a scaling back of the usual right of integrity. By international standards, however, the French Code enacts a moral right corresponding exactly to the norms of the Berne Convention. This approach is extremely interesting. Not only does France recognize a right of integrity in programs, but it also frames the right in accordance with the international standard of protection that is generally available for intellectual creation. But the French moral right in computer programs is restrictive by French standards. The French norm that presumes any intervention in a work to be a violation of the right of integrity seems too broad for the computer context, but the French legislature has not hesitated to apply the Berne standard as sufficiently balanced for software.

The right of withdrawal is completely discarded, and, given the characteristics of software, this seems to be a highly practical approach. Software changes rapidly; it is subject to updates, to modifications for new operating systems, and to countless other changes and improvements through time. A decision to withdraw software even a few months after its release could prove to be logistically impossible. Leaving the option open could paralyze producers who want to issue improved versions of programs.

iii. Moral Rights Reforms

The latest changes to France's moral rights code include some noteworthy modifications. Provisions added in 2006 and 2009 make changes in two areas. The first of these deals with moral rights in the employment context and restricts an employee's right of disclosure when the work is created for the employer. The employee still enjoys a right of integrity, but he can only object to modifications that threaten his honor or reputation. His right of withdrawal can only be exercised with the agreement of his employer.[126] The change is important where technological creation is concerned, because much creativity in the realm of software and other new technologies occurs in the context of company employment. It also represents a movement towards common law systems, which typically recognize an employer's copyright in the work of his employees.[127]

A more recent change involves the use of works in compilations and allows journalists to retain their right to authorize the inclusion of their works in edited collections. The right is interesting because it allows for collections in many different formats, including online publication. The new rules entered into effect on June 14, 2009, and replaced earlier provisions on the re-publication of an article in a magazine or periodical which stipulated that the new publication must not compete with the original news publication.[128]

The change reflects a valuable new definition, in Article L132–35 of the French Code, of "*titre de presse,*" which can be translated as "press publication." The definition attempts to extend the traditional understanding of news publications to the Internet environment and includes online communication of works within its ambit, while excluding works that are "broadcast" in the traditional sense. It invokes a principle of neutrality towards the transformation of the publication into new formats ("*support[s]*").[129] The French Code identifies editorial control as the key criterion for determining whether a work is, in effect, the transformation of the old work into a new medium, or a new work in its own right. This determination will decide the issue of whether or not a work has been "re-published," and therefore, whether or not the author's permission is once again required for publication.[130]

iv. Defenses to a Moral Rights Claim: Parody and Pastiche

While it is not included in the chapter on moral rights, the parody defense in French copyright law deserves special mention. Inhibiting the creation of parodies is among the dangers associated with moral rights, and, to commentators from common law countries, this represents a significant argument against the moral rights of integrity and attribution.[131]

---

126. *See* CPI, *supra* note 3, art. L121-7-1.
127. *See, for example,* see Article 13(3) of the Canadian Copyright Act, R.S., 1985, c. C-42.
128. *See* See CPI, *supra* note 3, art. 121–8.
129. The Canadian Supreme Court would call this media neutrality. *See Robertson v. Thomson Corp.* [2006] 2 S.C.R. 363, 2006 SCC 43 (Can.).
130. *See id.* In the *Tasini* case, the United States Supreme Court found that the use of freelance work in the online publication of newspapers did qualify as a new publication, and therefore, required permission from the original authors. *See New York Times Co. v. Tasini*, 533 U.S. 483 (2001).
131. In a recent Belgian case, the creation of a parody could not exempt its creator from a finding that the moral rights of the original author had been violated. *See* Joris Ghent, *Parody Exception Again Denied in Belgium: NV Code v. BV Mercis/Dick Bruna*, Hof van Beroep

France makes comprehensive provision for the art of parody. The parody defense is defined in the French Code; it is included in France's list of public interest exceptions to authors' rights, as a separate defense in its own right.[132] Crucially, proving a parody defense depends on being able to show that the work in question is a true work of parody. Intention is important. There are two possible rationales for a parody: humorous intent, and critical intent. The parody must be created in good faith. If the parodist intends to harm the author of the parodied work, or to cause harm by revealing facts of the author's personal life, the defense cannot be invoked. In an interesting parallel with trademark law, the risk of confusion with the works of the original author must also be avoided—much as trademark censures the creation of confusion in the mind of the consumer about the origin of goods.[133]

In the light of this framework, it should also be noted that the author of a work of parody in France should be entitled to enjoy the full extent of his moral rights. The parody may legitimately qualify as a copyright work in its own right. The copyright in the parody is not subject to any special limitations—except, of course, that the intent of the parodist should not be to harm the author.

e. Conclusions

France offers the world a comprehensive and sophisticated example of moral rights legislation. The extent of protection for the rights is beyond what they enjoy in any other jurisdiction. While many countries implicitly recognize

---

(Court of Appeal) of Antwerp, May 2, 2006, 1(11) OXFORD J. INTELL. PROP. L. PRAC. 694 (Current Intelligence) (2006). Ghent notes that the decision "confirms the tendency in Belgian jurisprudence to be very cautious in its application of the parody exception to copyright infringement"—and, presumably, to moral rights, as well. For example, an American perspective is provided by Geri J. Yonover, *The Precarious Balance: Moral Rights, Parody, and Fair Use*, 14 CARDOZO ARTS & ENT. L.J. 79 (1996). The analysis suffers from some misapprehensions about non-U.S. legal systems—for example, European jurisdictions do not have American-style "fair use" principles, but they approach the issue of fair uses, or fair dealing, in other ways. Notable among these is the citation defense.

132. *See* CPI, *supra* note 3, art. L122-5(4). In contrast to Germany and Japan, there is no need to consider parody as a special form of the citation defense. Civil law countries often rely on "citation" of the work in much the same way that common law countries invoke "fair use" (United States) or "fair dealing" (the UK and Canada), allowing for certain activities, treatments, and uses of a work to be exempt from copyright restrictions. Quoting or "citing," a work for the purpose of research would be a classic example of fair use in both systems. In the French Code, a citation defense is listed separately, in art. L122-5(3)(a).

133. The similarities between moral rights and trademark have often been noted; Vaver refers to this as the protection of "truth-in-marketing." *See* D. Vaver, *Moral Rights Yesterday, Today and Tomorrow*, 7(3) INT'L J. TECH. AND L. 270, 276 (1999); he notes that "attributions function like trade marks." Of course, a number of common law countries rely upon tort to protect authors' moral interests, including the United States and the United Kingdom. Vaver, at 271, remarks on the presence of "*misattribution*" in the UK Copyright Act of 1956; he describes it as "passing-off, writ large."

rights such as disclosure, France has codified them, and it has done so in straightforward and simple terms. Indeed, the framing of all of the rights is notable for its simplicity.

The right of integrity is a cornerstone of the French moral rights system. It grants to an author the right to object to any changes to his work, and is unclouded by references to reputation or—the curious nineteenth-century term entrenched in the Berne Convention—honor.[134]

France is not unique in this respect. Other countries have also recognized a right of integrity that focuses exclusively on damage to the work, leading some jurisdictions to adopt a clear distinction between a moral right of integrity and a moral right of "reputation." Damage to reputation is perhaps a more precise way of characterizing the integrity right in Article 6*bis* of the Berne Convention, as, without it, and no matter what the treatment of the work in question, no offense has occurred. Indeed, India codified a pure right of integrity in 1957, the same year the French *Code de la Propriété Intellectuelle* came into existence.[135]

In relation to technological works, French law embraces the protection of moral rights. It does so in relation to both the creation and the dissemination of works in a digital environment, offering moral rights protection to computer programs and films, and adapting the moral rights of journalists to the online environment. The French provisions have just begun to address technology, and the solutions that they express are incomplete. But the fundamental point of principle, that moral rights are appropriate to a technological society, is an interesting approach from a country that represents, at once, the heartland of the moral rights idea, and leadership in a European Union that aims to be the world's foremost digital society. The rights of programmers are subject to Berne-style constraints, and the works of journalists, to caveats about the use of works in news publications. The attempt to organize, and coordinate moral rights in films is impressive and suggests a starting point, at least, for the recognition of moral rights in movies at the international level, of which the Hollywood lobby should be more aware.

The French approach to moral rights in the digital context establishes three points of principle. First, moral rights may have to be flexible in order to adapt to technology. Second, a single moral rights regime may need to include different types and levels of protection for different types of works.

---

134. The concept of honor is discussed in Elizabeth Adeney, *The Moral Right of Integrity: The Past and Future of "Honour,"* 22 INTELL. PROP. Q. 111 (2005). *See* Chapter 3, *infra*, "A Theory in Flux," notes 246–49 and accompanying text.

135. India modified its right to fit the Berne formula in 1994, in response to an interim judgment that held the government responsible for violating the integrity of a work of sculpture in its possession. In the event, the court that issued the final ruling preferred to read the provisions, in effect, as if no substantive change had occurred. *See Sehgal* and Sundara Rajan, *Amar Nath Sehgal, supra* note 37.

Third, and most important, the moral rights doctrine is capable of evolving to meet these needs. The doctrine originated in Romanticism, but it remains vibrant in the Digital Age. Society has changed a great deal since the era of the Romantics, but the French seem to think that our attitudes towards our work have a few things in common with the past.

D. German Moral Rights: Romance of a Theory

Like France, Germany and the German-speaking countries make moral rights a focus of their copyright laws.[136] German tradition must also be recognized as a source of moral rights, but in a somewhat different sense from France. As Stig Strömholm observes, French courts were developing moral rights in practice throughout the course of the nineteenth century, while German scholars became interested in the theoretical justifications for the rights.[137] Among other things, the eventual recognition of moral rights in the Berne Convention, as reflected in the 1928 revisions to the agreement, represents a synthesis of German theory and French "practical solutions." Strömholm concludes:

> Certain writers have considered the theories of the nineteenth century from this historical perspective without, however, analyzing them in detail. Hoffmann goes so far as to affirm that the moral right as it is found in the Berne Convention (art. 6 bis) is a creation of [German legal theorists] Dambach, Klostermann and Kohler, imported into France by [French legal commentator] Morillot.[138]

---

136. Urheberrechtsgesetz, 9.9.1965, Bundesgesetzblatt, Teil I [BGBl. I] at 1273, last amended by Gesetz, 10.8.2004, BGBl. I at 1774, sec. 13, *available at*, http://www.iuscomp.org/gla/statutes/UrhG.htm#13 (last visited Oct. 5, 2010). [German Copyright Law]; Federal Law BGBl No. 111 of 1936 on Copyright in Works of Literature and Art and on Neighboring Rights (Copyright Law), as amended by BGBl 1949/206, 1953/106, 1963/175, 1972/492, 1980/321, 1982/295, 1988/601, 1989/612, 1993/93, 1996/151 and by 1998/25, *available at* http://www.wipo.int/wipolex/en/details.jsp?id=204 (last visited Oct. 5, 2010) [Austrian Copyright Law]. The translation is provided by WIPO.
137. Strömholm 1967, vol. 1, *supra* note 54, at 239.
138. *See* Strömholm 1967, vol. 1, *supra* note 54, at 239: "Quelques auteurs ont considéré les théories du XIXe siècle de ce point de vue historique sans toutefois les analyser en détail. HOFFMANN va jusqu'a affirmer que le droit moral (*Urheberpersönlichkeitsrecht*) tel qu'il se trouve dans la Convention de Berne (art. 6 bis) est une création de DAMBACH, de KLOSTERMANN et de KOHLER, importée en France par MORILLOT." Strömholm goes on to comment: "However, this judgment relates to the theory of moral rights as opposed to the solutions of [expressed by] positive law, because Hoffmann comments elsewhere that it is only in 1928 that the *Reichsgericht* finally adopted the moral right." ["Toutefois, il faut que ce jugement se rapporte à la théorie du droit moral par opposition aux solutions du droit positif, car HOFFMANN déclare ailleurs que ce n'est qu'en 1928 que le *Reichsgericht* a

What has German legal theory contributed to the international under-standing of moral rights?

1. The Birth of Monism

The analysis of moral rights undertaken by Strömholm in his classic 1967 study showcases the sheer exuberance of German thinking on moral rights. He makes a convincing case that this area has held interest for German jurists from the early years of the nineteenth century. The rigor of German theories is impressive. It seems that almost every imaginable approach to moral rights is explored, from authors' rights to personal rights and personality rights, to the idea of "innate rights," a variety of natural rights[139]—to the rejection of moral rights as a legal concept altogether.[140]

Groups of German theorists favored the French approach; others diverged from it, developing, in particular, their own understanding of the relation-ship between moral and economic rights. German theorizing in the nine-teenth and early twentieth centuries eventually led to a distinctive school of thought on moral rights, defined by its approach to this relationship and known as "monism."

German monism developed its understanding of the character of moral rights as a result of its deeper exploration of their origins. Where the French saw the moral and economic rights of authors as two categories of rights with differ-ent and distinct bases, first called "dualism" by the French writer Morillot,[141] German theorists saw moral interests and economic interests as essentially two aspects of a single right.[142] The right was simply an author's right. The theory

---

enfin adopté le droit moral."] For an interesting overview of the work of André Morillot, see *Primary Sources on Copyright 1450–1900*, ARTS AND HUMANITIES RESEARCH COUNCIL (Universities of Cambridge and Bournemouth), *available at* http://www.copyrighthistory.org/cgi-bin/kleioc/0010/exec/ausgabe/%22f_1878%22.

139. Droits innés or *angeborene Rechte*. See Strömholm 1967, vol. 1, *supra* note 54, at 242–43.

140. Strömholm discusses the concept of innate rights. *See* Strömholm 1967, vol. 1, *supra* note 54, at 242–43.

141. Strömholm 1967, vol. 1, *supra* note 54, at 226, noting: "What is strange is that Morillot, in his eagerness to acquaint his fellow countrymen with German ideas, he failed altogether to investigate the–by that time abundant–French case law which could be cited in support of his ideas."

142. Morillot's writing was largely based on the work of German theorists of his time. *See* Strömholm 1967, vol. 1, *supra* note 54, at 239, and Strömholm IIC, *supra* note 2, at 226–27. In fact, Strömholm notes the curious process whereby the work of German theorists was exported to France via Morillot, and found its way back into Germany theory from Morillot, *unrecognized* by German theorists of the later generation.

that came to be known as "monism" reflects the unity of all interests of the author, whether economic or personal in nature.[143]

The distinction between French dualism and German monism presents an imperfect contrast—shades of grey, rather than black and white. As Adolf Dietz observes, German and French law share the approach of dividing authors' rights into the two large groups consisting of economic and moral interests. He asks:

> Why does this apparently dual structure of copyright lead in one case to a dualistic and in the other case to a monistic interpretation of copyright? The answer to this delicate question is that the apparently dual structure of the content of copyright is only half of the truth.
>
> ... [I]t is copyright as a whole which serves to protect intellectual and moral as well as economic interests of authors. This could also be called [a] ... unitary or synthetic concept of copyright .... [144]

For Dietz, it seems that the difference between monism and dualism is a subtle one. Dualism is based on the idea that moral rights are "chronologically and systematically primordial." Accordingly, the key to dualism is not the division between economic and moral rights, so much as the establishment of a hierarchy between them. In a dualist system, moral rights are pre-eminent; their status is superior to that of economic rights.

2. Monism in Practice

Why was monism the outcome of such diverse German theorizing? The intellectual power of the theorists expressing this perspective, leading to an enduring recognition in German legal history, was surely an important factor.[145] From a modern perspective, the theoretical foundation that led to monism is exceptionally interesting. Strömholm identifies the key to the system as a focus on the work, the "object" of protection in both economic and personal terms. In a rather Hegelian twist, the work itself includes two elements: the

---

143. Strömholm traces monism to the earlier theories of Harum, Dambach, and Stobbe. *See* Strömholm 1967, vol. 1, *supra* note 54, at 205–07.

144. Adolf Dietz, *Legal Principles of Moral Rights (Civil Law) General Report, in* THE MORAL RIGHT OF THE AUTHOR 54, paras. 16 & 17 (Association littéraire et artistique internationale 1993).

145. The names of Kohler, Gierke, and, writing at the turn of the twentieth century, Allfeld, find prominence in Strömholm's study. *See* Strömholm 1967, vol. 1, *supra* note 54, at 330, and Strömholm IIC, *supra* note 2, at 225–27. Allfeld, in particular, is an important theorist of monism.

work in its realized form, and the will of the author, which is responsible for making it available to the public.[146] He comments:

> Until the author decides to publish it, the work would not be, according to Allfeld, the object of a *patrimonial* right; it is the *will* of the author that brings it into the world of commerce. On this basis, Allfeld establishes his own definition: the author's right, he says, "has its roots in the personality of the author and its foundation in the fact of intellectual creation; it is the exclusive right to decide if, when, in what form and to what end the results of his creativity should be communicated to a third party." As a result of the duality of interests involved, the author's right is neither patrimonial nor personal; it is a law of its own kind, valid against a third party, impossible to forfeit, but alienable at the author's will and transmissible upon his death.[147]

As suggested in this paragraph, monism has a number of practical consequences that are interesting, and help to distinguish German moral rights from the French approach. Two considerations are important: the first concerns the inalienability of moral rights, and the second relates to the duration of protection for moral rights.

While German law accepts the principle that moral rights are inalienable, it differs from French law in ceding to authors the ultimate right of decision when it comes to waiving one's own moral rights. Notwithstanding some specific provisions, as noted below, there is no general prohibition on the waiver of moral rights in German law. Indeed, the absolute prohibition on waivers of moral rights, which is normal in French law, raises the hackles of some French commentators. They feel that it is an illustration of the French state's paternalistic attitude towards authors, which seems to assume that authors are ill-qualified to protect their own interests.[148]

The availability of waivers leaves open the practical question of how to address the weakness of bargaining power that characterizes many, possibly

---

146. On Hegel, see the useful entry in the Stanford Encyclopedia of Philosophy, *available at* http://plato.stanford.edu/entries/hegel/.

147. Strömholm 1967, vol. 1, *supra* note 54, at 330. Strömholm further states that "Tant qu[e l'auteur] . . . n'aurait pas décidé de la publier, l'oeuvre ne serait pas, d'après ALLFELD, l' *objet* d'un droit patriomonial; c'est la volonté de l'auteur qui la fait entrer dans la sphère des biens. Sur ces bases, ALLFELD établit sa propre définition: le droit d'auteur, dit-il, 'a ses racines dans la personnalité de l'auteur et son fondement dans le fait de la création intellectuelle; c'est le droit exclusif de décider si, quand, sous quelle forme et dans quel but le résultat de cette création doit être communiqué aux tiers.' Il résulte de la dualité des intérêts engagés que le droit d'auteur n'est ni patrimonial ni personnel: c'est un droit particulier, opposable aux tiers, insaissable mais aliénable à la volonté de l'auteur et transmissible à cause de mort."

148. *See, for example,* see Pierre Recht, *Le Droit d'Auteur, supra* note 86; he is extremely skeptical about moral rights.

most, relationships between authors and their publishers. In Germany, the issue is addressed through an interesting combination of legislative measures designed to protect the author from unfair treatment. A number of provisions are to be found in the Copyright Law itself. In keeping with the monist theory at its core, the German Copyright Law will not allow the outright transfer of copyright,[149] and it includes specific limitations on the content of licenses.[150] German law allows moral rights to be waived, but only in circumstances that are tightly controlled. Specifically, the German law provides that the person granted an exploitation right may not make alterations to the author's work, unless they have been specifically agreed;[151] at the same time, certain aspects of the authors' rights cannot be waived at all. The author retains a right to revoke his work for reasons of changed conviction, which cannot be taken from him by contractual or other means.[152] Similarly, no agreement committing an author to the exploitation of future works can be valid for more than five years, and the author cannot extend these rights of exploitation over his yet-to-be-created works by the indirect means of waiving his right to terminate such an agreement.[153] These rights are not specifically identified as moral rights in the German Law; but the right of revocation, or withdrawal, is usually considered to fall under the rubric of moral rights. The provision on future works seems to involve moral interests, particularly the prerogatives of disclosure, and the moral element of free control over one's future earnings—which, in the case of artists, are often unforeseeable. It is perhaps closest to a recognition of an "innate right" to one's own future freedom, something like a right against slave labor. Again, its explicit recognition in the German law seems to fit well with the general emphasis on the principle of disclosure as the essence of the German system for authors' rights.

Interestingly, Germany has recently adopted a new law that specifically addresses the problem of inequality of bargaining power between authors and their publishers. It is a "Law to Strengthen the Contractual Position of Authors and Performing Artists,"[154] and as such, it seems particularly

---

149. The German Copyright Law, *supra* note 136, Section 29 provides that the only way in which copyright can be transferred is by inheritance.

150. *See, for example*, see Chapter IV on the *Right to Use a Work: German Copyright Law, supra* note 136. Copyright as a whole "shall not be transferable": Art. 23(3).

151. German Copyright Law, *supra* note 136, sec. 39(1); the author must not refuse to consent to alterations "which he cannot reasonably refuse."

152. *Id.*, sec. 42: "The right of revocation may not be waived in advance. Its exercise may not be precluded."

153. *Id.*, sec. 40. Section 41 also includes a "right of revocation for non-exercise," which can be invoked where the publisher's insufficient exploitation of a work "causes serious injury to the author."

154. Gesetz zur Stärkung der vertraglichen Stellung von Urhebern und ausübenden Künstlern vom 22. März 2002, BGBl. I S. 1155 [Law to Strengthen the Contractual Position of Authors and Performing Artists of March 22, 2002, amending the Copyright Law of Sept. 9, 1965, as

important in a digital environment where, once they have released it to the public, authors have less control than ever over their works. As Jens Schovsbo points out:

> A recent and most interesting development . . . has taken place in Germany, where special legislation in the context of copyright law to strengthen the legal position of (individual) authors (and performing artists) was introduced in 2002. Interestingly, from the e-consumer's point of view, the background for this legislation was also . . . changing market condition[s] and [the] increased risks of misuse of market power in the contractual relationship as a consequence of . . . new technologies and changing market conditions (fewer and stronger publishers and other producers). The German law aims in part to make sure that producers would not use their bargaining power to secure for themselves all the fruits of the copyright expansion.[155]

Interestingly, Schovsbo observes that there is a new identity of interests between authors and their public in the digital environment. He comments:

> *In many ways the individual author of books, music etc. would seem to be in a position similar to that of the consumer.* The present fixation in copyright on the investment interests of corporations is bad news to consumers and individual authors alike and an initiative like the German one certainly suggests a more active role . . . [for] copyright law to regulate the distribution of the copyright reward and to intervene in a contractual relationship to protect the weaker party.[156]

For Schovsbo, the digital context translates into new vulnerabilities. As corporations seek and acquire unprecedented new powers over the digital transformation of works—through copyright law reform—authors, as well as members of the public who want to have access to copyright works, become subject to a new level of exploitation.[157] The same idea can be expressed in more positive terms, in the recognition of a relationship of new closeness and more direct communication between authors and their public. In effect,

---

last amended by Article 16 of the Law of Dec, 13, 2001.], *available at* http://www.wipo.int/clea/docs_new/pdf/en/de/de094en.pdf.

155. Jens Schovsbo, *Integrating Consumer Rights into Copyright Law: From a European Perspective*, 31(4) J. Consumer Pol'y 393, 403 (2008) (footnote omitted).

156. *Id.*, at 403–04 (emphasis added; footnote omitted).

157. This is a quick summary of the dynamics behind the adoption of the American Digital Millenium Copyright Act, 112 Stat. 2860 (1998) [DMCA]. A summary of the DMCA is provided by the U.S. Copyright Office, *available at* http://www.copyright.gov/legislation/dmca.pdf.

digital technology has led to the "democratization" of their relationship.[158] Authors increasingly depend on the public for the recognition of their rights. The ability of corporations to compel respect for copyright ownership through new laws and new punishments is only one variable in an incredibly complex equation affecting the ability to enforce rights.[159] A copyright law without credibility can hardly be considered a law at all—at least, not in a democratic sense.

A second consequence of monism arises in relation to the duration of rights. The French dualist system allows the duration of protection for moral rights to differ from the term of economic rights. Under French law, the result is to grant a longer term of protection for moral rights than for economic rights. Moral rights are valid in perpetuity under French law. They will never expire.[160] In contrast, German monism links the duration of the rights to each other. Moral rights in Germany are protected only for the duration of economic rights.[161]

It is clear that a dualistic approach would make it easier to accord perpetual protection to moral rights. In the monist system, a separate duration for moral rights would break the fundamental concept of unity between moral and economic interests.[162] However, dualism does not require perpetual protection. All that dualist theory really accomplishes is to open up the possibility of choice on the important question of duration. Dietz observes that "there is no necessary correlation of dualism and perpetuity," and points out the

---

158. *See, for example,* the comments in Mira T. Sundara Rajan, *Moral Rights in the Digital Age: New Possibilities for the Democratization of Culture,* 16(2) INT'L REV. L. COMPUTERS & TECH. 187 (2002).

159. Indeed, the successful enforcement of copyright is likely to depend on much more than the improvement of police and customs powers. This approach is cosmetic; practical powers of enforcement are only the tip of the iceberg, but deeper problems involving the credibility of law, the absence of democratic infrastructure in societies where piracy is common, and a growing public distaste for copyright reform in many countries are other relevant factors. *See, for example,* the discussion of the situation in post-socialist countries in Sundara Rajan, *Copyright and Creative Freedom, supra* note 7, especially Chapter III, "Copyright Law in Transition," 47–71. An updated version of this chapter is also available in Mira T. Sundara Rajan, *Introduction in* INTELLECTUAL PROPERTY: EASTERN EUROPE AND THE CIS (Mira T. Sundara Rajan ed. Oxford Univ. Press 2008).

160. The perpetual duration of French moral rights was recently affirmed by the *Hugo* case, *supra* note 88, although the case was not decided in favor of the writer's heirs.

161. Article 64 of the German Copyright Law, *supra* note 136, provides that economic copyright lasts for the lifetime of the author and seventy years after his death. By the dualist theory, moral rights endure for the same period under German law.

162. But Dietz observes that "[i]f the German and, perhaps, also the Swiss example demonstrate that monistic or unitary interpretation of copyright shows a natural tendency to stop moral right protection together with copyright as a whole, there exists no necessary correlation. Duration of moral rights longer than the period of protection of the economic rights is rather a question of culture and policy." Dietz, *supra* note 144, para. 37.

great diversity of moral rights duration in countries that would categorize themselves as dualist.[163]

3. The Modern Moral Rights: Germany and Austria

In keeping with the theoretical tradition developed by German-speaking jurists, German copyright law protects three moral rights: disclosure, authorship, and integrity. German law treats the right of revocation separately in the Law, and it also includes the quasi-moral rights—in keeping with the flavour of the law, perhaps moral "interests" might be a better term—of access to one's own work, and an artist's resale right.[164]

The right of disclosure is a right of "publication" within the terms of the German law. It is comprehensively protected in the German provision, including communication of both the work and any attempt to "publicly communicate or describe the content of . . . [the] work."[165] The right of attribution is framed in broad terms, and it includes the right to be recognized as the author of one's work as one chooses, or to claim anonymity.[166] The integrity right is called a right against "Distortion of the Work." However, it is neither an unlimited right, as in France, nor a right framed according to the Berne formula. Instead, the German legislator opts for a prohibition against a "distortion or any other mutilation which would jeopardize [the author's] . . . legitimate intellectual or personal interests."[167] The German law does not enter into the question of reputation. Instead, it focuses on the author's

---

163. Dietz's list includes Belgium, Denmark, Italy, Netherlands, Spain, and Sweden. Dietz, *supra* note 144, para. 32. Canada should also be considered a dualist country, but one with lower levels of protection for moral rights, overall, than economic rights, and not only in relation to the question of duration. See the comments of the majority of the Supreme Court in *Théberge v. Galerie d'Art du Petit Champlain Inc.* [2002] 2 S.C.R. 336, 2002 SCC 34 (Can.), although the Supreme Court makes the ambiguous suggestion that Canada's copyright law is monist—"The Canadian legislation therefore recognizes the overlap between economic rights and moral rights in the definition of copyright"—in the subsequent case of *Desputeaux v. Éditions Chouette (1987) Inc.* [2003] 1 S.C.R. 178, 2003 SCC 17, para. 57.

164. The artist's resale right, or *droit de suite*, is now harmonized at the European level. *See* Directive 2001/84/EC of the European Parliament and of the Council on the resale right for the benefit of the author of an original work of art, 27.09.2001, *available at* http://ec.europa.eu/internal_market/copyright/documents/documents_en.htm.

165. German Copyright Law, *supra* note 136, art. 12.

166. *Id.*; art. 13 on the "Recognition of Authorship" provides: "The author shall have the right of recognition of his authorship of the work. He may decide whether the work is to bear an author's designation and what designation is to be used."

167. *Id.*; art. 14 on "Distortion of the Work" provides: "The author shall have the right to prohibit any distortion or any other mutilation of his work which would jeopardize his legitimate or personal interests in the work."

"interests," and it considers these in both their professional and personal dimensions.[168] Practically speaking, it seems a more general matter to attempt to show damage to one's "interests" than to have to prove damage to one's reputation. The language opens the door to a wider notion of proof where a violation of the integrity right is alleged.

A comparison with modern Austrian provisions is instructive.[169] The closeness of German and Austrian law reflects their shared theoretical heritage, but the Austrian law is a more ambiguous expression of the theory. On the one hand, Austrian law maintains the nontransferability of copyright, but, on the other hand, it does not explicitly recognize the right, or principle, of disclosure as a moral right. Rather, the author has an exclusive right to exploit his work.[170] However, a notion of disclosure is embedded in Article 14(3) of the Austrian law, which states a special rule in relation to "work[s] of literature or cinematography." The communication of the work to the public, or of its contents, "shall be reserved to the author, for as long as neither the work nor its substance has been published with his consent." As in the German law, the emphasis on substance is also noteworthy—it presents a contrast to the usual emphasis on communication of the *form* of knowledge rather than its substance, usual in copyright law and known as the distinction between unprotected idea and protected expression.[171] The provision is well adapted to the digital context, where transformations of a work can result in significant changes to the form while the content remains essentially unchanged. In the digital era, the economic and moral aspects of the work seem to converge in the fundamental principle of disclosure, illustrated, once again, by the emphasis on communication to the public in the Austrian law. Requiring an author's consent to communicate the work is clearly a moral right of disclosure; yet the Austrian act refuses to recognize it as such. In this sense, Austrian law makes a break from earlier Germanic theories of moral rights.

---

168. The inclusion of "personal" interests here seems reminiscent of the Berne emphasis on an author's "honor." *See* art. 6*bis* of the Berne Convention.

169. Federal Law BGBl No. 111 of 1936 on Copyright in Works of Literature and Art and on Neighboring Rights (Copyright Law), as amended by BGBl 1949/206, 1953/106, 1963/175, 1972/492, 1980/321, 1982/295, 1988/601, 1989/612, 1993/93, 1996/151 and by 1998/25, *available at*: http://www.wipo.int/clea/en/text_pdf.jsp?lang=EN&id=204 [Austrian Copyright Law].

170. *See* Austrian Copyright Law, *supra* note 136, Part 1, Exploitation rights, secs. 14–18.

171. The fixation requirement is another term expressing the same idea—that the form in which ideas are recorded can be protected by copyright law, but not the information contained therein. *See, e.g.,* TRIPs Agreement, *supra* note 11, Art. 9.1, and US Copyright Act, 17 U.S.C. §102 (b). Canadian law is noteworthy in that it odes not have a fixation requirement. This feature could have led to a potentially useful degree of flexibility when dealing with both traditional culture and new technology, but Canada's courts have read it into Canadian legislation. *See* DAVID VAVER, COPYRIGHT LAW, ESSENTIALS OF CANADIAN LAW SERIES (Irwin Law 2000).

The attribution right is comprehensive, allowing an author to protest any situation where his or her name is not associated with the work.[172] This is accomplished by splitting the right into two provisions, on the "Protection of Authorship" and the "Designation of Author," with the first empowering the author to protest against any situation of misattribution or failure to attribute.[173] The right cannot be waived. The combined effect of these provisions is to circumvent possible doubts about whether an author can protest against the association of his name with another person's work—the problem of forgery. As noted earlier, some commentators feel that this issue is not addressed by the language of the Berne Convention.[174]

The Austrian approach to the integrity right is to create a right for the "Protection of Works," which does not allow any alteration to the work without the author's consent. Interestingly, even if the author's consent is given, he may sue in the case of "distortions, mutilations or other alterations of the work which seriously violate his moral interests in the work." Once again, the broad language of "interests" replaces the specific issue of damage to reputation, and the provision is strong in effectively placing limits on the contractual relationship between author and publisher.

Finally, the Austrian law has been less willing to recognize quasi-moral rights than its German counterpart. It instituted an artist's resale right only in 2005, in order to bring Austrian law into conformity with the European Union Directive dealing with this issue. Its reluctance to recognize the resale principle may well have to do with the importance of Vienna as a market for art sales; a similar concern about the fate of London as the world's leading art market led to British reluctance to implement the right.[175] The Austrian law

---

172. Austrian Copyright Law, *supra* note 136, "Protection of Authorship 19.—(1) Where the authorship of a work is contested or the work is attributed to a person other than its creator, the latter shall be entitled to claim authorship. After his death, the right to safeguard the authorship of the creator of the work shall, in such cases, be held by the persons upon whom the copyright devolves.

(2) Waiver of this right shall be without effect."

173. *Id.*, arts. 19 & 20. Article 20 is on the "Designation of Author." Art. 20.—(1). The author shall determine whether and in what manner the work is to bear a designation of author.

(2) An adaptation may not bear a designation of author in a manner that would make the adaptation appear to be an original work.

(3) Copies of works of art may not bear a designation of author that would make the copies appear to be originals."

174. *See, e.g.*, von Lewinski, *supra* note 4, para. 5.99

175. The British fear was that London would cease to be competitive in relation to New York, which does not recognize an artist's resale right. *See* Nobuko Kawashima, *The Droit de Suite Controversy Revisited: Context, Effects and the Price of Art*, 3 INTELL. PROP. Q. 223, 227 (2006). In the United States, California is unique in instituting such a right. *See* the web pages of the California Arts Council, http://www.cac.ca.gov/resaleroyaltyact/resaleroyaltyact.php (last visited Aug. 22, 2010). For a general consideration of some of the moral rights issues involved in art forgery, *see also* Mira T. Sundara Rajan, *Moral Rights and Forgery*,

does include a provision on the "Obligations of Owners of Works," which provides for a limited right of access to one's own work even after it is sold. But the law also states that there is no obligation on an owner to "preserve" the work, effectively releasing him from the specter of an integrity claim for improper preservation.[176] This reference raises the interesting general question of whether Austrian law extends to prohibit destruction of a work, particularly at the hands of its owner.[177]

4. Historical and Cultural Context: The Nazi Past and the Significance of Reputation

In relation to culture, German law presents one difficult contrast with the law of France: the legacy of World War II and Nazi oppression. A discussion of cultural law, which moral rights represent, should not remain entirely silent on this issue. In its complex relationship with the arts, the Third Reich resembled its sister regime in totalitarian Russia rather closely. As the Soviet Union was actively preoccupied with the role of authors and artists, Hitler, too, had a well-known concern with art. He wanted art to serve in the cause, monstrous in his hands, of nation-building. The War was followed by the split between East and West, and East Germany, through its open lines of communication with the Soviet Union, mirrored the policies, practices, and problems of its "protector" state. But as Gladys Engel Lang and Kurt Lang observe:

> Over the years differences developed between the Federal Republic of Germany (FRG), closely tied to the West, and the German Democratic Republic (GDR),

---

in Original und Fälschung: Im Spannungsfeld von Persönlichkeitsschutz, Urheber-, Marken-und Wettbewerbsrecht 71–96, Schriftenreihe des Ludwig Boltzmann Institutes für Europarecht Herausgegeben von Gerte Reichelt, Band 25 (G. Reichelt ed., Manzsche Verlags-und Universitätsbuchhandlung, Vienna 2007). For some statistics on the importance of Vienna's art market to the Austrian economy, see http://departure.at/jart/prj3/departure_website/main.jart?rel=en&reserve-mode=active&content-id=1160330080281&presse_id=1243582751563.

176. A similar provision was added to the Indian copyright law in 1994. *See* Indian Copyright Act (*supra* note 39), and Copyright (Amendment) Act, 1994 (No. 38 of 1994). The immediate objective may have been to protect the government, as a significant owner of important Indian works, from liability for improper preservation. *See Sehgal* case, *supra* note 37.

177. Austrian Copyright Law, *supra* note 136:

> 3. OBLIGATIONS OF OWNERS OF WORKS
> 22. On request, the owner of a work shall be required to afford the author access to the work where necessary for the reproduction of the work: in such case, the author shall show due consideration for the interests of the owner. The owner shall not be required to surrender the work to the author for such purpose: neither shall he have an obligation towards the author to ensure the preservation of the work.

which quickly moved toward a state patronage system modeled on the one in the USSR. "Socialist realism" became the officially approved style but the actual degree of freedom for artists fluctuated with shifts in party policy. . . . Despite some cases of serious intimidation, especially through the 1960s, party leaders generally preferred—to quote an artist we interviewed—"to tame the recalcitrants, to keep them, so to speak, like domesticated animals." None of the measures during the near half-century of communist reign came even close to matching the ruthlessness and zeal with which the Nazis had pursued their purge of the past.[178]

These two authors define the problem as one of reputation, and, in particular, the flux of reputation with the political currents of the times. In many jurisdictions, the protection of reputation is, of course, the essence of the moral right of integrity: it is expressed as such in the Berne Convention. Modern German law prefers the terminology of moral or intellectual "interests," a term that is even broader than reputation. The German right of integrity is not an open-ended right, as in France, but it is framed as a right to "prohibit any distortion or any other mutilation of [the author's] . . . work which would jeopardize his legitimate intellectual or personal interests in the work."[179] It is a very strong right, and one that clearly encompasses reputation as a legitimate interest in one's work.

A comparison with modern Russian law is interesting. In its first post-socialist copyright law, the Copyright Act of 1993, Russian law created a right of reputation. In the 1993 Law, reputation was protected in lieu of the right of integrity. This is no longer the case, as the new provisions of Russia's Civil Code dealing with intellectual property from 2008 provide for comprehensive moral rights. The 2008 Russian Civil Code includes both a right of "name" and a right to the "inviolability" of the work. Russia also has a more general preoccupation with reputation, extending economic rights for new terms to compensate for the loss of reputation during Soviet rule. These measures do not find a parallel in German law.

But German copyright law has one distinguishing feature which changes the context for its interpretation. It is based in the German Constitution. Germany's Basic Law includes two provisions that are relevant to copyright. First, the right of the German federal government to legislate on copyright is noted in Article 73.9; unlike the American constitutional provision on copyright, the German clause is silent on policy.[180] However, the second relevant section is more interesting. It falls under the German provisions on freedom

---

178. Gladys Engel Lang & Kurt Lang, *Banishing the Past: The German Avant-Garde and Nazi Art*, 19(3) Qualitative Soc. 323, 325–26 (1996) (in-text references omitted).

179. German Copyright Law (*supra* note 136), art. 14.

180. The German provision finds a parallel in the Canadian Constitution, which contains a purely functional clause on "copyrights." *See* the British North America Act, 1867, art. 91.23,

of expression, and provides that, "Art and scholarship, research, and teaching shall be free."[181]

The German framework for moral rights arises in this context. Moral rights are seen as compatible with the constitutional prerogative for artistic and intellectual freedom. Indeed, they are, in some sense, an expression of these rights.[182] The Constitutional context in Germany reflects the progress of human rights in the post-World War II period, and it signifies a human rights rationale, or environment, for German copyright.

The differences from the American Constitutional framework for copyright should, once again, be noted. The U.S. approach treats copyright as a practical matter, simultaneously involving the provision of incentives to authors and the protection of the public interest in knowledge that is acquired by access to copyright works.[183] The logic of individual rights is not apparent in the U.S. Constitutional provision. Its focus is, rather, on the development of society.[184] It is interesting that this most individualistic of nations may have the most collectivist copyright system in the world.

---

available at http://laws.justice.gc.ca/en/const/3.html#anchorbo-ga:s_91> (last visited Aug. 22, 2010).

181. German Basic Law (Grundgesetz, May 23, 1949), art. 5(3), *available at* http://www.iuscomp. org/gla/statutes/GG.htm (last visited May 2, 2010). The German original may be seen on the website of the German Parliament at http://www.bundestag.de/dokumente/rechts-grundlagen/grundgesetz/index.html (last visited May 2, 2010).

182. German Basic Law (Grundgesetz), art. 5(3). *See* the interesting comments on the Compendium (Cultural Policies and Trends in Europe) website: Germany/5.3 Sector specific legislation
5.3.1 Visual and applied arts. As is the case in other artistic fields, visual and applied art activities are covered under the Freedom of Art Guarantee of the Federal Constitution (Article 5.III GG). This provision guarantees everyone the right to freely work in the artistic domain and to strive for recognition of his/her work by the public, that is: the guarantee includes not only the "sphere of the creative work," but also the "sphere of impact" of that work via its publication and distribution. *See* http://www.culturalpolicies.net/web/germany.php?aid=531 (last visited July 13, 2010). It is also worth noting that this constitutional provision could be interpreted to impose limits on copyright protection, particularly where the freedom of expression of members of the public might be threatened by the inaccessibility of published materials.

183. U.S. CONST., art. I, § 8, cl. 7: "The Congress shall have power . . . to promote the progress of science and useful arts, by securing for limited times to authors and inventors the exclusive right to their respective writings and discoveries." *See* http://topics.law.cornell.edu/constitution/articlei#section1 (last visited July 13, 2010).

184. *See* Ginsburg, *supra* note 70, at 991. Both Ginsburg and Carla Hesse argue that the opposition of individualistic French law and public-oriented American law is generally overstated—at least, prior to the development of "personalist doctrines, such as moral rights" in the nineteenth century (Ginsburg, *supra* note 70, at 995). Hesse's work shows that the concept of author as public servant is important to the development of French copyright law. *See* Hesse, *supra* note 32, at 110 & n.6.

5. Conclusion

Germanic law offers an appealing theoretical rigor in its approach to moral rights. The law of Germany, itself, has maintained remarkable consistency in its theoretical approach from the origins of German moral rights. Deriving its principles from a concentration on the basic principle of disclosure, the original and ultimate prerogative of the author, Germany offers a comprehensive and logically satisfying approach to moral rights. The German tradition provides both a complement and a contrast to French law.

The emphasis on disclosure as the foundation of copyright law has new implications in the Digital Age. These are consequences of a practical kind: in an environment of easy manipulation and communication, few aspects of authors' or owners' rights can claim the same validity as the right of disclosure. In a sense, concepts of attribution and integrity have become ambiguous—is a digital rights management (DRM) scheme equivalent to attribution? And what constitutes distortion in relation to new forms of art, media, and entertainment? But the basic idea that the author has a right to choose how, whether, and when he releases his own work to the public remains fundamentally valid. The challenge of digital copyright law is to determine how far to build above a bare foundation, or whether this particular brand of minimalism signifies the best of all possible tastes.

E. Great Britain: Second Thoughts—The Reasons Behind an Early Rejection of Moral Rights[185]

In relation to moral rights, as in many other respects, the contrast between Great Britain and the Continental countries is striking. European countries place moral rights at the heart of their legal systems. The legal culture of England, however, is considered a hostile environment for moral rights. They are, it is said, incompatible with the common law.

This position is a curious one. A study of moral rights in the French and German traditions shows that the character of the law is essentially informal and precedent-based. This is so in spite of the fact that each of these two legal cultures is built on codification. German theorizing about the law occurred

---

185. This section refers to Great Britain to capture the reach of copyright law throughout England, Scotland, and Wales—as described below, the struggle to define the scope of copyright law in the wake of the Statute of Anne had an interesting intra-British dimension, pitting the enterprise of Scottish booksellers against the entrenched interests of London monopolists.

while French courts were already engaged in a practical exploration of the idea. In France, codification of the law did not take place until the late date of 1957, nearly a century and a half after moral rights were already well established in French legal practice. English law and moral rights may be incompatible; but that incompatibility has little to do with the structure of the common law. On the contrary, the flexibility and pragmatism of the common law are closely analogous to the processes by which moral rights actually emerged in European countries. If anything, the common law would appear to be especially well adapted to the recognition of moral rights.

In fact, despite the common belief, English law had developed an early appreciation of authors' moral interests. This fact is all the more remarkable in that the English recognition of moral rights preceded the era of the French Revolution and its newfound rhetoric of individual rights.[186] English judges recognized moral rights as early as 1769, in the landmark case of *Millar v. Taylor*;[187] however, they rejected the idea in the follow-up ruling of *Donaldson v. Beckett* in 1775.[188]

A consideration of how and why the moral rights concept was purged from English law is illuminating in two ways. First, it helps to deflate the myth that English law is inherently biased against the noncommercial interests of creators. Secondly, it shows that the history of copyright is one of cyclical repetition. The problems of copyright in the eighteenth century have close parallels in the conflicts of the twenty-first. The eighteenth-century solution led, as a side-effect, to the banishment of moral rights; a viable twenty-first century approach may be to revisit this once-discarded idea.

In the final analysis, the reasoning behind the British attitude to moral rights is as much cultural as legal. The complexity of the common law position can be distilled into two propositions, each potentially unattractive in its own way. First, moral rights were never recognized in English copyright statutes. Copyright in England is, fundamentally, a creature of statute, and their absence from the statutory scheme is a clear indication of their lack of legal status. The incompatibility, therefore, is not between moral rights and the common law; ironically, it arises between moral rights and the drive towards codification in English copyright history.

Secondly, legal parochialism must bear some blame. The concept of moral rights is not an English concept. It is an alien idea, an import from French law, and when it was received into the British tradition through amendments to the Berne Convention, of which Great Britain was an original signatory, it was considered with profound misgiving.[189] To some extent, the attitude is

---

186. *See* Desbois' comments on the venerable laws of the 1790s in France. Desbois, *supra* note 27.
187. *Millar, supra* note 29.
188. *Donaldson, supra* note 29.
189. The United Kingdom has been a member of the Berne Convention since December 5, 1887. *See* http://www.wipo.int/treaties/en/Remarks.jsp?cnty_id=1043C (last visited May 2, 2010).

justified—not in its ready condescension to the foreign, which should be instantly condemned,[190] but in its implicit grasp of the complexity of legal translation. The problem of translating *droit moral* into English is not just a linguistic one; it requires the translation of legal and cultural principles from one tradition to another.

Culture is a nebulous sphere. In one of W. Somerset Maugham's novels, the different significance of authorship to the French and the English draws comment from him, a brilliant English writer whose background and training were distinctly French. Writers are important in France, not in England, he claims; at least not in the same way. Writing about Elliot Templeton, the "arch-snob" and one of his most memorable characters–

> I knew that with his perfect sense of social relations he had realized that in English society as an author I was not of much account, but that in France, where an author just because he is an author has prestige, I was.[191]

The cultural factor translates equally into different levels of prestige in the authors' law of the two countries. One of the consequences is, no doubt, a greater willingness to recognize an author's moral rights in the French context.

From a legal point of view, this fact is slightly frustrating. It is difficult to account for cultural sensibilities in a legal analysis. How can we build a meaningful comparison of moral rights in two jurisdictions of such distinct cultural bias? What is normal in France may not be feasible in England; what is right for one society may be irrelevant to the other.

The much-maligned concept of harmonization may hold the key to resolving this conundrum. Harmonization has come to mean many things in the international regulation of copyright, and it is often misrepresented as a call for identical laws in different countries. Given the different soil and climate of copyright systems around the world, such crude legal transplantation is bound to fail. The prevalence of copyright "piracy" in so many countries is undeniable evidence of this problem. The global reality of economic inequality underlying copyright piracy is underplayed—so, too, is its legal counterpart, inadequacy of imagination.

Moral rights were adopted into Berne in 1928, and Ricketson describes the circumstances in which England and other common law jurisdictions acquiesced. *See* Ricketson, *Berne Convention, supra* note 2, paras. 3.28 & 3.60.

190. Ugo Mattei and other comparative scholars use the appropriate terminology of "legal transplants" to discuss this issue. *See* Ugo Mattei, *Three Patterns of Law: Taxonomy and Change in the World's Legal Systems*, 45 Am. J. Comp. L. 5 (1997).

191. W. Somerset Maugham, The Razor's Edge 9 (Vintage Books, Random House 1944).

The word harmonization comes from music, and music provides invaluable guidance on global law:

> Harmonization finds its natural context, not in law, but in music. In the legal analogy, it seems to have gained currency as meaning a process of revision that makes laws broadly similar to one another. In music, however, this is not what it means. The very notion of harmony depends on difference. Two identical notes cannot "harmonize" with one another—the essence of harmony has been brilliantly described as a juxtaposition of the disparate.[192] Harmony means that two different notes enjoy a relationship of compatibility within the terms of a defined musical language.[193] What is more, harmony arises when individual notes are colored by the larger context defined by sequences of different notes. If the legal analogy is to be well-drawn, legal "harmonization" should embrace some concept of a mutually complementary relationship, a level of consensus in the international sphere, however slowly it may be achieved. Harmonized laws will work in concert with other laws, in the context of a wider legal environment.

---

192. *See* Carl Dahlhaus's historical discussion of harmony in "Harmony," part 1, *Historical Definitions, in* NEW GROVE DICTIONARY OF MUSIC AND MUSICIANS (Stanley Sadie & John Tyrrell, eds., 2d ed. Oxford Univ. Press 2001); he goes on to comment, "harmony considered as a structural principle is just as much an intrinsic part of ancient and medieval music as it is of the tonal system of modern times. The two-note consonance constituted the foundation of the old tonal system, the three-note consonance that of the new." *See* Sundara Rajan, *Copyright and Creative Freedom, supra* note 7, at 10–11 & nn. 13–14: "To satisfy musicians, it may be worth noting that the closest thing to two identical notes making 'harmony' is an octave—the sounding of a note with the tone that, in scientific terms, is exactly twice the frequency of the original note. The listener would hear this as 'the same note' sounded above or below the original note. In his entry on the octave in the New Grove Dictionary of Music, William Drabkin clarifies its nature: 'To Western and most non-Western musicians, two notes an octave apart are in a sense alike, being different only in their relative registers and often seeming to blend into one another. This acoustical phenomenon has made the division of the frequency spectrum into octaves fundamental to both the understanding and the notation of music. The ancient Greeks, who recognized this phenomenon, called the octave *harmonia*, later *diapasōn*; Ptolemy, writing in the 2nd century, distinguished the octave from the other perfect intervals, calling it *homophōnia* (the 5th and 4th were called *symphōnia*).'"
193. The use of the term "musical language" is applied here in the sense of a musical genre—for example, the different "musical languages" of jazz or classical music. Technically, however, genres often share the same musical language—classic jazz makes use of the same musical language, based on harmony, as Western classical music. On the other hand, Indian classical music is based on a "modal" language, which does not use the concept of harmony as it is usually understood in Western music. Modal music was the dominant form of medieval Europe, and it was largely replaced by harmonic systems based on the relative pitch of notes by the mid-seventeeth century—J.S. Bach's "Well-Tempered Clavier" was a response to this transformation. Modal music might be familiar to modern listeners in the West through experimental works like Eric Satie's "Gnossiennes' of "Gymnopédies," or modal jazz like Miles Davis's "Milestones." For an excellent summary of the issues, see Catherine Schmidt-Jones's web pages on "Connexions," *available at* http://cnx.rice.edu/content/m11639/latest/#s22.

Indeed, introducing "an identically phrased rule" into two different legal contexts may actually lead to legal differences, rather than the desired effect of sameness.[194]

In the area of moral rights, English culture could benefit from a consideration of the French approach, especially where the rejection of moral rights places English law in a position of world minority. But it must also be said that the French might benefit from the craftier English approach to authors' motives . . . The fact seems to receive covert acknowledgment in the recent ruling of the French *Cour de cassation* on the moral rights of Victor Hugo.[195]

1. Early History and the Statute of Anne, 1710

The Statute of Anne was the first British law to recognize an author's right in his own work.[196] Prior to this Statute, printing was regulated by a "privilege" granted directly to the printer by the Sovereign. Printing privileges were the sole province of the Stationers' Company, a group of printers who enjoyed the exclusive right to print works. Through the tightly controlled membership of the Stationers' group, it was the Sovereign who effectively acquired the power to supervise all publications appearing in the realm. The Stationers' monopoly made it easy for the monarch to monitor printed literature; the result was censorship. The recognition of individual rights of authorship in the Statute of Anne represented the culmination of a decades-long struggle for freedom of the press in England.[197] The same process was mirrored in France, where the breaking of the Paris Printers' Monopoly supported the genesis of an authors' right, into which, the French Revolution would ultimately blow the breath of life.

The recognition of authors was also a breakthrough in concepts, and this achievement should not be understated. It was made possible by influential thinkers: John Locke's labor theory of property was easily transferred to literary creation, and John Milton's arguments for freedom of the press were based

---

194. Sundara Rajan, *Copyright and Creative Freedom, supra* note 7, at 10–11. The point was emphasized in a statement by Professor Colin Tapper (personal communication with the author, 2006).

195. *See Hugo, supra* note 88: the symbolic award of one Euro was given, where 635,000 Euros were sought. But it seems doubtful that money was the only motivation for this lawsuit, given the history of Pierre Hugo's apparent involvement in Victor Hugo's work.

196. Statute of Anne, 8 Anne, c. 19 (1710). The text of the Statute of Anne is available on the website of the Lillian Goldman Library at Yale Law School, http://avalon.law.yale.edu/18th_century/anne_1710.asp. A facsimile copy of the book can be seen online at http://www.copyrighthistory.com/anne.html

197. *See* Lyman Ray Patterson, *Free Speech, Copyright and Fair Use*, 40(1) VAND. L. REV. 1 (1987).

on his understanding of the relationship between a work and the personality of its creator.[198] Indeed, paragraphs of Milton's famous pamphlet on free speech, "Areopagitica," read like an exposition of moral rights philosophy–

> For books are not absolutely dead things, but do contain a potency of life in them to be as active as that soul whose progeny they are; nay, they do preserve as in a vial the purest efficacy and extraction of that living intellect that bred them.[199]

The Statute represented a political breakthrough in another sense: it broke the economic monopoly enjoyed by the Stationers and, in particular, by the formidable printers' oligopoly known as the Conger, who had come to dominate eighteenth-century printing.[200] Prior to the Statute, the Stationers acquired the right to print a work from its author, and continued to exercise it without practical limitations in time. Moreover, as Lyman Ray Patterson points out, an entire industry had grown up around the printing of classics, whose authors were deceased, and where the question of the author's consent was irrelevant.[201] The Stationers recognized each others' prerogatives, and the printing right of each was in effect the exercise of a "copyright" that fellow members of the oligopoly would respect.

The Statute of Anne shattered this system. Under the terms of the new law, the right to print was no longer a right of the Stationers: it was a right of the author, to be allotted to the printer for a fourteen-year period, after which time, it would return to the author.[202] At the same time, the Stationers themselves could no longer benefit from the exclusive right to print. Instead, printing was thrown open to the world at large, and the Stationers had to compete

---

198. Milton's Areopagitica is a manifesto of the movement for a free press. *See* JOHN MILTON, AREOPAGITICA (AMS Press 1971), with a commentary by Sir Richard C. Jebb, and with supplementary material. [Areopagitica]. The text is available on the website of the St. Lawrence Institute at http://www.stlawrenceinstitute.org/vol14mit.html (last visited May 1, 2010).

199. *Id.*

200. *See* LYMAN RAY PATTERSON, COPYRIGHT IN HISTORICAL PERSPECTIVE 151 (Vanderbilt University Press 1968) ("In 1710, copyright was the right of a publisher to the exclusive publication of a work, and functioned to prevent literary piracy; by 1774, copyright had come to be the right of an author, and still functioned to protect the exclusive right of publication.") Patterson draws attention to the power of the Statute of Anne, which effectively established the notion of an *author's* copyright over this period. It is worth noting that the thinkers who lobbied for the right over the preceding half-century, such as Milton and Locke, also offered a conceptual basis for the grant of the right. It was a reflection of an individual's property right in his own labour.

201. *See Id.*, at 151–52; *see also* LAWRENCE LESSIG, FREE CULTURE: HOW BIG MEDIA USES TECHNOLOGY AND THE LAW TO LOCK DOWN CULTURE AND CONTROL CREATIVITY ch. 6 (Penguin Press 2004).

202. Statute of Anne, *supra* note 196.

in an open market. Finally, the Stationers would no longer have exclusive rights—*de facto* privileges—in classic works. On this last issue, the Statute relented slightly: it did include a transitional provision for the continued protection of Stationers' printing rights in classic works for 21 years. But under this "grandfather" clause, too, privileges would expire. After 21 years, the works would fall into the public domain, and then could be printed by anyone.

How could the Stationers and their collaborators allow the passing of their lucrative monopoly without a struggle? The issue came to a head in two celebrated cases, *Millar v. Taylor*, decided in 1769, and *Donaldson v. Beckett*, which settled the issue finally in 1774.[203] Both cases involved rights to print a celebrated long poem by James Thomson, "The Seasons," and the struggle arose between the booksellers of London, who wanted to hold on to their monopoly, and Scottish booksellers, represented by Alexander Donaldson of Edinburgh, who began to print inexpensive editions of classic works, arguing that the expiry of the grandfather clause in the Statute of Anne laid these works open to the public in 1731. In their struggle to hold on to power, the Stationers did something that was to be precedent-setting on a grand scale: in a strategy that is weirdly familiar in the Digital Age, the booksellers donned the mask of the author to argue for the promotion of their own interests.[204] The rejection of their suit by the English courts dealt a death blow to the formidable monopoly that they had enjoyed.

In this clash, however, there was an unexpected casualty: moral rights. As the *Miller* and *Donaldson* cases were decided, the possibility of legal recognition for the natural, noncommercial, or moral interests of authors was raised, and then definitively eliminated from English law. The concept of a moral right for British authors was not to be revisited for more than two hundred years.[205]

a. Early Recognition of a Moral Copyright: *Millar v. Taylor* (1769)

When the Stationers first went to court to vindicate their monopoly, they framed their arguments with care, using the very language of the Statute of

---

203. *Millar* and *Donaldson*, *supra* note 29.
204. In this regard, Patterson observes: "[C]opyright did not come into existence until the printing press facilitated the reproduction and widespread distribution of books. To protect the right to exclusive distribution, publishers created copyright. From this protection the author who created the work gained at best a reward secondary to that of the publisher. Copyright, therefore, originally functioned to encourage not creation, but distribution. In this regard, copyright's function is essentially the same today." *See* Lyman Ray Patterson, *Free Speech, Copyright and Fair Use*, 40(1) Vand. L. Rev. 1 (1987) at 8 (footnotes omitted).
205. Moral rights provisions were finally adopted as Chapter IV of the Copyright, Designs and Patents Act of 1988, c. 48, *available at* http://www.opsi.gov.uk/acts/acts1988/ukpga_19880048_en_1.htm (last visited May 1, 2010).

Anne to a new purpose. The Statute of Anne had recognized an author's copyright for the first time, but in doing so, the Stationers argued, the Statute did not extend authors' rights at all. Rather, the statutory copyright was a limited one. Indeed, the limitation of rights of printing to fourteen years, with the possibility of a renewal for fourteen more, was severely restrictive. Instead, authors actually enjoyed a copyright at common law. Unlike the statutory copyright, the common law right would be valid in perpetuity, and need not be subject to any limitation in time.

What was the basis for the Stationers' argument? As Patterson points out, the Stationers' familiarity with copyright was of long standing. The copyright, or right of printing, enjoyed by the Stationers was one which *they* had enjoyed, at least in theory, as a perpetual right. From the Stationers' perspective, perpetual protection was both an advantageous and, therefore, natural way of looking at copyright.[206]

But the introduction of the author brought a new dimension to the right. From the Stationers' perspective, copyright should be perpetual because it had always been so. But the recognition of a perpetual copyright for authors had to be based on some public policy rationale that fit with the Statute of Anne. This rationale found voice as the idea of a natural right of authorship, and it was easily derived from the humanistic arguments of Milton, Locke, and their contemporaries, dealing not only with authorship, but also, with property. The argument was accepted by the court in *Millar v. Taylor*, and Lord Mansfield affirmed the continued existence of authors' natural rights at common law, notwithstanding the presence of the Statute of Anne.

The author's right described by Lord Mansfield is mysterious. What common law principle was its source? As Mark Rose points out, Lord Mansfield relies on "the author's prepublication right" as the origin of common law rights. Lord Mansfield cites two precedents in support of the idea that the copyright in a book is something different from the possession of the book itself, a position that supports the idea of copyright as something more than physical property, and beyond mere physical control of the work.[207] But this search for the origin of the concept ultimately proves fruitless. As Rose observes, in none of these cases, "nor in immemorial custom

---

206. On the Stationers' practices, L. Ray Patterson comments: "The second compromise—giving the assignee all the rights of the author—played an even more important and ultimately determinative role in creating the confusion in copyright law. This provision enabled publishers to use authors as foils in their quest for recognition of a perpetual common-law copyright. *This perpetual common-law copyright, ostensibly for the benefit of authors, could be assigned to the publisher and, therefore, would effectively supersede the statutory copyright.*" Patterson, *supra* note 200, at 151–52 (emphasis added).

207. *See* MARK ROSE, AUTHORS AND OWNERS: THE INVENTION OF COPYRIGHT 79 (Harvard Univ. Press 1993): the cases are *Pope v. Curll* (1741) 2 Atk. 342, 26 Eng. Rep 608 (Ch.), involving the rights to print letters written by Pope but in physical possession of the person

because the introduction of printing was itself within living memory," can we pinpoint a source.[208] In Ronan Deazley's view, common law copyright never existed; there was truly no such thing as a common law copyright, but Lord Mansfield advocated for one with certain objectives in mind:

> The decision, handed down by Lord Mansfield's court, represents no less than a triumph of creative historical revisionism and legal advocacy. Notwithstanding the reality of the Statute of Anne ... the history of the first four decades of lawful book publishing in Britain had been carefully re-crafted. The London monopolists had picked a number of disparate legal-historical threads, bound them together within a compelling ontological framework, and created a new, altogether different, coherent form. The perpetual common law right had literally been written, talked and argued into existence.[209]

Clearly, Lord Mansfield was engaged in a creative legal enterprise: he wanted to redefine the law of copyright while relying upon the pedigree supplied by recent copyright judgments. He acknowledges his own comments as the product of long experience with the issue. His judgment is also strikingly impractical: the recognition of a common law copyright would have meant a re-establishment of the booksellers' monopoly. As Rose observes, "So far as [Lord Mansfield] ... was concerned, evidently, the justness of the fundamental principle rendered all other considerations secondary."[210]

From a moral rights perspective, Mansfield's comments on the actual substance of the common law copyright are riveting. His view of the author's right is comprehensive: the author's right originates in principles of "just[ice]." A failure to recognize the enduring nature of this right will lead to ill effects—

> He is no more master of the use of his own name. He has no control over the correctness of his own work. He can not prevent additions. He can not retract errors. He can not amend; or cancel a faulty edition. Any one may print, pirate, and perpetuate the imperfections, to the disgrace and against the will of the author; may propagate sentiments under his name, which he disapproves, repents and is ashamed of. He can exercise no discretion as to the manner in which, or the persons by whom his work shall be published.[211]

---

to whom they were addressed, and *Duke of Queensberry v. Shebbeare* (1758) 2 Eden 329, 28 Eng. Rep. 924 (Ch.).

208. *See id.*, at 79–80.
209. Ronan Deazley, On the Origin of the Right to Copy: Charting the Movement of Copyright Law in 18th-century Britain 178–79 (Hart Publishing 2004).
210. Rose, *supra* note 207, at 84.
211. This passage is quoted by Mark Rose, *supra* note 207, at 80.

This paragraph could not be a clearer statement of the moral rights approach. Mansfield recognizes every fundamental moral right later described by French and German writers—not only attribution—"use of his own name"—and integrity—"correctness," "additions," "errors"—but also, a right of withdrawal—the implication that "perpetuation" of the work in circumstances where the author "repents" or feels "ashamed" should be disallowed. The principle of disclosure occupies a central position in Mansfield's understanding of the author's rights and prerogatives: he defines it as the author's "discretion as to the manner in which, or the persons by whom his work shall be published."

Patterson points out the presence of moral rights in Mansfield's approach, and he goes on to a key observation: the *Millar* case makes it clear that the idea of an author's moral right, in English law, was inextricably linked with the recognition of a common law copyright. The Statute of Anne did not accommodate the idea of a comprehensive right for authors. Rather, it sought to protect the rights of both authors—an innovation—and publishers—a transitional measure in relation to the existing rights of booksellers, but also, an approach that laid the groundwork for the publishing regime of the future. Patterson concludes:

> Mansfield skillfully conflated the rights of the author and bookseller and invested copyright with the author's moral rights. The end result was to foreclose the future development of the author's rights in his work independent of copyright because copyright pre-empted the field. If a copyright encompassed all the rights in the work, the author's rights would become inextricably bound with the publisher's rights in accordance with the publisher's claims. Ironically, this development was detrimental, not beneficial, to the author. It eliminated the opportunity for courts to distinguish between the work and the copyright of the work. By embracing this conflation of rights, common-law jurisdictions forfeited the development of the doctrine of moral rights by default.[212]

Nothing in the Statute of Anne suggests a moral right. The most that could be said is that the Statute established an author's personal right to control the publication of his own work—implicit recognition of the principle of disclosure. Disclosure is the right to decide upon the publication of one's own, unpublished manuscripts, and William Patry asserts that

> [t]he United States' earliest statutes and case law were imported from England, where, under the common law, an author's right to prevent the unauthorized publication of his or her manuscript appears to have been recognized on the

---

212. Lyman Ray Patterson, *Free Speech, Copyright and Fair Use*, 40(1) VAND. L. REV. 1, 30–31 (1987) (emphasis added and footnotes omitted).

principle of natural justice, the manuscript being the product of intellectual labor and considered as much the author's own property as the physical substance on which it was written. Sir William Blackstone, English jurist and writer on law, associated such protection with the law of occupancy, which involves personal labor and results in "property," something peculiarly one's own (as implied by the Latin root "proprius").[213]

Patry's comment is slightly controversial, in the sense that the disclosure principle is not a common law doctrine, and the very existence of common law copyright is questionable. But the right of disclosure is clearly a feature of statutory copyright, expressed in the Statute of Anne, which "vest[ed] the Copies of Printed Books in the Authors or Purchasers of such Copies." As far as "Purchasers," or publishers, are concerned, the right is a transitional right; the focus of the new system is to give to authors a right to control publication of their own, unpublished manuscripts. But it is not a common law right; it is a statutory right established by the Statute of Anne. The policy rationales behind the right of disclosure are apparent in the preface of the Statute, which states

> Whereas Printers, Booksellers, and other Persons, have of late frequently taken the Liberty of Printing, Reprinting, and Publishing, or causing to be Printed, Reprinted, and Published Books, and other Writings, without the *Consent of the Authors or Proprietors* of such Books and Writings, to their very great *Detriment*, and too often to the *Ruin of them and their Families*: For Preventing therefore such Practices for the future, and for the *Encouragement of Learned Men to Compose and Write useful Books . . .*[214].

The Statute clearly articulates three policy rationales: the importance of consent from the author or owner of a copyright before reprinting of the work can be lawful; the financial difficulty suffered by authors—and owners!— and their families, and the availability of legal action against unauthorized reprinting in order to correct it; and, finally, the provision of an incentive to "encourage" the creation of "useful Books."

Bringing in moral interests was undoubtedly a common law affair. In doing so, however, common law adjustment of the rights of authors would have a practical impact on publishers. This was a reflection of the historical circumstances of the time, perfectly mirrored in the language of the Statute of Anne. The Statute was, in some sense, a transitional statute, marking the boundary between censorship—of which, the printers' monopoly was an artefact—and a free press. As such, the Statute was compelled to address the

---

213. William F. Patry, *Copyright Law and Practice* 3 (Bureau of National Affairs 1994), *available at* http://digital-law-online.info/patry/patry2.html (last visited May 1, 2010).

214. Statute of Anne, *supra* note 196, at I (emphasis added).

rights of both authors and publishers, whose position in the new regime, and relationship to one another, was to be redefined. Accordingly, any modification of the statutory treatment of authors through common law interpolations entailed changes to the rights of publishers, as well. The all-inclusive language of the Statute made it so.[215]

After the *Millar v. Taylor* case, how can the moral rights idea be said to be alien to English law? It was not. On the contrary, the *Millar* case shows that an English judge recognized the moral rights aspect of copyright law more than half a century before it became a matter of serious interest for the French. However, practical concerns about the implications of a common law copyright became an imperative reason to purge the moral rights concept from British law, as accomplished in the subsequent case of *Donaldson v Beckett*. In truth, a common law copyright presented dangers to freedom of the press. But there was nothing inherently incompatible about the relationship of moral rights with the common law. On the contrary, in Lord Mansfield's hands, the common law accommodated moral rights convincingly, and with ease.

b. Protecting Free Speech: Moral Rights Revisited in *Donaldson v. Beckett* (1774)

The subsequent failure of the moral rights concept in the *Donaldson* case had very little to do with objections of principle, or flaws in legal doctrine. The question was how the recognition of a common law copyright would affect the publishing regime established by the Statute of Anne. The Statute's purpose was to break the printing monopoly of the booksellers, and, through it, to strike at the heart of censorship. If a common law copyright beyond the Statute was to be recognized, would this purpose be accomplished?

Clearly not. Invoking rights beyond the Statute would have allowed publishers to do two things. First, they could continue to enjoy monopoly rights in works that they were already printing—classic works which, in modern terminology, belonged in the public domain. The literary heritage of England would become the property of the booksellers, and access to those works would be permanently controlled by them. Secondly, the booksellers might

---

215. Patterson, himself, blurs the distinction between common law copyright and moral rights. He states, "Finally, by limiting the rights of the copyright owner to rights that were economic in nature, it gave the user freedom to use the work for the purpose of learning." But this effect was achieved by limiting the rights of the copyright-holder to the Statute. Lord Mansfield's recognition of the moral rights as part of a "common law copyright" was not the reason behind the rejection of the common law copyright. Rather, the reason was to prevent the re-establishment of the booksellers' control over printing, a fact that Patterson has already pointed out in his detailed historical study. *See* Lyman Ray Patterson, *Free Speech, Copyright and Fair Use*, 40(1) VAND. L. REV. 1, 26 (1987).

be able to lay claim to printing rights in new works beyond fourteen years, the period stipulated by the Statute. What would happen after an author's death, and who would prevent the printer from enjoying the exclusive right to publish an author's work after his time? If the booksellers colluded, as was the norm at the time of the Statute of Anne, the mutual recognition of each other's printing "rights" could, in practice, generate new monopolies in valuable works. At the same time, the supposed supremacy of the author's will would be relegated to irrelevance by the printers.

The seriousness of these concerns led to a definitive ruling in the *Donaldson* case, which found that the principle established in *Millar* was untenable. No common law copyright existed beyond the Statute of Anne: to recognize one would be to thwart the very objectives of that Statute and to destroy the possibility of a free press while it was yet newborn. The ruling was accomplished on controversial terms, and Lord Mansfield abstained from judgment in the case;[216] but there could be no doubt that the concept of a common law copyright was destroyed. In the process, however, another idea became a covert casualty of the open conflict between common law and statutory copyright: moral rights.

No statutory basis for moral rights existed. Lord Mansfield's brilliant exposition of the moral rights theory associated it with its only possible legal source, the common law. As expounded by Lord Mansfield, the common law copyright reflected elements of natural law and, indeed, this was more or less the genesis of the moral rights concept in France and Germany. Judges and scholars gave voice to theories of natural rights that had infiltrated their cultures at an important moment in history. In Great Britain, however, the problem of the booksellers meant that common law copyright was abolished wholesale. The proprietary rights of copyright-owners needed to be limited; at the same time, limits were imposed on the natural rights of authors. The problem was not one of cultural incompatibility; it was one of practical necessity. British law acquired an almost phobic dislike for the idea of rights of authorship beyond the well-limited language of the copyright law. Yet this was a product of hatred for censorship, and had little to do with natural rights theories *per se*.

c. Modern Approach

The formal enactment of moral rights in British copyright law finally occurred at the relatively late date of 1988. International copyright relations provided the catalyst for reform. Great Britain had been a signatory to the Berne

---

216. *See* MARK ROSE, AUTHORS AND OWNERS: THE INVENTION OF COPYRIGHT (Harvard University 1993) for a description of what happened; *see also* DAVID SAUNDERS, AUTHORSHIP AND COPYRIGHT (Routledge 1992).

Convention since 1887.[217] But a review of British law by the Gregory Committee, in 1952, had found that British law met its obligations under the Berne Convention without the need for any amendments.[218] In an ironic twist, Britain was deemed to provide adequate protection for moral rights through common law remedies, particularly the torts of defamation, passing off, and injurious falsehood. The common-law copyright, it seems, was revisited and found to be alive and well in relation to one issue, at least—the moral rights of authors.

However, a subsequent review of the very same British law in 1986 reached the startling conclusion that British law was *not*, in fact, in conformity with international requirements.[219] Since the Berne provisions on moral rights had not expanded since 1928, it would appear that a fundamental change occurred in British attitudes towards these rights over the intervening quarter-century. The Paper assessed Britain's moral rights protection as deficient, and incompatible with British obligations under the Berne Convention.[220]

The finding is all the more surprising when considering the evolution of moral rights in the Berne Convention between 1928 and 1986. Not only were the rights no more than they had been at the time of the 1952 study; the level of protection had actually been reduced. When international copyright law entered a crisis during the 1960s, the language of Article *6bis* was again scaled back. The 1967 Stockholm text of moral rights expressly accommodated the legal systems of common-law countries. It stated that, if a given country had not yet enacted moral rights at the time of its accession to Berne, the protection of "some" moral rights in that country could be restricted to the lifetime of the author. The link with common-law systems can be found in tort law. Personal torts cannot be protected after a person's lifetime. While a proper reading of the Berne article does raise a troubling question about the proviso that only "some" rights may cease with the death of the author, common-law countries have generally read the provision leniently, and allowed "all" of the quasi-moral rights at common-law to lapse with the author's death. American caution in approaching the Berne provisions presents an interesting contrast in this respect, and reflects a justifiable concern about the extent of the moral rights required by Berne.[221]

---

217. The UK acceded to the Berne Convention as of Dec, 5, 1887: *see* WIPO website, *available at* http://www.wipo.int/treaties/en/Remarks.jsp?cnty_id=1043C.

218. *See* Gregory Committee Report (1952) (Cmd 8662), paras. 219-226. For a detailed discussion, *see* Gerald Dworkin, *The Moral Right of the Author: Moral Rights and the Common Law Countries*, 19 COLUM.-VLA J.L. & ARTS 229, 237–38 (1995); *see also* Stamatoudi, *supra* note 36, at 479.

219. Whitford Commission Report/The White Paper//United Kingdom, Department of Trade and Industry, *Intellectual Property and Innovation* (HMSO, London 1986) (Cmnd 9712).

220. *See* Stamatoudi, *supra* note 36, at 488.

221. Article *6bis* of the Berne Convention, setting out protection for the moral rights of attribution and integrity, was agreed upon at the Rome revision conference of 1928. A proposal to

The timing of the 1988 revision project leaves no doubt that international forces played an important role in raising awareness among British legislators of the importance of moral rights.[222] For example, the ambiguous position of the United States in relation to moral rights became a source of international disapproval when the United States joined the Berne Convention in 1988. As the United Kingdom had previously done, the U.S. argued that authors' personal interests were effectively protected in American law without the adoption of special provisions. The dynamic structure of American law means that tort protections do play a significant role in that country.[223] However, the power of the copyright industry groups lobbying against moral rights, and the subsequent enactment of a *Visual Artists Rights Act* (VARA) for the limited protection of moral rights in the visual arts, have created an ambiguous situation.[224] The United States decision to join Berne was itself a precursor of much larger changes to come in international copyright, which were already developing in the Uruguay Round of GATT trade negotiations, and led to the establishment of the WTO, with unknown consequences for moral rights.[225] The growing importance of copyright harmonization in the European Union was also a factor influencing British reform.

At this crucial juncture, Britain seemed explicitly to reject the common-law tradition of a primarily economic copyright. Instead, the United Kingdom adopted a posture of acceptance towards the growing internationalization of intellectual property rights, recognizing the need to modernize its approach to moral rights to keep pace with international standards. However, progressive

---

extend moral rights to prevent outright destruction of a work was put forward in the 1948 Brussels conference; the text of the Article remained unchanged, the conference expressed its clear intention to encourage member countries to "introduce, in their domestic legislation, some dispositions prohibiting the destruction of literary and artistic works." *See* Ricketson, *supra* note 2, para. 8.109, citing a *"voeu"* adopted at the conclusion of the conference.

222. David Nimmer, *Conventional Copyright: A Morality Play*, 3 ENT. L. REV. 94, 95–97 (1992) discusses this issue in detail.

223. Cornish draws attention to the contrast with the UK, commenting: "The United States has now joined Berne, without directly providing moral rights in its copyright statute, but with other provisions which make legal protection somewhat stronger than that arising under English common law." *See* W.R. Cornish, *Moral Rights Under the 1988 Act*, 11(12) EUR. INTELL. PROP. REV. 449, 449 (1989). Cornish's argument was stronger before the *Dastar* case of 2003, which seems–partly as a result of overzealous application in subsequent cases—to have closed off many of these alternate avenues for moral rights at US law. *See* discussion of moral rights in the United States in Chapter 3, *infra*, "A Theory in Flux."

224. Visual Artists Rights Act of 1990, Pub. L. No. 101-650, 104 Stat. 5128, 17 U.S.C. § 106A [VARA]. *See* Nimmer, *supra* note 222.

225. The Uruguay Round of multilateral trade negotiations spanned eight years, from 1986 to 1994, and was concluded with the establishment of the World Trade Organization from January 1, 1995. For a comprehensive assessment of its accomplishments, see the seminal work by MICHAEL J. TREBILCOCK & ROBERT HOWSE, THE REGULATION OF INTERNATIONAL TRADE (3d ed. Routledge 1995).

thinking in this area proved to be difficult to implement in practice. The end result is characterized by Cornish as "a highly pragmatic outcome," in which, as in the United States, "the pressures of interest played a noteworthy part."[226]

In its modern form, the British protection of moral rights is striking in its complexity—one could say, obscurity. In contrast to other aspects of British copyright law, known for its "compressed drafting style," moral rights are drafted with an emphasis on attention to legislative detail.[227] The rights are laboriously explained, and the exceptions are listed in fairly comprehensive provisions.[228] For all this attention to detail, the act can boast neither clarity nor precision in its treatment of moral rights. A lawyer trying to understand these rights is rather like a physicist puzzled by the location of an electron: the more precise he wants to be, the more indeterminate is the result. In this case, the final form of Britain's moral rights legislation suggests hesitation about the policies they are supposed to implement, and uncertainty about how to do so.

A question remains: does the scheme in the 1988 Act move Britain forward in complying with the Berne Convention? On certain key issues, the provisions seem deficient. Notably, authors can only enjoy their right of attribution if the right has been asserted.[229] The purpose of this unusual section seems to be the provision of adequate notice that any attribution claims will be linked to the person making the assertion. As Cornish observes,

> The right to be identified (unlike the right against derogatory treatment) requires as a pre-condition that it be asserted by the person entitled. This is a form of warning which is necessary, at least in the Government's view, if authors and directors are not to take undue advantage of the right.[230]

Yet, Article 5 of Berne provides that, "The enjoyment and the exercise of [authors'] . . . rights shall not be subject to any formality . . ." The requirement of assertion is a clear violation of this principle.

---

226. Cornish, *supra* note 223, at 449.
227. *Confetti Records v. Warner Music UK Ltd.* [2003] EWHC 1274 (Ch).
228. *See* Copyright, Designs and Patents Act 1988 (c 48), secs. 79 (exceptions to the attribution right) and 81 (exceptions to the integrity right), Office of Public Sector Information, *available at* http://www.opsi.gov.uk/acts/acts1988/UKpga_19880048_en_1.htm (last visited May 2, 2010) [Copyright, Designs and Patents Act, CDPA].
229. *See id.*, secs. 77(1) and 78. This has led to the practical result that most books first published in Britain bear the legend, "The author asserts the right to be recognized as the author of the work," on the inside cover, or copyright page, of the book.
230. Cornish, *supra* note 223, at 449–50. The assertion can be made at any time, but a delay may affect claims for an injunction or damages.

i. Moral Rights in the Copyright, Designs and Patents Act 1988[231]

At first glance, the provisions in the *Copyright, Designs and Patents Act 1988* (CDPA) appear to create four distinct moral rights: a right to be identified as the author of a work, a right to object to the derogatory treatment of a work, a right to be protected from association with someone else's work, and a right of privacy in relation to photographs and film.

In reality, the Act protects the two moral rights provided for in the Berne Convention. The right to be identified as the author of a work—or, in the case of a film, as its director—corresponds to the right of attribution in Article *6bis*. A right against false attribution in section 84 is simply another aspect of the attribution right, although this aspect of the right can only be implied into Article *6bis*.[232] In effect, this section appears to be a codified version of the common-law tort of passing off.[233]

At the same time, the right to protest derogatory treatment of the work is an expression of the integrity right. The formulation of this right is somewhat narrower than its Berne counterpart—it only covers "addition, deletion, alteration or adaptation" of the work, as opposed to the broad brush stroke of "modification." The section defines the key idea of "derogatory treatment" with a separate analysis of each word. Section 80 (2) (b) provides that "the treatment of a work is derogatory if it amounts to distortion or mutilation of the work or is otherwise prejudicial to the honour or reputation of the author or director." The provision is now confirmed to be limited to cases that cause prejudice to the reputation of the author, but the point was creatively contested in the *Confetti Records* case.[234] Given the placement of the clause "prejudicial to the honour or reputation of the author," the plaintiffs argued that any "distortion or mutilation" of a work would qualify as a violation of the right of integrity under the new British provisions. The court concluded that the "compressed drafting style" of the Act meant that the clause should apply to each word in this section, and a contrary interpretation would have expanded the scope of British moral rights far beyond what could have been foreseen by the drafters.

The provisions defining the integrity right are noteworthy for their systematic approach to each category of protected work, characteristic of the UK Copyright Act. Among other points of interest, the Act offers special provisions for film, extending moral rights explicitly to the soundtrack, and architecture,

---

231. CDPA, *supra* note 228.
232. Stamatoudi, *supra* note 36, at 490–91. Ricketson, *supra* note 2, para. 8.105 argues that the language of Berne effectively excludes this possibility.
233. See the case of *Moore v. News of the World Ltd.* [1972] 1 QB 441 (QB), Lord Denning on false attribution.
234. See *infra* note 224.

which allows an architect's name to be removed from his work if it is displayed in conditions that he finds unsuitable.[235]

An interesting addition to the list of moral rights in the British legislation is the right of privacy in relation to photographs and film taken in a domestic context.[236] The purpose of such a right would seem to be to protect the subject of a photograph from unwanted commercial exploitation by the photographer. As such, a privacy right could effectively balance the interests of the author and his subject. But the right is actually granted to the person who commissioned the photograph, and not directly to the subject himself. The availability of the right to protect the subject's privacy will therefore depend on the initiative of the person commissioning the image.[237] Clearly, this right cannot be considered a moral right in the classic sense.[238] Instead, it deals with a situation where the interests of someone other than the photographer—the author in this case—supersede the photographer's right. The person commissioning the author may well be the owner of the photograph, and therefore the holder of the copyright in it; but a moral right depends on authorship, not ownership. It is perhaps more accurate to call this right of privacy an exception to the right of disclosure or communication to the public, which attempts to balance the subject's personal privacy—or, as it may be, the privacy of the person commissioning the photo—against the moral right of the author.

ii. Practical Difficulties

The British provisions on moral rights are subject to a number of practical requirements that largely function as limitations restricting their scope.

---

235. Copyright, Designs and Patents Act 1988, sec. 80 (6): In the case of a film, the right is infringed by a person who—(a) shows in public, broadcasts or includes in a cable programme service a derogatory treatment of the film; or (b) issues to the public copies of a derogatory treatment of the film, or who, along with the film, plays in public, broadcasts or includes in a cable programme service, or issues to the public copies of, a derogatory treatment of the film sound-track. *Id.,* sec. 80(5): Subsection (4) does not apply to a work of architecture in the form of a building; but where the author of such a work is identified on the building and it is the subject of derogatory treatment he has the right to require the identification to be removed.

236. *Id.,* sec. 85: "private and domestic purposes."

237. *For example,* this situation arose in a recent Canadian case involving photos of the pianist Glenn Gould. *Gould Estate v. Stoddart Publishing Co.* (1996), 39 OR (3d) 545 (CA). The photographs had been taken in the 1950s for a journal article on his playing, but they were never published. When the photographer, Jock Carroll, assembled the photographs into a book on the pianist, the Gould estate sued, arguing under tort law, that his privacy had been violated. Here, the subject of the photos and the person who commissioned them are different; provisions like those in the UK Act would therefore not succeed in protecting the privacy of the subject.

238. Stamatoudi, *supra* note 36, at 491 argues that "the privacy right does not confer any additional right of the author of copyright. In this perspective is not a genuine moral right."

The striking requirement that the attribution right must be asserted has already been noted. In addition, the attribution and integrity rights are both subject to a series of elaborate and comprehensive exceptions. Interestingly, the question of what happens to moral rights in a technological context is a central concern.

Exceptions to the rights of attribution[239] and integrity[240] extend to several categories of technological works. Neither moral right can be claimed in relation to computer programs, computer-generated works, works created in the course of employment, news publications, or "collective works of reference"—all important types of new works, and works with new connotations, in a digital society.[241] Exceptions to the integrity right also include a particularly wide exception for modifications made by BBC broadcasting authorities. The provision responds to the scenario illustrated by the *Frisby* case, where the author of a play brought a case against the BBC to protest the deletion of a crucial line in the broadcast of his work.[242] The exception is noteworthy for its contribution to maintaining the sanctity of the BBC as British broadcasting authority.

The British treatment of moral rights in a technological environment is the very antithesis of the French approach. While the French have attempted to extend existing moral rights to technological creation, the British have preferred to exclude moral rights from technological works altogether. This approach was probably motivated by concerns about the implications of moral rights, but it is a legislative shortcoming that will almost certainly have to be reconsidered in due time.

iii. Inalienability and Waiver

The theoretical foundation of moral rights lies in the idea of a personal right of the author. Since moral rights are vested in the personality of the author, they are inalienable by definition. In the interest of consistency, it would be awkward to allow or to compel authors to use moral rights, a personal privilege, as a bargaining tool in negotiating professional matters.

However, it is not necessary for moral rights to be fully subject to alienation for this conflict to arise: it is also implicated in the narrower problem of waivers. Here, too, the issue is one of unequal bargaining power. When authors and publishers meet, the publisher typically enjoys vastly superior market clout. If the law allows moral rights to be waived, publishers may be in a position to take advantage of their greater bargaining strength by

---

239. Listed in Copyright, Designs and Patents Act 1988, *supra* note 225, sec. 79.
240. Listed in *id.*, sec. 81.
241. *Id.*, sec. 79(2)(a) & (c), and sec. 79 (3)–(6); sec. 79(2)(b) also provides an exception for typefaces; Section 79(7) also mentions Crown copyright.
242. *Frisby v. BBC* [1967] Ch 932 (Ch).

introducing standard form waivers into authors' contracts. In these circumstances, the formal possibility of waiving moral rights may seriously limit the practical significance of these rights.[243] The theory of moral rights does not require waiver to be completely banned, but, in consonance with the concept, the availability of the right must be subject to careful consideration in the interest of the author. With this proviso in mind, waivers are allowed to an extent even in a traditionally strong moral rights jurisdiction such as Germany; but, as noted, the author can invoke a waiver only in specific and well-defined circumstances.[244]

In principle, moral rights in Britain are inalienable. They cannot be assigned, but only inherited after the death of the author.[245] However, waivers are allowed, and, in contrast to the German model, the British provisions on waivers are especially broad.[246] The British Act allows any or all moral rights to be waived, and it also allows waivers of moral rights in relation to future works yet to be created—a provision that incites especially strong criticism from William Cornish.[247] Section 87 leaves open the possibility of standard waivers of moral rights in contracts between authors and publishers, and this probably explains why the provision "has induced a sense of relief in many entrepreneurs who deal with authors and directors."[248]

It is true that waivers will be subject to contract doctrines such as unconscionability and duress, which have developed to remedy situations of unequal bargaining power between the contracting parties. Whether they will be applied in disputes over moral rights in copyright contracts remains to be seen. To invoke them would require outright judicial activism based on an independent sense of justice and social priorities. Little legislative basis exists for a larger reading of moral rights beyond the text of copyright codes.

iv. Conceptual Confusion

In terms of theory, British legislation appears to be divided on moral rights. In dealing with the issue of duration, it follows the monist, German model.

---

243. This is the practical situation in Canada, as well as in the UK: see the comments in David Vaver, *Authors' Moral Rights in Canada*, 14 INT'L REV. INDUS. PROP. & COPYRIGHT L. 329, 349–52 (1983) [Vaver, *Authors' Moral Rights in Canada*].

244. *See* S. Fraser, *Berne, CFTA, NAFTA and GATT: The Implications of Copyright Droit Moral and Cultural Exemptions in International Trade Law*, 18 HASTINGS COMM. & ENT. L.J. 287, 292–95 (1996).

245. Copyright, Designs and Patents Act 1988, *supra* note 235, secs. 94 & 95: moral rights are not assignable, but, with the exception of the right of false attribution in section 84, they are inheritable upon the death of the author.

246. *Id.*, sec. 87.

247. Cornish, *supra* note 223, at 452.

248. *Id.*, at 451.

The duration of moral rights is generally equivalent to the term of copyright, although, in recollection of tort principles, the right of false attribution expires earlier, only twenty years after the author's death.[249] In spite of the appearance of this monist characteristic, however, the Act distinguishes strongly between economic and moral rights. The provisions on remedies, in particular, seem to establish a hierarchy between economic rights, or copyright proper, and moral rights. A violation of economic rights is considered an "infringement" of copyright, whereas a violation of moral rights is simply a breach of statutory duty. The possibility of an injunctive remedy for a violation of the integrity right is recognized in section 103, but there are no specific provisions regarding damages.[250]

This point leads to an interesting problem. For a civil law country, the award of injunctive relief is a normal remedy against moral rights violations. But in a common law country, damages are the usual remedy for copyright infringement. By excluding damages where moral rights are concerned, common law countries are reducing the status of those rights within their own legal systems—although injunctive relief is normal in the civil law. The problem that confronts common law countries is how to accord status to moral rights while preserving, to whatever extent appropriate, the availability of injunctive relief.

It is also not clear that the 1988 Act is informed by an understanding of the character of moral rights as a specific vision of authorship translated into law. The provisions distinguish between authors, film directors, and the commissioner of a work, all of whom enjoy moral rights independently of copyright ownership. However, the true purpose of moral rights is to protect the relationship between the author and the work. Whoever may actually assert the rights, their purpose remains the protection of this special relationship—a focus that may be lost when other interests, such as those of the subject in a photograph, are also expressed in moral rights language. In this respect, at least, the terminology of the Act is misleading.

v. Conclusions: The Birth of the Common Law Approach

It is clear that moral rights in Britain have not kept pace with technological developments. The legislation of 1988 explicitly excludes the possibility of moral rights in key kinds of technological works. Film is a notable exception, with the British law identifying the director as the "author" of a film, and endowing him with moral rights.[251] More generally, the British legislative

---

249. Copyright, Designs and Patents Act 1988, *supra* note 235, sec. 86. Personal torts expire with the lifetime of the person affected.
250. *See* Cornish, *supra* note 223.
251. *See, for example*, CDPA, *supra* note 228, sec. 77 on the right of attribution and sec. 80 on integrity.

provisions lack the conceptual and legal clarity required to deal with techno-logical pressures on authorship. The complexity and restrictiveness of the law seem almost intentional, and reflect political ambiguity. A lack of commit-ment and direction at the level of policy is clearly apparent in the first British provisions on the protection of authors' moral rights.

In many respects, the protection of moral rights in the *Copyright, Designs and Patents Act 1988* falls short of internationally accepted practice, at least as it is reflected in the Berne Convention. Moral rights protection in Britain appears to be significantly narrower in scope than the moral rights set out in Article *6bis* of the Berne Convention. In this respect, it would appear that the revision process failed to meet the immediate objective of raising UK stan-dards to the level of Berne. Rather, the latest provisions may be characterized, in many respects, as a codification of the informal protections known before 1988. It is worth noting that the moral rights provisions do not seem to offer a great deal of practical improvement from the pre-1988 situation in the UK, where the protection of authors' moral interests fell largely to the courts through accepted common law devices.[252]

Why is this significant? The question of whether common law torts pro-vide protection equivalent to a moral rights code is of fundamental impor-tance to the international community. Beginning with the UK, common law countries have continued to claim that informal protections through the mechanism of the common law address many moral rights concerns. Looking at moral rights through the lens of harmonization, the point is credible. It seems clear that different types of legal approaches will probably be appropri-ate in different legal systems. Indeed, the ability to recognize moral rights through the legal instruments peculiar to different systems will be one test of their adaptability to different environments. As noted above, the common law perspective is recognized in the revised Berne Convention of 1967 where the Stockholm text affirms:

> The rights granted to the author . . . shall, after his death, be maintained, at least until the expiry of the economic rights. . . . However, those countries whose legislation, at the moment of their ratification of or accession to this Act, does not provide for the protection after the death of the author of all the rights set out in the preceding paragraph may provide that some of these rights may, after his death, cease to be maintained.[253]

---

252. As Stamatoudi reports, case law on moral rights in the UK since 1988 has been very limited; it appears that the only successful claim has been made in the unreported decision of *Morrison Leahy Music Ltd. v. Lightbond Ltd.*, (1991), [1993] EMLR 144 (Ch. Div), under the right to object to derogatory treatment, section 80. See Stamatoudi, *supra* note 36, at 498.
253. Berne Convention for the Protection of Literary and Artistic Works (revised July 14, 1967) 828 U.N.T.S. 305.

This provision allows the protection of moral rights to cease upon the death of the author in certain circumstances. As such, it is an attempt at recognizing common law torts, which cannot be claimed against a deceased person. However, two points about the Berne formula for common law moral rights should be noted.

The first is an implicit inequality between economic and moral rights. All common law systems which rely on tort must, by definition, accord less protection to moral rights than to economic rights. This is because the Berne Convention itself requires protection of the author's copyright for a minimum of fifty years after the death of the author, and all common law countries who are Berne members must grant economic copyright in accordance with this rule.[254] Moral rights, however, may not be protected after the death of the author.[255]

A second point relates to the vagueness of the Berne provision itself. Article *6bis*(2) provides that, where extra-legislative means of protection are relied upon for moral rights, "*some of these rights may . . . cease to be maintained*" after the author's death.[256] The provision does not say "all of these rights," or even, simply, "these rights." The use of the word "some" seems to indicate that there are always other moral rights which will be protected after the author's death. Indeed, the provision seems to require, in parallel, that "at least some of these rights" must be protected after the death of the author. It is therefore doubtful, under Article *6bis*(2), that tort protections, alone, will be sufficient to protect moral rights in common law countries. Since personal torts uniformly expire upon the author's death, they will not be adequate to meet the requirements of this section.

F. Conclusion

The moral interests of authors have been recognized for at least as long as their economic rights. They are usually associated with the copyright practice of countries in Continental Europe. In France and Germany, a theory and practice of moral rights was well established by the end of the nineteenth century.

---

254. *See* art. 7 of the Berne Convention, *supra* note 9. This has been the case at least since the Berlin revision of 1908.

255. In this regard, an interesting point arises about the U.S. VARA framework, and whether it is in keeping with Berne requirements. According to sec. 106A(d), the duration of the visual artist's moral rights will be either the lifetime of the artist (where works are created on or after the effective date of VARA), or the duration of copyright protection in the work, for works created before that date.

256. Emphasis added.

But a striking fact of history arises when we consider the English example. Moral interests were not unknown in English law. On the contrary, they were recognized nearly a century before French judges began to deliver their rulings. The expulsion of moral rights from British copyright law occurred under the tremendous pressure generated by the booksellers' monopoly, which threatened to replace official censorship with a regime of press control through the private sector. The monopoly had to be destroyed; the era of censorship had to be brought to a close. In the process, moral rights fell before the powerful historical forces that were afoot in England of that time.

Not only the birth of moral rights, but also, the manner of their growth, is remarkable. The concept of literary property, or copyright, was largely a creature of statute; moral rights, however, were first recognized by judges. Accordingly, the development of the moral rights doctrine occurred in an environment of informality and flexibility. They were, in effect, a sort of common law within legal systems based on legislation, and from this position, they ultimately grew into equality with—perhaps supremacy over—the economic rights in the Continental systems. While rulings on moral rights were developing in France, German writers were exploring the conceptual implications of moral rights from almost every conceivable angle. The theories of moral rights that emerged proved to be extraordinarily rich, linking this aspect of authors' rights with considerations of personality, culture, and human rights.

In the environment of nineteenth-century France and Germany, however, a new perfume suffused the air of the times, and made itself felt even in the dry doctrines of the law. Romanticism! While the idea of moral interests existed in the European systems of law before Romanticism, the impact of Romanticism became a new lens through which moral rights have ever since been viewed. The new historical movement meant that moral rights were seen as an element in the recognition of individual rights of authorship, and it was in this form that they came to be enacted in the French and German laws of the twentieth century.

Strömholm speaks of "the cult of genius and originality characteristic of pre-Romanticism and the '*Sturm-und-Drang*' period [which] resulted in the final discrediting of the hitherto prevailing conception of creation . . . ." Creation was no longer divinely inspired, or at least, inspiration required a worthy vessel to contain it.[257] The author was the ultimate source of the work, an independent genius whose mind was at the origin of intellectual worth,

---

257. "Indwelling" is the poem from which this phrase is derived. The poet describes the personality in which there is no room for the divine spirit to enter—"replete with very thou." It seems that the poem, by T. E. Brown, is often misattributed to Sir Thomas Browne; it can be found in Louise Collier Willcox, A Manual of Mystic Verse: Being a Choice of Meditative and Mystic Poems 232 (E. P. Dutton & Co. 1917).

creative excitement, and, inevitably, social value. If this was the Romantic perspective, what will happen to moral rights under the influence of new historical currents?

The moral right of the Digital Age will reflect another social perspective. As befits the digital context, with its seemingly endless layering and overlap of works and interests, authorship in our times has also acquired multiple layers and shades of meaning. One of those meanings, clearly, will be found in the remnants of the Romantic spirit, which now coexists incongruously with postmodern approaches to culture. This marriage of opposites is reflected in conflict at the heart of copyright law, about the place of moral rights within it, and about the meaning and significance of moral rights themselves.

The postmoderns believed that Romanticism had died, but, to paraphrase—"Le Romantisme est mort. Vive le romantisme!" Although we may little realize it, Romanticism lives on in our society, albeit in an altered form.[258] The "cult" of Romanticism now lies embalmed deep within our collective psyche. For the moment, the poststructuralist view seems to have won out: since authorship is a mere social function, the author is no more than a glorified public servant, and talk of personal or spiritual interests is senseless.[259] The consequences of this view in a digital environment are not yet fully apparent, but, just as post-structuralism brilliantly destroyed concepts, digital technology has the potential to shatter the framework of copyright law.

Digital technology consumes works and regurgitates them as "content." In such an environment, there is every likelihood that the personal, individual, and humanistic aspects of copyright law will disappear, to be replaced by commercial rules, in their purest form, regulating "content." In the Digital Age, "content" may be adulterated, or so completely severed from its author that it becomes unrecognizable as the work of an individual human being. But this process of transformation has one undeniable and powerful attribute: economic value. The benefit arises at three stages in the life of a work: out of its initial creation, from its transformation into digital format, and in its potential to generate future transformations into new media. Some of these transformations will represent the knowledge and creativity developed by new authors, whose work, in turn, will become "content," and fuel the circuit of digital technology. The economic potential of "content" explains the bitter struggles of copyright holders to maintain an old-fashioned advantage out of

---

258. The attitude of mingled fascination, contempt, and respect for the arts seems like nothing but the hero-worship of the nineteenth century in a new guise. Ellen Dissanayake, *supra* note 31, comments on the continued associations of grandeur that cling to the arts.

259. *See* Foucault's brilliant essay, "What Is an Author?" where the philosopher argues that "authorship" is a social construct that embodies a certain perspective on creativity and its role in society. Michel Foucault, *What Is an Author?*, *in* THE FOUCAULT READER 101 (Paul Rabinow ed., Pantheon Books 1984).

the copyright works that they own, without understanding that new technology and existing models of copyright may be fundamentally incompatible.

Notwithstanding the seductive power of Foucault and his followers, and despite the digital reality, a human author still exists. Whatever the power of digital technology, the fact remains that it depends absolutely on the creative work made by a human author for its sustenance. Without the author, the technological circuit would grind to a halt. In this scenario, what happens to him, or to her, is one of the great unanswered questions of the twenty-first century.

CHAPTER

3

A Theory in Flux

The Evolution in Progress of Moral Rights

Les lois politiques et civiles de chaque nation . . .
doivent être tellement propres au peuple pour lequel
elles sont faites, que c'est un grand hasard si celles
d'une nation peuvent convenir à une autre.

–Montesquieu[1]

There is today what Mr. Justice Holmes might have
called a far reaching free trade in legal ideas.

—Otto Kahn-Freund[2]

---

1. "The political and civil laws of each nation . . . must be so fitting for the people for whom they were made that it is a great coincidence if those of one country can be suitable for another." *De l'Esprit des Lois*, Book I, ch. 3, 32 (Des lois positives); an electronic version of the 1758 text is made available by the website of the University of Quebec at Chicoutimi, Classics of the Social Sciences, based on an edition prepared by Laurent Versini, Professor at the Sorbonne (Editions Gallimard, Paris 1995), *available at* http://classiques.uqac.ca/classiques/montesquieu/de_esprit_des_lois/partie_1/esprit_des_lois_Livre_1.pdf (last visited Apr. 28, 2010).

2. *See* Otto Kahn-Freund, *Uses and Misuses of Comparative Law*, 37(1) MOD. L. REV. 1, 10 (1974), referring to the dissent of Justice Oliver Wendell Holmes in *Abrams v. United States*, 250 U.S. 616, 630 (1919).

A glance at the world's copyright systems reveals a surprising fact: moral rights are among the most widely accepted aspects of copyright law. Countries from Mali to Bulgaria, Azerbaijan to Tunisia, all include provisions on moral rights in their copyright laws.[3] Societies at all levels of development, and representing diverse cultures, recognize the moral right of the author. In many cases, moral rights in new jurisdictions also take a refreshingly new approach to the law. Moral rights are not limited to the scope of French or German law. Instead, international approaches expand the theory and practice of moral rights. Moral rights metamorphose into cultural rights, communal rights, national rights. Neither the rhetoric of Romanticism nor the gravity of European tradition has limited the imagination beyond Europe's borders.

New jurisdictions for moral rights were effectively created by three historical movements: colonialism, decolonization, and the end of Soviet Communism. Each of these movements brought its own color to the treatment of moral rights in the countries concerned.

The colonial era saw the preferences and prejudices of European powers exported to their colonies. The United States, Canada, and Australia all absorbed and perpetuated the anti-moral rights bias born in England. But the common law of moral rights was also subject to new pressures, leading to new legal approaches. Sometimes, restrictions were established. Extreme caution has led to a muddying of the doctrine in Canada, and tension over moral rights in the United States has even led to arguments for a differential regime that would treat foreigners more favorably than U.S. citizens on U.S. soil—a perversion of the sacrosanct principle of national treatment.[4] At the same time, the cultural wealth of the colonies has led to new opportunities, with

---

3. *See, e.g.,* arts. 15–17 and art. 75 of Bulgaria's Copyright Act; and arts. 14–16 and 33 of the Azerbaijani copyright legislation. English versions of both laws are available in Intellectual Property: Eastern Europe & the CIS (Mira T. Sundara Rajan ed., Oxford Univ. Press 2008). For online versions, see http://www.wipo.int/clea/en/text_pdf.jsp?lang=EN&id=450 (last visited May 2, 2010), and http://www.wipo.int/clea/en/text_pdf.jsp?lang=EN&id=5436 (last visited May 2, 2010). The Azerbaijani law receives a short overview by the government at http://www.mct.gov.az/?/en/culturehistory/2677/152 (last visited May 2, 2010).

4. National treatment has been a cornerstone of international copyright relations from the beginning. The Berne Convention codifies it in Article 5, and the TRIPS Agreement also does so in Article 3. *See* Berne Convention for the Protection of Literary and Artistic Works (adopted Sept. 9, 1886) 1161 U.N.T.S. 3, *available at* http://www.wipo.int/treaties/en/ip/berne/trtdocs_wo001.html (last visited Apr. 28, 2010); also available in a useful format at the Legal Information Institute, Cornell University Law School, http://www.law.cornell.edu/treaties/berne/overview.html [Berne Convention] (last visited Apr. 28, 2010); Agreement on Trade-Related Aspects of Intellectual Property Rights (opened for signature Apr. 15, 1994, entered into force Jan. 1, 1995) (1994) 33 I.L.M. 1197, *available at* http://www.law.cornell.edu/treaties/berne/overview.html [TRIPs Agreement] (last visited Apr. 28, 2010). On the U.S. twist, see the discussion about the parallel arguments that were, ironically, made when the Soviet Union contemplated joining the Universal Copyright Convention in 1976, in Mira T Sundara Rajan, Copyright and Creative Freedom: A Study of Post-Socialist Law Reform 102–07 (Routledge 2006) [Sundara Rajan, *Copyright and Creative Freedom*]; *see also* Michael A. Newcity, Copyright Law in the Soviet Union 152–57 (Praeger 1978).

Australia—and, to a lesser extent, Canada—becoming seriously interested in a moral right for Aboriginal culture.[5]

If a single factor can be held responsible for the expansion of moral rights in the post-World War II era, it is probably decolonization. The end of the colonial era brought legislative independence to a majority of the world's population, and encouraged new directions in cultural policy. The mood was one of optimism and urgency—the goal, to rebuild self-esteem, and to restore prestige to downtrodden cultures.[6] For these countries, moral rights were linked to the issue of cultural preservation—indeed, cultural survival in the post-colonial era. The moral right of the author was one instrument in a larger cause, and as such, it was subject to much experimentation and manipulation with the underlying objectives in mind.

Finally, the fall of the Berlin Wall reopened the gates of communication between Western and Eastern Europe after a half-century of hostility. For many ex-socialist jurisdictions, moral rights signified a return to pre-Soviet culture, as well as law. By an interesting paradox, Russia counts itself among these examples. Its approach to authors' rights offers interesting ways of thinking about the relationship between authorship and the rehabilitation of culture after a devastating experience of self-abuse.

Taken together, these developments suggest that the theory and practice of moral rights have touched new dimensions in the twenty-first century. A consideration of moral rights in the international community at large not only shows how they have evolved in response to social change throughout the twentieth century; it also proves the flexibility and malleability of the doctrine, features which point to its continued relevance in the Digital Age.

A. Spread of the Doctrine: Moral Rights and the Common Law

British legal history reveals that common law judges were well aware of a natural rights element in copyright, brilliantly articulated by Lord Mansfield

---

5. Australia's proposal for a moral right in Aboriginal culture is discussed in detail, *infra*. In Canada, Aboriginal peoples have become interested in asserting intellectual property rights to protect their traditional knowledge in the form of copyright and trademark; the area of Aboriginal rights is recognized as a priority in Canadian copyright reform, but, as yet, no movement has occurred on this issue. For an overview of concerns and cases to date, see Mira T. Sundara Rajan, Intellectual Property and Aboriginal Peoples: Conflict or Compromise? (Scow Institute Research Paper, Jan. 2008), *available at* http://scowinstitute.ca/library/documents/Intellectual_Property_Rights_Paper.pdf (last visited Apr. 19, 2010) [Sundara Rajan, *Intellectual Property and Aboriginal Peoples*].
6. *See generally* Claude Masouyé, *Décolonisation, indépendance et droit d'auteur*, 36 RIDA (Revue Internationale du Droit d'Auteur) 85 (1862).

in the pathbreaking case of *Millar v. Taylor.*[7] However, social forces of the time led to antipathy. Rejection of moral rights was an inevitable by-product of overpowering concerns about the deadening effects of natural rights of authorship on a free press. When moral rights eventually found their way into the common law, it was through international copyright law: the *Berne Convention for the Protection of Literary and Artistic Works* introduced moral rights in a new Article 6*bis* in 1928.[8] The provision was initiated by Continental European countries, and the rights therefore registered in the common law consciousness as a foreign import.[9]

The package of moral rights in the Berne Convention was approached in different ways by the different common law countries. For the UK, conformity with Berne was assumed; for the United States, moral rights were one more reason to remain aloof from Berne, whose requirement of "automatic" copyright protection upon the creation of a work sat uneasily with the registration-based approach to copyright that it favored.[10] Of all the common law jurisdictions, only Canada enacted moral rights in its copyright law as a result of Berne membership, for diverse reasons, and with mixed results.[11]

Negotiations for the World Trade Organization (WTO), established in 1995, led all of the common law countries to revisit their approaches to moral rights. The WTO included an Agreement on Trade-Related Aspects of Intellectual Property Rights (TRIPs) as one of its founding agreements.[12] TRIPs dealt with moral rights in an oblique formula, making acceptance of the moral rights in Article 6*bis* a requirement for WTO member countries,

---

7. *Millar v. Taylor* (1769) 4 Burr. 2303, 98 Eng. Rep. 201 [*Millar v. Taylor*].
8. Berne Convention, *supra* note 4; *see also* the Rome Act, 1928, Berne Convention for the Protection of Literary and Artistic Works (revised June 2, 1928), 123 L.N.T.S. 233, art. 6*bis*.
9. The discussions surrounding the adoption of Article 6*bis* at the Rome revision conference of 1928 are summarized by Ricketson. *See* Sam Ricketson, *The Berne Convention for the Protection of Literary and Artistic Works: 1886–1986* paras. 8.92–8.101 (Centre for Commercial Law Studies, Queen Mary College, Kluwer 1987); *see also* paras. 3.28 & 3.31.
10. In fact, the automatic enjoyment of copyright was not part of the Berne Convention until the Brussels revision conference of 1948, when Article 4(2) of the Brussels Act finally introduced a provision that, "The enjoyment and the exercise of these rights shall not be subject to any formality. . . ." *See* Brussels Act, Berne Convention for the Protection of Literary and Artistic Works (revised June 26, 1948).
11. *See* the brief comments in David Vaver, *Moral Rights Yesterday, Today and Tomorrow*, 7(3) INT'L J. TECH. & L. 270, 275–76 (1999) [Vaver, *Moral Rights Yesterday, Today and Tomorrow*].
12. Agreement on Trade-Related Aspects of Intellectual Property Rights (opened for signature Apr. 15, 1994, entered into force Jan. 1, 1995), Annex 1C to the Marrakesh Agreement Establishing the World Trade Organization, 1869 U.N.T.S. 299, 33 I.L.M. 1197 (1994), *available at* http://www.wto.org/english/docs_e/legal_e/27-trips_01_e.htm (last visited Apr. 28, 2010).

while providing that those moral rights could not be enforced through the newly established trade-dispute settlement mechanism at the WTO.[13]

Why were moral rights not simply excluded from TRIPs? The reason probably has to do with the political background to the WTO. The United States was the single most important motivating force behind the TRIPs system.[14] Although the U.S. copyright system did not recognize moral rights, the United States clearly needed to demonstrate solidarity with Berne principles as part of its larger agenda to establish leadership in the international copyright arena. Credibility demanded it.

Ultimately, the American interest in moral rights since its acceptance of the Berne Convention in 1989, however ambivalent, has had ripple effects throughout the international community. Despite the fact that the TRIPs Agreement provides only partial endorsement for the protection of moral rights as envisioned by Berne, moral rights have been considered with a new seriousness by common law countries.[15] Britain examined its moral rights scheme and found it deficient, leading to the adoption of moral rights provisions for the first time in 1988.[16] New Zealand has had moral rights since 1994, in a version of the rights that adheres closely to the British model.[17] Australia introduced moral rights protection for the first time in 2001, in complex provisions that are, nevertheless, models of clarity and balance.[18] In Canada, which made legislative provision for moral rights shortly after the original adoption of Article 6*bis* of the Berne Convention, the turn of the millennium has seen a number of attempts to redefine the rights in the Canadian context through Supreme Court rulings and law reform initiatives.[19]

---

13. *See* TRIPs Agreement, art. 9.1. Dreyfuss and Lowenfeld discuss the extraordinary significance of uniting intellectual property rights with trade-based enforcement measures at the WTO. Rochelle Cooper Dreyfuss & Andreas F. Lowenfeld, *Two Achievements of the Uruguay Round: Putting TRIPs and Dispute Settlement Together*, 37 Va. J. Int'l L. 275 (1997).

14. *See generally* Intellectual Property Rights: Global Consensus, Global Conflict? (R. Michael Gadbaw & Timothy J. Richards eds., Westview Press 1988) [Gadbaw & Richards].

15. Unlike other aspects of copyright law, moral rights cannot be enforced through the dispute settlement system of the WTO, and they are therefore not subject to the exercise of trade-based penalties against countries that do not provide adequate recognition or enforcement of the rights.

16. *See* the Gregory Committee, Report of the Copyright Committee, 1952, Cmd. 8662, which reevaluated Britain's protection of moral rights in 1986.

17. Copyright Act 1994 (New Zealand), secs. 94–110. As in the UK, the right of attribution must be asserted by an author in order to be claimed.

18. *See* Copyright Act 1968, *available at* http://www.austlii.edu.au/au/legis/cth/consol_act/ca1968133/ (last visited Apr. 30, 2010); Copyright Amendment (Moral Rights) Act 2000, *available at* http://www.comlaw.gov.au/ComLaw/Legislation/Act1.nsf/0/D25408DC39D0C132CA257434001EEDAE/$file/1592000.pdf (last visited Apr. 30, 2010).

19. In relation to law reform, the creation of moral rights for performers has been a priority; this change would bring Canadian law into conformity with the WIPO Performances and

In the process of reconsidering moral rights, common law countries have developed both new restrictions and new practices. Importantly, there is significant variation in their approaches to moral rights. With the progress of years, despite their common heritage, it will become increasingly difficult to identify a unified common law treatment of moral rights. The starting points are different. At one extreme, Australia's 2001 implementation of moral rights represents a straightforward, monist approach to the rights that is very similar to Germany's. At the other extreme, the United States has only enacted one provision on moral rights *per se*, the *Visual Artists Rights Act* of 1990, and its recognition of moral rights is exceptionally limited.[20] The common law countries now represent distinctive variations on the theme of moral rights that will clearly influence the global operation of the doctrine in the digital context.

1. Canada: A Country in Transition

Canada, legally and otherwise, is a more or less happy combination of French and English traditions. However, the now relatively smooth surface of French-English relations should not obscure the fact that Canadian legal practice is built on the shifting sands of an alliance between two potentially conflicting cultural traditions.[21] In no area of the law could this be more true than moral rights.

A closer look at the treatment of moral rights in Canadian law reveals the deep divisions on this issue between French- and English-Canadian jurists. The latest ruling of the Supreme Court of Canada, in the case of *Théberge*, resulted in a decision where the court was split precisely along linguistic

---

Phonograms Treaty, one of the two WIPO Internet Treaties to which it is a signatory. WIPO Copyright Treaty (adopted Dec. 20, 1996, entered into force Mar. 6, 2002) (1997) 36 I.L.M. 65 [WCT], *available at* http://www.wipo.int/treaties/en/ip/wct/trtdocs_wo033.html; WIPO Performances and Phonograms Treaty (adopted Dec. 20, 1996, entered into force May 20, 2002) (1997) 36 I.L.M. 76, *available at* http://www.wipo.int/treaties/en/ip/wppt/trtdocs_wo034.html [WPPT] (last visited Apr. 28, 2010). *See* Chapter 4, *infra*, "Moral Rights in the International Copyright Regime," notes 102–34 for a discussion of moral rights in the Treaties.

20. *Visual Artists Rights Act* of 1990, Pub. L. No. 101-650, 104 Stat. 5128, 17 U.S.C. § 106A [VARA].

21. French-English relations in Canada have a turbulent history. Throughout the 1960s, French-Canadians saw themselves as a "*peuple colonisé*" who had more in common with developing countries than with the English-Canadians with whom they shared a country. The specter of separatism has long hung over political relations between the "two solitudes," as Hugh MacLennan famously called them: Hugh MacLennan, Two Solitudes (McGill-Queen's Univ. Press 2009) (1945). The violent October Crisis of 1970 was informed by this perspective. *See* Louis Fournier, Histoire d'un movement clandestin (Editions Michel Brûlé Inc. Les; Nouvelle édition 1998).

lines.[22] What is the status and authority of a majority ruling in a case such as this? The observation that Canadian law must be more accepting of moral rights because of its French roots is appealing in theory, but a consideration of the facts shows it to be fundamentally untrue.

a. A Common Law Pioneer

Canada holds the distinction of being the first common law country to adopt provisions on moral rights into its copyright law. It did so in 1931, only three years after moral rights were first adopted in the Berne Convention.[23] It is equally significant that moral rights became a part of Canadian law a mere decade after the country's first independent copyright law came into effect, the Canadian *Copyright Act* of 1921.[24] Interestingly, rights akin to moral rights enjoyed formal recognition even before the legislative amendments of 1931, but they were not in the Copyright Act—the Canadian Criminal Code provisions of 1915 included recognition for attribution and integrity.[25] Still earlier, the doctrine of moral rights had been recognized by the Supreme Court of Canada in the 1911 case of *Morang v. Le Sueuer;* Chief Justice Fitzpatrick commented that, "[a]fter the author has parted with his pecuniary interest in the manuscript, he retains a species of personal or moral right in the product of his brain."[26]

---

22. *Théberge v. Galerie d'Art du Petit Champlain Inc.* [2002] 2 S.C.R. 336, 2002 SCC 34 (Can.) [*Théberge*].

23. Vaver, *Moral Rights Yesterday, Today and Tomorrow, supra* note 11, at 275.

24. The Copyright Act, 1921, S.C. 1921, ch. 24 (entered into force in 1924) Prior to 1921, copyright in Canada was governed by the British Imperial Copyright Act of 1842, which applied to all British dominions. The Canadian government did try to enact a Canadian copyright law at various points, but the idea received serious consideration only after a British reform led to a new UK and imperial copyright act in 1911. The Canadian Copyright Act of 1921 was in part a reaction to taxes imposed on American books by British legislation; Canadian legislation enacted for this purpose also created a tax on American imports, but it was far less than the tax collected by the British. The reason for taxation of American products was the flourishing US practice of re-printing copyright-protected works from other jurisdictions, an industry norm that was only limited by bilateral conventions on copyright initiated by the US, as the United States was not a party to the Berne Convention of 1886.

25. DAVID VAVER, COPYRIGHT LAW 159 (Essentials of Canadian Law Series, Irwin Law, 2000). Vaver is right to note this landmark: although the provisions were not in the Copyright Act, codification in the Criminal Code shows that the law had already achieved a significant level of acceptance. Formal recognition in criminal legislation certainly represents something beyond the informal recognition of a tort. Given the current emphasis on criminalizing copyright infringement, it is interesting to note that the idea is not a new one; indeed, other laws of the world have called infringement a criminal offense for even longer. See, for example, the discussion of the Russian copyright law of 1911, in Sundara Rajan, *Copyright and Creative Freedom, supra* note 4, Chapter IV, "Copyright and Tyranny", 82–85.

26. *Morang & Co. v. LeSueur*, 45 S.C.R. 95 (1911) at 98, *available at* http://scc.lexum.umontreal.ca/en/1911/0scr45-95/0scr45-95.html (last visited Aug. 23, 2010).

Canada's reasons for enacting moral rights were simple: it had signed the Berne Convention, and, Canada being a good international citizen, the Canadian government immediately set about enacting provisions to meet its international obligations.[27] More than a desire to meet copyright obligations *per se*, the Canadian government was probably influenced by two other considerations—its peculiar awareness of cultural issues as a close neighbor of the United States, and a growing commitment to human rights.[28] The language of the provision adopted in 1931 exactly mirrored the terms of Article 6*bis* of the Berne Convention.[29] However, the adaptation of the Berne provision into Canadian law led to an awkward and ambiguous result. Which aspects of attribution were protected?[30] Did the right of integrity require proof of damage to reputation, or not?[31] In comparison, a still subtler ambiguity in the drafting of

---

27. The contrast with the present must be duly noted. Canada has been a signatory to the WIPO Internet Treaties since 1997—the Treaties were themselves finalized only in 1996—but it has yet to implement them in its domestic law. The failure to do so has strained U.S.-Canada relations. Canada is not entirely at fault; the attempts of successive governments to reform Canadian copyright law have met with intense public controversy, and copyright reform has been affected by broader political uncertainty since 2004. For a consideration of the response to the proposed Bill C-60, An Act to amend the Copyright Act, 1st Sess., 38th Parl., 2005, cl. 29 [Bill C-60 (2005)], see IN THE PUBLIC INTEREST: THE FUTURE OF CANADIAN COPYRIGHT LAW (Michael Geist ed., Irwin Law 2005). The essays are also available for free download under Creative Commons licenses at http://www.irwinlaw.com/store/product/120/in-the-public-interest (last visited Apr. 28, 2010). On July 20, 2009, the Canadian government, led by the Conservatives, initiated a public consultation process on copyright reform, with a view to introducing new legislation. The proposed Bill C-32 was tabled by the government on June 2, 2010. *See* http://www2.parl.gc.ca/HousePublications/Publication.aspx?DocId=45 80265&Language=e&Mode=1 (last visited Aug. 19, 2010). A forthcoming sequel to the Geist volume addresses the plans in this Bill.
28. The instrumental role of Canadian lawyer and professor, John Peters Humphrey, in preparing the initial draft of the Universal Declaration of Human Rights, G.A. Res. 217A, U.N. GAOR, 3d Sess., U.N. Doc A/810 (Dec. 12, 1948) [Universal Declaration of Human Rights], should be noted.
29. *See* David Vaver, *Authors' Moral Rights in Canada*, 14 INT'L REV. INDUS. PROP. & COPYRIGHT L. 329, 341 (1983) [Vaver, *Authors' Moral Rights in Canada*].
30. *See* Vaver's discussion of the aspects of the attribution, or "paternity" right. *Id.*, at 352–55.
31. So subtle a change as the removal of a comma from the Berne phrase leads to this doubt. The Canadian section, quoted in *id.*, at 341, states that the author may "restrain" "any distortion, mutilation or other modification of the said work that would be prejudicial to his honour or reputation." In fact, prior to the latest amendments in 1994, the copyright law of India provided for moral rights in much the same language as the Canadian Act, but it divided the phrase in its sec. 57, into two parts. "Any modification" could lead to a violation of the right of integrity, but it would depend on the artist's ability to show "damage to his honour or reputation." *See* IJCP art. 83-84, and old sec. 57 of the Indian Copyright Act 1957, Act 14 of 1957, sec. 57; the Act is published by the Government of India, *available at* http://copyright. gov.in/Documents/CopyrightRules1957.pdf [Indian Copyright Act] (last visited Apr. 28, 2010). The Indian Copyright Act is available in many online versions, some of which are out of date; for example, the pre-1994 sec. 57 provisions can still be found on the website of the Commonwealth Legal Information Institute, *available at* http://www.commonlii.org/in/

the integrity right in the 1988 British provisions required judicial clarification of the issue by the High Court. The question arose in the very first integrity claim under the new rules, the "hip" and sparkling *Confetti Records* case.[32] David Vaver points out

> the folly of transporting virtually verbatim a provision from an international Convention into a domestic statute, without elaborating the provision in the manner intended by the Convention and without adapting it to the existing structure of domestic laws . . . .[33]

Subsequent amendment of the Canadian law waited a half-century and more. Reform in 1988 brought some clarification to the moral rights of authors, and the Canadian government took the additional step of codifying a right of publicity which protects authors from the commercial association of their works with products in advertising.[34] However, the greater precision of the 1988 provisions on moral rights was achieved at a cost. It is true that ambiguities in the earlier enactment were resolved, but the solutions invariably took the form of explicit restrictions on the exercise of moral rights.

Two noteworthy examples of these new limits arise in relation to the integrity right, and on the question of waivers. As noted above, the drafting of the integrity right in the 1931 amendments created a degree of ambiguity about the need to show proof of damage to reputation. When Canadian copyright law was reviewed by Claude Brunet and A. A. Keyes in 1977, they recommended that proof of damage to reputation should not be required under the new Canadian law.[35] The provision was indeed clarified, but the new version

---

legis/num_act/ca1957133/ (last visited Apr. 28, 2010). Vaver's criticism of the integrity right focuses on the question of whether personal reputation, as well as literary interpretation, is involved, and he concludes that both are legitimately touched by the integrity right. The critique could apply equally to the Berne Convention itself, which has also enshrined the term "honor," of uncertain legal connotations in modern copyright law. Vaver also draws attention to the use of the term "restrain," clearly intended to invoke the court's power to grant an injunction. *See* Vaver, *Authors' Moral Rights in Canada, supra* note 29, at 355–60.

32. *Confetti Records v. Warner Music UK Ltd.* [2003] EWHC (Ch) 1274. The case involved hip-hop music, known as "Garage" in the UK.

33. Vaver, *Authors' Moral Rights in Canada, supra* note 29, at 330.

34. Section 28.2(1)(b) of the Canadian Copyright Act, R.S.C. 1985, c. C-42, *available at* http:// laws.justice.gc.ca/en/C-42/index.html [Canadian Copyright Act]. Vaver, *Authors' Moral Rights in Canada, supra* note 29, at 331–40, mentions this protection of the conditions in which a work receives public exposure as part of the common law of moral rights in Canada. Accordingly, codification in this case represents a further degree of formalization for a pre-existing right, rather than the creation of a new right at Canadian copyright law.

35. ANDREW A. KEYES & CLAUDE BRUNET, LE DROIT D'AUTEUR AU CANADA: PROPOSITIONS POUR LA RÉVISION DE LA LOI (Consommation et Corporations Canada 1977) [Keyes and Brunet]. At that time, the Ministry of Consumer and Corporate Affairs had an Intellectual Property bureau. Responsibility for copyright law in Canada is now shared by two ministries,

actually went against the recommendation, and added a new requirement of proof of damage to reputation. The right was transformed from, potentially, a pure right of integrity, into a limited right of reputation.[36]

In relation to the question of whether moral rights could be waived in Canadian law, the changes of 1988 made waivers fully and comprehensively available to authors.[37] Interestingly, the practical consequence of this approach was to transform waivers into a standard feature of Canadian copyright contracts.[38] The example is an important one: it illustrates one of the ways in which the influence of the law is felt far beyond the confines of the courtroom. The language of the law can fundamentally shape the terms on which industries deal with copyright works. Litigation is only the final, most narrow, and most extreme consequence of legal provisions on moral rights.

As for the level of general clarity, an area where improvement was needed, the drafting of specific provisions was clarified, but an overall problem remained.[39] The issue concerned the structure of the Act. Canadian moral rights are dispersed throughout the Copyright Act, and it is difficult to piece together the complete jigsaw puzzle of the scheme. The rights are expressed in sections 14 and 28 of the Act, and they are separated from each other by a variety of unrelated provisions. The rationale for doing so may be that section 14 defines the rights, while section 28 defines infringement. The placement of the infringement offense in section 28 may reflect the fact that other parts of the Act dealing with the infringement of copyright may be found in the same

---

Heritage and Industry Canada. Splitting the development of copyright policy between two ministries with fundamentally different portfolios has led to chronic bureaucratic failures, and is probably one of the structural obstacles to copyright reform in Canada.

36. Brunet and Keyes made two types of recommendations in relation to Canadian moral rights: the first, a general call for clarification, and the second, specific proposals for the treatment of moral rights in amended legislation. For a quick overview of the proposals, see R. J. Roberts' review of the report, in 4(2) CANADIAN PUBLIC POLICY 264 (1978). The tone of the review is somewhat overwrought, but in fact, the proposals made by Keyes and Brunet reflect common practices in civil law countries—including damages and an accounting of profits among the remedies available for a moral rights infringement, for example. The damages awarded in a moral rights case are highly discretionary, and could be symbolic: the recent *Hugo* case resulted in damages of one Euro to the plaintiff. Roberts is also mistaken when he says that the report would allow authors to "force the copyright owner to withdraw from publication the author's work." In fact, the French model underlying this proposal recognizes that withdrawal could entail serious economic consequences for the copyright holder, and is subject to strict limitations.

37. *See* sec. 14(4) of the Canadian Copyright Act, R.S., 1985, c. C-42, *available at* http://laws.justice.gc.ca/en/C-42/index.html [current to Dec. 14, 2009] (last visited Apr. 28, 2010) [Canadian Copyright Act].

38. The Writers' Union of Canada now advises Canadian authors to refuse to sign publishing contracts that include waivers of moral rights. The warning may be found under *Hot Topics: Danger Clauses, Dubious Practices & Cautions* on the Union website, *available at* http://www.writersunion.ca/ht_clausecautions.asp (last visited Apr. 28, 2010).

39. Keyes and Brunet, *supra* note 35.

area of the Act. But these explanations are not fully satisfactory. The provisions in section 28 also serve to define the integrity right, and to clarify the definitions of other moral rights which are introduced in the earlier set. The two sections need to be read together to make sense.

b. Innovation and Convention: Attribution, Integrity, and Association

Section 14 of the Copyright Act defines two rights: attribution and integrity. The attribution right is comprehensive, and represents an innovative aspect of the Canadian moral rights scheme. It not only affirms the author's right to be "associated with the work . . . by name," but it also protects the author's right to maintain a pseudonym, and to protect any chosen anonymity. With regard to integrity, this section only tells us that "The author of a work has, subject to section 28.2, the right to the integrity of the work." For the substance of the integrity right, it is necessary to refer to the latter provision directly.[40] The definition of integrity in section 28.2 exactly parallels Article 6*bis* of the Berne Convention. It states that infringement of the integrity right will occur when the work is "distorted, mutilated or otherwise modified" in such a way as to "prejudice . . . the honour or reputation of the author."[41]

But this provision has a second part. It affirms that the author's right of integrity will be infringed if his work is "used in association with a product, service, cause or institution" in such a way as to "prejudice the honour or reputation of the author." This right could be considered an aspect of the integrity right, or a third Canadian moral right, known as a right of association. Given the presence of the right of association within a provision defining integrity, the first view seems more accurate. In the Canadian context, the unauthorized use of a work for commercial or endorsement purposes is not only a violation of the author's copyright. Additionally, if the author can show that the association has caused damage to his reputation, it may also involve a violation his or her moral right of integrity.

---

40. It is worth noting that the electronic version of the Act does not correct this inconvenience, by offering the facility of a hyperlink to connect directly between sections 14 and 28. *See supra* note 37, http://laws.justice.gc.ca/eng/C-42/index.html (last visited Apr. 28, 2010).

41. Canadian Copyright Act, *supra* note 37, sec. 28.2(1)(a). The intrinsic vagueness of this expression can be traced to its origins in the Berne Convention, which does not clarify the nature or standard of the proof required. *See* the interesting comments in *See* Silke von Lewinski, International Copyright Law and Policy (Oxford Univ. Press 2008), para. 5.104: "It is not entirely clear whether an actual prejudice must be established or whether the threat of a prejudice would be sufficient. There are better reasons for the second option— in particular the wording 'would be prejudicial'. It is also established today that the potential prejudice refers both to any modification and to any derogatory action" (footnotes omitted).

c. Opportunities and Limitations: The Visual Arts

It is striking to note that, in one specific case, Canadian law does not require proof of damage to an author's honor or reputation. This will arise where the author is an artist in the literal sense of the word—the creator of a work of visual art, such as painting, sculpture, or engraving. Any "distortion, mutilation or other modification" is "deemed" to be prejudicial to the author's reputation; rather than eliminate the need for proof of damage to reputation, the Canadian Act tells us to infer it. In practice, this means that, in the case of a work of visual art, any modification is, *prima facie*, an infringement of the artist's right of integrity.[42]

This provision accomplishes the important result of shifting the burden of proof from artist to audience, owner, or user. The formula by which this is done is not as straightforward as it could be. The right of integrity could have been left open-ended, with no mention of reputation. This would allow the artist to protest any modification of his work that he found objectionable— the usual practice in civil law jurisdictions.[43] Regardless, the moral right of integrity is much stronger for visual artists than for others. The special status of visual artists is reminiscent of the American situation, where the *Visual Artists Rights Act* of 1990 enacted moral rights for this class of artists alone.[44] Why the distinction? It may be justified by the unique nature of an artwork. In contrast to other art forms, there is one, and only one, original work of visual art. In this sense, visual art is quite unlike a book, music, or any other type of copyright work. Damage to an original artwork can never be set right.

But if, in fact, this is the rationale behind the separate regime for visual art, the Canadian law then goes on to impose two unexpected limits.[45] The first of these involves the conditions of display: controversially, the circumstances in

---

42. But note that in Canadian law, "modification" will have to be read *ejusdem generis*, in the context of a phrase beginning with "distortion . . . [and] mutilation," and it is conceivable that an artist might have to show that the modification is inherently damaging or likely to cause damage to the work.

43. *See, for example,* the French Intellectual Property Code, art. L121-1: *Loi N° 92-597 du 1er juillet 1992 relative au code de la propriété intellectuelle (partie législative), Journal officiel de la République française du 8 février 1994; Légifrance: Le service public de la diffusion du droit, available at* http://www.legifrance.gouv.fr/affichCode.do?cidTexte=LEGITEXT00000060694 14&dateTexte=20100412 (last visited Apr. 28, 2010) [Intellectual Property Code, CPI, *Code de la Propriété Intellectuelle*].

44. VARA, *supra* note 20.

45. Canadian Copyright Act, *supra* note 37, sec. 28.2(3).

which an artwork is exhibited will not give rise to a moral rights claim.[46] Secondly, conservation is addressed: "steps taken in good faith to restore or preserve the work" will also be exempted from an infringement claim. The purpose of the latter provision is clear: the goal is to avoid discouraging or penalizing valuable conservation work. The rationale for exempting the conditions of display from liability is harder to discover. It seems rather arbitrary—a way to limit the liability of galleries, companies, and perhaps government, for the mistreatment of artworks in their possession.[47]

d. Inalienability and the Canadian Penchant to Waive

If the framing of moral rights by Canadian legislators seems generally more favorable than the UK approach, the treatment of waivers in the Copyright Act is a caveat to the success of the endeavor. Canadian law follows the British approach of allowing extensive waivers. Indeed, under Canadian law, the only meaningful restrictions on the scope of waivers would appear to be those found in the common law principles governing the interpretation of contracts. Short of a finding of unconscionable dealings, or waiver under duress, nothing compels an author to retain his moral rights or restores them to him once they are waived.

Canadian law includes a most controversial provision on waivers. Article 14.1(4) provides:

> Where a waiver of any moral right is made in favour of an owner or a licensee of copyright, it may be invoked by any person authorized by the owner or licensee to use the work, unless there is an indication to the contrary in the waiver.

In other words, should an author waive his moral rights when he sells or offers to license his copyright to a publisher, he cannot then claim a violation of moral rights by anyone who is subsequently authorized by the *publisher* to use the work. An example helps to understand the implications of this provision. The author of a book signs a contract with a publisher, waiving his

---

46. The "Explanation" to India's sec. 57 states:

    > *Explanation.*—Failure to display a work or to display it to the satisfaction of the author Shall not be deemed to be an infringement of the rights conferred by this section.

    See Indian Copyright Act, *supra* note 31.

47. A similar approach is taken in Indian law; most probably, the goal is to protect the Indian government from liability for damage to artworks that it owns. In the context of a developing country, the fear is understandable: government is a major owner, and sponsor, of works. At the same time, the importance of the government's role in protecting culture should not fail to attract an obligation to do so with adequate care. See the comments of the Delhi High Court in the landmark case of *Amar Nath Sehgal v. Union of India* 2005 (30) PTC 253 (Delhi High Court) [*Sehgal*].

moral rights. The publisher authorizes another publisher to produce a chapter of the book as an article in a volume of essays. The author may object to the division of his work into separately published fragments. However, he cannot object to the re-publication by a third party as a violation of his moral right of integrity. The practical utility of the provision is clear: it allows the publisher to exploit his own rights without any inhibition because of the possible consequences of moral rights. In effect, the provision is a kind of negative assignment—an alienation in fact, if not in name. The author agrees to forego his moral rights, but the publisher effectively conveys that protection to any person who acquires the authority to use the work. At the same time, Canadian law specifies that authors cannot assign their moral rights; they can only be inherited upon the author's death.[48] In this sense, moral rights are formally "inalienable;" but can they truly be considered inalienable when they can be waived in favor of a third party with whom the author has no contract?

e. A Drought in the Courts

Although litigation is but one measure of the effectiveness of moral rights, the paucity of cases on moral rights in Canada is remarkable. In the entire history of Canada's moral rights provisions to 1988, only one successful case was ever brought.[49] It was the well-known case of Michael Snow, the artist whose sculpture of Canada geese decorating Toronto's Eaton Centre found itself adorned, one fine winter day, with festive ribbons for the Christmas season.[50] Snow argued that this was a violation of his integrity right. A sympathetic court ruled in his favor, issuing an injunction for the immediate removal of the ribbons. The case also established the principle of reliance on expert evidence as a way of proving the requisite damage to reputation in Canada:

> The plaintiff is adamant in his belief that his naturalistic composition has been made to look ridiculous by the addition of ribbons and suggests it is not unlike dangling earrings from the Venus de Milo. While the matter is not undisputed, the plaintiff's opinion is shared by a number of other well respected artists and people knowledgeable in his field.[51]

---

48. *See* Canadian Copyright Act, *supra* note 37, secs. 14.1(2) & 14.2(2).
49. *Snow v. The Eaton Centre Ltd.* (1982), 70 C.P.R. (2d) 105 [*Snow v. The Eaton Centre*]; *see also* sec. 12(7) of the old Canadian Copyright Act (pre-1988).
50. *Id.*
51. *Id.*, para. 6 (emphasis added).

f. Theoretical Confusion and its Practical Effects: Monism vs. Dualism

The Canadian Copyright Act defines the duration of moral rights as the minimum required by Berne: it protects them for the same duration as the economic rights enjoyed by the author, his lifetime and fifty years after his death. In this sense, the practice of the Act is in keeping with the "monist" theory, whereby economic and moral rights are protected for the same duration. The monist theory is additionally in evidence in the Canadian Act, because no formal distinction is made between an infringement of copyright and an infringement of moral rights.[52] In a country whose law is said to be of French origin, it is noteworthy that German theory is favored over the French model.

In Canada, however, the relationship between economic and moral rights is problematic in a much deeper sense. If moral rights and economic rights are seen as two branches of the same tree, the logical possibility of a potential overlap between the two arises. In other words, depending on the facts, an infringement claim could be made on both economic and moral grounds. In a truly monist system, the same facts could give rise to both moral and economic claims. On this theory, it should matter little to Canadian courts whether a claim is framed in terms of economic rights or moral rights. It may matter to the plaintiff, because the nature of the remedies available in the two cases may be different. Moral rights can lead to the practical solutions offered by injunctive relief, while economic rights lead to damages. And, again, in a single case, on a single set of facts, a plaintiff may be entitled to both.

This conclusion is of little concern to the French-speaking judges of the Supreme Court, who seem prepared to move seamlessly between the economic and moral dimensions of author's rights. For the English-speakers, however, the point needs to be resolved. The judges appear to be concerned that a monist approach implies a degree of equality between moral and economic claims which they are unwilling to recognize. In their view, it is not supported by the Act. As a result, in the recent ruling of *Théberge*, a majority of the Canadian Supreme Court affirmed that Canadian law is based on a dualist approach, where moral and economic rights are distinct. In particular, under Canadian law, the hierarchy between the two places economic rights above moral rights. Accordingly, facts that appear to contain the potential for a successful claim on both economic and moral grounds may nevertheless fail to generate a viable claim for the infringement of moral rights. A claim that would succeed as an economic rights claim, if approached as a moral rights issue, may fail.

The reason for this duality, as affirmed by the Supreme Court, is that the nature and standard of proof required for a moral rights infringement in Canada is higher than that required for an infringement of economic rights. The Court takes its cue from the legislation. The key phrase is to be found in

---

52. But note that infringement of copyright and of moral rights are dealt with in two separate sections of the Act, secs. 27 and 28.1.

"damage to honour or reputation," which appears as a prerequisite for moral rights claims in relation to all works except for the visual arts. No such evidence of an effect on reputation is required to show a violation of economic rights. On the contrary, any unauthorized action is, by definition, a violation of the author's economic copyright.

A consideration of the facts of *Théberge* illustrates this point, and shows how precariously balanced is the majority's reasoning. The case involved paintings by a Canadian painter, Claude Théberge, who authorized a company to make posters and art cards of his work for sale to the public. Unexpectedly, an art gallery which purchased the cards decided to make a further reproduction—this time, as a canvas-backed copy of the original image. The technique, on which the case turned, was to lift the ink from the postcard and superimpose it onto the canvas. The card was left blank, and the ink was transferred to the canvas.

Was this a reproduction of the work? The majority of the Court found that, in fact, no reproduction of Théberge's work had occurred. Rather, there was merely a transfer of ink from one medium to another. There was no increase in the overall number of copies of the work. The element of multiplication, required to constitute a reproduction, was missing.[53] This statement is somewhat reminiscent of the notion of media neutrality in a digital environment articulated by the Canadian Supreme Court in the 2006 case of *Robertson*,[54] affirming that the conversion of a piece of writing from print to data—newspaper to CD-Rom—would not qualify as a reproduction of the work.

No unauthorized reproduction under section 3(1) had occurred, but something else was at stake: a potential violation of the artist's moral rights and, in particular, an infringement of the artist's right of integrity under section 28 (1) of the Act. The artist, himself, had alerted the Court to this fact. In his testimony, Théberge affirmed that the canvas-backed reproductions could be confused with his original works, leading to what he considered "a dilution of my work."[55] Owners of Théberge originals might misunderstand the artist's intentions.[56]

However, Justice Binnie, writing for the majority, points out that there is an additional onus of proof that must be satisfied in relation to a moral right.[57] In the case of economic rights, any unauthorized reproduction is a *prima facie* violation of copyright, and this is clearly indicated by the language of the

---

53. *Théberge, supra* note 22, paras. 42–50.
54. On the other hand, the re-publication of a work in an online newspaper, subject to a new format and regular updates, would. *Robertson v. Thomson Corp.*, [2006] 2 S.C.R. 363, 2006 SCC 43 (Can.) [*Robertson*].
55. *Théberge, supra* note 22, para. 20.
56. *Id.*, paras. 17–21, and, especially the statements of M. Théberge himself, reproduced at para. 20.
57. *Id.*, para. 17.

Act.[58] But this is not the case in relation to moral rights. The Act explicitly requires that prejudice to reputation be shown, and Théberge had evidently failed to satisfy this additional requirement of proof. Instead, the artist was asserting a moral right in the guise of an economic right. The right, said Justice Binnie, was a *droit de destination*—a right to control the use of the work, one of the moral rights recognized in civilian jurisdictions.[59] A clear distinction is drawn between economic and moral rights, with different standards of proof coming into play in relation to each. This is a dualist theory of copyright—although, in the Canadian context, the application of the term "dualist" is slightly jarring. French dualism implies a higher status for moral rights in the legal hierarchy, and leads to protection for moral rights beyond the scope of economic rights.[60] In Canada, it is just the reverse. Dualism means that moral rights are limited in scope.

A brief consideration of the dissent in *Théberge* is instructive. Writing for the minority—all of the Francophone judges of the Court—Justice Gonthier argues that the majority approach is artificial. The claim may well involve a moral interest, but it is also a clear violation of the author's copyright. His observations emphasize the peculiar nature of reproduction in a digital environment:

> [I]t is clear that multiplication of the number of copies of a work is not an essential element of the act of "reproduc[ing it] . . . in any material form whatever." It does not matter that the process which produces a new materialization eliminates another; all that matters is that a new act of fixation occurs. Therefore, what we must *count* in order to determine whether a work has been reproduced

---

58. *See* Canadian Copyright Act, *supra* note 37, sec. 3(1).
59. Interestingly, it may be more accurate to characterize the *"droit de destination"* as an economic right. In French law, the *droit de destination* is recognized as an aspect of the right of reproduction, and it allows an author to exercise some control over the treatment of a work in circulation by a third party who is neither author nor *exploitant*. The reference to a moral rights aspect seems unusual; it could be considered a follow-on to the right of disclosure, by allowing an author some control over the fate of a published work. *See* Pascal Kamina, Film Copyright in the European Union, Cambridge Studies in Intellectual Property Rights, para. 1.97 (Cambridge Univ. Press 2002); he defines the right as "an expression of the right of the author to limit uses of copies of his work (droit de destination)." Kamina does not mention the moral aspect of the *droit de destination*, but he makes an interesting comment in relation to Belgian law, reformed to include specific aspects of *destination* within its provisions on economic rights; he says "that the theory could still be valid to justify a control over the resale of copies of copyright works or other acts of distribution not covered by the rental and lending rights." This could be interpreted as the (continued) existence of moral aspects of *destination* under Belgian law. Online sources also emphasize the economic nature of the right. *See, e.g.,* http://www.cabinetaci.com/le-droit-moral-et-patrimonial-de-l-auteur.html (last visited Apr. 28, 2010). The right is the subject of a thesis by Frédéric Pollaud-Dulian, *Le droit de destination: le sort des exemplaires en droit d'auteur*, ed LGDJ, Bibliothèque de droit privé Tome 205 [ISBN: 978-2-275-00791-5], 1989.
60. *See* the discussion *supra* in Chapter 2, "Moral Rights: History of an Idea," on French dualism, notes 111–19 and accompanying text; and notes 141–42 and accompanying text.

is not the total number of copies of the work in existence after the rematerialization, *but the number of materializations that occurred over time.*[61]

In an interesting afterword to the case, the 2003 *Desputeaux* decision is the latest ruling from the Supreme Court touching on moral rights. It supports the monist idea in Canadian law. The case involved arbitration proceedings, and the interesting question of whether copyright lies sufficiently within the ambit of personal rights to fall outside the jurisdiction of arbitrators. The Supreme Court states:

> Parliament has indeed declared that moral rights may not be assigned, but it permits the holders of those rights to waive the exercise of them. The Canadian legislation therefore recognizes the overlap between economic rights and moral rights in the definition of copyright. [62]

Ironically, this very paragraph concludes with a reference to Justice Binnie's comments in *Théberge*, while the different theory on which *Théberge* is based, passes unremarked. As Justice Binnie affirms:

> The [Copyright] Act provides the respondent with both economic and "moral" rights to his work. The distinction between the two types of rights and their respective statutory remedies is crucial.[63]

g. Canadian Copyright Reform: Moral Rights for Performers and an Opportunity Missed?[64]

On June 2, 2010, the Canadian government introduced a much-anticipated copyright reform bill, intended, among other things, to bring Canada into

---

61. *Théberge, supra* note 22, para. 149 (emphasis added).
62. *Desputeaux v. Éditions Chouette (1987) Inc.* [2003] 1 S.C.R. 178, 2003 SCC 17 (Can.), para. 57, *available at* http://csc.lexum.umontreal.ca/en/2003/2003scc17/2003scc17.pdf (last visited Apr. 30, 2010). The Court goes on to say: "Parliament has indeed declared that moral rights may not be assigned, but it permits the holders of those rights to waive the exercise of them. The Canadian legislation therefore recognizes the overlap between economic rights and moral rights in the definition of copyright. This Court has in fact stressed the importance placed on the economic aspects of copyright in Canada: the Copyright Act deals with copyright primarily as a system designed to organize the economic management of intellectual property, and regards copyright primarily as a mechanism for protecting and transmitting the economic values associated with this type of property and with the use of it. (See Galerie d'art du Petit Champlain inc. c. Théberge, 2002 SCC 34 (S.C.C.), at paras. 11–12, per Binnie J.)."
63. *Théberge, supra* note 22, para. 11.
64. For a parallel discussion of Canadian moral rights in view of Bill C-32, which draws heavily on this research, see *Culture Matters: Why Canada's Proposed Amendments to its Copyright Law Should Revisit Moral Rights*, in M. Geist forthcoming (*supra* note 27).

conformity with the WIPO Internet Treaties.[65] The proposed Canadian bill establishes moral rights for performers in the Canadian *Copyright Act.* The move should be viewed as generally positive, in two senses. First, Canada joins the ranks of countries that are signatories of the WIPO Internet Treaties, and have chosen to enact performers' moral rights as part of their implementation of the international accords. Notably, both the UK and Australia, sister common-law jurisdictions, have created moral rights for performers in their copyright laws. Australian implementation, like its overall regime for moral rights, is a model of legislative reform.[66] The UK position, like its general approach to moral rights, is ambiguous, and has been criticized by commentators.[67] Nevertheless, the simple fact of adopting moral rights for performers means that each country, within its respective limits, has signaled its commitment to the international community—to the belief that obligations assumed in the international arena are to be taken seriously by member states. To whatever extent possible, their position helps to enrich international discussions and support better compromises on international copyright issues. Canada has done the right thing by respecting the letter of the law where international copyright matters are concerned.

Secondly, moral rights for performers are to be implemented into Canadian law on exactly the same terms governing the protection of authors' moral rights under the Canadian Copyright Act. This aspect of performers' moral rights must be cited as a strength, because it emphasizes the equality of performers with authors under Canadian law. The approach confirms that Canada will be at least as serious about performers' moral rights as it is about the moral rights of authors.

But this last point undoubtedly leads to what must be a serious and fundamental critique of the proposed reforms. The problem of implementing the WIPO Internet Treaties in Canadian law presents a valuable opportunity to reconsider Canadian copyright practice—to examine Canada's approaches to copyright problems, and perhaps, improve the sophistication of the solutions generated by Canadian law. Unfortunately, where moral rights are concerned, this opportunity appears to have been wasted. Instead, performers' moral rights in Canada are a copy of authors' moral rights; and the flaws and dissatisfactions generated by the treatment of authors are now perpetuated in the new legislative scheme for performers.

Ironically, this problem must have arisen quite naturally. A similar approach was followed by the WPPT in its presentation of performers' moral rights: they closely resemble the moral rights of authors framed in Article 6*bis*

---

65. Bill C-32, *supra* note 27.

66. *See* Australian Copyright Act, *supra* note 18.

67. *See, for example*, Ilanah Simon Fhima, *The Introduction of Moral Rights for Performers*, Part 1 [2006] European Intellectual Property Review 552 & Part 2 [2006] European Intellectual Property Review 600.

of the Berne Convention. No doubt, Canadian drafters took their lead from the practices at WIPO itself. However, the significance of following the Berne approach is rather different – its provisions on authors' moral rights represented a series of compromises established over five decades, and it could be argued that the WPPT had little scope to move beyond the norms established by Berne. On the other hand, the Canadian treatment of moral rights may render them largely unprotected in practice. A consideration of how moral rights have evolved in Canadian law shows that, if the current bill is adopted, persistent difficulties will plague performers' moral interests much as they have afflicted authors' moral rights over the past eighty years. The Canadian government has an opportunity to reform Canadian moral rights in their totality. It should make use of the chance.

h. Conclusions

By introducing moral rights into the common law tradition, Canadian law has played a pioneering role in the spread of the doctrine. Its shared French and English traditions may help to account for the receptiveness of Canadian law to the concept, but the extent of French influence on Canadian copyright law remains doubtful.

Indeed, the relative surge of interest in moral rights, with two cases reaching the Supreme Court in recent years, raises the troubling prospect of a divide between English and French judges. There is confusion about Canada's moral rights framework, and the flexibility of the Francophone bench is mirrored by the strictness of the Anglophones. The status of a precedent such as *Théberge* is uncertain, and the perspective of a more united Court is to be welcomed.

The key to this dilemma may lie in Canada's commitment to human rights. In the context of a deeply entrenched culture of human rights, moral rights are bound to appeal to Canadian judges. It seems equally likely that the public will be willing to accept them, as a way of supporting the human rights of Canada's authors and artists. Human rights can ultimately help to define both the potential and the limits of moral rights. In this light, Canada is best understood as a hybrid system, with elements of French and American culture superimposed upon an English base, and animated by a prevailing rhetoric of human rights.

With these considerations in mind, Canadian copyright reform should make the rationalization of Canada's moral rights regime a priority of its larger agenda on the digital society. Canada's scheme as a whole needs re-examination. The criterion of "reasonableness" should be removed from the attribution right. The allowability of partial waivers of moral rights makes sense in the Canadian context, but the provision that authors may waive moral rights in their entirety should be removed from Article 14.1 (2) . Similarly, the controversial measures that allow a third party to claim the benefit of waiver arrangements between the author and his or her publisher, expressed in Article 14.1 (4) should be eliminated. Above all, the introduction of performers' moral rights should not be allowed to mirror the weaknesses of the existing regime for authors. The time for a serious legal commitment to moral rights in Canada has arrived.

A solution is urgently needed. Canada has not amended its copyright legislation since 1997, and digital issues remain practically unresolved. The current government claims that it wants to make Canada the world's leading digital society.[68] Without an up-to-date copyright law, it simply cannot be done.

2. The United States: A Difficult Future?

It is sobering to reflect that the world's most technologically advanced country, with the most *avant-garde* copyright law in the world—the Digital Millennium Copyright Act of 1998 predated the rival Copyright Directive of the European Union by three years[69]—does not protect moral rights in its copyright law. This is not to say that the United States does not recognize the moral interests of authors. On the contrary, the landmark case of *Shostakovich* dates from 1948, and suggests that the interests involved are quite well-known in American law.[70] But, as compared to other jurisdictions, the idea of moral rights protection is underdeveloped. Even among the common law countries, the United States is an outlier: the remainder have all enacted moral rights in their copyright laws.[71] In the United States, the *Visual Artists Rights Act* of 1990 remains the only federal legislation on moral rights.[72]

---

68. *See* Statement by Industry Minister Tony Clement at the Canadian Copyright Roundtable held in Vancouver, July 2009. The Vancouver session was the first of a series of public sessions held across Canada to consult experts and stakeholders on copyright reform. Attendance was, of course, by invitation only.

69. Directive 2001/29/EC of the European Parliament and of the Council of May 22, 2001 on the harmonization of certain aspects of copyright and related rights in the information society, *available at* http://eur-lex.europa.eu/LexUriServ/LexUriServ.do?uri=CELEX:32001L0029:-EN:NOT (last visited Apr. 28, 2010) [Copyright Directive, Information Society Directive].

70. Shostakovich v. Twentieth Century-Fox Film Corp., 80 N.Y.S.2d 575 (N.Y. Sup. Ct. 1948), *aff'd*, 87 N.Y.S.2d 430 (N.Y. App. Div. 1949) [*Shostakovich*].

71. All of the developed common law countries have done so: Canada, the UK, New Zealand, and Australia. India represents moral rights in a developing country that is also a common law state. However, the United States is not alone on the question of conformity with the Berne Convention. It also remains questionable whether other common law countries meet the Berne standard. From the perspective of Berne conformity, legislative reform in this area has met with mixed reviews in the UK, whose legislation is reflected in the New Zealand provisions. Canada's moral rights legislation dates from 1931, but various practical considerations, including the general and widespread availability of waiver in copyright contracts, throws doubt upon their practical importance. Australia's provisions on moral rights are well drafted and comprehensive, and in this sense, Australia is perhaps a model for how to enact moral rights in a common law system.

72. VARA, *supra* note 20.

The possible reasons behind the U.S. position are interesting, and two considerations seem compelling.[73] The first of these lies in a constitutional framework supporting U.S. copyright law. In contrast to other jurisdictions, where copyright might be seen as part of a framework for individual rights or human rights, American copyright law is an engine of the free market—a monopoly that is tolerated only insofar as it "promote[s] the progress of science and useful arts."[74] From an international perspective, a constitutional framework might hold the key to understanding certain aspects of the law as human rights-based law; but this is definitely not the American approach to the United States Constitutional framework for copyright. Rather, the limits of copyright norms have been set by the Constitution; and the acceptance of new measures such as an extended duration of copyright has depended on the approval of the United States Supreme Court. In the *Eldred* case,[75] a new copyright term found support; but the Constitutional tension remains, and it could certainly be seen as relevant to moral rights. In the U.S. discourse surrounding moral rights, they seem to be understood as an extension of copyright principles, and not as a form of recognition for underlying principles of individual or human rights.

A second consideration is cultural. The United States is the home of the digital revolution; it is the heartland of "remix" culture. The passion for engaging with digital information is an integral part of the U.S. cultural scene. Restricting the right to remix does not fit well with the *zeitgeist*. And the understanding of moral rights in American discourse seems to focus on their role in restricting the ability to use works. On the other hand, the role of moral rights in maintaining attribution seems to fit quite well with the public ethos of self-made reputations and the creative commons, but this aspect of moral rights is not well publicized in the United States.

In lieu of copyright law, the United States relies on a combination of consumer protection statutes, common law torts, and trademark legislation—the Lanham Act[76]—to protect the personal interests of its authors.[77] However, the progressive development of U.S. copyright law since it joined the Berne Convention in 1989 has tended to close off these alternative forms of recognition for moral rights, while the introduction of moral rights legislation

---

73. I am indebted to Professor Rochelle Dreyfuss of NYU Law School for drawing attention to these points.
74. *See* U.S. Const., art. 1, § 1, cl. 8, available online, Legal Information Institute, Cornell University School of Law, at http://www.law.cornell.edu/constitution/ (last visited Apr. 28, 2010).
75. Eldred v. Ashcroft, 239 F.3d 372 (2001), *aff'd*, 537 U.S. 186 (2003).
76. Lanham Act, 15 U.S.C. §§ 1051–1129 (2000), especially § 1125 on false designations of origin; Legal Information Institute, Cornell University Law School, <www.law.cornell.edu/uscode/15/usc_sec_15_00001125--000-.html> (last visited Apr. 28, 2010).
77. Of course, the changes made to the U.S. copyright act by VARA, *supra* note 20, protect the moral rights of visual artists.

becomes politically ever-more untenable. In view of these trends, where does the future of American moral rights lie? And, in particular, can the United States afford to ignore the implications of moral rights for new technology?

a. Moral Rights and the Berne Convention: Chronic Dissatisfaction

When the United States joined the *Berne Convention for the Protection of Literary and Artistic Works* in 1988, the event was one of immense magnitude for the world of copyright.[78] For the first time, it signified full-fledged American membership in the international copyright community. Structural features had made it difficult for the United States to join Berne and, hoping to find a viable alternative to its isolation, it joined the Universal Copyright Convention (UCC) in 1976. Limited international acceptance of the UCC made it nothing better than a temporary solution.[79] Indeed, by the 1980s, membership in Berne was perceived as an essential step towards defining a leadership role for the United States in the international copyright arena. Above all, Berne membership was a legal prerequisite to the adoption of the Agreement on Trade-Related Aspects of Intellectual Property Rights (TRIPs) at the WTO,[80] the leading new copyright agreement of its age. Negotiated by the United States and its trading partners, TRIPs exploited the knowledge of copyright acquired in more than a century of the Berne Convention, by requiring member countries of the WTO to adhere to its provisions.[81]

---

78. The United States officially became a member of the Berne Convention on November 17, 1988. *See* http://www.wipo.int/treaties/en/html.jsp?file=/redocs/notdocs/en/berne/treaty_berne_121.html (last visited Apr. 30, 2010).

79. Universal Copyright Convention, Sept. 6, 1952, as revised at Paris July 24, 1971, 943 U.N.T.S. 178 (entered into force July 10, 1974) [Universal Copyright Convention, UCC]. *See* the United Nations information page on this Convention, *available at* http://portal.unesco.org/culture/en/ev.php-URL_ID=1814&URL_DO=DO_TOPIC&URL_SECTION=201.html (last visited Apr. 28, 2010). The genesis of the Convention is discussed in EDWARD W. PLOMAN & L. CLARK HAMILTON, COPYRIGHT: INTELLECTUAL PROPERTY IN THE INFORMATION AGE 57–60 (Routledge & Kegan 1980) [Ploman & Hamilton]. They also comment that the "abolition of all formalities for the establishment of copyright was one of the reasons why many countries, particularly in the Western hemisphere, felt unable to accede to the Berne Convention": Ploman & Hamilton at 59. Both the United States and the Soviet Union, from 1974, have acceded to this treaty. *See* the discussion of Soviet accession to the UCC in Sundara Rajan, *Copyright & Creative Freedom, supra* note 4, at 102–07.

80. Agreement on Trade-Related Aspects of Intellectual Property Rights, Apr 15, 1994, Annex 1C to Marrakesh Agreement Establishing the World Trade Organization, 1869 U.N.T.S. 299; 33 I.L.M. 1197 (1994), *available at* http://www.wto.org/english/docs_e/legal_e/27-trips_01_e.htm (last visited Apr. 28, 2010) [TRIPs Agreement].

81. Dreyfuss & Lowenfeld assess the combination of trade penalties with intellectual property rights as one of the two most significant achievement of the WTO. *See* Rochelle Cooper Dreyfuss & Andreas F Lowenfeld, *Two Achievements of the Uruguay Round: Putting TRIPs and Dispute Settlement Together*, 37 VA. J. INT'L L. 275, 277 (1997).

At the time of American accession to Berne, there were at least two glaring inconsistencies between the United States copyright system and Berne practices. The two represent related issues. In the first place, the U.S. had a registration-based system of copyright. The origins of this system lie in the American Constitution, which defines copyright in primarily utilitarian terms—its purpose is to "promote the progress of science and useful arts," and the "limited monopoly" granted to authors and inventors was justified for this reason alone.[82] In contrast, the Berne Convention approaches copyright as a matter of natural rights. It requires automatic protection for authors' works: copyright arises out of the act of creation, and must be provided "without formalities."[83] In keeping with this natural rights approach, the Berne Convention also requires that member countries must protect the moral rights of authors. Taken together, these two features of the Berne system could not be reconciled with American copyright tradition.

United States accession to the Berne Convention necessarily entailed copyright reform. As far as registration is concerned, the United States has gracefully moved from a registration-based system to one where copyright is now recognized automatically.[84] However, implementation of a commitment to moral rights in American copyright law has proven to be more complicated.

In fact, there are at least three possible routes to achieving this goal: comprehensive legal reform, specialized law reform, and case precedent. The first, and most straightforward, solution would be general reform of the U.S. Copyright Act to include moral rights protection. From a purely legal perspective, this might be the simplest alternative; from a political perspective, however, it has proven to be untenable. Instead, a second approach has been feasible: limited legislative reform leading to the adoption of specialized provisions on moral rights, the *Visual Artists Rights Act* of 1990, which protects moral rights in works of visual art only.[85]

Is the scheme sufficient? It depends on how we assess it. In relation to the Berne Convention, the defining aspects of moral rights can be summarized in three statements. First, the interests to be protected are attribution and, to the extent that an author's reputation may be harmed, integrity. Secondly, the rights are to be protected automatically, and without the need for any formalities. Rather, they arise directly out of the act of creating a work—a principle that is violated by the UK requirement that an author must assert the

---

82. Art. 1, § 1, cl. 8, available online, *at* Legal Information Institute, Cornell University School of Law, http://www.law.cornell.edu/constitution/ (last visited Apr. 28, 2010).

83. Berne Convention, *supra* note 4, art. 5(2).

84. But it should be noted that the combination of automatic protection with American mechanisms for the automatic transfer of copyright from individuals to corporations translates into a significant new standard of corporate power in American copyright law.

85. VARA, *supra* note 20.

right of attribution to enjoy it.[86] It should be noted that the same holds true for copyright as a whole. Indeed, the fundamental right to release one's work to the public has both an economic aspect—the right to authorize first publication of one's work—and a moral dimension—the right of disclosure. Thirdly, at least "some," if not all, moral rights must be protected after the death of the author.[87] The provisions of the *Visual Artists Rights Act* limit the duration of protection to the lifetime of the author, and in this sense, they closely resemble personal tort protections which expire with the death of the affected person.[88]

A key feature of the U.S. regime for moral rights is its complexity. Here, the contrast with the French approach is at its most striking: the French *Code de la propriété intellectuelle* lists and describes the moral rights of the author in a single set of provisions,[89] while U.S. law requires us to search in many places, including the nebulous common law. In order to understand the U.S. scheme, it is necessary to determine how the different aspects of the U.S. legal system relate to one another. Is there any overlap between the different parts of the legal framework? Or, does the diversity of legal sources for moral rights in the United States imply that the regime is based on mutually exclusive principles?

The reliance on common law precedent, in particular, can be problematic. Given the relative novelty of the moral rights concept in U.S. law, American courts seem to have some difficulty in deciding how moral rights can merge with U.S. copyright doctrines. Their uncertainty leads to vagaries of interpretation that look like errors. Indeed, in the wake of the U.S. Supreme Court ruling in the *Dastar* case of 2003, U.S. case precedents on moral rights seem to be becoming more problematic with time, rather than helping to clarify the harmonization of U.S. copyright practices with the Berne Convention.[90]

Following the ruling of the U.S. Supreme Court in the 2003 case of *Dastar*, the approach appears to be one of strict separation among the different parts of the U.S. legal system dealing with moral rights. The protections of VARA,

---

86. Copyright, Designs and Patents Act 1988 (ch. 48), Office of Public Sector Information, sec. 78, *available at* http://www.opsi.gov.uk/acts/acts1988/UKpga_19880048_en_1.htm (last visited Apr. 28, 2010) [CDPA].

87. *See* the difficult provision in Berne Convention, *supra* note 4, art. 6*bis*(2).

88. But note that VARA seems to continue to recognize a perpetual copyright at American common law in unpublished works. *See* 17 U.S.C. § 106A(2). ("Duration of Rights— . . . (2) With respect to works of visual art created before the effective date set forth in section 610(a) of the *Visual Artists Rights Act* of 1990, but title to which has not, as of such effective date, been transferred from the author, the rights conferred by subsection (a) shall be coextensive with, and shall expire at the same time as, the rights conferred by section 106."

89. In France, moral rights are comprehensively covered in arts. L121-1–L121-9 of the CPI, *supra* note 44.

90. Dastar Corp. v. Twentieth Century-Fox Film Corp., 539 U.S. 23 (2003) [*Dastar*].

the Lanham Act, and other torts are parallel lines that run alongside one another, and will never meet. Moreover, there appears to be no overlap among the different legal regimes—not because statute prohibits it, but because judicial interpretation chooses to limit the availability of protection in this way. Eligibility for protection under one part of the U.S. legal regime implies limitations on the availability of protections under every other part. In itself, the approach is sound; it promotes a coherent and efficient approach to the law. However, in a situation where precedents on moral rights are not reconciled by an overarching doctrine, the rule eliminates possibilities for recognizing moral rights in U.S. law without allowing any alternative means for their protection.

i. From *Shostakovich* to *Dastar*: The Moral Rights Landscape in the United States[91]

The two cases of *Shostakovich* and *Dastar* represent benchmarks in U.S. copyright protection. *Shostakovich* was the first recognition of the moral rights principle in U.S. law; it saw an open-ended exploration of the idea of moral rights. The *Dastar* case, decided after U.S. membership in the Berne Convention, effectively restricts the scope of moral rights within very narrow limits.

(a) *Shostakovich:* The Integrity of the Public Domain

The concept of moral rights has been known in the United States since at least 1948, when the landmark case of *Shostakovich* was decided by a New York court.[92] This classic case in moral rights jurisprudence revolves around the use of music by a number of prominent composers from the Soviet Union in an anti-Soviet film. The film, called *The Iron Curtain*, explored the activities of Soviet spies in Canada.

The facts make for uneasy reading. The case was brought in the United States by the Soviet government, acting "on behalf of" the composers, and not by the composers themselves.[93] As its reason for doing so, the Soviet government offered the argument that the works in question were in the public domain and therefore depended on the government to intervene for their protection. All of the four composers—Prokofiev, Khachaturian, and Miaskovsky, as well as Shostakovich—were still alive at the time. Soviet copyright protection at that date had just moved from a historic low of 25 years from the first

---

91. *Shostakovich, supra* note 70, and *Dastar, supra* note 90.
92. *Shostakovich, supra* note 70.
93. Referring to the French litigation about this film, William Strauss notes that the plaintiff, French music company Société le Chant du monde, was acting as "assignee" of the composers. In fact, the French company sold these works under agreement with Soviet record labels which were, presumably, government-controlled. *See* William Strauss, *The Moral Right of the Author*, 4(4) Am. J. Comp. L. 506, 534–35 & n.56 (1955).

publication of the work, touched in legislation of 1925, to reestablishing the principle of copyright protection for the lifetime of the author and 15 years after his death, in 1928.[94] The moral right of integrity enjoyed strong protection in sections 18 and 11 of the Soviet legislation of 1928.[95] Soviet law of this period was in constant transition; but, assuming that the 1928 Act applied to these works, Soviet copyright in the works had not expired.[96] Rather, there was no legal basis for recognizing Soviet copyright in the United States, and, for this reason, the New York court eventually ruled that the works in question were effectively in the public domain in the United States. In fact, in the very year 1948, Shostakovich was denounced in the infamous Zhdanov decree; his visit to the United States a year later at Stalin's command, as part of a Soviet delegation to the United States, placed him in a most awkward position.[97]

The Soviet government wanted to suppress the film, on the grounds that the moral rights of the composers had been violated by the association of their music with political views which did not represent them. The case was brought both as a defamation suit and as a claim for the moral right of integrity. Ruling that defamation could not apply to works in the public domain, the American judge was willing to explore the idea that moral rights might be a viable option under American law.

His judgment does not dismiss the idea out of hand. Instead, the judge's reasoning suggests that, in certain cases, a violation of moral rights could be found under U.S. law. The two instances that he identifies are important. In the first case, direct mistreatment of the work could lead to a violation of the right of integrity in the United States.[98] The second point is more controversial: a moral right of integrity could be recognized for the purpose of protecting works in the public domain, bringing to the right of integrity the character of an instrument for protecting valuable cultural heritage from harm.[99]

The obstacles involved in acknowledging these rights are, in his view, too substantial to overcome. In particular, three practical problems arise: the standard of proof to be applied to an integrity claim, the effective balancing of the moral right against other rights and interests, and the nature of the remedies that would be appropriate to a moral rights violation. On the question

---

94. *See* Sundara Rajan, *Copyright and Creative Freedom, supra* note 4, at 94–97.

95. *See id.*, at 97.

96. *See id.*, at 94–97.

97. *See* L. E. FAY, SHOSTAKOVICH: A LIFE 171–73 (Oxford Univ. Press 2000). The decree condemned the works of a number of leading Soviet composers; they were rehabilitated in 1958, after Stalin's death and in the loosening of restrictions on intellectual life known as the "Thaw."

98. There is an interesting parallel with *Frisby v. BBC* [1967] Ch. 932 (Ch) [*Frisby*], decided on the interpretation of a contractual term. Moral rights were not then part of British copyright legislation, but on the other hand, the UK was a signatory to the Berne Convention.

99. This argument was made by the Delhi High Court in the *Amar Nath Sehgal* case. *Sehgal, supra* note 47.

of standards, he is eloquent—"Is the standard to be good taste, artistic worth, political beliefs, moral concepts or what is it to be?"[100] If such a right were to be recognized in American law, he concludes that it would be so vague as to cause troublesome uncertainties, especially in relation to acceptable evidence and correct standards of proof. As an interesting afterword, the same case brought in France, in 1953, won.[101]

(b) *Dastar:* Limits on Alternate Legal Mechanisms for Moral Rights

United States membership in the Berne Convention created a new opportunity for the recognition of moral rights in U.S. case law. While the provisions of Berne cannot be used directly in American copyright claims, the principle that domestic law should be interpreted in ways that harmonize with international obligations is well established in U.S. law.[102]

The applicability of this principle to moral rights was tested in the *Dastar* case of 2003. In *Dastar*, an attempt was made to apply section 43(a) of the Lanham Act to a dispute over the failure to attribute authorship to the original creators of a television program about World War II.[103] On the face of it, the Lanham Act provision has nothing to do with moral rights: it deals with false advertising. Nevertheless, the analogy between a "false designation of origin," as identified by the Lanham Act, and a moral right of attribution is a striking one.[104] Indeed, a well-known earlier case saw this kind of argument put forward with some success. A severely edited version of television skits by the famed British comedy troupe, Monty Python, was aired in the United States, and found to violate the comedians' rights.[105] The Lanham Act protected

---

100. *Shostakovich, supra* note 70, at 578.
101. Soc. Le Chant du Monde v. Soc. Fox Europe, Cour d'appel, Paris, Jan. 13, 1953, Dalloz, Jurisprudence 16, 80.
102. This rule is known as the "Charming Betsy" principle. *See* Graeme W. Austin, *The Berne Convention as a Canon of Construction: Moral Rights after Dastar*, 61 N.Y.U. ANN. SURVEY OF AM. L. 111 at 111 (2005).
103. Trademark Act of 1946 (Lanham Act), Pub. L. No. 79-489, 60 Stat. 427 (1946) (codified as amended at 15 U.S.C. §§ 1051–1129 (2000)) [Cite § 43(a), corresponding cite to 15 U.S.C. § 1125(a)].
104. *See* Vaver, *Moral Rights Yesterday, Today and Tomorrow, supra* note 11, at 276: he emphasizes "truth-in-marketing" as one acceptable basis for moral rights protection.
105. Gilliam v. Am. Broad. Cos., 538 F.2d 14 (2d Cir. 1976) [*Gilliam*], available on the website of Open Jurist, http://openjurist.org/538/f2d/14 (last visited Apr. 28, 2010). It is worth quoting at length from the decision.

> It also seems likely that appellants will succeed on the theory that, regardless of the right ABC had to broadcast an edited program, the cuts made constituted an actionable mutilation of Monty Python's work. This cause of action, which seeks redress for deformation of an artist's work, finds its roots in the continental concept of droit moral, or moral right, which may generally be summarized as including the right of

artists from potential damage to their reputations, at the very least, because of the potential economic consequences. As the Court in *Gilliam* noted:

> Nevertheless, the economic incentive for artistic and intellectual creation that serves as the foundation for American copyright law cannot be reconciled with the inability of artists to obtain relief for mutilation or misrepresentation of their work to the public on which the artists are financially dependent.[106]

However, the *Gilliam* case also succeeded through another device—the notion that the editing of the program was so extreme as to create a "derivative work." Under the usual copyright rules, the making of a derivative work must be authorized by the owner of the copyright in the work. A derivative work prepared against the owner's will simply violates the original copyright. Under U.S. law, the rules surrounding derivative works can successfully

---

the artist to have his work attributed to him in the form in which he created it. *See* 1 M. Nimmer, *supra*, at § 110.1.

American copyright law, as presently written, does not recognize moral rights or provide a cause of action for their violation, since the law seeks to vindicate the economic, rather than the personal, rights of authors. Nevertheless, the economic incentive for artistic and intellectual creation that serves as the foundation for American copyright law, *Goldstein v. California*, 412 U.S. 546, 37 L. Ed. 2d 163, 93 S. Ct. 2303 (1973); *Mazer v. Stein*, 347 U.S. 201, 98 L. Ed. 630, 74 S. Ct. 460 (1954), cannot be reconciled with the inability of artists to obtain relief for mutilation or misrepresentation of their work to the public on which the artists are financially dependent. Thus courts have long granted relief for misrepresentation of an artist's work by relying on theories outside the statutory law of copyright, such as contract law, *Granz v. Harris*, 198 F.2d 585 (2d Cir. 1952) (substantial cutting of original work constitutes misrepresentation), or the tort of unfair competition, *Prouty v. National Broadcasting Co.*, 26 F. Supp. 265 (Mass. 1939). *See* Strauss, *The Moral Right of the Author*, 128–138, *in* STUDIES ON COPYRIGHT (1963). Although such decisions are clothed in terms of proprietary right in one's creation, they also properly vindicate the author's personal right to prevent the presentation of his work to the public in a distorted form. *See* Gardella v. Log Cabin Prods. Co., 89 F.2d 891, 895–96 (2d Cir. 1937); Roeder, *The Doctrine of Moral Right*, 53 HARV. L. REV. 554, 568 (1940).

Here, the appellants claim that the editing done for ABC mutilated the original work and that consequently the broadcast of those programs as the creation of Monty Python violated the Lanham Act § 43(a), 15 U.S.C. § 1125(a). This statute, the federal counterpart to state unfair competition laws, has been invoked to prevent misrepresentations that may injure plaintiff's business or personal reputation, even where no registered trademark is concerned. *See* Mortellito v. Nina of California, 335 F. Supp. 1288, 1294 (S.D.N.Y. 1972). It is sufficient to violate the Act that a representation of a product, although technically true, creates a false impression of the product's origin. *See* Rich v. RCA Corp., 390 F. Supp. 530 (S.D. N.Y. 1975) (recent picture of plaintiff on cover of album containing songs recorded in distant past held to be a false representation that the songs were new); Geisel v. Poynter Products, Inc., 283 F. Supp. 261, 267 (S.D.N.Y. 1968).538 F.2d, at 23–24 (footnote omitted).

106. *Gilliam, supra* note 105, at 24 (citations omitted).

accommodate a moral right within the traditional parameters of copyright infringement.

The reasoning is reminiscent of a well-known British case, *Frisby v. BBC*.[107] This case about the author's moral right of integrity arose out of a dispute over the deletion of a single line from a radio play broadcast by the BBC.[108] It turned on the interpretation of a license agreement between Frisby and the BBC. The agreement was only partly contained in their contract. Importantly, the contract functioned with in the larger context of a "guild agreement" between the Screenwriters' Guild—of which, Frisby was a member—and the BBC, governing the alteration of scripts. Because of these background rules, the license to use the work granted by Frisby to the BBC had to be construed narrowly, limiting the changes that the BBC could make. In *Frisby*, the court decided that the removal of a single line amounted to a significant, "structural alteration" of the work, in contravention of the guild agreement. Accordingly, the court was able to impose limits on what the BBC could do with the work under the terms of the contract.[109] Significantly, the court accepted Frisby's own sense of the gravity of the deletion, a precedent that is interesting in the sense that it favored the author's subjective view of harm to his work — an unusual approach within the British common law tradition.

As in the *Shostakovich* case, the facts in *Dastar* are unappealing. Indeed, *Dastar* is a case that seems to exemplify the well-known cliché that "hard cases make bad law." *Dastar* involved the re-release of a television program. The original program was based on a memoir of World War II, written by then-General Dwight D. Eisenhower, and entitled, "Crusade in Europe." The program aired in 1949, and the copyright was registered by 20th-Century Fox. The copyright was not renewed by Fox, however, and in 1977, the program entered the public domain. In 1995, Dastar released a video series, entitled "Campaign in Europe," which copied substantially from the earlier program. But, in its marketing for the new program, Dastar mentioned neither Fox nor Eisenhower's original work.

In this scenario, the theory of moral rights tells us that there are two potential claims. The first would involve attribution to the makers of the original program; but, in this case, the original human creators of the program would have standing to sue, and not the corporate owners of copyright. In the event, the corporation responsible for commissioning the original program sued; neither the company responsible for its creation, nor the human authors behind it, were involved. In addition, the attribution rights of the author of the original book could have been raised, but these were not part of the litigation.

---

107. *Frisby*, *supra* note 98.
108. The line was: "My friend, Silv, said it was safe standing up."
109. *See* Robin Ray v. Classic FM Plc [1998] FSR 622, 641–44 (English HC, Ch. Div.) [*Ray v Classic FM*]. The scope of a license is generally thought to be much more limited than the rights enjoyed through a transfer of copyright.

At first instance, the claim succeeded on the grounds that the program was re-released under a "false designation of origin." The ruling was made under section 43(a) of the Lanham Act, and, as Graeme W. Austin notes in his insightful commentary, led to an award of damages for "double Dastar's profits, a decision that the U.S. Court of Appeals for the Ninth Circuit affirmed in an unpublished opinion."[110] This decision was subsequently overturned by a unanimous Supreme Court.[111]

The case failed before the U.S. Supreme Court on two grounds. First, the Court was troubled by the prospect of a multiplicity of authors who could potentially claim to be responsible for the true "origins" of the work, making the facts a poor fit with the Lanham Act provisions. From the perspective of moral rights theory, too, the Court's instinctive discomfort with the uncertainty of the work's origin makes sense: it is almost always the human creator behind the work who sues.[112] Secondly, the fact that the work in question had fallen into the public domain presented a difficult obstacle to the recognition of attribution rights. Under U.S. copyright law, the public domain is supposed to be entirely free of access. In contrast to the judgment in *Shostakovich*, the Supreme Court ruminated that recognizing the right of attribution in these circumstances could invalidate the American concept of public domain.[113]

The Court's intuitions on both of these issues seem well-founded. Under moral rights theories, the plaintiffs in this case had no right to claim attribution.[114] Similarly, the recognition of moral rights in the public domain implies perpetual protection for those rights. The prospect was one that received favorable consideration in *Shostakovich*, and it is certainly possible to imagine a legal regime that would provide moral rights for works in the public domain without establishing their protection for living authors. For example, the tort protections offered to living authors might be sufficient to protect name and reputation. Nevertheless, the idea of recognizing moral rights exclusively in public domain works seems unnatural—at least in the sense that it appears never to have been tried. Even to fulfill a special policy goal, perpetual recognition for moral rights in the public domain seems like a huge

---

110. Austin, *supra* note 102, at 118.
111. The lower court's decision was overturned by a vote of 8–0, "Justice Breyer recused." *See id.*, at 119.
112. The one notable exception is Japanese recognition for corporations. *See* the discussion of Japanese law, *infra*, notes 253–54 and accompanying text. In this respect, Korean law follows Japanese law.
113. *See Dastar, supra* note 90, at 37: Justice Scalia comments that "To hold otherwise would be akin to finding that §43(a) created a species of perpetual patent and copyright, which Congress may not do."
114. But note the empowerment of corporations under Japanese, and Korean, law: notes 253–54 and accompanying text.

step forward for a country that has yet to recognize moral rights in the works of living authors.

Subsequent interpretation of the *Dastar* case may have extended the application of the ruling beyond what the Supreme Court intended. The facts of *Dastar* turned on the issue of public domain; yet the ruling has been enlarged to apply to works still within the term of copyright protection in the United States. The distinction between works within copyright and works in the public domain is important everywhere, but this boundary seems to be marked with special clarity in the United States. It is therefore questionable to claim that *Dastar* establishes a principle for both.[115]

The case is also presumed to stand for an idea that is controversial in a different sense. It identifies the difficulty of locating a proper "origin" for a work as a practical problem. But subsequent interpretation seems to see this difficulty as insurmountable.[116] On this view, *Dastar* would invalidate all claims for moral rights protection under the Lanham Act provisions on false designations of origin. Accordingly, there could be no recourse to the Lanham Act to vindicate a claim for the moral right of attribution.

This conclusion is disturbing, and brings the analysis full circle. The United States does not have moral rights provisions in its Copyright Act. Within the terms of the Berne Convention, it may not need them: Berne requires that moral rights be protected, but it does not specify the manner of doing so. Rather, the Convention recognizes the diversity of the world's legal systems. It embraces the flexibility of different jurisdictions to enact the rights as each sees fit. But enact moral rights, they must. If the United States does not have moral rights in its copyright provisions, where can we find them? The *Dastar* case appears to close off two possible sources of law for American moral rights: the Lanham Act provisions on false designations of origin and, more generally—at least temporarily—case precedents. What else remains?

ii. Better to be Foreign: National Treatment as a Way Out?

In the wake of *Dastar*, proposals for implementing the Berne Convention in the United States should be reconsidered. The ruling considerably weakens claims that American law is in conformity with the requirements of the Berne Convention for the protection of moral rights. By introducing further restrictions on the ability of plaintiffs to rely on alternate legal mechanisms for the protection of their moral rights, it stirs the smoldering uncertainties surrounding the issue. By limiting the availability of the Lanham Act, in particular, the case ends what could have been an interesting alternative, expressed

---

115. *See* Austin's insightful comments on this issue: Austin, *supra* note 102, at 103–05.
116. *See* the comments in Austin, *supra* note 102, at 108–09, 110–14.

through commercial law principles, to the cultural model of moral rights found in civil law jurisdictions.

Indeed, with respect to moral rights, the United States could find itself in an anomalous position. National treatment requires that nationals of all member countries of the Berne Convention be treated in a non-discriminatory manner. At the same time, however, the Berne Convention also sets out minimum standards of copyright protection that are supposed to be recognized in all of the member countries. In a landmark 1998 ruling from the United States Court of Appeals for the Second Circuit, *Itar-TASS Russian News Agency v Russian Kurier,* these principles unite in a powerful way.[117]

Russian Kurier explored the meaning of national treatment under the Berne Convention. In this fascinating case, an American court found itself applying Russian law in order to determine whether, and on what basis, plaintiffs from Russia would have a right to claim ownership of the copyright in their works in the territory of the United States.[118] The question was important, because, without standing, the plaintiffs in this case—publishers, the Itar-TASS press agency, and the Russian Union of Journalists—would not be entitled to put forward a claim for infringement of copyright on behalf of the authors of news articles which they had published. The court relied on the principle, drawn from the rules governing conflicts of laws, that the law of the country which has the closest connection to the works should be applied.[119] The resolution of the case showed that American courts will have recourse to foreign law if they feel they need it in order to determine questions of copyright ownership. In this case, fairness may have demanded it; a sense of international obligation because of Berne membership could very well amount to another valid reason to defer to foreign law. Following *Russian Kurier,* where issues of copyright ownership are concerned, a French plaintiff claiming a violation of his or her moral rights on American soil could ask the court to apply French rules; an American plaintiff would have no such recourse.

The Court also notes that the distinction between ownership and infringement issues might not always be perfectly clear. It comments:

> The division of issues, for conflicts purposes, between ownership and infringement issues will not always be as easily made as the above discussion implies. If the issue is the relatively straightforward one of which of two contending parties owns a copyright, the issue is unquestionably an ownership issue, and the

---

117. Itar-Tass Russian News Agency v. Russian Kurier, Inc., 153 F.3d 82 (2d Cir. 1998) [*Russian Kurier, Kurier*].
118. The court was assisted in this daunting undertaking by expert evidence from distinguished American experts on Russian law, including Professors Peter B. Maggs and Michael Newcity.
119. "[T]he law of the country with the closest relationship to the work will apply to settle the ownership dispute." *Russian Kurier, supra* note 117, at 91.

law of the country with the closest relationship to the work will apply to settle the ownership dispute. But in some cases, including the pending one, the issue is not simply who owns the copyright but also what is the nature of the ownership interest. Yet as a court considers the nature of an ownership interest, there is some risk that it will too readily shift the inquiry over to the issue of whether an alleged copy has infringed the asserted copyright. Whether a copy infringes depends in part on the scope of the interest of the copyright owner. Nevertheless, though the issues are related, the nature of a copyright interest is an issue distinct from the issue of whether the copyright has been infringed . . . The pending case is one that requires consideration not simply of who owns an interest, but, as to the newspapers, the nature of the interest that is owned.[120]

Could the United States be moving towards a moral rights regime that recognizes the moral rights of foreign authors, but not of Americans?[121] The idea is a perversion of the concept of national treatment. National treatment is not only meant to protect foreign authors from discrimination throughout the territories of the Berne Convention, but it also aims to ensure minimum standards of copyright protection among its members. Granting additional protections to foreign authors cannot be a satisfactory solution to this American problem.[122]

b. Conclusions

In relation to the Berne Convention, it is clear that the United States has fallen short of its stated goal of implementing provisions that will bring it into conformity with moral rights requirements. In order to satisfy the requirements of Berne, the United States needs one of two things: law reform to enact moral rights provisions beyond the sphere of the visual arts, or openended principles of interpretation to guide existing law. A combination of both would be ideal. However, reluctance to expand the interpretation of existing laws throws the United States back to the initial difficulty of a legislative shortfall in relation to moral rights. The fault may not lie with the Supreme Court decision in *Dastar* only, but it may also be traced to the casual misinterpretation of the *Dastar* case beyond the reasonable limits that seem built into its unattractive facts.

---

120. *Id.*, at 91–92 (citation omitted).
121. The opposite problem—that Americans may have more rights outside their own country than within it—has already been illustrated in relation to the moral rights of film directors. *See* Judgment of December 19, 1994 (*Turner Entertainment v. Huston Heirs*), Cour d'Appel, chs. Réunies (Versailles), 164 RIDA 389 (1995) (Fr.), on remand from Judgment of May 28, 1991, Cass. Civ. lre, 149 RIDA 197 (1991) [*Huston*].
122. Austin draws attention to this "solution" to the problem, but, for the reasons discussed herein, it would be a highly unsatisfactory one. Austin, *supra* note 102, at 135–36.

As in the case of other common law countries, the deficit is a product of both legal traditions and political realities. In the digital context, however, the absence of adequate protection for moral rights signifies something entirely new—a careless approach to the protection of knowledge, culture, and information in an environment of rapid technological change where they are most vulnerable. When it comes to moral rights in a digital world, conformity with international law will be the least of America's problems. The real issue is to maintain the integrity of intangible heritage. It is a formidable problem, and, unlike doctrinal questions, attempting to argue our way out of it will accomplish nothing beyond delaying the inevitable.

3. Australia and a Moral Right in Indigenous Culture

Moral rights were enacted in the Australian Copyright Act at the late date of 2000;[123] with their implementation, the United States became the only common law country in the world with no general recognition for moral rights in its copyright law. Australia's implementation of moral rights is a model for the enactment of the doctrine. It is a straightforward approach to the principles of attribution and integrity, framed along Berne lines. Australian law provides for the moral rights, not only of authors, but also, of performers, making Australia the first common law country to implement the moral rights provisions of the WIPO Performances and Phonograms Treaty.[124]

The Australian treatment of moral rights also resolves certain long-standing issues about the substance of these rights. Attribution encompasses false attribution, defined simply as the attribution of someone else's name to one's work.[125] In the case of film, attribution rights are protected in relation to the director, producer, and screenwriter.[126] The Australian law defines the right of integrity as a "right of integrity of authorship."[127] It rejects any "derogatory treatment" of the work, and derogatory treatment is considered to be any treatment of the work that causes, in the Berne formula, damage to an author's

---

123. Copyright Amendment (Moral Rights) Act 2000 (Austl.), *supra* note 18. The moral rights provisions entered into force on as of Dec. 21, 2000. *See* Virginia Morrison, *Moral Rights Legislation in Force*, Copyright World (Jan. 8, 2001), *available at* http://www.copyright. org.au/pdf/acc/articles_pdf/A01n01.pdf> (last visited Apr. 28, 2010).

124. The UK implemented moral rights for performers in 2006. *See* Statutory Instrument No. 18 of 2006, Office of Public Sector Information, *available at* http://www.opsi.gov.uk/si/ si2006/20060018.htm (last visited Apr. 28, 2010). Despite its accession to the WPPT, Canada has yet to implement moral rights for performers. *See* Mira T. Sundara Rajan, *Center Stage: Moral Rights in the WPPT*, Case W. Reserve L. Rev. (forthcoming 2010).

125. Australian Copyright Act, *supra* note 18, secs. 195AC–195AHC.

126. *Id.*, sec. 195AF.

127. *Id.*, sec. 195AI.

honor or reputation.[128] The Australian scheme specifically identifies the destruction of an artwork as a violation of the right of integrity.[129] So, too, is the display of an artwork in unpropitious circumstances.[130] The duration of moral rights in Australia is equivalent to the duration of copyright, but film remains a notable exception: moral rights subsist only until the death of the director.[131] It is also striking that Australian legislators decided against the possibility of waiver: the Copyright Act provides that moral rights cannot be assigned, and the only exception to this rule allows coauthors to make arrangements for moral rights among themselves—no real exception at all.[132] Australia appears to be the only country in the world which addresses the problem of conflicting moral rights among those involved in the making of a film, by allowing coauthors to waive moral rights in their individual contributions in favor of a moral right in the work as a whole.[133] After the author's death, an heir or a legal executor may exercise moral rights on his or her behalf.[134]

In 2003, soon after the enactment of these provisions, the Australian government introduced a bill for the recognition of moral rights in indigenous culture.[135] The right was called an "indigenous communal moral right," and its purpose was to maintain the attribution and integrity of works of Aboriginal culture. Australia has been a pioneer in confronting indigenous cultural issues. Its test cases on copyright and indigenous culture have yielded important insights on the relationship of Aboriginal cultures and intellectual property, even where the findings may have been disappointing for indigenous cultural interests.[136] It is therefore no surprise that Australian legislators have made an attempt at recognizing indigenous interests through the device of

---

128. *Id.*, sec. 195AJ.
129. *Id.*, sec. 195AK (a). Section 195AT provides for safeguards where the destruction of a work will not be considered a violation of the right of integrity, including situations where the author cannot be located, or where the author has been given an opportunity to remove the work. Attempts made in good faith to restore the work will also not lead to a violation of the right of integrity. Canada has a similar provision in its law: *see* the Canadian Copyright Act, sec. 28.2(3)(b).
130. Australian Copyright Act, *supra* note 18, 195AK(b).
131. *Id.*, 195AM.
132. *Id.*, 195AN on the "Exercise of Moral Rights."
133. *Id.*, 195AN(4).
134. *Id.*, 195AN(4).
135. Copyright Amendment (Indigenous Communal Moral Rights) Bill 2003 (Cth) (Austl.). *See* Jane Anderson, *The Politics of Indigenous Knowledge: Australia's Proposed Communal Moral Rights Bill*, 27(3) U. New S. Wales L.J. 585 (2004).
136. *See, e.g.*, Yumbulul v. Reserve Bank of Australia, 21 Intell. Prop. Rev. 481 (1991) [*Yumbulul*].

moral rights, and that they have pre-empted both Canada and the United States in doing so.[137]

However, as introduced, the 2003 Bill raised serious concerns about the Australian legal perspective on indigenous culture. As Jane Anderson points out,

> [T]he power of the title *Copyright Amendment (Indigenous Communal Moral Rights) Bill* is that unless one actually reads the draft Bill (and there are only a few that have been distributed) it would superficially appear to break new ground in the field of Indigenous rights to cultural knowledge.[138]

Ultimately, the Bill did not become part of Australia's law. But the provisions are well worth reviewing: they reveal the underlying difficulty of recognizing indigenous moral rights, which are both legal and political in nature. Given that the idea progressed so deep into the Australian copyright reform process, it also seems likely that the Australian government will revisit this important cultural issue.[139] Indeed, it appeared that the rights might receive consideration in the 2006 round of Australian copyright amendments, but a rumored new proposal seems to have evaporated.[140]

Apart from its content, the process surrounding the introduction of the 2003 Bill was one that generated controversy in its own right. As Anderson notes, the Bill was not made available to the Australian public, and only a small number of copies were circulated to interested groups.[141] Among these groups, which included the Arts Law Centre of Australia,[142] the Australian Copyright Council,[143] and the Aboriginal Board of Study of New South Wales, the Bill generated strong criticism.

Two fundamental problems are apparent in the Bill. First, the posture adopted by the Bill was one of extreme caution in relation to the recognition of indigenous rights. The Bill was more concerned with clarifying boundaries

---

137. India is another country where recognition of indigenous, or "tribal," contributions to traditional culture is important. The issue is neglected in India, and the position of "tribals" remains one of general disadvantage.

138. Jane Anderson, *Indigenous Communal Moral Rights: The Utility of an Ineffective Law: Who Benefits from the Bill*, 5(30) INDIGENOUS LAW BULL. 8 (2004).

139. In fact, the idea of introducing an indigenous moral right resurfaced in 2006. *See* the comments by Molly Torsen, *IP Watch*, http://www.ip-watch.org/weblog/2006/12/04/inside-views-indigenous-communal-moral-rights/ (last visited Apr. 28, 2010).

140. *See* Samantha Joseph & Erin Mackay, *Moral Rights and Indigenous Communities*, ART+law (2006), *available at* http://www.artslaw.com.au/artlaw/archive/2006/06MoralRightsAndIndigenousCommunities.asp (last visited Apr. 19, 2010), Arts Law Centre of Australia.

141. A copy of the Bill was also, apparently, made available to one individual.

142. *See* http://www.mca.org.au/web/content/view/75/6 (last visited Apr. 28, 2010).

143. *See, for example*, Ian McDonald, *Article for Australian Intellectual Property Law Bulletin: Indigenous Communal Moral Rights* (July 16, 2003), *available at* www.copyright.org.au/pdf/acc/articles_pdf/A03n24.pdf (last visited Apr. 28, 2010).

for the users of Aboriginal artworks than protecting the works from misuse. This focus led to a second, and still more disturbing, problem. The Bill was based on a distorted picture of Aboriginal culture, observed through the lens of a Western copyright framework. It required Aboriginal cultural relations to be structured according to copyright norms.

The Aboriginal moral right could only be invoked in cases where the Aboriginal artist and his or her community had entered into an agreement prior to any transactions involving the work. This Agreement would need to clarify the mutual responsibilities of creator and community in relation to the work; but, as Jane Anderson points out,

> The presumption here is that at the time of executing a work the individual artist will first attend to . . . legal affairs and formally consider the question of communal moral rights management, presumably in anticipation of commercial potential in the reproduction of the work.[144]

This requirement seems like a crude response to the landmark Australian case of *Yumbulul.* Mr. Yumbulul was an Aboriginal artist, skilled in the art of making a sacred object known as a "Morning Star Pole." Yumbulul eventually entered into an agreement with the Australian government to allow an image of his pole to be featured on an Australian banknote. However, Mr. Yumbulul's community was unhappy with the dissemination of this sacred knowledge, and asked him to withdraw from the agreement.[145] In the eventual lawsuit, Yumbulul tried, unsuccessfully, to withdraw his permission from the Australian government for the use of his artwork on the banknote.[146] The case failed, for the simple reason that there was nothing wrong with the contract between Yumbulul and the government. In its finding, a highly sympathetic Australian Federal Court, though unable to understand that the Aboriginal group *did not want* this image circulating on a banknote,

---

144. *See* Anderson, *The Politics of Indigenous Knowledge, supra* note 135, at 598.
145. *See Yumbulul, supra* note 136, para. 12: "There was evidence that Mr. Yumbulul came under considerable criticism from within the Aboriginal community for permitting the reproduction of the pole by the bank. It may well be that when he executed the agreement he did not fully appreciate the implications of what he was doing in terms of his own cultural obligations. Certainly, it appears to be the case that neither Mr. Wallis, nor anyone else at the agency, felt a need to explore these ramifications with him. Mr. Wallis saw that as a matter which was Mr. Yumbulul's responsibility. It may be that greater care could have been taken in this case. And it may also be that Australia's copyright law does not provide adequate recognition of Aboriginal community claims to regulate the reproduction and use of works which are essentially communal in origin. But to say this is not to say that there has been established in the case any cause of action."
146. *Yumbulul, supra* note 136. The Court found that a valid copyright agreement existed between Yumbulul and the government, and it did not have the authority to intervene on the grounds of community objections by Mr. Yumbulul's clan.

expressed its distress about being unable to find a copyright solution for the conflict:

> [T]he question of statutory recognition of Aboriginal communal interests in the reproduction of sacred objects is a matter for consideration by law reformers and legislators. For what it is worth, I would add that it would be most unfortunate if Mr. Yumbulul were to be the subject of continued criticism within the Aboriginal community for allowing the reproduction of the Morning Star Pole design on the commemorative banknote. The reproduction was, and should be seen, as a mark of the high respect that has all too slowly developed in Australian society for the beauty and richness of Aboriginal culture.[147]

A possible solution to these kinds of conflicts would be an agreement between artist and community. But this approach presents an utterly artificial context for the creation of Aboriginal art. It presumes to impose the framework of Western contractual relations on relationships that have been defined by cultural rules, probably since time immemorial. It also identifies the physical creator of the work as its author, exactly in keeping with the Western copyright approach to creativity, without a consideration of the community's contribution to the work. Why, for example, could the Bill not introduce joint or communal authorship as an alternate model of authorship for the purposes of this right? Anderson is right to emphasize the impracticality of the rule. Indeed, the fluidity of relationships is not unique to Aboriginal cultures. On the contrary, many relationships involving the transfer of knowledge in Western society also take place without written contracts, leading to disputes about their scope.[148]

The requirement of a pre-existing contract was one of a number of prerequisites to moral rights in the proposed Bill. The Bill also specified that a

---

147. *Id.*, para. 20: "By its defence, the agency invoked ss 65 and 68 of the Copyright Act 1968, contending that the Morning Star Pole is either a sculpture or a work of artistic craftsmanship on display other than temporarily at the Australian Museum. On this basis, it was said, the allegation that the Reserve Bank had infringed Mr. Yumbulul's copyright, and that the infringement was authorised by the agency, could not be made out. In the event, it is not necessary for me to make any finding on the validity of this defence. But if it be correct, then it may be the case that some Aboriginal artists have laboured under a serious misapprehension as to the effect of public display upon their copyright in certain classes of works. This question and the question of statutory recognition of Aboriginal communal interests in the reproduction of sacred objects is a matter for consideration by law reformers and legislators. For what it is worth, I would add that it would be most unfortunate if Mr. Yumbulul were to be the subject of continued criticism within the Aboriginal community for allowing the reproduction of the Morning Star Pole design on the commemorative banknote. The reproduction was, and should be seen, as a mark of the high respect that has all too slowly developed in Australian society for the beauty and richness of Aboriginal culture."

148. *E.g., Robertson, supra* note 54.

copyright work should exist—clear enough in relation to artworks, but potentially too restrictive to accommodate traditional knowledge in the form of stories or other oral traditions.[149] The work had to show a link with Aboriginal traditions. This requirement generated little controversy, although the possibility of a disagreement between an individual artist and his or her community about the "traditional" nature of the work seems significant in the modern context. The third requirement had to do with agreement between artist and community, as noted above. Fourth, the Aboriginal community's association with the work needed to be acknowledged.

Finally, as Anderson points out:

> [I]nterested parties in the work need to have consented to the rights arising, and this consent must be provided through written notice. There is no clarification in the legislation of who constitutes an 'interest holder.'

As in the case of the agreement, this requirement, too, is problematic. Does it mean that any contributor to the work, including members of the community at large, must consent to the moral right before it can be asserted? The position is in contrast with the general Australian approach to moral rights, which recognizes them automatically upon the creation of a work, and rejects the possibility of waiving or assigning them. In contrast, the effect of this provision is that the proposed indigenous moral right would need to be asserted before it could exist. To make matters still more confusing, these requirements apparently need to be met "before the first dealing with the work, otherwise no rights arise."[150]

The idea of providing moral rights protection for Australian Aboriginal culture is an exciting prospect. Because of their inalienable, perpetual, and personal nature, the links between moral rights and traditional culture are readily apparent.[151] However, the form in which the Australian government attempted to express this moral right was disappointing. In practical terms, it is difficult to see how the preconditions for its exercise could ever have been met. From a conceptual point of view, the right offered little insight or enlightenment.

To be truly effective, an indigenous moral right would have to accomplish many things. At a minimum, it would need to accommodate the reality of shared authorship between an individual and his or her community. The joint authorship option is one; communities could also be asked to designate a claimant as and when an infringement suit is filed. The moral right should

---

149. The need for a copyright work to exist could imply a protection against misappropriation— for example, a rule that copyright in any work which can be shown to be derived from indigenous traditions must be shared with the culture from which it is drawn.
150. Anderson, *The Politics of Indigenous Knowledge, supra* note 135, at 598.
151. The relationship between moral rights and Aboriginal culture is explored in Mira T. Sundara Rajan, *Intellectual Property and Aboriginal Peoples, supra* note 5.

be available without formal requirements of assertion or registration, just as it is available to individual authors under Australian law. Moral rights in Aboriginal culture should not be restricted to copyright works. Traditional cultures are known for oral works and other, diverse forms of knowledge, all of which could potentially be protected by moral rights. And a moral right for indigenous culture would have to operate outside time limits, which are fundamentally incompatible with traditional heritage.

These considerations are only the beginning. They show how truly innovative a moral right in indigenous cultural heritage would have to be. Meeting these challenges may not be impossible, but the development of a viable moral right for indigenous cultures will require considerable legal ingenuity, and a commitment to learning from past failures.

At a fundamental level, the purposes behind the indigenous communal moral right should be clearly articulated. The protection of Aboriginal cultural heritage is the goal, but protection from what? Misappropriation by those who use traditional culture to create copyright works? The public release of sacred or restricted knowledge? And what about the separate goal of seeking recognition and prestige for Aboriginal culture itself?[152] All of these purposes could be fulfilled through moral rights. But the Australian attempt, sadly, reflects the desire to give nominal recognition to Aboriginal culture without the political will to translate that recognition into practical power. Above all, the proposed Australian right failed to treat Aboriginal ways of knowing and seeing their own culture on a par with the copyright framework. Any attempt at justice must first be able to acknowledge the right of Aboriginal people to define their own cultural practices, a crucial element in cultural self-determination.

B. Growth of the Doctrine: Moral Rights and Developing Jurisdictions

In developing countries, moral rights present an enigma. These countries hold a general attitude of suspicion towards copyright law. Where moral rights are concerned, however, their approach is entirely different. Moral rights are warmly embraced in the developing world, and they enjoy widespread and whole-hearted recognition in an astonishing range of countries.

---

152. For a useful and interesting summary of "[t]he major concerns for Indigenous people," see TERRI JANKE, OUR CULTURE, OUR FUTURE: REPORT ON AUSTRALIAN INDIGENOUS CULTURAL AND INTELLECTUAL PROPERTY ch. 3, 19–42 (Michael Frankel & Company 1998). The Report was prepared by Janke as Principal Consultant for Michael Frankel & Company, Solicitors, for the Australian Institute of Aboriginal and Torres Strait Islander Studies and the Aboriginal and Torres Strait Islander Commission (1998).

Why does copyright law bring out Jekyll and Hyde personalities in the developing world? The reasons are deeply rooted in the history of international copyright relations. International copyright law is defined by a fundamental schism between developed and developing countries. Developing countries favor access to knowledge over authors' rights—at least, where the works of foreign authors are concerned. No doubt, developing countries face a special need for knowledge from the outside world. To some extent, however, their dependence on external sources of education also reflects the persistence of a colonial mentality. From the onset of the colonial period, foreign works were perceived as essential for development. Valuable knowledge was thought to come from outside the country, and not as a product of one's own society.

Over the past two decades, this perception has slowly shifted with the empowerment of developing countries through technology. A notable example is India, which has long been a champion of developing countries' interests in the international copyright arena, but is now also a world leader in the software industry. As a result, India is no longer just a receiving country when it comes to copyright works; it is also a producing country, with a strong interest in promoting its software industry.[153] Moreover, India experiences conflict over copyright priorities in a new way—not only as a distinction between domestic and international priorities, but also, as a conflict between internal priorities. The goals of its software industry and the needs of its 700 million-odd people who fall under global standards of poverty may be quite different.

It would be suitably ironic if the growth of technology in developing countries, largely a product of education required from outside, proved to be a necessary prerequisite to the exploration of indigenous knowledge that has developed within these traditions.[154] In fact, this is exactly what has happened. As developing countries enjoy a new sense of self-worth through technological success, they are encouraged to turn towards their own traditions. At the international level, the new prominence of developing jurisdictions has brought publicity to the debates over traditional knowledge, which fundamentally question accepted ways of defining and valuing knowledge in the West.[155]

---

153. The issue of whether or not a strong copyright system promotes the software industry is highly contentious. *See* Chapter 5, *infra*.

154. The training of Indian scientists in the Soviet Union from at least the 1970s was one method by which India acquired scientific expertise. *See* the information on the website of the Indian Embassy in Moscow, *available at* http://www.indianembassy.ru/cms/index.php?option=com_content&task=view&id=60&Itemid=520 (last visited Apr. 28, 2010).

155. The problem of valuing traditional knowledge (TK) is closely related to the issue of how to value Aboriginal cultures, noted above in relation to *Yumbulul*. Both issues involve alternative frameworks of knowledge that in many respects differ fundamentally from the

Finally, it should be noted that the copyright concerns of developing countries reflect structural features of the international copyright regime which lead to built-in biases. The status of developing countries in the international copyright system is a peculiar one. As former colonies ruled by European "Great Powers," many of these countries found their way into the international copyright regime via membership in the Berne Union. When independence was won, they elected to stay, hoping that a system made by their rulers could expand to accommodate their needs.

The period of decolonization that followed proved to be a rude awakening. Developing countries felt that they were in need of information and knowledge from the developed world; ever-increasing copyright restrictions, and the costs obtaining materials from abroad, interfered. Policies such as the compulsory licensing of works for translation went against Western copyright norms.[156] By the 1960s, conflict between developed and developing countries had escalated to the point where the viability of the international copyright system was at stake. The result was the 1967 Stockholm revision of the Berne Convention, which modernized the Convention in a number of ways.[157] The Stockholm document included a new protocol with special provisions for developing countries, but, as Sam Ricketson notes, "These generous provisions in favor of developing countries . . . were destined never to come into force."[158] The Protocol regarding Developing Countries was revisited at the Paris meeting of 1971, and, in the course of a "salvage operation," a new and "less rigorous regime" was established.[159]

In the debates surrounding copyright in developing countries, moral rights were invariably seen in a different light. While developing countries fought against copyright standards that they perceived as inappropriate or excessive, they had few reservations about moral rights. Countries as widely

---

copyright/intellectual property system. *See* Mira T. Sundara Rajan, *Intellectual Property and Aboriginal Peoples*, *supra* note 5.

156. But it is worth noting that the United States was the country with the world's first provisions on compulsory licensing, in the Copyright Act of 1909. The license was "to allow for the use of nondramatic musical works," and it was initially established in response to an unprecedented new technology: piano rolls. *See* Statement of Marybeth Peters, The Register of Copyrights before the Subcommittee on Courts, The Internet and Intellectual Property of the House Committee on the Judiciary, Mar. 11, 2004, *available at* http://www.copyright.gov/docs/regstat031104.html#N_1_ (last visited Apr. 28, 2010). Peters also comments that the "stringent requirements for use of the compulsory license did not foster wide use of the license."

157. *See* Ricketson, *supra* note 9, paras. 3.49–3.67.

158. *Id.*, para. 3.64.

159. *Id.*, para. 3.67. *See also* Chapter 11 of *id.*, for a detailed treatment of the place of developing countries in the Berne system, including the events of the Stockholm and Paris conferences.

divergent as India,[160] Brazil,[161] Tunisia,[162] and Mali[163] were eager to embrace moral rights.

When moral rights migrated to the developing world, it was not just the law of developing countries that was affected. Rather, moral rights, themselves, were transformed. In the exotic landscape of the developing world, moral rights inhabited, not only a new geographical space, but also, a new cultural environment. Their ties with European Romanticism were severed, and they were set free from the models of creativity associated with that era.

Accordingly, developing countries do not stop at the recognition of moral rights as embodied in the Berne Convention, or even as envisioned by French and German legal theorists. They approach the implementation of moral rights in expansive and creative ways. The treatment of moral rights by legislators and judges in developing countries has led to new directions in the evolution of the doctrine. Apart from large developing countries like India or Brazil, the protection of moral rights in underdeveloped countries is impressive, at times exceeding accepted levels of protection in Continental jurisdictions.

---

160. Indian Copyright Act, *supra* note 31, sec. 57.

161. *See* Law No. 9610 of Feb. 19, 1998, on Copyright and Neighboring Rights Arts. 24–27 (entered into force June 20, 1998), *available at* http://www.wipo.int/clea/en/text_pdf.jsp?lang=EN&id=514 (last visited Apr. 28, 2010) [Brazilian Copyright Act]. A number of features make these provisions interesting. The state is under an obligation to check the attribution and integrity works in the public domain; in relation to film, directors are clearly designated as the sole moral rights holder, and architects have a special right to repudiate authorship if a building design is modified against their will. The law states clearly that the rights are "inalienable and irrevocable." These provisions are not fully up-to-date, as the Brazilian law has been amended since 1998; but the updated law is not yet available in English translation. *See* J. Carlos Fernández-Molina & Eduardo Peis, *The Moral Rights of Authors in the Age of Digital Information*, 52(2) J. Am. Soc'y Information Sci. & Tech. 109, 112 (2001), *available at* http://www.scimago.es/publications/jasist-01b.pdf (last visited Apr. 28, 2010).

162. Tunisia's 1966 Copyright Act included protection for folklore as a type of work eligible for copyright protection. For an analysis, see Edward W. Ploman & L. Clark Hamilton, Copyright: Intellectual Property in the Information Age 130 (Routledge & Kegan Paul 1980) [Ploman & Hamilton]. They comment that "[t]he purpose of these restrictions is to regulate teams which frequently tour Africa to record performances by local musicians and artists and secure exclusive world rights in the exploitation of the records for minuscule sums." They also note that, in the absence of international recognition for these rights, their effectiveness would be limited.

163. *See* Ordinance Concerning Literary Artistic Property No. 77-46 CMLN, of July 12, 1977, arts. 29 and, specifically, 30, *available at* http://www.wipo.int/clea/en/text_pdf.jsp?lang=EN&id=5331 (last visited Apr. 30, 2010): Malian law calls moral rights "attributes of an intellectual and moral nature." *See* the interesting perspective on piracy in the Malian context by Alex Duval Smith, *Mali's Radio Stations to Fall Silent in Protest over Tape Piracy*, Independent (Feb. 5, 2000), *available at* http://www.independent.co.uk/arts-entertainment/music/news/malis-radiostations-tofall-silent-in-protest-over-tape-piracy-726275.html (last visited Apr. 30, 2010).

When developing countries first adopted independent copyright laws, they were in a special situation. Their approach to the law was characterized by urgency and passion. They were poor countries, yes, but with such impossible cultural riches—cultural property, folk arts and folk lore, traditional medicine, ancient laws, and ancient languages—and an intense desire to recover dignity and self-esteem. More than a half-century after Indian independence, it is not easy to understand the mindset of the Freedom Fighters. They, and the first generation of Indian political leaders after them, approached the world with passionate idealism.[164] Any and every instrument that could improve the situation of the country should be deployed. In such an environment, under such pressures, moral rights could metamorphose into something quite new.

And indeed, moral rights in developing countries were transformed. Developing countries chose to implement extensive protections for moral rights in their laws, favoring such measures as perpetual protection, broad principles of attribution, the recognition of integrity without any need to prove damage to reputation, and moral rights in folklore.[165] In doing so, they drew upon two kinds of resources.

The first was the political idealism of decolonization. The second impulse behind moral rights in these jurisdictions was the availability of traditions of law that preceded colonization. For example, the aesthetic theories of ancient India apparently supported the protection of "ideas" as well as works, an approach to copyright that is more inclusive than Western norms.[166] More importantly, it is an approach that appears interesting again in the digital age. The significance of "fixation," the requirement that a work must be recorded in a tangible medium before it becomes eligible for copyright protection, may not hold the same power in an environment defined by the intangible exchange of information.[167]

It seems an enduring irony that "palm tree justice" signifies arbitrary and case-by-case decision-making disapproved in the Western concept of justice.[168] No doubt, in parts of the world where palm trees grow, humanity has

---

164. *See generally* Louis Fischer's classic biography of Mahatma Gandhi, Louis Fischer, Gandhi: His Life and Message for the World (Penguin Books 1954).
165. *See, for example,* Ploman & Hamilton, *supra* note 162, at 130, on Tunisia; Brazilian Copyright Act, *supra* note 161.
166. *See* T. S. Krishnamurti, *Copyright—Another View*, 15(3) Bull. Copyright Soc'y USA 217, 218 (1968); *see* Chapter 2, *supra,* "Moral Rights: History of an Idea," note 21 and accompanying text.
167. The protection of performers' moral rights in the WIPO Performances and Phonograms Treaty includes live performances. *See* WPPT. The provisions of the Treaty are limited to "live aural" performances and apparently do not extend to visual elements, audiovisual works, or audiovisual recordings.
168. Ironically, the phrase has been used to characterize the approach of one of the most brilliant of British judges, Lord Denning: *see* Wilfrid J. Waluchow, *Hart, Legal Rules and Palm Tree Justice*, 4(1) Law & Phil. 41 (1985). It is not clear whether the term might be used to

had its share of arbitrary rulership and lawlessness. However, developing countries also have legal traditions of their own. These traditions might take the form of custom, but customary law is increasingly given its rightful due as a valid form of law.[169] There were also circumstances where the laws of developing countries were manifest in written traditions that predated, or coincided with, colonial times.

Writing about the South Pacific, Sue Farran comments:

> When Pacific Island countries gained independence in the latter part of the 20th century some colonial laws were abolished, others were retained as interim measures pending their replacement by national laws. The place of custom and customary law was reassessed and in some cases strengthened as part of the assertion of independence and national identity, a process which has continued. In some cases, foreign laws have been introduced or have served as a model for national laws. Elsewhere colonial or imperial laws remain unaltered. In addition[,] participation in the family of nations by Pacific Island countries has seen the introduction of international law into domestic law. Today it would be difficult to claim that the law of Pacific Island states neatly fitted into any one of the major legal families of the world.[170]

India is a perfect example of a post-colonial legal system. In the case of India, defining the country's legal tradition is a problem of awesome complexity. Prior to British rule, India ran the full gamut of sources of law, from written Sanskrit codes, often of controversial content, to social customs which, in their turn, ranged from flexible and progressive to rigid and repressive.[171] In some sense, the influence of British law was superficial—little more

---

condemn the colonial administration of justice, also conducted, after all, "under palm trees." The term appears to have originated with Bucknill L.J. in the 1950 case of *Newgrosh v. Newgrosh* (unreported).

> Section 17 of the Married Women's Property Act 1882 (UK) gives the judge a wide power to do what he thinks under the circumstances is fair and just. I do not think it entitles him to make an order which is contrary to any well-established principle of law, but, subject to that, I should have thought that disputes between husband and wife as to who owns property which at one time, at any rate, they have been using in common are disputes which may very well be dealt with by the principle which has been described here as "palm tree justice." I understand that to be justice which makes orders which appear to be fair and just in the special circumstances of the case.

169. *See* the interesting discussion of the interplay between British law and Indian law, including its customary aspects, in Marc Galanter, *The Displacement of Traditional Law in Modern India*, 24(4) J. Soc. Issues 65 (1968).

170. Sue Farran, *Palm Tree Justice? The Role of Comparative Law in the South Pacific*, 58 Int'l & Comp. L.Q. 181, 182 (2009) (footnotes omitted). The article is an extremely useful exploration of how comparative law works in the context of law reform and legal modernization.

171. Werner F. Menski, Hindu Law: Beyond Tradition and Modernity (Oxford Univ. Press 2003).

than a common law façade superimposed upon a many-layered palimpsest of traditional law and culture. And, during colonial times, subtle influences from France and Portugal were also felt—bit-players in the great drama of the British Raj in India. The complexity of India's post-colonial legal reality plays itself out in relation to copyright and moral rights, aspects of the law that are inextricably intertwined with cultural realities and practices.

1. India and Other British Colonies: Common Law, or Not?

India is a striking example of how the moral rights principle has been transformed in a developing country. It illustrates the case of a common law jurisdiction which acquired its common law heritage through colonization, flirted with European civil law concepts during the British period, and ultimately drew upon the twin forces of decolonization and the revival of indigenous legal ideas to expand the availability of moral rights for its authors.

The presence of Continental European legal traditions outside the common law should also be noted, although their role in modern Indian law is indeterminate.[172] India's exposure to European civil law occurred in the course of expeditions to India run by the Portuguese, who set up a colony at Goa, and the establishment of a major French territory in Pondicherry. While the legal traditions of these civilian jurisdictions had little direct impact on India's national legal framework after British rule, it is interesting to consider the possibility of legal or cultural affinities between these European cultures and India. India's ancient jurisprudence knew and recognized codification, precedent, and custom as sources of law.[173] The French territory of Pondicherry was home to an important colony of nationalists in exile, although the French administration assuredly had its own reasons for tolerating their presence on "French" soil, and French models of culture and authorship were popular with the nationalists.[174] These factors could be cited as eventual influences on Indian moral rights.

---

172. The influence of civil law systems in India would be an interesting area for further research.

173. The most famous example of codified Sanskrit law is the ancient *Laws of Manu*, and has been frequently translated into English. *See* THE LAW CODE OF MANU (Patrick Olivelle trans., Oxford World's Classics, Oxford Univ. Press 2009) (paperback); see the classic discussion of ancient Indian law in Menski, *supra* note 171.

174. Subramania Bharati was among the exiles in Pondicherry; Aurobindo Ghosh was another member of the community and a good friend of the poet. Bharati's case is interesting because his move to Pondicherry was followed by the reestablishment of INDIA, a magazine originally published in British India, which now came under Bharati's *de facto* editorship. The motto of the magazine was "Liberté; Egalité, Fraternité." *See* S. VIJAYA BHARATI, SUBRAMANIA BHARATI (New Delhi: Government of India 1974); Statement by Dr. S. Vijaya Bharati (personal communication with the author, Apr. 27, 2010).

However, India's initial empowerment of authors eventually took an unexpected twist. In the early 1990s, the Indian government realized that it could become responsible for moral rights violations in relation to cultural works in its own possession. Apparently concerned about liability, it moved to modify the law of 1957, restoring it to more conventional bounds.

This shift in the official policy towards moral rights was firmly rejected by India's powerful and independent judiciary. Indian judges feel a responsibility for protecting Indian culture, even safeguarding it, where necessary, from India's political leadership. In the landmark 2005 case of *Amar Nath Sehgal v. Union of India*, the Delhi High Court ultimately turned to the international community for support, invoking international agreements on cultural property to trump legislative amendments to moral rights in the Indian Copyright Act that it perceived as ill-advised.[175] The decision builds on a tradition of recognition for moral rights in India, initiated in the *Mannu Bandhari* case,[176] but it moves into a new area by connecting moral rights doctrine with cultural property. The case has important implications for both legal theory and moral rights. Not only is it a pioneering guide to the interpretation of moral rights law in India—and, potentially, elsewhere—but it also points to the relevance of moral rights for the protection of cultural property and other elements of the public domain.

2. Moral Rights and the Protection of Culture: Indian Copyright Law[177]

India adopted its first independent Copyright Act in 1957, and this statute continues to regulate Indian copyright matters.[178] The 1957 Act included protection for the author's moral rights of attribution and, in a broad interpretation reminiscent of France, integrity. The Act has been amended five times since its adoption,[179] but 1994 was a benchmark year. A series of major revisions to India's copyright law were undertaken, and among these, significant amendments to India's moral rights were enacted.[180]

---

175. *Sehgal, supra* note 47.
176. Smt. Mannu Bhandari v. Kala Vikas Pictures Pvt. Ltd. (1986) 1987 A.I.R. (Delhi 13) [*Mannu Bhandari*]. A consideration of the seminal case may be found in Mira T. Sundara Rajan, *Moral Rights in Developing Countries: The Example of India*, 8(5) & 8(6) J. Intell. Prop. Rights, 357, 449, (2003), *available at* http://nopr.niscair.res.in/bitstream/123456789/4907/1/JIP%208(5)%20357-374.pdf, and http://nopr.niscair.res.in/bitstream/123456789/4911/1/JIPR%208(6)%20449-461.pdf (last visited Apr. 28, 2010) [Sundara Rajan, *Moral Rights in Developing Countries*, Parts I & II].
177. An earlier treatment of these issues may be found in *id.*
178. Indian Copyright Act, *supra* note 31.
179. *See* the Copyright Office of the Government of India, *available at* http://copyright.gov.in/ (last visited Apr. 28, 2010).
180. The amending Bill is available on the Parliament of India website at http://parliamentofindia.nic.in/ls/bills/1994/1994-31.htm> (last visited Apr. 28, 2010) [1994 Amendment Bill].

India's amended provisions on moral rights clearly meet the minimum standards set out in the Berne Convention, but they represent a scaled-down version of the moral rights originally set out in the Copyright Act of 1957. The old section 57 provided protection for moral rights that was both more comprehensive and more nuanced than the current provisions. As such, the postcolonial legislation could be said to demonstrate the significant influence of national cultural priorities, indigenous customs, and, possibly, exposure to European legal and cultural traditions. Taken together, these factors led to a treatment of moral rights that considerably exceeded international standards—and indeed, with case precedents taken into account, Indian law transcended the approach to moral rights even in France. The common law veneer was shown to be little more than a cosmetic layer disguising the true attributes of Indian cultural law.

In a section entitled "Special Rights of the Author," section 57 of the Indian Copyright Act protects the author's rights of attribution and integrity. In keeping with the provisions of the Berne Convention, moral rights are "independent" of economic copyright, and they are retained by the author even after he may have sold the work, or assigned his copyright in it.[181]

Section 57 demonstrates an impressive attention to technological matters. As part of the amendments of 1994, an early date by international standards, the issue of moral rights in computer programs received attention in the Indian Act.[182] The Act provides that the making of copies or adaptations of a computer program by the owner of that copy cannot be held to violate the moral right of the author. Moral rights are not addressed directly; but the

---

181. Section 57(1) states:

> Independently of the author's copyright and even after the assignment wholly or partially of the said copyright, the author of the work shall have the right—

> (a) to claim authorship of the work; and
> (b) to restrain or claim damages in respect of any distortion, mutilation, modification or other act in relation to the said work *which is done before the expiration of the term of copyright* if such distortion, mutilation, modification or other act would be prejudicial to his honour or reputation:

>> Provided that the author shall not have the right to restrain or claim damages in respect of any indication of a computer programme to which clause (aa) of sub-section (1) of section 52 applies. . . .

> (2) The right conferred upon an author of the work by sub-section (1), *other than the right to claim authorshipof the work*, may be exercised by the legal representatives of the author. (emphasis added).

182. France was the first country to recognize moral rights in programs; it did so, at first, by excluding the rights of integrity and withdrawal in software, while in theory leaving attribution available. France modified the provision two years later to institute a Berne-style integrity right for software. *See* CPI, *supra* note 43; the Légifrance service provides a history of Art L121-7. India, too, was among the first to address moral rights in software, and its method of recognition, as in France, was purely indirect; *see* 1994 Amendment Bill, *supra* note 180.

suggestion that certain acts will *not* lead to a violation of moral rights seems to imply that other acts could lead to the infringement of moral rights. The Indian provision coincides with limited recognition of the moral right of integrity computer programs in France, and probably reflects India's preoccupation with information technology as an engine for growth and prestige. Any right prohibiting modifications to computer programs could clearly have major implications for the software industry, whose development depends to a great extent on the ability to build on existing efficiencies, including those specifically achieved by the language of programming code.[183] In an interesting comparison to the world's other pioneer in information technology, the United States, India chose to address the question of rights more comprehensively than its chief competitor. The United States has yet to consider the issue of moral rights in information technology, a question that is now especially pertinent in view of its membership in the Berne Union.[184]

The right of attribution is, quite simply, the right "to claim authorship of the work." As in French law, there is no explicit attempt to define the scope of this right in India.[185] Rather, it is left to the courts to decide on the extent of protection for the author's right to publish on an anonymous basis, or under a pseudonym. The application of the right to the attachment of one's own name to someone else's work is also left open.

As in the Berne formulation, a finding that the author's right of integrity has been violated will turn on the question of damage to the author's "honor

---

183. Section 57 (1)(b), to be read in conjunction with sec. 52(1)(aa).

184. It is worth noting that Japan also addresses moral rights in software to an extent, providing that the modification of a program in order to make it usable, or in order to improve its functioning, will not amount to a violation of the programmer's moral right of integrity; *see* art. 20(2)(iii) of the Japanese Copyright Act, available in English translation on the website of the Copyright Research and Information Center at http://www.cric.or.jp/cric_e/clj/clj. html (last visited Apr. 28, 2010) [Japanese Copyright Act]. Interestingly, Jonathan Band and Edward Durney comment: "This last phrase may make the exception eat up the rule, since it is hard to imagine any modification that could not be justified as having been made to make more effective use of the program. However, the drafters of the amendments may have intended this result, since there is little need for the moral rights in the case of program works." (footnotes omitted) *See* Jonathan Band & Edward Durney, *Protection of Computer Programs under Japanese Copyright Law, available at* http://www.policybandwidth.com/doc/JBand-JapaneseSoftware.pdf (last visited July 16, 2010). This may be overstating the case; the provision is definitely designed to cover fair uses, or private uses, of the work, and it may also allow modifications that improve the functioning of a program. Nevertheless, destructive interference with the program is still prohibited. For example, changes to a program that introduce questionable issues, from bugs to advertising features, should qualify as a violation of the right of integrity under Japanese law. *See also* the comprehensive overview of Japanese moral rights in Tatsuhiro Ueno, Chapter V, "Moral Rights," *in* PETER GANEA, JAPANESE COPYRIGHT LAW: WRITINGS IN HONOUR OF GERHARD SCHRICKER 41–50 (Christopher Heath & Hiroshi Saito eds., Kluwer Law International 2003).

185. CPI, *supra* note 43, art. L121-1, provides only that the author has the right to "respect for his name." Presumably, he has the right to choose whether and how to use his name as part of this provision.

or reputation." Unless the author can prove that his reputation is in danger, mistreatment of the work is not considered to be an infringement of the integrity right under Indian law.[186] The Indian legislation also includes a special provision on the conditions in which works of visual art are displayed, to the effect that the failure to display a work properly cannot lead to an infringement of the moral rights of authors.[187] This provision seems to respond directly to influential Indian case law on moral rights in works of visual art.[188]

a. History of the Indian Right of Integrity

But it was not always so. Prior to the crucial amendments of 1994, the old section 57 of the Copyright Act dealt differently with the moral right of integrity. The Indian Copyright Act did not require proof of damage to reputation. Instead, it allowed an author to make a claim, quite simply, in relation to "*any* distortion, mutilation or other modification of the . . . work."[189] The terms were directly comparable to French law, which "treat[s] . . . [the right of integrity] as an absolute right against alteration."[190]

A closer examination of the language and structure of the earlier Indian provision shows it to be completely unambiguous in affirming that an integrity violation would not depend on proof of prejudice to the author's honor or reputation. In the old section 57, the integrity right was dealt with in two parts. The first clause, section 57(1)(a), defined the integrity right as "any distortion, mutilation or modification of the . . . work." It was then followed by section 57(1)(b), which protected the author against "any other action in relation to the . . . work which would be prejudicial to his honour or reputation."[191] In this way, the old section 57 accomplished two distinct

---

186. It is advisable to keep in mind that the appropriate standard of proof is, of course, the non-criminal standard of a balance of probabilities.

187. Explanation to Section 57(1)(b) of the Indian Copyright Act, *supra* note 31.

188. See *Sehgal, supra* note 47, discussed in detail below, notes 209–228 and accompanying text.

189. Still available on the website of the Commonwealth Legal Information Institute at http://www.commonlii.org/in/legis/num_act/ca1957133/ (last visited July 16, 2010); *see also* note 31, *supra*.

190. *See* Staniforth Ricketson, The Law of Intellectual Property, para. 15.57, n.53 (The Law Book Company 1984); this view is particularly French, as is generally exemplified in the commentary of Henri Desbois, Le Droit d'auteur en France (3rd ed. Dalloz 1978).

191. *See* the original sec. 57, *supra* note 31, available on the website of the Commonwealth Legal Information Institute, http://www.commonlii.org/in/legis/num_act/ca1957133/ (last visited Apr. 28, 2010). It is interesting to note that the structure of sec. 57 is consistent with the traditional importance accorded to the work, independently of its creator, in Indian thinking on the arts. On the relationship between the artist and his creation in Indian thought, see Sneh Pandit, An Approach to the Indian Theory of Art and Aesthetics 134 (Sterling 1977).

objectives, in two specific provisions. The first was to preserve the integrity of the work; the second, to protect the author's reputation.

In keeping with Continental traditions, the old Indian legislation implicitly recognized the author as the ultimate judge of how his own work was treated. Judges did not need to assert their preference for subjective evidence of how the author felt about the treatment of his work; the legislation required it. To provide a blatant illustration of this principle, the old Section 57 could never support a defense to an integrity claim based on the argument that changes to an author's work, though against his will, made improvements to the original. Unless the author agreed, the issue would be completely irrelevant. The theory of the Indian law was clearly what French scholar Henri Desbois characterizes as "individualist" in the context of French law.[192]

b. Independence from Economic Rights

In keeping with the Berne Convention, section 57 of the Indian Copyright Act continues to affirm the "independence" of economic and moral rights. An author can assert his moral rights even after the assignment of the economic copyright in his work.[193]

At first glance, therefore, moral rights in India are inalienable. But the question of inalienability receives imperfect treatment in the Indian law. The Copyright Act does not address the question of whether moral rights may be waived. Accordingly, in keeping with common law tradition, Indian lawyers generally accept the possibility of waiver under section 57.[194]

India's judicial landscape makes the implications of waiver different from other common law countries. In particular, India should be distinguished from the extreme case of Canada, where waivers of moral rights are both usual and comprehensive. In the UK, the *Frisby* case showed a willingness to read copyright contracts with authors' interests at heart. But no British precedent, to date, can tell us whether a British court would be willing to overrule a waiver of moral rights on similar grounds.[195] Given the proven sympathy of the Indian judiciary for creators, it seems likely that Indian judges would readily overturn comprehensive attempts to waive moral rights in artists' contracts. This is all the more probable in view of the difficulties and delays faced by Indian authors who attempt to sue, of which, judges in that country are well aware. Persistence in a lawsuit means different things in India than elsewhere—the stamina to wait for redress, determination in the pursuit of it,

---

192. Desbois, *supra* note 190.
193. Indian Copyright Act, *supra* note 31, sec. 57(1).
194. *See* Pravin Anand, *The Concept of Moral Rights under Indian Copyright Law*, 27 Copyright World 35, 36 (1993). Anand argues that, "[m]oral rights under Indian law are not transferable, although under an agreement an author may waive his rights under section 57."
195. *Frisby, supra* note 98.

and a level of financial success that probably reflects prominence, even eminence, in one's field. In India, where moral rights are concerned, enduring litigation may very nearly justify a presumption of guilt!

c. Term of Protection and Inheritance of Moral Rights

Like the right of integrity, the approach to term of protection for moral rights has evolved in Indian law from the time of Indian independence to the present. The initial approach was to leave the question of duration open. Accordingly, the old section 57, by implication, allowed the possibility of perpetual protection for moral rights. There can be little doubt that this openness was a product of concerns about the status of Indian culture in the post-colonial period. The perpetual protection of moral rights could provide a valuable means of protecting important cultural works from harm, and of preserving the integrity of the historical record which they represent.

If moral rights are to be protected forever, who should exercise them? Should these interests and obligations be entrusted to the author's descendants, his legal representatives, cultural organizations, the government, or some combination of these? Indian law resolves this issue very conventionally, by assigning a right of action to the author's heirs.[196]

Subsection 57 (2) of the Indian Copyright Act provides that the author's moral rights can be exercised on his behalf by his legal representatives. This provision is meant to address the exercise of moral rights after the author's death, and as such, it is considered to be in keeping with the theory of inalienability. Death, of course, is unavoidable; but the relationship between author and work is permanent, and someone must therefore be placed to protect the work after the author's death. Since this provision deals generally with the assertion of moral rights after the author's death, all of the moral rights protected in Indian law, presumably, must continue to be protected after the author's death.[197]

However, the Act generates some confusion with respect to the fate of attribution after an author's death. An obscure clause in section 57 states that the author's legal representatives may assert his moral rights on his behalf, but that they may not "claim authorship of the work."[198] The provision appears to draw a distinction between the assertion of the author's moral rights by his

---

196. Indian Copyright Act, *supra* note 31, sec. 57(2).
197. *See generally* S. Ramaiah, *India, in* PAUL EDWARD GELLER & MELVILLE B. NIMMER, INTERNATIONAL COPYRIGHT LAW AND PRACTICE (Matthew Bender 1998), and STIG STRÖMHOLM, LE DROIT MORAL DE L'AUTEUR EN DROIT ALLEMAND, FRANÇAIS ET SCANDINAVE AVEC UN APERÇU DE L'ÉVOLUTION INTERNATIONALE: ETUDE DE DROIT COMPARÉ, vol. 1, *Première Partie: L'Evolution historique et le mouvement international* 420 (PA Norstedt & Söners Förlag 1967).
198. Indian Copyright Act, *supra* note 31, sec. 57(2).

descendants or legal representatives on his behalf, and the capacity of these agents to claim authorship of his work for themselves. It is difficult to see the need for this provision. Within the logic of the Indian scheme for moral rights, there is no real reason to restrict the capacity of the author's descendants or representatives to assert attribution on his behalf.[199] Rather, the law seems to reflect some policy concern that the descendants of an author could claim attribution in a more personal sense. . . . As a matter of folk culture, the theory of reincarnation is popularly believed to support the idea that a great person will be reborn in his own family. Could the special relationship between family members in Indian culture possibly be a factor affecting Indian copyright law?

In his comparative work on moral rights, Stig Strömholm attempts to explain this problem as a question of whether the author's descendants act in their own name, or as agents of the author. He argues that the proper interpretation will ultimately depend on the general position of the Indian law on inheritance. Regardless, the practical implications of this section have never been explored, and there can be no doubt that the descendants of Indian authors are entitled to protect the attribution right of their ancestors. As Strömholm observes:

> As for the rule which provides that the right to assert paternity of the work may not be exercised by the [author's] descendants, its precise meaning appears to depend on the proper answer to the question of whether the descendants are perceived to be acting in their own capacity against offences to the moral right, or if they are considered to be acting as representatives [of the author]. To resolve this question, it would be necessary to have exact information on the Indian concept of the right of successors mortis causa. If the first possibility is correct, the provision is perfectly logical: the descendants cannot claim for themselves paternity of the work. In this case, it would appear to be possible to allow them, on the other hand, the right to oppose at least some attacks on the right of paternity and, notably, to intervene where the author's name does not appear on copies of a work [first] published during his lifetime under his name.[200]

---

199. Strömholm, *supra* note 197, at 420, points out that, "[I]l serait singulièrement arbitraire de refuser aux héritiers le droit de défendre la paternité du de cujus en leur laissant le droit de s'opposer aux modifications, car si celles-ci deviennent souvent désirables après la mort de l'auteur, . . . l'usurpation de la paternité ne paraît pas justifiée par le fait que le créateur de l'oeuvre est mort." ("It would be exceptionally arbitrary to deprive the descendants of the right to vindicate the paternity of the deceased author ['de cujus'] while allowing them to retain the right to oppose modifications [of the work]. . . . While modifications often become desirable after the author's death, . . . taking over the right of paternity does not seem to be justifiable on the grounds that the creator of the work is dead.").

200. *Id.*, at 420. ("Quant à la règle suivant laquelle le droit de revendiquer la paternité de l'oeuvre ne passe pas aux héritiers, son sens exact paraît dépendre de la réponse qu'il convient de donner à la question de savoir si les héritiers sont censés agir en leur propre nom en

This provision is confusing, and it is not surprising that recent proposals for reform would remove these words from section 57.[201]

The current Section 57 still fails to specify a precise duration for moral rights. However, since 1994, the provision includes a new requirement: any act infringing the moral right of integrity must be "done before the expiration of the term of copyright."[202] This is not quite to say that the term of protection for the integrity right is thereby restricted to the term of copyright in Indian law—the lifetime of the author and sixty years after his death. This language does not preclude the possibility that a claim for the infringement of moral rights could still be brought forever. But the facts on which the claim is based would have to originate within the period of copyright protection. Once copyright has expired, no treatment of the work can be considered a violation of the integrity right within the current terms of Indian law. The provision may represent an attempt to define the public domain in India as the period following the term of copyright protection—without, however, imposing a limitation period on the right to bring a claim for the infringement of moral rights.

---

intervenant contre les atteintes portées au droit moral ou s'ils sont considérés en quelque sorte comme des mandataires. Pour trancher cette question, il faudrait posséder des informations précises sur la conception indienne du droit des sucesseurs *mortis causa*. Si la première alternative est la correcte, la disposition est parfaitement logique: les héritiers ne peuvent pas réclamer *pour eux* la paternité de l'oeuvre. Dans cette hypothèse, il paraît possible de leur accorder, en revanche, le droit de s'opposer au moins à certaines atteintes portées au droit à la paternite et notamment d'intervenir contre la suppression du nom de l'auteur sur les exemplaires d'une oeuvre publiée pendant la vie de son créateur sous sa signature.").

201. At one point, the Indian government made copyright reform proposals available in an online document, organized by section, which was very useful; this document showed the government's intent to remove these words. In December of 2009, the government initiated a new round of reform discussions, and the document has since been removed from its website.

202. *See* Indian Copyright Act, *supra* note 31, sec. 57(1)(b):

(b) to restrain or claim damages in respect of any distortion, mutilation, modification or other act in relation to the said work which is done before the expiration of the term of copyright if such distortion, mutilation, modification or other act would be prejudicial to his honour or reputation:

Provided that the author shall not have any right to restrain or claim damages in respect of any adaptation of a computer programme to which clause (aa) of subsection (1) of section 52 applies.

Explanation.—Failure to display a work or to display it to the satisfaction of the author shall not be deemed to be an infringement of the rights conferred by this section.

d. Remedies

Under Indian law, the breadth of remedies available for an infringement of moral rights is noteworthy. The Indian Act provides that the author has "the right to restrain, or claim damages in respect of" any violation of the integrity interests in his work.[203] The fact that Indian courts have the explicit authority to impose damages, as well as ordering injunctions, is a power that would be associated with moral rights in the civilian tradition. It is hardly typical of the common law approach.

e. Judicial Chivalry: The Practical Dynamics of India's Moral Rights

To a significant degree, amendments to Indian moral rights represent a reaction to the expansive treatment of moral rights by the Indian judiciary. The tension between legislative and judicial perspectives has exerted a powerful influence on the shape of Indian law. In case after case, on copyright law and beyond, Indian courts invariably choose to define themselves as guardians of civil liberties and individual rights.[204]

This is not to say that the Indian government's concerns about moral rights are nefarious. On the contrary, they reflect real and important issues. In developing countries, governments often play an especially important role as sponsors of culture. They may commonly be owners of culturally-important works. India's government is known for its role in the arts. Not only does the government own artworks, but Indian state governments have also taken the unusual step of assuming the ownership of copyright in the works of important authors.[205] Extensive provisions on moral rights could translate into liability, affecting the government's ability to support culture. Indeed,

---

203. *Id.*, sec. 57(1).
204. *See* the interesting article by S. P. Sathe, *Judicial Activism: The Indian Experience*, J.L. & Pol'y 29 (2001), *available at* http://www.wulaw.wustl.edu/journal/6/p_29_Sathe.pdf (last visited Apr. 28, 2010).
205. Subramania Bharati's case is probably the most famous such example in India, but many others exist. In Bharati's case, ownership of his copyright was acquired by the state government, but the copyright rests in the hands of the Indian people overall: the circumstances are discussed in Mira T. Sundara Rajan, *Moral Rights in the Public Domain: Copyright Matters in the Works of Indian National Poet C. Subramania Bharati*, Singapore J. Legal Stud. 161 (2001) [Mira T. Sundara Rajan, *Moral Rights in the Public Domain*], and an update on recent purchases of copyright by Tamil Nadu state (2009) may be found in Mira T. Sundara Rajan, *The Lessons of the Past: C. Subramania Bharati and the Nationalisation of Copyright*, 6(2) SCRIPTed 201 (2009), *available at* http://www.law.ed.ac.uk/ahrc/script-ed/vol6-2/rajan_editorial.pdf (last visited Apr. 28, 2010) [Sundara Rajan, *Nationalization*]. From a strictly legal point of view, the process by which state governments acquire copyright is rather obscure, as copyright is a matter for federal legislation in India. The issue was once in doubt, as an early case on copyright seemed to suggest state-based jurisdiction, but that decision was clearly in error.

the actions of the Tamil Nadu state government in Subramania Bharati's case have led directly to violations of the author's moral rights, and a good case could be made for government liability on both legal and ethical grounds. Where public resources are scarce, the prospect of liability could be overwhelming. Even if a court did not levy financial damages against the government, the intimidating costs of a legal defense might be incurred.

The international consequences of a strong moral rights regime could also be a concern for India. India's membership in the Berne Convention will compel it to extend any moral rights protections which it grants to its own authors to foreign authors, as well. Two negative consequences could follow. First, a classic concern: Indian access to foreign materials could be restricted, because Indian users would be obliged to observe additional precautions when using foreign works. Secondly, and on a grander scale, moral rights might make India a less attractive destination for foreign investment in creative enterprises, such as film, by increasing both the costs of "doing business" and the risks of liability for investors. Indeed, the extension of moral rights protection to Indian authors would bring new considerations to bear on a number of activities which are likely to be important, culturally and economically, in the environment of new media. Transformation of existing works into new media, adaptation of foreign works into Indian media,[206] translation, and many other kinds of activities could be affected. Indeed, the same concerns arise in the domestic context, where moral rights could have a negative impact on investment into industries like film and software. But the international dimension would mean that India's ability to compete for investment with countries where moral rights are less important would, at least in theory, be affected.

None of these arguments necessarily leads to the conclusion that reducing moral rights protection would be the right choice for India. Should labor standards be reduced in India and China because it makes these countries more competitive for international investment into industries such as clothing manufacture? . . . Should the moral rights of individuals be limited in order to promote investment into knowledge industries?

While it is possible to understand the concerns that may be at the heart of the Indian government's reluctance to support moral rights, the approach of India's courts is ultimately more satisfying. Indian judges are firmly grounded in an appreciation of the dynamics of Indian society, and they can lay claim to greater objectivity and foresight. In upholding moral rights protections, Indian courts have, in a sense, become the champions of individual creative

---

206. Here, the practice of Bollywood producers who commonly produce Indian remakes of Hollywood films is noteworthy. Citing a 2003 article by Subhash K. Jha, Rachana Desai claims that "In recent years, nearly eight out of every ten Bollywood scripts have been 'inspired' by one or more Hollywood films." *See* Rachana Desai, *Copyright Infringement in the Indian Film Industry*, 7 VAND. J. ENT. L. & PRAC. 259 (2005).

efforts and noncommercial artistic endeavor—arduous and undervalued activities in modern India. Judges have protected individual authors against the titans of the Bollywood industry,[207] and artists against the prestige of government.[208] Through moral rights, their focus on the relationship between authors and their works has also allowed them to avoid the pitfalls of attempting to assess artistic quality in the courtroom. Instead, Indian judges prefer to accept the evidence of artists where the treatment of their own work is concerned.

f. *Amar Nath Sehgal*: Duties of the Government[209]

The case of *Amar Nath Sehgal v. Union of India* extended over three decades to establish a groundbreaking precedent on the interpretation of the moral right of integrity in Indian law. The case involved the work of Mr. Amar Nath Sehgal, a celebrated Indian sculptor who died in 2007.[210] In the 1960s, Mr. Sehgal was invited by the government of India to create a mural cast in bronze for the decoration of Delhi's Vigyan Bhavan.[211] The mural was an extraordinary piece of work, massive in scale and scope, and represented several years of Sehgal's creative effort.[212] It eventually came to be considered a national treasure of India.

In 1979, the government of India dismantled the mural and placed it in storage. Carelessness and neglect in the process of moving and storage led

---

207. But the courts can also be nationalistic; they have not hesitated to protect Bollywood productions against the claims of individual authors from outside India. The *Bradford* case, involving an Indian television serial based on a novel by American author, Barbara Taylor Bradford, is a case in point: see *Bradford v. Sahara Entertainment* (2004) 28 PTC 474 (Cal.). Interestingly, the Indian courts seem more willing to find infringement between India's national film industries, producing films in different languages. For a case of Bollywood versus the Bengali film industry, known as "Tollywood," see *Shree Venkatesh Film v. Vipul Amritlal Shah*, Civil Suit No. 219/2009, Calcutta High Court, Sept. 1, 2009. The litigation was eventually settled, but the Calcutta court made a number of important points about film copyright at the interim stage of the process. *See* Arpan Bannerjee, *Film Copyright Infringement: Bypassing the "Carbon Copy" Handicap*, 5(1) Oxford J. Intell. Prop. L. & Prac. 17 (2010). *See also* the interesting comments on the *Unwilling Lawyer* blog, *available at* http://theunwillinglawyer. blogspot.com/2009/08/namaste-copyright-calcutta-high-court.html.
208. *Sehgal, supra* note 47.
209. The *Amar Nath Sehgal* case receives a detailed treatment in Mira T. Sundara Rajan, *Moral Rights and the Protection of Cultural Heritage*: Amar Nath Sehgal v. Union of India, 10(1) Int'l J. Cultural Prop. 79 (2001) [Mira T. Sundara Rajan, *Moral Rights and the Protection of Cultural Heritage*].
210. *See* Vandana Kalra, *Renowned Painter, Sculptor Amarnath Sehgal Is No More*, ExpressIndia (Dec. 29, 2007), *available at* http://www.expressindia.com/latest-news/Renowned-painter-sculptor-Amarnath-Sehgal-is-no-more/255494/ (last visited Apr. 28, 2010).
211. The facts are described in detail in Mira T. Sundara Rajan, *Moral Rights and the Protection of Cultural Heritage, supra* note 209. *See also* Anand, *supra* note 194, at 36.
212. Anand, *supra* note 194, at 36, describes it as being 140 feet long and 40 feet high.

to damage. Some parts of the mural were lost, including the piece where the sculptor had plaed his name.[213] Sehgal brought a suit against the government, asking for an injunction to prevent further harm to what was left of his work. When the Delhi High Court reached its final verdict in the case, in 2005, the harm suffered was severe enough to be considered outright destruction of the work.[214]

i. Interim Ruling: 1992

In a country where it can take decades to receive a final judgment in a case, interim rulings can be powerful indicators of the direction of the law. In Mr. Sehgal's case, the interim ruling itself took 13 years to emerge, but it clarified two important points about the scope of Indian moral rights. These points were supported and further developed in the final judgment of 2005.

(a) *Right to Prevent Destruction*

The *Sehgal* decision established that the moral right of integrity under Indian law can protect an artistic work from outright destruction. This determination goes against the influential international school of thought which holds that the right of integrity can only protect a work from being mistreated while it remains in existence; it cannot intervene to prevent a work from being destroyed.[215] The rationale for this position may be found in the language of the legal bridge joining the integrity and reputation interests. In most jurisdictions, following Article 6*bis* of the Berne Convention, the integrity right can only be invoked if the author's reputation has been harmed. Given the fact that the Indian moral rights scheme of 1992 did not require proof of damage to the author's reputation, the court did not need to consider this argument. The comments of the Delhi High Court in 2005, though made in a different legislative context, continued to support this position. It affirmed that, under Indian law, the moral right of integrity can, at the very least, prevent the destruction of works of cultural importance.[216] The issue turned on the idea of a "creative corpus"—a body of work. The destruction of any single work would have an undeniable impact on the reputation of the artist by reducing his creative output as a whole.[217]

---

213. *Id.*, at 36.
214. *Sehgal, supra* note 48.
215. *See* Ricketson, *Berne Convention, supra* note 9, para. 8.109. Anand, *supra* note 194, at 36, points out that the rationale underlying this view is that, once the work is destroyed, "there would be no subject-matter left to affect the author's reputation."
216. Anand, *supra* note 194, at 36.
217. The phrase originates in Mira T. Sundara Rajan, *Moral Rights and the Protection of Cultural Heritage, supra* note 209, and was invoked by both Mr. Pravin Anand, counsel for Mr. Sehgal, and the Delhi High Court judge.

(b) *Duty of Care of the Government*

The interim judgment also established the important principle of a governmental duty of care towards artworks in its possession. This finding is especially significant in the context of a developing country like India, where the government represents a concentration of power and national resources. Where the powers of government are extensive, there is great potential for both good and evil in government action.[218] In countries like India, the judiciary can play an important role in defining the extent and nature of governmental power, and this responsibility was duly borne by the court in its interim judgment. Pravin Anand, a leading Indian intellectual property lawyer and counsel for Mr. Sehgal in this litigation, emphasizes this aspect of the case:

> [T]his case raised . . . [an] important issue, namely, the right of every citizen to see that works of art which belong to the government, being national wealth, are treated with respect and not destroyed by the government.[219]

(c) *Amendments to the Copyright Act*

The interim ruling in the *Sehgal* case must have given the Indian government food for thought. Jagdish Sagar, an exceptional Indian lawyer involved in drafting the 1994 amendments to section 57 of the Copyright Act, comments that the primary motivation behind reform was conformity with the language of the Berne Convention.[220] Nevertheless, the new provisions look like a direct response to the *Sehgal* judgment.[221] Given the adjustments to the Indian integrity right that followed, it would seem that any case brought today would have to be pleaded differently.

In particular, an injured party would need to be able to show that the damage to his work would also be prejudicial to his honor or reputation. Not only does this change signify a shift in the burden of proof from defendant to plaintiff, with the plaintiff now required to show that the treatment of the work would injure his reputation, but it also has implications for the

---

218. Frazier points out the power of governments and their ability, not only to generate cultural developments, but even to define what is and is not art. Following Frazier's line of argument, it is equally true that governments may influence social attitudes towards art. *See* Jimmy A. Frazier, *On Moral Rights, Artist-Centered Legislation, and the Role of the State in Art Worlds: Notes on Building a Sociology of Copyright Law*, 70 TUL. L. REV. 313, 330–54 (1995).

219. Anand, *supra* note 194, at 36.

220. Statement by Mr. Jagdish Sagar (personal communication with the author, Feb. 2009), who, as of February 2009, was working as a consultant with Anand & Anand. Mr. Sagar's profile is available on the website of Asia Law at http://www.asialaw.com/Article/1989296/Channel/16712/Anand-and-Anand-hires-Jagdish-Sagar.html (last visited July 16, 2010).

221. *Id.*, comments that conformity with Berne was a concern.

extension of the integrity right to prevent destruction. In the interim decision on Sehgal's case, the judge was ready to accept that the destruction of a work of art is a violation of the author's right of integrity. This argument was legally bolstered by the separation of integrity and reputation into two distinct principles by the language of the Indian Copyright Act. This position could now be altered by the new legal language. If integrity depends on damage to reputation, it may be that destruction of a work is no longer covered by the Act. Moreover, under the new legislation, there would be no chance of objecting to a failure to display an artwork, or to display it in proper conditions. This possibility was specifically eliminated in the amendments to the law.[222]

It is interesting to note one further change in the Indian law related to moral rights—the introduction of a resale right in works of visual art, also enacted in 1994. According to section 53A of the amended Indian Copyright Act, the sale of a work of art for more than 10,000 rupees will attract a royalty of up to 10 percent of the price.[223] This provision resembles a moral right, in the sense that it is inalienable.

The resale right lasts for the duration of copyright—the lifetime of the author and 60 years after his death. It is worth noting that this clarity about duration presents a contrast to the treatment of true moral rights. The Indian Copyright Act does not indicate any limit on duration for the right of attribution. The duration of integrity, however, is described by an indirect formula: the author has the right "to restrain or claim damages in respect of any distortion, mutilation, modification or other act" that is harmful to the author's reputation, as long as it is " done before the expiration of the term of copyright." In practical terms, it looks like the integrity right terminates with the expiry of copyright, though the method of achieving this result leaves the question somewhat open to interpretation. [224]

An innovation that is unique to India involves the extension of this resale right to authors' original manuscripts, as well.[225] The provision seems to recognize the manuscript as an entity in its own right, independent of the copyright in a literary work. It is a very practical response to the reality that authors' original manuscripts may be valued in much the same way as

---

222. Indian Copyright Act, *supra* note 31, sec. 57(1), Explanation.
223. Ten thousand rupees is approximately US$215 (as of this printing); but the sum is more significant in India than it seems from outside.
224. Indian Copyright Act, *supra* note 31, sec. 22. The Copyright Amendment Act 1992 extended the term in order to prolong copyright in Tagore's works for the benefit of the University founded by him at Shantiniketan. The case of Tagore presents an interesting contrast to Bharati, whose copyright was terminated early for the benefit of society. *See* Mira T. Sundara Rajan, *Nationalization, supra* note 205.
225. In contrast, the European resale right, for example, does not apply to original manuscripts: see EUROPA, Summaries of EU Legislation, http://europa.eu/legislation_summaries/internal_market/businesses/intellectual_property/l26049_en.htm last visited August 8, 2010.

an original work of art, appreciating considerably in value over time as artworks do.[226]

ii. Final Ruling: 2005

When the moment for a final ruling was at last reached in 2005, the Delhi High Court faced a number of challenges in the interpretation of Indian law. In particular, the court had to address the issue of a significant legislative amendment which occurred at the midpoint of Mr. Sehgal's case, threatening to invalidate the principles that had been set out in the interim ruling.

This problem of legal interpretation could have been approached in a number of ways. In the absence of transitional provisions in the Indian Act, the determination of which law to apply was an immediate threshold that had to be crossed. On this point, the judge had at least two clear choices. He could have argued that the old provisions of the Indian Copyright Act would apply in Amar Nath Sehgal's case, because they governed the time when the acts of destruction occurred, and when the action was initially brought. Alternatively, he could have said that the new provisions should apply because they were in force at the time of the final judgment, and expressed the current policy of the Indian government.

In the event, and with the creative flair for which Indian judges are known, he did neither. Rather, he adopted a completely different approach. Where outstanding works of art are concerned, he argued, there is an overriding obligation to protect their integrity. In this sense, it makes little difference whether the old or the new provisions of the Indian Copyright Act are applied. In either case, the letter of Indian law must be read in the light of a higher objective of public policy—the protection of cultural treasures.

How did the judge identify this superior public policy interest? He did so by considering international law. In particular, the policy that he identified was derived, not from intellectual property laws, but from the provisions of international conventions on cultural property. As a signatory to these Conventions, India had to respect its obligations under them. Accordingly, its provisions on moral rights should be read in such a way that Indian law remained in harmony with the objectives of the Conventions.

Not only does this approach to Indian law address the temporal dimension of Amar Nath Sehgal's case, but it also allows for a clean resolution of the destruction issue. Clearly, it would be incompatible with the objectives of cultural property conventions to allow the destruction of a work of art. And, additionally, the judge was moved by the argument that the overall reputation of an artist is affected by damage to the quantity and quality of his

---

226. Indian Copyright Act, *supra* note 31, sec. 53A (as amended 1994).

"creative corpus" taken as a whole. The ruling leaves little ambiguity. Even if the new Indian provisions on moral rights mirror the language of the Berne Convention, and even if doubts are raised by international commentators, India's provisions on moral rights do prohibit the destruction of a work. When transplanted into the context of Indian law, the language of the Berne Convention means something different. Justice Jaspal Singh concludes:

> [T]he various declarations by the international community in the conventions [on cultural property] noted above, lift the moral rights in works of Art if the same acquire the status of cultural heritage of a nation. India is a signatory to the conventions and it would be the obligation of the State to honour its . . . declarations.[227]

g. Proposed Amendments: The Copyright Bill of 2010

India's proposed new amendments involve a comprehensive overview of Indian copyright law, with a view to technological updating of the Copyright Act.[228] Changes to the Indian moral rights scheme would improve the drafting of section 57. In particular, the proviso that an act infringing the moral right of integrity should be "done before the expiry of the term of copyright" is to be removed. Similarly, the apparent restriction on the right of an author's heirs to assert the right of attribution is also to be deleted from the Act.

Another significant change, from a moral rights perspective, is that the proposed amendments will make the director of a film a coauthor of the work alongside the producer. This change would generate some confusion in Indian law, because producers and directors will each have moral rights in the film. Given the historic absence of directors from Indian copyright law, the Copyright Act provides no guidance as to how the sharing of these rights is to be managed.

---

227. *Sehgal*, *supra* note 47, para. 55. Under the terms of this ruling, it is still possible to argue that a work is not culturally important, and would therefore not qualify for protection from destruction. The likelihood of success with this argument seems very slight, for two reasons: the Indian judge's emphasis on the concept of "creative corpus," or body of work as a whole; and, as a practical matter, the persistence that would be required of an artist to pursue a claim, financially and otherwise, supporting his or her status as a professional and creative success.

228. The Bill was introduced on April 19, 2010. *See* Indian Copyright Amendment Bill, available on the website of PRS Legislative Research at http://prsindia.org/uploads/media/Copyright%20Act/Copyright%20Bill%202010.pdf (last visited May 2, 2010).

3. Conclusion

The Indian example illustrates the curious fate of moral rights in the hands of a developing country. Transplanted from Continental law, the doctrine has experienced significant growth and transformation on Indian soil. From a private-law doctrine of limited application, it has grown to assume the stature of a public-law principle of widespread cultural and moral significance, in the broadest sense of the word. According to the pioneering case of *Amar Nath Sehgal*, moral rights are an instrument for the protection of important cultural works in India. As such, they must be read in conjunction with other national and international instruments which aim at the same target. The case opens up a universe of interesting questions and problems. What is to be the treatment of moral rights in works in the public domain? And, to take this question one step further, does India now recognize a moral right in works of cultural property?[229]

Most interesting of all, and in a striking throwback to French tradition, the evolution of moral rights in India is occurring through the intervention of judges. But there is something utterly new and different about the judicial development of moral rights in India. This is the fact that, in India, judicial decision-making has been resolute in resisting the currents of change initiated by the Indian government.

This situation is at once inspiring and troubling. In India, the independence of judges functions as a counterweight to political corruption. By an interesting irony, judicial activism helps to build a democratic connection between law and the people that government cannot provide. The problem is not unique to India: in a different context, American judges were asked to decide on the fairness of George W. Bush's claim to the U.S. presidency.[230] At the same time, India can hardly be expected to dispense with government leadership on copyright issues. Given India's position in the vanguard of technological change, government initiatives should be an important part of addressing moral rights in a digital environment. To an impressive degree, both the past and future of Indian culture may depend on the fundamental principles of disclosure, attribution, and integrity.

The classic copyright dilemma of balancing control and use is poignant in the Indian context. India's is a deeply divided society, and a fundamental challenge faced by Indian law is how to reconcile the interests of a technological superpower with the needs of a desperately impoverished population. The

---

229. *See* Bumper Development Corporation v. Commissioner of Police for the Metropolis, [1991] 1 W.L.R. 1362, 4 All E.R. 368. The case receives an interesting treatment in RICHARD H. DAVIS, THE LIVES OF INDIAN IMAGES, ch. 7, *Loss and Recovery of Ritual Self*, at 222–60 (Princeton Univ. Press 1997).
230. *See* Bush v. Gore, 531 U.S. 98 (2000).

secret may lie in the protection of creative individuals. By helping to generate legal conditions which favor the creative freedom of individuals, the Indian government could promote development at a grass-roots level, helping to build confidence and self-esteem among the masses of the Indian people. For India and other developing nations, it is not enough to deal with copyright as a business model; they also need to explore the implications of copyright as a human right.[231]

Whatever copyright may mean to industrialized countries, the principles of copyright law have a special role to play in the developing world. For the sake of development, it is imperative to protect authors' rights. In conditions of general poverty and uncertainty, the position of creators must be stabilized, and a base of local knowledge and culture firmly established. India's culture is diverse and Indians have traditionally held works of the intellect and spirit in great esteem. Indian traditions provide a solid foundation for the protection of individual creativity. The ambition of India's artists and intellectuals is undeniable, and it has always been one of the most important forces underlying the country's drive to modernize. In the words of India's National Poet:

> "What has been shall yet be." Her music will yet be recognized as the most marvellous in the world; her literature, her painting and her sculpture will yet be a revelation of beauty and immortality to the wondering nations; her life and acts will yet be ennobling examples for a grateful humanity. . .[232]

C. Moral Rights and "Honor" in a New Technological Society: Japan

In relation to moral rights, special mention must be made of Japan. Historically remote, Japan's membership in the international copyright system came about as part of its broader engagement with its trading partners at the end of the nineteenth century. Its opening to international influences was compelled by the United States after more than two centuries of seclusion known as the Edo era, and it was in the subsequent period of the Meiji Restoration that

---

231. For a discussion of the relationship between copyright and human rights, see Sundara Rajan, *Copyright and Creative Freedom*, *supra* note 4, Ch IX, "Copyright and Human Rights: The Post-Communist Experience and a New International Model," at 205–33.

232. *See* C. Subramania Bharati, *Rasa—The Key-Word of Indian Culture*, *in* Agni and Other Poems and Translations & Essays and Other Prose Fragments 69 (A. Natarajan 1980).

Japan was first exposed to European law.[233] In 1896, the country adopted a civil code derived from German law;[234] the copyright law was adopted in 1899, the same year in which Japan joined the Berne Convention.[235]

Japan's copyright law was initially based on the German model, and a look at the current law shows its continued influence. Japanese law protects three moral rights—disclosure, attribution, and integrity—and the concept of disclosure, as in the German law, is central to the Japanese appreciation of these rights.[236] Attribution includes protection for those writing under a pseudonym, but the right is somewhat restrictive. In particular, it allows the omission of attribution in certain circumstances—when "it is found that there is no risk of damage to the interests of the author in his claim to authorship in the light of the purpose and the manner of exploiting his work and in so far as such omission is compatible with fair practice."[237] In contrast, the integrity right is almost completely open-ended, and the law even goes so far as to specify that any change made "against [the author's] . . . will" is a violation of the right.[238] The Japanese law seems to invert international practice in a curious way, making attribution subject to proof of damage to reputation, while integrity is protected without limit. Japanese moral rights are inalienable, although the economic rights in a work may be "transferred in whole or in part."[239]

At first glance, the problem of the duration of moral rights seems basically resolved by protecting moral rights for the term of copyright—under Japanese law, the relatively short duration of fifty years after the death of the author.[240] But the Japanese formula for accomplishing this is unusual. Japanese copyright

---

233. *See* the website of the Copyright Research and Information Centre, *History of Copyright System in Japan*, at http://www.cric.or.jp/cric_e/csj/csj2.html (last visited Apr. 28, 2010).

234. Civil Code, Law no. 89 of 1896. *But see* the interesting discussion in Charles P. Sherman, *The Debt of Modern Japanese Law to French Law*, 6(3) Cal. L. Rev. 198, 200–01(1918). Sherman shows the interplay of French and German influences that eventually led to the adoption of a Civil Code modeled on German law, but still a strong reflection of French legal principles.

235. Copyright Law of 1899. *See* Sherman, *supra* note 234, and *History of Copyright System in Japan*, *supra* note 233. Japan originally acceded to the Berne Convention on July 15, 1899; *see* WIPO website at http://www.wipo.int/treaties/en/documents/pdf/berne.pdf (last visited April 28, 2010).

236. Japanese Copyright Act, *supra* note 184, secs. 18–20.

237. *Id.*, art. 19(1)(3): "It shall be permissible to omit the name of the author where it is found that there is no risk of damage to the interests of the author in his claim to authorship in the light of the purpose and the manner of exploiting his work and in so far as such omission is compatible with fair practice."

238. *Id.*, art. 20(1); special exceptions to the open-ended integrity principle, including the cases of architectural works and computer programs, are listed in art. 20(2).

239. *Id.*, art. 61.

240. The term is short when compared to the international standard set by the European Union, which is now life plus seventy years. India's term of protection is ten years shorter, at life plus

law provides for the protection of moral rights, either for this duration, or until the author's immediate family members, defined as the "bereaved family," have all died.[241] The "bereaved family" extends from grandparents to grandchildren, and if any of these family members survives the fifty-year period after the author's death, he or she will continue to hold the moral rights until his or her own death.[242] The effective term of protection for moral rights could thereby extend considerably beyond the statutory term of copyright protection, fifty years after the author's death. Interestingly, while the "bereaved family" members are alive, they can make a claim, not only against mistreatment that has occurred, but also, in order to prevent *potential* damage.[243]

But moral rights do not end with the family. Even after the expiry of the copyright term, it is prohibited to do anything that would be against the author's moral rights. Article 60 of the Japanese copyright law states:

> Even after the death of the author, no person who offers or makes available a work to the public may commit an act which would be prejudicial to the moral rights of the author if he were alive; provided, however, that such act is permitted if it is deemed not to be against the will of the author in the light of the nature and extent of the act as well as a change in social situation and other conditions.

Explicit provision is not made for who is to enforce moral rights after the grandchildren of the author have also passed away. Two implications of this omission should be noted. First, family members in subsequent generations will continue to have a right to assert the author's moral rights, but their rights will not be unlimited. Rather, they will be subject to two tests: ascertaining the "will of the author," a key concept in Japanese moral rights, and determining whether the act complained of is appropriate in the light of a "change[d] . . . social situation and other conditions." Secondly, it is obvious that assertion of the moral right is no longer an exclusive prerogative of the authors' descendants. Presumably, any interested person should have the right to assert the author's moral rights on his behalf under this provision.[244]

---

sixty years. *Id.*, art. 51, provides for this basic term of protection, with variations for certain types of subject-matter.

241. *See id.*, art. 116(3).

242. *See id.*, art. 116(1).

243. *Id.*, art. 112, refers to both "cessation" and "prevention" of infringement; *see also* art. 116(1).

244. *Id.*, art. 62, provides for copyright to revert to the National Treasury if the author has no heirs, but it is not clear that this applies to moral rights.

In all of these measures, Japanese law impresses with its pragmatic approach to protection. The Japanese rationale for maintaining moral rights recognizes the close connection between authors and their descendents; it is reasonable to think that grandchildren may have known the author, while great-grandchildren most likely would not have had this opportunity. At the same time, one of the frustrations with moral rights law, as apparent in India's *Sehgal* case, is that the remedy comes too late to prevent damage to cultural heritage. By providing that authors may "demand . . . prevention" of harmful acts, Japanese law makes an attempt to forestall this result.[245]

Two unique features of Japanese moral rights deserve special mention. The first of these has to do with the role of honor and reputation in Japanese law. The concept of "honor" has become quite nebulous in Western countries, and, in recent amendments to its law, the Republic of Ireland decided to remove it altogether from the legislative formulation of moral rights.[246] Elizabeth Adeney argues that this is a mistake. For all its archaism, the use of the word "honor" signifies that the integrity right extends to something more than the protection of reputation alone.[247] In Adeney's view, this "something more" is the recognition of a subjective element in moral rights—the idea that an author's own feeling about the treatment of his work should be acknowledged and accepted as legal evidence of infringement.

This conclusion is curiously unsatisfying. In fact, the question of subjectivity really seems to hinge upon the language of a given provision on the integrity right. If the law requires "proof" of damage to honor or reputation, and the author's feelings are said to furnish adequate proof, any assertion by the author that his integrity has been violated will be a sufficient demonstration of proof. If this is the case, why do we need the requirement at all? The same result could be accomplished by an open-ended right of integrity in the French or German style. Adeney argues that the Canadian case of *Snow* provides the example of a common law court accepting subjective standards; but the *Snow* case introduced the evidence of experts on Snow's reputation, thereby satisfying the requirement that the complaint of damage to the author's reputation should be "reasonable."[248]

---

245. *See id.*, art. 112.

246. Irish Copyright and Related Rights Act, 2000 (No. 28 of 2000), entry into force Jan. 1, 2001. Section 109(1) states: "Subject to the exceptions and qualifications specified in sections 110 and 111, the author of a work shall have the right to object to any distortion, mutilation or other modification of, or other derogatory action in relation to, the work which would prejudice his or her reputation and that right shall also apply in relation to an adaptation of the work." Despite this apparent modernization in terminology, Ireland also continues to refer to the attribution right as the "paternity right": *see* Irish Copyright Act, sec. 107(3).

247. *See* Elizabeth Adeney, *The Moral Right of Integrity: The Past and Future of "Honour,"* 2 INTELL. PROP. Q. 111 (2005).

248. Judge O'Brien states: "It is conceded that the sculpture is a 'work' within the meaning of the Copyright Act. I believe the words 'prejudicial to his honour or reputation' in s. 12(7)

The answer may lie, instead, in the idea that integrity accommodates two different types of affronts to an author's "reputation"—his professional reputation and his personal "honor." Adeney draws attention to the statement of the Italian delegate to the Rome revision conference of the Berne Convention in 1928, at which moral rights were first adopted:

> The Italian delegate referred to " . . . the [author's] right to prevent his work being altered, deformed, transformed or abridged to the prejudice, not only of his patrimonial interests, but of the even more delicate interests of his scientific, literary or artistic personality, a personality represented by this very work, doing little here to clarify the notion of the intérêts moraux.[249]

Adeney's assessment of the Italian statement seems a bit pessimistic. In fact, the key word in the Italian statement is "personality," and the idea of damage to the personality, or personal harm, could indeed help to clarify the meaning of honor. Nevertheless, Adeney's instinct that "honor" still matters seems sound.

The Japanese approach to honor accords greater substance to this ancient concept. Notably, Japanese scholarship discusses the suitability of a "public apology" as a remedy for damaged honor or reputation.[250] Indeed, Japan's focus on practical remedies to a violation of moral rights is impressive. The Japanese approach is informed by an awareness that, all too often, it will be impossible to restore the status quo once a violation of moral rights has occurred. *Amar Nath Sehgal* is a case in point: when Mr. Sehgal sued, the best he could do was to ask for an injunction to prevent further damage to his work. Nothing could undo the damage that had already been caused by the mistreatment of his sculpture. In any event, it took him 13 years to obtain a "preliminary" injunction!

A second point relates to a striking difference between Japanese law and other legal systems of the world: Japan appears to be one of a very small minority of countries to allow companies to hold a moral right.[251] This peculiarity of Japanese law is accomplished by including corporations within the Japanese definition of authorship.[252] But it would be difficult to interpret this provision as a legislative attempt to separate moral rights from the personality

---

involve a certain subjective element or judgment on the part of the author so long as it is reasonably arrived at": *Snow v. The Eaton Centre* (n. 49, at para.7); Adeney (n. 247, at 128) feels that the case evidences a particular concern with honour, rather than reputation.

249. Adeney, *supra* note 247, at 118 (footnote omitted).

250. *See* Naoya Ichimura's fascinating discussion of this subject, *Restoration-of-Status-Quo Relief to Redress Infringement of Authors' Moral Rights*, available on the website of the Copyright Research and Information Center at http://www.cric.or.jp/cric_e/cuj/cuj.html (last visited July 16, 2010).

251. Korea also allows corporations to hold moral rights. *See infra* notes 253–54.

252. *See* Japanese Copyright Act, *supra* note 184, Chapter II, sec. 2, arts. 14–16.

of a human author. Rather, it probably reflects Japan's corporate culture, which places unique human responsibilities upon the leaders of companies. Corporate honor is a real phenomenon in Japan. Corporate leaders in Japan have even been known to respond to professional disgrace by suicide. Executives cannot live with the damage to their honor.[253] Rather than an example of moral rights supporting corporate power, the Japanese law, when seen in cultural context, is more properly understood as an argument for extending the concept of honor to corporate conduct.[254]

D. Moral Rights and Creative Freedom: Post-Socialist Countries and the Example of Russia

Post-socialist countries offer a unique window onto moral rights. Their experience shows an interesting link between the moral rights of authors and the struggle to overcome political repression. The reason for this connection lies in ideology. By a bitter irony, the ideological aspect of socialism imbued all human expression with powerful political connotations. When superimposed upon societies with instinctive respect for culture, the combination of politics and creative expression proved to be a deadly cocktail. As Russian poet, Osip Mandelstam, commented: "Only in this country is poetry respected—people are killed for it."[255]

The repression of free speech and thought could be considered an intrinsic feature of totalitarian government. In this process, rights of authorship, like

---

253. *See "Modest" Japanese CEOs Escape Wrath*, Taipei Times 11 (Mar. 23, 2009), *available at* http://www.taipeitimes.com/News/biz/archives/2009/03/23/2003439154 (last visited Apr. 20, 2010). It is an interesting question as to whether the moral right extends to companies in Korean law, as well, both because of Korea's historical domination by Japan and because of the similarity of corporate cultures in the two countries. A fascinating overview of Korean moral rights is provided by Ilhyung Lee at http://www.aals.org/documents/2006intprop/ LeeAbstract.pdf. Article 14 of the Korean copyright law, affecting the duration of moral rights, shows the close relationship between Japanese and Korean law. *See* Korean Copyright Act, http://portal.unesco.org/culture/en/files/37872/12221640381KOREAN_COPYRIGHT_ ACT.pdf/KOREAN_COPYRIGHT_ACT.pdf (last visited Apr. 28, 2010).

254. A similar provision may be found in the Korean copyright law, art. 9; an English version, updated to December 1995, may be found in the WIPO Collection of Laws for Electronic Access, *available at* http://www.wipo.int/clea/en/text_pdf.jsp?lang=EN&id=2743 (last visited Apr. 28, 2010). The structure of Korean copyright law closely resembles Japanese law and, through it, German law. For a fascinating discussion of the colonial history between Japan and Korea, and Korea's distinctive cultural affinity with moral rights, see Ilhyung Lee, *Culturally-Based Copyright Systems?: The U.S. and Korea in Conflict*, 79 Wash. U. L.Q. 1103 (2001).

255. Mandelstam's comment, to his wife, is quoted in Geoffrey Hosking, A History of the Soviet Union 1917–1991 408 (Fontana Press 1992).

every other aspect of the law, became an instrument of state power against the people. But a study of legislation and its evolution can only provide a partial illustration of this dynamic. This is because socialist law was characterized by another, pernicious feature—the separation of the letter of the law from the actual practice surrounding authors' rights. This is probably the underlying explanation for the difficulty of enforcing intellectual property rights in post-socialist countries today. The problem of enforcement points to a fundamental failure of the rule of law, experienced by these societies over an extended period of their history.

Perhaps more than any other system of law, socialist law promoted the enactment of laws with no real intent to enforce them. Indeed, it would be fair to say that socialist governments had no capacity to enforce authors' rights in the usual sense of the term, because the structural features of socialist government imposed practical limits on free expression. In particular, publication in socialist countries was generally controlled by the state. In the Soviet Union, the state was both the publisher of most works and the overseer of private publishing initiatives such as the famed literary journal, *Novy Mir*.[256] It is no accident that anti-state activists in Soviet countries called for practical observance of the law as a first step in lifting repression. "Respect the Constitution!" was the rallying-cry of dissidents in Stalin's time.[257]

The copyright framework that emerges from the post-socialist experience is characterized by a number of unique features distinguishing it from Western norms. In particular, post-socialist copyright represents an expansion of expansion of moral rights into new areas. New moral principles address the mistreatment of dissident authors in Soviet times, attempting to compensate for the practical inability to enjoy the benefits of copyright by providing for a renewed term of protection for many rehabilitated authors.[258] Moral rights not only arise in relation to copyright works, but they are also recognized in scientific innovation, represented by patents.[259] The protection

---

256. Hosking, *supra* note 255, describes the curious relationship of give-and-take between the editor of *Novy Mir*, Alexander Tvardovsky, and the government: 410–11.

257. *Id.*, at 414–26; see also the comprehensive discussion of this issue in Sundara Rajan, *Copyright and Creative Freedom, supra* note 4, Chapter V, "Revolution and Reform," 107–20.

258. The circumstances in which this protection is allowed are discussed below.

259. *See* arts. 1345 (right of authorship) and 1356 of the Russian Federation Law on Copyright and Neighboring Rights (No. 5351-I of July 9, 1993), sec. 15 [Russian Copyright Act 1993, 1993 Copyright Act, Law on Copyright]; as of January 1, 2008, the law has been superseded by Part IV of the Russian Civil Code on intellectual property: *Grazhdanski Kodeks Rossiiskoi Federatsi, Chast' Chetvërtaya* [Civil Code of the Russian Federation, Part IV], Federal Law No. 230-FZ of December 18, 2006, *Rossijskaja Gazeta* No. 289 (4255) of Dec. 22, 2006 = *Sobranie zakonodatel'stva RF* (SZ RF) No. 52 (Part I) of Dec. 25, 2006, Item 5496, at 14803 [2008 Civil Code]. The new Part IV is not yet available in English; it may be found in the original Russian on the website of Rospatent, the federal agency of the Russian Federation

of works in the public domain through moral rights is a definite priority. And, finally, moral rights are generally considered relevant to new technological creation.

The level of protection for moral rights fluctuates with the general ebb and flow of social reform processes active in these countries. Times of greater sympathy between the government and the people translate directly into improved protection for the moral rights of authors. When the historical wheel comes full circle, and a new cycle of repression rises and subsides, moral rights principles from the past are revisited and, most often, reinstated in reformed laws.

1. Russia's Place in the Post-Socialist World

Like developing countries, post-socialist countries, too, represent a hybrid legal tradition. The socialist law common to them since the latter half of the twentieth century is known for its extreme emphasis on codification, surpassing even civil law jurisdictions in their affinity for codified laws.[260] Their shared political heritage brings a surface veneer of similarity to their law. So, too, does the behemoth of received Russian law, a product of Soviet expansion into the region, and an omnipresent background reality. As I noted in an earlier work:

> It is well-known that Central and East European countries experienced Soviet expansionism in the political arena; what is less obvious is that they were also subject to a form of Russian imperialism in the legal sphere. Any in-depth study of socialist law inevitably turns towards Russian law. Many copyright laws in the "Eastern Bloc" were closely based on Soviet copyright statutes; as for free speech, it was conditioned by the physical or psychological presence of the Soviet Union in Eastern Europe, as well as whatever indigenous patterns of repression developed.[261]

---

responsible for intellectual property matters at http://www1.fips.ru/wps/wcm/connect/content_ru/ru/documents/russian_laws/codeks_rf/gkrf_ch4 (last visited Apr. 28, 2010).

260. The characteristics of Soviet legal systems are usefully summarized in GENNADY M. DANILENKO & WILLIAM BURNHAM, LAW AND LEGAL SYSTEM OF THE RUSSIAN FEDERATION 1–10 (Parker School of Foreign & Comparative Law, Columbia Univ. Juris Publishing 1999).

261. Mira T. Sundara Rajan, *Copyright and Free Speech in Transition: A New International Perspective, in* COPYRIGHT AND FREE SPEECH: COMPARATIVE AND INTERNATIONAL ANALYSES 315, para. 13.09 (J. Griffiths & U. Suthersanen eds., Oxford Univ. Press 2005) [Mira T. Sundara Rajan, *Copyright and Free Speech in Transition*]. *See also* Mihály Ficsor, *The Past, Present and Future of Copyright in the European Socialist Countries*, 118 RIDA 33 (1983): this comprehensive article includes a discussion of how the European socialist countries traced their copyright laws to Soviet, and through it, Russian law.

But if we scratch this polished surface, the extraordinary diversity of post-socialist countries becomes apparent. The socialist era exaggerated similarities by painting over the colors of the region with the uniform grey of the "Iron Curtain." The post-socialist period promotes diversity in all its forms—both positive and negative, from cultural reawakening to social disintegration. The region is affected by a great variety of political affiliations and social trends. Oppression was experienced differently by each country, both at the hands of the Soviet powers and under its own rulers. The re-assessment of the past has also been approached differently by different countries. The diversity of pre-socialist cultural traditions in Central and Eastern Europe, denied by Soviet imperialism, has come to be acknowledged. Factors from European unification to Islamic resurgence affect the area of Eastern Europe and Western Asia roughly known as "post-socialist."[262]

In this shifting landscape, moral rights have been a surprising historical constant. Virtually all of the countries of Central and Eastern Europe have recognized moral rights in their copyright laws. In some cases, the recognition predates Soviet times—Russia has recognized copyright in the form of an "author's right" since 1828, and protected a very strong moral right of integrity from 1911.[263] This tradition later led to the recognition of a right of "inviolability," first named in the 1961 Soviet legislation, which continues to be mirrored in the post-socialist laws of the region.[264] The Czech Law of April 2000 provides that "[t]he author shall have the right to the inviolability of his work . . . ."[265] Hungary and other socialist countries were members of the Berne Convention from pre-socialist times. For Hungary, the adoption of moral rights at the 1928 Berne revision conference led to problems of compatibility between Hungarian copyright law and the Berne Convention; they were resolved through the intervention of Hungary's Supreme Court, the Kúria, which recognized moral rights in a series of

---

262. The Russia-Europe agreement marked a thawing point in Russian relations with the EU, but, of course, it falls far short of membership in the EU. For a discussion of the Agreement on Partnership and Cooperation between the EU and Russia and its impact on Russian copyright law, see Michiel Elst, *The Interaction of European Community and Russian Copyright Law: A Matter of Partnership and Cooperation*, 22(3) REV. CENT. & E. EUR. L. 267, 276–85 (1996).

263. Indeed, even the structure of the 1828 legislation lays open the possibility that Russian law implicitly recognized a moral right of disclosure. *See* Sundara Rajan, *Copyright and Creative Freedom, supra* note 4, at 79–87. Interestingly, the moral right of integrity recognized in the reforms of 1911 sought to protect an author against his or her own publisher—a theme that resurfaced in Soviet legislation and legal theory, which saw the publisher, crudely, as the "capitalist" exploiting the author.

264. *See* Sundara Rajan, *Copyright and Creative Freedom, supra* note 4, at 98–99; the language of inviolability dates from 1961.

265. *See* Czech Copyright Act art. 11(3). The Czech copyright law is available in English translation in the Collection of Laws for Electronic Access, WIPO, *available at* http://www.wipo.int/clea/en/text_html.jsp?lang=en&id=962 (last visited July 16, 2010).

rulings post-1928.[266] Russia's decision to abstain from membership in Berne was exceptional, and reflected domestic policy issues of various kinds. Concerns arose about "opening Russia to an influx of foreign literature," with "political and cultural as well as economic" implications; even the endorsement of eminent Russian writers was not enough to push Russia into Berne membership.[267] Russia finally joined the Berne Convention in 1995, a mere six years after the United States became a member.

But legislative recognition in socialist countries must be seen in context. The primacy of legislation as a source of law is undeniable; but the practical context in which that legislation functioned must be taken into account. The landmark Soviet law of 1961 is a case in point.[268] The law recognized an author's right to the "inviolability" of his work, and at first glance, it appears that earlier and more limited language protecting the author's right of integrity has been expanded by the new right of inviolability.[269] Yet no author could expect to take action against state bodies which controlled the publication of his work and, invariably, measured its print-worthiness against political criteria. By 1961, the reality was that the identity of publisher and government had essentially merged, and the idea of an author being able to act against a publisher was largely meaningless.[270] Perhaps this is why it made sense to remove the terminology of "exclusivity" from Soviet law: under article 98 of the Russian Civil Code of 1961, the rights of authors were not exclusive in any real sense of the term. The ability of the author to exercise them depended on government cooperation. In other words:

> There can be no doubt that the shape of moral rights in socialist countries, like driftwood caught in the tides, bent under the pressure of political flux. Complex currents were at work. After a brief period of revolutionary *élan*, when nationalization dominated the copyright landscape, copyright rules were swiftly reinforced as part of a state strategy to win the support of authors and artists.[271]

---

266. *See Copyright Law in Hungary, in* Intellectual Property: Eastern Europe & the CIS (Mira T. Sundara Rajan ed., Oxford Univ. Press 2008; forthcoming 2010).

267. Sundara Rajan, *Copyright and Creative Freedom, supra* note 4, at 85–87.

268. Fundamentals of Civil Legislation of the Union of Soviet Socialist Republics and the Union Republics, c. IV, VVS SSSR, 1961, No. 50, Item 525. An English translation is available in Newcity, *supra* note 4, at 181–87.

269. In fact, in keeping with theories about the "bourgeois" nature of relations between the publisher and the author, the earlier right protected the author explicitly against the unauthorized intervention of the publisher.

270. Sundara Rajan, *Copyright and Creative Freedom, supra* note 4, at 85–87, 79–88, 89–97, 99–100.

271. For a discussion of the nationalization of copyright in the Bolshevik period, see *id.*, at 89–93. Nationalization has also been tried in India, with various results: *see* Mira T Sundara Rajan, *Moral Rights in the Public Domain, supra* note 205, and Mira T. Sundara Rajan, *Nationalization, supra* note 205.

At different times in Soviet history, copyright and moral rights were improved—for example, to support reconciliation at the crucial time of reassessment after Stalin's death, known as the "Thaw"—or eviscerated, as in the post-Thaw period when the very idea of "exclusive" rights in one's own work was purged from the legislation, a consideration that was poorly balanced by the introduction of the terminology of "personal" rights for the first time in Russian copyright law.[272]

In summary, socialist copyright law was fundamentally shaped by two influences, clearly illustrated by the Russian example. The first, as noted above, has to do with the peculiarities of the socialist system of government. In the Soviet Union, publishing was inextricably linked with government approval, and, as a result, the idea of a meaningful relationship between an author and his or her publisher was little more than fiction.

The second influence was also political, but in a much larger sense. The Soviet government always felt a need for the work of authors. Sometimes, as in the early period of the Revolution, the clarion call for support was messianic and full of enthusiasm, and it was heeded by great and rising voices—Mandelstam, Blok, Mayakovsky, among others. At other times, as under Stalin's rule, it was a crude manipulation of authors for the promotion of state policy, and its victims were just as eminent—Akhmatova, Pasternak, Shostokovich. But, whatever its reasons—the promotion of ideology in an ideology-based regime, or the demands of development in a "backward" society[273]—the Soviet state always needed authors and artists.

In keeping with this pattern, Gorbachev's ascent brought new vitality to authors' rights. Gorbachev wanted the support of creative people, and the late 1980s and early 1990s saw reforms that introduced the most pro-author copyright rules in Russian history.[274] In temporary reforms to Russian law, adopted in 1991, moral rights were considerably expanded, and the concept of exclusive rights of authorship was reinstated. Changes to moral rights introduced in Russia's Copyright Act of 1993, valid until 2008, represented new forces which were afoot—the creation of the World Trade Organization and its adoption of the Agreement on Trade-Related Aspects of Intellectual Property Rights (TRIPs), signifying a practical and conceptual shift towards an economic, or commercial, model of copyright law.[275] The amended approach

---

272. *See* Sundara Rajan, *Copyright and Creative Freedom*, *supra* note 4, at 98–99.

273. *See id.*, at 100.

274. For a detailed discussion of the politics behind copyright changes of this period, see *id.*, at 150–69.

275. Russian Copyright Act 1993, *supra* note 258, sec. 15; *see* 2008 Civil Code, *supra* note 258. The 1993 Act is still *available at* http://en.wikisource.org/wiki Russian_Federation._Law_ on_Copyright_and_Neighboring_Rights (last visited Apr. 28, 2010). In 2008, the Russian government adopted a new Chapter IV of the Russian Civil Code on intellectual property rights, which was said to supersede all previously existing legislation in the field of intellectual property. The speed with which the changes were adopted, their comprehensiveness

to moral rights in the 1993 legislation was closely, though not perfectly, aligned with the Berne Convention provision on moral rights.

The adoption of new provisions in 2006 represents, once again, a shift in the Russian approach to moral rights. There is a new sense of historicity about the treatment of moral rights in the Civil Code. Characteristically Russian terminology such as "inviolability" is restored from the 1961 Soviet law. The terminology of exclusivity is retained, but it refers only to an author's economic interests in his work. Provisions on the copyright of rehabilitated authors are retained in the new law. However, the general trend in the new provisions is actually to scale back Russian protection for moral rights from the levels in the 1993 Copyright Act. In this sense, the Russian legislation is, once again, an enigma—a law that is, in fact, highly Westernized, though it appears in the guise of an orthodox legal framework.

2. Moral Rights in Transition: The 1991 USSR Fundamentals of Civil Legislation[276]

The first Russian foray into modern copyright law occurred at a true moment of transition: the 1991 Fundamentals came into effect just as the Soviet Union was on the brink of collapse. The Fundamentals, *osnovy* in Russian, were a type of model code used by the member states of the Soviet Union to develop laws; as such, they could be compared to European harmonization directives on copyright at the EU level.[277] Profound changes were made. The terminology

---

in repudiating previously existing law, and the relative secrecy in which these provisions were developed have all led to controversy. A quick overview of the new legislation may be found in Sergey Budylin & Yulia Osipova, *Legislative Developments—Total Upgrade: Intellectual Property Law Reform in Russia*, 1(1) Colum. J. E. Eur. L. 1 (2007). Budylin and Osipova do not draw attention to the novel conceptualization of intellectual property rights in the Code—for example, the very idea of intellectual "property" is eliminated, and the Code is much closer to a *sui generis* conception of the rights. It is also interesting to note that the new provisions seem to represent some sort of effective compromise between two bureaus of the Russian government which have been charged with intellectual property regulation and have struggled with each other for supremacy: the Private Law Institute of the Russian Federation, reporting directly to the President of Russia, and Rospatent, the Russian patent agency. For a consideration of the Code from a patent law perspective, see Adolf Dietz, *Incorporation of Patent Law into Part Four of the Russian Civil Code—A Structural Analysis*, *in* Patents and Technological Progress in a Globalized World: Liber Amicorum Joseph Straus 687, MPI Studies on Intellectual Property, Competition and Tax Law Series, Vol. 6 (Wolrad Prinz zu Waldeck und Pyrmont, Martin J. Adelman, Robert Brauneis, Josef Drexl, & Ralph Nack eds., Springer 2009) [Dietz, *Incorporation of Patent Law into Part IV*].

276. Fundamentals, *supra* note 268.

277. But it should be noted, perhaps in contrast to the European situation, that the Russian *osnovy* were often adopted unchanged into the legislation of the Soviet republics. *See* Dietz, who feels that this is generally the case in the area of patent law, with greater diversity in the

of "exclusive" rights for authors was revived for the first time since 1928.[278] Moral rights included authorship, "the right to his or her name," a right to the integrity of the work, a right of publication, and a right of use with an important "moral" dimension.

a. Publication and Use

The right of use should be read in conjunction with the right of publication, which is identified explicitly. Open recognition of this right is especially meaningful in a country where political obstacles to publication imposed silence on generations of writers.

The author's right of use specifically included the right to produce translations and revised editions of one's own work.[279] It is interesting, in the sense that it emphasizes authorship over ownership: a publication contract, for example, could not prevent an author from developing a revised edition of his own work.

The right of use presents a contrast to both the long-standing principle of freedom of translation that dominated early Russian copyright, and the idea of government control that became the accepted norm after Soviet accession to the Universal Copyright Convention in 1973. The "right to compensation for the consent to use, and the use of, the work"[280] was part of a comprehensive scheme to remove the possibility of compulsory purchase of an author's work by the state, which was a key feature of the legislation of the 1960s and a focal point of the controversy when the Soviet Union attempted to join the international copyright community by joining, not the Berne Convention, but the Universal Copyright Convention (UCC), in 1973.[281] Article 138 of the Fundamentals of 1991 reiterates that any use of an author's work "can only be done with the consent of the author or his successors, and with payment of compensation." The only exceptions to this rule arise in relation to uses of works by the public that are considered to be exempt from copyright restrictions. The list of fair uses, or fair dealings, in Article 138.2 closely resembles similar provisions in Western copyright laws, and it also provides specifically that "making one copy of a computer program by the owner of the copy" may be lawful.[282]

---

implementation of copyright. Dietz, *Incorporation of Patent Law into Part IV, supra* note 275, at 691.

278. Fundamentals, *supra* note 268, art. 138.
279. *Id.*, art. 135.2.
280. *Id.*, art. 135.2.
281. *See* Sundara Rajan, *Copyright and Creative Freedom, supra* note 4, Chapter V, "Revolution and Reform," at 100–07.
282. *See* 1991 Fundamentals, *supra* note 268, art. 136.2(6); this was permitted "under the conditions specified by legislation"—meaning, presumably, that specific provisions in legislation on computer programs could inform, and possibly override, this section. Permitted free uses

b. Authorship and Name

In relation to the moral rights of publication and use, the 1991 Fundamentals either introduced new protections or significantly improved upon existing ones. In contrast, the right of authorship and the right to one's name are new rights. They respond to characteristic problems confronted by authors in Soviet times, such as the appropriation of works and manuscripts, and the systematic defamation and destruction of authors' reputations for political reasons.[283]

c. Integrity as Inviolability

The integrity right is defined in precise and unusually strong terms in the 1991 Fundamentals, as the right of the author "to keep his or her work intact." This right evokes the memory of "inviolability," the strong language used to frame the integrity principle in the Soviet law of 1961. If anything, it seems even more powerful: the general idea of inviolability is extended into the absolute clarity of keeping a work "intact." According to this rule, any alteration of the work without the author's consent, even if it is undertaken by a publishing house, is prohibited.

The omission of "prejudice to honour or reputation," an important departure from Article 6*bis* of the Berne Convention, is retained from the Soviet legislation, but given new life in the 1991 Fundamentals. This formula for the right of integrity responds fundamentally to censorship under the Soviet regime and, as such, could be even more significant than it is in jurisdictions with traditionally strong moral rights, such as France.

d. Inalienability and Inheritance

The Fundamentals of 1991 are generous to the author in their treatment of the inalienability and inheritability of moral rights. Article 135.6 provides that both the author's right to the integrity of the work and his right of publication shall be inherited by his "successors." In view of the following provision that restricts the rights of the "other successors" to inheriting a right of use only, it is clear that the moral rights, in keeping with their "personal" character, can descend only to the author's heirs, rather than his successors in title.[284] Once

---

included quotation, news reporting, reproduction for research, and reproduction for the blind. The subsequent article 136.3 also allowed use "for exclusively personal purposes."

283. *See, e.g.,* Sheila Fitzpatrick, THE CULTURAL FRONT: POWER AND CULTURE IN REVOLUTIONARY RUSSIA 183–215 (Cornell Univ. Press 1992). The case of *Shostakovich* is described by Sheila Fitzpatrick, who offers an analysis of his situation within the broader context of government control, manipulation, and repression of the musical world. Fitzpatrick concludes her discussion by noting that "his disgrace on each occasion proved temporary and his status as an acknowledged 'great Soviet composer' survived these debacles."

284. The moral right of the author, in contrast to the property rights, is considered to be vested in the author, rather than in the work; it is for this reason that, in the purest application of the doctrine, his personal heirs can inherit the right, but not his successors in title.

again, in an environment where it may not have been possible to publish an author's works during his lifetime, it seems well-advised to make specific provision for the continued exercise of the right of first publication by an author's descendants.

e. Duration

For the first time in Russian or Soviet copyright law, Article 137 of the Fundamentals sets out a specific duration for authors' moral rights. Article 137.3 provides that the rights of authorship, name, and integrity "shall be protected permanently." In this respect, the transitional legislation follows the tradition of protection in strong moral rights jurisdictions, especially France.[285] Presumably, since the moral rights are inherited by the author's heirs, it is their prerogative to enforce them after the author's death. However, in contrast to the current Russian Code, Section IV of the Fundamentals does not specifically address the methods of enforcing moral rights after the author's death.[286]

f. Performers

Finally, the Fundamentals took the unusual step of protecting the moral rights of performers, eleven years before an international moral right for performers was established by the WIPO Performances and Phonograms Treaty. Article 141.1 provides that performers, actors, stage managers, and conductors all have a right to the protection of their name, as well as a right to the protection of their "performance or rendition" from distortion. The right to be named is protected "without limitation in time."[287] Performers have traditionally been viewed as "disseminators" of the works of composers, rather than creators in their own right. The decision to protect performers' moral rights carried the Soviet Union forward into the vanguard of a new approach to moral rights.

In addition, an area of ambiguity in the Fundamentals arises in relation to works which are expressed orally, but not fixed. In keeping with the Russian tradition expressed in the landmark Copyright Act of 1911,[288] works of oral expression are entitled to copyright protection under the Fundamentals.

---

285. *See* art. L121-1 of the CPI, *supra* note 43.
286. It should be noted that Article 135.6 of the 1991 Fundamentals, *supra* note 269, provides for the author's heirs to inherit the moral rights of integrity and publication, but it does not mention the author's right to his name. Given the general framework of protection, it seems consistent with the logic of the legislation to infer that the right to a name is also inherited by the author's heirs, and that its protection falls to them after his death.
287. 1991 Fundamentals, *supra* note 276, art. 141.5.
288. Russian Copyright Law of March 20, 1911, Polnoe Sobranie Zakonov Rossiiskoi Imperii (Sob III) [Third Complete Collection of Laws of the Russian Empire], Sanktpeterburg 1914, Vol. XXXI, Item No. 34, 935, sec. 2 [Copyright Act 1911].

However, the provision seems designed to address specific kinds of public appearances and "performances"—a speech, or music featuring improvisation—as the protection of folklore is specifically excluded.[289] The Fundamentals depart from earlier Russian policy in this respect: although Section 1 of the 1911 Act listed only "speeches, lectures, essays, reports, sermons" in the section on oral works, it included other provisions on folklore. For example, Section 13 provided for the copyright protection of "combinations of folklore, melodies, details, short stories and similar folk works that exist in aural forms" for fifty years from the date of publication—without, however, precluding others from making their own compilations of the same folk culture. The exclusion of folklore from the Fundamentals may have signified the intention of the Russian government to explore separate legislation on cultural heritage.

3. International Influence: The Copyright Act of 1993

The moral rights provisions in the Russian Copyright Act of 1993 reveal a strong Western influence, superimposed upon the post-socialist orientation established by the transitional Fundamentals. Like the measures of 1991, the Act retained a number of features that responded to Soviet-era abuses, although their presence was somewhat subtler and less overt than in the earlier law.

Both the structure and substance of the 1993 Act reflect the influence of Article 6*bis* of the Berne Convention. The distinctiveness of earlier expressions of moral rights in Russian laws was largely abandoned. A general reduction in their legal stature from 1991 is evident and can probably be attributed to the secondary importance of moral rights, as opposed to economic rights, in the climate for international copyright reform surrounding TRIPs.

However, the Russian Copyright Act of 1993 also retained some unique features to place its moral rights scheme above the minimum level required by Berne. In particular, the Act created a "paying public domain" for the protection of cultural works.[290]

a. Dualism

For the first time in the history of Russian copyright law, the Act of 1993 introduced a clear separation between the moral and economic rights of

---

289. 1991 Fundamentals, *supra* note 276, art. 134.5.

290. The schemes are commonly known as "*domaine public payant*" and refer to the imposition of a royalty on the use of public domain works. The royalty can then be used to support cultural causes. *See* Adolf Dietz, *Term of Protection in Copyright Law and Paying Public Domain: A New German Initiative*, 22(11) EUR. INTELL. PROP. REV. 506 (2000) [Dietz, *Term of Protection*].

authors. The two areas are dealt with in two separate articles. Article 16 on "Economic Rights," like the Fundamentals of 1991, creates an exclusive right. Article 15 on "Moral Rights" provides simply for the "enjoy[ment]" of five moral rights. These include a "right of authorship," which protects the right of the author to be acknowledged as the author of his own work; a "right to be named," which allows the author to exploit his work, not only in his own name, but also, under a pseudonym, or anonymously;[291] a "right of disclosure," which allows the author to determine the circumstances of first publication; as part of disclosure, a distinct right to "disavow or withdraw" the work from circulation; and, finally, a "right to the protection of the author's reputation" that replaces the right of integrity, and allows the author to protect his work from any distortion or derogatory act that is "liable to prejudice his honour or dignity."[292] The right of use is not carried over from the Fundamentals. It is interesting to note that the right of withdrawal receives extensive treatment: Article 15.2 provides a detailed description of the circumstances in which the right may be exercised, including the author's obligation to compensate the user of the work for any damages resulting from his decision to withdraw.

Article 15 also specifies that moral rights are independent of economic rights, and may continue to be exercised by the author even after he has relinquished his economic rights. The suggestion of inalienability in this provision is not further clarified by provisions on the possibility of waiving moral rights.[293]

The broad and extensive list of rights in the Fundamentals, which is inclusive and not limited to the rights listed in Article 135.2, has been replaced by an apparently "closed" list of moral rights in Article 15 of the Copyright Act. Article 15 provides, simply that "[t]he author shall enjoy the following moral rights in relation to his work." The combining of moral and economic rights in one section on the author's rights in the Fundamentals helped to emphasize the overlapping implications of moral and economic interests arising from the creation and use of creative works—for example, in relation to translations. The perspective was lost in the 1993 Act.

---

291. Clearly, the right to exploit the work under a pseudonym, or anonymously, is the crux of the distinction between this right and the preceding right to be acknowledged as the author of the work.

292. *See* I. Pozhitkov, *Copyright and Neighbouring Rights Protection in the Russian Federation*, 20(1) Rev. Cent. & E. Eur. L. 53, 62–63 (1994).

293. For example, the widespread availability of waivers is considered to weaken substantially the moral rights provisions in the United Kingdom Copyright, Designs and Patents Act of 1988. *See* William R. Cornish, *Moral Rights Under the 1988 Act*, 11(12) Eur. Intell. Prop. Rev. 449, 452 (1989); *see also* Vaver, *supra* note 11, at 274–78, who comments on both the British and Canadian contexts.

b. Duration of Protection: Perpetual Moral Rights and the Question of Inheritance

The Copyright Act of 1993 provides that the right of authorship, and the author's right to his name and the protection of his reputation, "shall be protected without limitation in time."[294] While Soviet jurisprudence generally interpreted the duration of moral rights as unlimited,[295] the Copyright Act of 1993 followed the 1991 Fundamentals in providing an explicit answer to the question of duration.

The related question of whether moral rights may be inherited receives a detailed treatment. Article 29, on the "Transfer of Copyright by Succession," refers to "succession," like the Fundamentals, in the specific sense of succession in title. In keeping with their "personal" character, the three principal moral rights of authorship, name, and reputation cannot be transferred by succession; they can only be inherited by the heirs of the author.

The Copyright Act took the laudable step of addressing the potentially problematic issue of who is to enforce an author's moral rights after his death. Presumably, this problem was beyond the scope of the transitional copyright provisions in the Fundamentals of 1991. Article 27.2 of the Copyright Act provides that the right to be named as the author of one's own works and the author's right to the protection of his reputation can be enforced by an executor appointed for this purpose by the author. In the absence of such an appointment, the author's own heirs or "an agency of the Russian Federation especially empowered to do so" could assert these moral rights after the author's death. It is interesting to note the implied legislative preference for an "executor of moral rights." Practical problems may well arise from entrusting moral rights to the author's heirs. Conflict can arise among the author's descendents, or they may not be sufficiently knowledgeable about the author's work to assert moral rights effectively.[296] However, it may be even more awkward to entrust moral rights to the state. For much of the Soviet period, the state was foremost in failing to respect the moral rights of authors.

In any event, a state agency for administering moral rights after the author's death was never created during the lifetime of the 1993 Copyright Act.[297] Doing so would almost certainly have raised issues of credibility in the

---

294. *See* Russian Copyright Act 1993, *supra* note 258, art. 27.

295. *See* Bella Karakis, *Moral Rights: French, United States and Soviet Compliance with Article 6bis of the Berne Convention*, 5 Touro Int'l L. Rev. 105, 133–34 (1994). Karakis' view is in accordance with the interpretation of the well-known Soviet legal scholar, Serge Levitsky.

296. This issue is discussed in Mira T. Sundara Rajan, *Moral Rights in the Public Domain*, *supra* note 205, at 177–80.

297. Writing in 1993, Elst mentions the Russian Agency for Intellectual Property, which may have been the natural agency to exercise these rights. *See* Michiel Elst, *New Developments in the Copyright Legislation of the Russian Federation: Part I*, 15(3) Eur. Intell. Prop. Rev. 95, 103 (1993). However, the Agency was abolished by an Edict of October 7, 1993, and a "new"

Russian Federation. After all, Russia does not have a tradition of respecting press freedom, and creative writers have historically paid a very high price for exercising their profession in this restrictive political environment. It now seems incongruous for the post-Soviet state to become responsible for safeguarding authors' moral rights. In the past, the Union of Soviet Writers was charged with the implementation of authors' rights; at the time of Soviet accession to the UCC, the Writers' Union was revamped to deal with the enforcement of Soviet copyright abroad. However, the history of the Union was one of antagonism to the dissident community, and indeed, it often became an instrument of repression against its own members.[298]

c. Moral Rights in the Public Domain: *Domaine public payant*

The Russian Copyright Act of 1993 included a number of provisions geared towards the recognition of the public interest in copyright works. In this, it diverges from the individualistic or corporate character of Western copyright law, particularly as illustrated by the American and common law models.[299] It might be tempting at first glance to assume that the sense of a collective interest in copyright works is a product of the socialist mentality. However, if we think back to the socialist and Soviet approaches to copyright law—for example, in the nationalization decrees and, later, the Soviet Civil Code—we cannot fail to note that the public or collective interest, though identified, was poorly protected. Rather, the state enjoyed the benefits of copyright in more

---

authors' society—what Pozhitkov calls "an independent public organization"—was established. However, as Pozhitkov points out, the society actually reflects the structure and leadership of both the Agency and the earlier VAAP. *See* Pozhitkov, *supra* note 292, at 82–83.

298. *See* the discussion of the role played by the Union of Soviet Writers (VOUAP) in maintaining ideological conformity between its members and the Communist Party in Hosking, *supra* note 255, at 222–25. The functions of VOUAP are described in Newcity, *supra* note 4, at 25–26, and suggest an outstanding level of state support through the agency for the activities of writers favored by the state. A generally positive view of the agency, in its later incarnation as the Copyright Agency of the USSR (VAAP), may be found in an article written shortly after its establishment, from within the Soviet Union: N.S. Roudakov & I.A. Gringolts, *L'agence de l'URSS pour les droits d'auteur (VAAP)*, 81 RIDA (Revue Internationale du Droit d'Auteur) 2, 3 (1974). *See also* the informative article by Elena Muravina, *Copyright Transactions in Russia Part I. The VAAP Era: 1973–1991*, 17 NEW MATTER 4 (1993).

299. The term "corporate" is used here in the sense of relating to an incorporated business, and not as referring to a group. In Canada, current amendments to bring Canadian law into conformity with the WIPO Internet Treaties have moved it towards fewer allowable public uses. The trend was the subject of a book of critical commentary by Canadian lawyers and professors. *See* IN THE PUBLIC INTEREST: THE FUTURE OF CANADIAN COPYRIGHT LAW (Michael Geist ed., Irwin Law 2005); the essays are also available for free download under Creative Commons licenses, *available at* http://www.irwinlaw.com/store/product/120/in-the-public-interest (last visited April 28, 2010). Geist is planning a second edition of this book of essays, to address copyright reform bill C-32, introduced in June of 2010. The book is forthcoming in the Fall of 2010.

or less the same way that private copyright owners enjoy them in market-driven societies—except that the rights of the state extended to expropriation, which is, of course, practically forbidden in modern jurisdictions.[300]

In specific terms, the Russian Copyright Act of 1993 was quite original in addressing the vulnerability of authors' moral rights in the public domain. The importance of moral rights does not evaporate when copyright in creative works expires and they enter the public domain. On the contrary, moral rights in public domain works assume a broader significance for cultural heritage—a point suggested even in the American context by the decision in the *Shostakovich* case.[301] In a country like the Soviet Union, where the integrity of works as well as authorship, attribution, and reputation were all vulnerable to attack by the state, the continued protection of moral rights in the public domain may have considerable value.

Article 28.2 of the Copyright Act states that the three main moral rights of authorship, name, and reputation must be respected when using works in the public domain. Article 28.3 established a *domaine public payant* scheme for collecting a special royalty from public domain works to be paid into "an authors' professional fund or to an organization for the collective administration of the economic rights of authors." The scheme could contribute to the welfare of the post-Soviet creative community; it also had the symbolic value of representing a benefit flowing from the repression of past writers to future generations of authors. However, practical details of the plan, including who would receive the funds and how they would be spent, were never worked out, and the scheme for a paying public domain was not implemented while the Copyright Act of 1993 was in force.[302]

d. Reputation vs. Integrity

The recasting of the integrity right as a right of reputation in the Copyright Act of 1993 is striking. The right of reputation clearly shows the imprint of Article 6*bis* of the Berne Convention, which prohibits only those acts that

---

300. In very rare cases, the expropriation of copyright may be used to support public policy. In Britain, the *Spycatcher* case saw the House of Lords ordering th at copyright royalties from the sale of a book be relinquished to the government. But the reason was extreme: the book, written by a British double agent who had worked in the Soviet Union, represented a flagrant violation of the public trust. The House of Lords was keen to disallow an apparent incentive for this kind of breach of public policy, in the unusual form of copyright royalties. *See* A-G v. Guardian Newspapers Ltd. (No. 1) [1987] All E.R. 316; A-G v. Guardian Newspapers Ltd. (No. 2) [1988] All E.R. 545.

301. *Shostakovich, supra* note 70.

302. An interesting discussion of a *domaine public payant* scheme proposed in Germany may be found in Dietz, *Term of Protection, supra* note 290, at 508–11. See also the related discussion of *domaine public payant* in Mira T. Sundara Rajan, *Moral Rights in the Public Domain, supra* note 205, at 183–85.

would negatively affect an author's "honour or reputation". But the provisions of Article 15 go beyond Article 6*bis*, making reputation the actual focus of the right. Indeed, it is questionable as to whether Article 15 actually met the standard of protection set by the Berne Convention.

Article 6*bis* prohibits "any distortion, mutilation or other modification of, or other derogatory action in relation to, the . . . work"; Article 15 prohibited only "any distortion or other derogatory act." The language seems sufficiently precise to imply an intentional restriction on the scope of Article 6*bis*, but much would have depended here on the interpretation of the Russian courts. Although Article 15 protected a right of "reputation," it did not explicitly provide for recourse in the case of damage to an author's reputation; it was only concerned with the possibility of prejudice to his "honour or dignity." However, it did seem to allow a flexible standard of proof, since the derogatory act need only be likely— "liable"—to cause damage. If, indeed, Article 15 did not meet the standard of protection required by Article 6*bis*, the exclusion of moral rights from the TRIPs Agreement meant that the Russian Federation did not face any overwhelming international pressure to improve the protection of the integrity right.

As Pozhitkov, writing in 1994, commented:

> The right to integrity was rescinded and substituted by the right to protection of an author's reputation [in the 1993 Copyright Act] which permits him to object to any distortion of a work or any derogatory action in relation thereto [that is "liable to prejudice his honour or dignity"]. It remains to be seen how broadly the courts will interpret this provision.[303]

When viewed in the context of Russian copyright history, the narrowness of the integrity right in the 1993 Copyright Act is surprising. The right to the "inviolability" of the work is a long tradition in Russian copyright law—it was even paid lip-service in the copyright jurisprudence of Soviet times. The 1991 Fundamentals reflected this tradition, and arguably strengthened it by assuring authors that they had the right to keep their work "intact." It is quite probable that the change, once again, was a result of the American influence on Russian law reform. The integrity right is generally acknowledged to be the most powerful moral right of the author, and the American film industry, which has already faced moral rights problems in France, may well have feared the implications of a strong Russian right of integrity for their exports

---

303. Pozhitkov, *supra* note 292, at 63. However, he goes on to observe: "Since in the past there was no concept of monetary compensation for moral damage, authors did not usually submit the issues of violations of their moral rights to courts." This analysis of why moral rights claims did not find their way into the Soviet courtrooms is slightly surprising in the Soviet context. What seems more likely is that authors were fearful of bringing cases, or thought of legal actions as being pointless.

to Russia.[304] In contrast to the integrity right, however, the rights of authorship and name were retained in Article 15 of the Copyright Act, perhaps out
of sensitivity to the Soviet-era treatment of authorship.

e. Performers' Moral Rights

Like the earlier Fundamentals, the Copyright Act predated the international
community by a number of years with its recognition of moral rights for
performers.[305] It recognized the performer's right to be named, and to ensure
the protection of his performance "against any distortion or other derogatory
act liable to prejudice his honour or dignity." These protections could be
found in Article 27 of the Copyright Act on the "Rights of the Performer."
However, these moral rights were applicable only to the performer, and,
unlike the 1991 Fundamentals, did not offer protection to actors or stage
managers. The provisions mirror the concerns of the American film industry
about the consequences of allowing actors to claim moral rights. Moreover,
Russia, too, may have wanted to protect its historically important film
industry from complications arising out of moral rights.

f. *Droit de suite* for the Visual Arts

In addition to extensive provisions on moral rights, the Copyright Act of
1993 made provision for protection of the *droit de suite*, the right of a visual
artist to a royalty from the resale of his work after he initially parts with it to
a first buyer. Again, Russian legislation on this issue predated the European
initiative, which led to the adoption of a copyright harmonization directive
on *droit de suite*, over British objections, in 2004.[306] The right is an accepted
method of responding to the tendency of works of visual art to appreciate in
value over time, sometimes substantially. Accordingly, where a work is sold
at a price that is at least 20 percent greater than that of the previous sale, the
seller is required to pay its creator a resale royalty of five percent of the resale
price. Although the *droit de suite* is not technically a "moral right," it is supported by the rationale of a lasting connection between an author and his
own work which is at the heart of moral rights doctrine. Russian law did
indeed seem to conceive of the *droit de suite* as a kind of moral right: it was

---

304. *See* the *Huston* case, *supra* note 121, where the colorization of *The Asphalt Jungle* was pro-
    hibited by French courts as a violation of the directors right of integrity. It is, of course, likely
    that moral rights issues may be of concern to other U.S. copyright industries, as well.
305. The WPPT provisions to this effect were drafted in 1996, but only came into effect in 2002.
306. The concern was that London would lose its competitiveness as a major art center, particu-
    larly *vis-à-vis* New York. *See* Will Bennett, *Art Sales: New Headache for Dealers*, TELEGRAPH
    (Dec. 20, 2005), *available at* http://www.telegraph.co.uk/culture/art/3648899/Art-sales-new-
    headache-for-dealers.html.Or (last visited Apr. 28, 2010).

protected under Article 17, in conjunction with an additional right of visual artists to continue to have access to their work after it is sold.[307]

g. Disclosure in the Post-Socialist Context

Finally, it is important to note that the issue of disclosure is fundamental to both the economic and moral rights in the Act. Indeed, the Act seems to address the problem of expropriation of authors' works, legally and practically tolerated in the Soviet Union, by creating and providing a detailed elaboration of an author's specific right to disclose his own work.[308] Disclosure of a work cannot occur without the author's consent, while the author's right to disclose his own work is stated in Article 15 on Moral Rights.

4. Programmers' Moral Rights: The Law on Computer Programs and Databases and the Recognition of Scientists[309]

Until the adoption of the Civil Code provisions of 2008, the Russian intellectual property system included a number of laws dealing with copyright in addition to the Copyright Act of 1993. The difficulty of locating an authoritative source for the treatment of copyright has been one of the post-socialist problems associated with Russian law. The Civil Code provisions address this problem in two ways. First, the Civil Code consolidates Russian law on copyright into a single source. By doing so, it contributes to the clarity and accuracy of Russian provisions. Secondly, the Civil Code does what previous reforms should have done, but did not do: it explicitly cancels other legislation dealing with copyright law.[310]

Prior to the Civil Code, other legislation dealing with copyright issues seems to have been adopted to meet the needs of specialized industries, as in the case of computer software, or to address broader social concerns, such as cultural heritage, information, and privacy.[311] A glance at the legislation that formerly dealt with computer programs—the Law on the Legal Protection of

---

307. Law on Copyright, *supra* note 259, art. 17.1.
308. *Id.*, Basic Concepts, art. 4.11, "disclosure of a work."
309. Law No 3523-1 (Sept. 3, 1992), as amended by Federal Law No. 177-FL (Dec. 24, 2002) [Law on Computer Programs].
310. Dietz, *Incorporation of Patent Law into Part IV*, *supra* note 275, at 689–90, explains the process by which previous legislation was invalidated, noting that it occurred in several steps; and, indeed, it cancels all other legislation dealing with intellectual property rights overall.
311. See, for example, the comments on privacy law, analogous to intellectual property in many ways, in Mira T. Sundara Rajan, *The Past and Future of Privacy in Russia*, 27(4) REV. CENT. & E. EUR. L. 625, 627–36 (2001). In particular, the "complexity of Russia's legal framework surrounding information" is cited as a general problem in this area. *Id.* at 628.

Computer Programs and Databases of 1992, last amended in 2002—[312] is helpful. It shows how the moral rights aspect of computer programs has been dealt with in the past, gives us a point of comparison on the terms of their inclusion within the new Civil Code.

The Law on Computer Programs supplemented provisions for the copyright protection of software that were already quite extensive in the Russian Copyright Act of 1993. It is therefore not surprising that, in some respects, the provisions of this special law overlapped with the Copyright Act. In others, however, the legislation succeeded in a more laudable objective—the introduction of specific measures directed towards the software industry. In these areas, the coverage of the special law was extraordinarily comprehensive. In effect, the law not only allowed for computer programs to be recognized as a form of literary work on par with every other; it also conferred upon computer programmers a status more or less equivalent to that of authors, more generally, in Russian copyright legislation. Notably, the Law on Computer Programs and Databases created an exclusive right of authorship for programmers, extended to the creators of databases, reserved for "the natural person whose creative effort has brought about the creation of the computer program or database."[313]

In fact, the Russian law established a range of moral rights for computer programmers, providing for rights of authorship, name, disclosure, integrity, and even withdrawal, which matched their general availability to authors of other kinds of works under the Copyright Act.[314] A comparison with the French approach is useful. The Russian provisions for programmers' moral rights occurred in the same year when French rules on moral rights in computer programs were elaborated, and they matched the model for protection in France established at that time. Subsequent amendments to the French *Code de la Propriété Intellectuelle* in 1994 recast the programmers' right of integrity to match the Berne scenario; modifications of the program must cause damage to the programmer's reputation before they can qualify as a violation of his right of integrity.[315]

---

312. Law on Computer Programs, *supra* note 309.
313. *Id.*, art. 8.
314. *Id.*, art. 9.
315. *See* art. L121-7 of the CPI, *supra* note 43, amended in 1994: "In the absence of provisions which are more favorable to the author of a computer program, he may not: (1) object to the modification of the program by the right holder mentioned in Article L122-6 (2), unless it causes prejudice to his honour or reputation; (2) Exercise his right of withdrawal."
    Article L121-7—Modifié par Loi n°94-361 du 10 mai 1994, art. 3 JORF 11 mai 1994:
    "Sauf stipulation contraire plus favorable à l'auteur d'un logiciel, celui-ci ne peut 1° S'opposer à la modification du logiciel par le cessionnaire des droits mentionnés au 2° de l'article L. 1226, lorsqu'elle n'est préjudiciable ni à son honneur ni à sa réputation; 2° Exercer son droit de repentir ou de retrait."

Nevertheless, the right of software corporations in the work of their employees was simultaneously protected by Article 12 of the Russian computer law, which specifies that exclusive rights in a program or database created by an author who is an employee "shall [in the absence of contractual provisions] belong to the . . . employer." Interestingly, the rights of disclosure and recall were added to the law on computer programs in 2002, along with the rights of employers. The overall logic of the scheme is not entirely clear, as the existence of moral rights independently of the economic—or, in the language of the Russian law, "exclusive"—rights would not have facilitated the dealings of companies with information technology. However, the provisions were consonant with the objectives of protecting free speech and scientific reputations. Oppression of free speech in the Soviet Union affected scientists in much the same way as it affected artists, and the Soviet scientific community can claim its own share of outspoken and courageous dissenters.[316]

5. Return to the Future: The 2008 Civil Code Provisions on Copyright

In 2008, a surprising new set of Russian provisions on intellectual property rights was introduced. The new Part IV of the Russian Civil Code was prepared in an environment of relative secrecy, with little input from the outside world. However, its pedigree can be traced to a draft version of the Civil Code that has been circulating since 2001, and upon which, many of its provisions are closely based.[317]

Russia has not had a Civil Code section on intellectual property law since 1961.[318] By purporting to overrule all pre-existing intellectual property legislation in this field, the Civil Code creates post-socialist Russia's first unified system of intellectual property rights. The new Civil Code deals cleanly with old legislation, explicitly invalidating the Copyright Act of 1993 and related legislation such as the Law on Computer Programs and Databases of 1992.[319]

With respect to copyright law, Part IV signifies a fundamentally new approach. The very theory on which copyright is based is dramatically altered. Copyright is no longer considered a proprietary right. Instead, something akin to the operation of a software license occurs: transactions involving

---

316. Andrei Sakharov, the physicist, is probably the best known of these to outsiders.
317. The draft Civil Code provisions of 2001 are discussed in detail in Sundara Rajan, *Copyright and Creative Freedom*, *supra* note 4, Chapter VIII, "The Future of Post-Communist Copyright," 188–98.
318. Before that, Russia included copyright in the Civil Code of 1887. *See* Sundara Rajan, *Copyright and Creative Freedom*, *supra* note 4, at 98–99.
319. *See* Dietz, *Incorporation of Patent Law into Part IV*, *supra* note 275, at 689–90.

works take place without any real shift of ownership. Property rights subsist in the media in which works are recorded; those "copies" can be owned, but the underlying work remains attached to the author.[320] Dmitry Golovanov points out that, under the new Code,

> the results of intellectual activities as such may not be alienated or transferred. Only economic rights to such results as well as property rights to the material carriers of such results shall circulate on the market. Art 1227 of Part 4 of the Civil Code stipulates that "intellectual rights" shall not be interrelated with ownership rights concerning material carriers. Thus so far the concept of [the] proprietary nature of intellectual property is definitively rejected by the Russian lawmakers.[321]

In keeping with this approach, three different types of interests may arise: moral rights; economic rights, now known as "exclusive rights" in the Civil Code;[322] and what Galavanov calls "other rights blending together both economic and personal elements."[323]

In this last category, the most important right must certainly be the concept of disclosure. Disclosure involves the communication of a work to the public, and signifies something larger than the concept of publication. Publication specifically means the distribution of a work through professional channels, whereas communication of the work to the public can be accomplished by a variety of methods and technologies. The disclosure concept under the Civil Code extends to both economic and moral rights in a special sense: after the author's death, the current publisher of the work has a right to continue publishing the works unless the author has clearly indicated that this should not be the case.[324]

---

320. *For example*, Article 1227 of the 2008 Civil Code, *supra* note 259, supports this view.

321. D. Golovanov, Moscow Media Law & Policy Centre, *Transformation of Authors' Rights and Neighbouring Rights in Russia*, IRIS Legal Observations of the European Audiovisual Laboratory (Strasbourg Feb. 2008), *available at* http://www.obs.coe.int/oea_publ/iris/iris_plus/iplus2_2008.pdf.en (last visited April 28, 2010).

322. The terminology of "exclusive rights" was also distinguished from moral rights in the 1993 Copyright Act. The use of the term "exclusive" to designate economic rights is clarified in the current provisions of Part IV of the Civil Code.

323. Golovanov, *supra* note 321, at 5.

324. *Id.*, says: "After an author's death his or her heirs as well as the publisher (after the work entered the public domain) shall have the right to publish the works unless the author clearly expressed his wish to the contrary (art. 1268, paras. 2, 3)." Presumably, Golovanov is referring to two different scenarios: the persistence of the publisher's right for the duration of copyright protection—the life of the author plus seventy years (*see* 2008 Civil Code, *supra* note 259, arts. 1281 & 1282)—and the right of the heirs to publish works as they subsequently enter the public domain (art. 1282). Article 1338 concerns the right of the publisher in works that have never been made public. *See also* 2008 Civil Code, *supra* note 259, arts. 1268.2 & 1268.3: the right to publish the works after the author's death is also granted

A second hybrid right is closely related to disclosure: it is the right to withdraw a work from circulation after it is published, which, as in the French model, entails an obligation on the author to compensate the publisher for its loss. The exceptions to the right of withdrawal are interesting ones. The authors of computer programs and of "works integrated into complex works (including audiovisual ones)" are denied the right to withdraw their works from circulation.[325] Once again, in different ways, software and film test the practical limits of moral rights.

Finally, the *domaine public payant* scheme set out in the Copyright Act of 1993 is not carried over into the Civil Code provisions. This decision appears to be based on the practical issue that the paying public domain was never actually implemented under the Copyright Act. If the scheme could not be implemented in the thirteen-year tenure of the Act,[326] it seems clear that the idea was not workable in the Russian context—whether for lack of political will, or because of the practical difficulty of collecting royalties in public domain works in a post-socialist state. It is perhaps more significant that, in keeping with the logic of the 1993 Act, moral rights continue to be protected in public domain works.[327] As in the earlier law, any "interested person" can assert moral rights in a work that is in the public domain.[328] This is a potentially important tool for the protection of culture, but it leaves open the practical question of how to determine whether or not, under this broad provision, a given party has standing to sue on behalf of the moral rights in a work.

a. Moral Rights in the Civil Code: General Provisions[329]

The intellectual property section of the Civil Code opens with Chapter 69, which sets out General Provisions relating to intellectual property rights.[330] This choice of structure is somewhat controversial in its own right. Presumably, a general section like this should aid in the interpretation of the specific chapters of the Civil Code dealing with particular kinds of intellectual property rights, and help to clarify their content. In fact, there is considerable overlap

---

to the heirs of the author. *See* Golovanov, *supra* note 321, at 5, Concept of "Intellectual Rights," Other Rights.

325. Golovanov, *supra* note 321, at 4–5, Concept of "Intellectual Rights."

326. Chapter IV of the Civil Code was concluded in 2006, although it did not enter into force until 2008. *See supra* note 259.

327. *See* Golovanov, *supra* note 321, at 4–5, "Concept of Intellectual Rights."

328. *See* 2008 Civil Code, *supra* note 259, art. 1267 (2). An author may appoint a person to protect his moral rights after his death. Should he have failed to do so, or should the appointed person be unable to act—or, himself, be deceased—the heirs, as well as other interested persons may act.

329. For a complementary analysis of Russian patents under the new Civil Code provisions, see Dietz, *Incorporation of Patent Law into Part IV*, *supra* note 275.

330. *See id.*, at 688.

between the Chapter 69 provisions and the Chapters of the Code dealing with specific intellectual property rights. Rather than clarifying their interpretation, the presence of Chapter 69 provisions may actually complicate the interpretation of the Code. From the perspective of transparency, it is not clear why provisions dealing with copyright law should be found in both the general provisions and the chapter on copyright—especially when the copyright provisions in the General section apply to copyright only, and not to all areas of intellectual property rights covered by the Code.

The usefulness of a section on general provisions is a question of general interest to civil lawyers, and it is considered by Adolf Dietz in his examination of Patents under the new Russian Code. In relation to moral rights, the General Provisions do accomplish the interesting objective of extending moral rights to inventors. Dietz comments:

> [T]he interplay between those "General Provisions" in Chapter 69 and the "special" patent law provisions in Chapter 72 must always be kept in mind. That is particularly true for the general provisions concerning personality rights of "authors" since in Russian terminology an inventor is also called an author (of the invention). The inventor consequently profits from the personality rights granted to authors in general in the introductory Chapter (especially in Article 1228 Point 2).[331]

Chapter 70 deals specifically with copyright, and Chapter 71, with "Copyright Neighbouring Rights." Mirroring the General chapter of the Code, both chapters contain provisions on moral rights.

The protection of moral rights in the Russian Civil Code departs substantially from the formula adopted in the 1993 Copyright Act. Indeed, this eventuality has been apparent since at least 2001, when a detailed "draft" version of what has now become Chapter IV was circulating. Interestingly, it is possible to identify a degree of continuity between the Civil Code provisions, the 2001 Draft, and the 1991 Fundamentals; but there is a definite break with the moral rights provisions of the Copyright Act of 1993.[332]

---

331. Dietz, *Incorporation of Patent Law into Part IV*, *supra* note 275, at 695 (footnote omitted). But note that art. 1228.2 also provides that the moral rights of "name and other personal non-property rights" are available "in the cases provided by the present Code—presumably, as identified in the special sections of the Code." The right of authorship is not subject to this proviso. *See also* art. 1255.2, in the Copyright section of the Code, which provides for moral rights in relation to the author of "products of science, literature and art."

332. *See* Sundara Rajan, *Copyright and Creative Freedom*, *supra* note 4, Chapter VIII, "The Future of Post-Communist Copyright," 188–98. The discussion of the Draft in this book is based on a version of the Draft Civil Code which was translated into English by Oksana M. Kozyr, a drafter of the 1993 Russian Copyright Act, and E.V. Luchits. I am grateful to Professor David Lametti of the Faculty of Law, McGill University, who provided me with a copy of this document. In 2001, Gainan Avilov of the Private Law Research Centre was able to

b. General Principles

Chapter 69 seeks to elaborate the general philosophy of intellectual property rights in the Code, and establishes principles to guide the interpretation of the specific provisions in subsequent chapters. It specifies the "exclusive" nature of the author's economic rights, and the special nature of his moral rights.[333]

Moral rights are set out in Article 1228, which defines an author as, "[a] citizen . . . whose creative efforts have produced a result of intellectual activity." Article 1228.2 provides for the protection of an author's "personal non-property rights," such as a "right of name."[334] All of the author's personal rights, including the rights of authorship and name are inalienable and non-transferable, and the Code provides that they cannot be waived by any means. These rights are protected in perpetuity—"without term"—and, in certain circumstances after the death of the author, they may be asserted by "any interested person" on his behalf.[335]

Since these provisions appear in the "General" part of the Code, they are presumably applicable to all areas of intellectual property rights in the special sections. Accordingly, moral rights are not unique to copyright works; as appropriate, they will extend into the areas of patents and neighboring rights, as well.

The reference to the right of "interested persons" to act is noteworthy. How will the courts interpret it? Would a member of the general public qualify as an "interested person" in relation to moral rights issues?[336] Alternatively, would it be restricted to people who had personal or business dealings with the author, or would it extend to the artistic community in which he was involved? In any case, Article 1228.2 represents a substantial commitment to the protection of works in the public domain, their integrity and historical accuracy; it achieves this protection by opening the door onto a greatly augmented possibility of moral rights disputes arising out of alterations to the works of deceased authors. The term has a pleasing democratic air—in Russia, any person has the

---

suggest that a revised Civil Code could be adopted at any point over the next decade. (Personal communication from Gainan Avilov, Sept. 2001). In previous conversations, Dr. Kozyr indicated that a completely new draft was in the making, and the new 2008 Civil Code provisions are presumably the result of these efforts.

333. 2008 Civil Code, *supra* note 259, art. 1228. The "inalienable and nontransferable" quality of these rights is noted. The article specifies that "[w]aiver of these rights is void," and that moral rights are "protected in perpetuity." *See id.*, art. 1228(2).

334. *See id.*, art. 1228(2). The Article states that the author has "the right of name, the right of authorship, and other non-property rights in cases established by this code." Also "*inie lichnie neimushestvennie prava.*"

335. *See id.*, arts. 1267(2) & 1316(2).

336. *See id.*, art. 1266(2). In these circumstances, interested persons may request the protection of the author's moral rights. The interested person must be granted standing to sue by the court.

right to act on behalf of culture, which does, after all, become the treasure of the public after the expiry of copyright term. In practice, however, "interested person" may prove to be self-defining. With the possible exception of wealthy art-lovers, only institutions such as museums or universities are likely to have the resources to pursue a moral rights case in Russia.

In the copyright context, an author's right to the protection of his name is protected in Article 1265,[337] and his right to the inviolability of his work is described in Article 1266.

The Civil Code also considers several aspects of the problem of implementing and enforcing moral rights effectively. Article 1251, on the protection of authors' rights and liability for their infringement, deals specifically with moral rights. It provides that a number of specific remedies will be available for the "violation of [the] personal non-property rights of the author." These include the cessation of infringing activities, compensation for "moral harm"—a new concept in post-Soviet civil law, though it is well-known to the civil law of Western Europe—[338]and, in general, an attempt to restore "the situation that existed prior to the violation of the right." Among the remedies available is "publication of a court decision on the committed infringement," a usual remedy against infringement in civilian jurisdictions. Publication of decisions has several implications for moral rights. It allows precedents to develop, which have both legal and practical value, in this civil law system, for the injured parties who may wish to make a claim. Reformers who prepared the Code may also intend to emphasize the importance of shining the light of publicity on infringements of authors' rights. Public information is a sure antidote to the culture of secrecy and persecution historically endured by Russian authors.

In contrast to the old Copyright Act, the Civil Code deals directly with the issue of moral rights infringement. Article 1251 addresses the "violation of personal non-property rights of the author."[339] The remedies provided include, but are not limited to, "recognition of the right, restoration of the situation that existed prior to the violation of the right, stopping effects that are infringing the right or creating the threat of its infringement, compensation for moral harm, [and] publication of a court decision on the committed infringement."

Finally, it is worth noting that moral rights in "complex objects"—works with multiple components, such as film or databases—are also recognized.

---

337. An interesting feature of this Article is that it allows the publisher to protect works in cases where publication is anonymous, or carried out under a pseudonym. *See id.*, art. 1265(2). The right will expire if the author chooses to declare himself.

338. *See* the discussion of indemnification for moral harm in transitional and post-Soviet law, in M. I. Braginskii, *The General Part of Civil Codification in Russia, in* THE REVIVAL OF PRIVATE LAW IN CENTRAL EASTERN EUROPE: ESSAYS IN HONOUR OF FJM FELDBRUGGE, Vol. 99, 109–10 (G. Ginsburgs, D. D. Barry & W. B. Simons eds., Kluwer Law International 1996).

339. 2008 Civil Code, *supra* note 259, art. 1252, is concerned with "Protection of Exclusive Rights and Liability for Their Infringement."

Article 1240 provides for the recognition of rights of authorship, name, and inviolability in relation to multi-faceted works such as motion pictures and dramatic productions. Article 1240(3) provides that the author of an under-lying work that is used in a "complex object," such as a film, enjoys moral rights in his contribution, and it clearly specifies that those rights persist through the "process of use" of the contribution.[340] However, in none of the sections where this information should logically fall does the Code specify who should be considered the author of the work. Authorship is not defined in Article 1240, itself, the general provision on authorship; in Article 1228(4), which simply provides for the possibility of recognizing coauthorship; or in Article 1258 the provision on coauthorship in Chapter 70 on copyright, which only provides for equal recognition of authors of a joint work whether or not the work an be separated into its parts.[341]

The issue receives a partial response in Article 1263, in the Copyright chapter of the Code, on copyright in audiovisual works. This provision states that, in the case of films, the "director, author of scenario, and author of the [original] music [for the film]" will be deemed its coauthors.[342] The problem requires further clarification in relation to "complex" works which may give rise to competing moral rights claims in the absence of adequate legal measures clarifying their relationships.

c. Copyright

Chapter 70 of the Civil Code, on copyright, reunites the economic and personal rights of the author in a single section. Under the heading, "Authors' Law,"[343] Article 1255 provides for the recognition of rights in "science, literature and art."[344] It goes on to identify five rights of authorship: an "exclusive" right, the term by which economic rights are implied under the new Code; a right of authorship; a right to one's name; the right to the invio-lability of one's work; and a right of first publication.[345]

i. Moral Rights Defined

The five moral rights are given a detailed treatment in three separate articles. The right of authorship and the right of name, being especially closely related, are dealt with together in Article 1265. The right to one's name includes the

---

340. *Id.*, art. 1240(3), states: "In the process of the use of a product of intellectual activity as a part of a complex object, the author of that product has the authorship rights and other personal non-property rights to that product."

341. *Id.*, art. 1258(1).

342. *Id.*, art. 1263(2).

343. Like civil law systems, copyright in Russia is known as *droit d'auteur*, "*avtorskoye pravo.*"

344. 2008 Civil Code, *supra* note 259, art. 1255(1).

345. *See id.*, art. 1255.2(5).

right to work under a pseudonym, or anonymously. If the author does not choose to identify himself by name as the author of his works, the publisher is charged with protecting his interests as the author's representative until the author chooses to reveal his name. In keeping with the general part of the intellectual property provisions, Article 1265 confirms that the rights of authorship and name are inalienable and non-transferable, even if the "exclusive" economic right is transferred to another person.

Article 1266 deals with the right of inviolability of the work, which is restored to all of its formal expansiveness in Soviet copyright law. Indeed, it is a striking feature of the moral rights scheme in the Civil Code that the author's right of "inviolability" is reinstated; it had been drafted down to a "right of reputation" in the 1993 Copyright Act. The principle of inviolability represents a return to the foundations of moral rights in Soviet jurisprudence, and exceeds the standard set by Article *6bis* of the Berne Convention.[346] The right of inviolability offers very strong protection to the integrity of creative works, especially during the lifetime of the author.

In effect, however, this right is actually split into two parts, an outstandingly strong right of inviolability for living authors, and a strong right of reputation after the author's death. During the lifetime of the author, alterations, abridgments, editions, illustrations, forewords or afterwords, commentaries, and "[any] other explanations whatsoever" are permitted only with the consent of the author. However, after the author's death, previously prohibited changes will be allowed, provided that the person who holds the economic rights during this period consents to them. The alterations will only be allowed if the author has not expressly indicated that changes to the work should not be undertaken after his death, and provided that they do not "distort the conception of the author . . .[or] derange the integrity of [the audience's] perception of the work." In an interesting overlap with trademark principles, Article 1266 (2) also makes it possible for an author to protect the inviolability of his work as part of his honor, dignity, and "business reputation." The wording of the provision may help to distinguish between "reputation," as it refers to the professional standing of the author, and "honor" and "dignity" as matters of personal reputation.[347]

---

346. The terminology of "inviolability" dates from the reforms of 1961, which led to the adoption of a new set of Fundamentals in that year. However, the idea of a very strong integrity right, at least against the publisher, goes further back, at least to the early Soviet law of 1928. *See* Sundara Rajan, *Copyright and Creative Freedom*, *supra* note 4, Chapter V, "Revolution and Reform," 97–100. *See generally* Serge L. Levitsky, *Continuity and Change in Soviet Copyright Law: A Legal Analysis*, 6 Rev. Socialist L. 6 425 (1980).

347. Under this provision, the author is entitled to seek the protection of his "honor" or "dignity," as well. The idea is reminiscent of an interesting moral rights case from India, where the author of a novel sued a filmmaker for distorting her story; in finding for the author, the judge specifically made mention of the damage to her reputation that might result from her

The right of disclosure is set out in Article 1268. These detailed provisions seem to respond directly to the pressures faced by Soviet writers and dissidents in relation to publication. Article 1268(1) protects the author's right to decide "independently" whether or not his work should be disclosed to the public. It is worth noting that this article distinguishes between disclosure and publication: it considers publication as only one form of a possible disclosure, including disclosure of the work by electronic means. But article 1268(3) provides for the publication of posthumous works, which is permissible by the holder of the exploitation rights unless the author has expressly provided otherwise elsewhere in his writings—whether published or unpublished, public or private—or in his will. This provision addresses the possibility that an author may assign rights to a work, but not live to see the publication.[348]

The Code also protects an author's right to withdraw his work from publication, but in a limited sense: the author has the right to withdraw a published work from circulation, but he must publicly announce his decision, and provide financial compensation to the publisher for any potential losses.[349] Despite these safeguards, the right of withdrawal is not granted to the authors of computer programs. The treatment of withdrawal, and its placement in the Code immediately after the Article elaborating the right of first publication, suggests that the drafters of the Code saw it as a limited, but definite, counterpart to disclosure.

ii. Special Features

The duration of copyright is specified as the lifetime of the author and seventy years after his death. In contrast, the term of moral rights protection is explicitly provided for in Article 1267 (1): the rights of authorship, name, and inviolability are protected "indefinitely," or, in other words, in perpetuity. Moral rights cannot be waived, but they may be asserted after the author's death by his heirs.[350]

The treatment of works in the public domain becomes a key issue, and is dealt with in Article 1282. As in the 1993 Copyright Act, the use of public domain works must continue to preserve the author's rights of authorship,

---

association with the commercial film industry. *See* Smt Mannu Bhandari v. Kala Vikas Pictures (1986), 1987 AIR (Delhi 13).

348. It also suggests that contracting for the future publication of the work is acceptable under the Code.

349. 2008 Civil Code, *supra* note 259, art. 1269, provides that, in the case of still unpublished works, the author must compensate "a person who has the exclusive right to the product or who has the right to use the product." If the work has been published, the author is liable for damages resulting from his decision to withdraw.

350. *Id.*, art. 1267(2).

name, and inviolability. According to Article 1267, the author's moral rights in a work that has fallen into the public domain may be asserted by "other interested persons." Finally, according to Article 1260, it should be noted that translations, compilations, or derivative works must be created while respecting the rights of the original author.

As in the earlier legislation, copyright is extended to oral works, but the provision later specifies that works of folklore shall not be protected by copyright where the authorship of the folkloric creation is indeterminate.[351]

iii. Moral Rights vs. Exclusive Rights

The terminology of "exclusive" rights is worth closer consideration. Russian authors enjoyed "exclusive" rights in their work from the time of the landmark Russian Copyright Act of 1911; when the term was eliminated from the reformed Soviet Civil Code provisions dealing with copyright in 1961, the change of wording dealt a blow to the legal status of authors' rights.[352] "Exclusivity" in the 1993 Copyright Act refers only to the economic rights of authors and owners, but there is no reason to think that an inferior status for moral rights is implied. Rather, given the history of the term in Russian copyright law, the association between exclusivity and economic rights is of long standing. The use of the term in the current Civil Code is perhaps a way of distinguishing between rights that are vested in the author and those that can be controlled by owners. In this sense, the terminology is quite effective. It captures the nature of copyright prerogatives in a way that achieves an effective distinction between the qualities of authorship and the rights of ownership.

iv. Moral Rights and Technology

The Civil Code provisions offer the most detailed treatment of technological issues in any Russian law, to date. In fact, the Civil Code consolidates the treatment of technology in the Russian Copyright Act of 1993 and related legislation, such as the 1992 Law on Computer Programs and Databases. The Civil Code includes explicit recognition of computer programs and databases as copyright works, in whatever language they are expressed, and on par with literary works.[353] The Code implicitly provides for moral rights in computer programs and databases, but certain restrictions apply. Notably, the right of withdrawal, already limited for non-technological works, does not apply to

---

351. *Id.*, art. 1259(6) (3).

352. Sundara Rajan, *Copyright and Creative Freedom*, *supra* note 4, at Chapter V, "Revolution and Reform," 98.

353. *See* 2008 Civil Code, *supra* note 259, art. 1259 (computer programs and databases protected as literary works).

computer programs or databases, to "complex objects," which would include film, or to employment scenarios.[354]

It is worth noting the circumstances in which the free reproduction of computer programs and databases is allowed: this right is extended even to enable the completion of computer programs, and cannot therefore be considered a violation of the right of integrity.[355] Alterations made in the interest of improving the program's functioning or correcting errors are permitted, as is copying for the purposes of making an archive or a replacement. The decompilation of programs is also tolerated, but only with a view to making possible, or improving, the functioning of software, and not "for the performance of any . . . act prejudicial to copyright." This provision closely resembles India's approach to the same issue. It is worth noting that India has faced considerable criticism from the United States over its treatment of software, and will probably be amending its Copyright Act to remove the allowance for decompilation within the next year or two.[356]

v. Fair Use and Parody

Provisions on fair use, as in the Law on Copyright of 1993, are extensive, and they parallel the approach of Western laws.[357] Special protection is offered to the creators of works of parody, whose works will not constitute violations of the author's moral rights or, indeed, of his "exclusive," economic rights.[358] The creator of a parody is under no obligation to compensate the author for his "use" of the original work.[359] However, the Civil Code provisions offer a contrast to Western law by providing for the possibility of compulsory licensing.[360] The idea is not unusual by international standards, however, as it reflects similar provisions in developing countries, and it provides for courts, rather than the government, to exercise their judgment about the conditions of the license.

---

354. *Id.*, art. 1269.

355. *Id.*, art. 1280.

356. The current round of copyright reform came as a surprise, with the Indian government introducing a so-called "secret bill" in December of 2009. The bill, Bill No. XXIV of 2010, is now *available at* http://prsindia.org/uploads/media/Copyright%20Act/Copyright%20Bill%-202010.pdf (last visited Apr. 28, 2010). For helpful coverage of the current amendment process and other Indian intellectual property issues, see the *Spicy IP* blog http://spicyipindia.blogspot.com/2010/04/copyright-amendment-bill.html (last visited Apr. 28, 2010).

357. *See* the list of permitted "free uses" in arts. 1273, 1274, 1275, 1276, 1277, 1278, 1279, 1280.

358. 2008 Civil Code, *supra* note 259, art. 1274(3).

359. *Id.*, art. 1274(3).

360. *See id.*, arts. 1238 and 1239.

vi. Visual Art

The provisions of the Civil Code include special treatment for works of visual art. Article 1291 distinguishes between the physical possession of an original work and the ownership of its copyright. The purpose of the right may be to allow artists to control the making of reproductions; the following article provides for artists to enjoy a right of access to their work for the purpose of reproducing it.[361] But the effect of the provision in Article 1291 is to emphasize the effective inalienability of copyright as a whole, drawing attention, once again, to the fact that physical possession of a work is not the same thing as owning its copyright.

In addition to the moral rights identified in the Code, Article 1293 of the Russian law also codifies the visual artist's *droit de suite*, or right to a resale royalty. The Russian *droit de suite* shows its kinship to moral rights in the fact of its inalienability. With the exception of a transfer to the author's legal heirs, the artist's resale right cannot be transferred to anyone while copyright in the work subsists. Unlike true moral rights, which are perpetual in Russian law, the artist's resale rights last for the duration of the exclusive right—the lifetime of the author plus seventy years.[362]

d. Neighboring Rights

Like corresponding provisions in the 1993 Copyright Act, Chapter 71 of the Civil Code on "copyright neighboring rights" consists of various provisions that create comprehensive rights for performers, the makers of sound recordings, and broadcasting and cable distribution agencies.[363] In addition to providing standard protection for neighboring rights, this Chapter also offers recognition for the moral rights of performers.

The Code provides for performers' moral rights of name and integrity, on the same terms on which they are enjoyed by authors.[364] Article 1315 protects the performer's right of attribution—his name or pseudonym must be associated with the performance—as well as his right to protect the performance against "distortion" when it is recorded, reproduced, or broadcast. It is not clear whether the Russian provisions, like the WIPO Performances and Phonograms Treaty, exclude protection for performers' moral rights in audiovisual recordings. An important provision is made by Article 1316(2), which specifies that the performer has a right to designate a person who will be responsible for performers' moral rights after his or her death.

---

361. *Id.*, art. 1292. This article also allows "demonstration" of a work without the artist's consent, and without the payment of a commission to him.
362. *Id.*, art. 1293(3).
363. *Id.*, ch. 71.
364. *Id.*, arts. 1315 & 1316.

e. Patents

Interestingly, the 2008 Civil Code includes an unusual moral right in patents. In Chapter 72, Article 1418 protects the "right of authorship" of plant or animal breeders. Article 1419 allows that the author of the new variety can "determine . . . its denomination," subject to statutory requirements and the approval of the federal agency for the protection of new plant and animal varieties.

6. Continuing Improvements to Moral Rights in Russia

While the Copyright Act of 1993 left something to be desired in the protection of authors' personal interests, the moral rights provisions of the Civil Code have set a significantly higher standard of protection. The new law is strongly oriented towards creative authorship and the protection of culture. Its provisions on moral rights reflect concerns about the status of authors and their work in a society that has long suffered the consequences of political oppression. At the same time, it recognizes that moral rights have a contribution to make to the protection and preservation of cultural heritage, and the reach of moral rights is not limited to the protection of individual authors and works. By ensuring that someone will be entrusted with the protection of moral rights in public domain works—an author's legatee, his heirs, or, eventually, any "interested person"—Russian reformers have made a laudable attempt to realize their cultural and democratic potential.

Despite the generally positive picture of moral rights that emerges from the Civil Code, a number of questions remained unanswered. For example, Article 1248 of the Civil Code provides that "a court" shall deal with copyright claims, including the assertion of moral rights. However, Russia's court system is complex, and it is not immediately apparent which forum will be most appropriate for dealing with authors' moral rights. Copyright matters are usually dealt with in the *arbitrazh* courts, the branch of the Russian judicial system concerned with copyright matters. It is true that moral rights have important commercial implications; nevertheless, their main purpose is personal and noncommercial, and commercial courts may therefore not be the best forum for adjudication. If not, who should make decisions on moral rights? Would a specialist tribunal dealing with intellectual property rights—such as the Supreme Patent Chamber, for example—be the ideal forum? Or would the Constitutional Court, which should be building expertise on the protection of individual rights, ultimately be more suited to dealing with authors' personal interests?

The role of government in copyright matters is also far from clear. Both the Copyright Act of 1993 and the Civil Code make provision for the active involvement of government agencies in protecting authors' moral rights. But how will it be possible to entrust the Russian government with the protection of authors' rights when it has been the main instrument of their oppression in the past? A similar question arises in relation to the role of writers' or artists' unions in Russia's new copyright system. How can the collective administration of rights be made into a viable proposition in a country where the writers' union was essentially a tool of government oppression, rather than an authentic mouthpiece for writers' needs?[365]

Another area of concern is the question of how moral rights relate to technology. The Civil Code, like the Copyright Act before it, allows moral rights in computer programs and databases. When is the right of integrity in a computer program infringed? When can the author claim a right of attribution? For example, if an author produces a computer program and this work is used by insurance companies to collect personal data about health-related matters, can the author object that the use is against his principles, and therefore, violates his honor and his right to the integrity of his work? Previous Russian tradition recognized a moral right related to the use of a work, but this concept now seems to have been purged from Russian law.

The application of moral rights raises serious concerns about the ability of information technology to develop, and to be used to its full potential. For this reason, India, with its dynamic information technology industry, imposes certain limits on the availability of moral rights for computer programs.[366] What are Russia's interests in relation to information technology, and how does its approach to moral rights support them?

A number of questions concerning moral rights also arise in relation to works of art whose creation has been made possible by technology. For example, in a computer-generated artwork, where the only creative activity of the author is to write the computer program, should the complete range of moral rights be available? What happens in the case of a multimedia work that is composed of images, sound, and text from a variety of sources which have now been compiled and reworked in an innovative way through digital technology? To what extent should attribution and integrity in relation to the original works be preserved? For artists and creative people, the question of how digital technology will affect their creative potential is the key to their future in the Digital Age. Yet questions like these are not addressed in the Russian Civil Code provisions on moral rights.

---

365. An interesting perspective on this issue arose in the *Russian Kurier* case, *supra* note 117. The Russian journalists' union was unable, or perhaps unwilling, to provide the New York appeals court with a list of its members, making it impossible for the court to grant it standing to sue on their behalf.

366. Pravin Anand suggests that the idea was developed in *Statart Software Pvt Ltd. v. Karan Khanna, cited in* Pravin. Anand, *The Concept of Moral Rights under Indian Copyright Law*, 27 COPYRIGHT WORLD 35, 35–36 (1993), and later, became the subject of a legislative amendment. *See* The Copyright (Second Amendment) Bill, 1994, Bill No. 105C of 1992, Parliament of India, *available at* http://parliamentofindia.nic.in/ls/bills/1994/1994-31.htm (last visited Apr. 28, 2010).

7. A New Moral Right in Russian Law: The Renewal of Copyright Terms for Rehabilitated Authors[367]

In Russia, the importance of moral rights is immediately apparent in two features of the copyright law. The first is the prominent place of moral rights in the copyright legislation. Russian moral rights in the 1991 Fundamentals of Civil Legislation[368] gave explicit protection to a great variety of interests, including new rights not featured in previous Russian law or in the Berne Convention, and framed in expansive language. The rights were scaled back in the Copyright Act of 1993, introduced after the collapse of the Soviet Union in 1991; but the Copyright Act simultaneously continued to recognize certain rights which may not be traditionally classified as moral rights themselves, but support moral rights in a broader sense. This broad preoccupation with the ethics of copyright continues to characterize the latest provisions in Part IV of Russia's Civil Code. In this context, a second feature of Russian copyright law should be noted: the attempts of Russian copyright law in the post-socialist era to redress the injustices of the past.

It is well-known that the Soviet government had a policy of bringing calumny on authors and artists who fell afoul of its policies. To offer but one well-known example, the life of the composer, Shostakovich, was a microcosm of the general situation in one individual case: over his lifetime he endured unimaginable ups and downs in his official reputation, due to the direct intervention of Stalin.[369] Accordingly, post-Soviet law, from the transitional Fundamentals of 1991 to the present Civil Code, has always included provisions for the "rehabilitation" of authors.[370]

Rehabilitation was not only a matter of official apologies and recognition; there was also a copyright dimension. In the case of authors who had been victimized by the state and were posthumously rehabilitated, the term of copyright protection in their works would run anew from the time of rehabilitation.[371] This amounts to an extension of copyright term for humanitarian

---

367. 2008 Civil Code, *supra* note 258, art. 1281(4).
368. Fundamentals of Civil Legislation of the USSR and the Republics, ch. IV, *Copyright, VSND i VS SSSR*, 1991, No. 26, Item 773 (invalidated by Resolution of the Supreme Soviet of the Russian Federation No. 5352-1 of July 9, 1993) [1991 Fundamentals].
369. *See* Fitzpatrick, supra note 268, at 183-215. Fitzpatrick offers an analysis of his situation within the broader context of government control, manipulation, and repression of the musical world. She concludes her discussion by noting that "his disgrace on each occasion proved temporary and his status as an acknowledged 'great Soviet composer' survived these debacles."
370. 2008 Civil Code, *supra* note 258, art. 1281(4).
371. *See* 1993 Copyright Act, *supra* note 258, art. 27(5): "Copyright in a posthumous work shall have effect for 50 years following the publication of the work. If the author has been rehabilitated posthumously after having been the subject of repressive measures, the period of

reasons: it effectively allows the term of copyright protection after an author's death to be reinstated for rehabilitated authors.

There is still a slight issue of prejudice in distinguishing between those who were rehabilitated posthumously and those who were rehabilitated during their lifetimes. The point is illustrated by the case of Andrei Siniavsky and Yuli Daniel, two writers who were prosecuted for their writings by the Soviet Union in a notorious "show trial" of the 1960s.[372] Siniavsky lived to see their rehabilitation in 1991, but Daniel died in 1988. Siniavsky himself died in 1997, six years after his official rehabilitation. Accordingly, the Russian provision on the extension of copyright for rehabilitated authors would apply to Daniel, but not to Siniavksy. In effect, Siniavsky's copyright would endure for 50 years after his death in 1997; but Daniel's would endure for 53 years after his death in 1988. Is the extra duration a form of compensation for the especially egregious wrong of allowing a man or woman to die before the restoration of his or her name? If so, the families of these authors received a benefit through prolonged copyright protection in honor of their ancestors.

The fact that the provision is limited to cases of "posthumous" rehabilitation may be a simple recognition of the tragedy that most authors and artists did not live to see it occur: the persecution of writers in the Stalinist period occurred decades before the end of the Soviet regime was in sight. But, in the interest of fairness, the Russian government probably should have framed the provision to include both posthumous rehabilitation and the rehabilitation of living authors. Otherwise, the provision reads faintly like a penalty: if you enjoyed any of your copyright without persecution during your lifetime, you would forfeit any possible extension of copyright term.

The extension of copyright term in the case of posthumous rehabilitation, though not a moral right itself, certainly has the flavor of a moral right. At least three interpretations seem possible. Is it a new aspect of the right of integrity, to the effect that an author is entitled to enjoy copyright protection provided by law without inhumane interference? Indeed, as noted below, the Russian Copyright Act of 1993 recognized a right of reputation even in preference to the usual formula represented by the Berne Convention, where reputation and integrity are linked. In the Russian Act, the reputation

---

protection of rights under this Article shall begin on January 1 of the year following that of the said rehabilitation."

In keeping with general improvements to the term of copyright protection under Russian law, the current provision is for life of the author plus seventy years: 2008 Civil Code, *supra* note 258, art. 1281(3).

"If the author worked during the Great Patriotic War or took part in that War, the period of protection of rights under this Article shall be prolonged by four years." 2008 Civil Code, *supra* note 258, art. 1281(5), continues this traditional extension. The 1960s "show trial" of Andrei Siniavsky and Yuli Daniel comes to mind.

372. *See* Sundara Rajan, *Copyright and Creative Freedom*, *supra* note 4, at 133 and Chapter VI, "Creative Freedom on Trial," 123–49.

right was simply an author's right to protect oneself from damage to one's reputation.[373] Alternatively, is it a new dimension of disclosure? The idea that an author should not be forced to disclose his works in an environment of abuse seems apt, since publication in such a context would be damaging, rather than beneficial, to the author's career. Finally, it could also represent a response to an implicit right against excessive or unreasonable criticism. In this case, because the criticism is propagated by the state and the state is also responsible for copyright protection, the remedy seems most appropriate.

8. Conclusion

The evolution of moral rights in Russian legislation shows increasing reliance on Russian legal tradition, which is generally preferred to international law in the Civil Code provisions on moral rights. The influence of the Berne Convention in Russia has actually translated into a scaling back of Russian protection for moral rights, reflected in the Copyright Act of 1993. It meant fundamental readjustments to the Russian concept of moral rights, particularly in relation to the right of integrity. Known as the right of "inviolability" since 1961, the right of integrity was finally implemented into the 1993 Act in a modified form that converted it into a simple right of reputation. The 2008 Civil Code has now re-instated the Russian right and the associated terminology of "inviolability".

The history behind this situation reflects an interesting experience of translating international norms into domestic laws. Golovanov suggests that this interpretation of the integrity right reflected "an incorrect translation of Art. 6bis of the Berne Convention." He points out that Professor Gavrilov, a senior expert on Russian copyright, has argued for the right of adaptation as the true legal mechanism for the protection of the integrity of a work in Russia. Golovanov points out that the right of adaptation has been amended in Article 1266 of the new Code to prevent any modifications to a work that would violate the author's wishes or ideas. However, it is difficult to agree with Golovanov's hope that the adaptation right could compensate for a shift from integrity to reputation. The problem is not only that adaptation is fundamentally an economic right, now defined with moral dimensions in the new Civil Code. Rather, any change to a work would also have to meet the definition of adaptation to qualify as a violation of moral rights. The rule is reminiscent of the American approach, which, in the Monty Python case, converted an edited version of the work into an unauthorized adaptation in

---

373. Russian Copyright Act 1993, *supra* note 258, art. 15(1).

order to establish that the edited version violated the authors' copyright.[374] This was not a finding that the moral right of integrity had been violated, but it offered a solution to the moral rights problem in American law.[375]

In the Russian Civil Code, key elements of a post-socialist approach remain intact. The Russian law recognizes both traditional moral rights and new rights with moral dimensions, such as the special rights of rehabilitated authors. It gives precedence to the protection of moral rights over economic rights, in the sense that it requires the protection of moral rights in almost every circumstance of individual authorship, and even extends these requirements into the public domain where economic rights have completely expired. Russian law is also in the vanguard of technological change, recognizing moral rights in software and scientific inventions. Its very emphasis on the concept of disclosure has powerful technological resonance—disclosure, whether moral or economic, is a key concept for the copyright law of the Digital Age. In practical terms, disclosure may be the one act which remains unequivocally within an author's control in an environment of digital technology.

E. Conclusion: The Modern Doctrine

In both space and time, moral rights have traveled a great distance from their origins in Continental Europe. The rights have spread around the globe to diverse countries, representing an immense variety of legal traditions and cultures. In this process of global migration, moral rights have themselves been transformed.

In their original form, moral rights were an individual right of the author. In French law, they were a form of recognition for the author's creative powers, while German jurisprudence emphasized respect for the personality of the author. In both of these traditions, moral rights were independent of all other rights, including economic rights in a work. They were inalienable, and could not be waived. The duration of moral rights was at least equivalent to the duration of economic rights in a work, as in the German system, but the rights could also last forever, as in France.

The spread of moral rights to new jurisdictions has led to a startling variety of new interpretations of the doctrine. The basic principles of independence and inalienability have been universally maintained. However, moral rights

---

374. *Gilliam, supra* note 105.

375. The Canadian case of *Théberge* presents the reverse scenario: a moral rights concern claimed as a violation of economic rights failed because of the additional standard of proof required for moral rights, which, the majority of the Canadian Supreme Court said, should not have been evaded by the plaintiff. *Théberge, supra* note 22.

in the common law countries show relaxation of the theory in various ways. Waivers of moral rights are possible in some circumstances.[376] Different approaches to duration have been explored. An extreme insistence on the separation of economic and moral rights in Canada seems to imply that the same set of facts probably cannot lead to litigation on both grounds: one set of rights must be preferred.[377] The possibility of protecting moral rights through tort law is one that American lawyers, in particular, are interested in exploring. Among other things, this approach implies that protection for moral rights will be limited to the lifetime of the author. Common-law countries have also considered the applicability of practical formalities to the enjoyment of moral rights, including the controversial UK and New Zealand requirement that the moral right of attribution must be asserted. The proposed Australian bill on an "indigenous communal moral right" would have established moral rights in works of indigenous culture, but it also imposed certain formalities on the enjoyment of this special right.

The recognition of moral rights in developing and post-socialist jurisdictions has raised interesting possibilities for their expansion. Moral rights are said to exist in cultural heritage; they can also help to address the problems of political repression, to protect an author's reputation from destruction, and to compensate an author for the abuse of his reputation. These countries, follow more traditional moral rights jurisdictions like France, by recognizing moral rights in works of new technology such as computer programs and film—although questions surround the management of the complex relationships between the different personalities involved in the making of a film. The general trend is to exclude at least some aspects of moral rights where employment situations arise, as is often the case in relation to computer programs. The special case of Japan seems to have generated new principles in its own right: a moral right for companies, restoration of the status quo as a principle guiding compensation, and moral rights that may be time-limited in name, but perpetual in practice.

The near-universal recognition of moral rights is convincing proof of their relevance to diverse countries and cultures. They are not limited by the contours of European Romanticism. Similarly, the willingness to explore and extend the doctrine of moral rights in "new" jurisdictions is convincing evidence of its flexibility and malleability—its potential for growth. This feature of moral rights is a key element in determining whether or not the rights hold any true relevance for the digital environment.

In addressing this fundamentally important question, a distinction should also be drawn between the suppleness of moral rights doctrine and the

---

376. But note that waivers are also permitted, under limited circumstances in German law. *See* the discussion in Chapter 2, "Moral Rights: History of an Idea," *infra*, notes 148–159 and accompanying text.

377. *Théberge, supra* note 22.

relative rigidity of copyright norms. In relation to all of the different policies that moral rights have helped to serve—the protection of individual rights, the preservation of cultural heritage, the recognition of oppressed cultures, the accommodation of technological creativity, and the validation of human rights—the doctrine has proven to be an instrument, at once subtle and powerful, for the achievement of social goals.

This analysis of moral rights in a number of the world's major jurisdictions shows beyond doubt that the doctrine of moral rights will continue to be both relevant and valuable in an environment of new technology. It has demonstrated its ability to adjust to new realities. The moral right of the Digital Age will draw upon the many strands of theory and practice that have proven themselves in different parts of the world. It is also certain that moral rights will expand and adjust in new ways, subjecting them to transformation yet again in the digital context.

The current international climate is one of skepticism about rights in the intangible—information, knowledge, culture. This mood has been generated by the politics behind law-making. Powerful corporations in the copyright industries are grasping at copyright law in the hope that the enforcement of long-established copyright principles will help them to survive the radical transformation of their world. The strategic mistake, natural as it is, has been to look beyond survival and seek a simultaneous expansion of rights and privileges through the exploitation of copyright laws. Moral rights are not part of the stakes in this political game. They should not be left open to manipulation in order to serve the needs of industry.[378]

Indeed, moral rights have little to do with the economics of the copyright *per se*: their implications for commerce, even where significant, are little more than an inadvertent side-effect of protecting non-economic concerns.[379] In all their permutations, global and historical, moral rights remain personal and cultural rights. Their purpose is to recognize and protect authorship and, through it, cultural heritage. Whether that heritage offers itself in the form of paintings or poems, ancient bronzes or computer programs, is of little importance. If it is worth protecting, as shown by the experience of moral rights around the globe, moral rights can probably adapt to embrace this new need.

---

378. The circumstances in which the WPPT was adopted suggest that the American music industry saw moral rights as one more layer of copyright protection which could help record companies to regain control over the dissemination of music. This outcome is certainly one of the possible results of introducing a moral right for performers, but it depends entirely on the approach of performers to their own moral rights. Record companies cannot exercise moral rights on behalf of performers, and should not be allowed to do so.

379. See Henry Hansmann & Marina Santilli, *Authors' and Artists' Moral Rights: A Comparative Legal and Economic Analysis*, 26 J. LEGAL STUD. 95 (1997), for a discussion of moral rights from an economic perspective.

The role of moral rights in the protection of culture may vary greatly according to social context. The protection offered by moral rights may be comprehensive or narrow—moral rights can fulfill some objectives better than others, and their contribution must be guaged accordingly. But there can be no doubt that moral rights have grown into a global instrument of cultural policy to contend with. The moral right of the author is nothing less than the human face of copyright law. Like the human author herself, it is here to stay.

CHAPTER

4

Moral Rights in the International Copyright Regime

In an era when international forces seem to dominate every aspect of copyright law, moral rights stand apart. Their position is a strange one. The global system for copyright protection defines the environment for moral rights, but the results are strikingly ambiguous. The web of international copyright agreements somehow enmeshes moral rights without quite ensnaring them. From the perspective of copyright policy, their status as partial rights within the international system is at once a strength to be exploited, and a weakness to overcome.

A. The International Copyright Regime: An Overview

By an interesting irony, modern copyright law is largely a product of international agreements. When we consider the long and distinguished tradition, in the common law world, of celebrating copyright as "purely statutory" law, the irony is striking. Copyright originates with national law-making bodies; the rights that fall under this rubric are derived from national copyright laws, and copyright's reach remains confined within national borders. If international agreements have now become a primary source of copyright rules, the continued supremacy of domestic statutes, and their sovereignty over domestic matters in the area of copyright, is far from assured.

The conflict is potentially intense. The need for international norms and practices regarding copyright is clear, as copyright-protected material moves across international borders with ever-greater ease. Without measures for addressing the international movement of works, the very notion of copyright protection seems meaningless.

However, the broad social impact of copyright in a technological environment is undeniable. Copyright law is an important and growing part of national policy affecting such sensitive areas as culture and economic development. At times, control of copyright policy seems synonymous with cultural sovereignty, which, most countries would argue, can hardly be entrusted to the international community.

The peculiar quality of the tinder feeds this flame. In themselves, international copyright agreements are nothing new—the *Berne Convention for the Protection of Literary and Artistic Works* dates from 1886[1]—but the power that they have acquired over the past decade is unprecedented. Moreover, the

---

1. Berne Convention for the Protection of Literary and Artistic Works (adopted Sept. 9, 1886), 1161 U.N.T.S. 3, *available at* http://www.wipo.int/treaties/en/ip/berne/trtdocs_wo001.html (last visited Apr. 26, 2010); also available in a useful format at the Legal Information Institute, Cornell University Law School at http://www.law.cornell.edu/treaties/berne/overview.html (last visited Apr. 26, 2010) [Berne Convention].

nature of the accords has changed. A system that was once based on "consensus," however flawed and unsatisfactory it may have been, has now moved overtly towards "coercion."[2]

This metamorphosis of values is clearly apparent in the movement of international copyright law from the public law arena to what has come to be known as "private" international law.[3] A glance at the old and new leading documents of international copyright law confirms the transition. "Soft" law, based on consensus and not enforced through any practical method of coercion, has been transformed into the economic law of world trade, enforced through the availability of powerful trade sanctions against offenders.[4]

The Berne Convention was a classic instrument of public international law. Administered by the United Nations, it represented a negotiated approach, at times more successful than others, to international copyright norms.[5] The copyright rules in the Berne Convention represent minimum standards to which all member countries are expected to conform. Their effectiveness in doing so, however, depends on the priority given to copyright in each jurisdiction. Indeed, the Convention is clear in allowing member countries to undertake measures for the legislative enactment of Berne principles, and to facilitate their practical interpretation and enforcement in accordance with national approaches. Talk of the "enforceability" of Berne provisions would probably have been considered un-neighborly. No doubt, disagreements and conflicts were common, even characteristic, of the Berne Union.[6] But the system, at least nominally, was built on consensus.

---

2. *See* Martine de Koning, *Why the Coercion-Based GATT Approach Is Not the Only Answer to International Piracy in the Asia-Pacific Region*, 19(2) Eur. Intell. Prop. Rev. 59, especially 59–61 (1997).

3. *See* Graeme B. Dinwoodie, *Developing a Private International Intellectual Property Law: The Demise of Territoriality? The Boundaries of Intellectual Property Symposium: Crossing Boundaries*, 51 Wm. & Mary L. Rev. 711, 716–65 (2010). *See also* Rochelle C. Dreyfuss, *The ALI Principles on Transnational Intellectual Property Disputes: Why Invite Conflicts?*, 30 Brook. Int'l L.J. 819 (2005).

4. On the classic problem of "enforceability" in public international law, see Elena Katselli Proukaki, The Problem of Enforcement in International Law: Countermeasures, the Non-Injured State and the Idea of International Community (Routledge Research in International Law Series, Routledge 2009).

5. Administration of the international copyright framework was initially entrusted to the United International Bureaux for the Protection of Intellectual Property (BIRPI). In 1967, as part of the Stockholm revision conference program, the functions of BIRPI were taken over by the newly established World Intellectual Property Organization (WIPO), a specialist agency of the United Nations. WIPO arguably remains the most important international focus of knowledge and information about international copyright matters. *See* Sam Ricketson, The Berne Convention for the Protection of Literary and Artistic Works: 1886–1986, paras. 3.50–3.52, 3.65 (Centre for Commercial Law Studies, Queen Mary College, Kluwer 1987) [Ricketson, *The Berne Convention*].

6. *See* Ricketson's discussion of the Berne revision conferences and, in particular, his notes on the Stockholm revision conference of 1967: Ricketson, *The Berne Convention*, *supra* note 5, paras. 3.49–3.65, especially para. 3.64 on the role of developing countries.

Consensus may be desirable, but it often requires great patience. The ability of developing countries to block changes to the Berne Convention through the United Nations system of bloc-voting was one of the practical reasons why, by the mid-1980s, the creation of a new intellectual property system was thought to be desirable. Naturally, the initiative came from technologically advanced countries, with the United States assuming a leadership role.[7]

With the creation of the World Trade Organization, the international copyright regime experienced a fundamental shift. As one of its founding agreements, the WTO adopted an Agreement on Trade-Related Aspects of Intellectual Property Rights, known as TRIPs,[8] and made disputes on intellectual property matters subjects to the general dispute-settlement mechanism of the WTO.[9] The brilliance of the TRIPs concept should not be understated. Rather than attempt to develop new copyright standards, negotiators preferred to retain the copyright principles in Berne, which embodied the experience of more than a century. TRIPs ultimately achieved this by the simple and straightforward means of incorporating the Berne Convention into itself.

The truly innovative character of TRIPs lay, instead, in its practical approach to the norms found in Berne. Through TRIPs, "soft" law—international conventions that are typically criticized as "unenforceable"—was transformed into "hard" law. And how truly "hard:" the provisions of TRIPs were available for enforcement in a novel way, by the powerful deterrent of economic penalties.[10] Membership in the WTO meant that member countries would have to achieve the levels and kinds of intellectual property protection described in TRIPs. Failure to do so could lead directly to economic sanctions—trade penalties which could be ordered by the dispute-settlement panel hearing the case. The past decade has shown the "enforcement"

---

7. *See, generally* the contemporaneous account in INTELLECTUAL PROPERTY RIGHTS: GLOBAL CONSENSUS, GLOBAL CONFLICT? (T. J. Richards & R. M. Gadbaw eds., Westview Press 1988).

8. Agreement on Trade-Related Aspects of Intellectual Property Rights (opened for signature Apr. 15, 1994, entered into force Jan. 1, 1995), Annex 1C to the Marrakesh Agreement Establishing the World Trade Organization, 1869 U.N.T.S. 299; 33 I.L.M. 1197 (1994), *available at* http://www.wto.org/english/docs_e/legal_e/27-trips_01_e.htm (last visited Apr. 29, 2010) [TRIPs Agreement].

9. Understanding on Rules and Procedures Governing the Settlement of Disputes, Annex 2 to the Marrakesh Agreement Establishing the World Trade Organization, *id., available at* http://www.wto.org/english/docs_e/legal_e/28-dsu_e.htm (last visited Apr. 29, 2010) [DSU].

10. The combination of intellectual property with dispute settlement has been called one of the two most significant achievements of the WTO. The importance of this "linkage" was already apparent in the early days of the Agreement. *See* Rochelle Cooper Dreyfuss & Andreas F. Lowenfeld, *Two Achievements of the Uruguay Round: Putting TRIPs and Dispute Settlement Together*, 37 VA. J. INT'L L. 275, 277 (1997).

mechanism of the WTO to be strong, effective, and sought after by the member states.[11]

Notwithstanding its coercive character, distasteful to many at first glance, it is difficult to condemn the TRIPs Agreement outright. Indeed, even developing countries, whose complaints against TRIPs would be well-justified, have preferred to join the system and work for change within its parameters, with some success.[12]

The Agreement cannot be evaluated in black and white terms. Clearly, it represents a landmark in copyright regulation; it has succeeded in achieving what the Berne Convention could not, establishing recognized minimum standards for copyright protection throughout the world. In this sense, the TRIPs system could be considered a successful attempt at harmonizing international copyright norms. But the term "harmonization" should be used with care: it misrepresents what international copyright rules actually achieve. Harmony evokes consensus, yet the TRIPs Agreement represents standardization that was achieved in non-consensual circumstances.[13] A better way to characterize TRIPs might be to say that it represents, not the harmonization of laws, so much as an effective force for "internationalization" in this area of the law.[14]

At the same time, the very strengths of the TRIPs system—the power to coerce, and its grandiose, all-inclusive reach—are also its weaknesses. Ironically, the Agreement, which was a product of the impatience of advanced countries about the ability of copyright practices to keep pace with

---

11. The WTO dispute-settlement website is constantly updated, and bears witness to the vigor of the dispute-settlement process. Especially useful is the "map" of disputes, which graphically displays the engagement of each country with the dispute-settlement mechanism. For example, a map of U.S. involvement at the WTO can be found at http://www.wto.org/english/tratop_e/dispu_e/dispu_maps_e.htm?country_selected=USA&sense=e. Interestingly, the map shows that developing countries use the system extensively, and against both developed and developing countries. This situation has developed in spite of an inauspicious beginning; the first-ever case under TRIPs was a complaint brought by the United States against India's pharmaceutical patent provisions, now amended. See the information page on Dispute DS50, at http://www.wto.org/english/tratop_e/dispu_e/cases_e/ds50_e.htm (last visited July 17, 2010).

12. The Doha declaration represents one of the most highly publicized efforts of developing countries to reframe the TRIPs Agreement with their concerns in mind. In particular, the issue of making HIV drugs available in Africa has been a rallying cry. *See* the comprehensive discussion in Frederik M. Abbott, *The Doha Declaration on the Trips Agreement and Public Health: Lighting a Dark Corner at the WTO*, J. INT'L ECON. L. 469 (2002). *Also see* the WTO website, the Doha Declaration Explained, at http://www.wto.org/english/tratop_e/dda_e/dohaexplained_e.htm (last visited Apr. 29, 2010).

13. For an exploration of the musical analogy underlying legal "harmonization," see Mira T. Sundara Rajan, COPYRIGHT AND CREATIVE FREEDOM: A STUDY OF POST-SOCIALIST LAW REFORM 10–11 and accompanying notes (Routledge 2006) [Sundara Rajan, *Copyright and Creative Freedom*].

14. *Id.*, at 7–16.

technological growth, had effectively become obsolete by the time of its adoption in 1994. WIPO stepped in to address this gap, issuing its two Internet treaties in 1996, and in the process, reinventing itself as the leading world forum for digital copyright issues.[15] The WIPO Internet Treaties now represent the benchmark for copyright protection in a digital environment. These Treaties, and not TRIPs, are the defining copyright agreements of the Digital Age. The importance of TRIPs, lies, rather, in its refashioning of intellectual property rights into norms of international trade.

Given their benchmark status, the perspective on digital issues in the WIPO Treaties is highly controversial. WIPO's perspective lends aggressive support to the existing, pre-digital framework of copyright law. The main treaty of the two, the WIPO Copyright Treaty, advocates the enlargement of copyright's umbrella to cover all of the new ways known, so far, of obtaining and using copyright works in a digital environment.[16] However quietly they may be framed, the aims of the WIPO Treaties are radical: to make private what was once public, and to restrict what has always been free within the very terms of modern copyright law.[17]

---

15. WIPO Copyright Treaty (adopted Dec. 20, 1996, entered into force Mar. 6, 2002) (1997), 36 I.L.M. 65 [WCT], http://www.wipo.int/treaties/en/ip/wct/trtdocs_wo033.html (last visited Apr. 29, 2010); WIPO Performances and Phonograms Treaty (adopted Dec. 20, 1996, entered into force May 20, 2002) (1997) 36 I.L.M. 76, http://www.wipo.int/treaties/en/ip/berne/trt-docs_wo001.html (last visited Apr. 29, 2010) [WPPT].

16. *See, for example*, art. 8 of the WPPT, *supra* note 15, known as the "making available right." For an overview of art. 8, see Mira T. Sundara Rajan, Moral Rights and Copyright Harmonisation: Prospects for an "International Moral Right"?, at 6–7, paper presented to the 17th BILETA Annual Conference in 2002, available in draft form online at http://www.bileta. ac.uk/Document%20Library/1/Moral%20Rights%20and%20Copyright%20Harmonisation %20-%20Prospects%20for%20an%20%27International%20Moral%20Right%27.pdf (last visited Aug. 11, 2010). The article receives a detailed and authoritative analysis by Mihály Ficsor, The Law of Copyright and the Internet: The 1996 WIPO Treaties, their Interpretation and Implementation 493–510 (Oxford University Press 2002).

17. The language of the treaties is concise and relatively simple. While these are generally positive features, one of the unintended consequences may be that the implications of joining the treaty are not immediately apparent. Implementation has been a contentious issue in Canada, where at least two potential bills for implementation, Bills C-60 and C-61, have been thrown out by successive governments. Bill C-61 continues to be available on the Government of Canada website at http://www2.parl.gc.ca/HousePublications/Publication.aspx?Docid= 3570473&file=4 (last visited Apr. 28, 2010). For an interesting response to Bill C-60, see collection of essays by Canadian legal academics published in In the Public Interest: The Future of Canadian Copyright Law (Michael Geist ed., Irwin Law 2005); the essays are also available for free download under Creative Commons licenses at http://www.irwinlaw. com/store/product/120/in-the-public-interest? (last visited Apr. 28, 2010).

B. First Principles: International Copyright in Practice

In view of this global framework, international copyright law is clearly an unusual phenomenon. It is not law in the domestic sense of the term, because it is not governed by a law-making body, represents no specific jurisdiction, and commands no enforcement power beyond the economic mechanisms related to trade at the WTO. At the same time, it can be distinguished from other areas of public international law in its focus on specific rules and principles, and in the combination of economic and non-economic, public and private elements encompassed by copyright. In fact, international copyright law functions very much as a *sui generis* system, driven by rules and practices specific to its role. These can be summarized as three basic principles: minimum standards, national treatment, and, since the adoption of the TRIPs Agreement, most-favored-nation treatment.

1. Minimum Standards

The international copyright framework provided by the Berne Convention sets out the basic norms that must be respected by member countries of the Berne Union. But these norms are not comprehensive. Rather, the Berne Convention specifies the minimum standards of protection that must be observed. Any member country of Berne can choose to exceed these minimum standards by implementing a higher level of protection in its domestic copyright law.

A simple example lies in the question of copyright term. The Berne Convention establishes a minimum duration of copyright protection, for the lifetime of the author and fifty years after his death.[18] However, nothing in the Berne Convention precludes a country from increasing the term of copyright protection; and, indeed, Article 19, entitled "Protection Greater than Resulting from Convention," states:

> The provisions of this Convention shall not preclude the making of a claim to the benefit of any greater protection which may be granted by legislation in a country of the Union.

Many countries now exceed this minimum term of protection. The European Union has set a new benchmark for copyright term, life of the author plus seventy years after his death; India has a term of life plus sixty years, specially extended in 1992 to accommodate copyright in the works of

---

18. Berne Convention, art. 7.

Indian Nobel laureate in literature, Rabindranath Tagore.[19] Article 7.6 of the Berne Convention also makes specific provision for this general rule, stating that, "The countries of the Union may grant a term of protection in excess of those provided by the preceding paragraphs." The provision is not strictly necessary; it reinforces the general rule that countries can exceed Berne requirements, as noted above.[20] But duration of copyright is a slightly unusual issue, in that the Berne Convention also makes an exception to the principle of upward harmonization by legislating a "rule of the shorter term." This special rule allows the duration of copyright to be generally limited to the term of protection in the country of origin of the work.[21]

This system of minimum standards leads to certain practical consequences. Notably, it is clearly not a legal regime that promotes the standardization of copyright norms around the world. On the contrary, there is considerable scope for variation in the copyright practices specific to different countries. What Berne does provide is an assurance that no country will fail to guarantee the minimum levels of protection offered by the Convention. Accordingly, the protection enjoyed by authors will vary, in practice, depending on the

---

19. The Copyright (Amendment) Bill, 1992 (Bill No. 35-C of 1992) is available on the Parliament of India website at http://parliamentofindia.nic.in/ls/bills/1992/1992-06.htm (last visited Apr. 29, 2010). For a full explanation of the story behind the change, see KRISHAN ARORA, ed., The Copyright Act, 1957 (14 of 1957) along with The Copyright Rules, 1958 & International Copyright Order, 1999, Bare Act with Short Comments (Professional Book Publishers, New Delhi 2006), Amendment Act 13 of 1992, Statement of Objects and Reasons, at 4. It is ironic that copyright term was extended by ten years in order to prolong the copyright in Rabindranath Tagore's works—"in view of their national importance"—when the same reason was given for the early termination of Subramania Bharati's copyright in 1949.

20. *See* Ricketson, *supra* note 5, for a discussion of why this was done.

21. The provision is beautifully explained by Paul Edward Geller, *Zombie and Once-Dead Works: Copyright Retroactivity After the E.C. Term Directive*, 18(2) ENT. & SPORTS LAW. 7, 7–9 (2000). Geller points out that the nondiscrimination principle established by the 1993 *Phil Collins* decision at the European Court of Justice signifies that European Union member states can no longer apply the Berne rule of the shorter term and comply with EU requirements. *See* Phil Collins v. Imtrat Handelsgesellschaft mbH; Patricia Im-und Export Verwaltungsgesellschaft mbH and Another v. EMI Electrola GmbH, Joined Cases C-92/92 and C-326/92, *available at* http://eur-lex.europa.eu/smartapi/cgi/sga_doc?smartapi!celexplus!prod CELEXnumdoc&lg=en&numdoc=61992J0092 (last visited Apr. 29, 2010). *See also* Ricketson, *supra* note 5, para. 3.13, on the adoption of the minimum term of protection as life plus fifty years in the Brussels Act of 1948.

Article 7.8 of the Berne Convention, *supra* note 1, states: "In any case, the term shall be governed by the legislation of the country where protection is claimed; however, unless the legislation of that country otherwise provides, the term shall not exceed the term fixed in the country of origin of the work." *See also* art. 7.7: "Those countries of the Union bound by the Rome Act of this Convention which grant, in their national legislation in force at the time of signature of the present Act, shorter terms of protection than those provided for in the preceding paragraphs shall have the right to maintain such terms when ratifying or acceding to the present Act." Taken together, these two subsections limit the duration of protection to the term in the country of origin.

country where an infringement of copyright is asserted, and protection is claimed.

2. National Treatment

National treatment is a cornerstone of the Berne copyright system. Codified in Article 5.1 of the Berne Convention, national treatment simply means that an author who is a national of any Berne member country can expect to be treated on par with the nationals of the country where copyright protection is claimed.[22] For example, a Canadian author claiming infringement of her copyright in the United States will be treated in exactly the same way as any U.S. national where her copyright status is concerned.

In practice, the law of the country where infringement is claimed is usually applied to copyright cases. This represents a pragmatic approach to litigation, as it is likely to be the best way to ensure that the defendant can be brought to justice. This principle is also articulated in Article 5.2 of the Berne Convention, which states:

> The enjoyment and the exercise of these rights shall not be subject to any for-mality; such enjoyment and such exercise shall be independent of the existence of protection in the country of origin of the work. *Consequently, apart from the provisions of this Convention, the extent of protection, as well as the means of redress afforded to the author to protect his rights, shall be governed exclusively by the laws of the country where protection is claimed.*[23]

a. Practical Implications

It now becomes apparent that the combination of national treatment with the practice of minimum standards can create certain anomalies in practice. Let us take the exaggerated case of moral rights for an example.

With the exception of visual arts, U.S. law only provides for protection of moral rights through common law actions or, potentially, economic rights, which, it argues, is in conformity with Article 6*bis* of the Berne Convention. An American author who wants to claim the protection of his moral right of integrity under Article 6*bis* of the Berne Convention can, of course, make a claim under American law like any other American author—on the grounds

---

22. Article 5.1 of the Berne Convention, *supra* note 1, states: "Authors shall enjoy, in respect of works for which they are protected under this Convention, in countries of the Union other than the country of origin, the rights which their respective laws do now or may hereafter grant to their nationals, as well as the rights specially granted by this Convention."
23. Berne Convention, *supra* note 1, art. 23 (emphasis added).

that the modification of the work is sufficient to create an unauthorized adaptation, for example.[24] However, if the alleged infringement were to occur in France, an American author could claim the protection of his integrity right in a French court, where he would expect to be treated on par with any French national. By relying on moral rights provisions in French legislation, an American author could expect his right of integrity to be upheld by the French court. Yet this is more than he could expect in the United States. This situation arose in the case of *Huston*, where the broadcasting of colorized versions of films by the famed American director, John Huston, on French television was found to violate the moral rights of the director.[25] In the United States, however, the existing framework for moral rights was inadequate to protect film directors from colorization.[26]

The contrast between France and the United States is extreme; but similar situations can arise in relation to many aspects of moral rights. For example, Canada offers protection for the moral rights of attribution and integrity, but it does not protect an author's right to withdraw his work from circulation. French law does; and if a Canadian author were to ask a French court to withdraw his work from circulation in France, he would be legally entitled to have his claim upheld. Once again, the situation is anomalous in the sense that an author would enjoy more rights in a foreign country than in his own home country.

Of course, this kind of situation would be routinely experienced by "stateless" people. For example, members of certain Aboriginal communities are not granted citizenship by the states controlling the territory where they live.[27] The Berne Convention clearly provides that recognition of copyright depends, not on one's country of origin, but on the law of the country where protection is claimed. In these circumstances, the fact that a work has been published, or communicated to the public, in another country should be sufficient to meet the requirements for the subsistence of copyright under the Berne Convention.[28] The Berne Convention also imposes a requirement that

---

24. *See* the well-known case of *Gilliam v. American Broadcasting Companies*, 538 F.2d 14 (2d Cir. 1976), about the modification of television skits by the famed British comedy troupe, Monty Python [*Gilliam*].

25. Judgment of Dec. 19, 1994 *(Turner Entertainment v. Huston Heirs)*, Cour d'Appel, chs. Réunies (Versailles), 164 RIDA 389 (1995) (Fr.), on remand from Judgment of May 28, 1991, Cass. Civ. lre, 149 RIDA 197 (1991).

26. For a powerful comment on the colorization issue from a film director's perspective, see the short article by Woody Allen, *The Colorization of Films Insults Artists and Society*, New York Times (June 28, 1987).

27. *See* the summary of concerns regarding "Nationality and Statelessness" by Human Rights Watch, http://www.hrw.org/campaigns/race/nationality.htm (last visited Apr. 29, 2010).

28. *See* Article 5.2 of the Berne Convention, *supra* note 1: "The enjoyment and the exercise of these rights shall not be subject to any formality; *such enjoyment and such exercise shall be independent of the existence of protection in the country of origin of the work.* Consequently,

non-nationals be treated as nationals within the country of origin of the work.[29]

b. Choice of Law

Where multiple countries are involved in the publication and dissemination of a work, the Berne Convention rules have historically avoided conflicts over the choice of law. The rule seems simple: the law of the country where protection is claimed must be applied. Once again, this is a practical rule. It avoids at least two potential problems: the highly practical issue of bringing a defendant to justice in his own home jurisdiction, and the more legalistic concern, that the judges of a given jurisdiction should not be asked to locate, interpret, and apply the laws of a foreign country when deciding the outcome of a copyright case.

But this well-established approach to international copyright problems was questioned in a landmark American judgment—*ITAR-Tass v. Russian Kurier*, decided in 1998 by the United States Court of Appeals for the Second Circuit.[30] In this case, a number of articles and accompanying graphics were lifted from publications in Russia, to be re-published in the *Kurier*, a Russian-language newspaper circulating in New York. The question of standing to sue was crucial: the case was brought by a press agency, a journalists' union, and the publishers of the original newspapers. Rather than apply the American rule to decide who was entitled to sue, which would simply have involved the assignment of copyright to the employer of the journalists whose articles were reprinted, the Appeals Court felt that it had to take a more nuanced approach to this problem. Accordingly, the court explored the question of whether the Russian copyright law should be applied to the problem of establishing ownership of copyright.

What was the court's motivation? A number of possible reasons come to mind—fairness, and subtlety in the application of the law in an increasingly global environment for copyright transactions. The court dealt with the awkwardness of assessing foreign laws very sensibly, by calling upon the opinions of experts. In the *Kurier* litigation, plaintiff and defendant offered the opinions of outstanding U.S. experts on Russian law, including Professors Michael Newcity and Peter B. Maggs, to clarify the interpretation of the relevant sections.

---

apart from the provisions of this Convention, the extent of protection, as well as the means of redress afforded to the author to protect his rights, shall be governed exclusively by the laws of the country where protection is claimed." (emphasis added).

29. Article 5.3 of the Berne Convention, *supra* note 1, states: "(3) Protection in the country of origin is governed by domestic law. *However, when the author is not a national of the country of origin of the work for which he is protected under this Convention, he shall enjoy in that country the same rights as national authors*." (emphasis added).

30. Itar-Tass Russian News Agency v. Russian Kurier, Inc., 153 F.3d 82 (2d Cir. 1998).

A second question then becomes interesting: in taking this approach, was the court acting in conformity with the rules of the Berne Convention on choice of law? In fact, there are two reasons to think that the court's approach was clearly in harmony with Berne. First, Article 5.2 is the only section of the Berne Convention dealing with general concerns about choice of law.[31] This Article does provide that the law of the state where protection is claimed should apply, but it specifies that it will apply to two issues: "the extent of protection, as well as the means of redress afforded to the author to protect his rights." These cases describe the application of copyright, and remedies for infringement; they do not, however, address the question of subsistence of copyright. To say that the law of the place of infringement applies to the subsistence of copyright, as well, is to extrapolate from what is actually in these words—to apply an extension of the principle to this additional question. One further point should be noted: the application of American law principles to decide that Russian law can govern the subsistence of copyright would arguably qualify as an application of the rules of American law to this particular copyright problem.

c. Most-Favored-Nation

Finally, the TRIPs Agreement adds the international trade rule of "most-favored-nation" treatment to the basic principles of copyright protection established by the Berne Convention. The rule means that, normally speaking, any trade privilege granted to one country must be granted to all member countries of the multilateral trading system. The practice could potentially be in conflict with provisions of the Berne Convention that allow member countries to enter into bilateral copyright agreements in order to improve upon the baseline standards established by the Convention. The point is clarified by Article 4 of the TRIPs Agreement, which creates two exceptions to the most-favored nation rule: agreements authorized by the Berne Convention to provide that "the treatment accorded be a function not of national treatment but of the treatment accorded in another country," and the circumstance of bilateral arrangements predating the adoption of TRIPs.[32]

---

31. It should be noted that art. 14*bis* (2)(a) of the Berne Convention, *supra* note 1, deals with the specific case of the subsistence of copyright in films, providing that: "Ownership of copyright in a cinematographic work shall be a matter for legislation in the country where protection is claimed." *See* the discussion of this view, as developed by Paul Torremans and discussed in Phillip Johnson, *Which Law Applies? A Reply to Professor Torremans*, 1(1) J. Intell. Prop. L. Prac. 71, 72 (2005).

32. The relevant sections of Article 4 of the TRIPs Agreement, *supra* note 8, state:

> With regard to the protection of intellectual property, any advantage, favour, privilege or immunity granted by a Member to the nationals of any other country shall be accorded immediately and unconditionally to the nationals of all other Members.

C. The Global Status of Moral Rights

Within this global framework, moral rights occupy an uncertain place. Originally brought into international copyright law at the 1928 Rome Revision Conference of the Berne Convention, the subsequent development of the rights has been limited. Their presence in international copyright law has been at once strengthened and weakened by the progress of global regulation. At the same time, they are among the most widely recognized aspects of copyright law in the world's different jurisdictions, enjoying exceptionally strong protection in diverse countries. An assessment of this complex state of cumulative affairs requires a closer look at each of the pieces composing the modern puzzle of moral rights.

1. The Berne Convention: An Uneasy Compromise

Moral rights first became part of the international system with their inclusion in the Berne Convention, which was established during the 1928 revision conference in Rome.[33] The text has been subject to amendment only twice—in 1948, at the Brussels revision conference of the Berne Convention, and again, at the landmark Stockholm conference of 1967. It is telling that the amendments did not introduce substantial change into the provisions, unless it was to reduce their scope. Their focus, rather, was on clarifying limitations on moral rights which previous generations of negotiators may well have taken for granted as built into the system.

a. The Age of Authorship: The Original Text of 1928

The 1928 provisions on moral rights in the Berne Convention stated as follows:

> Independently of the author's copyright, and even after transfer of the said copyright, the author shall have the right to claim authorship of the work, as

---

Exempted from this obligation are any advantage, favour, privilege or immunity accorded by a Member: . . . (b) granted in accordance with the provisions of the Berne Convention (1971) or the Rome Convention authorizing that the treatment accorded be a function not of national treatment but of the treatment accorded in another country; . . . (d) deriving from international agreements related to the protection of intellectual property which entered into force prior to the entry into force of the WTO Agreement, provided that such agreements are notified to the Council for TRIPS and do not constitute an arbitrary or unjustifiable discrimination against nationals of other Members.

33. International Convention for the Protection of Literary and Artistic Works Signed at Berne on the 9th September, 1886, Revised at Berlin on the 13th November, 1908, and Revised at Rome on the 2nd June, 1928, Article 6*bis*, *supra* note 1 [Rome Act, 1928].

well as the right to object to any distortion, mutilation or other modification of the said work which would be prejudicial to his honour or reputation.[34]

From the great range of possible moral rights, the 1928 provision envisioned the protection of two which were universally recognized among Continental European countries.[35] The first of these was the author's right of attribution, and the second, the author's right to protect his work from harm, generally known as the integrity right. In relation to integrity, the focus was on circumstances where damage to the work affected the author's reputation, or "honor," negatively. This formula presents its share of ambiguities, but one is particularly worth noting: although the meaning of the concept of honor may have been quite clear in nineteenth-century Europe, the term is not one that modern claims usually rely upon.[36] The right of attribution is also known as the right of paternity,[37] now unfashionable. In some jurisdictions, the right of integrity, reflecting the limits of Berne language, is known simply as a right of reputation.[38]

The presence of moral rights in the Berne Convention represented a significant achievement. A compromise had been reached between the civil law countries of Continental Europe and the United Kingdom and its colonial possessions on an issue of fundamental difference. However, the compromise did not imply a consensus. Rather, the addition of moral rights to Berne signified the inclusion of civil law principles within the Convention, which the common law countries were willing to accept.

---

34. Rome Act, 1928, *supra* note 33, art. 6*bis*(1). Article 6*bis*(2) deals with the practical exercise of the rights, and in 1928, it provided: "The determination of the conditions under which these rights shall be exercised is reserved for the national legislation of the countries of the Union. The means of redress for safeguarding these rights shall be regulated by the legislation of the country where protection is claimed."

35. Adeney mentions the right "to decide if the work should appear"—*divulgation*—which is arguably implied in art. 6*bis*. *See* Elizabeth Adeney, The Moral Rights of Authors and Performers: An International and Comparative Analysis: New Edition, para. 6.30 (Oxford University Press 2006).

36. The meaning of honor is discussed by Elizabeth Adeney, *The Moral Right of Integrity: The Past and Future of "Honour,"* 2 Intell. Prop. Q. 111 (2005). Her interpretation of "honor" is not entirely satisfying; *see* the discussion in Chapter 3, *supra,* "A Theory in Flux," note 241-43 and accompanying text.

37. In French, "*droit à la paternité.*"

38. This was formerly the case in Russia, under Article 15 of the Russian Federation Law on Copyright and Neighboring Rights (No. 5351-I of July 9, 1993); *see* WikiSource, a public domain source for legislative documents: http://en.wikisource.org/wiki/Russian_Federation._Law_on_Copyright_and_Neighboring_Rights#Article_15._Moral_Rights; this provision receives a detailed treatment in Sundara Rajan, *Copyright and Creative Freedom, supra* note 13, at 173–79. The situation has changed under the Russian Civil Code, ch. IV, which came into effect on January 1, 2008, and in which, following a well-established legislative tradition under the Soviet regime, the right of integrity is restored to a right of "inviolability." A pure right of reputation fails, of course, to consider the implications of honor.

In the civilian tradition, moral rights are considered an essential part of the author's copyright, and indeed, some of the classic commentaries on French copyright law go so far as to suggest that moral rights are the *raison d'etre* of copyright itself.[39] This position is the very antithesis of English law—at least since 1774, when the landmark judgment of *Donaldson v. Beckett* conclusively dismissed the idea that moral rights could be a feature of English copyright protection, by eliminating the possibility of a common law basis for the doctrine.[40] The history of moral rights in the common law countries is one of suspicion, if not outright hostility. The moral right of the author is considered a foreign import, usually perceived as originating from the French *droit moral*, a legal concept based on cultural sensitivities that are of dubious relevance to the common law tradition.[41]

However, the *Donaldson* case should be read with care. The judgment was essentially a response, not to the moral rights idea, but to a different type of claim: the assertion by British publishers of the day that the existence of a common law copyright, separate from the Statute of Anne of 1710, entitled them to rights beyond the statutory provisions.[42] Prior to the adoption of the Statute, the publishers enjoyed a monopoly on printing in the realm, and this was one of the most straightforward ways for the monarch to exercise his, or her, power of censorship in practice—by controlling publishing directly. The purpose of the new Statute was to break the monopoly of the publishers, and in so doing, loosen the grip of the monarch on free speech. The Statute of Anne was a response to concerns about freedom of speech articulated by writers from John Milton to John Locke, and the prospect of rights, for the Stationers beyond those contained in the Statute was unnerving. Had the courts agreed to this proposition, the effectiveness of the Statute in arresting censorship, achieved by the manipulation of exclusive printing rights, would have been frustrated. The exclusion of moral rights for authors, which could have been derived from a common law copyright expressing natural rights theories, was a side-effect of this process—a casualty among onlookers. Beliefs are powerful, however, and the conviction that moral rights are a foreign import to copyright law fits well with the current focus on copyright as commercial law in the common law countries, particularly the United Kingdom and the United States.

---

39. *See, for example,* Henri Desbois, Le Droit d'auteur en France vii paras. 380–83 (3d ed. Dalloz 1978). Not all the French commentators agree; at least one writer, Pierre Recht, argues that the position of moral rights in French law is both overstated and undesirable, representing a paternalistic approach to authors by the state. *See* Pierre Recht, Le Droit d'Auteur, une nouvelle forme de propriété: histoire et théorie (Editions J. Duculot, Gembloux 1969).

40. Donaldson v. Beckett (1774) 2 Brown's Parl. Cases 129, 1 Eng. Rep. 837.

41. *See generally* the discussion in Chapter 2, *supra,* "Moral Rights: History of an Idea," notes 185–216 and accompanying text.

42. Statute of Anne (1710), 8 Ann., c. 19.

Given these circumstances, it seems surprising that moral rights found their way into international copyright regulation at all. To shed light on their success, two factors are worth considering: first, the contribution of authors to the establishment of an international copyright framework, and the historical context in which it was made; and secondly, the specific legal basis on which common law countries accepted the protection of moral rights.

i. Literary Language

The nineteenth and twenty-first centuries resemble each other closely, in the sense that both are periods of upheaval for copyright law. In one key respect, however, the dynamics of reform are strikingly different. In the nineteenth century, authors, in contrast to their current state of near-invisibility, played a pivotal role in establishing international copyright rules.

If the present century is considered the Digital Age, the nineteenth century probably deserves to be known as the Century of the Book. The spread of literature during this period was without precedent in the Western world, and it was based on the development of a mass publishing industry as one of the by-products of the Industrial Revolution.[43] The mass-market for books of all kinds made authors a prestigious and powerful group.

With the rise of international trade and travel, the unhappiness of many authors with the protection of their rights outside their countries of origin was a key factor in promoting the idea of international copyright.[44] High profile cases arose, including the example of Charles Dickens, who was profoundly unhappy about the unauthorized printing of his works in the United States. Dickens attempted to draw attention to the issue of literary piracy by undertaking a tour of the United States in 1842, but his efforts bore little fruit, and he remained embittered about the situation until his death.[45] In another twist, Russian authors were keen to encourage the printing of their works in European countries, believing that the popularity and prestige of Russian authors had attained historic heights in Western Europe.[46] In 1878, the

---

43. *See* the comments in Martha Woodmansee, *The Genius and the Copyright: Economic and Legal Conditions of the Emergence of the "Author,"* 17 Eighteenth-Century Stud. 425, 425 (1984).
44. Noted by Sam Ricketson, *The Berne Convention, supra* note 5.
45. Charles Dickens was a notable victim. See the interesting review of his situation on *The Victorian Web, Literature, History and Culture in the Age of Victoria, available at* http://www.victorianweb.org/authors/dickens/pva/pva76.html, http://www.jhtl.org/BookReviews/2004-05/Horbaczewski.pdf (last visited Apr. 29, 2010). F. Kaplan, Dickens: A Biography 91 (Morrow 1988), notes Dickens' support for the improvement of copyright protection in the UK and abroad.
46. Ricketson and Ginsburg note the growing interest in Berne membership over the early years of the twentieth century in Russia: Sam Ricketson & Jane Ginsburg, International Copyright and Neighbouring Rights: The Berne Convention and Beyond, para. 3.09 (2d ed. Oxford University Press 2005).

Association Littéraire et Artistique Internationale was founded in France with the goal of promoting authors' rights. It had no less a luminary than Victor Hugo at its head.[47]

These authors certainly recognized the idea of moral rights and were familiar with its significance as a legal concept in French and Continental law. Given the divergence of world legal traditions on this account, however, the idea needed time to gain momentum. The presence of moral rights in the 1928 document was clearly a product of their efforts.

ii. Legal Language

A consideration of the legal terms on which moral rights were eventually articulated in the Berne Convention is telling, and leads to more sobering reflection. In particular, the significance of the language in the Berne Convention becomes clear when we consider the evolution of Article 6*bis* from its first adoption in 1928, to its clarification at Brussels in 1948, and its final modification thirty-nine years later, at the important revision conference of 1967 held in Stockholm.[48]

The communiqués surrounding the 1928 discussions show that the common law countries may have been partly persuaded to accept moral rights because they believed that they were not agreeing to anything new. Instead, the rights were apparently perceived by the UK and Australian delegations to the Rome conference as a codification of rights that were already enjoyed by their authors—presumably, through the common law of tort and statutory provisions outside copyright law that addressed related issues. Overall, it was to the advantage of common-law countries to accept moral rights in the Berne Convention because of Berne's reliance on the principle of national treatment. Authors from the common-law countries would enjoy moral rights abroad, while the common-law countries were only constrained to apply the minimum standards in Berne within their own borders.[49]

Elizabeth Adeney refers to the Canadian delegation's silence on the issue. She attributes it to the unwillingness of Canada to stir up controversy, which would certainly be characteristic; but her suggestion that Canada had a deeper understanding of moral rights because of the presence of French law in

---

47. *See* the website of the ALAI at http://www.alai.org/index-a.php?ch=pubAcc-historique-a&sm=1 (last visited Aug. 16, 2010), which notes: "The ALAI's main objective was the creation of an international agreement aimed at protecting literary and artistic copyright."

48. The clarifications which occurred at Rome are worth noting. *See* Adeney, *supra* note 35, para. 7.15.

49. I am indebted to Colin Tapper for pointing this out (personal communication with the author, June 4, 2010).

Canadian legal tradition seems more uncertain. David Vaver refers to such claims as "folklore."[50]

A more cynical truth may be in evidence. Canada's moral rights measures, though enacted at the early date of 1931, included extensive, indeed comprehensive, provisions on waivers. The adoption of waivers as a feature of standard form copyright contracts in Canada would render it practically impossible for the great majority of Canadian authors and artists, wielding limited bargaining power, to exercise their moral rights in practice. Canadian jurisprudence can only boast one unequivocal victory for moral rights in its history: the well-known, colorful, and very brief judgment on Michael Snow's sculpture of Canada geese.[51] The most recent comments of the Supreme Court of Canada on moral rights suggest that, in fact, Canadian courts will be extraordinarily cautious in recognizing and applying moral rights principles.[52] Rather than expanding appreciation of moral rights to Canada's English-law community, the French influence seems to have produced a schism among judges from both traditions at Canada's Supreme Court.

b. The Era of Trade: Moral Rights in a Commercial Age

The 1948 text of the moral rights provisions, concluded at Brussels, saw an attempt to clarify the relationship between moral rights and the legislation of common law countries. In particular, the duration of moral rights is specified as follows:

> In so far as the legislation of the countries of the Union permits, the rights granted to the author in accordance with the preceding paragraph shall, after his death, be maintained, at least until the expiry of the copyright, and shall be exercisable by the persons or institutions authorized by this legislation . . . .[53]

---

50. *See* David Vaver, *Moral Rights Yesterday, Today and Tomorrow*, 7(3) Int'l J. Tech. & L. 270, 275–76 (1997).

51. Snow v. The Eaton Centre Ltd. (1982), 70 C.P.R. (2d) 105 [*Snow v. The Eaton Centre*]; *see also* sec. 12(7) of the old Canadian Copyright Act (pre-1988). Vaver, *supra* note 50, at 275–76, provides a survey of Canadian case law on moral rights to 1999. Since then, two Canadian Supreme Court decisions have dealt with moral rights, both of which occur in unusual contexts. The first, *Théberge*, involved in economic rights claim which, the court said, should have been framed as a moral rights claim; the second, *Desputeaux*, commented on the place of moral rights in an arbitration problem. *See* Théberge v. Galerie d'Art du Petit Champlain Inc. [2002] 2 S.C.R. 336, 2002 SCC 34 (Can.), and Desputeaux v. Éditions Chouette (1987) Inc. [2003] 1 S.C.R. 178 para. 57, 2003 SCC 17 (Can.).

52. *See id.* Interestingly, the court in *Théberge* was exactly split along linguistic (and cultural?) lines, with English judges agreeing in their restrictive interpretation of moral rights and securing a victory of one. The law is open to change in Canada, but a pro-moral rights bench would have to contend with badly drafted law and nearly a century of industry practice combining to weaken them.

53. Excerpt from Article 6*bis* (2), Brussels Act, 1948, Berne Convention for the Protection of Literary and Artistic Works (signed on the 9th September, 1886, completed in Paris on

In a sense, the new formulation improved upon the old by establishing a definite minimum duration for the protection of moral rights. Under the Brussels Act, the rights had to be protected until the expiration of copyright. But the reach of the Article was severely limited by the proviso that this minimum duration of protection would only apply "[i]n so far as the legislation of the countries of the Union permits." The new provision was not so much an improvement in protection as a paring down, whittling, or shaping of the loose and open-ended language of 1928 in Article 6*bis* (2) of the Berne Convention. The change occurred in an environment where copyright was increasingly seen as an economic matter, and the cultural sensitivities engendered by a nineteenth-century worldview were becoming obsolete. As Ezra Pound observed, "They will come no more,/The old men with beautiful manners."[54] The world of 1948 had new priorities. As Elizabeth Adeney points out, "[T]he UK Delegation stated that this country would prefer that the Convention not contain any provision for moral rights, given that the Convention was, in the delegation's view, an economic agreement."[55]

In 1967, at a revision Conference rife with conflict and overshadowed by the fear that developing countries would abandon the international copyright system altogether and trigger its collapse,[56] the common law understanding of moral rights was codified into the Berne Convention in the following words:

> The rights granted to the author in accordance with the preceding paragraph shall, after his death, be maintained at least until the expiry of the economic rights, and shall be exercisable by the persons or institutions authorized by the legislation of the country where protection is claimed. However, those countries whose legislation, at the moment of their ratification of or accession to this Act, does not provide for the protection after the death of the author of all the rights set out in the preceding paragraph may provide that some of these rights may, after his death, cease to be maintained.[57]

Against this historical backdrop, the new clause enacted in Article 6*bis* (2) of the Convention, incomprehensible to the uninitiated, makes perfect sense.

---

the 4th May, 1896, revised at Berlin on the 13th November, 1908, completed at Berne on the 20th March, 1914, revised at Rome on the 2nd June, 1928, and revised at Brussels on the 26th June, 1948).

54. Ezra Pound, *Moeurs contemporaines*, *in* Quia Pauper Amavi (Egoist Press 1919). The passing of the era, for Pound, was marked by the onset of the first World War.

55. Adeney, *supra* note 35 (citing *Documents de la conférence de Bruxelles 5–26 juin 1948* 194–95 (Berne: Bureau de l'Union internationale pour la Protection des Oeuvres littéraires et artistiques 1951)).

56. Ricketson, *The Berne Convention*, *supra* note 5, para. 3.64, provides a quick overview of the situation; for a detailed discussion of the evolving role of developing countries in the Berne Union, see Ricketson, Chapter 11, on *Developing Countries*.

57. Stockholm Act, 1967 (revised at Stockholm on July 14, 1967).

The objective was to limit moral rights protection in the common law countries, which did not previously protect moral rights in their copyright laws, to the lifetime of the author. In other words, moral rights were transformed into a personal tort which, like all other personal torts and in contrast to all other aspects of copyright law, could not be exercised by the author after his death. It is also worth noting that the Berne provision entered into force at a time when the principle of protecting authors' rights after the time of death was well-established in international copyright law.

As drafted, however, the accommodation was imperfect. Article 6*bis* states that "some" of these rights may cease to be protected after the author's death—not "all." It seems that the drafters of the provision were not quite able to relinquish the idea of recognizing moral rights after an author's death, although it is stated as subtly as possible. Ricketson suggests that

> [T]his formulation now imposes a specific obligation on these countries to protect "some [one]" of these rights after the author's death, and this is a significant advance on the position under the Rome and Brussels Acts.[58]

Perhaps, after all, the United States was most sage in its approach. Its commitment to a registration-based system of copyright protection and its concerns about moral rights were behind the American decision to abstain from Berne membership until the late date of 1989.[59] By an interesting irony,

---

58. Ricketson, *supra* note 5, para. 8.114. Ricketson's interesting discussion seems to emphasize the idea that Berne signatories which did not offer protection for moral rights after the author's death were effectively undertaking an additional obligation under this section. He notes: "There is an apparent gap in the formulation of this clause, as it might be taken to imply that a country which did not provide for the *post mortem auctoris* protection of either of the moral rights referred to in para (1) is now obliged to protect both rights *post mortem auctoris* if it accedes to or ratifies the Paris Act. This is on the basis that the precondition that 'all [both] the rights set out in the preceding paragraph' are not protected *post mortem auctoris* means that nonetheless 'some [one]' of them must be protected in this period. This would be a problem for countries such as Australia which, prior to 1967, did not accord *post mortem auctoris* protection to either of the rights set out in para (1). However, the records of the Stockholm Conference indicate that this would be too restrictive an interpretation, as Australia was a co-sponsor of the amendment which embodies the present wording, and it seems clear from the discussion in Main Committee I that its purpose was to accommodate the position of those countries which did not at that time provide *post mortem auctoris* protection for any moral rights. On the other hand, this formulation now imposes a specific obligation on these countries to protect 'some [one]' of these rights after the author's death, and this is a significant advance on the position under the Rome and Brussels Acts." (square brackets in the original.)

59. *See* David Nimmer, *Conventional Copyright: A Morality Play*, 3(3) ENT. L. REV. 94 (1992); he discusses the paradox of U.S. accession to Berne. Interestingly, Adeney, *supra* note 35, suggests that concerns about American "alienation" had compelled the British delegation to resist the expansion of moral rights as early as 1948. One suspects that the American position offered convenient support for a view that the British already held.

the two former Cold War enemies, the United States and the Soviet Union, were actually two of the last major powers to accede to the Berne Convention.[60] They did so within six years of each other, in 1989 and 1995.[61] In this respect, at least, the ghost of Dickens can at last rest in peace.

c. The Technological Era: Moral Rights and the Unknown

It is interesting to consider the implications of the Berne Convention for the moral rights aspect of technological creation. The Berne Convention has been saved from technological obsolescence by its *modus operandi*: the agreement represents a codification of the classic copyright logic of expansion by analogy, allowing it to extend copyright protection to new kinds of intellectual creation with relative ease. The method has proven its worth. It has allowed modern copyright law to embrace new types of human creativity, from music, whether written down or performed,[62] to visual arts and photography,[63] to film.[64] These processes of expansion have been remarkably effective in bringing diverse worlds of new creativity within copyright's scope.

---

60. China joined the Berne Convention in 1992. *See* Berne Notification No. 140, Dated July 15, 1992, entry into force October 15, 1992, *available at* http://www.wipo.int/treaties/en/html.jsp?file=/redocs/notdocs/en/berne/treaty_berne_140.html (last visited Apr. 29, 2010).

61. United States, Notification number 121, dated 1988, entry into force 1989, *available at* http://www.wipo.int/edocs/notdocs/en/berne/treaty_berne_121.html (last visited Apr. 29, 2010); Russian Federation, Notification number 162, dated 1994, entry into force 1985, *available at* http://www.wipo.int/edocs/notdocs/en/berne/treaty_berne_162.html (last visited Apr. 29, 2010).

62. In both Canada (1993) and India (1994), the definition of music was altered to include its unwritten form.

63. The extension of literary copyright to the fine arts was accomplished in 1862 with the Fine Art Copyright Act, London (1862); *see* http://www.copyrighthistory.org/cgi-bin/kleioc/0010/exec/ausgabe/%22uk_1862%22 (last visited Apr. 29, 2010) (responsible editor: Ronan Deazley). The abstract notes that the Act "was . . . innovative . . . in providing artists with a new form of 'moral rights' protection."

64. The history of film protection in the common law tradition is interesting. *See* Pascal Kamina, Film Copyright in the European Union, Cambridge Studies in Intellectual Property Rights, paras. 15 & 22 (Cambridge University Press 2002). Kamina describes how, under the landmark 1911 Copyright Act, British law protected film indirectly, as a series of photographs, or as a dramatic work—by analogy. When the 1956 Copyright Act recognized film as a new category of copyright work, it did so in a new way, removing the requirement of originality. Kamina notes: "According to section 13(10) of the Act, the author of the 'cinematograph film' was 'the person by whom the arrangements necessary for the making of the film were under taken,' i.e., the producer. The Gregory Committee Report shows that the rationale behind this new subject-matter was both to avoid multiple claims for authorship in what are, in essence, composite works, while complying formally with the provisions of the Berne Convention, and to avoid the problems of the determination of originality." (footnotes omitted).

The same principle is key to understanding how and why computer programs came to be protected as copyright works. Although the technology was new, there was clearly no special innovation in extending copyright to the protection of a new type of intellectual creation. The controversy surrounding the move was, instead, a question about the appropriateness of doing so. Was the expansion of copyright to computer programs good policy? Was it beneficial to the community of programmers, or to the public?[65]

Since computer programs were written down, albeit in code, they were considered to be analogous to literary works. This shared attribute was superficial, but undeniable. Indeed, Colin Tapper observes that "the whole terminology of programming is literary; it is perhaps even more surprising that 'instructions' or 'commands' are 'read.'" He notes "the metaphoric use of 'libraries,' 'files,' 'documents,' 'words,' and 'characters'."[66]

A number of features of copyright law within the Berne framework also encouraged the software industry to look at copyright as their right of choice. The deliberate informality with which the Berne copyright system operated was a factor encouraging the extension of copyright to computer programs. The enjoyment of copyright did not depend on the satisfaction of any administrative formalities, such as registration, and as such, the creators, or owners, of computer programs could expect to enjoy a swift and easy form of control over their works.[67] Similarly, the extensive duration of protection—lifetime of the author plus fifty years after his death, or fifty years from publication for a corporate work—was attractive.[68] The same points can, of course, apply to the copyright protection of databases.[69]

The one difficulty arises in relation to moral rights. This was not an issue that was likely to attract a great deal of attention in the United States, the

---

65. *See generally* Jane Ginsburg's analysis of copyright protection of programs and possible alternatives, in Jane C. Ginsburg, *Four Reasons and a Paradox: The Manifest Superiority of Copyright over Sui Generis Protection of Computer Software*, 94 Colum. L. Rev. 2559 (1994).

66. (Personal communication with the author, June 4, 2010).

67. Berne Convention, *supra* note 1, art. 5 (2) ("The enjoyment and the exercise of these rights shall not be subject to any formality").

68. Berne Convention, *supra* note 1, art. 7. ("The term of protection granted by this Convention shall be the life of the author and fifty years after his death"). Note that Article 7 is subject to the rule of the shorter term.

69. The case of databases is complicated by the problem of trying to decide whether the database represents an "original" contribution on the part of the creator, or his or her labor only. The approach in the European Union Databases Directive is to offer protection to investment in the creation of databases through a *sui generis* right. The right has been controversial; as Estelle Derclaye comments, "It has been said that the database sui generis right is 'one of the least balanced and most potentially anti-competitive intellectual property rights ever created.'" *See* Estelle Derclaye, The Legal Protection of Databases: A Comparative Analysis Part I, Chapter II, 43–50 (Edward Elgar 2008); a detailed analysis of the right follows; at 43, she cites Reichman & Samuelson 1997.

home of computer innovation. However, as a look at the early development of the Berne Convention reveals, the Berne system fundamentally reflects a civil law picture of copyright. Under Berne, copyright is a right that includes, by definition, both economic and moral components. The divergences of civil law theories, reflected in the different practices of Continental European countries, generally have to do with how these concepts relate to each other. Some jurisdictions think of copyright as a single right with economic and moral dimensions, while others see it as two, fundamentally distinct kinds of rights. But the moral dimension is always present; that is undeniable.[70]

In particular, the Berne Convention makes little provision for treating different classes of copyright works differently. As long as works fall within the same overall category, they are expected to be treated alike. An artistic work, whether it is a painting by Van Gogh or the simple drawing of a "a hand carrying a pencil and in the act of finishing a cross enclosed in a square,"[71] is entitled to the same kind and level of protection. Different categories of works may elicit different rights—for example, poems, songs, and photographs may each enjoy differential protection. But here, too, there are limits: no category of copyright work is simply exempt from moral rights. This lack of discrimination has often been regarded as one of copyright's strengths. The law has been successful in extending protection to works without venturing too far into the terrain, where angels fear to tread, of attempting to define artistic quality.[72]

---

70. It is interesting to consider the relationship between moral rights and, more generally, the notion of moral damage or moral harm—well established in the civil law countries, but firmly rejected in the English common law tradition. For an illuminating comparison of the two positions, with some special insight into the unique position of German law, see P. R. Handford, *Moral Damage in Germany*, 27(4) INT'L COMP. L.Q. 849 (1978). Handford points out the development of the notion of *persönlichkeit*, (personality), in German law, which is also the basis of German moral rights, and draws attention to the work of legal theorist, von Gierke, who "believed that the individual ought to be able to complain of any unauthorised interference not merely with his person, his property or his reputation, but also with the social, intellectual and economic activities, opportunities and amenities, which combine to form the sum total of his existence." (footnote omitted). Interestingly, in a case involving the posthumous publication of letters to a friend written by Nietzsche, the German courts were unwilling to recognize the doctrine of personality rights, arguing that it was not (yet) part of German law. *See* Handford, at 856; he cites the Nietzsche case as (1908) 69 R.G.Z. 401, and also refers to (1912) 79 R.G.Z. 397; (1926) 113 R.G.Z. 413. For an interesting twist on the issue of moral rights in civil law countries, see the comments by Article 19, a public-interest organization supporting free speech, regarding proposed changes to Moldovan law in 2008; *see* http://www.article19.org/pdfs/analysis/moldova-moral-damages-proposal.pdf (last visited Apr. 29, 2010).

71. *See* the landmark case of *Kenrick v. Lawrence* [1890] 25 Q.B.D. 99; the purpose of the drawing was to show illiterate voters how to vote.

72. *See* Hensher (George) Limited v. Restawile Upholstery (Lancs.) Limited [1974] F.S.R. 173 (H.L.). In multiple opinions, the Lords had various ideas of what would constitute "artistic" creativity. The case considered the question of whether a prototype of furniture would

From a technological perspective, the Berne Convention, like the civil law traditions on which it is partly based, implies an interesting result. If copyright is to be extended by analogy to new types of technological creation, the proper approach to those works will be to treat them as other works in the same class are treated. A computer program should be treated as any other literary work. Accordingly, if literary works in general enjoy moral rights, we must assume that moral rights also arise in relation to technological creation—literary works that happen to be technological in nature. This possibility has somehow failed to receive serious consideration in international copyright discussions, and the correction of an ambiguity that could be potentially awkward was not addressed in the movement from the Berne Convention to the TRIPs Agreement. Indeed, the point was overlooked in spite of the fact that one of the avowed purposes of TRIPs was to update the Berne Convention with new technologies in mind. Instead, moral rights are present in TRIPs, but in a phantom sense. Their situation is one of great uncertainty, and they bring a sense of ambiguity to copyright protection in the international trade regime.

2. The TRIPs Agreement: Reality or Illusion?

American membership in the Berne Convention was a prelude to the development of the TRIPs Agreement. It was a decision that responded to an important policy shift: the United States intended to undertake a new role of international leadership in the field of copyright. Acceptance of the Berne framework was an essential part of bringing credibility to its leadership.

Inevitably, the decision to join Berne generated intense debate in the United States on the issue of moral rights protection.[73] In particular, questions surrounded the natural problem of what the United States needed to do to bring its copyright law into conformity with the international

---

qualify as a work of "artistic craftsmanship" within the meaning of UK copyright law. Nevertheless, there are limits on the inclusiveness of the "sweat of the brow" principle. *See, e.g., Exxon Corp. v. Exxon Insurance Consultants International Ltd.* [1982] Ch. 119, where the court found that copyright will not usually subsist in a single word, even an invented one, and used the example of Lewis Carroll's fantastic poem, "Jabberwocky," to anchor its argument. The trial judge comments, as approved by the Court of Appeal: "Such a word would, however, I think, have to have qualities or characteristics in itself, if such a thing is possible, which would justify its recognition as an original literary work rather than merely as an invented word."

73. *See* the discussions in the U.S. Congressional Committee on the Judiciary and Subcommittee on Patents, Copyrights, and Trademarks. U.S. Adherence to the Berne Convention: Hearings before the Subcomm. on Patents, Copyrights, and Trademarks of the Comm. on the Judiciary, 99th Congress (May 16, 1985 & Apr. 15, 1986) (U.S. GPO, Washington, DC 1987) [U.S. Congress].

standard articulated in Berne. The response, surprising even after twenty years, was—nothing. A consideration of the 1986 debates in Congress shows that the United States believed in the strength of its tort protections, while remaining careful about the expansion of copyright law.[74] Indeed, similar arguments had surfaced when the United Kingdom first assessed its conformity with Berne.[75] But the American position seems more convincing, perhaps because of the particularly dynamic nature of its case law, relatively newer and more flexible than its British counterpart.[76]

Interestingly, the 1948 case of *Shostakovich* had seen an American judge searching in U.S. common law to find a basis for moral rights protection in that country.[77] The case eventually failed—not because of any special antipathy to the moral rights concept in the United States, but instead, due to the practical difficulties of providing proper evidence for a moral rights claim.[78]

Political concerns may also have played a role. *Shostakovich* raised the issue of the rights of Soviet composers to protest the use of their music in an anti-Soviet film. It was brought by the Soviet government "on behalf of" the composers, a highly questionable legal approach to rights that are supposed to be inalienable.[79] Recognizing moral rights on these facts may simply have been too risky.

What is astonishing is the tenacity with which the United States has persisted in its view. To date, the only significant legislation on moral rights remains the *Visual Artists Rights Act* of 1990. As David Nimmer comments:

> The Visual Artists Rights Act of 1990 is of limited scope. It does not apply across the board to copyrightable works; rather, it applies only to works of art, namely photographs, sculptures, paintings, and what in the United States would

---

74. U.S. Congress, *supra* note 74.
75. The argument was later reversed and the need for moral rights legislation recognized. THE WHITFORD COMMITTEE, THE WHITFORD COMMITTEE REPORT ON COPYRIGHT AND DESIGNS LAW, 1977, Cmnd. 6732.
76. Briefly noted by W. R. Cornish, *Moral Rights Under the 1988 Act*, 11(12) EUR. INTELL. PROP. REV. 449, 449 (1989).
77. This aspect of the case is generally not given adequate emphasis. *See* Shostakovich v. Twentieth Century-Fox Film Corp., 80 N.Y.S.2d 575 (N.Y. Sup. Ct. 1948), *aff'd*, 87 N.Y.S.2d 430 (N.Y. App. Div. 1949) [*Shostakovich*]. The court's comments about rights in the public domain are especially interesting; the judge comments: "Conceivably, under the doctrine of Moral Right the court could in a proper case, prevent the use of a composition or work, in the public domain, in such a manner as would be violative of the author's rights." But he goes on to note, "The application of the doctrine presents much difficulty however." *Shostakovich*, 80 N.Y.S.2d at 578.
78. *Id.*, at 578–79.
79. The legality of the Soviet Union's actions in claiming to assert moral rights on behalf of its citizens, generally alive at the time of the claims, is discussed in Sundara Rajan, *Copyright and Creative Freedom*, *supra* note 13, at 104–05.

traditionally be called "fine art": it is further limited to fine art that is either the original, signed by the artist, or issued in a limited edition of 200 or fewer, and only those limited editions that are signed and numbered by the artist. By contrast, moral rights, as they are envisioned in the Berne Convention, apply across the spectrum of copyrightable compositions. Moral rights apply to novels, plays, movies and songs; two artworks to, indeed, but certainly not only artworks, as in the US law that took effect on June 1, 1991.[80]

The uneasiness surrounding the moral rights provisions in the Berne Convention now had to be addressed in a larger, truly global context. How would moral rights be dealt with in the TRIPs Agreement? The general approach to copyright in TRIPs was to incorporate the Berne Convention into the new Agreement in a structure resembling the famous Russian *matrioshka* dolls. Members of the TRIPs Agreement would be required to adhere to the substantive provisions of the Berne Convention. Article 9.1 of the TRIPs Agreement is the first article on copyright, and it is entitled, "Relation to the Berne Convention." It begins:

9.1. Members shall comply with Articles 1 through 21 of the Berne Convention (1971) and the Appendix thereto.

With respect to Article 6*bis*, however, the new Agreement adopted a special formula. Article 9.1 goes on to state:

However, Members shall not have rights or obligations under this Agreement in respect of the rights conferred under Article 6*bis* of that Convention or of the rights derived therefrom.

The practical significance of this curious phrase is simple: since member countries do not enjoy moral rights under the TRIPs Agreement *per se*, but only under the Berne Convention, dispute-settlement measures are not available in relation to moral rights. In theory, a moral rights dispute under the Berne Convention could certainly be referred to the International Court of Justice. In the history of the Berne Convention, however, this has never been done.

The impact of TRIPs on the international protection of moral rights is important. Practically speaking, no country can complain of inadequate recognition of moral rights at the WTO; and, of course, no penalty can be assigned. For example, French film directors could not petition the French government to sue the United States government on the grounds that the moral rights of French directors are not adequately protected in the United

---

80. David Nimmer, *supra* note 59, at 96. Nimmer goes on to critique other aspects of the Visual Artists Rights Act as a tool for Berne implementation.

States.[81] In fact, moral rights are the only area of copyright law that has remained beyond the reach of the WTO dispute-settlement system. Every other aspect of copyright, from the notion of fixation to the issue of enforcement is, as far as possible, addressed by TRIPs. Clearly, the negotiators of TRIPs perceived moral rights as an area that was distinct from other aspects of copyright law, and one that should be excluded from the operation of ordinary copyright rules.

The exclusion of moral rights from WTO dispute-settlement leads to interesting questions about the interaction of legal provisions within TRIPs. Although the focus of TRIPs was not on generating new copyright norms, which were largely satisfactory within Berne, the TRIPs Agreement did introduce a few substantive sections on copyright protection. These provisions dealt with technology, and attempted to update Berne with copyright terminology that addressed technological creation directly. Notably, Article 10.1 cements the protection of computer programs as literary works by specifically classifying them as such, while Article 10.2 accomplishes the same objective in relation to databases.[82] The statement on computer programs is especially interesting, because the aim is clearly to protect them at a level on par with other "literary works." If literary works enjoy moral rights—not under the TRIPs Agreement, but through it, under the Berne Convention—the legal implication is that moral rights must also arise out of the creation of computer programs and databases. Without explicit clarification, this approach leads to some ambiguity about the nature and extent of rights in these new kinds of works under TRIPs.[83]

The international fall-out of excluding moral rights, not from TRIPs *per se*, but from the dispute-settlement procedures of the WTO, have been interesting to observe. The situation has both a bright side and a dark side. On the one hand, the decision to exclude moral rights from the normal operation of the WTO system makes sense: these are noncommercial, individual, and cultural rights that, apart from shared roots in the prerogatives of authorship, do not have much in common with the economic aspects of copyright law.[84] The exclusion may be to the advantage of national policy-makers who want to use moral rights as an instrument of cultural policy.

---

81. *See supra* note 25 and the facts of the *Huston* case.
82. "Compilations of data," in the language of the article.
83. *See* the detailed discussion of this issue in Chapter 5, "The Programmer as Author," notes 12–42 and accompanying text.
84. This is not to suggest that moral rights do not have economic implications—quite the contrary. The potential economic costs of moral rights, such as withdrawing or reprinting works, may be highly significant. For an analysis of moral rights from an economic perspective, see the pioneering work by Hansmann & Santilli: H. Hansmann & M. Santilli, *Authors' and Artists' Moral Rights: A Comparative Legal and Economic Analysis*, 26 J. Legal Stud. 95 (1997); *see, for example*, the interesting comments on the economic and "mixed" implications of the right of integrity, 104–08.

On the other hand, however, there is a concern: the exclusion of moral rights from TRIPs could also be interpreted as lack of interest on the part of an international community that no longer thinks of them as being particularly important. In this case, moral rights could lose the international status and prestige that were secured for them in Berne. As other areas of copyright law move forward to meet technological change, moral rights could be left behind.

Interestingly, this is not what has happened. Rather, the period surrounding the adoption of TRIPs has been an extraordinarily active time for moral rights—particularly in the common law countries. All of the common law countries have now enacted some form of moral rights legislation, and each one has done so in its own way, accepting the rights to varying degrees. The abstruse provisions of the UK law of 1988,[85] developed in response to the Whitford Commission's landmark reassessment of the state of UK copyright law in anticipation of TRIPs, stand in contrast to the comprehensive Australian law of 2001.[86] The U.S. has enacted only one statute for moral rights, the *Visual Artists Rights Act* of 1990, and it continues to consider the issue of Berne implementation.[87] Canada is, once again, the relatively quiet country: it has had moral rights legislation since 1931, and therefore, did not face the problem of potential non-compliance with Berne. But Canada's moral rights provisions were amended in 1988, and the changes accomplished two things. They confirmed the closeness of Canada's integrity right to the reputation-based model in Berne, and, controversially, expanded the right to waive moral rights into a global and comprehensive provision.[88]

Among the developing countries of common law heritage, India undertook a major reform of its moral rights in 1994. In fact, its revisions were controversial, involving the scaling back of extensive protection for moral rights in that country, with reformers offering the rationale that it was thought to be a good idea to make the language of Indian law conform to Berne.[89] The comments seem rather tongue-in-cheek, in the sense that moral rights were an active area of litigation in the pre-TRIPs period in India, and, seen in the context of litigation that was ongoing during the early 1990s, the

---

85. Copyright, Designs and Patents Act 1988 (c. 48), Office of Public Sector Information, *available at* http://www.opsi.gov.uk/acts/acts1988/UKpga_19880048_en_1.htm (last visited Apr. 29, 2010) [CDPA, *Copyright, Designs and Patents Act 1988*].

86. *See* Copyright Act 1968 (Cth), http://www.austlii.edu.au/au/legis/cth/consol_act/ca1968133/ (last visited Apr. 29, 2010). The moral rights legislation was the Copyright Amendment (Moral Rights) Act 2000.

87. Visual Artists Rights Act of 1990, Pub. L. No. 101-650, 104 Stat. 5128, 17 U.S.C. § 106A [VARA].

88. Vaver.

89. Private comments of Jagdish Sagar, February 2009. *See* the Copyright (Amendment) Act, 1994 (No. 38 of 1994).

changes had the specific effect of limiting government liability for moral rights violations.[90]

By excluding moral rights, TRIPs seems to have had an unanticipated effect: the progress of internationalization of a different kind. TRIPs has played a role, perhaps inadvertently, in promoting moral rights, by bringing a higher profile to the Berne Convention. Ironically—despite their absence from the international trade arena, or because of it?—the concept of moral rights is now among the most widely accepted and up-to-date aspects of copyright law in the world.

The uncertain place of moral rights in the international trade arena raises questions about their role in a technological environment. The essence of digital technology is its power to dissolve borders. Indeed, technology over-comes borders by its very nature; the mere fact that technology exists is enough to transform borders from real into notional frontiers. No decisions are needed, no actions or policies need to come into play, to "use" technology for cross-border communication. Marshall McLuhan famously stated that the "medium is the message," and the technologies of our generation have brought new meaning to his words.[91]

Technology is behind the urgency of new international copyright rules. In the same way, and for the same reasons, the moral rights concept, like every other aspect of copyright law, demands to be harmonized across borders. This does not necessarily lead to the conclusion that moral rights without harmonization are meaningless: such a position would be an overstatement of the case for harmonization. The moral rights concept is powerful. It is not devoid of significance at the national level. But in the absence of inter-national harmonization, there are definite limits to what moral rights can accomplish for the protection of authors and their works. Without inter-national protection, the status of a work can never be assured once it is exported to other countries—a virtually automatic occurrence in the digital environment.

Works of visual art, which are relatively more fixed than other intellectual creations, are a slightly special case.[92] Nevertheless, the international dimension

---

90. *See* the case of *Amar Nath Sehgal v. Union of India*, where the courts found the Indian government negligent of a sculptor's moral rights in work commissioned by it. *Amar Nath Sehgal v. Union of India* 2005 (30) PTC 253 (Delhi High Court) [*Sehgal*]. The litigation seems to have had a direct effect on moral rights legislation in India. For details of the case, see Mira T. Sundara Rajan, *Moral Rights and the Protection of Cultural Heritage:* Amar Nath Sehgal v. Union of India, 10(1) INT'L J. CULTURAL PROP. 79 (2001) [Sundara Rajan, *Amar Nath Sehgal*]. This article informs the decision of the Delhi High Court and is quoted in paragraph 41.

91. *See* MARSHALL MCLUHAN, UNDERSTANDING MEDIA: THE EXTENSIONS OF MAN (MIT Press 1994) (1964).

92. As there may be only one "original" of a work of visual art, moral rights in the visual arts often receive a more sympathetic treatment than other types of works. The VARA, *supra* note 87,

of moral rights is important even to these, and grows in significance in a digital environment. The making of digital archives by museums and libraries is increasingly common. Digital repositories of knowledge like these raise questions which are both legal and moral, in the general sense of the term, about rights, ownership, and control.[93] The status of public art is changing in a digital environment, where photographs and other images have a new significance.[94]

In relation to technological works, the lack of international harmonization may be a more serious issue. By nature, these works are different from traditional copyright works. They are more easily transported across borders; indeed, where information technology is concerned, international movement is a fundamental indicator of its success. The problem of moral rights in these kinds of works lends itself to a variety of practical solutions. For example, a decision to exclude moral rights from technological works could translate into a successful way of dealing with moral rights in the world's major jurisdictions. But the exemption from moral rights would have to be consistent across all jurisdictions where technological works are disseminated. Even one deviant country with different norms could compromise the scheme. Alternatively, an accepted set of moral rights could be established for technological creation—for example, by recognizing the moral rights that they already enjoy, in law if not in fact, by virtue of Article 6*bis* of the Berne

---

is one notable example. Canada's copyright act also features a more favorable treatment for visual art, in relation to which there is no need to prove damage to the author's honor or reputation: it is presumed. *See* Canadian Copyright Act, R.S.C. 1985, c. C-42, sec. 28.2(1), *available at* http://laws.justice.gc.ca/en/C-42/index.html (last visited Apr. 29, 2010) [Canadian Copyright Act]: "(2) In the case of a painting, sculpture or engraving, the prejudice referred to in subsection (1) shall be deemed to have occurred as a result of any distortion, mutilation or other modification of the work." Note that the following subsections exempt certain types of treatment, such as good-faith attempts at restoration of an artwork, from becoming a violation of the artist's integrity right.

93. Efforts by Oxford's Pitt Rivers Museum to build a digital archive of Tibetan images with a "map" to encourage users to view the images in cultural context are also critiqued by Tibetan collaborators as an assertion of "ownership" over the images, works, and culture they represent. *See* Dr. Clare Harris, *The Tibet Album, available at* http://tibet.prm.ox.ac.uk/tibet_prm-collections.html (last visited Apr. 29, 2010). *See* the illuminating and thought-provoking comments in Clare Harris & Tsering Shakya, *Seeing Lhasa: British Photographic and Filmic Engagement with Tibet in 1936–47*,1–78 (Serindia Publications 2003); statement by Dr. Clare Harris (personal communication with the author, May 2009).

94. An interesting example concerns the totem poles of Duncan, British Columbia, Canada. The poles, on display in the town center, became the focus of controversy when the city government attempted to prohibit photography of these public works of art, subject to the payment of a copyright fee. The city eventually developed a new policy on photography that emphasized, among other things, the moral rights of the artists. *See* Shannon Moneo, *Do You Have a Permit to Take That Photo?*, photos by Deddeda Stemler (Oct. 4, 2007), *available at* website of News Photographers Association of Canada, http://npac.ca/?p=47 (last visited July 17, 2010).

Convention.[95] Once again, if moral rights in these works were not harmonized across jurisdictions, their significance would be limited. Anomalies would arise: a computer programmer could expect to have his work attributed to him by name in India, for example, but not in the United States. A composer of electronic music could expect to protect the integrity of his work in France, but not in England. In a right that is supposed to protect an author's "fame," does it make sense that the recognized extent of "fame" in technological innovation should be enclosed within national borders?

Harmonization, itself, is a concept that requires careful scrutiny. It can mean many different things. A baseline standard, like the practice under the Berne Convention, could represent a harmonized approach to the law. But the experience of the Berne Convention suggests that minimum standards, alone, are not sufficient for harmonization. At the other extreme, harmonization is often taken to mean the protection of identical rights in different jurisdictions. This is a cruder and less satisfying approach, not least because it goes against the fundamental meaning of the word "harmonization," itself. It is well worth noting that difference is built into harmony, and the idea of legal "harmony" as identical laws is slightly perverse.[96]

Words have power. As every lawyer knows, finding the right terminology is one of the keys to the success of any legal concept. In this sense, the concept of the "moral right," as a result of its birth in French territory, carries the heavy burden of a contradiction in terms in the English-speaking world. *Droit moral* succinctly conveys the idea of personal, intellectual, or even spiritual rights;[97] but a "moral right" implies a problem between general principles of morality and legal rights that are enforced by the state. If the English had taken their terminology from the eminently sensible German term, *persönlichkeitsrecht*, "personality" right, the history of moral rights in the common law world might have been different![98]

Determining the content and scope of harmonized moral rights would be a vast undertaking. The implications are cultural, economic, and even political in nature. Perhaps most important, the recognition of an author's moral right is, fundamentally, a matter of human rights. The moral right of the author is a reflection of society at large, and a well-respected moral right would be incompatible with authoritarianism and political repression.[99]

---

95. Of course, the rights are notional if they are not translated into legal provisions in the countries where authors seek to exercise them. But conceptual recognition in Berne is still powerful and has proven its significance over the past two decades of moral rights reform in the world.

96. For a discussion of harmonization and the analogy between law and music, see Sundara Rajan, *Copyright and Creative Freedom*, *supra* note 13, at 10–11.

97. *See* Adeney, *supra* note 35, para. 7.26.

98. *See* Handford, *supra* note 70.

99. *See* Mira T. Sundara Rajan, *Copyright and Free Speech in Transition: A New International Perspective*, *in* J. Griffiths & U Suthersanen, eds., Copyright and Free Speech:

Harmonizing moral rights may imply a broader commitment to recognizing freedom of speech, individual rights, and cultural objectives around the world.[100]

The potential injustice involved in discriminating between technological and traditional works to exclude moral rights from technology are disturbing. On what basis can we justify depriving a computer programmer of moral rights in his work, while we allow a writer of cookbooks the moral right in his? How do we address the problem, likely to become pervasive, of works that are somehow both traditional and technological at the same time? Is electronic music to be defined as a technological work, and therefore, is its composer to be denied a moral right? Or is it a traditional work where moral rights apply, regardless of their implications for the computer software and hardware underlying its creation?

And, finally, how do we address the psychological element involved in moral rights? Is the programmer's pride in his creation a real factor? Should we fail to recognize his human right to be known as the creator of his work, simply because his creativity happens to be "technological" in nature?

Although the devil may confound us in these details, it seems clear that the proper solution to the moral rights conundrum should involve some form of recognition for them in the technological context. Indeed, given the current state of economic copyright, there is every possibility that the moral right may ultimately overtake the economic right as the essence of copyright protection for the coming century. Moral rights have one undeniable strength: moral appeal. In an increasingly jaded copyright arena, the naïveté of the doctrine may surprise us with a refreshing and rejuvenating perspective on the law.

3. Moral Rights in the Digital Age: The WIPO Treaties

The WIPO Internet Treaties represented the first attempt, at the international level, to re-fashion copyright with digital concerns in mind. Notwithstanding TRIPs, this honor belongs to WIPO and not to the WTO. By the time of its adoption, the TRIPs Agreement was already becoming obsolete—a reflection of the gargantuan scope of the WTO system, which was beginning to collapse under its own weight. Given its place within the WTO, TRIPs was a slow-moving entity, and the fact that each of its provisions was won by hard negotiation meant that amendment would be a slow and laborious process.

Comparative and International Analyses 315 (Oxford University Press 2005) [Sundara Rajan, *Copyright and Free Speech in Transition*].

100. *Id.*

The contrast between the TRIPs Agreement and the quicksilver world of technology could not be greater.

The WIPO Internet Treaties were drafted to address this concern. There are two treaties, of unequal weight: the groundbreaking WIPO Copyright Treaty, or WCT, and the more specialized WIPO Performances and Phonograms Treaty, the WPPT.[101] The Treaties were the product of a landmark exercise in treaty-making. Concise and to the point, they focus directly, and purely, on digital issues.

a. The WCT: A Digital Right of Disclosure

The single major innovation in the WCT is its creation of a right of "making available." It brings every Internet transaction involving a copyright work within the ambit of copyright restrictions. It confirms that Internet privacy is an illusion: once we accept the WCT concept of infringement, there is no inviolable privacy of Internet use.[102] Data on Internet use must be collected to furnish the necessary evidence of copyright infringement. This issue has been uneasily avoided by Canadian courts in the *BMG v. John Doe* litigation, and the European Court of Justice has collided with it in the *Promusicae* case. As Fanny Coudert and Evi Werkers succinctly conclude:

> The ECJ decided that it cannot be derived from European legislation that Member States are obliged to install a duty to provide personal data in the context of a civil procedure to ensure the effective protection of copyright. It did not however provide guidelines on how the balance should be made. In sum, the "hot potato" was passed on to the Member States.[103]

The place of moral rights in the WIPO Copyright Treaty is difficult to assess.[104] The Treaty makes no reference whatsoever to moral rights, which is straightforward enough. However, there is a subtext of possibilities for moral rights which should not be missed. As is often the case where moral rights

---

101. *See supra* note 15.
102. The potential conflict between a need for data on Internet usage in order to secure evidence in copyright infringement cases and individual privacy has become a theme of the discussions surrounding the liability of Internet Service Providers for illegal file-sharing. For examples, see *BMG Canada Inc. v. John Doe*, 2005 F.C.A. 193 [2005] 4 R.C.F. 81 and *Productores de Música de España (Promusicae) v. Telefónica de España SAU (Telefónica)*, Judgment of the Court (Grand Chamber) of Jan. 29, 2008, Case C-275/06, *available at* http://eur-lex.europa.eu/LexUriServ/LexUriServ.do?uri=CELEX:62006J0275:EN:HTML (last visited Apr. 29, 2010).
103. Fanny Coudert & Evi Werkers, *In the Aftermath of the Promusicae Case: How to Strike the Balance?*, 18(1) Int'l J. L. Info. Tech. 50, 51 (2010).
104. An earlier version of this analysis of the WCT was presented at the Seventeenth BILETA Annual Conference in 2002. *See* BILETA, *supra* note 16.

arise in a digital context, the concept of moral interests seems to arise out of the text as a by-product of some of its other objectives. This observation is important, because it reminds us of one of the characteristics of moral rights—their informal quality. Although they are, of course, legal rights, they share with human rights their origins in naturalistic theories of both rights and creative expression. The relevance of the WCT to moral rights lies in the evocative power of its language. The potential significance of the WCT in laying the foundation for a future accommodation of moral rights at the international level means that these linguistic allusions should not be ignored.

The language of the WCT is different from that of other copyright conventions, and suggests at least two interesting things. First, the Treaty's preoccupation with technology seems to be carrying copyright law towards a new conceptual orientation. The model of copyright law articulated by the WCT points towards a merging of economic rights with what might be called authorship interests. This observation is supported by a second point, the evident focus of the Treaty's language on authorship rather than ownership.

The Preamble of the WCT points out that it is largely a response to "the profound impact of the development and convergence of information and communication technologies on the creation and use of literary and artistic works." The most significant innovation that it introduces in this regard is the creation of a new "right of communication to the public." Not present in any other international copyright instrument, this right is a pure innovation. Defined in Article 8, it introduces the concept of "making [a work] available," specifying that

> authors of literary and artistic works shall enjoy the exclusive right of authorizing any communication to the public of their works, by wire or wireless means, including the making available to the public of their works in such a way that members of the public may access these works from a place and at a time individually chosen by them.[105]

In common law copyright systems, the right of communication to the public is considered a fundamental economic right. While the right of reproduction is the essence of copyright protection, the right of communication to the public was initially considered necessary, as Sam Ricketson observes, for

---

105. *See* WCT, *supra* note 15: "Article 8 Right of Communication to the Public Without prejudice to the provisions of Articles 11(1)(ii), 11*bis*(1)(i) and (ii), 11*ter*(1)(ii), 14(1)(ii) and 14*bis*(1) of the Berne Convention, authors of literary and artistic works shall enjoy the exclusive right of authorizing any communication to the public of their works, by wire or wireless means, including the making available to the public of their works in such a way that members of the public may access these works from a place and at a time individually chosen by them."

copyright works that are disseminated to the public through non-material representation, such as dramatic or musical performances.[106] It may be helpful to think of the right as being closely aligned with neighboring, or performers', rights.[107] This history of the right is an interesting one; it suggests that an active fusion of copyright with neighboring rights has occurred in the WCT—a reaction that has been precipitated by digital technology.

The character of the economic "communication" right is perhaps reflected more precisely in its French name, the right of "*représentation*."[108] With the growth of digital reproduction technologies and technologies of instantaneous communication, the scope of the communication right, or right of representation, has become much broader. It is no longer performance alone that presents a challenge; a vast array of other means and methods for conveying and communicating works exists. The language of Article 8 clearly visualizes the prospect of disseminating works via broadcasting, cable, and satellite technologies, and, of course, the Internet.

As noted, Article 8 of the WCT does not make explicit reference to moral rights. However, the new right of communication to the public bears a striking resemblance to the moral right of "*divulgation*," or disclosure. The idea that an author should be able to control the circumstances in which his work first appears before the public is the very foundation of moral rights. For example, confiscating an unpublished work from its author and publishing it would clearly be a violation of the author's moral rights, and is recognized as such in most jurisdictions where they are protected.[109] Although the right of *divulgation* was not explicitly included in Article 6*bis* of the Berne Convention, some commentators believe that the right is nevertheless built into the provisions of Berne.[110]

---

106. Ricketson, *Berne Convention*, *supra* note 5, para. 8.63.

107. Neighboring rights are known by this term because their scope is less ambitious than an author's copyright. They have been a form of protection for performers, whose status is generally inferior to that of authors, but they also extend to other types of broadcasting and dissemination activities. As a group, they are considered "secondary," or "neighboring," to copyright.

108. J. M. Pontier, J. C. Ricci, & J. Bourdon, Droit de la culture, para. 347 (2d ed. Dalloz 1996).

109. On the other hand, it is common practice in developing countries to allow translations to be made on the basis of a compulsory license issued by the government. In a sense, this could amount to a trespass on an author's right of disclosure—for example, the practice, observed in India, of translating a work written in English, or translated into the language, by a writer whose primary language is one of the Indian national languages, back into the writer's native language. This example arose in relation to the publication of S. Vijaya Bharati, C. Subramania Bharati (Government of India Publications 1974); this biography, written in English by a Tamil writer was subsequently translated into Tamil and published by the Government of India without the author's permission.

110. *But see* Adeney, *supra* note 35, para. 6.34, who shows that the idea of a right of disclosure was deliberately excluded from Berne.

The right of communication in Article 8 of the WIPO Copyright Treaty aims to protect—indeed, secure—economic gains to the author from the dissemination of his work by digital means. However, it is also apparent that the Article emphasizes the author's right, in more general terms, to present his work to the public. The right represents legal protection for the personal choice of the author. The language of Article 8 is entirely open-ended—"the exclusive right of authorizing any communication to the public of [the authors'] . . . works"—and it does not distinguish between the economic right and the moral right, at all. The only important characteristic of the right is that it is "exclusive" to the author.

Once again, it is worth noting that initial communication of a work to the public is the essence of the moral rights idea. And indeed, this observation brings us full circle, in the sense that the right to choose the conditions of first publication is also the essence of economic copyright. Whether we call it communication, *représentation*, or *divulgation*, there can be no doubt that the concept lies at the origin of the author's economic and moral rights alike. As Claude Colombet observes:

> It is the right of divulgation which, chronologically, precedes the other [moral rights], as it is through the exercise [of this right that] the work, removed from its author, enters into the economic circuit, and becomes an economic good on the basis of which the other attributes of the author's right, both moral and economic, can be exercised.[111]

If, indeed, Article 8 of the WIPO Copyright Treaty can serve the purpose of helping authors to cope with the erosion of their moral interests in a digital environment, it is disappointing that the right of disclosure should not have found expression alongside the right of communication. Its absence is undoubtedly rooted in the preference of common law countries to avoid the language of moral rights—perhaps, especially, in view of the active participation of the United States in drafting the WCT.[112] However, the curious convergence of economic and moral interests in the language of the WCT shows that any attempt to separate the moral and material concerns of authors in

---

111. C. Colombet, Grands principes du droit d'auteur et des droits voisins dans le monde: Approche de droit comparé 42 (2d ed. Unesco Paris 1992): "C'est le droit de divulgation qui, chronologiquement, précède les autres, car c'est à partir de son exercice que l'oeuvre, arrachée à son auteur, entre dans le circuit économique, devient un bien patrimonial sur lequel pourront s'exercer les autres attributs, tant moraux que pécuniaires, du droit d'auteur."

112. Nevertheless, as discussed in the following section, U.S. leadership favored the creation of a performer's moral right. No doubt, the addition of a moral right for performers was seen as desirable because it would impose an additional layer of protection on music in the online file-sharing environment. *See* Pamela Samuleson, *The U.S. Digital Agenda at WIPO*, 37 Va. J. Int'l L. 369 (1997).

the Digital Age will be an increasingly artificial exercise. It seems inevitable that the moral interests of authors, just like their economic rights, will be implicated in new technology.

b. The WPPT: Dissemination is the New Creation

The WPPT presents a different scenario, rather puzzling at first glance. Negotiated and finalized alongside the WCT, any assertion of an American influence in that Agreement must equally apply to this one.[113] In this light, the WPPT offers what is simply a tremendous surprise. It deals with moral rights; and, not only does it address them, but it also takes steps forward that are radical and new at the level of both concept and practice of the law. It creates moral rights of attribution and integrity for performers, just as the Berne Convention articulates them for authors in the text of Article 6*bis*.

The WPPT scheme for moral rights is innovative and important for a number of reasons.[114] First and foremost, at a time when conceptual discussion of copyright issues has become distressingly rare, a performer's moral right represents a fundamental innovation in the theory of the law. In fact, WPPT represents the first international progress on moral rights since they were added to the Berne Convention in 1928. A moral right for performers has never existed before in international copyright law.[115] The moral rights in the WPPT are limited in some important ways—in particular, the Performances Treaty excludes the possibility of moral rights claims arising out of performances in audiovisual works, thereby maintaining the exclusion of moral rights from films.[116] Nevertheless, the presence of performers' moral rights in international copyright regulation signifies a fundamental shift in our understanding of performance.

The new moral rights are set out in Article 5 of the WPPT. The rights created by the Article closely resemble those established in Article 6*bis* of the Berne

---

113. *Id.*
114. For a discussion of moral rights in the WPPT, *supra* note 15, see Mira T. Sundara Rajan, *Center Stage: Moral Rights in the WPPT*, CASE W. RESERVE L. REV. (forthcoming 2010).
115. The Rome Convention, the first international agreement dealing with performers' rights, makes no mention of performers' moral interest. *See* International Convention for the Protection of Performers, Producers of Phonograms and Broadcasting Organizations, Oct. 26, 1961, 496 U.N.T.S. 43 [Rome Convention].
116. This has been a key issue for the Hollywood film industry. *See* Samuelson, *supra* note 112, at 371–72 (and footnotes 15 & 16), who comments: "Although the U.S. and European delegations were allied on almost all other intellectual property issues at the diplomatic conference, they were bitterly divided on a proposal to universalize European norms about rights of performers of audiovisual works which the U.S. motion picture industry regarded as an anathema. After the Europeans finally agreed to put off to another day the debate over international rights for audiovisual performers, the New Instrument could be finalized. The final treaty provides a much improved framework for protecting the rights of producers and performers of sound recordings."

Convention, though they are not identical. Berne articulates two fundamental moral rights for authors: a right of attribution and a right of integrity. Article 5 of WPPT creates the same two rights for performers. However, in its formulation of the performers' integrity right, the WPPT is slightly more conservative than Berne. It removes the possibility that any "other derogatory action" could violate integrity, and it eliminates the concept of "honor." Of these modifications, Mihály Ficsor sees the second as potentially significant.[117]

The WPPT imposes one significant limitation on moral rights: the language of the Treaty specifies that the rights will apply only to "aural" performances. Performances used in audiovisual works are, therefore, excluded. Within their application to aural performances, however, the moral rights in the WPPT are quite broad, extending both to live performance and to recorded, or "fixed," performances. Once again, this feature of the WPPT is responsive to technology. We see the emergence of a new kind of freedom in relation to the orthodox copyright precept that a work must be "fixed" in a tangible medium before it can enjoy protection, in order to accommodate the new realities of the performer's art in the digital context.

The second part of Article 5 seems to maintain some interesting flexibilities in relation to the statutory enactment of moral rights. Here, too, the formula follows the compromise established by Berne. The idea that common law protection, especially through tort, may offer an adequate substitute for statutory provisions on moral rights is derived directly from Article 6*bis* (2) of the Berne Convention.

As in the case of Berne, however, a careful reading of this article of the WPPT suggests that some protection beyond tort law, some kind of statutory enactment, however minimal, remains a requirement in relation to performers' moral rights. The key distinction lies in the statement that "some, but not all of these rights . . . may cease to be protected." The extent of the obligation is far from clear; but some kind of obligation to maintain moral rights after the performer's death appears to have been created.

The moral rights in the WPPT inaugurate a new status for performers. Copyright law has traditionally understood performers to be engaged in the dissemination of information or culture, rather than creating works of art in their own right. Accordingly, the status of performers has always been distinctly inferior to that of "true" authors. This situation is reflected in historically lower levels of protection for performers' rights, usually known as mere "neighboring" rights to copyright, and delayed recognition for them at the international level.

---

117. *See* Mihály Ficsor, The Law of Copyright and the Internet: The 1996 WIPO Treaties, Their Interpretation and Implementation 617–18 (Oxford University Press 2002). The issue is discussed in more detail in Chapter 6, *infra*, notes 103–05 and accompanying text.

By recognizing that performers may, in fact, be as deeply implicated in their work as authors, the WPPT moves copyright into a new era. Like authors, performers, too, may be vulnerable to harm from the failure to acknowledge them as the creators of their own performances, or to preserve the integrity of their interpretations. While performers were traditionally considered mere mouthpieces for composers, the role of the performer has grown dramatically over time. The change is long overdue. But it is worth noting that the nineteenth-century perspective on performance held its own inherent contradictions, as an era that promoted virtuoso musicianship still clung to the idea of a nobler calling in composition.[118]

Practically speaking, the new moral rights reflect the process of cultural adaptation by which copyright law is finding its way into the digital world. Moral rights for performers imply a recognition of the growing cultural importance of performers and their creative activities. In a sense, performance is the most powerful art form of the digital era. The WPPT seems to recognize this new reality by elevating performers to the status of creators in their own right.

If the first contribution of WPPT is to offer a new theory of performance, a second point worth noting about its moral rights scheme has to do with the general affirmation of moral rights in a digital environment, signified by their inclusion in the WPPT. The moral rights in the WPPT are specifically adapted to digital activities—for example, directly addressing the possibility of having access to performances through sound files that may be obtained via the Internet. In many situations involving the communication of performances through digital technology, a moral rights dimension could now be involved. The WPPT accommodates this new possibility.

This leads to a third feature of the WPPT measures, which is noteworthy and has to do with one of the broader problems of copyright in a digital environment. A practical concern raised by the creation of a new moral right is the fact of its introduction into an environment where copyright restrictions have become generally difficult to enforce. Existing rights are poorly observed, yet the WPPT creates further rights. These rights are not only new factors to contend with in their own right, but they also interact with existing rights in various ways.

Like other dimensions of copyright, moral rights for performers bring additional complexity to a problem that is frequently encountered in the digital context, and is perhaps best described as the "layering" of rights. Because of the potential confluence of multiple works, layers of rights have always tended to accumulate in the copyright sphere. A song with words serves as a

---

118. For an in-depth introduction to the virtuoso piano tradition, see KENNETH HAMILTON, AFTER THE GOLDEN AGE: ROMANTIC PIANISM AND MODERN PERFORMANCE 3–32 (Oxford University Press 2008).

simple example: two copyright works, lyrics and musical score, combine to form a larger whole.

In a digital environment, there is an exaggerated tendency for layers of rights to develop. The potential for incorporating, or "re-using," existing copyright works, or parts of them, in new creation is a characteristic feature of the digital landscape. A database is perhaps the most obvious example; but re-use can happen in countless ways. When dealing with performances, copyright "layers" present a complex problem because of the great number and variety of interests that may be involved in creating, recording, and publicizing a performance. We may be concerned with the interaction of a performer, a composer, possibly a lyricist, a sound engineer, a producer, the owner of the sound recording and, of course, the public that ultimately receives, enjoys, and "uses" that recording. These interests may be shared and overlapping in some instances, but at other times, they will clearly be in conflict. Copyright law must confront the difficult task of finding an effective solution to these problems.

There can be no doubt that the presence of moral rights in the WPPT is a significant innovation in international copyright law. It is also rather mysterious: how did they get there? In a world which appears to be consistently cautious about moral rights, why does the WPPT advance the idea of a performer's moral right? The result is all the more surprising in view of the fact that negotiations for the Treaty were largely driven by discussions between the United States and European Union countries.[119]

The support of Europeans for moral rights is hardly surprising. Countries like France, Germany, Italy, and Austria have been stalwarts for moral rights since the inception of the Berne Convention and before.[120] Most EU member states have a long tradition of protection for authors' moral rights, and indeed, even the new member states of Central and Eastern Europe offered strong protection to authors in the earlier history of their laws.[121] These states would readily have accepted a moral right for performers as the logical extension of a well-established and useful doctrine.

It is the American position that complicates things. U.S. feelings about moral rights are ambivalent. The difficulty of protecting moral rights on American soil has both legal and political roots. The origins of U.S. copyright policy in the American Constitution have always implied restrictions on the

---

119. *See* Samuelson, *supra* note 112.

120. *See* Ricketson, *supra* note 5, paras. 8.92–8.101.

121. For an interesting overview of Hungarian copyright history, see Péter Munkácsi, *Copyright Law in Hungary*, in Intellectual Property: Eastern Europe & the CIS (Mira T. Sundara Rajan ed., Oxford University Press 2008). Regarding moral rights, he notes: "the 1921 Act did not provide for moral rights, creating a problem when Hungary adhered to the 1928 Rome Act of the BC. The 'Kúria,' the Supreme Court at that time, adopted a series of decisions of principle recognizing Berne moral rights."

scope of copyright protection. The Constitutional culture helps to explain why the American copyright system once developed as a registration-based system while authors virtually everywhere else enjoyed automatic rights.[122] Constitutional limits on copyright are usually invoked in the name of freedom of speech or its alter ego, freedom of access to knowledge and information.[123] In the past, the concern has undoubtedly been one of creating powerful monopoly rights whose effect would be anticompetitive in the worst sense of the term.

The same rationale that restricts the scope of copyright protection on Constitutional grounds could signify limits on the protection of moral rights, as well. Indeed, until and unless copyright came to be acknowledged as some variety of natural right—either a labor-based right or a human right—the possibility of expanding legal protection for them within a Constitutional framework would seem to be excluded.

In political terms, the industries implicated in American moral rights include two powerful lobbies: music and film. On the one hand, there has been great resistance to moral rights at home, largely because of the Hollywood film industry. On the other hand, there appears to be an awareness on the part of the music industry that moral rights offer an additional layer of protection for performances, leading to a consideration, or hope, that they could be of help in the fight against Internet piracy of copyright-protected music. In the final analysis, the overall impact of the new moral rights of performers is, indeed, to create an additional layer of rights in performances.

This new layer of moral rights involves a number of practical implications for American industry players. First, where moral rights arise, there is an additional level of permissions which would have to be obtained by anyone who wanted to use the work. In the case of the WPPT, permission would have to be obtained from the performer, as well as the producer of the recording. Moral rights are generally inalienable, so that a "user" will consistently confront the challenge of having to obtain the permission of an author who may

---

122. *See* U.S. CONST., art. I, § 8, cl. 8, which states: "The Congress shall have power . . . to promote the progress of science and useful arts, by securing for limited times to authors and inventors the exclusive right to their respective writings and discoveries." The clause has been widely discussed in U.S. copyright literature; it was the basis for a Constitutional challenge to the extension of copyright term in the United States, in *Eldred v. Ashcroft*, 239 F.3d 372 (2001), *aff'd*, 537 U.S. 186 (2003); *see* Legal Information Institute, Cornell University Law School, http://www.law.cornell.edu/supct/html/01-618.ZS.html (last visited Apr. 29, 2010). The argument failed, as the U.S. Supreme Court identified other safeguards within U.S. copyright law that provided adequate protection to the public interest in access to knowledge. For a critique of the decision and surrounding commentary, see Jack M. Balkin, *Digital Speech and Democratic Culture: A Theory of Freedom of Expression for the Information Society*, 79 N.Y.U. L. REV. 1, 12–26 & n.46 (2004).

123. *See* the arguments against the extension of copyright term in *Eldred v. Ashcroft*, *supra* note 120.

not have any other rights in his work at all, and to do so *in addition to* securing economic rights to use the work. Although the moral right would be asserted by performers, it could help music corporations to strengthen their hold on works indirectly. As a practical matter, the rights would create an additional onus, a further legal obligation for the public to satisfy when attempting to use works.

The consideration of inalienability leads to a second point: the problem of balancing interests that are potentially competing in our reformulation of moral rights for the Digital Age. In addition to introducing another layer of rights into the use of performances, moral rights may emphasize the potential for antagonism between the creator of a work and those involved in its exploitation. Moral rights do not create this hostility, but they give legal expression to the divergent interests of performer and publicist for the first time in copyright statutes. The effect is to shift the balance of bargaining power between them.[124] Given the number of individual copyright claims that may be implicated in a performance, this change could play a significant role in redefining a number of key relationships—performer and composer, performer and sound engineer, performer and producer, performer and record label. And, inevitably, our final consideration must be the relationship between performer and public, made more complex by the articulation of moral rights, and in which, the public will have a new responsibility to be aware of performers' moral interests.

This issue of balance is clearly a problem of many dimensions, and merits closer examination. First, let us consider the balance between creators of works and those who exploit them commercially: performer versus record label.

Given the drafting history of the WPPT—and, in particular, potential corporate support for performers' moral rights—it is of the utmost importance to emphasize the connection between moral rights and the individual performer. This relationship, like that between an author and his work, is personal, unbreakable, and permanent. It is not eligible to be acquired by someone other than the performer. Except in the event of the performer's death, it cannot be exercised by anyone "on his behalf." This was one of the peculiarities of international moral rights cases brought by the Soviet

---

124. Interestingly, early Soviet copyright was explicitly based on the theory of an inherent tension between publisher and author, with publisher exploiting the relative weakness of the author. The 1938 commentary states, "[It] is characteristic that, except for a small group of bourgeois authors, the author's right is the property, in bourgeois society, not of the author, but of the publisher, of a big capitalist, an industrialist. . . . [T]he author's right in capitalist countries is made into a tool of the interests of the monopolist-publisher, a means of exploiting the author and retarding the cultural growth of the masses of the people." MATERIALS ON SOVIET LAW 35 (J. N. Hazard trans., Columbia University 1947). *See also* Sundara Rajan, *Copyright and Creative Freedom, supra* note 13, at 96.

government in the 1960s: the cases were litigated by the government "on behalf of the author," but this is something that no government would have the right to do in the absence of legislated rules.[125] Certainly, Soviet law of the time did not grant the government rights to claim moral rights for its authors.[126] Given the ever-expanding reach of copyright law, it would not be helpful if moral rights now became vulnerable to a new type of exploitation— co-opted by industry as one more tool in its struggle for power in a digital environment. The prospect that a standard practice might develop, whereby industry seeks to assert moral rights "on behalf of" performers, is disturbing.

Apart from the fact that it would be inconsistent with the theory of the law, the idea of a corporate moral right raises serious concerns of public policy. It would be a dangerous development. Through moral rights, corporations could acquire the power to restrict freedom of expression. We may be able to justify giving the performer a say in the treatment of his or her own work on humanitarian grounds; what justification can we offer for transferring the exercise of these personal rights to corporations?[127]

In terms of balancing the needs of performer and public, once again, we face a complex issue. The freedom of expression of the public is at stake; so, too, is the freedom and independence of the performer. We may be talking about a net benefit in the long term—a more humane cultural environment for performers. But this benefit is more obviously cultural than economic in nature. It is difficult to articulate, and vague. As in the case of authors' moral rights, the economic consequences of a moral right for performers remain largely unknown.

All of these implications of the WPPT remain abstract until the principles in the Treaty find their way into national legislation. The challenge of drafting and interpreting these rights in domestic laws is to achieve the benefit of including performers in the copyright process. It would be ideally satisfying to be able to acknowledge the creative contribution of the performer as an

---

125. One possible exception to this principle would be government intervention in copyright in extreme cases of public interest. *See* Attorney General v. Blake and Another, [2000] 4 All ER 385; [2000] 3 WLR 625 (27th July, 2000), *available at* http://www.bailii.org/uk/cases/UKHL/2000/45.html (last visited Aug. 17, 2010). In this case, the British Crown acquired proceeds from the author's copyright because it was strongly against the public interest to encourage a double agent to profit from his illegal actions. Allowing the author to profit from his wrongful actions would have been condoning a form of unjust enrichment.

126. On Soviet moral rights at that period, see the overview in Sundara Rajan, *Copyright and Creative Freedom, supra* note 13, Chapter V, "Socialist Copyright Law," 97–100.

127. Japan, along with Korea, is one of the very few countries in the world that does allow corporations to claim moral rights; it does so by including corporations within the definition of "author" under its copyright law. But the cultural context of Japan is very different. In particular, the role of corporations in Japanese society is distinct, as is the idea of corporate responsibility. Korea, whose law is closely based on Japanese copyright, follows the same practice. *See* the discussion in Chapter 3, *supra*, "A Theory In Flux: The Evolution in Progress of Moral Rights," notes 244–246 and accompanying text.

individual, while developing a workable relationship among the different interests involved in the process of making a performance available to the public. The WPPT has pioneered the recognition of the performer as a creative individual involved in the copyright equation. This is a surprising, yet important, achievement of the Treaty, in an environment where copyright is usually thought of as a right-owner's prerogative.

The moral rights of performers in the WPPT present a new quandary for countries engaged in the task of harmonizing their laws with international agreements. Can moral rights be incorporated into national legal frameworks that are an imperfect reflection of the provisions of the Berne Convention? In other words, in countries where authors' moral rights are not yet protected, or recognition for them is inferior to Berne standards, the introduction of moral rights for performers could create an anomalous situation where performers enjoy better protection for their moral rights than authors.

Canada presents an interesting illustration of this scenario. Blanket provisions allowing moral rights to be waived comprehensively are a well-known feature of the moral rights scheme in the Canadian Copyright Act.[128] Canada is a signatory to the WIPO Internet Treaties, but it has yet to ratify them by enacting appropriate amendments to Canadian copyright law.[129] Two rounds of amendments to implement the WCT and the WPPT have been proposed and rejected in Canada;[130] but it is telling that both proposals reproduced the existing formula for the moral rights of authors in the Canadian Copyright Act, including the controversial provisions on waivers. A third round of proposed changes is currently pending, and the new Bill takes the same position on performers' moral rights as the previous two.[131] Accordingly, if these provisions eventually become law, performers' moral rights in Canada will operate under long-familiar constraints. The Canadian government had an opportunity to reform the entire scheme for moral rights, and nothing less

---

128. *See supra* note 91; the provisions on waiver of moral rights may be found in sec. 14.1(2). Note especially the controversial provision of sec. 14.1(4), which allows a third party to benefit from a waiver of moral rights executed by the author in favor of the person exploiting his work. Arguably, this amounts to permitting the alienation in fact of moral rights under Canadian law.

129. Canada acceded to both treaties on December 22, 1997. The accession notifications can be seen on the WIPO website, WPPT Notification No. 1 WIPO Performances and Phonograms Treaty, *available at* http:/www.wipo.int/treaties/en/html.jsp?file=/redocs/notdocs/en/wppt/treaty_wppt_1.html (last visited Apr. 29, 2010); and WCT Notification No. 2 WIPO Copyright Treaty, *available at* http://www.wipo.int/treaties/en/html.jsp?file=/redocs/notdocs/en/wct/treaty_wct_2.html (last visited Apr. 29, 2010).

130. For details, see *supra* note 17.

131. Bill C-32 was tabled by the government on June 2, 2010. *See* http://www2.parl.gc.ca/HousePublications/Publication.aspx?DocId=4580265&Language=e&Mode=1 (last visited Aug. 19, 2010).

than this is required if Canada is to enact a credible regime. But change is not on the horizon.

The United States presents another case in point. With the exception of the *Visual Artists Rights Act* of 1990,[132] there is no American legislation dealing specifically with the moral rights of authors.[133] Despite the pivotal role of the United States in the adoption of the WPPT, the country has no statutory regime for the protection of performers' moral rights. If the United States were to enact moral rights for performers, would this be another specialty scheme like VARA? If so, on what legal or theoretical grounds could such a scheme be justified in the absence of moral rights for authors?

These examples draw attention to a conceptual issue. Moral rights in a digital environment can be seen in one of two ways—as an expression of historical continuity with the laws of the past, or as a departure from past legal theories. If the second perspective eventually dominates, it should be recognized that there are dangers in a break with the past. In particular, if we cut moral rights loose from their moorings in natural rights theory, they may become open to commercial exploitation. If this were to happen, moral rights could generate serious problems for freedom of speech, creativity, and access to knowledge. Ironically, a corporate moral right in performances could work to the detriment of creative individuals in a digital environment—a contradiction in terms. Moral rights in a technological environment have benefits to offer, but they also present dangers to be avoided. Maintaining a pristine theory of the relationship between creator and work will be important. But the problem should not be underestimated. The integrity of this relationship is fundamentally challenged by new technology.[134]

---

132. *See supra* note 86.
133. Historically, the Lanham Act, which protects consumers against false designations of origin, has been proposed as a possible stand-in for the moral right of attribution; this possibility now appears to have been closed off by the U.S. Supreme Court's decision in the *Dastar* case and subsequent interpretation of this precedent. *See* Lanham Act, 15 U.S.C. §§ 1051–1129 (2000); Dastar Corp. v. Twentieth Century-Fox Film Corp., 34 Fed. Appx. 312 (9th Cir. 2002), *rev'd and remanded*, 539 U.S. 23 (2003). *See* the interesting commentary by Graeme W. Austin, *The Berne Convention as a Canon of Construction: Moral Rights after Dastar*, 61 N.Y.U. Ann. Surv. Am. L. 111 (2005).
134. *See* the discussion of this theme in Mira T. Sundara Rajan, *Moral Rights in the Digital Age: New Possibilities for the Democratisation of Culture*, 16(2) Int'l Rev. L., Comp. & Tech. 187 (2002); an earlier version of this paper was presented to the Sixteenth BILETA Annual Conference, *available at* http://www.bileta.ac.uk/Document%20Library/1/Moral%20Right s%20in%20the%20Digital%20Age%20-%20New%20Possibilities%20for%20the%20Demo cratisation%20of%20Culture.pdf (last visited Apr. 29, 2010).

4. The European Union: Unfulfilled Promise

An assessment of moral rights in the international copyright system would not be complete without a consideration of the European experience. Although the EU copyright Directives are a regional system, their achievements in copyright harmonization are, in many respects, pioneering. The EU is a unique international group in relation to copyright because of the exceptional drive towards harmonization within its borders. The WTO and WIPO represent the full complement of international diversity, implying competing copyright goals., But the EU, at least when it comes to copyright policy, is a remarkably unified group. It is no exaggeration to say that all countries of the Union, including the new member states, see improvements in copyright as an important commercial, and possibly cultural, goal. Harmonization in the EU is watched closely by countries and regions throughout the world, from Canada to India, because the EU has also achieved another, subtler victory: the brokering of effective compromises between the copyright systems of continental Europe and the UK, and among countries at different levels of economic development.[135] Success has been achieved even in as controversial an area as the *droit de suite*, or artist's resale right, which the UK believed would threaten the vitality of the London art market.[136] As such, the EU example can illuminate broader issues of harmonization with international agreements.

In contrast to both the WTO and WIPO, the European Union copyright harmonization process involves a much greater potential for developing a Europe-wide appreciation of moral rights for authors and performers. The most powerful members of the EU, France and Germany, are also the heartland of moral rights doctrine. American objections to moral rights at the WTO resulted in a half-hearted treatment in the TRIPs Agreement. However, the United Kingdom, Europe's only common law jurisdiction, has perhaps been more prepared to adapt to a changing copyright landscape, at least in principle, by adopting legislative protections for moral rights. The treatment of moral rights in the UK Copyright, Designs and Patents Act of 1988 leaves much to be desired; but their presence in British copyright law, for the first time in the history of UK legislation, is itself an important sign of progress.[137]

---

135. The problem is of direct relevance to Canada, which has always faced the issue of balancing French and English traditions where copyright is concerned. See, in particular, the recent moral rights case of *Théberge*, which raises the specter of persistent differences in the interpretation of moral rights. Théberge v. Galerie d'Art du Petit Champlain Inc. [2002] 2 S.C.R. 336, 2002 SCC 34.

136. Directive 2001/84/EC of the European Parliament and of the Council on the resale right for the benefit of the author of an original work of art. 27.09.2001, *available at* http://ec.europa.eu/internal_market/copyright/documents/documents_en.htm (last visited Apr. 29, 2010).

137. Copyright, Designs and Patents Act 1988, *supra* note 84, Chapter IV on Moral Rights.

An additional factor that may make the EU a viable candidate for the development of an international moral rights standard is the role of adjudication. At the WTO, moral rights are excluded from the adjudicative capacity of the Dispute Settlement Body. In the EU, however, the European Court of Justice is a strong force to be reckoned with where the trans-border movement of intellectual property is concerned. A number of cases from the ECJ have established seminal principles on the recognition and enforcement of copyright in the EU, and moral rights, though little clarified, are uniformly included in the Europe-wide concept of the law. Notable among ECJ judgments is the *Phil Collins* decision of 1993, which established that copyright within the European Union must apply on a nondiscriminatory basis to the nationals of all EU member states,[138] and the *Magill* case of 1995, which recognized the need to "protect the moral rights in the work" as a part of the "essential function" of copyright law.[139] Still deeper in the history of ECJ decisions, the seminal *GEMA* case of 1981 found that the presence of moral rights in copyright law did not require the differential treatment of copyright subject-matter within the EU. As Catherine Seville observes:

> The ECJ acknowledged that copyright comprised moral rights, but held that this was no reason to make a distinction between copyright and other industrial and commercial property rights with regard to economic rights, which were the subject of the case. It therefore confirms that copyright, like other intellectual property rights, could not be used to entrench the isolation of national markets or restricting parallel imports.[140]

These cases show that the European Court of Justice has considerable potential to implement harmonized copyright practices across its member states. It may also be worth pointing out that the European concept of legal harmonization is different from the approach of the WTO. Coercion has been a consistent theme of WTO dispute settlement; in the European context, however, if coercion exists, it plays a more subtle role in European dynamics. Though imperfectly realized, the basic European ideal is consensus. This difference in character may imply a subtle potential for recognizing

---

138. *See* Phil Collins v. Imtrat Handelsgesellschaft mbH; Patricia Im-und Export Verwaltungsgesellschaft mbH and Another v. EMI Electrola GmbH, Joined Cases C-92/92 and C-326/92, *available at* http://eur-lex.europa.eu/smartapi/cgi/sga_doc?smartapi!celexplus!prod CELEX numdoc&lg=en&numdoc=61992J0092 (last visited Apr. 29, 2010); this case receives an excellent analysis, alongside other ECJ decisions on copyright, *in* CATHERINE SEVILLE, EU INTELLECTUAL PROPERTY LAW AND POLICY 324–25 (Edward Elgar 2009).

139. *See* Radio Telefis Eirann and Independent Television Publications Ltd. v. Commission, [1995] 4 CMLR 718; [1995] ECR 1-743. The case receives a detailed and helpful commentary in I. Stamatoudi, *The Hidden Agenda in* Magill *and its Impact on New Technologies*, 1(1) J. WORLD INTELL. PROP. 153–76 (1998).

140. Seville, *supra* note 138, at 324–25.

moral rights in the EU. The TRIPs Agreement is perhaps more accurately characterized as an experiment in legal "standardization" at the international level, rather than "harmonization" *per se*. The objective of the WTO system is to achieve a uniform level of protection across borders; the nature of the dispute settlement mechanism also lends itself to greater uniformity in standards. The purpose of European legal harmonization is to favor freedom of movement across borders in the Internal Market. Its attempt to bring national standards into congruity across such a diverse region cannot avoid the problem of accommodating cultural sensitivities. European attempts at harmonization have been mired in controversy, but they have at least generated discussion about the implementation of copyright norms across jurisdictions of great cultural and economic diversity.

In a 1995 Green Paper on Copyright and Related Rights in the Information Society, the European Commission made a number of statements about the need to include moral rights in the process of copyright harmonization.[141] It observed:

> With the arrival of the information society the question of moral rights is becoming more urgent than it was. Digital technology is making it easier to modify works. The Commission believes there is a need for an examination of the question whether the present lack of harmonization will continue to be acceptable in the new digital environment.[142]

In 2000, a second study on moral rights in the EU was completed.[143] This study concluded that there was no need to pursue the goal of moral rights harmonization in the EU, as harmonization was only desired by two countries, Italy and Greece, which enjoyed higher levels of moral rights than the others.[144] However, the general tone of the study is surprisingly complacent towards the impact of digital technology on copyright law. Given the thoroughness of the research, it seems likely that the study conclusions have simply become outdated in the years since the new millennium. In particular, the experience of the past decade has taught us that new technology creates both practical and conceptual challenges to copyright law, and this has occurred to an extent that would have been impossible to anticipate before

---

141. Commission of the European Communities Green Paper on Copyright and Related Rights in the Information Society (19.07.1995), COM (95) 382 final, VII [EU Green Paper]; *see also* the interesting and more recent work by Marjut Salokannel & Alain Strowel, with Estelle Derclaye, Study Contract Concerning Moral Rights in the Context of the Exploration of Works through Digital Technology: Final Report, Study contract n° ETD/99/B5-3000/E°Apr. 28, 2000, *available at* http://ec.europa.eu/internal_market/copyright/docs/studies/etd1999b53000e28_en.pdf. [Salokannel & Strowel].

142. EU Green Paper, *supra* note 138, at 67.

143. *See* Salokannel & Strowel, *supra* note 141, at 242.

144. Salokannel & Strowel, *supra* note 141.

the year 2000. Since the appearance of this study, there has been no further investigation of the issues, although one would certainly appear to be warranted. The expansion of the European Union to the post-socialist jurisdictions of Central and Eastern Europe would be reason enough to reconsider the issue of harmonizing moral rights. These countries bring many types of new concerns to the European copyright arena, ranging from the need for access to technology, to the promotion of innovation and the progress of freedom of speech.[145] The reconstruction of historical truth and the restoration of authors' reputations is a special concern, ongoing at least since 1989.[146] The presence of these countries in the EU, many of whom showed an early commitment to moral rights, creates an opportunity to re-examine them from a pan-European perspective.

Lack of commitment at the level of policy in recent years is reflected in the state of European moral rights. When the EU has not made significant progress on policy development, which is severely out of date, progress on harmonization is not to be expected. To date, none of the eight harmonization directives has dealt with the problems of moral rights in a digital environment. For example, the Computer Programs Directive addresses only the economic rights in computer programs.[147] The Term Directive states that it "shall be without prejudice to the provisions of the Member States regulating moral rights"[148]—presumably, in order to accommodate jurisdictions where moral rights enjoy perpetual protection. A similar approach is taken in the Database Directive, which specifies that "the moral rights of the natural person who created the database belong to the author and should be exercised according to the legislation of the Member States and the provisions of the Berne Convention . . .; . . . such moral rights remain outside the scope of this

---

145. *See* Sundara Rajan, *Copyright and Creative Freedom, supra* note 13, Chapter I; an updated version appears as Mira T. Sundara Rajan, *Introduction, in* Intellectual Property: Eastern Europe and the CIS (Mira T. Sundara Rajan ed., Oxford University Press 2008).

146. The notorious Soviet show trial of Andrei Siniavski and Yuli Daniel illustrates some of the ignominies to which writers were subject; for an in-depth analysis of the case, see Sundara Rajan, *Copyright and Creative Freedom, supra* note 13, Chapter VI, "Creative Freedom on Trial."

147. Directive 2009/24/EC of the European Parliament and of the Council of Apr. 23, 2009 on the legal protection of computer programs (codified version) (text with EEA relevance); Original version Council Directive 91/250/EEC of May 14, 1991 on the legal protection of computer programs, *available at* http://eur-lex.europa.eu/LexUriServ/LexUriServ.do?uri=OJ:L:2009:111:0016:0022:EN:PDF (last visited Apr. 19, 2010).

148. Directive 2006/116/EC of the European Parliament and of the Council of Dec. 12, 2006 on the term of protection of copyright and certain related rights (codified version); Council Directive 93/98/EEC of Oct. 29, 1993 harmonizing the term of protection of copyright and certain related rights, *available at* http://eur-lex.europa.eu/smartapi/cgi/sga_doc?smartapi!celexapi!prod!CELEXnumdoc&numdoc=32006L0116&model=guichett&lg=en. n 57 (last visited Apr. 19, 2010).

Directive."[149] This statement confirms that moral rights, at least in the European view, are not automatically excluded from technological creations such as databases.

The 2001 Directive on Copyright in the Information Society is the most ambitious harmonization initiative to date.[150] It deals with copyright comprehensively, and it could have provided an ideal opportunity to address the issue of moral rights. The Directive attempts to harmonize the reproduction right—what Michael Hart aptly calls the "very core of copyright law"[151]—as well as the rights of distribution and communication to the public. However, moral rights appear only in Recital 19 of the Directive, which provides as follows, in a formula that closely resembles Article 9.1 of the TRIPs Agreement:

> The moral rights of right holders should be exercised according to the legislation of the Member States and the provisions of the *Berne Convention for the Protection of Literary and Artistic Works*, of the WIPO Copyright Treaty and of the WIPO Performances and Phonograms Treaty. Such moral rights remain outside the scope of this Directive.[152]

The directive on Copyright in the Information Society is generally based on the WIPO Copyright Treaty. As such, it emphasizes the changing quality of authors' rights in a digital environment, especially in relation to the issue of *représentation*, or communication to the public. Article 3 of the Directive sets out details of the right, including, in broader language than the WIPO Copyright Treaty, an "exclusive right to authorize or *prohibit* any communication to the public . . . including the making available to the public of their works in such a way that members of the public access them from a place and at a time individually chosen by them." (emphasis added). In Article 3.2, the right is explicitly extended to performers in the case of a fixation of their performances, and to phonogram producers in their phonograms.

---

149. Directive 96/9/EC of the European Parliament and of the Council of Mar. 11, 1996 on the legal protection of databases, Official Journal L 077, 27/03/1996 P. 0020–0028, *available at* http://eur-lex.europa.eu/LexUriServ/LexUriServ.do?uri=CELEX:31996L0009:EN:HTML, Preamble, para. 28 (last visited Apr. 19, 2010).

150. Directive 2001/29/EC of the European Parliament and of the Council of May 22, 2001 on the harmonization of certain aspects of copyright and related rights in the information society, *available at* http://eur-lex.europa.eu/LexUriServ/LexUriServ.do?uri=CELEX:-32001L0029:EN:NOT (last visited Apr. 29, 2010) [Copyright Directive, Information Society Directive].

151. Michael Hart, *The Proposed Directive for Copyright in the Information Society: Nice Rights, Shame about the Exceptions*, 20(5) Eur. Intell. Prop. Rev. 169, 169 (1998).

152. Copyright Directive, *supra* note 150.

As in the case of the WIPO Copyright Treaty, it seems difficult to divide this digital-era right of representation into neat economic and moral compartments. Indeed, the explicit right of the author to prohibit communication of the work to the public seems, if anything, to make this right even more powerful and significant than it is in the WIPO Copyright Treaty.

Despite the greater potential for harmonizing moral rights at the level of the EU, the copyright harmonization directives have not succeeded in confronting the issue directly. Rather, the latest Directive on Copyright in the Information Society seems to grant tacit recognition to an author's moral right of disclosure in the form of an extended right of communication to the public, or *représentation*—without, however, any explicit acknowledgement of authors' moral interests. In this sense, the Directive closely follows the WIPO Copyright Treaty, though its treatment of the communication right is somewhat broader than the WIPO approach.

In terms of the moral rights of attribution and integrity, the European process has not made any progress to date. On the basis of EU policy pronouncements and long-standing European tradition, it seems reasonable to expect a greater degree of openness towards moral rights than may be found in other international fora. The failure of the harmonization process in this regard is surprising, and disappointing.

5. Bilateral Agreements: A Deceptive Way Forward

An analysis of moral rights in the international copyright arena would not be complete without some consideration of their place in bilateral agreements. Agreements between countries that deal with copyright issues of mutual interest are an increasingly prominent feature of international copyright arrangements. There is something disturbing about their resurgence: they represent a throwback to the pre-Berne era, when bilateral agreements offered the only possibility of recognition for copyright beyond national borders. But the nineteenth-century system of bilateral accords which pre-dated the Berne Convention ultimately led to chaos. Authors were faced with tremendous uncertainty about the protection of their rights in different jurisdictions.[153] This situation was the antithesis of legal clarity, and the uncertainty that it generated could only be detrimental to authors' interests. History suggests that the temptation of a return to bilateral accords today should be approached with caution.

Most bilateral agreements are now a product of U.S. negotiations with jurisdictions that are perceived to be important for American interests—notably, those like Brazil and Thailand, where copyright piracy is a serious

---

153. Ricketson, *supra* note 5, Chapter 1.

problem.[154] The Agreements reflect an international situation that can still be perceived as unresponsive by American copyright interests. Since the WIPO Internet Treaties came into force in 2002, there has been no further movement on international copyright; even the new directives emanating from the EU are essentially instruments to facilitate the implementation of the WIPO Treaties in the European Union and its member states.[155] For the United States, bilateral agreements are part of an arsenal of anti-piracy strategies, including the Special 301 Watch List and reports of the U.S. Trade Representative's office, which identify and try to exert pressure upon countries where copyright piracy is common, and various public information campaigns in U.S. embassy offices around the world.[156]

Bilateral agreements present an interesting example of new legislative forces in the international copyright arena. Berne specifies that additional agreements are allowed between member states of the Berne Union, with the avowed goal being the improvement of copyright protection in like-minded countries.[157] In this light, bilateral agreements could also be used to promote the clarification of moral rights in a digital environment. However, the effectiveness of an agreement between, for example, the United States and Canada

---

154. *See* the interesting guide on America's international copyright relations published by the U.S. Copyright Office, *International Copyright Relations of the United States*, Circular 38a, *available at* http://www.copyright.gov/circs/circ38a.pdf (last visited Apr. 29, 2010).

155. For an example, see the Directive 2004/48/EC of the European Parliament and of the Council of Apr. 29, 2004 on the enforcement of intellectual property rights (text with EEA relevance), Official Journal of the European Union L 157 of Apr. 30, 2004, *available at* http://eur-lex.europa.eu/pri/en/oj/dat/2004/l_195/l_19520040602en00160025.pdf (last visited Apr. 29, 2010) [Enforcement Directive].

156. *See, for example,* Press Release, U.S. Embassy, New Delhi, Intellectual Property Rights and Film on the Agenda at the American Library (Apr. 24, 2009), *available at* http://newdelhi.usembassy.gov/pr042409a.html; and Intellectual Property Rights (IPR) Enforcement Training Program in Chennai, May 4–6, 2006 (U.S. Embassy, New Delhi), *available at* http://newdelhi.usembassy.gov/iprconfenftrainchen.html (last visited July 13, 2010). See also the annual 2009 Special 301 Report of the U.S. Trade Representative's Office, Apr. 30, 2009, *available at* http://www.ustr.gov/about-us/press-office/reports-and-publications/2009/2009-special-301-report (last visited July 17, 2010). Interestingly, Canada was placed on the Priority Watch List; the Report comments: "The United States continues to have serious concerns with Canada's failure to accede to and implement the WIPO Internet Treaties, which Canada signed in 1997. We urge Canada to enact legislation in the near term to strengthen its copyright laws and implement these treaties. The United States also continues to urge Canada to improve its IPR enforcement system to enable authorities to take effective action against the trade in counterfeit and pirated products within Canada, as well as curb the volume of infringing products transshipped and transiting through Canada. Canada's weak border measures continue to be a serious concern for IP owners."

157. Berne Convention, *supra* note 1, art. 20 provides that: "The Governments of the countries of the Union reserve the right to enter into special agreements among themselves, in so far as such agreements grant to authors more extensive rights than those granted by the Convention, or contain other provisions not contrary to this Convention. The provisions of existing agreements which satisfy these conditions shall remain applicable."

on moral rights would be of limited value to authors in these two countries. New technology brings a global dimension to moral rights. Bilateral agreements may be helpful in initiating movement on this issue in the international arena, but they will probably require follow-up in multilateral discussions.

D. Conclusion

Moral rights are a well established presence in international copyright law. International agreements have included some form of protection for moral rights since 1928, when they first appeared in the Berne Convention. Since then, their international presence has grown.

It has done so in two ways. First, there is the paradox of the TRIPs Agreement. The Agreement excludes moral rights from the practical possibility of enforcement through the trade-based dispute-settlement mechanism at the WTO, but the adoption of TRIPs also signified a powerful new commitment to the copyright norms found in the Berne Convention. Of these two competing forces, the second appears to have won out. Moral rights have been adopted and modernized in an unprecedented number of jurisdictions, including a historic number of common law countries.

Secondly, the specific question of how moral rights should respond to new technology has begun to be addressed by the WIPO Internet Treaties. The Treaties make an explicit attempt to create digital moral rights, in the form of a new moral right for performers. They also move towards a tacit fusion of the moral and economic aspects of copyright in a new right of "communication to the public," which closely resembles the "moral" concept of disclosure.

At the same time, the international framework for moral rights leaves much to be desired. Current international agreements are poorly adapted to the needs of technology. The open-ended approach of Berne to the protection of new technological works allows it to bring them under the copyright umbrella, but the Convention cannot help to clarify broader questions. The issues are intensified rather than relieved by TRIPs, which affirms that technological creation should not be treated differently from "traditional" copyright works. There is also another sense in which TRIPs represents continuity rather than change: it is committed to well-established copyright concepts, such as fixation, which may prove to be fundamentally incompatible with digital realities.[158] Fixation is but one example; notions of originality and authorship, cornerstones of the copyright edifice, are also in flux.

The international copyright regime confronts a fundamental question: should moral rights be part of digital copyright law? If so, what are the

---

158. *See* TRIPs Agreement, *supra* note 8, art. 9.2.

nuances of rights in technological creation, and to what extent should moral rights be a feature of protection? The question demands an answer in at least three different avatars: moral rights as they appear in pure works of technology, such as computer programs; moral rights arising out of hybrid works that include a technological dimension, such as new artistic forms, computer-generated works, or performance-based art; and, finally, moral rights issues in the communication of works through digital reproduction and the Internet.

If moral rights are to adapt to technological change, the international community needs to address two legal issues—whether harmonization of moral rights is necessary in a digital environment, and, if so, what specific legal reforms would be involved in the international harmonization of moral rights. In answer to the first question, it appears likely that international harmonization will prove to be a practical necessity; and even the achievements of bilateral agreements, which could be interesting for countries who hope to improve their relationships with trading partners, will be of limited use without a supportive international framework.

The basic tools for the establishment of an "international moral right" are already available in existing international fora, and of these, both the European Union and WIPO, in that sequence, may be well placed to move forward. The missing catalyst is political will. In the world of copyright lobbying and diplomacy, the relevance of moral rights has been superseded by urgent practical concerns about the enforcement of economic rights. At some point, however, the international community needs to arrive at the understanding, unpleasant but real, that enforcement is a long-term project. The enforcement of intellectual property rights cannot succeed without the right kind of investment in what is, essentially, its "infrastructure"—law reform and the development of public policy, education, and open debate. The practical ability to enforce copyright rulesdepends on the viability of the underlying concept. Once again, ideas, and words, have power.

By itself, an international legislative framework will never be enough to harmonize moral rights. Harmonization requires something more—the ability to implement norms, in both their legal and cultural dimensions, across jurisdictions. Here, too, the solutions will need to address long-term problems—deeply ingrained legal biases, and deep-seated cultural prejudices. Experience shows that identical laws are not likely to work well in diverse jurisdictions because their weak connection with the culture of the new country will emphasize their most unattractive qualities. This approach to "harmonization" is subtle coercion; it leads to poor adaptation to the new environment and a chronic inability to respond to its needs. Above all, the paradoxically outmoded character of reformed laws can often be characterized as, for lack of a better expression, post-colonial. This final factor should not be underestimated: it destroys the credibility of Western-inspired law reform in the very jurisdictions where copyright piracy is a most serious problem, and where change is pursued most urgently by the West.[159]

In terms of its adaptation to new technology, the moral rights concept, like copyright itself, has much further to travel. However, these early steps are, in a sense, "giant" ones. They show that moral rights will not only be relevant to a technological environment, but also, pivotal in defining the future shape of the law. In a post-digital world, there is every chance that copyright as it is now known will become an outmoded concept. But the moral right, and all that it represents, may prove to be more important than ever.[160]

---

159. In relation to the example of post-socialist countries, see the comments in Sundara Rajan, *Copyright and Creative Freedom*, *supra* note 13, at 53–59.
160. In this regard, Hector MacQueen's comments on the proposed Google Book Settlement continue to have a visionary quality. *See* H. MacQueen, *The Google Book Settlement*, 3 Int'l Rev. Indus. Prop. & Copyright L. 247, 249 (2009).

The Programmer as Author

Moral Rights in Information Technology

The fox knows many things, but the hedgehog knows one big thing.

–Archilocus, as translated by Isaiah Berlin[1]

---

1. THE HEDGEHOG AND THE FOX: AN ESSAY ON TOLSTOY'S VIEW OF HISTORY (Elephant Paperback ed. 1993), first published *in* RUSSIAN THINKERS (revised text, Henry Hardy & Aileen Kelly eds., Hogarth Press 1978) (first published George Weidenfeld & Nicolson 1954).

In many ways, information technology represents a test case for moral rights in the digital context. Computer software has been integrated wholeheartedly into copyright law. At the same time, software and related technologies challenge copyright at a fundamental level, raising a number of questions that will need to be answered before the relationship between copyright and software can be called harmonious.

The concept of moral rights takes us straight to the heart of this dilemma. Moral rights can provide the basis for a better model of intellectual property protection for software. In the process, they can also help us to navigate the waters of an entirely uncharted cultural transition, where technology occupies a new place in the human creative psyche.

This chapter considers moral rights in two contrasting manifestations of information technology. First, it examines the place of moral rights in works of new technology that are now accepted subject-matter for copyright protection. The focus is on the paradigmatic case of computer software and, to a limited extent, databases. Secondly, this analysis explores the collision of new technology with the world of the arts and considers three aspects of the problem. What are the moral rights implications of new kinds of artistic works; creative works that are created by new technological methods; or, as is increasingly the case, artistic creation that represents some combination of the two?

A. Computer Software

When considering moral rights in software, it is useful to remember that there is nothing inevitable about the protection of computer software by copyright law. On the contrary, computer programming developed in an environment that was largely devoid of regulation. When the question of offering legal recognition to programs arose, lawmakers confronted the difficult task of how to classify a previously nonexistent and novel technology under established legal terminology.

In fact, there were at least three possible options. The first was to recognize computer programs as a form of intellectual property. However, once again, this does not mean that copyright was the preferred approach. Rather, computer programs seemed to fit more naturally with the legal understanding of scientific inventions, making them eligible for protection under patent law. The patent option was initially rejected by legislators, but it later found favor with the courts, who saw it as a logical approach to intellectual property in software. In the landmark 1998 decision of *State Street Bank*, computer programs were found to be patentable as "business methods."[2]

---

2. State Street Bank & Trust Co. v. Signature Fin. Group, Inc. 149 F.3d 1368 (Fed. Cir. 1998), *cert. denied*, 525 U.S. 1093 (1999). The recent ruling in *Bilski* has compelled a reassessment of the

But the principle of software patentability recognized at that time caused a curious problem. By recognizing that computer programs were entitled to patent protection, it effectively allowed patent and copyright protection to overlap in software—two forms of intellectual property protection simultaneously coexisting in the same work. Concerns about overlapping intellectual property rights in software later contributed to the downfall of the proposed Directive on software patents at the European Union, where excessive levels of intellectual property protection in software were seen as a danger to the public good.[3]

Recent developments in the United States suggest that the pendulum is swinging towards the exclusivity of copyright protection in software under U.S. law, as well. The issue of whether business method patents should be allowed was recently reconsidered in the important case of *Bilski,* where the United States Supreme Court expressed caution about these kinds of patents without quite disallowing them.[4]

A second possibility for the legal protection of software was to accept the novel character of computer software and proceed to recognize it as a new form of intellectual creation in its own right. This would lead, naturally, to a new form of legal recognition peculiar to this kind of work.[5] According to this logic, a *sui generis* right in computer software would be appropriate.

In fact, two *sui generis* regimes for the protection of intellectual creation currently exist in international law. One protects plant varieties and is set out in the UPOV (International Union for the Protection of New Varieties of

---

State Street Bank case by imposing severe limits on what will qualify as a patentable business method. *See* In re Bilski, 545 F.3d 943, 88 U.S.P.Q.2d 1385 (Fed. Cir. 2008), *aff'd*, No. 08-964 (U.S. June 28, 2010) [*Bilski v Kappos*], *available at* http://www.supremecourt.gov/opinions/09pdf/08-964.pdf (last visited Aug. 17, 2010). The Federal Court of Appeal ruling was largely approved by the Supreme Court, but its decision is more nuanced than the appellate ruling. Under the earlier decision, it was widely believed that business method patents would be disallowed; according to the final ruling, the patentability of business methods may or may not be permissible, depending largely on case by case assessments. The case is usefully summarized online by the Electronic Frontier Foundation (EFF) at http://www.eff.org/cases/re-bilski? (last visited Aug. 17, 2010).

3. *See, e.g.,* the overview of the proposed Software Patents Directive, in Robert Bray, *The European Union "Software Patents" Directive: What Is It? Why Is It? Where Are We Now?*, DUKE L. TECH. J. 11 (2005). *See also* the coverage in *Vote Looms for EU "Software Law": European Lawmakers Preparing to Vote on a Directive Which Could Protect Companies' Computerized Inventions,* BBC News (July 5, 2005), *available at* http://news.bbc.co.uk/2/hi/technology/4651585.stm (last visited Apr. 28, 2010); and *Software Patent Bill Thrown Out: European Politicians Have Thrown Out a Controversial Bill That Could Have Led to Software Being Patented,* BBC NEWS (July 6, 2005), *available at* http://news.bbc.co.uk/2/hi/technology/4655955.stm (last visited Apr. 28, 2010).

4. *See supra* note 2.

5. But the argument receives a spirited rejection in Jane C. Ginsburg, *Four Reasons and a Paradox: The Manifest Superiority of Copyright over Sui Generis Protection of Computer Software,* 94 COLUM. L. REV. 2559 (1994).

Plants) Convention of 1961.[6] The UPOV scheme is essentially a specialized type of patent regime for plant varieties, offering more limited protection than a patent, and, as befitting this area of innovation, protection that is more easily obtained.

The second *sui generis* regime governs databases, and traces its origins to the European Union Database Directive of 1996.[7] The Database Directive established protection for "non-original" databases—databases in which the assembly of pre-existing information did not represent a higher level of creative input, and would not, therefore, be eligible for copyright protection. The right represents an attempt to reward the labor of those who build databases. In contrast to the system for plant varieties, the database right is widely considered unsuccesful. In a 2005 report, the European Commission voiced concerns about the failure of the Directive to stimulate the creation of new databases. It also aimed direct criticism at the language of the Directive for instituting a right that was lacking in clarity, and potentially infringed upon the right of the public to have free access to information.[8]

Finally, there remains the important argument that regulation could be rejected outright, leaving computer programs freely available to both the scientific community and the general public. This perspective eventually developed into open-source movements, with Richard Stallman's Free Software Foundation being the original and most philosophically powerful of them all.[9] While there is a range of open-access movements, with subtle shades of variation among them, they all share the general conviction that

---

6. For information on UPOV and the development of the Convention, see http://upov.int/index_en.html (last visited July 18, 2010).

7. Directive 96/9/EC of the European Parliament and of the Council of Mar. 11, 1996 on the legal protection of databases, Official Journal L 077, 27/03/1996 P. 0020-0028, http://eur-lex.europa.eu/LexUriServ/LexUriServ.do?uri=CELEX:31996L0009:EN:HTML (last visited Apr. 28, 2010) [Database Directive]. For a helpful assessment of the Database Directive, see ESTELLE DERCLAYE, THE LEGAL PROTECTION OF DATABASES: A COMPARATIVE ANALYSIS (Edward Elgar 2008).

8. Commission of the European Communities, First evaluation of Directive 96/9/EC on the legal protection of databases (Working Paper) (Dec. 12, 2005). The report is available on the website of the European Commission, *available at* http://ec.europa.eu/internal_market/copyright/docs/databases/evaluation_report_en.pdf (last visited Apr. 28, 2010). A summary of the EU position on databases is provided at http://ec.europa.eu/internal_market/copyright/prot-databases/prot-databases_en.htm (last visited Apr. 28, 2010). *See also* Estelle Derclaye, *Database Sui Generis Right: The Need to Take the Public's Right to Information and Freedom of Expression into Account, in* NEW DIRECTIONS IN COPYRIGHT LAW, Vol. 5, at 3 (Fiona Macmillan ed., Edward Elgar 2007).

9. Larry Lessig acknowledges Stallman's pioneering role in his book, *Free Culture;* he identifies Stallman as the main inspiration behind the Creative Commons movement as well. LAWRENCE LESSIG, FREE CULTURE: HOW BIG MEDIA USES TECHNOLOGY AND THE LAW TO LOCK DOWN CULTURE AND CONTROL CREATIVITY XV (Penguin Press 2004). Appropriately, the book is also available for free download, http://www.free-culture.cc/freeculture.pdf (last visited Apr. 28, 2010).

software should be available for modification on an unrestricted basis. Stallman's Free Software movement elevates this premise to the status of a moral imperative.

The eventual victory of copyright as the chosen form of legal recognition for software occurred for a number of reasons. Not least among these was the active lobbying of the software industry, which had become well established by the beginning of the 1990s and wanted to enjoy the benefits of copyright. From an industry perspective, copyright presented a number of advantages, particularly over its rival in the intellectual property field, patent law. In contrast to patent protection, copyright was available instantaneously, without any formalities or need to fulfill an extensive review process,[10] and it offered a prolonged duration of protection, at least fifty years from the date of creation.

The practical decision to extend copyright protection to software was easily justifiable in legal terms. Copyright had always functioned by the analogical method, extending protection to new kinds of works on the basis that they resembled the existing subject-matter of copyright in some essential way. On this basis, rights in literary property were extended to musical and artistic works.[11] Software was nothing more, or less, than one more example of this circumstance. Just as it had accommodated many new kinds of intellectual works in the past, copyright could adapt to the protection of computer programs.

However, the moral rights aspect of copyright law was neglected in these discussions. In a sense, the omission seems entirely natural. Software was really an American phenomenon. United States accession to the Berne Convention only occurred in 1989, and even after that date, American law did not recognize the concept of moral rights outside the narrow sphere of the visual arts. How has the legal situation since evolved to address the moral rights of programmers?

1. Legal Position: A New Kind of "Literary Work"

Computer programs are now widely accepted as a kind of intellectual creation protected by copyright law. The informal recognition of programs as a form of "literary work" is mirrored at the international level in the language of the Berne Convention. The Convention provides for the copyright

---

10. It should be noted that the claims of the software industry to copyright protection followed upon U.S. membership in the Berne Convention, which removed the need to register copyright(s) under U.S. law.

11. *See, for example,* the UK Fine Arts Copyright Act of 1862, 25 & 26 Vict., c. 68. An insightful Commentary on Fine Arts Copyright Act 1862 is provided in Ronan Deazley, Primary Sources on Copyright (1450–1900), http://www.copyrighthistory.org/cgi-bin/kleioc/0010/exec/ausgabeCom/%22uk_1862%22 (last visited Apr. 28, 2010).

protection of "every production in the literary, scientific and artistic domain, whatever may be the mode or form of its expression." It easily accommodates computer software within its terms.

Accordingly, computer programs enjoy protection in international copyright law as "literary works." Programs are written in the language of computer code, and as such, they can be considered analogous to written works in the more usual sense of the term. This approach fits particularly well with the treatment of literary works in common law countries, where the requirement of originality in copyright works simply means that a work should not be copied, and that it should exhibit a certain degree of "skill and labour."[12] Protecting computer programs as literary works is somewhat more problematic in Continental European countries which have traditionally required an element of creative originality for copyright protection—what is known in German law, for example, as the *Schöpfungshöhe*, or "level of creativity."[13] Nevertheless, the European Software Directive of 1991, applicable to member countries of the European Union, specifically avoids this problem, providing that:

> A computer program shall be protected if it is original in the sense that it is the author's own intellectual creation. No other criteria shall be applied to determine its eligibility for protection.[14]

---

12. But see the most recent decision of the Supreme Court of Canada on the issue, *CCH Canadian Ltd. v. Law Society of Upper Canada* [2004] 1 S.C.R. 339, 2004 SCC 13 (Can.) [*CCH*]: Chief Justice McLachlin uses the term "skill and labour" to indicate a new and slightly higher standard of originality in Canadian law than a traditional emphasis on labor, "sweat of the brow." The terminology is confusing, because in English law, the expression "skill, judgment and labour" usually indicates a *de minimis* standard of originality, equivalent to "sweat of the brow": *Ladbroke (Football) v. William Hill (Football)*, 1964 1 All E.R. 465 (HL). Nevertheless, the *CCH* standard has been extended internationally by the effective adoption of the Canadian standard in Indian law *See* Eastern Book Company & Ors. v. D.B. Modak & Anr. (Dec. 12, 2007) (Supreme Court of India) [*Eastern Book Co.*], *available at* Supreme Court of India judgments http://judis.nic.in/supremecourt/chejudis.asp (last visited Apr. 28, 2010). However, it is important to note that the United States copyright law, at least, has made a definite move away from the common law conception of originality as the "sweat of the brow," to a Continental-style standard involving a "modicum of creativity." *See* the landmark decision of the U.S. Supreme Court in *Feist Publications, Inc. v. Rural Telephone Service Co.*, 499 U.S. 340 (1991) [*Feist*].

13. The issue is discussed in Gerhard Schricker, *Farewell to the "Level of Creativity" (Schöpfungshöhe) in German Copyright Law?*, 26(1) INT'L REV. INDUS. PROP. & COPYRIGHT L. 41 (1995).

14. Directive 2009/24/EC of the European Parliament and of the Council of April 23, 2009 on the legal protection of computer programs (Codified version) (Text with EEA relevance); original version Council Directive 91/250/EEC of May 14, 1991 on the legal protection of computer programs, *available at* http://eur-lex.europa.eu/LexUriServ/LexUriServ.do?uri= OJ:L:2009:111:0016:0022:EN:PDF (last visited Apr. 28, 2010) [Software Directive, Computer Programs Directive]. Article 1.3., para. (8) of the preface to the Directive also states: "In

The protection of computer programs as literary works means that they are entitled to the same protection as any other kind of literary work. Notably, the creator of a program enjoys the same rights as any author of a literary work. The creator of the program has the right to control the reproduction and dissemination of the program, and the duration of protection should be equivalent to the lifetime of the author and at least fifty years after his death.[15] In many cases, due to the operation of "work-for-hire" rules, computer programs are initially owned by corporations. In this case, rights are determined as they are in any other circumstance where a literary work is owned by a corporation.[16]

Crucially, the recognition of computer programs as a form of literary work was subsequently formalized in the TRIPs Agreement of the WTO.[17] The approach to the protection of computer programs in TRIPs is somewhat different from the Berne Convention. Rather than inferring the copyright protection of computer programs by analogy, Article 10.1 of the TRIPs Agreement makes explicit provision for protecting them as literary works.[18] At the same time, TRIPs, as usual, yields to Berne's substantive authority in copyright matters, with the formula:

> Computer programs, whether in source or object code, shall be protected as literary works under the Berne Convention (1971).[19]

---

respect of the criteria to be applied in determining whether or not a computer program is an original work, no tests as to the qualitative or aesthetic merits of the program should be applied."

15. The normal term of protection for an author's copyright in both the United States and the European Union is now the lifetime of the author plus seventy years. The extension of copyright term was fought in the United States on Constitutional grounds, and lost. *See* Eldred v. Ashcroft, 239 F.3d 372 (2001), *aff'd*, 537 U.S. 186 (2003); *see also* Legal Information Institute, Cornell University Law School, http://www.law.cornell.edu/supct/html/01-618.ZS.html (last visited Apr. 28, 2010).

16. The U.S. work-for-hire provision can be found in 17 U.S.C. § 101, available on the website of the Legal Information Institute, Cornell University Law School at http://www4.law.cornell.edu/uscode/17/usc_sec_17_00000101—000-.html (last visited Apr. 28, 2010).

17. Agreement on Trade-Related Aspects of Intellectual Property Rights (opened for signature Apr. 15, 1994, entered into force Jan. 1, 1995), Annex 1C to the Marrakesh Agreement Establishing the World Trade Organization, 1869 U.N.T.S. 299; 33 I.L.M. 1197 (1994), http://www.wto.org/english/docs_e/legal_e/27-trips_01_e.htm (last visited Apr. 28, 2010) [TRIPs Agreement]. *See* Article 10.1 on Computer Programs and Compilations of Data:

    Computer programs, whether in source or object code, shall be protected as literary works under the Berne Convention (1971).

18. TRIPs Agreement, *supra* note 17, art. 10.1.

19. More generally, the TRIPs Agreement provides that member countries of the WTO must respect the substantive standards of copyright protection in the Berne Convention. *See* TRIPs, *supra* note 17, art. 9.1. For a detailed discussion of this structure, see Chapter 4, "Moral Rights in the International Copyright Regime," *supra*, notes 1–17 and accompanying text.

TRIPs was not the first international instrument to specify this approach; a precedent for doing so had already been set by the EU Software Directive, which states:

> In accordance with the provisions of this Directive, Member States shall protect computer programs, by copyright, as literary works within the meaning of the *Berne Convention for the Protection of Literary and Artistic Works* . . . .[20]

2. Moral Rights: An Awkward Silence

Do moral rights apply to these new kinds of literary works? The Berne Convention provides for moral rights in its Article 6*bis*, and it does so without drawing any distinctions between different classes of copyright works. Rather, moral rights arise in all copyright works. There is no special provision in the Berne Convention regarding moral rights in computer programs, but there is also no explicit exclusion of moral rights protection for them. It must therefore be presumed that moral rights would subsist in computer programs, as they do in every other type of literary work.

The potential for a more restrictive interpretation of Article 6*bis* could be found in its association of moral rights with "authors." In the case where it could be shown that a computer program had no author—for example, if a program were generated by another computer program and was sufficiently removed from the first programmer's input—an argument might be made for excluding moral rights under the Berne Convention. But this would represent a situation that would have to be both unusual and quite specific.

Like Berne, the TRIPs Agreement makes no explicit provision regarding moral rights in computer programs—neither extending the rights to them, nor prohibiting their recognition. Presumably, the general approach to moral rights under Article 9.1 of the Agreement would therefore apply to software, as well.[21] If moral rights did exist in computer programs, TRIPs makes it clear that no possibility exists for a moral rights claim on behalf of programmers through the dispute-settlement body of the WTO.[22]

In view of the strong tradition of moral rights protection in European countries, and the central position which they occupy in civilian authors' rights systems, the European Software Directive seems like the most natural

---

20. *See* art. 1.1 of the Software Directive, *supra* note 14.
21. TRIPs Agreement, *supra* note 17, art. 9, on Relation to the Berne Convention. Article 9.1 states: "Members shall comply with Articles 1 through 21 of the Berne Convention (1971) and the Appendix thereto. However, Members shall not have rights or obligations under this Agreement in respect of the rights conferred under Article 6*bis* of that Convention or of the rights derived therefrom."
22. *Id.*, art 9.1.

place to search for a reference to moral rights in computer programs. However, the Directive makes no direct reference to moral rights. Rather, Article 2.3 of the Directive refers to them obliquely, in another context—the relationship between employer and employee. In this scenario, Article 2.3 provides that the creation of a program by an employee "in the execution of his duties" allows the employer to exercise "all economic rights in the program so created." Since only the economic rights in the program are mentioned, is it possible to read in an implication that there is a moral right of the author which continues to rest with the employee—the human author of the program—after the economic rights have been relinquished?

The failure to address moral rights explicitly creates great ambiguity about the extent and nature of rights in computer programs. The uncertainty arises in both the broader international regime and in the EU copyright system. In both of these international contexts, we are left to draw the general conclusion that, if computer programs are to be treated as literary works, then moral rights in software must be recognized. In fact, this is the only way to maintain a truly nondiscriminatory approach to programs vis-à-vis the treatment of other literary works under copyright rules. Software is a literary work like any other; therefore, moral rights apply. If, for some reason, moral rights cannot, or should not, apply to software, then something quite important must be acknowledged: the basic premise that programs can be treated as literary works for the purpose of copyright law cannot hold good. The proposition that copyright protection excludes moral rights might once have been tenable for common law countries, which have historically rejected moral rights, or had inadequate legislation in place. But the post-TRIPs era is one in which all common law countries have joined Berne, and bear a universal obligation to recognize moral rights. In these circumstances, barring an explicit exception, moral rights in software exist—at least, at the international level.

3. National Approaches: A Search for Balance

The European approach to moral rights in software confirms the belief that there is no outright prohibition on moral rights for programmers in European law. On the contrary, most European countries make specific provision for moral rights in software in their copyright laws. In these provisions, a comparison of moral rights for software with general provisions on moral rights reveals a somewhat restrictive approach to their availability under national legislation.

France's *Code de la Propriété Intellectuelle* provides a useful point of departure. Article L121–7 of the French law was introduced in 1994, and it deals with moral rights in computer programs. In keeping with the general logic of the French scheme, moral rights are protected, but they are subject to two special limitations. The first relates to the rights protected. Attribution and integrity are granted to computer programmers, but the right of withdrawal is specifically excluded.

This exclusion surely reflects concern about the doubt that a right of withdrawal could throw onto the development of a sensitive industry. Much software is created in the employment context. How could commercial transactions function effectively under the looming shadow of the possible withdrawal of software from circulation? However, the moral right of withdrawal in French law is balanced by the requirement that a person who exercises the right must compensate the owner of the work for any potential losses that are likely to follow from his decision to withdraw the work. Why is this safeguard deemed inadequate by the French legislator where computer programs are concerned? Is it considered too difficult in practice to obtain the necessary compensation from an employee who may be able to shut down the distribution of software, but who may need to be sued into paying for his choice? Is it necessary, from a practical point of view, to exclude the right altogether in order to achieve the desired environment for commercial transactions in the software industry? Or, as Colin Tapper suggests, are there broader concerns about the impact of withdrawing software on crucial functions in areas like banking, defence, or health?[23]

The French model appears to have been followed in Chapter IV of the Russian Civil Code of 2008, which also excludes the right of withdrawal from computer programs.[24] Once again, the need for the exclusion is not obvious, since compensation of the owner is a required feature of the regime. The explanation may simply lie in the influence of the French Civil Code on Russian reformers, which is likely to have been considerable.[25] Perhaps there is a psychological element, as well: the withdrawal right may be among the most controversial aspects of moral rights, and the possibility of a "chilling effect" on software development may have been feared by Russian reformers.

Perhaps in anticipation of the problems that might arise from a situation of ambiguity, the United Kingdom *Copyright, Designs and Patents Act 1988* (CDPA) explicitly provides that neither the moral right of attribution nor the

---

23. (Personal communication with the author, June 4, 2010).

24. *See* art. 1269, Grazhdanski Kodeks Rossiiskoi Federatsi, Chast' Chetvërtaya [Civil Code of the Russian Federation, Part IV], Federal Law No. 230-FZ of December 18, 2006, *Rossijskaja Gazeta* No. 289 (4255) of Dec. 22, 2006 = *Sobranie zakonodatel'stva RF* (SZ RF) No. 52 (Part I) of Dec. 25, 2006, Item 5496, at 14803 [2008 Russian Civil Code]. The right of withdrawal is excluded in the case of both programs and databases.

25. At the time of the 2001 Draft Civil Code, international codes appear to have been an important resource for Russian copyright reform; for example, a Russian-language translation of the Civil Code of the Canadian province of Quebec, was part of the library of the Russian Private Law Institute. For a discussion of the provisions of the 2001 Draft, see MIRA T. SUNDARA RAJAN, COPYRIGHT AND CREATIVE FREEDOM: A STUDY OF POST-SOCIALIST LAW REFORM (Routledge 2006) [Sundara Rajan, *Copyright and Creative Freedom*], Chapter VIII, "The Future of Post-Communist Copyright," 188–98.

right of integrity shall apply to computer programs.[26] The exclusion is part of a generally restrictive approach to moral rights under British law. The UK Act includes a provision as stringent and unusual as the requirement that the moral right of attribution must be asserted before it can be recognized.[27] Since the CDPA fails to extend liberal protection to moral rights in more traditional areas of copyright subject-matter, it seems natural that the treatment of programs would be still more restrictive. However, the rationale behind the exclusion of moral rights in computer programs under the CDPA is not clear.

Notwithstanding UK law, it is not possible to infer a general reluctance on the part of common law countries to recognize moral rights in computer programs. In fact, New Zealand may be the only common law country to follow the UK approach. Australia, in its well-developed scheme for moral rights, has not done so; neither has Canada. The Canadian government's current reform bill does not indicate any plans to address the possibility of moral rights for programmers.[28] In contrast, India, another common law jurisdiction of note where software is concerned, does not exclude moral rights in computer programs. All indications are that it has no plans to introduce such an exemption in its current reform plans. On the contrary, Indian copyright law implicitly seems to recognize and support programmers' rights.[29]

To return to the French example, a second limitation on programmers' moral rights has to do with the drafting of the integrity right in the French Code. French law normally allows an author to enjoy an entirely open-ended

---

26. Copyright, Designs and Patents Act 1988, secs. 79(2)(a) & 81(2) (c. 48), Office of Public Sector Information, http://www.opsi.gov.uk/acts/acts1988/UKpga_19880048_en_1.htm (last visited Apr. 28, 2010) [CDPA].

27. *Id.*, sec. 78(1). This provision brings into question the British conformity with the Berne Convention, which provides that all rights must be available "without formalities." Berne Convention for the Protection of Literary and Artistic Works (adopted Sept. 9, 1886) 1161 U.N.T.S. 3, http://www.wipo.int/treaties/en/ip/berne/trtdocs_wo001.html (last visited Apr. 28, 2010); also available in a useful format at the Legal Information Institute, Cornell University Law School, http://www.law.cornell.edu/treaties/berne/overview.html (last visited Apr. 28, 2010) [Berne Convention], art. 5(2): "The enjoyment and the exercise of these rights shall not be subject to any formality."

28. The current copyright reform bill, Bill C-32 was tabled by the government on June 2, 2010. It is available online: http://www2.parl.gc.ca/HousePublications/Publication.aspx?DocId=458 0265&Language=e&Mode=1 (last visited Aug. 17, 2010). The previous proposals were Bill C-60, introduced in 2005, and Bill C-61, which appeared in 2008. *See* http://www2.parl. gc.ca/HousePublications/Publication.aspx?Language=E&Parl=38&Ses=1&Mode=1&Pub= Bill&Doc=C-60_1 and http://www2.parl.gc.ca/HousePublications/Publication.aspx? Docid=3570473&file=4 (last visited Aug. 19, 2010). Neither one made mention of the issue. A commentary on Bill C-60 is available at http://www2.parl.gc.ca/Sites/LOP/Legislative-Summaries/Bills_ls.asp?lang=e&source=library_prb&Parl=38&Ses=1&ls=C60 (last visited Aug. 17, 2010).

29. This conclusion is reached by reading sec. 57 on moral rights with sec, 52A. *See* Indian Copyright Act, 1957 (Act 14 of 1957) [Indian Copyright Act].

right of integrity. No demonstration of harm to the author's reputation is required; any assertion by the author that his right of integrity has been violated will be sufficient cause to sue. In the case of computer programs, however, the exercise of the integrity right is somewhat curtailed. Where the software is in the possession of the person entitled to the economic rights in the work, a violation of the programmer's moral rights can only be asserted if the treatment of the program is prejudicial to his honor or reputation.[30]

From the French perspective, this provision represents a restriction of the integrity principle. From an international perspective, however, the programmer's moral right against the copyright-owner in French law corresponds exactly to the moral rights generally enjoyed by every author of a literary work under Article 6*bis* of the Berne Convention. The French approach to programmers' moral rights represents a case of pure conformity with the requirements of Article 6*bis,* and it also respects the TRIPs requirement that computer programs are to be treated as literary works. Although the programmer's right of integrity is slightly deficient in terms of French practice, the French standard clearly conforms to international requirements for moral rights in literary works.

In all other circumstances, however, the programmer's moral rights are not restricted under French law. He does, indeed, enjoy rights equal to those granted to the author of every other kind of "literary work," not only by international standards, but also, according to French norms.

Like French law, Japanese law attempts a more thoughtful approach to integrity in the computer context. But the Japanese approach is slightly different.

---

30. Article L121-6(2) of the Code refers to "[l]a traduction, l'adaptation, l'arrangement ou toute autre modification d'un logiciel et la reproduction du logiciel en résultant" ["the translation, adaptation, arrangement or any other modification of a program and the copy of the program resulting therefrom"]. The article applies in the absence of contractual arrangements to the contrary that grant additional rights to the programmer, as art. L121-7 explicitly points out. The term used in art. L121-7 is *"cessionnaire"*—assignee of the rights. French Intellectual Property Code, art. L121-1: *Loi N° 92-597 du 1er juillet 1992 relative au code de la propriété intellectuelle (partie législative), Journal officiel de la République française du 8 février 1994; Légifrance: Le service public de la diffusion du droit, available at* http://www.legifrance.gouv. fr/affichCode.do?cidTexte=LEGITEXT000006069414&dateTexte=20100412 (last visited Apr. 28, 2010) [Intellectual Property Code, CPI, *Code de la Propriété Intellectuelle*]. It is also interesting to note that this article represents a movement towards greater precision in the programmer's moral right of integrity. The earlier provision in the 1985 law did not allow a programmer to exercise the integrity right at all. See Loi n°85-660 du 3 juillet 1985 relative aux droits d'auteur et aux droits des artistes-interprètes, des producteurs de phonogrammes et de vidéogrammes et des entreprises de communication audiovisuelle. The 1992 codification abrogated this provision, apparently without introducing an alternative, which would lead to the conclusion that the "default" position in French law—an open-ended right of integrity—would apply. The history can be traced online, on the Légifrance website: http:// www.legifrance.gouv.fr/affichTexteArticle.do;jsessionid=F878CE5FD503D7E4E3F9EA9D7 841EBCB.tpdjo16v_2?cidTexte=JORFTEXT000000693451&idArticle=LEGIARTI00000647 1277&dateTexte=19850704&categorieLien=cid#LEGIARTI000006471277 (last visited Aug. 17, 2010).

Japan is specifically concerned with protecting certain rights to modify a program. Rather than focusing on the relationship between author and owner, the Japanese law specifically addresses the modifications themselves. Any changes for the purpose of improving the functioning of a program will not amount to a violation of its creator's moral rights.[31] For users and owners of a program who may eventually be involved in developing it further, this solution is both practical and effective. It probably reflects the insight of a technological giant.

India is unique among the common law countries in addressing the issue of programmers' moral rights. It does so in a novel way, by considering the fair use of a computer program as a kind of exception to moral rights protection. In its definition of the integrity right, Section 57 of the Indian Copyright Act specifies that

> the author shall not have any right to restrain or claim damages in respect of any adaptation of a computer programme to which clause (aa) of sub-section (1) of section 52 applies.

The clause that is referenced here, section 52(1)(aa) of the Act, deals with the right to make copies of computer programs for noncommercial purposes, including regular use of the program and the making of backup copies.[32] The Indian Act seems to draw the right distinction between private and public uses of a work, and it understands these categories as a way of distinguishing between situations of potential harm to the author and those that are likely to be innocuous. Indeed, from another perspective, the very idea of a right of

---

31. Art. 20(iii) of the Japanese Copyright Act, Law No. 48 of 1970, available in English translation on the website of the Copyright Research and Information Center at http://www.cric.or.jp/cric_e/clj/clj.html (last visited Apr. 28, 2010) [Japanese Copyright Act]. The provision exempts any "modification which is necessary for enabling to use on a particular computer a program work which is otherwise unusable on that computer, or to make more effective the use of a program work on a computer" from a violation of the integrity right.

32. Indian Copyright Act, *supra* note 29, sec. 52, provides for "Certain acts not to be infringement of copyright."
   (1) The following acts shall not constitute an infringement of copyright, namely:
     (a) a fair dealing with a literary, dramatic, musical or artistic work 104[not being a computer programme] for the purposes of—
       (i) private use, including research;
       (ii) criticism or review, whether of that work or of any other work;
     (aa) the making of copies or adaptation of a computer programme by the lawful possessor of a copy of such computer programme, from such copy—
       (i) in order to utilise the computer programme for the purposes for which it was supplied; or
       (ii) to make back-up copies purely as a temporary protection against loss, destruction or damage in order only to utilise the computer programme for the purpose for which it was supplied . . . . (footnotes omitted).

"reputation" is to protect the opinion of the author *held by others*. In this sense, by making the fair use of a computer program an exception to the moral right of integrity, the Indian approach seems to confirm the idea that damage to an author's reputation is the key to software moral rights—adding a new twist to the French model of the programmer's integrity right.[33]

The use of the term "adaptation" in the Indian provision is interesting. It leads to the question of whether this section can address the concern that a moral right of integrity could interfere with the special flexibility required for development in the software industry. India, of course, has become one of the dominant players in software worldwide. It is probably fair to say that India's role in the software industry has been the single most important force behind skyrocketing Indian economic power and prestige in the international community.

In an interesting early case, *Statart Software Pvt Ltd. v. Karan Khanna*, Indian judges considered the issue of whether a company's modification of a computer program developed by two former employees to personalize templates of letters amounted to an infringement of their moral right of integrity.[34] The parties eventually reached a settlement without going to court; however, notice of the dispute was taken by the Indian government, which appears to have responded by introducing the exception to the integrity right in section 57, discussed above.

Once again, the relevant clause of section 52 provides that "making . . . copies or adaptation of a computer program by the lawful possessor of a copy" will be exempt from liability for copyright infringement. In particular, the exception applies in two kinds of circumstances. First, if the copying or adaptation is done "in order to utilise the computer programme for the purpose for which it was supplied," it will not be considered an infringement of copyright or moral rights. Secondly, the making of "back-up copies purely as a temporary protection against loss, destruction or damage in order only to utilise the computer programme for the purpose for which [it] was supplied" is also permitted.

What are the practical implications of this exception? Clearly, the normal use of a computer program by the purchaser of the software will not be an infringement of the author's moral rights.[35] What is not clear, however, is the extent to which an employer or commissioner of the program may be exempt from liability. The use of the term "adaptation" evokes the role of the person or company commissioning the work, as "adapting" the programs is perhaps not (yet) something that is commonly done by the purchaser, or "end-user,"

---

33. It also seems to codify the principle of "free" use in the sense understood by the Free Software Foundation. *See* Chapter 9, *infra*, "Friends or Enemies? Moral Rights and Open Access."

34. The case is summarized by Pravin Anand, *The Concept of Moral Rights under Indian Copyright Law*, 27 Copyright World 35, 35–36 (1993).

35. *See* Indian Copyright Act, *supra* note 29, sec. 52(1)(aa).

of the program. The use of the program "for the purpose for which it was supplied" by its commissioner could certainly include subsequent development of the program, in a situation such as the one presented by the *Statart* case.

However, if this was the ultimate aim of the section, the same purpose could have been achieved in a much simpler fashion by excluding the moral right of integrity from computer programs altogether. Instead, there are limits on what even the commissioner of the program can do. If he transgresses the limits of using the program "for the purpose for which it was supplied," he could conceivably be in violation of the author's moral rights. Contractual agreements between employer and employee, or commissioner and consultant, may help to clarify the extent of the employer's, or commissioner's, obligations. The general experience of moral rights in India suggests that the Indian courts will look upon the claims of individuals with sympathy, although software is different from art or film.

The Indian example raises the question of why a country with an important software industry has decided not to exclude moral rights outright from computer programs—especially when that industry is crucial for growth and international recognition. It must be concluded that the Indian government has not found it necessary to eliminate the moral right of integrity for the benefit of India's software industry.

4. Programmers: A Special Case?

These examples suggest that, in fact, the legal imperative to treat computer programs as literary works may be mistaken. In fact, it is entirely normal for copyright law to deal with different classes of subject-matter in different ways. Where computer programs are concerned, the obstacle to fashioning a special moral rights regime is a result, probably accidental, of the TRIPs Agreement, which specifies that they must be treated the same as other literary works.[36]

If there were some way to modify our understanding of TRIPs to allow computer programs to be recognized as different—even as a special subcategory of "literary works"—it would become possible to undertake a more complete exploration of moral rights in computer programs without offending obligations under international copyright agreements. The idea of differential treatment for different types of works could be applied to computer programs in two ways.

First, the fact that software is different could be used to exclude moral rights from programs, as has been done in the UK Act. However, this position

---

36. TRIPs Agreement, *supra* note 17, art. 10.1.

has not been favored by many jurisdictions, and a second alternative is preferable: framing moral rights in software in special terms, to reflect the peculiar characteristics of this type of literary work.

In doing so, some lessons can be learned from the approach to moral rights in software in a number of leading jurisdictions. From the examples noted above, it is evident that all countries choosing to address moral rights in software are motivated by their awareness that software is a different kind of work. Accordingly, the crucial differences between software and literary works deserve a closer examination.

First and foremost, given the vision of artistic creativity on which moral rights are based, is it inappropriate to consider applying them to technological works? In particular, legal protection for moral rights assumes that the work is an extension of its author's personality, so that any damage to the work will cause harm to the author. Is this the reality of the relationship between a programmer and his computer program?

It is important to resolve this question, as it holds the key to finding an effective balance between the interests of the programmer and the interests of those seeking access to the program.[37] Does the programmer have some sort of personal interest arising out of his creative involvement and, if so, what is the nature of that interest? Will the answers to these questions be different if the program is created by the efforts of a number of joint authors, or if it is produced in the course of an employment relationship rather than being primarily a product of individual effort?

In fact, it is possible to observe a fundamental difference between computer programs and works of artistic creativity. The issue is one of purpose. An artistic work is supposed to generate a certain kind of experience for both artist and audience. A computer program, on the other hand, is usually a means to an end; it seeks to facilitate technical possibilities in the use of computer hardware. Nevertheless, it seems unduly harsh to suggest that the programmer has absolutely no emotional investment in his work. If the program is especially successful, elegant, or effective in achieving the purpose for which it is designed, would it not be important to its creator to be personally identified with the work as its author? Would the same idea apply if a programmer created a part of a program that was exceptionally well-realized? Similarly, if technology created by the programmer came to be used for purposes that he or she found objectionable—for example, the distribution of pornography via the Internet—should the programmer not have a legal basis for raising an objection?

The idea that software is somehow "not creative" in the same sense as a work of literature should be dismissed as irrelevant. Many types of works that

---

37. The issue here is not only one of public access; the needs of the owner of the program, of course, must also be considered.

are not literary, in the sense of "works of literature," are nevertheless protected by copyright law—although, since the *Feist* decision, the standard for
protection has known a gradual but marked increase in the United States,
Canada, and India.[38]

But this issue should be examined at a deeper level: is the relationship
between programmers and their work fundamentally different from that
between creative authors and their works? This question is quite a complex
one, as it leads to the issue of what exactly is protected by moral rights in a
creative work, and why. Moral rights are often said to protect the author's
personality as it is expressed in his work. The work is a "reflection" of his
personality; harming it will effectively harm the author's personality, and
therefore, the author himself. This could be called the "aesthetic" rationale for
moral rights; but it is not the only rationale. Rather, the moral rights problem
also deserves consideration from a human rights perspective.

Any creative product that reflects the labor, talent, training, and ingenuity
of the author has the potential to lead to pride of achievement for the author
in his work. The fact that the object of his activity is a technological work
rather than a form of aesthetic expression does not necessarily mean that the
author will escape the personal impact of mistreatment or misattribution of
his work. Why should we discriminate against authors because their intelligence and creativity happen to be applied in scientific or technical fields
rather than aesthetic ones?

This is not to suggest that a computer program and a work of art are intrin-
sically the same. They are obviously, perhaps fundamentally, different. The
differences can be encapsulated in three points: the technical, rather than
artistic, nature of software; the extreme dependence of software innovation
upon earlier works, and the corresponding need to examine and re-use
earlier works for further development; and the fact that much software is
developed in a corporate environment where employment relationships
prevail. But these differences do not mandate the exclusion of programmers'
moral rights. Rather, they suggest a specific shape to them.

First, moral rights should be expansive enough to reach scientific creativity. This idea is already recognized in some jurisdictions. For example, Russia

---

38. In the United States, White Pages directories are now not considered sufficiently "original" to
    qualify for protection. *See Feist, supra* note 12. In the Canadian Federal Court of Appeal case
    of *Tele-Direct (Publications) Inc. v. American Business Information Inc.* (1997), 76 C.P.R. (3d)
    296 (F.C.A.), the Yellow Pages directory of a phone book, which undertakes the humble task
    of organizing the names and advertisements of merchants by subject-matter, is a case in
    point and fared no better. The decision is available online at http://www.canlii.org/en/ca/fca/
    doc/1997/1997canlii6378/1997canlii6378.html (last visited Apr. 28, 2010). *See also CCH,
    supra* note 12, and *Eastern Book Co., supra* note 12.

has a tradition of protecting moral rights in patents, which continues in the current Civil Code provisions on intellectual rights.[39]

In the software context, the line between acceptable use and infringement of the moral right of integrity can be drawn quite easily, by relying on established copyright concepts. The landmark U.S. case of *Altai* established the "abstraction/filtration/comparison" test to differentiate between copyright infringement of a computer program and copying that is permissible for the purpose of further innovation.[40] A similar idea is articulated in the Canadian case of *Delrina*, where the principle of functionality defines the parts of the program that are clearly situated beyond the bounds of copyright protection.[41] *Delrina* effectively establishes the principle that programmers should enjoy a right to *freedom of function*, which will allow them to make use of the functional elements of pre-existing programs. In other words, the functionality approach means that any "functional" elements of a computer program fall into the public domain, and cannot be restricted by copyright law.

With reference to the moral right of integrity, if a programmer makes "functional" use of another program, he should be exempt from the charge of violating the author's right of integrity. This result could be strengthened by framing the right of integrity to require proof of damage to an author's reputation or honor, as, indeed, the French law does.

Secondly, moral rights would not necessarily impede the ability of either programmers or software companies to use each others' works for the development of future work. It is true that moral rights would create an additional layer of obligations for the user of the work. However, these obligations are not especially onerous. Attribution should become a routine matter once the acceptable forms of attributing a computer program became established, something that would likely develop through industry practice rather than

---

39. 2008 Russian Civil Code, *supra* note 24, art. 1228. *See* the discussion in Adolf Dietz, *Incorporation of Patent Law into Part Four of the Russian Civil Code—A Structural Analysis, in* WOLRAD PRINZ ZU WALDECK UND PYRMONT, MARTIN J. ADELMAN, ROBERT BRAUNEIS, JOSEF DREXL & RALPH NACK, eds., PATENTS AND TECHNOLOGICAL PROGRESS IN A GLOBALIZED WORLD: LIBER AMICORUM JOSEPH STRAUS, MPI Studies on Intellectual Property, Competition and Tax Law Series, Vol. 6, 687, 700–01 (Springer 2009). The Russian provisions are discussed in detail in Chapter 3, *supra*, "A Theory in Flux," notes 317–75 and accompanying text.

40. Computer Associates International, Inc. v. Altai, Inc., 982 F.2d 693 (2d Cir. 1992).

41. The Ontario Court of Appeal states: "However, in this case the trial judge found that all of the alleged similarities between Sysview and Assess, including similarities in the arrangement of elements, were *dictated by functional considerations or otherwise not protectable by copyright*. Given this finding, it could hardly be concluded that Assess was a substantial reproduction of Sysview, even if the Sysview elements, by reasons of their collocation with other parts of Sysview, were part of a work which was entitled to copyright as a whole." (emphasis added). *See also* Delrina Corp. v. Triolet Systems Inc. (2002), 58 O.R. (3d) 339, 17 C.P.R. (4th) 289 (Ont. C.A.), para 29, *available at* http://www.canlii.org/en/on/onca/doc/2002/2002canlii11389/2002canlii11389.html (last visited Apr. 28, 2010) [*Delrina*].

legislative imposition. Maintaining the integrity of programs could actually help to protect the quality of programs and make them less vulnerable to weaknesses that could be exploited. An improvement in a program should not lead to litigation, but this issue can be well controlled by maintaining that the programmer must be able to show some damage to his reputation before an integrity claim can be made. Given the fact that the programming community, worldwide, is a rather tightly-knit group, claims about reputation make sense and should be feasible without too much difficulty or ambiguity on the facts.

The right of integrity could also be adjusted to meet the needs of the programming community to modify and re-use existing works. An attempt has been made to accommodate the needs of "users" in French, Japanese, and Indian law; but the sculpting of integrity should probably be more detailed. Specifically, the moral right of integrity should include a clear exception for the use of works to develop new features or new programs. The purpose of the exception would be to accommodate the creative development of software. Programmers should be required to exercise their rights in good faith, and, as appropriate,to respect the principle of attribution.

Finally, should moral rights in software be restricted because software development usually occurs in a corporate context? Quite the contrary. The fact that much programming occurs in a corporate context is a particularly strong argument for moral rights in this industry. Once again, moral rights are not just an aesthetic theory; they are a form of protection for the human rights of creators. In a technological environment, they should apply to programmers. They can help to maintain the connection between technology and the human beings who create it.[42]

Moral rights can help to establish a more humane environment in the software industry by offering better recognition to the contributions of programmers, and allowing greater value to be associated with the quality of their work. In a professional environment where reputation is important, moral rights could offer programmers a profoundly meaningful form of appreciation for their work. From the companies' point of view, moral rights might seem inconvenient; but so are labor standards and minimum wage payments. Modern society accepts the regulation of the workplace to a degree that Victorian industrialists, for example, might have found quite extraordinary. Moral rights in the workplace fit well with modern sensibilities. As part of a

---

42. *See, for example,* the tragic story of how software for the use of radiation treatments led to mishaps in Walt Bogdanich, with reporting by Simon Akam, Andrew Lehren, Dan Lieberman, Kristina Rebelo, & Rebecca R. Ruiz, *Radiation Offers New Cures, and Ways to Do Harm,* New York Times (Jan. 23, 2010), *available at* http://www.nytimes.com/2010/01/24/health/24radiation.html (last visited Apr. 29, 2010). This case illustrates some of the difficulties that can arise when a human being is no longer responsible for the functioning of technology.

general attempt to progress towards better recognition for human rights than what our ancestors could achieve, they make sense.

5. The Software Industry: Practical Fallout?

Strong arguments support the protection of moral rights in software. Nevertheless, the practical impact of moral rights in a dynamic and powerful industry remains a concern. Are moral rights likely to dampen software development by creating uncertainty and generating liability?

Perhaps for this reason, the failure to clarify moral rights in information technology is tacitly interpreted as a *de facto* exclusion under international copyright agreements. The UK decision to exclude computer programs seems to confirm this view. The reasons for restraining moral rights in software mainly reflect a public interest rationale, and in particular, the concern that excessive protection for programmers' rights in the computer industry will inhibit growth and development in this crucially important field. The development of the software industry depends on programmers being able to build on pre-existing programs. Software creation requires an especially high degree of freedom of access to existing works.

But the decision to exclude moral rights from programs is too hasty. On this issue, it may be helpful, once again, to consider the overall experience of software copyright. There can be no doubt that copyright rules affect the development of software, restricting and limiting an industry that has the potential to achieve spectacular growth and dissemination for its products. Regular litigation on software copyright issues in the United States, the UK, Canada, and India has helped to establish some limits to copyright protection. But this level of clarity has been achieved at a cost: expensive and time-consuming lawsuits. At the same time, the adoption of copyright protection for software has helped to establish the interests of well-entrenched companies, while creating difficulties for newcomers to make inroads into this area. It has been particularly difficult for new developers because of this technology's necessary dependence on established methods in the world of programming, which became protectable by copyright law.

Moral rights would establish a new layer of protection in software. But the kind of protection involved would be less intrusive than the economic rights have been, focusing on individual rights that can only be exercised by the programmer in the protection of his personal and professional interests. Indeed, open-source software thrives on the recognition of attribution and even integrity-type interests within its community.[43]

---

43. *See* the in-depth discussion of this issue in Chapter 8, *infra*.

6. Infringement of Moral Rights in Software

A serious question about software copyright has proven to be the practical difficulty of clarifying which aspects of software should be protected by copyright, and which should be left open to copying. Once again, the issue is triggered by the very nature of software, which combines functional and design elements in the creation of a program, and may often do so in practically inseparable ways. In relation to moral rights, this problem is compounded by the fact that copyright in most computer programs may be owned by corporations, who acquire copyright in them through the operation of work-for-hire rules governing ownership.[44]

As noted above, the problem of copyright subsistence in computer programs was recognized by the Ontario Court of Appeal in the 2002 case of *Delrina*.[45] A closer examination of the case is important for moral rights, and reveals a fascinating matrix of facts. The *Delrina* litigation was based on an allegation of copying between two competing companies who employed the same programmer to create software for them.[46] "[S]ome method must be found," said the trial judge, "to weed out or remove from copyright protection those portions [of the program] which . . . cannot be protected by copyright."[47] Exploring possible solutions, the trial judge had turned to U.S. precedents—in particular, the *Altai* decision, which established a new benchmark for the copyright protection of software in that country.[48] As noted above, *Altai* established an "abstraction," "filtration," and "comparison" test. Those elements of a program that reflect general knowledge in the field must be "abstracted," or isolated from the context of the original program and "filtered" out from it; the remainder of the program represents its "original" components, and should be compared with the "original" elements of the new program to assess infringement.

The judge in *Delrina* also called upon a second case—the judgment of the Supreme Court of Canada in *Apple Computers v. Mackintosh*,[49] which, in his view, expressed an idea that is similar to the *Altai* test, although it is stated somewhat differently. The *Apple* case developed the "merger" doctrine, borrowed from U.S. law, in the Canadian context. According to the merger

---

44. *E.g.*, sec. 13.3 of the Canadian Copyright Act, R.S.C. 1985, c. C-42, http://laws.justice.gc.ca/en/C-42/index.html (last visited Apr. 29, 2010) [Canadian Copyright Act]; U.S. Copyright Act, Pub. L. 94–553, 90 Stat. 2541 (1976) § 201(b).

45. *See supra* note 41.

46. Delrina Corp. v. Triolet Systems Inc. (1993), 47 C.P.R. (3d) 1 (Ont. Ct. (Gen. Div.)) [*Delrina* OCGD]; *Delrina*, *supra* note 41.

47. *Delrina* OCGD, *supra* note 46, at 37, *quoted by* the Ontario Court of Appeal in *Delrina*, *supra* note 41, para. 43.

48. *Altai*, *supra* note 40.

49. Apple Computers Inc. v. Mackintosh Computers Ltd. (1986), 10 C.P.R. (3d) 1 (F.C.T.D.), *aff'd*, (1988), 18 C.P.R. (3d) 128 (F.C.A.), *aff'd*, (1990), 2 S.C.R. 209 [*Apple*].

doctrine, if an idea can be expressed in "only one way, or in a very limited number of ways . . . the expression merges with the idea and thus is not copyrightable."[50] In this situation, a monopoly in the "idea or function itself" should not be granted to the holder of the copyright in the work. According to the doctrine, copying of these elements of a program cannot, therefore, qualify as an infringement of copyright in the work. The facts of the *Apple* case presented this question in "rather stark form," as Justice Morden of the Ontario Court of Appeal was to note, because it offered the argument that an entire computer program represents a merger of idea with expression, and is therefore not copyrightable. Justice Reed of the Canadian Supreme Court found that the application of merger "is a question of degree."[51] Upon the application of both the *Altai* test and the merger doctrine, as set out by the Canadian Supreme Court in *Apple*, no infringement could be said to have occurred in the *Delrina* case.

The approach of the trial judge was generally approved by the Ontario Court of Appeal. Justice Morden of the appeals court relied on the idea of functionality, which he described as key to answering the question of whether, and to what extent, copyright subsists in a computer program. In essence, if some aspect of a computer program is required in order for it to accomplish its functions, and if it is not realistic to attempt to accomplish those functions by any—or, indeed, many—other means, then that aspect of the program cannot be entitled to copyright protection. In copyright jargon, the "functionality" test can also be expressed as the concept that such elements of programming fall into the group of unprotectable "ideas," rather than "expression," which is eligible for copyright protection. This is exactly what the merger doctrine implies.

In the process of examining the case, the Ontario Court of Appeal in *Delrina* returned repeatedly to the disconcerting facts, as they had earlier drawn the attention of the trial judge. Similarities between the two programs were inevitable, because both had been created by one and the same person. The fact that the program came to be "owned" by the corporate employers of the programmer, Mr. Duncombe, led to the odd situation where one owner sued another in the hope of establishing a programmer's infringement of his own work. The trial judge had noted that "common similarities between two competing functional works are to be expected without one being a copy of the other."[52] But he also noted the similarities in approach dictated by the fact that the same author had made both. Would similarities of "programming style and experience" lead to infringement of copyright?[53]

---

50. Trial judge in *Altai*, *supra* note 40.
51. The expression is used by the British court in *Ibcos Computers Ltd. v. Barclays Finance Ltd.*, [1994] F.S.R. 275, 290–92 (Ch. D.) [*Ibcos*], and quoted by Justice Morden in *Delrina*, *supra* note 41, para 51.
52. *Delrina* (O.C.G.D.), *supra* note 46, at 40, *quoted in Delrina* (O.C.A.), para 17.
53. *Delrina*, *supra* note 41, para 18.

The British courts have considered the copyright status of "style" or "technique" in two important cases, with confusing results. The 1999 case of *Norowzian v. Arks* involved the copying of techniques used by a filmmaker to give a novel appearance to the figure of a man dancing; the House of Lords held that this style of image-making, known as "jump-cutting," could not be protected by copyright.[54] But in the 2004 decision of *Designers Guild v. Russell Williams*, the House of Lords found that the design of a fabric that looked similar to another pattern, but did not use any of the specific components of the original work, nevertheless amounted to infringement of the work.[55] In *Designers Guild*, Lord Hoffman broke an unspoken taboo and acknowledged an awkward truth: separating idea from expression is an artificial exercise.

Instead, Lord Hoffman suggested that copyright protection should more realistically be determined along a spectrum from general idea to specific work. Drawing from Isaiah Berlin's celebrated essay, *The Hedgehog and the Fox*, Lord Hoffman affirmed that a more detailed and fully realized work is likely to find itself closer to the "expression" end of the spectrum—"Copyright law protects foxes better than hedgehogs." The same concept was specifically upheld in the computer context in the earlier case, from 1994, of *Ibcos Computers v. Barclays Finance*, where it was found, once again, that the protection of detailed ideas is possible under UK law:

> It is a question of degree where a good guide is the notion of overborrowing of the skill, labour and judgment which went into the copyright work.[56]

Designers Guild has been viewed with skepticism in the United States. Ever since the U.S. Supreme Court's 1991 decision in *Feist*, the United States seems to be moving towards higher threshold requirements for protection under its copyright law. The issue is directly relevant to the case of *Delrina*, where the Canadian trial judge relied extensively on the American decision in *Altai*. The standard of originality in Canada appears to be lower than the *Feist* standard; this has continued to be the case even after the Canadian concept of originality was updated by the Supreme Court in its 2004 ruling in *CCH*. The Canadian Supreme Court made use of the *CCH* litigation to revisit originality, and found that a "modicum of creativity" is now required for copyright to subsist

---

54. The case pivoted on the fact that the technique was used to tell two different kinds of stories. In film copyright, copying of the narrative element was deemed to be crucial. But the ruling is controversial, as the director, Mr. Norowzian, clearly intended to showcase his technique with a view to using it toward the development of a new narrative, appropriate for the Guiness advertising campaign. *See* Norowzian v. Arks Ltd. (No 2) [2000] E.M.L.R. 67 [2000] F.S.R. 363.

55. Designers Guild Ltd. v. Russell Williams (Textiles) Ltd. [2000] UKHL 58, [2001] 1 All E.R. 700 [*Designers Guild*].

56. *Ibcos*, *supra* note 51, at 302.

in a work under Canadian law.[57] By giving pride of place to the higher requirements of copyright protection implied by *Altai*, did the *Delrina* court apply a standard for the subsistence of copyright in Mr. Duncombe's program that was too high?

In fact, at the trial level, the Canadian judge exemplified a growing trend: reliance on international precedents, particularly across the common law world, when dealing with technological copyright. In relation to copyright in computer programs, relying on a pioneering American precedent made sense. The technology originates within the United States, and U.S. law has had to confront technological issues before most other jurisdictions. Accordingly, on appeal, Justice Morden quickly dismissed the question of American precedents and their applicability in Canada as irrelevant. Regardless of variations in the standard of originality between Canada and the United States—or, indeed, among other common law countries—the Ontario Court of Appeal agreed that the American test of abstraction, filtration, and comparison could be applied to the problem of copyright infringement where computer programs were the works in question.

The conclusions reached in *Delrina* imply a startling new role for moral rights in computer programs. The ruling in *Delrina* can be summarized in two steps. First, in keeping with the American approach articulated in the *Altai* case, the Canadian courts agreed that not all elements of a computer program are, or should be, entitled to copyright protection. Only those that satisfy the requirements of the abstraction-filtration-comparison process showing themselves as authentic forms of "expression" rather than "ideas," will be eligible for copyright protection.

This determination is important in a field of technological innovation that depends on access to programming conventions for continued growth. All creation, whether artistic or scientific, is, in a sense, dependent on pre-existing work; but computer software presents an extreme example.[58] As Justice Walker states in the *Apple Computer v. Microsoft & Hewlett Packard* case:

> Merger means there is practically only one way to express an idea. But if technical or conceptual constraints limit the available ways to express an idea, even

---

57. The case is confusing because of the Supreme Court's reference to "skill and labour," which usually defines the "sweat of the brow" approach to originality, the lowest standard in the world, that is traditional to the UK and other Commonwealth countries. *CCH, supra* note 12, para. 16. Canada has historically been considered an extreme version of a "sweat of the brow" jurisdiction. The CCH case was considered persuasive enough to be followed by the Indian Supreme Court in a case dealing with very similar facts, the *Eastern Book Co.* ruling, *supra* note 12.

58. The idea is encapsulated in the phrase that we see farther, by "standing on the shoulders of giants." It has been used by Isaac Newton and is closely associated with him. A similar idea finds expression in the artistic context by T. S. Eliot, who brilliantly explores the question of how past literary tradition shapes the development of a writer. T. S. Eliot, *Tradition and the Individual Talent, in* T. S. ELIOT, SELECTED ESSAYS 3 (Harcourt, Brace and World 1964).

though there is more than one avenue of expression available, copyright law will abhor only a virtually-identical copy of the original . . . . Sometimes this is described as "indispensable expression," a term which is also used as a synonym for the scenes a faire doctrine. Scenes a faire originated in stock characters and features of dramatic works, . . . and now encompasses stereotyped expression, standard or common features in a wide variety of works, including audiovisual works generated by computers."[59]

But, secondly, even though certain parts of a program may qualify for copyright protection, it may still not be possible to establish infringement. The key lies in the moral right of attribution. Copyright in the program may be owned by two different companies; but if the same human author is behind the work, or indeed, any significant part of it, copying between the two programs will not amount to an infringement of copyright. It is, rather, an inevitable result of the programmer's personal involvement in both projects. The moral right functions as an exception to copyright protection. In this guise, the moral right of attribution bears more resemblance to a fair use or fair dealing exception than it does to copyright *per se*.

7. Should Waivers of Moral Rights be Allowed?

Where waivers are concerned, the software community confronts exactly the same dilemma that arises in relation to every other kind of copyright work. If waivers of moral rights are permitted, what prevents those entering into contracts for the creation, use, or purchase of the work from requesting waivers as a standard rule? For this reason, it generally makes sense to limit the availability of waivers for moral rights—not so much out of a paternalistic impulse towards the creators of works as in order to promote greater equality of bargaining power between creator and owner where copyright contracts are concerned. The key question would therefore seem to be whether the circumstances of computer programs are different, in any material way, from those of other copyright works. Is it necessary or desirable to allow waivers of moral rights in programs, and if so, how can the programmer be protected from the routine confiscation of his moral rights by industry standard-form contracts?

In fact, there is one immediately apparent reason why it may be more important to make waivers available for computer innovation than for other copyright fields. This has to do with the potentially large number of contributors to a given computer program. When continuing to work with a successful piece of software to make further improvements, both attribution and

---

59. Apple Computer, Inc. v. Microsoft Corp. & Hewlett-Packard, 799 F. Supp. 1006, 1021 (N.D.Cal. 1992) [*Apple v. Microsoft & HP*].

integrity could present difficulties over time. It may make sense to provide that rights of attribution and integrity can be waived once the number of authors involved exceeds a certain number. This approach is also consonant with moral rights theory because, as the number of authors grows, each author's contribution to the program becomes relatively smaller in scope, and the relationship between the program as a whole and each individual author becomes weaker. It is worth noting that this problem commonly arises where moral rights in collaborative works are concerned—film, for example.

A second, important task will be to frame moral rights with sufficient precision to accommodate the needs of software. As a simple example, companies should be given a sufficient opportunity to develop appropriate methods of attribution that reflect the special characteristics of their software.[60] In this way, the programmer's contributions could be made known without imposing any undue burdens on the functioning of the program.

8. Conclusions

The international copyright community seems to accept the tacit assumption that moral rights are not applicable to computer programs under existing copyright regimes, and that there is no need to extend them to software. Both conclusions are premature. They are not based on an adequate exploration of the issues involved.

In fact, as this relatively brief analysis seeks to demonstrate, programmers may well have moral interests in their technological creations. As individuals functioning largely in corporate environments, programmers are also vulnerable to exploitation in special ways. Rather than outright rejection of moral rights in software, the problem deserves to be considered from a comprehensive point of view, in terms of legal doctrine, economic consequence, the public policy of protecting adequate access to new technology, and broader concern for the human rights of programmers. Like India and France, many countries may ultimately reach the conclusion that software development is not promoted by eliminating programmers' moral rights. Instead, the exclusion of moral rights may bring inconsistency to copyright protection for software as a kind of literary work, while preventing programmers from receiving what is rightfully their due.

---

60. It is worth noting that, to date, norms of attribution for software seem to be more or less the same as in other kinds of works. For example, a popular program such as Adobe's Acrobat allows users to locate the names of contributors to the program in a special area, "About" the program, entitled "Credits." But different types of attribution practices may be appropriate for different types of programs.

B. Technology Meets Art: Moral Rights and New Artistic Creation

A computer program is a work of scientific innovation. There is a certain novelty—perhaps, incongruity—in the idea of applying moral rights, a doctrine which developed for the creative arts, to software. But what happens in the case of computer software that is designed to generate a so-called work of art? The issue of whether moral rights should arise out of the authorship of computer programs is here complicated by the mingling of information technology with artistic creativity, blurring the dividing line between science and art.

Indeed, new technology has broad implications for the creative arts; the case of computer-generated works is but one example. This section considers the effects of technology from two perspectives: first, the use of new technologies in the creation of artworks, and, second, the creation of works that are new kinds of works in themselves. Both situations present problems for established concepts of authorship and the creative work. These tensions are, in turn, reflected in moral rights.

1. New Technologies for Creation: The Computer-Generated Work

A variety of new technologies can be used in the creation of artworks. In some cases, these technologies are new means of accomplishing well-established goals. Simple examples include dictation software that allows text to be typed directly from dictation by a computer, or software that helps composers to generate musical scores. In other cases, new technologies have a direct impact on the nature of the final product—for example, where new means of creating and using sounds, colors, images, text, or video are concerned. It is worth noting that the range of creative possibilities generated by the digital revolution has yet to be explored fully by authors and artists. At times, the focus seems to be on "re-mixing" existing material rather than generating new work—a potential shift in the quality of the cultural domain.

All of these new technologies intervene between the author and his own creative work. Depending on the nature and extent of the technological intervention, the relationship between the work and its author may be altered fundamentally. Moral rights are based on the presumption of a personal, intimate, and unbreakable bond between the author and the creative work. Where the influence of technology is powerful, this relationship may become tenuous, and the connection between author and work may even be broken. In these circumstances, would the moral rights of the author continue to be relevant?

Computer-generated works are a case in point. They reveal the fluidity that new technologies bring to traditional conceptions of the author and the work, and the newly porous distinctions between once well-defined issues, such as the distinction between means and ends in artistic creation.

In the case of a computer-generated work, the "author" creates a computer program whose purpose is to generate a "work of art," whether it is visual art, sound, some combination of these, or some other kind of work altogether. When these elements are "generated" by a computer, uncertainty can arise at a number of levels.

First, who is the "author" of the work? It could be the human author of the computer program, of course; but where the computer-generated work is concerned, the program, itself, might also be the author. This scenario seems increasingly feasible in an artificial intelligence scenario where a computer program could grow and develop, "learning" on the basis of previous "experience." In such cases, it is easy enough to say that the author must still be the programmer, as the intelligence that designed the program is his; but what happens when the program is designed to generate a chaotic and unforeseeable series of events, which then coalesce into a work? Is it correct to call the programmer the author, even though he cannot predict the form of the final "work"? Can any author or artist truly predict the form of his final creation? Perhaps not; but the capacity of a computer program for truly aleatory creation is probably much greater than a human being's. If such a program were to be executed over an extended period of time, with ever more intricate variations, how strong does the connection of the human author with "his" work remain?

The difficulty of identifying the author is matched by uncertainty about the nature of the computer-generated work. What exactly is the "work"? Is it the computer program that generates the end product, the end product itself, or both? If the work is executed through time, at what stage of its existence does it become a final product rather than a work-in-progress, thereby becoming capable of protection by copyright? It is worth noting that this question is not unique to computer programs; rather, it can arise in many contexts where technology helps in the creative process. For example, deciding on the final version of a film can be an ambiguous issue.[61]

Where such uncertainty exists about the nature of the artist and the work, very little can be said about the relationship between the two. Yet moral rights postulate a strong and certain author-work relationship, with well defined characteristics. It may therefore prove to be exceptionally difficult to achieve a useful approach to moral rights in computer-generated works.

The UK *Copyright, Designs & Patents Act 1988* (CDPA) is one of the few examples of direct legislative treatment of the issue.[62] The CDPA provides

---

61. This is recognized in the French Intellectual Property Code, *supra* note 30, where it is a central issue in the regime for film copyright. *See* Article L121-5 and L113-7.
62. CDPA, *supra* note 26.

that the author of a computer-generated work that is literary, dramatic, musical, or artistic in nature will be "the person by whom the arrangements necessary for the creation of the work are undertaken." However, it explicitly excludes moral rights from computer-generated works.[63] Both attribution and integrity interests for computer-generated works are rejected under the UK scheme. Strangely, the issue of false attribution is not addressed directly and, as Simon Stokes points out, it could, in theory, lead to a valid claim under UK law.[64] A plausible explanation for this apparent oversight is that the UK drafters meant to exclude the right against false attribution of a computer-generated work from UK law by implication—since the right to attribution is itself not recognized in relation to computer-generated works.

The general issue of moral rights in computer-generated works is not dealt with in international copyright instruments, nor is it widely considered in other national laws.[65] As computer-generated works become a more common feature of the cultural landscape, neglecting this kind of creation may well lead to legal difficulties in the coming years.[66]

In the final analysis, the Indian Copyright Act may be the only copyright law to grant moral rights in computer-generated works. The Act specifically addresses the question of authorship in computer-generated works, providing, along UK lines, that the author of "any literary, dramatic, musical or artistic work which is computer-generated" is "the person who causes the work to be created." Section 57 of the Act then grants moral rights to authors, without any exception or exclusion related to computer-generated works. Moreover, the pending amendment Bill, while proposing some drafting improvements to section 57, does not introduce an exception to moral rights protection for the authors of computer-generated work.

---

63. CDPA, *supra* note 26, sec. 9(3); *see* the exceptions to attribution in sec. 79(2)(c) and the exceptions to the right to object to derogatory treatment, sec. 81(2).

64. *See* SIMON STOKES, ART AND COPYRIGHT sec. 5.7 (Hart 2003), *Implications of Moral Rights for the Digital Environment*, at 95.

65. Section 9(3) of the CDPA (*supra* note 26) states: "the person by whom the arrangements necessary for the creation of the work are undertaken." As noted earlier, see exceptions to attribution, sec. 79(2)(c), and exceptions to the right to object to derogatory treatment, sec. 81(2).

66. Interestingly, the point is noted as a concern in the African context. *See* Caroline B. Ncube, *Copyright Protection of Computer Programs, Computer-Generated Works and Databases in Zimbabwe*, J. INFO. L & TECH. (2002)(2), *available at* http://www2.warwick.ac.uk/fac/soc/law/elj/jilt/2002_2/ncube (last visited Apr. 24, 2010). *See* sec. 2.1.2 on *Computer-Generated Works*; Ncube observes, "Zimbabwean legislation is thus deficient as it fails to comprehensively cater for computer generated works, which are actually being produced on a significant scale."

2. New Kinds of Works: Appropriation Art

Where art is concerned, technology affects both means and ends, and even tends to break down the distinction between the two.[67] When the possibility of creating new kinds of artistic work arises, how are moral rights involved?

Once again, when it comes to the satisfaction of basic copyright requirements, works that incorporate digital technology present difficulties. Multimedia creations are an obvious example. If the multimedia work incorporates text, images, or sound from pre-existing sources, when does the new work cease to be original, and lose its entitlement to copyright protection? Are new kinds of work based on technology still sufficiently linked to the personality of the creator to generate moral rights?[68] Is the appropriation or alteration of these works likely to affect the digital author in the same way that these actions could affect an author in the traditional sense of the term?

Appropriation art introduces another type of conflict. By definition, this genre refers to the creation of a work of art out of a person's deliberate choice to use the work of another person in his own work. The use is direct, involving outright copying. There is nothing especially new about appropriation art—Warhol made his name as an appropriation artist during the 1960s—but the advent of digital technology has brought new connotations to appropriation. Appropriation can occur on a scale that was previously not known, and works of appropriation can achieve a level of technical polish that was never possible in the past.

Since appropriation art is based on copying, it seems clear that these kinds of works would infringe copyright—Warhol was on both sides of the issue, and fought off a number of lawsuits.[69] But would appropriation art also violate the moral rights of authors? Depending on the extent to which a work has been used, the failure to attribute the original author could indeed violate his or her moral rights. Potentially, the use of works, or even parts of works, in a new context could also violate rights of integrity and reputation.

---

67. *See, for example*, the provisions of the French CPI (*supra* note 30), art. L121-5 on film: establishing the final version of the film, which is the "work" for copyright purposes, is key to the French approach to film copyright.

68. Irini A. Stamatoudi, Copyright and Multimedia Products: A Comparative Analysis (Cambridge Studies in Intellectual Property Rights, Cambridge Univ. Press 2002).

69. For an interesting discussion of this aspect of Warhol's art and legacy from a slightly different angle, see Randy Kennedy & Carol Vogel, *Suit Claims a Warhol Is Not, Well, a Warhol*, New York Times (June 26, 2008), *available at* http://www.nytimes.com/2008/06/26/arts/design/26warh.html (last visited Apr. 28, 2010).

The very nature of appropriation art depends on taking from others. Appropriation is in vogue with art insiders in many parts of the world. Should appropriation art therefore be exempted from moral rights—and possibly, the operation of copyright law—in much the same way that parody is? Or should appropriation artists be required to respect these rules? Since much appropriation art would fall into the category of visual art, it is also interesting to note that this question is directly relevant to the United States, where the *Visual Artists Rights Act* of 1990 could apply to appropriation art.[70]

In an interesting parallel, the infiltration of literature by an appropriation mentality is described by Randy Kennedy, writing for the New York Times. In his coverage of teenage media sensation, Helene Hegemann, who has written a novel built largely out of passages from the works of other writers, Kennedy comments:

> A child of a media-saturated generation, she presented herself as a writer whose birthright is the remix, the use of anything at hand she feels suits her purposes, an idea of communal creativity that certainly wasn't shared by those from whom she borrowed. In a line that might have been stolen from Sartre (it wasn't) she added: "There's no such thing as originality anyway, just authenticity."[71]

Whatever the literary merit of appropriation, its impact on fairness should give us pause. Theft from a well-known writer could be considered a tongue-in-cheek form of homage. Can the same be said of words taken from an obscure or unknown person who may have hopes of achieving renown in his own right? In this case, it would seem that appropriation art should be compelled to abide by some form of attribution, for the sake of protecting the words of unknown authors and preventing others from making capital out of them. A similar issue arises in relation to integrity: should the distortion of unknown works be allowed, and if so, what are the human and cultural costs? Once again, the scope of appropriation is much different than what was possible in the past. Technology is invasive. Is it really fair to group T. S. Eliot and James Joyce, who did indeed use the work of predecessors to build new and "original" work, with the work of Helene Hegemann? Who is to decide? As Louis Menand points out:

> If something is really successful, then the law tends to get changed and society changes to allow it to happen . . . . The test has always been in the pudding.[72]

---

70. Visual Artists Rights Act of 1990, Pub. L. No. 101-650, 104 Stat. 5128, 17 U.S.C. § 106A [VARA].

71. Randy Kennedy, *The Free-Appropriation Writer*, NEW YORK TIMES (Feb. 26, 2010), *available at* http://www.nytimes.com/2010/02/28/weekinreview/28kennedy.html (last visited Apr. 24, 2010) [Kennedy, *The Free-Appropriation Writer*].

72. *Id.*

3. The Problems of Authorship

It is apparent that the most serious challenges to moral rights presented by technology occur at the level of authorship. In particular, there is a confusion of identity among the individuals—or entities—who are involved in artistic creation at every stage.

a. Programmer as Author

When a computer programmer creates a work of art through the medium of programming technology, he arguably becomes an "author" in the practical sense of the expression. However, does the programmer fit the copyright concept of an author as an independent and original being, whose work reflects his creative genius? Moral rights require an author. If we refuse to accord the status of author to the programmer, who will then fulfill this role?[73]

The work of a programmer seems intuitively different from that of an artist—all the more so if the creative work is the product of technological events that are, to some extent, self-propagating. How can authorship be associated with a machine, or an impulse of software, without continuous or continued human involvement?

There are many reasons why moral rights in the digital context should not deviate from their original purpose—the recognition of the author's prerogative over his own work. However, situations can arise where the recognition of a "moral right" in a work is important for reasons other than authorship *per se,* such as the preservation of information or knowledge. In these situations, rather like a moral right in folklore or Aboriginal culture, a "moral right" without an author may be both possible and desirable.[74] Indeed, it could be argued that moral rights doctrine is only superficially preoccupied with authors. Its concern with authorship may be somewhat cosmetic in nature, while the underlying focus of moral rights is actually on the status of the work.[75] But, at present, the idea of a moral right without an author remains the unusual case. In information technology, as in other areas, moral rights continue to crystallize around the author as a human individual.

---

73. In relation to moral rights in folklore, for example, there is no individual author in the usual sense; but someone else is there to be the "author," namely, a community or group. For an interesting exploration of the relationship between individual and communal creativity in works of folklore, see *Yumbulul v. Reserve Bank of Australia* (1991) 21 I.P.R. 481 (Austl.).
74. *See* Chapter 3, *supra,* "A Theory in Flux," notes 123–52 and accompanying text.
75. Indeed, the integrity right is often considered to be the heart of the doctrine.

b. Performer as Author

If the performance of an electronic work of art requires the involvement of a human being—for example, someone to manipulate the underlying computer program or to carry out required steps at different stages of its realization—how will the law define the role of this person in the artistic creation? Is he a performer, a performer-*cum*-author, or a coauthor of the program?

The merging of identities between performer and author is increasingly a feature of global culture. There are both technological and cultural reasons for this trend. It reflects the impact of technology on artistic creation, and the increasing emphasis on performance as an artistic activity in its own right. Interestingly, these changing identities are reflected in the latest international regulation on copyright in performances, the WIPO Performances and Phonograms Treaty (WPPT) of 1996, which entered into force in mid-2002.[76] Article 5 of the WPPT creates moral rights in performances, on terms that closely resemble the moral rights enjoyed by the authors of original works under Article 6*bis* of the Berne Convention. From the perspective of moral rights doctrine, this change is a radical one. However, it appears to reflect a determination at WIPO to ensure that moral rights are available to a broad range of creators—a new legal approach to situations where the distinction between performer and original author is, in practice, increasingly blurred.[77]

c. Audience As Author

The widespread ease and availability of technological means for intervening in ostensibly finished works of art allows so-called "end-users" an unprecedented role in reshaping, modifying, criticizing, and disseminating art. This trend is often portrayed as an indication of the "unenforceability" of moral rights—and indeed, of copyright law as a whole. The empowerment of the public to deal with artworks directly through technology—without the continued mediation of the author—has brought about a number of important changes in the relationship between authors and their public.

In particular, the supremacy of authorship is now curtailed by the power of the public to intervene. The protection of moral rights depends, to an increasing extent, on the support of the public. By an appropriate irony, the future protection of the personal and cultural interests involved in moral

---

76. WIPO Performances and Phonograms Treaty (adopted Dec. 20, 1996, entered into force May 20, 2002) (1997) 36 I.L.M. 76, *available at* http://www.wipo.int/treaties/en/ip/berne/trtdocs_wo001.html (last visited Apr. 28, 2010) [WPPT].

77. However, moral rights were excluded from performances that occur in an audiovisual context—films. This was largely due to the firm opposition of the Hollywood lobby. *See* Pamela Samuleson, *The U.S. Digital Agenda at WIPO*, 37 VA. J. INT'L L. 369 (1997).

rights depends upon the development of an attitude of responsibility and interest—"ownership," in the large sense of the term—towards artistic creation among the public. In effect, through technology, the audience, too, has become a potential "author." Realizing that potential will depend on combining technological power with cultural sensitivity.

C. Recommendations

Excluding moral rights is a hasty and ill-advised approach to the question of creators' rights in a technological environment. Information technology, in particular, implies a series of fascinating questions about the evolving nature of human creativity, and moral rights in this area deserve greater reflection. An honest attempt should be made to investigate the implications of technology for moral rights, and to develop the proper legal formulae for their recognition. Conversely, the potential impact of moral rights on technology, in its turn, deserves to be explored.

It is apparent that moral rights in information technology may differ in a number of ways from the moral rights protected in civil law jurisdictions such as France. Moral rights in software should include the "bundle" of rights protected in Article 6*bis*, but they may also lead to new and different rights and exceptions than attribution and a reputation-dependent integrity right. An exemption to the right of integrity based on the use of the work for further technological development might be one helpful idea.

The area of technology-based artistic creation is even more likely to generate new kinds of moral rights. For example, the relationship between the author and the work may not be as important in relation to these kinds of works. Moral rights in technological works might focus on the work without seeking to protect the author. In some cases, they might focus exclusively on attribution. Appropriation art, if it proved its worth, might justify an exemption from moral rights—at least, where the appropriated work is already well-known.

New moral rights should carefully seek to maintain a balance between the rights of authors and the right of the public to have access to technology. This is particularly important if moral rights are to serve the higher purpose of further technological development. Moral rights will certainly have to differentiate between different kinds of works, as the UK copyright law attempts to do, but the grounds on which this differentiation will occur must be clarified. The purpose of the work will probably be a key issue. Is the computer program intended to contribute to the creation of a work of art? Does it help to express a personal relationship between the person who develops the program and the final product or process?

Moral rights in information technology should be based on three guiding principles: the promotion of technological development, the protection of the relationship between a human author and his work, and the recognition of the human rights of programmers and, of course, artists working with technology. Respect for human rights deserves to become an overarching principle that informs the treatment of moral rights.

Several conclusions flow from these criteria. The first is that moral rights in information technology should be recognized. The primary objective of doing so is to respect the human rights of creators in a technological and, potentially, corporate environment. Secondly, it is also clear that special standards and limits may need to apply where moral rights arise in information technology. For example, functionality may be a useful concept.

In relation to computer programs, the principle of "functionality" can offer a concrete basis for determining how moral rights should apply. In particular, assessing functionality can help to balance the prerogatives of authorship against the needs of technological development. Elements of programs that are functionally essential, or contribute to the greater effectiveness of technology, should not be restricted from use. Properly speaking, they belong in the realm of a "software commons," where programming ideas and tools would remain generally available to the software community. It may still remain feasible, and important, for any useful innovation to be attributed to its creator. The author may hope to build professional renown from it, although the manner of the attribution is something that should be determined by industry practice.

Given the fast pace of the software industry and its dependence on the ability to re-use and modify existing code, the integrity right should probably be restricted to situations of damage to the programmer's reputation. The balance is effectively struck in French law, which scales back the programmer's right of integrity to the Berne formula.

The right of withdrawal presents lawyers with a quandary. In French law, it includes a built-in safety net. The withdrawal of a work from circulation must be accompanied by the payment of economic compensation to anyone who suffers as a result of the decision.[78] The right is reproduced, with little attempt at revision, in the Russian intellectual property code.[79] Given this safeguard, why does French law disallow the computer programmer's right to withdraw his work? Practical concerns may be at work—the difficulty of enforcing compensation, or of arriving at a figure for compensation when the number of people affected by such a decision could be very large. The right may also be politically untenable, and could be seen as having a chilling effect on the operation of the software industry.

The clash between moral rights and new artistic forms could be dramatic. Can the remix generation be persuaded to accept restrictions on its "right" to remix? The fate of remix culture will ultimately depend on the quality of

---

78. CPI, *supra* note 30, art. L121-4.
79. 2008 Russian Civil Code, *supra* note 24, art. 1269.

its products. If history's ultimate verdict is negative, what happens to the countless instances of moral and human rights violations that may have occurred in the process? If the creation of art is a kind of freedom within discipline, the necessity of moral rights may be one discipline that artists should learn to respect. It seems virtually certain that appropriation culture will lead to some deterioration in cultural heritage—changing contexts and repeated re-use seem to guarantee it. If so, the public may eventually pay a steep price for the notoriety of appropriation art. Is it worth it? Only time will tell.

D. Conclusion

The belief that moral rights are inappropriate for information technology is ill-informed. It is based on a spurious consideration of the issues. While it is true that some areas of new creativity are clearly removed from moral rights, in other respects, digital creation has only enhanced their value and importance. An all-encompassing conclusion about the appropriateness of applying moral rights to new creative endeavors cannot be drawn, particularly if that conclusion implies the complete exclusion of moral rights from technological creation. Rather, moral rights appear to be necessary and desirable in some areas, but may be inappropriate in relation to others.

The example of moral rights in information technology helps to establish a basic framework for the treatment of moral rights in a new technological environment. Three conclusions can be drawn. First, moral rights have a place in the world of technology; they should not be arbitrarily excluded from it. Second, there is no universal legal formula for moral rights; rather, the specifics of moral rights protection may vary according to the technological context in which they apply. Third, the framing of these moral rights may need to demonstrate delicate nuances that respond to the subtle needs of technology. Notably, technology's dependence on existing technology for its future growth is a sensitive issue that should never be neglected.

The moral right that meets the needs of human creativity in the digital age will reflect the variety of human experience as never before. In doing so, it will not only accommodate the cultural side of the digital revolution, but it will also help us to recognize the underlying breadth of human creativity. New cultural realities have always been there—in the villages of India, the grasslands of Africa, the rain forests of South and North America—and the modern era has always been plagued by the limited ability of Western and international copyright laws to reflect human cultural diversity. By an interesting irony, the challenges that technology brings to the concepts underlying copyright law may ultimately lead to a better accommodation of ancient models of creativity and culture that are found in non-Western societies.[80] The "very new" may help to recognize the "very old."[81]

There is much to be gained from a reassessment of moral rights, their purpose, scope, and content. The experience promises to be mind-expanding in much more than a legal sense. Technology confirms the apparently limitless potential of human creativity. However strange the products of new technology may seem, the creative impulse somehow remains identifiable, and entirely true to itself. The same thought can be expressed in the language of moral rights: it may no longer be entirely clear what an author or a work is, yet both of them undoubtedly continue to exist. Moral rights can help us to navigate the changing seas of cultural transition, and keep alive our sense of wonder at the richness of human possibilities.

---

80. *See* the related discussion in James Tunney, *E.U., I.P., Indigenous People and the Digital Age: Intersecting Circles?*, 20 (9) Eur. Intell. Prop. Rev. 335 (1998).

81. *See id.*

CHAPTER

6

More Than Musicians

Moral Rights and Digital Issues in Music

*The purpose of art is . . . the . . . lifelong construction
of a state of wonder and serenity.*[1]
–Glenn Gould

---

1. Geoffrey Payzant, Glenn Gould: Music and Mind 64 (Key Porter Books 1984).

Music may be the oldest form of art known to humanity. By an interesting irony, it has also become the emblematic creative expression of the digital era. Music is a complete reflection in microcosm of the digital revolution, an embodiment of the themes of unfettered creation and communication, new relationships between artists and their public, and, quite possibly, the death of an industry.

Perhaps surprisingly, the first musicians to recognize the potential of technology came from a classical background. While technology has since not penetrated far into the realm of classical music,[2] the initial collision of worlds was spectacular. The classical art is defined by its preoccupation with perfection. Johannes Brahms once said that he was not primarily concerned with whether his compositions were beautiful, but with the question of whether they were perfect.[3] Pianist Artur Schnabel famously commented that he was "attracted only to music which I consider to be better than it can be performed."[4] In a sense, the environment of the recording studio is undoubtedly better equipped for "perfection" than the concert hall.[5]

But technology also promised something more: the democratization of an art that was deeply mired in convention, not all of it serving the higher purpose of musical excellence. Technology could break down the barriers between an artist and his audience; it could transform the passive experience of the listener into active engagement with the music. The Canadian pianist Glenn Gould was in some sense the living embodiment of this dream.

Gould was the first prominent musician to become excited about the creative possibilities brought to classical music by technology, and he courageously reshaped his own career to reflect his vision. In 1964, he retired permanently from concert-giving. He was 32 years old. He preferred, instead, to focus on what he saw as the musical art of the future: recording. His manager, Walter Homburger, warned him that public tastes were fickle. Gould might be unable to maintain his livelihood as a classical artist through recordings.[6] But Gould's experiment proved to be a brilliant success. Not only did he craft some of the iconic recordings of the twentieth century—his early and late versions of the Goldberg Variations are but two examples from

---

2. But note the pathbreaking work of classical sound engineers, such as Steve Epstein; *see* the information on the program "Glenn Gould in Re-performance" developed by Epstein and his colleagues, *available at* http://www.zenph.com/sept25.html (last visited Apr. 25, 2010).

3. Jan Swafford, Johannes Brahms: A Biography 420 (Alfred A. Knopf 1997).

4. Glenn Gould comments that Schnabel was "a person who didn't really care very much about the piano as an instrument. The piano was a means to an end, for him, and the end was to approach Beethoven." Quoted in Payzant, *supra* note 1, at 6.

5. But note, nevertheless, that Schnabel is said to have disliked recording, perhaps because of his preoccupation with the environment in which his music was heard.

6. *See* the comments in Peter F. Ostwald, Glenn Gould: The Ecstasy and Tragedy of Genius 210, with a Foreword by Oliver Sacks (W.W. Norton and Co. 1997).

his peerless discography[7]—but he also wrote and lectured extensively on the theme of recording. He thought it the ultimate musical art form. Writing in 1966, Gould commented:

> In an unguarded moment some months ago, I predicted that the public concert as we know it today would no longer exist a century hence, that its functions would have been entirely taken over by electronic media. It had not occurred to me that this statement represented a particularly radical pronouncement. Indeed, I regarded it almost as self-evident truth and, in any case, as defining only one of the peripheral effects occasioned by developments in the electronic age.[8]

Gould's passion for technology was not limited to the joys of the recording studio, whose privacy, concentration, and opportunities for multiple takes provided the perfect setting in which to examine a work comprehensively, to approach it in a mode of consistent creative exploration.[9] Gould was also interested in digital music in its own right. He commented, controversially and with typical self-deprecation, that the Moog synthesizer produced the most perfect interpretation imaginable of Bach.[10]

Gould may have been the first person to see the "democratizing" potential of technology for the hierarchical and elite art of classical music. In Gould's view, technology offered new opportunities for the listener to intervene in a creative work—to change the sound of a recording, to alter the balance among multiple "voices" or performers, to adjust the speed of the music. The possibilities for intervention in a work of recorded music are much greater now than they were even in Gould's time.

The legendary jazz pianist Bill Evans, coincidentally a friend of Gould's, was also interested in technology.[11] He used it to accomplish something

---

7. GLENN GOULD, GOLDBERG VARIATIONS (Columbia Masterworks 1981) (1955). Both were recorded by Columbia Masterworks.

8. Glenn Gould, *The Prospects of Recording*, 16(4) HIGH FIDELITY 46–63 (1996), *available at* http://www.collectionscanada.gc.ca/glenngould/028010-4020.01-f.html (last visited Apr. 25, 2010). The online version appears with comments by a number of leading musical figures [Gould, *The Prospects of Recording*]. *See also* the extremely interesting comments on Gould's attitude to recording in the Canadian encyclopedia online, *Gould, Glenn*, THE ENCYCLOPEDIA OF MUSIC IN CANADA ("For Gould, recording had fundamentally altered the traditional relationship of composer, performer, and listener."), *available at* http://www.thecanadianencyclopedia.com/index.cfm?PgNm=TCE&Params=U1ARTU0001410#SEC883720 (last visited July 18, 2010)

9. Gould's creative process in studio is the subject of a book by his long-time producer, Andrew Kazdin. ANDREW KAZDIN, GLENN GOULD AT WORK: CREATIVE LYING (Dutton 1989).

10. The personality of the performer could not "interfere" with the integrity of the composition if the performer, as in the case of the Moog synthesizer, was a machine.

11. In his biography of Bill Evans, Peter Pettinger notes their friendship *See* PETER PETTINGER, BILL EVANS: HOW MY HEART SINGS 221 (Yale Univ. Press 1998).

slightly different—a pathbreaking record called *Conversations with Myself*, in which he used the then-novel technique of "overdubbing" his own playing, superimposing one recorded performance of a piece upon another, to achieve a new level in his exploration of musical ideas.[12] Recorded in 1963, the album won the young pianist a Grammy Award. Jason R. Laipply describes the work as an "instant classic." He comments:

> Overdubbing was sneered at by most jazz people, looked at as "gimmicky" and "synthetic." But Evans, one of the most lyrical musicians the jazz world has ever known, was intrigued with taking the "conversational" approach his trio had been practicing to the next logical level. If three musicians could practice and play together long enough to be able to carry on musical conversations during a song, then wouldn't the musical ideas expressed and explored by multiple tracks of the same musician be even closer to an "idealized" perfection?[13]

These early experiments were in the avant-garde of a phenomenon that has now become widespread: the manipulation of music through technology. For outstanding artists like Gould and Evans, technology allowed them to approach, more closely than ever before, the perfection of their artistic vision. But technology has had a broad impact on all genres of music. In relation to popular music, it has fundamentally redefined musical expression. Entire genres of new music are based on technological intervention, including the use of samples and mixing techniques that alter well-known sounds or songs, voices or riffs, presenting them in a new context. The DJ has become a musical creator in his own right.[14]

The democratic aspect of technology has taken on new meaning, as artists rely increasingly on direct connections with their public, through technology, to publicize their work. The YouTube service, which allows users to post their own videos online, has become one major vehicle for publicizing new talent. Singer Susan Boyle became an overnight sensation when her performance on the television program, *Britain's Got Talent*, posted on YouTube, made an unlikely star of the modest 47-year-old Scotswoman, defying a media environment hungry for youth and glamour.[15] To date, Boyle's YouTube video

---

12. Apparently, Evans used Gould's Steinway piano, CD 318, for the recording of the album CONVERSATIONS WITH MYSELF. *See id.*, and KEVIN BAZZANA, WONDROUS STRANGE: THE LIFE AND ART OF GLENN GOULD 88 (Oxford Univ. Press 2004).

13. Jason R Laipply, *Conversations with Myself: Bill Evans*, ALL ABOUT JAZZ (Oct. 1, 1997 review), *available at* http://www.allaboutjazz.com/php/article.php?id=2440 (last visited July 18, 2010).

14. An interesting program on this theme has been produced by Paolo Pietropaolo and colleagues at the CBC. Paolo Pietropaolo et al., THE WIRE (2005), *available at* http://www.cbc.ca/thewire/ (last visited Aug. 22, 2010).

15. *See* Scott Collins & Janet Stobart, *Talent Trumps All for YouTube Sensation Susan Boyle: An Appearance on "Britain's Got Talent" Propels the 47-Year-Old Singer onto the World*

has apparently received a staggering 300 million hits, and subsequent sales of her debut album have set new records.[16]

Another famous incident is the decision of rock band Radiohead to give away its album, "In Rainbows," on its website, with the stipulation upon downloading that, "You pay what you want."[17] This approach has raised the hackles of other performers. Robert Smith of the Cure, comments:

> You can't allow other people to put a price on what you do, otherwise you don't consider what you do to have any value at all. . . .[18]

As far as the economics of music are concerned, technology has made a dramatic impact. Two sets of issues have surfaced. The first, the general problem of securing an economic benefit from music, is illustrated by the case of Radiohead. The second problem is more specific, and subtle—where to draw the line separating restricted from free uses of music. This problem can be neatly encapsulated in copyright language: it is the issue of whether existing copyright rules should be extended to new technologies, and if so, to what extent. Should file-sharing of music files, for example, be subject to copyright restrictions or completely exempt from them? If copyright should apply, will every act of file-sharing attract copyright protection, or only certain acts?

At the level of principle, the first issue seems to have been settled; the music industry argues that copyright should apply, but the practical problem remains, of how to control the diffusion of music in a technological

---

Stage—with Nary a Speck of Glitz or Glamour. Los Angeles Times (Apr. 17 2009), *available at* http://www.latimes.com/entertainment/la-et-susan-boyle17-2009apr17,0,2767635.story (last visited July 18, 2010).

16. *See* Sarah Lyall, *Unlikely Singer Is YouTube Sensation,* New York Times (Apr. 18, 2009), *available at* http://www.nytimes.com/2009/04/18/arts/television/18boyle.html. An interesting update on Boyle's career appears in *Susan Boyle's New Album to Be Released November 24th,* Malaysia Star (Oct. 12, 2009), *available at* http:/www.star-ecentral.com/news/story.asp?-file=/2009/10/12/music/20091012152419&sec=music (last visited Apr. 25, 2010). Her celebrity has also translated into outstanding album sales. *See Susan Boyle Sets US Chart Record,* BBC News (Dec. 2, 2009), *available at* http://news.bbc.co.uk/2/hi/8391777.stm (last visited Apr. 25, 2010). The problems of attributing posted videos to their creators, and of maintaining the integrity of videos, are briefly noted by Damien O'Brien & Brian Fitzgerald, *Digital Copyright Law in a YouTube World,* 9(6 & 7) Internet L. Bull. 71 (2006).

17. *See* Josh Tyrangiel, *You Pay What You Want,* Time (Oct. 1, 2007), *available at* http://www.time.com/time/arts/article/0,8599,1666973,00.html (last visited Apr. 25, 2010). *See* the interesting follow-up by Greg Sandoval, *Radiohead Won't repeat "In Rainbows" Giveaway* (Apr. 30, 2008), *available at* http://news.cnet.com/8301-10784_3-9932361-7.html (last visited Aug. 11, 2010).

18. *See* Michael Leonard, *Robert Smith Blasts "Idiot" Radiohead: Pay What You Want? Not for The Cure* (Feb. 24, 2009), *available at* http://www.musicradar.com/news/guitars/robert-smith-blasts-idiot-radiohead-197836 (last visited Apr. 25, 2010). Leonard comments: "The Cure's frontman Robert Smith says he 'disagreed violently' with Radiohead allowing their fans to pay what they wanted for the band's last album, In Rainbows."

environment that allows information to circulate, more or less, unimpeded. But the second problem is a struggle over the details of copyright reform: depending on how copyright rules are redefined, the entire music industry as we know it may stand or fall. This is because copyright provides the missing moral imperative—the justification for restrictions on music that could be free-flowing and self-replicating without them. It offers the moral sanction implicit in the law to justify the dedication of resources to the "enforcement" of copyright laws as a major public policy initiative.

In the contest over music rights, moral rights have been almost entirely neglected. This remarkable oversight may be explained by the fact that the agenda for music copyright is largely set by corporations, whose focus falls naturally on economic rights. But the moral interests in music are as deeply implicated in technological change as economic rights. Indeed, in a fundamental sense, moral rights in music are of greater importance to society than economic rights. This is not to understate the drama of the economic issue— once again, there can be no doubt that the survival of an industry is at stake. However, this problem will find an eventual resolution. The music industry, willingly or unwillingly, conservatively or in the spirit of innovation, will find itself reshaped by the social forces at work; copyright law will both guide that process and respond to the perspectives of the public. Where moral rights are concerned, the issues are insidious, and the concerns that they raise include the creation and sustenance of artistic and professional reputations, the potential misappropriation of music, and the integrity of knowledge about musical traditions in a digital environment. Economic rights involve the fate of an industry. Moral rights are concerned with the human rights of authors and artists; they invoke the integrity of cultural heritage. What are the moral rights involved in musical technologies? And what kinds of strategies should be used to approach them in a digital environment?

A. Creation or Production? Moral Rights and New Musical Techniques

The use of new technologies in the creation of musical sound leads to questions about the moral rights of creators. The initial view is one of natural compatibility between new musical forms and moral rights—after all, whatever the intervention of technology, music remains fundamentally the same. However, the creation of music through technology challenges basic concepts on which moral rights are based. The confusion occurs in utterly existential terms. Who is an author?[19] What constitutes the integrity of a work?

---

19. *See* the seminal essay by Michel Foucault, *What Is an Author?*, *in* THE FOUCAULT READER 101 (Paul Rabinow ed., Pantheon Books 1984).

1. Sampling

Digital technology transforms our relationship with the past. One of the joys of musical creation through technology is the ability to explore pre-existing musical performances. Recorded music has allowed some access to the music of the past throughout the twentieth century, but the digital scenario is different. Recorded works can now be used in the creation of new works—not through inspiration or idea alone, but directly, through the actual use of recorded music.

The champion of this new creative act is the DJ, or disc jockey. When it was coined in the early twentieth century, the term initially meant a person who organized a radio program with many features, including recorded and live music, interspersed with the commentary of the announcer. John Peel, a British DJ famous for his work at the BBC, championed new music and helped to create careers for little-known bands that he found interesting.[20] Over the past century, the art of the DJ has expanded considerably, and it now includes "composition" and "performance" based on the use of segments from recorded music and artificial sound. The use of these "samples" can lead to a distinctive new style, and many DJs have become celebrity musicians through their work. Sampling gave birth to a new genre of popular music, hip-hop, which is extensively derived from the practice.[21]

A number of interesting cases have arisen in the United States on the use of music samples, particularly since the turn of the millennium. To date, litigation has been framed in terms of economic rights, with musicians arguing that the use of a sample is a straightforward example of copyright infringement. Two principles have emerged. The first is that the use of a sample may be justified as a "fair use" of the work. If so, it will be beyond the scope of copyright law. But in order to qualify as an exception to copyright rules, the use must fall into some special category, such as parody, recognized in U.S. copyright law. The rule is also an "old" one—it dates from a 1994 Supreme Court ruling on a parody of Roy Orbison's song, *Pretty Woman*, and, given the speed of technological change, the time for revision may have come.[22] In particular, the period since 2000 has been one of increasingly tight restrictions

---

20. *Legendary Radio DJ John Peel Dies*, BBC News (Oct. 26, 2004), *available at* http://news.bbc.co.uk/2/hi/entertainment/3955289.stm (last visited Apr. 25, 2010).

21. Ian Condry explores the world of Japanese hip-hop, considering, among other things, the fascinating question of how an American cultural export like the hip-hop genre can adapt to a new environment. He remarks, "For some, the presence of hip-hop implies a 'loss of Japanese culture.' But what if hip-hop is used to express one's Japaneseness?" *See* Ian Condry, Japanese Hip-Hop, *available at* http://web.mit.edu/condry/www/jhh/ (last visited Apr. 25, 2010); Ian Condry, Hip-Hop Japan: Rap and the Paths of Cultural Globalization (Duke Univ. Press 2006).

22. Moore's law, that the speed of the computer processor doubles every 18 months, is probably a good basic indicator.

on the scope of fair use in the United States, as well as counterpart doctrines such as "fair dealing" in Canada and the UK. The second principle is the *Bridgeport* rule: even a minimal use of a work for sampling purposes will trigger an infringement of copyright law.[23]

The question of moral rights has not been addressed directly, and this is in keeping with American tradition: in U.S. litigation, implicit recognition of moral rights has often been framed in terms of copyright infringement.[24] In the classic case of *Gilliam v. ABC*, a U.S. court found that altering the broadcast of Monty Python episodes on national television to exclude the "naughty bits" was an infringement of copyright law.[25] The reasoning? Changes to the program were so extensive that the edits had, in effect, created a new copyright work in its own right—a derivative work. The creation of a derivative work requires, of course, the permission of the original creator. A translation of a book into a foreign language, or the adaptation of a play into a film, cannot be legitimately carried out without the permission of the original author. In the *Gilliam* case, the question of whether the troupe's right of integrity in their creation had been violated was simply not discussed by the court. In similar terms, the use of a sample in a new musical work, especially if it were marketed for commercial purposes, could amount to an unauthorized reproduction of the original work. Tellingly, the *Bridgeport* decision of 2005 saw a U.S. appeals court deciding that a mere three notes was enough to constitute the taking of a substantial part of a musical work, leading to a finding of copyright infringement.[26]

Sampling has also provoked a degree of schizophrenia in the American music lobby. While the Recording Industry Association of America (RIAA) has generally been unrelenting in its quest for higher levels of copyright protection, sampling presents a quandary. Excessive restrictions could limit the expansion of a lucrative new genre, and the RIAA has accordingly resisted the temptation to condemn sampling outright. Nevertheless, the ruling in

---

23. Bridgeport Music, Inc. v. Dimension Films, 410 F.3d 792 (6th Cir. 2005).
24. Interestingly, this approach is ill-advised in the Canadian context: the Supreme Court of Canada has effectively ruled that a violation of moral rights cannot succeed as a claim for copyright infringement in Canada. *See* Théberge v. Galerie d'Art du Petit Champlain Inc. [2002] 2 SCR 336, 2002 SCC 34, *available at* http://csc.lexum.umontreal.ca/en/2002/2002scc34/2002scc34.html [THÉBERGE] (last visited Apr. 25, 2010).
25. Gilliam v. American Broadcasting Companies, 538 F.2d 14 (2d Cir. 1976).
26. *See* Bridgeport, *supra* note 23. It depends which three notes. For example, Rachmaninoff's famous first prelude for piano— Opus 3, No. 2, in C-Sharp Minor— is instantly recognizable by its first three notes. *See also* Frisby v. BBC [1967] Ch. 932. The deletion of a single line from a radio play was considered an effective violation of the dramatist's copyright; it was so significant as to require express contractual permission. As in the U.S. example, the UK court had to have recourse to copyright infringement doctrines in the absence of statutory protections for moral rights. If the case were to be considered today, it could be approached as a question of the violation of the author's moral right of integrity.

Bridgeport has led to a situation where any sampling is effectively deemed to require a license, a position that clearly favors established musicians who can afford to pay for the use of samples. In this sense, sampling may become an art of the establishment—a rich man's art that can no longer afford its status as an act of creative rebellion.

But sampling seems to raise a number of moral rights issues, as well. If a group samples the work of other musicians, should it be required to credit them for their work? Doing so in the body of the new song may not be possible, but the attribution could be provided on liner notes. This raises a separate issue—the fact that many songs are now purchased through online music services such as Apple's iTunes or Amazon.com. In this case, they are sold without liner notes, and attribution is often incomplete. A jazz recording might credit the soloist and not the other players in a trio; a classical recording might identify the orchestra and not the soloist.

The attribution aspect of sampling seems important for a number of reasons—not only to recognize the performers of the past, but also, to give due credit to new or obscure groups who develop music that could become popular through sampling. In these situations, attribution may ultimately be more important than proving copyright infringement. Assuming that the musicians could afford to launch a copyright suit, litigation could lead to the suppression of the new recording, and a payment of damages. On the other hand, if sampling were to be allowed, with a requirement of attribution, the result would be different: widespread circulation of the music and the establishment of a reputation through it. Sampling could bring publicity to music that might not have had a chance to become popular *unless* the work were championed by a famous name. The long-term benefit could be celebrity and success, in terms of both reputation and money. In spite of the "new" nature of these musical genres, they remain quite old-fashioned in their reliance on reputation. It is the bedrock of musical stardom.

2. Mixing

In relation to sampling, the integrity principle is more difficult to assess. The technique of mixing, or re-mixing, provides an opportunity to consider the difficult question of the integrity of the sampled work. Does the use of music in small segments result in a violation of the musician's right of integrity?

This problem can arise in any context, but it is perhaps most troublesome in relation to the works of artists who have come to be known as classics of their kind. To take a sample of Stan Getz's saxophone playing and mix it, or layer it, onto an urban beat changes the context of the music. To a jazz aficionado, Getz's style is instantly recognizable—even stronger examples of musical personality in the jazz world might be the muted sound of Miles Davis' trumpet, or a single chord voicing, notes famously clustered together, as played by Bill Evans. Would it be a violation of the artist's right of integrity to present his work in a new context? Or would it simply amount to a new perspective on the work—a new window through which to view it—in a sense, the most basic definition of creative listening?

Clearly, to recognize an integrity right in relation to mixing might spell the doom of this artistic genre. At the same time, respecting the context in which a work of music is presented may be an important new moral interest in the Digital Age. It is rather like the requirement that an artistic work should be displayed in appropriate conditions. This right is recognized as a moral right in France and Australia, but it is explicitly rejected in other jurisdictions, such as Canada and India.[27]

A cross-cultural dimension also exists, and here, remixing is perhaps at its most controversial. A DJ takes a vocal sample from a work of classical Indian music and superimposes it upon a hip-hop beat. From the perspective of Indian culture, this could amount to a complete misrepresentation of an art form that is thousands of years of old and steeped in a devotional tradition that has no real parallels in Western culture. For Indian *rasikas*, the association between the saint-composers and the music is so powerful that even when songs are heard in purely instrumental performances, the mood of the underlying poem is invoked.[28] How can it be justified to mingle the

---

27. Canadian Copyright Act, R.S.C. 1985, c. C-42, *available at* http://laws.justice.gc.ca/en/C-42/index.html (last visited May 2, 2010) [Canadian Copyright Act], sec. 28.2(3)(a): "a change in the location of a work, the physical means by which a work is exposed or the physical structure containing a work" will not violate the artist's right of integrity. *See* "Explanation" to sec. 57(1)(b) of the Indian Copyright Act, which states: "Failure to display a work or to display it to the satisfaction of the author shall not be deemed to be an infringement of the rights conferred by this section." The Australian Copyright Act, 1968 (Cth) (Austl.) provides, in sec. 195AK(b), that the integrity right can be invoked in the case of "an exhibition in public of the work that is prejudicial to the author's honour or reputation because of the manner or place in which the exhibition occurs." In the French case, the issue is not addressed explicitly in the Code de la Propriété Intellectuelle. *See* Loi N° 92-597 du 1er juillet 1992 relative au code de la propriété intellectuelle (partie législative), Journal officiel de la République française du 8 février 1994; Légifrance: Le service public de la diffusion du droit, *available at* http://www.legifrance.gouv.fr/affichCode.do?cidTexte=LEGITEXT000006069414&dateTexte=20100412 (last visited Apr. 29, 2010) [CODE DE LA PROPRIÉTÉ INTELLECTUELLE, CPI, Intellectual Property Code]. But the case of the refrigerator panels painted by Bernard Buffet, and later separated and sold without the artist's knowledge, confirmed that the "dismantling" of an artwork into its component parts would violate the right of integrity. *See* PIERRE SIRINELLI, SYLVIANE DURRANDE & ANTOINE LATREILLE, eds., CODE DE LA PROPRIÉTÉ INTELLECTUELLE COMMENTÉ, EDITION 2009, 101, para 43, Codes Dalloz, ed. Jeanne Daleau (Dalloz 2009) [Sirinelli et al.]; *see also* John Henry Merryman, *The Refrigerator of Bernard Buffet*, HASTINGS L.J. 1023 (1976).

28. The term, "*rasikas*," is used by Indians to denote the audience; it specifically means those who enjoy the music. It is derived from the word "rasa," called, by India's National Poet, the "key-word of Indian culture." *See* C. SUBRAMANIA BHARATI, AGNI AND OTHER POEMS AND TRANSLATIONS & ESSAYS AND OTHER PROSE FRAGMENTS 69 (A. Natarajan 1980).

composition of an Indian saint-composer such as Tyagaraja with hip-hop culture? On the other hand, is the result equally objectionable if the mix is between Carnatic music and gospel, or jazz?[29] After all, Ravi Shankar pioneered the popularization of Indian classical music in the West with his work with the Beatles. It seems fitting that his two daughters are leading musicians in each genre: Anoushka Shankar, the sitar player, and Norah Jones, the popular singer.

3. Production[30]

Sound recording is an activity of fundamental importance in the digital era. With digital technology, the role of the sound engineer has expanded dramatically. Sound engineers have always played an essential role in the quality of a recording, but the means and methods behind sound recording have grown. If art can be defined as the creative exercise of choice, artistry in sound engineering may now be possible as never before. In the digital environment, the sound engineer is much more than a technician; it is perhaps only a matter of time until he can lay claim to being an artist in his own right.

The transformation of the recorded music industry also supports the artist in the sound engineer, in a rather curious way. In the heyday of recording, teams of engineers worked as employees of a recording label, and the label would have its own "sound"—Decca or Deutsche Gramophon in the world of classical music, for example. As the recorded music industry has had to become more streamlined, it is now common for sound engineers to work as individuals under contract. The characteristic sound of the label

---

29. The mixing of jazz with the Carnatic, or South Indian, style of Indian classical music, is discussed in Gary Giddens, *A Passage to India: Rudresh Mahanthappa Chooses a Heritage*, New Yorker (Mar. 2, 2009), *available at* http://www.newyorker.com/arts/critics/musical/-2009/03/02/090302crmu_music_giddins (last visited Apr. 25, 2010). Kadri Gopalnath and Kanyakumari are pre-eminent artists in the genre; Mahanthappa found great good fortune to play with them.

30. This section makes use of the terms production, sound engineering, audio engineering, and making a recording, interchangeably. In relation to recording, the English language is somewhat lacking in precision; in contrast, consider the German term tonmeister, as opposed to tontechniker and toninegenieur, which specifically distinguishes the creative side of sound engineering from its hardware aspects. *See, for example,* the encyclopedia entry at Absolute Astronomy.com, *available at* http://www.absoluteastronomy.com/topics/Audio_engineering (last visited Apr. 25, 2010). *See* Industry Canada, Intellectual Property Policy—Assessing the Economic Impacts of Copyright Reform on Performers and Producers of Sound Recordings in Canada (Economic Impact Study), *available at* http://www.ic.gc.ca/eic/site/ippd-dppi.nsf/eng/ip01113.html (last visited Apr. 25, 2010).

may have vanished; but the sound of the individual engineer has a place in this new landscape.[31]

Paul Greene's definition seems apt: sound engineering is "the technological empowerment to engineer music, culture, soundscapes, and lifeways."[32] The work of a sound engineer involves myriad creative features, from the choice of equipment and the placement of microphones, to the mixing of sound to create a suitable environment for the music being recorded.[33] The emerging concept of "virtual recording" is interesting in a classical music culture obsessed with "authenticity." In classical music, history plays an important part in establishing authenticity, and this preoccupation probably explains the current interest in rebuilding instruments from historical periods to be used for performing the works of the composers of the times. Virtual recording seems to turn this ideal on its head, by focusing on the re-creation of a sound that exists somewhere in space and time, through technological means. It is certainly reminiscent of Glenn Gould's idea of "creative cheating" in his quest for musical perfection.[34]

If the art lags behind, at least the skill involved in creating a sound recording has been recognized for some time in copyright law. The special right in a sound recording exists independently of the matter recorded; it is an additional layer of rights beyond the rights of the composer and performer of the music. In most jurisdictions, the sound recording right is available for a period of fifty to seventy years after the making of the recording; in the UK and

---

31. I am indebted to sound engineer, Steve Epstein, for illuminating the world of sound engineering for me and sharing his vast knowledge of the recorded music industry (personal communication with the author, May 2010).

32. *See* Paul D. Greene, Engineering Spaces in Nepal's Digital Stereo Remix Culture (Paper delivered at the panel, "Sound Engineering as Cultural Production," Society for Ethnomusicology meeting (Austin), Nov. 19, 1999). Greene's website, dedicated to panel research on "Sound Engineering as Cultural Production," is an extremely useful resource that includes a helpful bibliography of this growing field. *See* http://pmssem.tamu.edu/greene.html (last visited Apr. 26, 2010).

33. For example, a current project undertaken by *tonmeister* Martha de Francisco, a leading classical sound engineer, and her colleagues at McGill University involves the creation of "virtual concert halls" based on the sound environments of well-known concert venues, which are effectively re-created using special speaker and microphone techniques. The project features performances by Tom Beghin, and engineering by Wieslaw Wozczyk at McGill's Center for Music, Media and Technology, and a description can be seen online at http://www.music.mcgill.ca/thevirtualhaydn/ (last visited Aug. 22, 2010). The recordings are produced by Naxos, and the set of blu-ray discs includes a 3-hour documentary film on the project. *See* http://www.naxos.com/catalogue/item.asp?item_code=NBD0001-04 (last visited Aug. 22, 2010). The project receives an interesting review by Paul Wells, *You've Never Heard Haydn Like This*, MACLEAN'S (Oct. 1, 2009), *available at* http://www2.macleans.ca/2009/10/01/you've-never-heard-haydn-like-this/ (last visited Aug. 23, 2010).

34. The expression "creative cheating" is used in Payzant, *supra* note 1, at 119. Note also the echo of the term in Andrew Kazdin's title, *supra* note 9.

Europe, a controversial move to extend the right to 95 years is still pending.[35] The right can be classified as a "neighboring" right, as performers' rights have traditionally been called, and it effectively recognizes a contribution made in creating a work that is derived from the original work of a higher-level creator—traditionally, the composer, but now, the performer as well.

An additional complexity arises because the sound engineering activity is one that often occurs in a corporate environment. Accordingly, companies acquire copyright in sound recordings through the operation of the work-for-hire rule, which makes an employer the first owner of copyright in a work that has been created in the course of employment.[36] A company might also require copyright through the purchase of a recording prepared by an independent sound engineer. However, copyright law does not have a general mechanism to recognize the creative contribution of the sound engineer. Notably, rights of attribution and integrity for sound engineers are not protected.

The contribution of sound engineers to the quality of a musical recording is unquestionably creative, and it is only likely to become more so as recording techniques become more sophisticated. However, it is worth noting that the labor of sound engineers on a recording might, in itself, suffice to invoke moral rights as a matter of justice. Moral rights are generally available for copyright works without any need to establish artistic quality.[37] This issue leads to another interesting point: moral rights have traditionally been important in civil law countries, but those countries also have a higher standard of originality for copyright works. In Continental Europe, labor, alone, is not enough to acquire copyright; creativity is required.[38] The 1992 decision of the U.S. Supreme Court in *Feist* also initiated a trend in the common law

35. *See* HECTOR L. MacQUEEN, CHARLOTTE WAELDE & GRAEME LAURIE, CONTEMPORARY INTELLECTUAL PROPERTY: LAW AND POLICY, para 7.5, 223 (Oxford Univ. Press 2008). A helpful comparison of the American, UK, and European positions on sound recording rights is provided by Susanna Monseau, *"Fit for a Purpose": Why the European Union Should Not Extend the Term of Related Rights Protection in Europe*, 19(3) FORDHAM INTELL. PROP., MEDIA & ENT. L.J. 629.

36. *See, for example,* 17 U.S.C. § 201(b); the corresponding Canadian provision provides for transfer of ownership in the case of a "work made in the course of employment": Canadian Copyright Act, *supra* note 27, sec. 13(3). *See* Stephen Fraser, *Who Owns the Copyright in a Canadian Film? Answer: It Depends (And That's the Problem)*," (2005), *available at* http://www.fraser-elaw.com/pdf/fraser_article_1.pdf (last visited Apr. 21, 2010) [Fraser, *Canadian Film*], who notes the important distinction between the two. The Canadian provision leads to some ambiguity about the circumstances in which the "employer's" copyright prevails.

37. *See* Nicholas Stuart Wood, *Protecting Creativity: Why Moral Rights Should be Extended to Sound Recordings under New Zealand Copyright Law*, VICTORIA UNIV. WELLINGTON L. REV. 8 (2001).

38. *See, e.g.,* Gerhard Schricker, *Farewell to the "Level of Creativity" (Schöpfungshöhe) in German Copyright Law*, 26(1) INT'L REV. INDUS. PROP. & COPYRIGHT L. 41 (1995). Schricker discusses the evolution of the creativity standard in the German context.

countries towards higher standards of originality. The latest rulings on this issue are the 2008 *Eastern Book Company* case decided by the Indian Supreme Court, and the Canadian case of *CCH*, decided in 2004, on which the Indian ruling was very closely based.[39] Both cases establish that some standard of originality beyond mere labor will now be required in these jurisdictions, although many questions remain about the extent of the change.[40] But the creative work of sound engineers would be comfortably grounded even in the new, "modicum of creativity," standard of originality established by *Feist*.[41] The work of sound engineers clearly reflects the additional feature of human imagination that would lead to the recognition of a creative copyright, as well as a moral right in the European context. Importantly, the creative nature of their work suggests that sound engineers, themselves, will ultimately want a moral right, and see it as relevant to their work.

The attribution right does not present any special difficulties, as a sound engineer's involvement in a recording project can be indicated on liner notes just as other album information is provided.[42] Where integrity is concerned, however, the scope of the sound engineer's prerogative is unclear. Just as in the case of copyright, moral rights in the Digital Age confront the issue of multiple claims, and, potentially, layers of coexisting, or competing, rights.

Sound recordings also highlight the importance of the fundamental relationship underlying this art form—that between the performer and the sound engineer. The sound engineer, of course, has no work without the performer. But the performer depends on the sound engineer in a different sense: he relies on the engineer to present his performance to the public in a proper light. "Proper" may mean different things to different artists. For Glenn Gould, it meant intimacy, detail, and clarity of sound; for another pianist, it may mean recreating the ambience of the concert hall.[43] One can imagine the recordings of Vladimir Horowitz in this light: some of his most celebrated

39. CCH Canadian Ltd. v. Law Society of Upper Canada, [2004] 1 S.C.R. 339, 2004 SCC 13 [CCH]; Eastern Book Co. & Ors v. DP Modak & Anr., 2008 (36) PTC 1, 2008 (1) SCC 1 [*Eastern Book Co.*].

40. The issue is a subtle one. Do the new standards apply to all copyright works, or to fact-based works alone, such as databases and telephone directories? And, how high is the new standard? Feist Publications Inc. v. Rural Telephone Service Co., 499 U.S. 340 (1991) [FEIST] moved all the way to "creativity," but CCH, *supra* note 39, only establishes that the standard is somewhere between labor and creativity. The exact point on the spectrum where the Canadian threshold coalesces is unclear, and the emphasis on "skill and judgment" at the Supreme Court of Canada is not entirely helpful.

41. *See* FEIST, *supra* note 39, and CCH, *supra* note 39.

42. But, once again, sale without liner notes will create a problem. This issue is discussed INFRA, in the context of downloaded music. *See infra* notes 69–70 and accompanying text.

43. *See* the fascinating analysis in Gould, *The Prospects of Recording, supra* note 8, *Change of Acoustic*.

recordings are of live performances, though the great pianist himself, does not seem to have commented significantly on the art of recording.

On the subject of a pathbreaking jazz record by the (first) Bill Evans Trio, *Live at the Village Vanguard*, Paul Motian, the drummer, comments:

> You know what I like best on that record? . . . The sounds of all those people, glasses and chatter—I mean, I know you're supposed to be very offended and all, but I like it. They're just there and all.[44]

Adam Gopnik observes that the record provides "[n]ot a timeless experience of a general emotion but a permanent experience of a particular moment."[45] Editing could "clean up" this recording, but it would go against the sensibility of the one surviving member of the trio. And, in the process, something irreplaceable would perhaps be lost.

Accordingly, the exercise of the moral right of integrity by performer and sound engineer should be mutually reinforcing. The possibility of a disagreement between performer and sound engineer about the mixing of a recording exists, but the nature of the art form lends itself to collaboration. Even differences in temperament seem to be superseded by the practical need for collaborative work.[46] The two moral rights coexist to protect the integrity of the recording.

For the same reason, it makes sense to limit the sound engineer's right of integrity by affirming that good-faith attempts at restoration should be free from complaints about the integrity of the original. This responds both to the reality of constant technical improvements that make restoration a growing industry, and to the increasing subtlety of restoration, which may transmute it to the level of an art. Once again, the surprising parallel between a work of visual art and a sound recording makes sense, and the exemption from moral rights for conservation efforts in the visual arts that is present in many laws of the world can help to define the engineer's integrity right in a sound recording.[47]

Finally, no discussion of moral rights in sound recording should neglect the issue of disclosure. Of the three basic moral rights, disclosure is perhaps the one that should not be extended to the maker of a sound recording. The performer's

---

44. The quote appears in a remarkable article by Adam Gopnik, *That Sunday*, NEW YORKER (Aug. 13, 2001), available on The Bill Evans Webpages at http://www.billevanswebpages. com/gopnik.html (last visited July 18, 2010).

45. Gopnik, *supra* note 44.

46. The working relationship between Glenn Gould and his sound engineer, Andrew Kazdin, seems to have been a case in point. Their collaboration yielded a number of outstanding recordings over a period of 15 years. *See* Kazdin, *supra* note 9.

47. *E.g.*, Canadian Copyright Act, *supra* note 27, sec. 28.2 (3)(b). *See also* the U.S. Visual Artists Rights Act of 1990, Pub. L. No. 101-650, 104 Stat. 5128, 17 U.S.C. §§ 106A, 106A(c)(2) [VARA], although this section provides that cases of "gross negligence" in restoration efforts will constitute a violation of the right of integrity.

right of disclosure already protects her right to present the work to the public; because it is the performance that is actually being released to the public, the role of the sound engineer should, in this circumstance, be recognized as a derivative one. At the same time, in situations where the recording of works is controversial—recordings of music from non-mainstream cultural groups in the "ethno-music" context, for example—granting a right of disclosure to the maker of the recording would reinforce existing biases against the rights and interests of the artists themselves. The right to disclose a performance must remain with the performer; only with his or her participation can the sound engineer's work be brought before the public at all. In this sense, there is something integral about the hierarchy between performer and engineer that should probably be preserved for the good of the music.

4. Electronic Music

Electronic music can mean many things. It is the use of electronic instruments in classical music, the creation of synthesized sounds in jazz or popular music, the development of computer programs or algorithms that generate sequences of sound.[48] The challenge of moral rights in electronic music is to determine how closely the musical work remains connected to its human creator. When the bond is strong, moral rights of attribution and integrity will continue to be appropriate.

When the connection between music and man becomes more tenuous, the validity of moral rights is questionable. If an algorithm creates musical sequences, should the creator enjoy a moral right in the algorithm on the same terms as a composer of a musical work in the traditional sense? The answer to this question lies, not in music *per se*, but in the broader issue of moral rights in technological creation. If the creator of a computer program is entitled to a moral right, so, too, is the creator of an algorithm that generates electronic music. Both efforts represent human ingenuity and, whether or not the work is a "reflection" of the author's personality in the earlier sense, the investment of personality in the creation of the work is apparent. Even the choice of electronic techniques reflects the personality of the composer.

A greater reality is also at work. It is a feature of the digital environment that the human expressive personality is likely to be influenced by technology. The technologies of the past, from printing press to piano, had an impact on creative expression. Now, however, the nature of technology is arguably different. New technologies function on a more individual basis, and are therefore

---

48. An example of the use of technology by a classical instrumentalist, well-known to aficionados of Indian classical music, would be violinist Kanniyakumari's "silent violin." For a brief note on her music, see Giddens, *supra* note 29.

more closely intertwined with the choices and preferences of individual personalities. This applies both to creators and "users" of musical works. New technologies also have a special relationship with human creativity because they depend on a continuous input of creative material for their own survival. Human creative works are, in a sense, the "raw material" that feeds technology.[49] This realization is exciting, but it should also give us a moment's pause. The engagement of the human being with technology can be a highly creative experience, yet it is also one in which the human personality can be completely effaced.

The intervention of technology need not make moral rights irrelevant. Rather, the presence of a technological element is increasingly to be expected in human creative endeavors. The role of technology should be acknowledged; it should not become a reason to adopt restrictive views, whether of creative expression or of human nature.

B. Communication

Of all aspects of the new music scene, new means of communicating music have come under closest scrutiny by copyright law. To date, the discussion about rights in music that is communicated over the Internet remains almost entirely focused on economic rights. The reasons for this commercial preoccupation are simple. The free movement of music files threatens the very existence of the music industry, and large music companies are engaged in a struggle for economic survival. At the same time, the size and importance of the American music market plays a role in the sidelining of moral interests: moral rights as they are known in other parts of the world are not recognized in the United States. American protection for moral rights remains largely limited to the visual arts[50] and, outside this field, to the availability of tort actions at common law.

Nevertheless, the moral rights of authors are closely implicated in the sharing of music online. First and foremost, moral rights remain important for defining and protecting the interests of musicians. But in this, as in so many respects, the music industry also represents a test case, and as such, music practices are well placed to generate baseline standards from which more general precedents and conventions can develop. The treatment of

---

49. *See* Jack Ralite, *Vers un droit d'auteur sans auteurs*, LE MONDE DIPLOMATIQUE 5 (1998), *cited in* MIRA T. SUNDARA RAJAN, COPYRIGHT AND CREATIVE FREEDOM: A STUDY OF POST-SOCIALIST LAW REFORM 37 (Routledge 2006).

50. VARA, *supra* note 47. Protection of the rights in this section is quite comprehensive, but weakened by issues such as the general availability of waivers. *See also* David Vaver, *Moral Rights Yesterday, Today and Tomorrow*, 7(3) INT'L J. TECH. L. 270, 274–75 (1999). Vaver's comments on written waivers are made in the UK context, but they are also relevant to this Act.

moral rights in music files can provide a model for practices around the sharing of information by Internet communication more generally.

This section considers two scenarios: the problems of moral rights in relation to file-sharing, an unregulated and possibly illegal activity,[51] and the treatment of moral rights in legal download environments. In relation to file-sharing, the question of whether or not downloading by individual users is a "public" act—a key issue in assessing copyright infringement—will also be crucial when exploring the implications of file-sharing for moral rights.

In the example of legal downloading, two possibilities are considered. First, the Apple iTunes framework is taken as a basic model. In recent years, the music industry seems to be moving towards acceptance of downloading through the contractual model favored by iTunes. The customer purchases a song or an album for money, valid "consideration" within the terms of contract law, and Apple bears the onus of assuring that it has the necessary copyright permissions to sell the files.

However, Apple's dominance of the legal download market is not universally viewed as positive. To some eyes, the exclusivity of iTunes, which formats its files for Apple machines such as iPods only, is seen as a burgeoning new monopoly. In 2006, France attempted to pass a new law that would require files downloaded from iTunes to be playable on any digital device. Had it passed, Apple would have had to change its business model, or abandon its operations in France. The law eventually passed in a modified form: whether or not a track will be made available exclusively in Apple's format now depends on the decision of the copyright-owner, who would specify this in his agreement with Apple. While the French bill was pending, the BBC commented:

> Under the bill, companies such as Apple, Sony and Microsoft could still be forced to share their proprietary copy-protection systems if the restrictions imposed went against what the copyright holder wanted.[52]

---

51. After the rulings in *MGM Studios, Inc. v. Grokster, Ltd.*, 545 U.S. 913 (2005) [GROKSTER] and *Sony BMG Music Entertainment v. Tenenbaum*, No. 03-CV-11661 (D. Mass. July 31, 2009) [TENENBAUM], file-sharing is clearly illegal in the United States. However, the issue is not as clear-cut in other jurisdictions, such as Canada, where the distinction between private and public activities may still be sufficient to define file-sharing as a private activity outside the scope of copyright law. *See, e.g.,* the ambiguous statements of the Federal Court, at both the trial and appeal levels in *BMG v. John Doe*, 2004 FC 488, [2004] 3 F.C.R. [BMG v. JOHN DOE, F.C.], *available at* http://www.canlii.org/en/ca/fct/doc/2004/2004fc488/2004fc488.html, (last visited Apr. 29, 2010); *see also* BMG Canada Inc. v. John Doe, 2005 FCA 193, [2005] 4 R.C.F. 81. The criteria for copyright infringement are discussed in James J. S. Holmes & Afigo I. Okpewho, *Transformative in the Eye of the Beholder,* 22(5) INTELL. PROP. & TECH. L.J. 12, 15 (2010). Of the four criteria that can meet the U.S. standard for a finding of infringement, the issue of the economic harm caused by music downloading is clearly satisfied.

52. *Apple Gets French iTunes Reprieve: The Future of iTunes in France Looks More Secure after MPs Watered Down a Draft of Its New Copyright Law,* BBC NEWS (June 22, 2006), *available at* http://news.bbc.co.uk/2/hi/5106400.stm (last visited Apr. 25, 2010).

As a second option, the alternative model of "global licensing" will be considered. Here, the payment of a flat monthly fee to an Internet service provider (ISP) would allow the subscriber to download as much music as desired.[53] In effect, the subscriber has purchased a "global license" to use music files. The obligation then rests on the ISP to ensure that the downloaded materials are obtained legally.

The iTunes and global licensing approaches each raise distinct concerns about moral rights. This leads to the further question of how to harmonize approaches to moral rights in music in an environment where multiple technologies coexist and are likely to diversify for some time into the future.

1. File-sharing: Moral Rights in the Grip of Illegality

The dissemination of music through technologies for file-sharing has widely come to be considered the ultimate challenge to the music industry. Music companies claim that it is a fight to the death: communicating music over the Internet effectively renders their role in music sales obsolete. Their response is to fight the technology "tooth and claw."

But the dynamics of the music industry are anything but straightforward. Not only do music companies want to reinforce existing copyright rules in their works; they are also attempting to expand copyright protection into new technological areas. Fundamentally, this strategy translates into copyright reform, as lobbyists seek to redefine Internet communication as a right restricted by copyright law.

The need for a redefinition not only reflects the fact that Internet communication is a new form of dissemination; it also has to do specifically with the type of communication involved. Communication via the Internet usually occurs in a private setting—in one's home, or in an office, or at an Internet terminal in a public place such as a library or café, where no other person is involved in the act. The communication often takes place for private purposes—one's private enjoyment or use of materials for reasons that have nothing to do with business or commerce. The tradition of copyright law is that private and noncommercial uses of a work will fall outside the scope of copyright protection.[54] The purpose of copyright is, rather, to protect a work

---

53. *See* Victoria Shannon, *Recording Companies Show New Interest in a "Global Music License,"* New York Times (Jan. 25, 2007), *available at* http://msl1.mit.edu/furdlog/docs/2007-01-25_iht_isp_billing.pdf (last visited July 18, 2010).

54. This argument was made by Professor Charles Nesson in the *Tenenbaum* case: it went against the U.S. copyright doctrine that significant economic loss to a right-holder is evidence that an infringing activity has occurred, and was widely disapproved of by Nesson's own peers in the U.S. copyright community. *See, for example,* John Schwartz, *Tilting at Internet Barrier, a Stalwart Is Upended,* New York Times (Aug. 10, 2009), *available at* http://www.nytimes.com/2009/08/11/us/11download.html (last visited Apr. 29, 2010).

from unauthorized commercial exploitation—a form of free-riding on an author's creative effort that would be unfair.

There is an aura of privacy about Internet communication, but it is an illusion. In fact, in the digital world, there is no longer any such thing as the purely "private." The United States Supreme Court affirmed this perspective in the landmark litigation surrounding Grokster, a popular file-sharing service, when it argued that a "private" activity carried on by millions of people had, in effect, transformed itself into a "public" use. Quantity, it said, is what draws the line between private and public. The volume of music file-sharing is so great that it has ceased to be a private activity and has become essentially public in nature.[55]

The U.S. Supreme Court had a well-established basis in American law for its position. Invoking the fair use defense depends on the ability to show, among other things, that the proposed fair use will not destroy the economic advantage of the copyright-holder.[56] Downloading on an individual basis may not do so; but if downloading as an individual act is pursued by millions of individuals, the collective activity can lead to the degradation and devaluation of the copyright in the work. The *Grokster* approach is solidly supported by the reasoning of the Federal District Court for Massachusetts in the *Tenenbaum* decision, which saw the award of $675,000 in damages against a 25-year old student at Boston University who admitted to downloading thirty songs from a file-sharing network. In *Tenenbaum*, Judge Nancy Gertner rejected the position of legendary Harvard professor Charles Nesson, who argued that downloading music for private use should be excluded from copyright's reach because of the need to maintain the catholicity of the distinction between private and public uses of a work under copyright law. The distinction was a part of U.S. law, Nesson argued, through the common law of copyright. A satisfying and convincing argument from the perspective of pure legal theory, the approach was completely out of tune with U.S. legal trends. It was widely criticized by Nesson's peers, including the doyen of "Copyleft" lawyers, Stanford professor Lawrence Lessig.[57]

Indeed, from the perspectives of both pure legal reasoning and global law, there is something deeply unsatisfying about the current U.S. approach. Should the nature of the transmission not play a determining role in separating private from public? In Canada, a decision from the 1950s considered the broadcast of a television program in a Montréal showroom, and the judge commented:

> I cannot see that even a large number of private performances, solely because of their numbers, can become public performances. The character of the individual

---

55. *See, e.g.*, GROKSTER, *supra* note 51, at 940, 948.
56. *See* Holmes & Okpewho, *supra* note 51, at 15.
57. *See, for example*, Nate Anderson, *Harvard P2P Lawyer; File-Swapping Is Fair Use—No, Really!*, ARS TECHNICA (Apr. 1, 2009), *available at* http://arstechnica.com/tech-policy/news/2009/04/harvard-p2p-lawyer-file-swapping-is-fair-use–no-really.ars (last visited Apr. 25, 2010).

audiences remains exactly the same; each is private and domestic, and therefore not "in public."[58]

The success of the music industry in bringing an essentially private activity into the public realm is likely to have broad implications for copyright law. Already, the notion of privacy is disintegrating. In the United States, Internet service providers are now expected to divulge information about the names of computer users associated with IP addresses—information that could allow a user to be prosecuted, for example, for downloading music files from the Internet, by providing much-needed evidence of infringement.[59] While there is nothing inherently wrong with this choice—access to users through IP addresses could be an important means of combating illegal behavior that is far more dangerous than music downloading, such as the dissemination of pornography or human trafficking—there is something incongruous about the apparently "private" setting in which the Internet is used. Internet privacy is an illusion; but if this fact is not more widely discussed and advertised, it may become a charade. The subversive uses of the Internet are not all criminal in nature; the Internet can also support free political speech and democracy in repressive climates.[60] Privacy should not be callously brushed aside where democratic values are involved.

On Internet privacy issues, Canada presents an interesting contrast to the United States. Notwithstanding the cultural similarities between the two countries, Canadian courts have been troubled by the apparently casual approach to privacy in the United States. The latest ruling on file-sharing from Canada's Federal Court, the 2004 case of *BMG v. John Doe*, affirms that Internet service providers in Canada cannot be compelled to divulge information about their users' identity.[61]

---

58. Canadian Admiral Corp. v. Rediffusion Inc. [1954] Ex. C.R. 382, 20 C.P.R. 75, para 73; the judge explicitly rejected the plaintiff's argument that his market might be reduced by the broadcast.

59. The "safe harbor" provisions of the Digital Millenium Copyright Act, designed to protect ISPs from unreasonable liability, can be found at 17 U.S.C. § 512. As Sonia Katyal argues, "the DMCA has led to the creation of a new kind of surveillance that enables content owners to search the Internet for unauthorized distributions of their products and creations—indeed, an entire industry has sprung up, seemingly overnight, that searches through individuals' hard drives, Web sites, and chat rooms to find evidence of infringement." *See* Sonia Katyal, *Privacy vs. Piracy*, YALE J.L. & TECH. 222, nn.200–220 & accompanying text (2004–05).

60. China's discomfort about free Internet communication is a case in point; it has also led to confrontations with Google about its activities in China. *See New York Times* coverage of the issue, *available at* http://topics.nytimes.com/topics/news/international/countriesandterrito-ries/china/internet_censorship/index.html (last visited Apr. 26, 2010).

61. *See* BMG, *supra* note 51; the Federal Court of Appeal is Canada's second court, after the Supreme Court of Canada, but no case on this issue has been heard, as yet, by the Supreme Court. The European case of PROMUSICAE affirms a similar principle. *See* Productores de Música de España (Promusicae) v. Telefónica de España SAU (Telefónica), Judgment of the

Interestingly, over the past three years, France has found itself on both sides of the issue. In its latest attempt to come to terms with the downloading phenomenon, the French government has passed a law which would create a new authority to investigate alleged cases of illegal downloading, with the ultimate power to seek the disconnection of Internet service to infringers through a court order. The law represents a watered-down version of a previously introduced bill. The earlier proposal would have allowed the body, itself, to disconnect Internet services, but the provision was declared unconstitutional by France's Constitutional Court.[62]

In 2006, the Socialist government had passed an altogether different kind of law—one that allowed unlimited downloading of files from the Internet upon payment of a monthly fee of seven euros to the subscriber's Internet service provider.[63] The law generated an infuriated response from the music industry, with EMI commenting that it would destroy the growing market for *legal* music downloads in France by neutralizing downloading from *illegal* sites. In other words, the availability of free music through illegal networks would pre-empt the development of a pay-per-download system.

In France, the music industry seems to have won an interesting victory. It is also worth noting that industry players are not the only proponents of restrictions on free downloads in France: French cultural figures have spoken out against them. When the 2006 law was adopted, film director Bertrand Tavernier protested, "By your calamitous decisions, you are torpedoing my profession, my livelihood."[64]

At the international level, the attempt to extend copyright protection to downloading has been largely successful. The WIPO Internet Treaties provide for a new right of "making available to the public" which explicitly places Internet communication into the realm of activities subject to copyright control.[65]

Court (Grand Chamber) of Jan. 29, 2008, Case C-275/06, *available at* http://eur-lex.europa.eu/ LexUriServ/LexUriServ.do?uri=CELEX:62006J0275:EN:HTML (last visited Apr. 25, 2010).

62. *See Revised French Download Law Passes Lower House*, REUTERS (Sept. 15, 2009), *available at* http://www.reuters.com/article/lifestyleMolt/idUSTRE58E5DE20090915 (last visited Apr. 25, 2010). For a discussion of the original law, see Fanny Coudert & Evi Werkers, *In The Aftermath of the Promusicae Case: How to Strike the Balance?*, 18(1) INT'L J.L. INFO. TECH. 50, 56 (2010). The basic features of the law remain the same, and this overview is very helpful. The law was struck down, in part, because of the lack of judicial oversight of its provisions, but the requirements for judicial review under the revised law are of questionable seriousness. *See* Eric Pfanner, *France Approves Wide Crackdown on Net Piracy*, NEW YORK TIMES (Oct. 22, 2009), *available at* http://www.nytimes.com/2009/10/23/technology/23net.html (last visited Apr. 25, 2010).

63. *See* Adam Sherwin, *France Condemned for Unlimited Download Law*, TIMES (Feb, 3, 2006), *available at* http://business.timesonline.co.uk/tol/business/industry_sectors/media/article 725510.ece (last visited Apr. 25, 2010).

64. Quoted in *id.*

65. WIPO Copyright Treaty (adopted Dec. 20, 1996, entered into force Mar. 6, 2002) (1997) 36 I.L.M. 65, *available at* http://www.wipo.int/treaties/en/ip/wct/trtdocs_wo033.html [WCT]

Notwithstanding this international dimension, the success of music companies in campaigning for increased copyright protection is a reflection of their lobby power in the United States. The WIPO Treaties reflect the role of U.S. trade negotiators in international copyright discussions.[66] Indeed, the WIPO example reflects the general process by which U.S. copyright norms and policies influence international copyright law and, through law reform geared towards conformity with international agreements, the domestic copyright laws of most countries in the world.[67]

Where moral rights are concerned, file-sharing illustrates the difficulty of attempting to enforce rights in a situation of illegality. Illegal behavior threatens moral rights as much as it harms economic rights. However, this does not necessarily imply that better protection of economic rights is the only, or best, solution to lack of recognition for moral rights. On the contrary, as discussed below, the benefits to moral rights from the legal downloading model are uncertain. The effectiveness of remedies will depend, rather, on who will be entrusted with the responsibility for recognizing moral rights, and on how effectively that responsibility will be exercised.

File-sharing has the potential to violate three moral rights: attribution, integrity, and, increasingly, disclosure. With no controls in place over file-sharing, the right of attribution cannot command respect. Once a file is posted on a peer-to-peer network, recognition of the attribution right depends on the willingness of users to honor it. Depending on the nature of the file, the person initially making the file available may have an incentive to specify the attribution—a song by a well-known band or artist may be in great demand. But the same perspective on motivations has a negative side: a song that becomes popular, but circulates on a non-attributed basis, could represent a missed opportunity for up-and-coming talent that has yet to build a reputation. In the music world, reputation is everything. The proper attribution of music is a key element in the construction of success.

Similarly, if a recording is released onto a file-sharing network by someone other than the performers—and perhaps, without their knowledge—the musicians' right of disclosure is violated. Once again, the decision could affect

---

(last visited Apr. 25, 2010); WIPO Performances and Phonograms Treaty (adopted Dec. 20, 1996, entered into force May 20, 2002) (1997) 36 I.L.M. 76, *available at* http://www.wipo. int/treaties/en/ip/berne/trtdocs_wo001.html [WPPT] (last visited Apr. 25, 2010I). *See, e.g.,* art. 8 of the WCT; art. 10 of the WPPT.

66. *See* Pamela Samuleson, *The U.S. Digital Agenda at WIPO*, 37 Va. J. Int'l L. 369 (1997).

67. Canada is a case in point; it has ratified the WIPO Internet Treaties, but has yet to implement them in its copyright law. This is one of the reasons behind Canada's placement on the Special 301 Priority Watch List of the U.S. Trade Representative's office, which identifies countries in the world that are in violation of their international intellectual property obligations. Implementation of the WIPO Treaties is cited as a key impediment in U.S.-Canada copyright relations. The 2009 Priority Watch List is available on the USTR website at http://www.ustr. gov/sites/default/files/Priority%20Watch%20List.pdf (last visited Apr. 26, 2010).

the success of their future careers. It could prove to be a strategic error, destroying the possibility of future earnings out of a song; on the other hand, a song that becomes an unexpected hit could translate into an exciting future career that the musicians could only have dreamed of without the unauthorized release of their music.

The integrity right is virtually impossible to protect in the file-sharing context. Few restrictions control the uploading of a music file onto a peer-to-peer service; certainly, these services do not require respect for the integrity of music from their users. But here, too, there is a self-policing aspect. The circulation of maligned music files may be of little interest to the peer-to-peer community.

Although the moral rights of attribution and integrity are not explicitly recognized in peer-to-peer transactions, in another sense, the concepts are very well-known. When music is transformed into data, concerns about the authenticity and the integrity of information arise. The reliability and security of the peer-to-peer network may depend on being able to verify that the source of a file is trustworthy—that the file is posted on a bona fide basis. The use of digital signatures, or other forms of digital identification, could be important—attribution. At the same time, from a *data* perspective, it is important to maintain the integrity of the file. Indeed, it may be essential to do so in order to protect the integrity of the network in a technical sense. The concepts of attribution and integrity are therefore familiar to the peer-to-peer community, and this point suggests another strategy for securing the moral rights in shared music files: education. Users of peer-to-peer networks have strong practical reasons to observe attribution and integrity; arguments based on moral rights might help to support actions which are, from a technical point of view, already in their own best interest.

2. Downloading: Moral Rights as a Corporate Obligation

Legal downloading is a very different lens through which to view the moral rights of musicians. File-sharing presents a sort of cultural Wild West, which remains at least partly beyond the reach of the law, even in the United States. Downloading music for payment, however, is a regulated activity. The corporations who are powerful on this scene are few—Apple controls just over half the global market in legal music downloads[68]—and their actions are closely scrutinized by governments and regulatory bodies throughout North America and Europe.

---

68. Other major players are Sony, Microsoft, and Amazon. For a UK list of legal download providers, *see, e.g., Where to Download Music Legally*, THE GUARDIAN (2010) (Special Report: Digital Music), *available at* http://arts.guardian.co.uk/netmusic/page/0,,1127237,00.html (last visited Apr. 26, 2010).

But recognition of moral rights remains uncertain. The origin of the music trade in the United States, where the law remains ambiguous on authors' moral rights, is probably at the heart of this reality. The purpose of the pay-ment-per-download services is to bring music file-sharing into the arena of legal activities. Accordingly, it seems likely that the failure to respect moral rights is anything but a situation of intentional neglect.

The global development of the market for music downloads could lead to better recognition for moral rights. Where music downloads are concerned, the countries of Europe are in the forefront of growth. The laws of the European Union member states, in particular, provide strong protection for moral rights. The availability of music downloads in these countries cannot be said to be legal unless the moral rights of composers and performers are respected.

While there is some variety in the levels and kinds of moral rights protected in European countries, the standard remains generally high. In France and Germany, both major European music markets, the moral right of integrity is protected in strong terms—in France, independently of any reputational issues, and in Germany, whenever the artist's interests, whether personal or intellectual, are threatened.[69]

The recent comments of SACEM, France's primary collective agency for the administration of music copyright, indicate its willingness to participate in building the legal download market.[70] The support of SACEM represents an important new resource for Apple, and for other companies involved in the legal download business. Access to SACEM's catalogue of members offers information that will greatly facilitate the process of obtaining copyright per-missions to make music available through Apple's iTunes store and other music download services. However, it seems clear that SACEM cannot allow this information to be used in ways that contravene French copyright law. Where moral rights are concerned, standards of communication that define

---

69. *See* CPI, *supra* note 27, art. L121-1; German Copyright Law, art. 14, on "Distortion of the Work," states: "The author shall have the right to prohibit any distortion or any other mutila-tion of his work which would jeopardize his legitimate intellectual or personal interests in the work." The standard of protection is higher than Berne: Berne requires "proof" of damage to "honor or reputation," but the German law only requires a showing of jeopardy—placing in danger—to an author's "interests"—a more general term than reputation—in his work. *See* Urheberrechtsgesetz, 9.9.1965, Bundesgesetzblatt, Teil I [BGBl. I] at 1273, last amended by Gesetz, 10.8.2004, BGBl. I at 1774 § 13, *available at* http://www.iuscomp.org/gla/statutes/UrhG.htm (last visited Apr. 26, 2010) [German Copyright Law]. The translation is provided by WIPO.

70. Société des Auteurs, Compositeurs et Editeurs de Musique, *available at* http://www.sacem.fr/cms (last visited Apr. 26, 2010). *See* Nathalie Vandystadt, *EU Exec Ups Pressure on Music Industry*, EUROPOLITICS (May 26, 2009), *available at* http://www.europolitics.info/business-competitiveness/eu-exec-ups-pressure-on-music-industry-art237884-7.html (last visited Apr. 25, 2010).

Apple's behavior in the United States will not be legally acceptable in France.[71] The spread of iTunes to Asian countries will also have to give face value to moral rights; countries like Japan and India will require it as part of their law.

Regulatory pressures are likely to generate better observance of moral rights in the legal download scenario. But there is another dimension to moral rights and music downloads—the question of whether the norms of music downloading are compatible with the interests protected by moral rights. The case of attribution presents mild symptoms of this disease. To some extent, attribution is respected, but the attribution interest appears to be seen through the lens of practicality. It is not respected as a matter of principle. Attribution of music tracks and albums makes it possible for customers to locate the works that interest them. However, attribution of music on iTunes is often unsatisfactory, including partial and incomplete credits for composers and performers.

Integrity reveals serious fault lines underlying this already irregular terrain. The iTunes model is built on the sale of single tracks, or songs. No doubt, this structure is inherited from the peer-to-peer file-sharing landscape, dominated by sales of individual songs.[72] However, many musical artists might see, not only the song, but also, the album as an integral artistic work. The problem is readily apparent in classical music, where splitting an album into its component parts can separate the movements of a symphony or concerto from one another. This is mildly ironic, because nineteenth-century conventions would favor the independent performance of movements; but the twentieth century preferred entire works. The same thing can occur in relation to multimovement instrumental works, and the results can be truly disconcerting. The three movements of Robert Schumann's *Fantasy* for piano cannot be found in recordings by a single performer on iTunes.[73] Individual variations

---

71. Interestingly, the same could be said of Canada, which is a major iTunes market; but there are various reasons Canadian law might have little power to influence Apple's behavior. In terms of population, Canada is a relatively small country, and its moral rights provisions are subject to many limitations. Apple could easily argue that copyright licenses obtained in Canada include implicit waivers of moral rights, an attitude that would not be possible in France.

72. Ironically, the file-sharing model also invokes the early era of rock music, when the release of singles was an important step. The single as cultural icon is explored by Andrew O'Hagan, *The Sad Death of a Pop Single*, TELEGRAPH (Jan. 29, 2005), *available at* http://www.telegraph.co. uk/culture/music/3635867/The-sad-death-of-the-pop-single.html. But his pessimism is not universally shared. *See Pop Single Still Hits Right Note*, SYDNEY MORNING HERALD (Aug. 24, 2004), *available at* http://www.smh.com.au/articles/2004/08/25/1093246622880.html (last visited Apr. 25, 2010). The idea of combining singles with ringtones in a CD format available for purchase was first explored Sony-BMG in 2007. The package, called a "ringle," is discussed by Ed Christman, *Music Industry Betting on "Ringle" Format*, REUTERS (Sept. 9 2007), *available at* http://www.reuters.com/article/idUSN0921673020070912 (last visited Apr. 25, 2010).

73. Opus 17; this work represents a landmark in Romantic music. For a fascinating discussion of its genesis, see NICHOLAS MARSTON, SCHUMANN: FANTASIE, OP. 17, Cambridge Music Handbooks (Cambridge Univ. Press 1992).

from Bach's Goldberg variations, as performed by Glenn Gould, could be made available for sale, completely destroying what he thought of as thematic unity throughout the piece.[74]

Interestingly, the first case on this issue has emerged, not from classical music, but from classic rock. Pink Floyd sued EMI records for splitting up an album and offering individual tracks for download, arguing that this treatment of their work violated its integrity. As Reuters news service summarizes:

> The judge in the case, Andrew Morritt, accepted arguments by the group that EMI was bound by a contract forbidding it from selling records other than as complete albums without written consent.
>
> The judge said the purpose of a clause in the contract, drawn up more than a decade ago, was to "preserve the artistic integrity of the albums."[75]

In the context of file-sharing, an interest in particular tracks makes sense; music is exchanged within a community of equals for private use and enjoyment. File-sharing is a game for amateurs. But the iTunes scenario is fundamentally different: music is sold in this form for Apple's profit. It is the professionalization of file-sharing. In these circumstances, why should the sale of individual tracks be allowed when it could compromise the integrity of an album?

In fact, two objectives are accomplished by a focus on individual songs. First, and necessarily foremost, the objective is to bring money to the corporation, and it seems plausible that more money can be earned from the sale of individual tracks than the sale of complete albums would allow. The gain is not only in pricing. The possibility of buying individual songs opens up a large potential market of people who could not afford an entire album, or would not want to buy it as a matter of taste.[76] The second benefit of selling individual songs—certainly in theory, possibly in practice—would be to forestall illegal sharing of individual songs through peer-to-peer networks where they are available. Here, legal download services would hope to tap into a market that has already proven its existence in the world of file-sharing, by finding the right price combinations to retain this frugal clientele. Whichever of the two rationales we choose to accept for the splitting up of albums, it

---

74. One of the reasons given by Gould for re-recording a work that had already received a classic treatment at his hands was the discovery of a unifying "pulse" throughout the variations which, he felt, had not been adequately reflected in his first version. It was very unusual for Gould to re-record a work.

75. Reuters, *Pink Floyd Wins Court Battle with EMI over Downloads*, NEW YORK TIMES (Mar. 12, 2010), *available at* http://www.nytimes.com/2010/03/12/business/media/12pink.html [*Pink Floyd Wins*] (last visited Apr. 25, 2010).

76. Songs on an album might be of uneven quality; the customer might also like one track, but not be serious about owning or hearing more performances by a given group or singer.

seems clear that the moral right of integrity plays second fiddle, so to speak, to the profit in a musical work.

This problem, too, could be handled at the licensing stage. If the overall regulatory scheme provides for respecting musicians' rights of attribution and integrity when files are exchanged on the Internet, artists and owners of copyright releasing their work to the music corporation should do so by the terms of a well-defined license. The copyright law of the country in question will specify that the right of integrity must be respected; the license can specifically indicate whether or not the separation of individual tracks from an album will constitute a violation of the right.[77] The other facilities offered by iTunes software—mixing and organizing tracks, generating recommendations for other music of interest available through iTunes—all fall into the realm of private use and enjoyment. These techniques may take desperate chances with user privacy, but they have nothing to do with respect for moral rights. Moral rights are a public affair; in the privacy of his home, however, the "new listener" can freely engage with music to the fullest extent. It is a democratic entanglement made possible by new technology.

3. Global Licensing: Moral Rights and Overgeneralizations

Global licensing offers a completely different solution to the problem of legalizing music downloads. The customer pays a flat fee to his or her Internet service provider, usually for the month; he or she then acquires the right to download music on an unlimited basis during that period. The global licensing scheme initially proposed as part of France's DADVSI law in 2005 would have involved a supplement of seven euros per month to an Internet subscription charge.[78] Of course, the amount of the levy could be set as a a

---

77. In the Pink Floyd case, the license between the group and its producer, EMI, specified that the songs should not be "unbundled." But the contract was several decades old. Since it was concluded before the Internet environment came into existence, EMI seems to have hoped that the provision would be considered inapplicable to the digital scenario. Justice Morritt disagreed. *See Pink Floyd Wins, supra* note 75.

78. The acronym stands for the law of Aug. 1, 2006, "relative au droit d'auteur et aux droits voisins dans la société de l'information." *See* Estelle Dumout, *Projet Dadvsi: la licence globale remplacée par les exceptions au droit d'auteur*, ZDNET.FR (Mar. 7, 2006), http://www.zdnet.fr/actualites/projet-dadvsi-la-licence-globale-remplacee-par-les-exceptions-au-droit-d-auteur-39317039.htm (last visited Aug. 23, 2010). The law was eventually updated by a new law, known as Hadopi, which established a "three-strikes" rule to cut off Internet access to individuals engaged in the illegal downloading of files. France's Constitutional Court struck down the measure as unconstitutional because it terminated Internet access to those *accused* of illegal downloading, a clear violation of the presumption of innocence, and erroneously allowed a non-judicial authority to impose this penalty. An amended version of the law is now in force. *See* MICHEL VIVANT & JEAN-MICHEL BRUIGUIÈRE, LE DROIT D'AUTEUR (Dalloz 2009) para. 12, for an excellent overview of DADVSI and the process leading to the

larger (or smaller) fee under such a scheme.[79] The proper price point for the fee would depend on successfully balancing the interests involved— for the public, what it sees as feasible and rightful, and for music companies, finding a comfort zone between survival and new profit motivations.

The resurgence of the global licensing approach in recent years has been linked to the tensions surrounding the inter-operability of music systems, particularly in Europe.[80] Apple has become a corporate focus for European regulators, who would like to see the iTunes system become an open market for music that can be played on any technical system, not just Apple's machines. At the same time, European governments have turned on collective licensing bodies, which traditionally enjoy great power and prestige in Europe, arguing that their nationalistic policies have inhibited the growth of a legal market in music downloads that could challenge the United States market. The statistics are impressive: measured in terms of legal downloads, the online music market in the United States appears to be as much as eight times larger than the European market.[81] This is the case in spite of the fact that Europe actually boasts a larger number of Internet users than the U.S.[82] While there are many aspects to this situation, the European intuition is that

---

Hadopi law. *See also Court Curbs French Net Piracy Law*, BBC News (June 10, 2009), *available at* http://news.bbc.co.uk/2/hi/technology/8093920.stm (last visited Aug. 23, 2010), and Nate Anderson, *French Court Savages "Three-Strikes" Law, Tosses It Out*, ArsTechnica (June 10, 2009), *available at* http://arstechnica.com/tech-policy/news/2009/06/french-court-savages-3-strikes-law-tosses-it-out.ars (last visited Aug. 23, 2010).

79. Roughly equivalent to US$8.89 at current rates.

80. *See, for example*, Shannon, *supra* note 53.

81. The European Commission provides this figure in a 2005 report. *See* Commission of the European Communities, Study on a Community Initiative on the Cross-Border Collective Management of Copyright (Commission Staff Working Document July 7, 2005), *available at* http://ec.europa.eu/internal_market/copyright/docs/management/study-collectivemgmt_en.pdf [EC Report] (last visited Apr. 25, 2010). The Executive Summary states: "This Study concludes that present structures for cross-border collective management of legitimate online music services–that are based on models developed for the analogue environment need to be improved for music to fulfil its unique potential as a driver for online services. Action is now required at EU level because revenue achieved with online content services in the US in 2004 was almost eight times higher than online content revenue produced in Western Europe. As music pervades European culture and society, only music has the real potential to kick-start online content services." *See* the useful article by Ana Eduarda Santos, *Experimenting with Territoriality: Pan-European Music Licence and the Persistence of Old Paradigms*, 2009 Duke L. Tech. Rev. 007; *see also EU-wide Copyright for Online Music under Consideration*, EurActiv (July 8, 2005), *available at* http://www.euractiv.com/en/infosociety/eu-wide-copyright-online-music-consideration/article-142190 (last visited July 18, 2010): "The Commission has compared the online music market in the US and the EU and found out that, in spite of the larger number of internet users in the EU, the online music market in the US was eight times as big in the US and will still be five times as big as in the EU."

82. EC Report, *supra* note 81.

the bureaucracy of national licensing schemes is part of the problem.[83] The European position is an interesting mix of propositions: illegal downloading may be bad for the economy, but legal downloading will be very good. The same activity in two different legal contexts leads to different economic results.

But the attraction of global licensing is much broader than this: it appears as a viable alternative to both illegal downloading and to the iTunes model of individual sales. The secret of its promise lies in the underlying wild card of human psychology. It would appear that the global licensing model lets people feel more or less the same attractions that they feel for illegal down-loading—it is limitless and free, as opposed to the clear and rather stark equa-tion between music and payment in the iTunes model. At the same time, the payment of a flat fee absolves the user of fear and guilt about potential liability. Writing for the *New York Times*, Eric Pfanner comments:

> Unlimited offerings give consumers the sense that they are getting music free because it can be bundled into the cost of a broadband subscription, in the way that many Internet providers already offer television programming.[84]

When it comes to moral rights, the global licensing model should give us pause. In fact, the situation of moral rights in this model more closely resembles illegal downloading than the iTunes approach. The iTunes model provides a degree of control over the use of individual songs and albums. The global licensing model essentially releases control over individual works of music, imposing a restraint, instead, at the level of the ISP. The global licens-ing model would allow music downloading through all available technolo-gies—including, perhaps primarily, peer-to-peer file-sharing. As in the illegal download scenario, individuals or companies making music files available online would have an incentive to respect the integrity of the file—in musical

---

83. *See* Ian Bell, *EU Pushes Music Industry to Open Up Online Rights*, DIGITAL TRENDS (May 26, 2009), *available at* http://news.digitaltrends.com/news-article/20025/eu-pushes-music-in-dustry-to-open-up-online-rights (last visited Apr. 25, 2010): "Internet music downloads in Europe lag behind those in the United States, pulling in just a fraction of revenues the record industry is losing from falling CD sales. Part of the problem in Europe is that music rights are sold separately in each country, which has prevented Apple Inc.'s iTunes from set-ting up a single store to service all of Europe. Instead, it has to seek licenses from each EU member state where it wishes to sell and to set up separate national stores with different music selections."

84. *See* Eric Pfanner, *Omnifone Nears Broadband Music Service in Europe*, NEW YORK TIMES (Feb. 16, 2009), *available at* http://www.nytimes.com/2009/02/17/technology/17digital.html (last visited Apr. 25, 2010). Pfanner also notes that there is some evidence about the limits to Apple's success as a legal alternative to the illegal music market: "Services offering unlimited listening are proliferating as the music industry tries to counter illegal file-sharing, which the record companies blame for billions of dollars in lost sales. Growth in sales of individual tracks, via online music stores like Apple's iTunes, has slowed."

terms, to maintain the interest of the file for users, and in technical terms, to protect the integrity of the systems. But larger questions of musical integrity remain unanswered. In a global licensing framework, the circulation of songs, albums, and parts of songs would all be common. Artists, while entitled to collect royalties, would have little control over the form in which their work circulates. The attribution interest would also remain in flux: users would sometimes have a built-in propensity to attribute, if it could increase the attractiveness of the exchange, but it is easy to see how the attribution of a work could fall by the wayside in online transactions with music.

The global license approach to music downloads would therefore require legislative intervention on behalf of moral rights—an expressed commitment on the part of European Union member states, in particular, to require respect for the moral rights of attribution and integrity in the pan-European circulation of music files. But the call to action comes at a time when the regulatory environment for moral rights is quite poor. Europe's focus is on increasing its download market; will moral rights frighten companies and individuals away?

Indeed, the idea of harmonizing moral rights has not been pursued with any commitment in the European Union, even as most other aspects of copyright law have been harmonized.[85] The harmonization of moral rights in music downloads across the Continent may prove to be particularly difficult because of discrepancies between UK and Continental approaches to moral rights; in practice, certain UK limitations may creep in. In order to avoid ambiguities about protection under British copyright law, European musicians will certainly choose to assert their rights of attribution in accordance with UK law. The additional requirement of showing damage to reputation for the integrity right under British law would mean that Continental musicians enjoy a stronger integrity right on the Continent, where large markets such as France, Germany, and Italy do not have such a requirement. On the other side of these arguments, one positive feature of global licensing for moral rights is that the approach would free Europe from dependence on American companies and technologies, such as iTunes, which are likely to be naturally slower to recognize and implement moral rights than their European counterparts in broadcasting and digital technology.

---

85. The success of harmonization has been mixed. *See* Michel M. Walter, *Updating and Consolidation of the Acquis: The Future of European Copyright* (June 2002), *available at* http://ec.europa.eu/internal_market/copyright/docs/conference/2002-06-santiago-speech-walter_en.pdf (last visited Apr. 26, 2010). For a detailed assessment of the harmonization project, see Mireille van Eechoud et al., Harmonizing European Copyright Law: The Challenges of Better Lawmaking, Information Law Series, Vol. 19, gen. ed., P. Bernt Hugenholtz (Kluwer Law International 2009).

C. Mobile Technology: Music in a New Form

The use of music in mobile technologies offers a rare puzzle—a truly new area for moral rights. Mobile technology raises two different issues. The first is relatively narrow: how are moral rights implicated in the transfer of files between different electronic media? For example, files may be moved from a computer to an iPod or similar device that stores a portable music library. The problem may seem sharply focused, but its implications are large. The future scope of mobile technologies—indeed, their very survival—may depend on the ability to transfer files between media. Without it, they may have little potential.

The second question is more complex. What happens when music serves new functions in mobile devices? An excerpt of a song can be used as a mobile ringtone to alert the owner of a call, and the excerpt itself may be reproduced as recorded by a given performer, digitized, or mixed in some other way. The moral rights implications of these transformations are well worth exploring. They offer guidelines, not only for the treatment of moral rights in the digital environment, but also, as a consideration of pioneering German case law on this issue shows, for the administration of rights by collective agencies.

1. Moral Rights and Media Neutrality

From the general perspective of copyright, digital technology generates a certain level of discomfort because of the ease with which a digitized work can be transferred from one medium to another. Traditionally, the very meaning of copyright is a right to restrict the making of copies. This factor is probably behind the extreme reluctance of music and media companies to support the right to transfer music from one format into another as a free use exempt from copyright restrictions. The issue was reformulated for the digital age by the Canadian Supreme Court. Speaking of visual art in the landmark case of *Théberge*, the Justices argued about whether reproduction in the digital context meant the creation of multiple copies or, alternatively, multiple acts of copying.[86] Simply put, copying CDs into an iPod to create a digital library could be an infringement of copyright. Considering that

---

86. THÉBERGE, *supra* note 24. The majority view held for multiple copies, but, writing for the minority, Justice Gonthier argued that the number of times a work had been copied was really the defining feature of a reproduction in the Digital Age. The case was decided on a vote of 5 to 4, and both opinions are therefore likely to be important for defining digital reproduction in Canadian law.

90 percent of music on iPods is said to be transferred from CDs, this activity would make criminals of many music lovers.

From a legal perspective, format shifting becomes a difficult problem because of the complexity of the web of regulation dealing with digital phenomena. The creation of one right leads to a need to adjust and rebalance the entire system of rights. The use of digital rights management and technological protection measures to protect copyright in a work will prevent anyone from copying it—unless, of course, the person manages to break through, or "circumvent," the secure technology. However, if an individual is empowered by the law to make a copy of the CD for the purposes of shifting the use to a different format, he or she will have to be able to open the digital lock. Copyright laws must therefore ensure that provision is made for allowing—and indeed, facilitating—the circumvention of the lock for the purpose of copying the work to a new device. The copying, itself, must be clearly confined to the allowable circumstances—private and noncommercial use, the payment of a fee for the music in its original form, and the promise not to circulate the copied work to others.

This issue is complicated by the fact that the fear of copying has encouraged industry to develop restrictions that have little to do with copyright law *per se*. These include region codes for DVDs and locks on the use of mobile phones. Mobile locks protect the association of phones with a particular company, and they are commonplace in an environment that is generally restrictive towards the use of digital technology. In relation to mobile phones, the power of communication companies in the North American market, where mobile locks are usual, should also be noted.

Region codes for DVDs essentially require a purchaser to buy the same product more than once because he or she wants to use it in different parts of the world. In theory, the technology may help to inhibit piracy by making it difficult to buy DVDs in a country or region known for piracy and take them to one's home country for viewing. Nevertheless, there are several problems with this argument. Region coding seems to operate on the premise that all items purchased in a country with piracy problems are somehow "contaminated": legal purchasers of the work are in no better position than those who bought pirated copies. Indeed, the region coding system may even create an incentive to acquire pirated goods, as a person who travels frequently is not rewarded for buying legitimate merchandise in a pirate zone. It would be simpler and cheaper to buy and use pirate copies while traveling, discarding them upon departure. Similarly, the logic by which the codes are imposed seems senseless. A DVD purchased in the UK, where it may be at its highest world price, cannot be viewed in the United States or Canada without code-breaking technology.

In relation to music, music companies claim that there is an economic value inherent in format shifting. This value accrues to the makers of new format technologies, such as Apple with its iPod, and music companies argue that copyright owners, too, should have a share in the benefit. The current trend is towards the legalization of format shifting, but at a price: the music industry would like the makers of the new technologies to accept a levy on their products so that a share of the economic benefits of new media can be returned to the owners of copyright.[87]

The eventual outcome of these discussions is almost certain to be some form of acceptance for format shifting—the practice is both more widespread and more innocuous than file-sharing. Without it, new media and mobile technologies will have little purpose, and an entire area of music innovation would be destroyed. The role of new media in developing the music industry is also a factor to take into account, although the music industry has established its tendency to amazing narrowness of vision in the search for profit. When it comes to new media, the developers of the technology may themselves be valuable partners in the fight against piracy. Apple, which pioneered the concept of legal downloads based on classic contract principles, is a case in point.

For moral rights, format shifting creates a new environment. When purchasers of musical recordings transfer them between different media, the act generates a clear potential for information to be lost. Liner notes are not usually fed into an iPod; complete track information about the composer, performer, and those technically involved in the making of a recording may not be transferred.

When it comes to moral rights, however, the line between acceptable uses and possible violations is much easier to draw than in the murky area of apportioning economic benefits. If failure to attribute, or modification of a work, occur in a purely private context, the artist is hardly threatened by these acts. On the contrary, as far as the creator of the music is concerned, the creative activity is no longer in his or her hands. In the sphere of personal pleasure, the ultimate judgment falls to the listener. Two creative spaces are involved: the cosmos of the original creative artist, and the sound-world of the listener who wants to engage actively with the music.

---

87. *See, for example*, on plans to revive the possibility of a copyright levy of $75 to be charged on every iPod sold in Canada, Nate Anderson, *Canada's $75 iPod Levy Returns (And Might Legalize P2P)*, Ars Technica (Mar. 2010), *available at* http://arstechnica.com/tech-policy/news/2010/03/canadas-75-ipod-levy-returns.ars (last visited Apr. 26, 2010). The position of the music industry is mixed: the question of how the proposed levy might address downloading of music files, or peer-to-peer file-sharing, is not clear. If the levy is intended to address file-sharing, Minister Angus, who introduced the proposal, has not made a statement to this effect. As Anderson comments: "The issue of how the levy applies to music obtained from P2P networks remains controversial in Canada, where industry has long claimed that the money only covers things like format-shifting." *See also* Charlie Angus, *Copyright Levy Would Protect Artists in a World of Downloads: Proposal Deserves More Serious Response than Derisive Tory Tweet, NDP Critic Argues*, Toronto Star (Mar. 30, 2010), *available at* http://www.thestar.com/opinion/article/787278–copyright-levy-would-protect-artists-in-a-world-of-downloads.

An iPod allows music to become integrated into the listener's life, in much the same way that earlier technologies brought mobility and individuality to the musical experience. Describing one of his early musical memories, Glenn Gould talks about hearing Beethoven as a small child, on a car radio while driving the snowy route from Lake Simcoe to Toronto:

> I remember, when I was a kid, I always associated the New York Philharmonic broadcasts, which we used to hear on Sunday afternoons, with great, vast fields of snow—white and grey. We used to go up north to the country for weekends and, about four o'clock in the afternoon, the Philharmonic would be on when we were on our way back to Toronto. And, in wintertime, it was usually grey—a sort of endless vista of snow, frozen lake, horizon, this sort of thing— and Beethoven never sounded so good.[88]

The issue of moral rights in format shifting deserves to remain unregulated. It is a form of recognition, and respect, for the listener as creator.

2. Moral Rights in Mobile Ringtones

The issue of moral rights in mobile ringtones presents several challenges. Attribution is not a normal feature of the mobile format. Similarly, integrity can be affected in many ways. The use of music in a mobile ringtone generally requires direct modification of the work—creating an excerpt, and possibly, modifying the performance of the work in some way.

The issue of how the excerpt is modified is interesting in its own right. The use of digitally altered versions of songs is common and has implications for moral rights. But "truetones," or mastertones, are unmodified versions of songs in accepted audio formats such as MP3s, which at one time represented the largest share of the market in ringtones—upwards of 86 percent.[89] Interestingly, the use of "truetones" in mobiles is also an increasingly valuable tool for the marketing of music, as popular musicians may choose to introduce a song as a ringtone before its release as a single. This points to the fact

---

88. Geoffrey Payzant, Glenn Gould: Music & Mind 2 (Goodread Biographies Canadian Lives Series 1984).

89. *See* Edna Gunderson, *Mastertones Ring Up Profits*, USA Today (Nov. 29, 2006), *available at* http://www.usatoday.com/life/music/news/2006-11-28-mastertones-main_x.htm (last visited Apr. 25, 2010). Other terms include "realtones." *See* Catherine Soanes, *Mobisodes, Mastertones and Micromoments*, AskOxford.com "World of Words" (June 25, 2005), *available at* http://www.askoxford.com/worldofwords/bubblingunder/archive/bubbling_06/?view=uk (last visited Apr. 25, 2010). A "mobisode" is a one-minute excerpt from a television program, and raises similar issues to moral rights in music.

that use in mobile ringtones involves issues of reputation for artists—a strong argument for the recognition of moral rights in ringtones.

Clearly, mobile music represents an important testing ground for moral rights. The practices that develop in the music world will be directly relevant to other mobile technologies that are still in their infancy.[90] In particular, the makers of television programs and films should be watching closely as moral rights in mobile music are explored.

a. Integrity of a Ringtone: Germany Leads the Way

In the first litigation on moral rights in mobile technology, Germany's Supreme Court, the *Bundesgerichtshof* (BGH) has delivered an authoritative ruling on the issue.[91] The German court's ruling makes a number of insightful points about moral rights in the mobile context, but it also leaves some fundamental questions unanswered. The case provides an excellent starting point to explore the implications of moral rights in mobile ringtones.

i. Excerpts

The creation of an excerpt is a necessary part of using a piece of music as a mobile ringtone. The nature of the new musical form is such that only an excerpt will do: a short and memorable part of the song is needed to create an effective and popular ringtone. Even the chosen excerpt will be heard differently at different times. Answering the call will interrupt the excerpt. Cutting off an incoming call would stop the excerpt even sooner, and more abruptly. For a musician, all of these factors could offend his sense of the integrity of the musical work. The injury could be felt by both the composer and the performer. What would be an appropriate legal response to this problem?

Without allowing the making of an excerpt, it would be impossible to use a work as a ringtone. The extent of the moral right of integrity therefore depends on the key issue of consent. The author's consent to the use of the work as a ringtone should be explicitly obtained by the producer of the ringtone. Once it is obtained, however, an author should no longer be able to object to the use of the work as a ringtone on the grounds that the use of an excerpt violates his integrity. This was the eminently sensible finding of the BGH.[92]

---

90. *See* Soanes, *supra* note 89, on "mobisodes."
91. Decision of the German Bundesgerichtshof (Supreme Court) of Dec. 18, 2008, I ZR 23/06 [Mobile Ringtones Judgment].
92. *Id.* The decisions of the BGH can only be reviewed on constitutional grounds, by the Federal Constitutional Court.

ii. Modifications

On the issue of modifications, however, the German court's position is somewhat ambiguous. Not only do the judges state that the use of excerpts is presumed for the conversion of music into ringtones; they also comment that " digital . . . process[ing]" of a work is to be assumed.[93] This second point is troublesome. The role played by digital modifications in ringtones is far from clear. Indeed, the trend appears to be just the opposite—a popular movement towards the use of ever more reliable reproductions of music that attempt to preserve the quality and characteristics of the original recording. The technical quality of a ringtone may also be prized by musicians. A high-quality ringtone could encourage subsequent sales of a song, and boost the artist's reputation.

In these circumstances, it seems important to clarify that the nature and quality of the reproduction used in a ringtone, from a purely technological perspective, is an important factor affecting the integrity of the work. A broad exception to the integrity right for modifications due to the needs of technology makes sense. But the exception should not automatically exempt all digital modifications of musical works from integrity considerations. In some cases, digital modifications will be far-removed from technological "necessity." If this is the case, they should not qualify for the exception.

By identifying technological necessity as one of the criteria for determining whether or not the integrity of a work has been violated, the BGH has applied an entirely appropriate standard to moral rights. If something is technologically "necessary," then that aspect of the transformation should be exempt from liability for violating the artist's right of integrity. In support of the court's approach, similar ideas can be found in other areas of copyright regulation. The tests for infringement of copyright in a computer program establish that "functional" features of a program cannot be protected by copyright, and copying these features cannot lead to infringement.[94] The issue is essentially one of where to draw the line between necessity and choice when deciding on questions of integrity in the mobile context.

Has the German ruling gone too far? Neither of the two criteria introduced by the court—the presumption of excerpting and the permissibility of digital modifications—entirely precludes success on an integrity claim. However, the idea of technological necessity sets a high threshold of proof for the claim that a ringtone violates the author's integrity. As lawyer Lutz Riede argues, the decision does not completely pre-empt moral rights in

---

93. Quoted in Lutz Riede, Mobile Ringtones: German Supreme Court Rules on the Licensing of Music as a Ringtone for Mobile Phones, unpublished article (personal communication with the author, April 2009).

94. *See., e.g.*, Delrina v. Triolet Systems Inc. (2000), 58 O.R. (3d), 17 C.P.R. (4th) 289 (Ont. C.A.).

mobile ringtones. Rather, the right of integrity can continue to be invoked in cases of egregious mistreatment. Riede states that:

> [T]he decision is certainly not expected to prejudice the rights of composers to object to mutilations of [their] . . . work in extraordinary cases, e.g. when the ringtone significantly varies from the original or puts . . . [the music] into a context detrimental to the composer's reputation.[95]

This point applies equally well to performers, of course. But the issue of reputation is exactly where the German court's ruling fails to provide insight—particularly in view of the fact that ringtones increasingly have a role to play in maintaining, reviving, and perhaps even building reputations for popular musicians.

b. Licensing: Who Speaks on Moral Rights?

In Germany, the issue of moral rights in mobile ringtones arose in the context of a general dispute about the powers of GEMA, the body responsible for the collective licensing of German music rights.[96] In particular, did the general license issued by GEMA, and signed by German musicians, extend to the use of musical works in mobile ringtones?

To this question, the BGH provided a mixed answer. Over the past decade, licensing practices at collective agencies such as GEMA have been evolving in response to technological change. The issue has affected the use of rights in many contexts; for example, in the United States and Canada, major rulings have had to examine the use of news articles in online archives.[97] The problem arises for an obvious reason: prior to the growth of new technologies, licensing agreements did not take new technological media into account. They could not. Even a global and comprehensive license for the use of a work made before the development of new media would not necessarily be honored by a court interpreting it after the fact.[98] The reach of digital technology was difficult to foresee. In the case of a dispute, a court might well find that the necessary meeting of minds between author and publisher on the issue of how the work would be disseminated never took place. Indeed, in the pre-digital era,

---

95. Riede, *supra* note 93.
96. *See* http://www.gema.de/ (last visited Apr. 26, 2010).
97. *See* Robertson v. Thomson Corp. [2006] 2 SCR 363, 2006 SCC 43, *available at* http://csc. lexum.umontreal.ca/en/2006/2006scc43/2006scc43.html [Robertson] (last visited Apr. 26, 2010); New York Times Co. v. Tasini, 533 U.S. 483 (2001) [Tasini].
98. One of the interesting points in the Pink Floyd ruling is that the British court considered the terms of a pre-digital license to be applicable in the digital context. But the license that continued to be honored was one that restricted certain treatments of the work; it was not, as in the Robertson case, the possibility of extending a contractual omission—in that case, the absence of a contract—into the digital environment.

relations between author and publisher were often informal, and this led to situations such as Canada's *Robertson* case, where no written contract existed to clarify the extent of the rights transferred into the hands of the publisher.[99] It was left to Canada's Supreme Court to determine the nature of the relationship between the two. With no contractual basis for the use of the work, the case embodied the ultimate nightmare of copyright lawyers everywhere.

In its ruling on mobile ringtones, the German BGH considered the different licensing agreements used by the collective agency in recent years. It concluded that composers who had made arrangements for music rights in 1996 or before had not, in fact, consented to the use of their work as mobile ringtones. The possibility was not covered by the terms of the GEMA license that was then current.

However, in the updated versions of 2002 and 2005, German composers who assigned their rights through GEMA had done what was necessary to allow for the use of their works in ringtones. Accordingly, in the case of works licensed after 2002, no additional permission had been sought to use the work as a mobile ringtone. If the work was licensed prior to 2002, however, special permission had to be sought before it could be used as a ringtone.

Prior to this ruling, the German music industry operated on the basis of what is known as a "two-step" licensing scheme.'[100] This arrangement reflects the moral rights orientation of German law. A company wanting to use German music would have had to seek permission from two sources: the authority empowered to deal with economic rights, such as GEMA, and the composer of the music, himself, who would personally have to authorize the use as being consistent with his moral rights.

The new German ruling seems to eliminate the need for this practice. It establishes two principles. First, the use of music in mobile ringtones is permitted under the current GEMA licenses. Secondly, the GEMA license effectively takes care of the moral rights in the work, as well. In other words, if an author agrees to the use of his work in a mobile ringtone, he implicitly agrees to the necessary modifications that will be made to transform the work into this format. In relation to current and new works, the case sets an important new precedent: it effectively eliminates the need to seek additional permission from the composer to use a musical work in a mobile ringtone. As moral rights are eventually extended to performers under German law, their rights, too, should be implicitly accommodated by a license to use a musical work as a ringtone.

This aspect of the ruling is controversial for two reasons. The first, as noted above, is the issue of how much technological modification is truly "necessary" for the use of music in a ringtone. But, secondly, a troubling administrative issue arises. The fundamental quality of a moral right is its personal

99. *See* ROBERTSON, *supra* note 97.
100. *See* Riede, *supra* note 93.

nature: it cannot be claimed by anyone but the author himself, or herself. This situation changes only at the point of death, when the heirs or executors of the author may exercise it, not in his stead, but on his behalf. On maintaining the personal connection between an author and his or her moral rights, German law is quite strict. Even waivers of moral rights through contracts are not generally allowed in German law.

When this is the case, there is something startling about the BGH ruling on moral rights. The decision effectively allows the German collective agency, GEMA, to exercise moral rights on behalf of its members. But there are two limiting factors. First, GEMA's dealing with moral rights is not explicit, because the involvement of moral rights in the GEMA licenses is implicit rather than overt. Secondly, as noted above, if modifications to the music exceed the requirements of technological "necessity," moral rights can be invoked. The effective waiver of moral rights, by authors in favor of GEMA, is partial; but the standard of damage that the author must show to invoke moral rights in the ringtone scenario will be very high. How is this position in keeping with the near-absolute tradition that moral rights are personal to the author at German law? Indeed, it is possible that reading moral rights into the general provisions of a GEMA license on music rights may invalidate that license as a whole. But the BGH chose not to address this issue, and it seems that moral rights present no practical obstacle to the use of German musical works in ringtones. In the current state of the law, only cases of egregious distortion will allow a composer, or performer, to raise any objection.

c. Attribution

German moral rights law covers attribution interests comprehensively, but the ruling of Germany's BGH on moral rights makes no direct mention of attribution. Rather, the court's consideration of the integrity interest leads to a general rule that is potentially applicable to all moral rights: technological necessity presents a valid exception to moral rights. This idea can be extended to the principle of attribution, as well. The format of ringtones does not usually allow for attribution to the composer—we hear only a brief excerpt of music, and there is no accompanying literature to clarify attribution—and it may be that the German ruling can be interpreted as excluding attribution in part of its broader attempt to define technological "requirements."

This is an easy answer to a difficult question. By no means is it obvious that musicians' attribution interest should, as a matter of policy, be excluded from the mobile environment. On the contrary, trends in the music industry seem to support the idea that mobile ringtones will play an increasing role, both in restoring economic value to music and in helping musicians to develop reputations. Attributing the use of music in ringtones could present artists with a distinct advantage in building their reputations, and it may be one that they should be entitled to claim.

The fact that current ringtone technology does not facilitate attribution does not mean that attribution is impossible. For example, most phones come equipped with video screens and movie cameras; when the phone rings, and the ringtone plays, the composer's name, picture, or trademark could flash on the screen. The composer's name could be included in his or her own voice at the beginning or end of a track; whether or not this was heard every time the phone rang would be irrelevant, as the use of an excerpt which is subject to interruption is clearly an inherent feature of mobile technology. In the terms defined by the BGH, excerpts and interruptions are technologically "required" for the use of music as a ringtone. Creative solutions to the problem of attribution are limited only by the imagination.

To what extent does mobile technology truly imply the exclusion of moral rights? To this fundamental question, neither the BGH nor any other court has, as yet, provided a fully satisfactory answer.

D. Performers: The New Authors

In 2002, the WIPO Performances and Phonograms Treaty (WPPT) introduced the first innovation in the international treatment of moral rights since their incorporation into the Berne Convention in 1928: it created a moral right for performers.[101] The WPPT's formulation of the right closely resembles the framing of the moral right of authors in Article 6*bis* of the Berne Convention.[102] Performers' rights of attribution and integrity are affirmed, and, as in Berne, they can either be included in the copyright laws of member countries or protected through alternate legal arrangements.[103] Like Berne, the WPPT limits the integrity right to circumstances where the author's reputation is endangered. Curiously, it drops the language of "honor" from this provision—an omission that Mihály Ficsor finds important, although it could be

---

101. *See* WPPT, *supra* note 65, art. 5.

102. *But see* MIHÁLY FICSOR, THE LAW OF COPYRIGHT AND THE INTERNET: THE 1996 WIPO TREATIES, THEIR INTERPRETATION AND IMPLEMENTATION 617–18 (Oxford University Press 2002). He notes that the reference to "other derogatory actions" affecting the artist has been eliminated; the word "honor" has also been left out of the WPPT formulation of performers' moral rights. The issue is discussed at note 105, below, and accompanying text. The important exception to the performer's moral right is that performances in audiovisual works—film—do not enjoy moral rights. As Article 5 of the WPPT states, moral rights apply only to "live aural performances or performances fixed in phonograms," and implicitly do not extend to performances in audiovisual works.

103. *See* WPPT, *supra* note 65, sub-sections 5(1), 5(2), & 5(3), mirroring the provisions of Article 6BIS of the Berne Convention.

argued that the sense of "reputation" is broad enough to encompass the personal dimension that "honor" seems to suggest.[104]

The moral right of performers was a dramatic step that raised performers to a new place in the musical hierarchy defined by Western tradition. Western culture has long emphasized the supremacy of the composer, at the apex of the musical pyramid, and the devotion of the audience below. The performer's place is between the two. He is a vehicle which transmits the greatness of the composer's larger genius to the world.

With moral rights, however, the performer is no longer a mere mouthpiece for the composer. Instead, the performer, too, is recognized as an original creator in his own right. The nature of the creation may be different, and the secret of the performer's art may find expression in more ethereal ways—style, touch, gesture. Without the aid of technology, the greatness of a performer passes away as gently as a cloud, and all that he or she has worked for becomes dependent on memory and word of mouth. In this sense, performance is perhaps the art that most closely mirrors life: its essential quality is impermanence. But the intervention of technology has altered this situation. What was impermanent has, in some sense, become permanent through the grace of recording.

In the case of improvisatory art forms like jazz, the performer is in a position of special poignancy. Here, the recording medium confirms, not only the special talent of performance, but the awesome genius of composition in action. As Bill Evans wrote, "Direct deed is the most meaningful reflection."[105] Technology makes a record of that reflection possible, and a moral right for performers is one attempt to recognize the close kinship between the compositional and performance aspects of the art.

The new moral right for performers seems more appropriate than ever in the modern environment, where performance-based music seems largely to have captured the public imagination. Most popular music depends, not primarily on the composition, but on the success of the performance in presenting it to the public. Performance in many musical genres—jazz, Indian classical music, rock, and hip-hop, also features moments of improvisation, sometimes brief, but often extended. In these circumstances, what are the practical implications of performers' moral rights?

---

104. *See* Ficsor, *supra* note 102, at 617–18.
105. *See* Bill Evans' classic liner notes to the pioneering jazz album, *Kind of Blue*, *available at* http://www.billevanswebpages.com/kindblue.html (last visited July 17, 2010). Evans elaborates: "There is a Japanese visual art in which the artist is forced to be spontaneous. He must paint on a thin stretched parchment with a special brush and black water paint in such a way that an unnatural or interrupted stroke will destroy the line or break through the parchment. Erasures or changes are impossible. These artists must practice a particular discipline, that of allowing the idea to express itself in communication with their hands in such a direct way that deliberation cannot interfere. The resulting pictures lack the complex composition and textures of ordinary painting, but it is said that those who see well find something captured that escapes explanation."

1. Live Performance: The Moral Rights of Composer and Performer

Music is a complex art form. Even in earlier historical periods, the potential for confusion about the creative roles of composer and performer was apparent. In the nineteenth century, the art of performance gained enormously in public prestige and visibility; composer and performer were often one and the same person, but the enlargement of the performer's role set the scene for later contests between the two.[106]

There was also an interesting gender dimension to this split. Composers were generally male, and the few women who tried their hand at composition faltered under early discouragement. Notable examples were Felix Mendelssohn's sister, Fanny, and Robert Schumann's wife, Clara Wiecke. A selection of Fanny's works was eventually published under her brother's name.[107]

In Clara's case, family life left her with little time for composition. The situation was a source of deep regret for her husband, who observed:

> Clara has composed a series of small pieces, which show a musical and tender ingenuity such as she has never attained before. But to have children, and a husband who is always living in the realm of imagination, does not go together with composing. She cannot work at it regularly, and I am often disturbed to think how many profound ideas are lost because she cannot work them out.[108]

Clara herself commented:

> I once believed that I possessed creative talent, but I have given up this idea; a woman must not desire to compose—there has never yet been one able to do it. Should I expect to be the one?[109]

---

106. *See* Kenneth Hamilton, After the Golden Age: Romantic Pianism and Modern Performance (Oxford University Press 2007). Examples included Johannes Brahms, who gave up his performance career to compose; Robert Schumann, whose early brilliance as a performer was terminated by a hand injury, self-inflicted in his effort to improve his technique; and Franz Liszt, who believed that his own career as a composer had been ruined by his excessive financial dependence on composition. The last in this line was twentieth-century composer-pianist, Sergei Rachmaninoff, whose concerts in the United States led to such a busy career that he had little time left for composing. No doubt, the sadness of exile also colored his attitude to composition in the United States, where he lived after 1918. Of course, given the variety of their output, there were many situations in which the works of these composers were also performed by other artists, from singers to orchestras.

107. *See* R. Larry Todd, Mendelssohn: A Life in Music (Oxford University Press 2003).

108. Joint diary of Robert and Clara, *quoted in* Nancy B. Reich, Clara Schumann: The Artist and the Woman 215 (Cornell University Press 2001).

109. Quoted from Clara Schumann's diary, 1839—when she was 20 years old—*in* Nancy B. Reich, *Clara Schumann, in* Women Making Music: The Western Art Tradition 1150–1950, 249, 267 (Jane Bowers & Judith Tuck eds., University of Illinois, 1987).

At the same time, the audience for classical music appears to have been even predominantly female. Playing the piano was a desirable accomplishment for women of the eighteenth century, and by the nineteenth, a significant number of amateur musicians—including students of the great composers—were female. Identifying the source of the creative impulse is therefore important as a matter of human rights. It not only establishes a certain equality between different kinds of artists; it also encourages the correction of a gender imbalance that has long placed the art of classic composition almost exclusively in the hands of men. The moral right of performers helps to recognize and value the contribution of women—as performers, students, and, in the elegant French expression, *amateurs éclairés*[110]—to the development of music.

The recognition of performers addresses another human rights concern. Many systems of world music, including the highly developed classical music of India, are not based primarily on written forms. In India, classical compositions are often created orally, memorized, and taught to students by an outstanding composer and his disciples.[111] In 1994, to accommodate this tradition, the Indian Copyright Act was modified to include protection for music that is not written down.[112]

The insistence of Western copyright laws on written forms for music reflects a cultural bias—one that places oral traditions consistently at a disadvantage. In Canada, one leading case found that the transmission of music by wire could not be an infringement of copyright because the musical score itself had not been copied—a judgment that eventually led to an amended definition of musical work to close this loophole in the Act.[113] With a performer's moral right, it becomes easier to accord status to oral and improvised music. It is a small step towards recognition for non-Western traditions

---

110. Enlightened amateurs, meaning nonprofessionals skilled in the art.
111. Statement by Dr. S. Vijaya Bharati (personal communication with the author, Apr. 27, 2010). Ravi Shankar notes, "The tradition of Indian classical music is an oral one. It is taught directly by the guru to the disciple, rather than by the notation method used in the West. The very heart of Indian music is the raga: the melodic form upon which the musician improvises. This framework is established by tradition and inspired by the creative spirits of master musicians." Ravi Shankar, *On Appreciation of Indian Classical Music, available at* http://www.ravishankar.org/indian_music.html (last visited Apr. 26, 2010).
112. The amending Bill is available on the Parliament of India website at http://parliamentofindia.nic.in/ls/bills/1994/1994-31.htm [1994 Amendment Bill]. *See* Amendment of sec. 2(p): "(p) 'musical work' means a work consisting of music and includes any graphical notation of such work but does not include any words or any action intended to be sung, spoken or performed with the music."
113. *See* Composers, Authors and Publishers Assoc. of Canada Limited v. CTV Television Network Limited [1968] S.C.R. 676, *available at* http://csc.lexum.umontreal.ca/en/1968/1968scr0-676/1968scr0-676.html (last visited Apr. 26, 2010). The amendment was enacted in 1993. *See* Canadian Copyright Reform Timeline, *available at* http://www.innovationlaw.org/archives/projects/dcr/reform/timeline.htm (last visited Aug. 22, 2010).

in music, whether they are found in developing countries or among Aboriginal cultures in the developed world.

The creation of moral rights for performers creates an interesting environment for live performance. In the past, the supremacy of the composer's interest in the presentation of the work was obvious, and it was he who was the final authority on how his own work should be performed. A performance that did not accord with the composer's view of his own music could amount to a violation of the composer's right of integrity. When the performer also enjoys a moral right to the integrity of the performance, the balance of power in this relationship shifts. The performer's art is recognized as creative and original; she is entitled to present her view of the composition. The hierarchy inherent in the relationship between composer and performer cannot be entirely removed, of course, and the performer should not be allowed to present the work of a composer in some way that circumvents his artistic intent. However, the threshold at which this determination will be made should be set at a much higher point than in the past. In particular, the composer should not be able to intervene in questions of style and expression that represent the performer's art, and to which she is entitled as a matter of preserving the integrity of her own performance.

This issue arose in the Netherlands in a slightly different context. A Dutch theater company, De Haarlemse Toneelschuur, decided to mount a production of Samuel Beckett's play, *Waiting for Godot*, with an all-female cast. This iconic play focuses on four male characters, but there are many reasons, both practical and idealistic, why a female production might be attempted. Theater scholar, David Bradby, sees it as a simple issue of gender equality:

> With the increasing empowerment of women in theater, many attempts have been made to perform *Godot* with an all-female cast. One such was in 1988, in Holland, a society where women's liberation was accepted earlier than elsewhere.[114]

This Dutch production aroused the ire of Beckett, who felt that women actors could not convey what he intended in his play. His explanation that "women do not have prostates" may offend at first glance, but the main character, Vladimir, actually suffers from an enlarged prostate that becomes known to the audience through his frequent visits offstage to relieve himself. Bradby comments:

> [H]is remark about prostates, although typically economical and rather puckish, deserves to be taken seriously because of its emphasis on the body. As Krejča

---

114. David Bradby, Beckett: Waiting for Godot 155–56 (Plays in Production Series, Cambridge University Press 2001).

pointed out, the play came to life when the actors were able to use their own flesh, avoiding "impersonating" in favor of "being."[115]

Beckett brought an action against the Dutch theater company through the French *Société des auteurs et compositeurs dramatiques*, (SACD) the collective agency responsible for dramatic rights. But the theater company received a sympathetic hearing from the Dutch judge, who commented that "the play was about the human condition in general," and therefore, " transcended the sexual identity of men and women." He also noted that the interpretation of the play by the female actors and director showed great fidelity to Beckett's text. For this reason, it was impossible to establish that the integrity of the work had been violated.[116]

Bradby feels that the judge's approach should have found sympathy with Beckett's artistic vision for the play, since Beckett himself rejected traditional conventions of location and, it could be added, traditional notions of plot. The innovative nature of the play lies in its ability to create a tremendous sense of indeterminacy. The extension of this aesthetic to the issue of gender would seem to be an important creative insight. Yet Beckett objected.

The case lays bare the interesting possibility of a schism within the artistic personality itself. Creative innovation and social conservatism may coexist in one mind. The resulting inner tension can lead to situations where moral rights are invoked by the author to the detriment of his own artistic work, as arguably happened in this case.

On the French theory of moral rights in its purest form, the artistic quality of the alteration is irrelevant: the fact that the author does not want it is reason enough to ban it. But the Dutch court took a broader perspective on moral rights, not only considering the author's right to control his own creation, but also giving weight to the broader social interest in culture. It may be helpful to see the issue as one of competing moral rights—dramatic author, theater director, and performers—and how to manage their coexistence. Bradby generally comments that the discussion surrounding the case in Holland did touch on the issue of "the director's creative freedom."[117]

Beckett's response to the court case was to ban all productions of his plays in Holland.

2. Recording and Broadcasting

Where recordings are concerned, the extension of moral rights to performers brings a new layer of complexity into the equation. Performers' moral rights

---

115. *Id.*, at 157.
116. *Id.*
117. *Id.*

coexist alongside an existing framework of both economic and moral rights. From the artists' perspective, the territorial borders of composition and performance must now be redrawn. From the perspective of the public, when it comes to use of the work, there is an additional layer of rights to recognize and negotiate—permissions to seek, payments to make.

The complex relationship between composer and performer means that, in most cases, the successful release of a recording will involve a degree of cooperation between the two. The purchase of music rights by the performer from the composer may not be enough to clarify matters. Notwithstanding the potential role of collective agencies, the moral rights will still be held personally by the composer, and must be dealt with as a distinct issue. At the same time, a composer's objections to the interpretation of his work should not be allowed to stray into areas of the art that are properly the domain of performers. As the area of performers' rights develops, courts are likely to find themselves in the awkward position of trying to determine and delimit the creative spaces inhabited by each. Prominent members of the musical community need to address this issue in their own writing, speaking, and collaborative work. It should not be left primarily in the hands of outsiders who may not be able to appreciate fully what is at stake.

The potential for conflict between composers and performers is likely to affect the largest and most powerful musical communities, represented by popular music in all its genres. They are built upon the work of living composers and recent composers. Classical music is also affected, to a lesser extent, when work by current composers is performed. Where perpetual protection for moral rights exists, as in France, moral rights issues could also arise in the performance of classic works, although this has yet to happen.[118] Given that classical music is struggling for an audience, especially among youth, the possibilities that technology brings to the performance of classic works could be exciting.[119] Performers may be tempted to exploit technology

---

118. *See* Sawkins v. Hyperion Records [2005] E.M.L.R. 29, an interesting UK case on moral rights that involved a record company's failure to attribute authorship to the editor of works by a French baroque composer, Richard de Lalande. The editor, Dr Sawkins, was a musicologist and authority on the works of Lalande, and his work on each of the 4 editions used extended over some 300 hours. Hyperion had thanked Dr Sawkins "for his preparation of performance materials for this recording." The English Court of Appeal noted that there was no fixed formula for attribution in circumstances such as these. Nevertheless, Mummery L.J., like the judge at first instance, felt that this was insufficient: "Although the CD sleeve named Dr Sawkins, it did not identify his authorship." (para. 69) Interestingly, Mummery L.J. commented that Hyperion's acknowledgement was in line with usual practice, but this did not excuse the failure to attribute authorship.

119. British violinist, Nigel Kennedy, was a pioneer, using video to accompany his performances. *See also The Sound of the Carceri*, a performance of Bach by cellist Yo-Yo Ma filmed in the virtual environment of an Italian prison based on drawings by architect Giovanni Battista Piranesi, Bach's contemporary. The challenge of designing the virtual sound environment fell to Steve Epstein. For a quick summary of the project, see http://www.bullfrogfilms.com/

in their search for an audience, but the moral rights of composers could present a sobering thought. Would it be a violation of the composer's moral rights to perform a work by a classical composer with an accompaniment of African drums? . . . To include a synthesizer in an orchestral recording?

Although this group represents a relatively small proportion of recording sales, it is interesting to note that a largely untapped market for Western classical music exists in far-flung regions of the globe—India and China are two cases in point. Music critic Norman Lebrecht, writing for Bloomberg news, comments:

> Taking a different measure, classical recording is bucking the industry slump in key areas, according to the International Federation of the Phonographic Industry. Sales are on the rise in France and Poland, where they constitute 9 percent of the market, in Austria and Hungary at 11 percent, and in Germany and Australia at 6 percent.

> The biggest surge is in China w[h]ere one in six recordings that are legally traded is of Western classical music, show figures just released by the IFPI. In South Korea, the share is 18 percent. In the U.S., the classical share of record sales is just under 1 percent.

> It's in the young tiger markets, more than at the mature American concert halls, that classical music is finding its future.[120]

3. "Audiovisual Works:" A Necessary Exception?

The performers' moral rights created by the WPPT retain one significant exception: performances in "audiovisual works" will not be eligible for moral rights protection. The exception simply means that performances on film will not give rise to moral rights. Musicians who perform on film will be affected; so, too, are actors, who will not enjoy moral rights in their performances in movies.

---

catalog/soc.html (last visited Aug. 23, 2010). Early in the twentieth century, Russian composer Alexander Scriabin explored the visual aspect of his compositions by performing them with a display of colored lights. The apparatus can be seen at his home in Moscow, now a museum. *See* the website of the Scriabine Foundation at http://scriabinefoundation.org/museum.html (last visited July 18, 2010).

120. He concludes, "The signs are that recession is once again accelerating the need for the spiritual consolation that only a symphony can deliver." *See* Norman Lebrecht, *Recession Blues Spurs Classical Music*, BLOOMBERG (June 8, 2009), *available at* http://www.bloomberg.com/apps/news?pid=20601088&sid=a_kEJSPKJ5ao&refer=muse (last visited Apr. 25, 2010).

The provision satisfies concerns about moral rights in film, which have long been an area of concern for America's Hollywood lobby.[121] The fears are understandable. The making of a film involves large numbers of people, both on and offscreen. If a significant proportion of the contributors is entitled to their moral rights, the resulting uncertainty could create a logistical nightmare for filmmakers and, of course, for the producers who invest in films.

As a matter of justice, the exception is more difficult to justify. Should a musical performer be banned from claiming his moral right of attribution if the film's director makes use of his performance in an unflattering way, possibly damaging the performer's reputation? Should an actor be forbidden from claiming a moral right in his performance if it is improperly used by the director? Does a performer not have a right to be identified in the film credits when his or her performance is one of the elements that has gone into the successful realization of the film?

These issues are difficult, because the art form, itself, is strongly hierarchical in nature. The producer pays for the film; the director is its *"auteur."*[122] Between the two of them, financial rights and responsibilities as well as artistic vision are accounted for.[123] In the Hollywood model, the producer, who finances the work, continues to hold the upper hand on final decisions. Choices about the different elements of the film, from actor's performance to screenplay, are ultimately in the hands of one or both of them. The *"auteur"* theory of filmmaking, originating in the French "new wave" cinema of the 1960s, goes a step further. According to this view, the director's personality contributes the unified vision necessary to the success of the film as an artistic work. In this sense, all of the actors' performances are merely the raw material with which the director works. This is true of all of the elements that are involved in the making of a film.

The time may not yet be right for a moral right in audiovisual performances. However, the possibility of expanding performers' moral rights to include performances on film ultimately deserves to be reconsidered. It is questionable whether a director's or producer's rights in his film need to be absolute. Conferring upon performers the right to protect their own reputations could actually help to improve the climate for filmmaking. Moral rights could encourage mutual respect between director and performer. A sense, in the performer's mind, that his contribution to the work is recognized and valued might make him a better collaborator in the director's artistic vision.

---

121. *See, for example*, the analysis in Stephen Fraser, *Berne, CFTA, NAFTA and GATT: The Implications of Copyright Droit Moral and Cultural Exemptions in International Trade Law*, 18 Hastings Comm. & Eng. L.J. 287 (1996).

122. The idea of filmmaker as author originated in French cinema of the 1960s. *See* below, and Chapter 7, *infra*, notes 76–8 and accompanying text.

123. Tensions between the claims of producer and director are considered in detail in Chapter 7, *infra*, on film moral rights.

Moral rights could help to promote these goals. But there is no doubt that they could also lead to conflict, and moral rights enjoyed by collaborators in a film would have to be managed with consummate skill.

E. Recommendations

Moral rights in music should be recognized and protected in the digital context. The recognition of moral rights should be subject to certain modifications which are appropriate to this environment. The form in which digital music rights develop will almost certainly help to frame policies around digital moral rights in other areas of interest, such as film.

The moral right of attribution should be respected, but it should be exercised with technological necessity in mind. Notably, in the context of specialized uses of music such as mobile ringtones, attribution in the sound of the ringtone would be unpredictable because of the nature of the ringtone. Different methods of attribution, such as video attribution or attribution in an attached file, should be explored. But the importance of attribution in the digital environment should be recognized. In the future, music is likely to be distributed primarily through online channels—pay-per-download services like iTunes, global licensing schemes, or new models that develop as a result of new experiences in the coming years. If the attribution of works is not maintained, we will experience a gradual loss of musical history. As the names of musicians disappear, so, too, do their stories. Much of our knowledge about music is derived from our knowledge of the lives, careers, and compositions of great musicians of the past. In this light, there can be no doubt that the principle of attribution needs to include, not only composers, but also, performers. The WPPT has set an important benchmark in this regard, although its recognition of performers excludes the world of film and is, therefore, incomplete.

The right of integrity remains an essential right in the environment of new music. It plays an important role in preserving musical culture, and it lends invaluable support to the establishment of artistic reputations, on which musical careers continue to be built. In most digital scenarios, the integrity right should be restricted to situations of damage to reputation. Given the extent to which music is "handled" in the downloading context, an open-ended right of integrity might prove counterproductive, and lead to an unwillingness to disseminate music via digital means.

In the digital context, it is particularly important to recognize a third, and fundamental, moral right: the right of disclosure. The principle of disclosure assumes a new significance in the digital world—indeed, it may be the only right that can be unequivocally protected in practice, and justified in theory, where digital technology is concerned. When it comes to moral rights in the

Digital Age, the right of disclosure should no longer be taken for granted, implied into the existing legal framework for moral rights.[124] It should be stated openly, alongside the author's economic right to release his work to the public. In the monist tradition, disclosure should be recognized as both an economic and moral prerogative of authorship.

Extending moral rights to technical musicians, such as sound engineers, makes sense in an environment where art and technology are ever more closely connected. The nature of the special relationship between performer and engineer must be considered, as the work of the engineer is dependent upon the performer for its raw material. This factor will affect the framing of moral rights for sound engineers. The rights that they enjoy may need to remain subordinate to the performer's rights; at the same time, sound engineers are entitled to attribution for their labor, creativity, and individuality in the creation of a sound environment appropriate for the performer's work. In a sense, the sound engineer is like the jeweler who places an exquisite gem in its setting—without the setting, the gem shows little splendor.

In order to acquire practical significance, moral rights must be recognized across a wide variety of jurisdictions. In this process, the countries of the European Union have a special role to play. Moral rights should be harmonized across European member states as part of a pan-European licensing scheme for music downloads. European countries are well placed, as a bloc, to demand compliance with moral rights from music companies. If European countries are determined to command respect for moral rights across the EU region, a level of corporate acquiescence is likely to be achieved. Given the size and importance of this pan-European market, it seems unlikely that respect for moral rights will dampen the European music market vis-à-vis the United States. On the contrary, if companies are required to respect moral rights in Europe, it seems likely that they will choose to circulate moral rights information in other jurisdictions, as well, rather than removing it for the U.S. market.

The European experience of both collective licensing and moral rights is extensive, placing European Union countries in a good position to develop rules on specific moral rights issues, such as the separation of individual tracks on an album. It should also be noted that respect for moral rights is in harmony with the legal systems of a number of powerful countries—India, Japan, Russia, and even China—and may actually help to open up further markets for the American music industry overseas.

---

124. For example, it is arguably implicit in Article 6*bis* of the Berne Convention. *See* Mira T. Sundara Rajan, Moral Rights and Copyright Harmonisation: Prospects for an "International Moral Right"?, nn.42–65 and accompanying text (paper presented to the Seventeenth BILETA Annual Conference), *available at* http://www.bileta.ac.uk/Document%20Library/1/Moral%20Rights%20and%20Copyright%20Harmonisation%20-%20Prospects%20for%20an%20%27International%20Moral%20Right%27.pdf (last visited Aug. 22, 2010).

F. Conclusion: The Public Interest in Music

As the first area of the arts to become intimately engaged with technology, music represents an important test case for the protection of moral rights in the digital context. From the DJ phenomenon to the composition of electronic music, technology brings new challenges to the principles of attribution and integrity. The practices that evolve through music are likely to serve as invaluable guideposts for recognizing moral rights in other contexts.

The importance of access to music is often invoked by advocates of the public interest. But why is the discussion of the public interest so narrowly circumscribed? The broader interest in the integrity of cultural heritage, which is ultimately the treasured possession of the public, also deserves attention. The integrity of cultural heritage is a vast question—it encompasses, not only the protection of material cultural property, but also, the general environment for culture. Only by encouraging interest in culture, education, and the creative ability of individuals who are alive today can cultural heritage as a concept continue to exist.

Protecting the moral rights of composers and performers upholds their human rights and helps to preserve an important part of our cultural heritage: musical history. Through technology, this ancient art form can extend its reach across time and space, and into individual hearts and minds. In this sense, technology mirrors the magic of music itself, which can transport us instantly into the intimate state of mind of the composer. Contact with music means contact with its creator, and moral rights can help to imbue this relationship with meaning. Without the musicians of our world—past, present, and future—the digital cosmos could prove to be a lonely place.

CHAPTER

7

Twenty-First Century Classics

Film and the Complexities of the Collaborative Work

I believe the people who are coloring movies have
contempt for the audience by claiming, in effect, that
viewers are too stupid and too insensitive to
appreciate black and white photography—that they
must be given, like infants or monkeys, bright colors
to keep them amused.

–Woody Allen[1]

---

1. Woody Allen, *The Colorization of Films Insults Artists and Society*, NEW YORK TIMES (June 28, 1987) [Allen].

Film is widely admired as the one truly original art form of the twentieth century.[2] Countless artistic elements merge in the creation of a film—images, drama, words, music, and, of course, the technology that binds all of these together and creates the look of the finished work. However spectacular in themselves, the whole is still somehow greater than the sum of these parts. The complex nature of this art form presents a fundamental challenge to the image of the artist as individual, whose work reflects a unified artistic concept, embodied in the nineteenth-century doctrine of moral rights. But moral rights have also proven their capacity to accommodate film. With the notable exception of the United States, moral rights in this medium are recognized in most countries of the world.[3]

Their practical relevance to film is beyond doubt.[4] A number of leading international cases on moral rights have arisen out of the treatment of films. In this process, something peculiar has happened: films originating in the United States, now the world's third largest producer of movies, have found themselves at the heart of international conflicts involving moral rights.[5] The colorization of black and white films has become the single most widely

2. James H. Billington, Librarian of Congress, has commented: "The moving picture is not so much the art form as the language of the twentieth century . . . . Future generations will wonder why so little of such a marvelously accessible and appealing record was ever preserved or seriously studied by the strangely transparent and otherwise exuberant society that produced it all." *See* National Film Preservation Board, *available at* http://www.loc.gov/film/studypr.html (last visited July 18, 2010).

3. Most Western European countries, including France, Germany, Italy, Austria, Spain, and Belgium, have special provisions on moral rights in film. For useful comparative analyses of the different regimes of film copyright in European countries, see Irini Stamatoudi, *Moral Rights of Authors in England: The Missing Emphasis on the Role of Creators*, 8(4) INTELL. PROP. Q. 478, 500–03 (1007) [Stamatoudi, *Moral Rights of Authors in England*], and for a more detailed treatment, PASCAL KAMINA, FILM COPYRIGHT IN THE EUROPEAN UNION 284–337 (Cambridge Studies in Intellectual Property Rights, Cambridge Univ. Press 2002).

4. This chapter uses the terminology of film, audiovisual works, and cinematographic works interchangeably; all of these appear in international laws dealing with copyright and moral rights in motion pictures. For a helpful analysis of their different uses and connotations, see IRINI A. STAMATOUDI, COPYRIGHT AND MULTIMEDIA PRODUCTS: A COMPARATIVE ANALYSIS, para 6.1, *Audiovisual Works*, 104–11 (Cambridge Studies in Intellectual Property, Cambridge Univ. Press 2002) [Stamatoudi, *Copyright and Multimedia Products*]. She notes (at 110), "There is no definite way of distinguishing between audiovisual works, films and cinematographic works, and most national copyright laws use one of the terms to include the others or use all or some of the terms interchangeably." (footnotes omitted).

5. The largest producer of films is India, which combines the Hindi language popular film industry, known as "Bollywood"—because it is based in Mumbai, formerly known as Bombay—with cinema in a variety of other national languages. Nigeria is in second place; its film industry is now known as "Nollywood." *See* UN News Centre, *Nigeria Surpasses Hollywood as World's Second Largest Film Producer—UN*, May 5, 2009, *available at* http://www.un.org/apps/news/story.asp?NewsID=30707&Cr=nigeria&Cr1# (last visited Apr. 28, 2010). This article notes: "Key to Nollywood's explosive success is Nigerian filmmakers' reliance on video instead of film, reducing production costs, and, as the survey points out, the West African

litigated conflict in film moral rights. The issue, essentially a dispute between the competing Hollywood interests of filmmakers and production companies, received a seminal legal treatment from the French courts in the case of *Huston*.[6] Moral rights issues have arisen in the creative products of a country that does not recognize moral rights in film, and, perhaps more importantly, where moral rights protection is vigorously opposed by the powerful Motion Picture Academy Association (MPAA), Hollywood's lobbying wing.[7] As a result, the contribution of American filmmakers to the art has been vindicated outside American borders, while little scope to recognize it exists under American law.

At the same time, American courts have built a certain familiarity with artistic and cultural issues in film. The classic case of *Shostakovich*, from 1948, involved the use of music by four celebrated Soviet composers in an anti-Soviet film. In a lawsuit brought in the New York Supreme Court, the composers argued that their right of integrity had been violated by the association of their works with the incompatible political views expressed in the film.[8] Despite the silence of U.S. copyright legislation on moral rights, the American judge gave an impressive assessment of the issues. His reasoning undertook the difficult task of determining whether moral rights could exist at American law even though the American copyright statute did not provide explicitly for them. The reasons for Justice Koch's eventual finding against a moral right were practical ones—he felt that the absence of legislative guidance on this issue would create intolerable uncertainty about the nature of the rights and the practical implications of protecting them. However, in the judge's view, there was no underlying reason of law or culture why moral

---

country has virtually no formal cinemas, with about 99 per cent of screenings in informal settings, such as home theatres."

6. Judgment of Dec. 19, 1994 (*Turner Entertainment v. Huston Heirs*), Cour d'Appel, chs. Réunies (Versailles), 164 RIDA 389 (1995) (Fr.), on remand from Judgment of May 28, 1991, Cass. Civ. lre, 149 RIDA 197 (1991) [*Huston*].

7. For an analysis of how the MPAA's role developed in the context of U.S. bilateral and international trade negotiations, see Stephen Fraser, *Berne, CFTA, NAFTA and GATT: The Implications of Copyright Droit Moral and Cultural Exemptions in International Trade Law*, 18 Hastings Comm. & Ent. L.J. 287, 308–11 (1996) (film and the Canada-U.S. Free Trade Agreement), 316–18 (film and U.S.-France discussions during the Uruguay Round of GATT negotiations leading to the establishment of the WTO) [Fraser, *Berne, CFTA, NAFTA and GATT*].

8. Given the copyright-related practices in the Soviet Union of the time, and Shostakovich's own precarious position, it seems clear that the Soviet government took it upon itself to act for the composers. William Strauss notes that the plaintiff was acting as "assignee" of the composers. William Strauss, The Moral Right of the Author, 4(4) 506, 534–35 (1955); the case is discussed in note 56. See also the discussion of this aspect of the case in Mira T. Sundara Rajan, Copyright and Creative Freedom: A Study of Post-Socialist Law Reform 104–05 (Routledge 2006) [Sundara Rajan, *Copyright and Creative Freedom*].

rights could not be accepted on the American scene.[9] Indeed, the judge found that, in certain circumstances, a moral right could be invoked to protect works in the public domain. In this respect, the ruling still represents a novel way of thinking about the public domain in the United States, where it is usually considered an area of near-absolute freedom.[10]

The twenty-first century transformation of film has brought many new possibilities to this art form. Digital images of personalities from film history can be used to re-create actors and characters from the past. Movies can be communicated to viewers by Internet, with access on an individual and near-instantaneous basis. Films can be copied and broken down into their component parts with relative ease, and potentially reused in the making of new videos or films.

A newly global film community has also come into being. India now surpasses the United States as the world's largest maker of films, and India's insatiable appetite for stories has translated into numerous "Bollywood" remakes of Hollywood films. In contrast to the United States, India has embraced moral rights in films. Indeed, its pioneering jurisprudence on film has paved the way for moral rights in other aspects of culture to be recognized by the Indian courts.[11] It is also interesting to note that Indian moral rights have kept alive a cultural discussion around film, although it is a poor counter to the deterioration of India's art-film tradition which parallels Bollywood's rise.

All of these new activities, and the many more that are certain to arise in the digital environment, involve questions about moral rights. In this context, will Hollywood continue to oppose moral rights in film? And if so, what will be the potential losses to American and international filmmakers?

---

9. A detailed discussion of the case can be found in Chapter 3, *infra*, "A Theory in Flux: The Evolution in Progress of Moral Rights", notes 91–101 and accompanying text.

10. See the comments on the U.S. Public domain in *id*.

11. For an overview of the development of moral rights jurisprudence in India, including the seminal case of *Mannu Bhandari*, which deals with moral rights in a film adaptation of a novel, see Mira T. Sundara Rajan, *Moral Rights in Developing Countries: The Example of India*, 8(5) & 8(6) J. INTELL. PROP. RIGHTS 357 and 449 (2003) [Sundara Rajan, *Moral Rights in Developing Countries*]; *Smt Mannu Bhandari v. Kala Vikas Pictures Pvt Ltd.* (1986) 1987 AIR (Delhi 13), *available at* http://www.cscsarchive.org:8081/MediaArchive/medialaw.nsf/1105fec5 535ec8ab6525698d00258968/9db260daa1f31d99652571160021775b/$FILE/LA030256.pdf (last visited Apr. 28, 2010) [*Mannu Bhandari*]. The *Mannu Bhandari* case is also discussed by American lawyer, Jeffrey Dine. *See* Jeffrey M. Dine *Authors' Moral Rights in Non-European Nations: International Agreements, Economics, Mannu Bhandari, and the Dead Sea Scrolls*, 16 MICH. J. INT'L L. 545 (1995).

A. Commerce Meets Creation: Authorship of a Film

The complexity of moral rights issues in film is unmatched by any other form of creative expression. The nature of the work, itself, is at fault. Film combines technological and creative elements in a way that no other form of intellectual creation attempts.

Film is the prototype of a technological work. It is a composite work that is largely compiled from the original work of a number of contributors. Those who contribute to a film include the writer of the screenplay or dialogue, the composer of film music and the arranger of the film score, the performers who act in the film, and the technicians responsible for physically creating and shaping the final product. Indeed, countless individuals are involved in the technical and cosmetic aspects of production that give a particular film its characteristic look, from costumes and set design, to cinematography.[12] The director requires special mention. He does not contribute a separate work, but his labor, vision, and editorial control are instrumental in realizing the final character of the work. The contribution of the producer is essential, but it is different from all others—financial in nature, but potentially creative, as well.

From a copyright perspective, it is not necessarily important to identify the author of the film. Copyright law, whatever its apparent protests to the contrary, is oriented towards the protection of owners of copyright, rather than authors *per se*. In relation to film, this focus is clearly apparent. The primary objective of copyright, particularly in the common law countries, is to protect the investment of economic resources into the making of a film, a rationale that fits well with the labor theory of copyright that traditionally holds sway in these countries.[13] But this approach is more than a common law tradition; it is pragmatic. A large investment of resources is required to

---

12. The use of costumes is a striking creative issue. Among major directors, Alfred Hitchcock is well-known for his attention to this detail; in just one example from his 1960 *Psycho*, the viewer watches the metamorphosis of a female character from white to black clothing to signify her moral corruption. For an unusual discussion of this and other aspects of the film, see *Psycho: Queering Hitchcock's Classic*, Bright Lights Film J., *available at* http://www. brightlightsfilm.com/61/61psycho.php (last visited Apr. 28, 2010).

13. The principle that copyright is available in practically any work involving the investment of labor into its creation is a classic proposition of English law. *See* the seminal cases *Kenrick v. Lawrence* [1890] 25 Q.B.D. 99 and *University of London Press v. University Tutorial Press* [1916] 2 Ch. 601. In recent years, this standard has slowly evolved upward, toward the creativity standard required for copyright protection in civil law countries. This trend was initiated by the U.S. Supreme Court in *Feist Publications Inc. v. Rural Telephone Service Co.*, 499 U.S. 340, 362–63 (1991) [*Feist*], which identified a "modicum of creativity" as a requirement for copyright and led to a reconsideration of standards of originality in other jurisdictions such as Canada, *CCH Canadian Ltd. v. Law Society of Upper Canada* [2004] 1 S.C.R. 339, 2004 SCC 13, [*CCH*], and India, *Eastern Book Co. & Ors v. DP Modak & Anr.*, 2008 (36) PTC 1, 2008 (1) SCC 1 [*Eastern Book Co.*]. Interestingly, the *Eastern Book Company* case relied explicitly on the Canadian ruling in *CCH* for its resolution of closely similar facts. *See*

make a film and, as a result of these financial stakes, the industry has acquired certain special characteristics. The focus on production makes sense. At its origins, film was a corporate product; but it has evolved progressively towards a higher identity, becoming an increasingly creative and individual art form.[14]

Where moral rights are concerned, the first question that needs to be addressed is that of authorship. The moral right is vested in the human author of a work, and its existence depends on the expression of creative personality in the work. The fact that a film is a composite work does not necessarily make moral rights inappropriate—indeed, moral rights may be relevant to many group phenomena, from folklore and traditional knowledge in India, to the corporate culture of Japan.[15] The rationales for recognizing moral rights in these kinds of works are diverse. Protection of the author is only one perspective on moral rights, and a consideration of moral rights in non-Western jurisdictions shows that the preservation of culture in its less individualistic forms can also be supported by the doctrine.

Is it possible to identify an author whose creative personality is expressed in a film? From a moral rights perspective, it is essential to be able to answer this question. Without an author, it is not clear who would benefit from the moral rights in a film, or why.

The legal response to this question is astonishingly vague. Major jurisdictions, including the United States, do not clarify the basic question of who can claim authorship in a film.[16] The British approach makes the producer the owner of copyright, but the director is entitled to moral rights even though he is not considered an author.[17] As William Cornish notes:

> The moral rights are in some cases given to film directors, who are not authors at all and so never acquire initial copyright. In consequence, qualification for

---

Supreme Court of India judgments, *available at* http://judis.nic.in/supremecourt/chejudis. asp. (last visited Apr. 28, 2010).

14. In the French context, the progress of film from corporate creation to individual art form is famously described in François Truffaut's landmark essay. *See* François Truffaut, *Une Certaine Tendance du cinéma français* [*A Certain Tendency in French Cinema*], trans. in Ginette Vincendeau & Peter Graham, The French New Wave: Critical Landmarks 17 (Palgrave Macmillan 2009). The original article appeared in Cahiers du Cinéma 31 (Jan. 1954) [Truffaut *Une Certaine Tendance*].

15. Japan includes moral rights for corporations in its copyright law. *See* art. 15(1) & (2), on the attribution of authorship to a legal person. The Japanese Copyright Act is available on the website of the Copyright Research and Information Center, *available at* http://www.cric.or. jp/cric_e/clj/clj.html (last visited Apr. 28, 2010) [Japanese Copyright Act]. *See* Chapter 3, *supra*, "Moral Rights:," notes 245–48 and accompanying text.

16. See the comments in F. Jay Dougherty, *Not a Spike Lee Joint? Issues in the Authorship of Motion Pictures under U.S. Copyright Law*, 49 UCLA L. Rev. 225, 269–70 (2001) [Dougherty].

17. *See, e.g.,* Copyright, Designs and Patents Act 1988 (c 48) secs. 77 (1), (6), (8) ("Right to be identified as author or director); 80 (1), (6) (Right to object to derogatory treatment of work).

moral rights does not necessarily depend, so far as the matter is one of status, upon the position of the person enjoying the right. Dualism on this scale opened the way, during the Parliamentary process, to a highly pragmatic outcome, in which the pressures of interest have played a noteworthy part.[18]

British law also offers the possibility that a film may be physically copied without infringing copyright. The case of *Norowzian v. Arks*[19] found that the essence of a film is to be found in its narrative aspect. If the narrative element is not copied, even the use of similar techniques to create a film that looks very much like the original will not lead to an infringement of copyright.[20] The implications for moral rights are interesting. Under British law, the physical treatment of a film may not be the only factor that can lead to a violation of the moral right of integrity. Acts that compromise the integrity of the film as a work of narrative art may also be a relevant concern. The use of images or excerpts in contexts that misrepresent the original narrative could constitute a violation of the right of integrity.

The French approach is to classify the film as a "collaborative" work of "co-author[ship]."[21] "Coauthors" are defined in the Intellectual Property Code as the scriptwriter, the author of any adaptation, the writer of the dialogue, the composer of music that is especially created for the film, and the director.[22] Coauthorship is the approach of choice in most civil law jurisdictions, including the post-socialist civilian systems of Central and Eastern Europe.[23]

French law has the most comprehensive approach to the problem of film authorship in any major jurisdiction. While production is underway, the relationship of the coauthors plays an instrumental role in shaping the film. Finalizing the film depends upon their mutual agreement and consent. After the final product is complete, the focus turns outward, to the relationship of the creators with the outside world. In this scenario, the producer is not an "author" or "coauthor" of the film, but his agreement is necessary in order to

---

18. William R. Cornish, *Moral Rights Under the 1988 Act*, 11(12) Eur. Intell. Prop. Rev. 449, 449 (1989). Cornish's use of the term "dualism" in this context is interesting.
19. Norowzian v. Arks Ltd. (No. 1) [1998] EWHC (Ch) 315; Norowzian v. Arks Ltd. (No. 2) [2000] EMLR 67, [2000] FSR 363 (CA) [*Norowzian*].
20. *Id.*, see, especially, the comments of Buxton LJ at 77–78.
21. *See* arts. L113-7 and L121–5 of the French Code de la Propriété Intellectuelle (Intellectual Property Code); *see Loi N° 92–597 du 1er juillet 1992 relative au code de la propriété intellectuelle (partie législative), Journal officiel de la République française* du 8 février 1994; *Légifrance: Le service public de la diffusion du droit, available at* http://www.legifrance.gouv.fr/affichCode.do?cidTexte=LEGITEXT000006069414&dateTexte=20100412 (last visited Apr. 28, 2010) [CPI, Intellectual Property Code, *Code de la Propriété Intellectuelle*].
22. *Id.*, art. L113-7.
23. *See, for example,* the provisions of the 2008 Russian Civil Code on intellectual property. Grazhdanski Kodeks Rossiiskoi Federatsi, Chast' Chetvërtaya [Civil Code of the Russian Federation, Part IV], Federal Law No. 230-FZ of Dec. 18, 2006, *Rossijskaja Gazeta* No. 289 (4255) of Dec. 22, 2006 = *Sobranie zakonodatel'stva RF* (SZ RF) No. 52 (Part I) of Dec. 25, 2006, Item 5496, at 14803 [2008 Russian Civil Code], art. 1263.2.

settle upon the final version of the film.[24] Under French law, this version is considered the *"version définitive,"* which will stand as the copyright work, and in which, moral rights subsist.[25]

The life of a film therefore unfolds in two phases. The first phase involves the period in which the work develops, and is based on the collaborative efforts of the various contributors to the film. This phase concludes with the establishment of the "final version" of the work. This version is a product of agreement between the producer and the coauthors, and, once it is decided upon, it becomes illegal to destroy the matrix of this version of the film.[26] It is certainly possible that moral rights issues could arise at this stage of the film's existence, in the form of conflicts between the coauthors about the artistic development of the work. French law does not seem to address the question of how to finalize a work when the coauthors have differences of opinion, except for the indirect assertion that the agreement of all is required before the final version of the film can be established.

In a sense, what this provision really specifies is a kind of *composite* right to disclose the film. If even one of the coauthors disagrees on the final version proposed by the other authors, that version cannot be established as the *"version définitive"* of the film.[27] In their commentary on the French Intellectual Property Code, Pierre Sirinelli and his colleagues point out that this "slight bending of the traditional rules" on moral rights can be understood in conjunction with the following provision, which sets out the procedures for the completion of a project in the case where one author drops out part-way.[28] It is also interesting to note that, in this phase, the treatment of the moral rights of the coauthors is egalitarian. The director's moral rights do not now have any precedence over the moral rights of the other authors. In the end, French law seems to visualize a practical solution to the problem of artistic conflicts: if the parties concerned cannot agree, the film cannot be released. From the producer's point of view, however, this result could present a highly undesirable outcome, and alternatives may not always be available to complete a work when one of the original

---

24. *See* CPI, *supra* note 21, art. L121-5.
25. Pierre Sirinelli, Sylviane Durrande, & Antoine Latreille, eds., Code de la propriété intellectuelle commenté, Edition 2009 at 120, para II.A.3, Codes Dalloz, ed., Jeanne Daleau (Dalloz 2009) [Sirinelli et al.].
26. The wording of the statute is that it is *"interdit,"* forbidden or prohibited, to destroy this version. *See* CPI, *supra* note 21, art. L121-5.
27. Sirinelli et al., *supra* note 25, at 119, Commentaire, call it "veto power," and they observe: "Il y aurait donc bien deux phases distinctes dans l'opposabilite du droit moral et l'articulation de l'ensemble fait que l'essentiel des debats ou risques de contentieux se manifesteront au moment d'etablir la version definitive puisque chacun des coauteurs aura alors un pouvoir de veto . . . ." ("Accordingly, there would be two distinct phases in the opposability of moral rights and the articulation of the whole such that points of debate or the risk of litigation will occur at the moment when the final version is established because each of the coauthors will have veto power . . . .").
28. Sirinelli et al., *supra* note 25, at 119, Commentaire: ". . . *léger infléchissement aux règles traditionnelles.*"

authors objects to its realization. No provision is made for the indemnification of the producer in the case of truly irreconcilable artistic differences.

In the second phase of a film's life, the film as a work has been finalized. Moral rights issues may arise, no longer in the course of production, but in the course of the *"exploitation,"* or commercial circulation, of the film. Not only must the users of the film respect moral rights; the producer must also respect the moral rights of the coauthors. It is clear that moral rights subsist in the final version of the film only. In this sense, although film is considered a work of coauthorship, the director is given a certain pride of place in the French system. This transition occurs as part of the movement from creative process to product in the life of the film.

But the interpretation of this rule is a subtle point. A moral right may continue to exist in the underlying work which has been made into a film, such as the script or the musical score, and this right would be held by the author of that work. In fact, each author would be the author of two works—his own component part and the film as a whole. He or she could therefore object to both the misuse of his own portion and to problematic uses made of the film as a whole.

In the final analysis, French law does not provide formal clarification about what is to happen in the case of disputes among the coauthors involving their respective moral rights. A practical solution seems implicit in this separation of a film into its pre- and post-production life: authors should have reconciled their artistic differences before the film is finalized. After that point, any one of the authors has a right to object to abuse of the film as a whole, or of any part that he or she created. However, the right to restrict the use of one's individual contribution cannot apply against one's own coauthors, or, indeed, be invoked by the authors against the producer: it is only a right against the outside world. The case of the film as a whole is different. For example, the conversion of a black and white film into a colorized version, authorized by its own producer, might amount to a violation of the moral right of integrity by him—this is roughly what happened in the *Huston* case, where Ted Turner was responsible for the colorization of films that he owned, which were regarded as masterpieces by the cinema community, including Huston's *Asphalt Jungle.*[29] The company that bought the rights to show the film, but wanted to broadcast it in a colorized version, was also responsible for violating the integrity of the film.[30] In this scenario, any of the coauthors should have standing to sue for the moral right of integrity.

The German approach can be said to defuse the potential tensions of producer-director relations through two features of the law. First, German

---

29. *Huston, supra* note 6. A number of well-known directors objected to colorization. See Woody Allen's article in the *New York Times, supra* note 1.

30. The case concerned the broadcast of the film by France's LaCinq network. It is interesting that over-dubbing of foreign films in French does not seem to attract the sanction of moral rights, and remains a common practice in France.

law does something important: it restricts the general rules on moral rights in order to accommodate the special nature of film. It does so through a number of special provisions. The law includes a special section on film rights,[31] and in this part, the possibility of distortion of a film is weighed against the requirements of commercial exploitation. In particular, where the "production and exploitation" of the film is concerned, the German provision will only allow "gross distortions" to be prevented. Importantly, "[e]ach author or right holder shall take the others and the film producer into due account when exercising the right."[32] As an additional point, the producer of the film, himself, is also granted a kind of quasi-moral right against distortion, which allows him "to prohibit any distortion or abridgment of the video recording or video and audio recording which may jeopardize his legitimate interests."[33] Of course, the producer's right against distortion is not a moral right in the usual sense—it is a right arising from economic considerations, and it may be transferred.[34] But the objective is clearly to achieve fair recognition of the producer's contribution to the production of a film. As a final point, it should be noted that the moral right of an author to withdraw his work from circulation, whether for a change of opinion or for concern about the inadequate exploitation of the work, is not available to those involved in the making of a film.[35]

Secondly, German law provides a useful criterion for evaluating the claims of potential coauthors of a film: "separability." The test to be applied is whether a contribution can be commercially exploited on its own as a "separate" work; if not, then the creators of those inseparable elements will be considered joint authors of the work.[36] The application of this criterion considerably reduces the claims of coauthorship, excluding, in particular, the possibility of scriptwriters and composers of musical scores being treated as joint authors of the film.[37] The device is a clever way of isolating the creative contribution of the makers of a film. If the creative contribution truly applies to the film as a whole, and not merely to a component part, then the person making that contribution is entitled to claim authorship. As Pascal Kamina observes, "[U]nder such a rule, only the director, the director of photography and possibly the editor could claim co-authorship in the film."[38]

---

31. *See* Part III of the German Copyright Law: Urheberrechtsgesetz, 9.9.1965, Bundesgesetzblatt, Teil I [BGBl. I] at 1273, last amended by Gesetz, 10.8.2004, BGBl. I at 1774 § 13, *available at* http://www.iuscomp.org/gla/statutes/UrhG.htm (last visited Apr. 28, 2010) [German Copyright Law]. The translation is provided by WIPO.

32. *Id.*, art. 93.

33. *Id.*, art. 93.

34. *Id.*, art. 94.

35. *Id.*, art. 90 on "Limitation of Rights."

36. *Id.*, art. 8.1.

37. Kamina, *supra* note 3, at 157.

38. *Id.*, at 157.

The contrast with the American approach could not be stronger. Insofar as rules on coauthorship apply to a film, as F. Jay Dougherty points out, "an independently copyrightable contribution is required."[39] If the logic of the German scheme is to isolate the original contribution of the filmmaker, American law looks, instead, at the substantiality—no doubt, in quality as well as quantity—of a given contribution to a work. If the contribution is sufficient to qualify for copyright on its own, the contributor may merit the title of "author."

American law is firmly anchored in an economic understanding of film. The producer can be identified as the owner of the film, and the issue of who is its author is therefore of nominal importance. The question is left open— American law does not identify any individuals as the author, or joint authors, of a film.[40] The solution to authorship problems in the U.S. context is generally thought to lie in the work-for-hire doctrine, with the practical realization that most of the contributors to a film work as employees of the producer. Contractual arrangements for the making of a film can also clarify matters; although contracts imply flexibility, the general practice is to assign all rights to the producer.[41]

These traditions have their roots in the studio system, which saw directors and other creative contributors to a film working as employees of the studio.[42] Conflicts between studio and artist are, of course, an integral part of Hollywood history; and, in a notorious chapter of American life, the McCarthy era blacklist tore apart these relationships as some studios condemned creative people suspected of Communist sympathies.[43] The blacklist episode was not only a clash between studio and artist; like all repressive movements, it also led to general contamination of the environment, with artists turning against one another under conditions of extraordinary pressure.[44] The potential for conflict is inherent in human relationships, but overwhelming evidence supports the power of environment to shape relationships. Legal norms can influence individual and collective behavior in extraordinary ways beyond the courtroom, and litigation is only one of the many

---

39. Dougherty, *supra* note 16, at 276–77; this rule has been upheld by the Ninth Circuit, in particular.
40. *Id.*, at 269.
41. *See id.*, at 269–71.
42. *See* United States Copyright Office, *Technological Alterations to Motion Pictures and Other Audiovisual Works: Implications for Creators, Copyright Owners, and Consumers* (A Report of the Register of Copyrights, Washington, DC 1989), 10 Loyola Ent. L.J. 1, 22–5 (1990).
43. A fascinating collection of notes and interviews from the people targeted on the blacklist can be found in Patrick McGilligan & Paul Buhle, Tender Comrades: A Backstory of the Hollywood Blacklist (St. Martin's Griffin 1999); Paul Buhle & David Wagner, Blacklisted: The Film Lover's Guide to the Hollywood Blacklist (Palgrave Macmillan 2003).
44. *See* McGilligan & Buhle, *supra* note 43.

measures of the "success" of a law.[45] A moral rights framework could alter the entire chemistry of film industry relationships, even with little or no increase at all in the number of lawsuits.

In the case of *Aalmuhammed v. Lee*,[46] the Ninth Circuit Court of Appeals showed extreme reluctance to grant the status of a coauthor to Mr. Aalmuhammed, a consultant who made an important contribution to Spike Lee's 1992 film on the controversial African-American Muslim activist, Malcolm X. Aalmuhammed was credited on the film as "Islamic Technical Consultant," but he felt that this designation did not provide fair recognition of his work. The situation was complicated by the fact that, unusually, there was no written contract between Aalmuhammed and either Spike Lee or the film's producers.[47] Dougherty describes Aalmuhammed's involvement in the film:

> There was evidence he suggested script revisions that were included in the film, directed [star Denzel] Washington and other actors in several scenes, created at least two entire scenes with new characters, translated material from Arabic for subtitles, provided voice-overs in his own voice, and edited parts of the film.[48]

Dougherty argues that Hollywood convention should have allowed Aalmuhammed to cross the threshold into coauthorship. Instead, in the absence of explicit contractual arrangements to that effect, it now appears that it will be exceptionally difficult to qualify as a joint author of an American film.

In the *Spike Lee* case, the court's consideration of film authorship in American law could have provided an interesting clarification of this point. But the court's comments generated further confusion on an already peculiar issue. Questions of authorship primarily arise in American law when the work-for-hire doctrine does not apply, or in the absence of specific contractual arrangements between the parties. Ownership of the work is what counts. Unless and until the authorship of a film implies concrete rights and obligations, the designation of author may have little importance. From a moral rights perspective, a clarification of these issues under American law is imperative, because the exercise of moral rights depends on establishing authorship. At the same time, it seems unlikely that the producer's contribution

---

45. It should be duly noted that lack of litigation can also indicate the success of a regulatory framework.

46. 202 F.3d 1227 (9th Cir. 2000).

47. *See* Dougherty, *supra* note 16, at 276, n. 277; Dougherty's informative comments about contract practices in the movie industry conclude with the remark that "Perhaps Aalmuhammed's arrangement was not formally documented because he did not fall into one of those categories at the inception of his relationship with the production company."

48. *Id.*, at 277 (footnotes omitted).

to a film will be sufficient for him to qualify as the holder of the moral right, leading, once again, to the classic potential for conflict between producer and director, owner of the copyright and author of the work.[49]

The court found that there was enough evidence of an authorial contribution to Spike Lee's film to justify its examination of the possibility of coauthorship, but it proceeded to find that the contribution of a coauthor must be more than simply a contribution that is "creative" in nature. According to Dougherty, the required contribution amounts to "an extreme expression of the romantic authorship concept."[50] The test established by the judge in this case was to assess two factors: the degree of "control" over the work exercised by the person claiming joint authorship, and the extent to which that person's contribution is ultimately responsible for the work's "public appeal." Dougherty is rightly skeptical about these tests:

> Judge Kleinfeld's laudable goal was to encourage authors' consultation with others during the creative process and to limit the risk of claims by overreaching contributors. His approach may encourage authors to consult, but it will arguably discourage other people from consulting with them. It does not solve the problem of overreaching contributors, because it may be considered entrenchment for the author to use any minimally creative expressive material a contributor provides. Also, it may not really benefit production companies because the tests of control and of audience appeal are inherently unpredictable and uncertain.[51]

Of course, the emphasis on contractual arrangements for film is not by any means unique to the United States, or to common law countries. Contractual arrangements also enjoy pride of place in regulating the relationships among different contributors to a film in the Continental systems. From one perspective, the role of contracts makes sense: contracts provide a measure of flexibility to deal with the complexities of individual relationships and circumstances involved in the making of a film. On the other hand, the issues that arise are likely to have many points in common from one film production scenario to the next, and some basic level of regulation to establish rules that reflect these commonalities would make sense. The failure to do so is little more than a form of tacit cooperation on the part of governments with the power of production houses, which are likely to enjoy the advantages of disproportionate bargaining power when film contracts are concluded.

---

49. Dougherty describes the transformation of the roles of producer and director through the history of film and concludes that "today, studio production executives focus more on business matters and the director's importance has correspondingly increased." (footnote omitted). *See id.*, at 312.

50. *Id.*, at 277.

51. *Id.*, at 281.

Money is important, but without creative input, how can a viable film be developed for either critical or mass-market tastes? In fact, both financial resources and creative skill are needed for any film venture to succeed. The problem of unequal bargaining power is recognized in both common law and European countries, but the specific issue of bargaining inequality in artistic relationships seems to receive greater attention in the European context. In particular, moral rights play a role in alleviating this inequality. In Europe, restrictions on the scope of artistic contracts, and on the allowability of waivers of moral rights, leads to a situation where film relationships function in an environment of greater legal rigidity, but in which, fairness for artists may become an achievable goal.[52]

Appropriately enough, the regulation of author-producer relationships receives interesting consideration in Italian law. Italy, a country with a brilliant tradition of intellectual cinema, has some of the most elegant provisions on film moral rights among the European Union countries. Italian law clearly identifies the "author of the subject-matter, the author of the scenario, the composer of the music and the artistic director" as joint authors of the film; rights of exploitation are, however, held by producers.[53] The Italian law provides that a producer has the right to make "necessary" modifications to the contributions for the purpose of "cinematographic adaptation," presumably with commercial viability in mind.[54] Importantly, any disagreement between an author and a producer about modifications to the film are subject to adjudication by a government panel.[55]

---

52. An example of how this occurs in the Russian context is discussed by Elena Muravina & Karina Ayrapetova, *Making the Twain Meet: Cross-Border Entertainment Transactions between Russia and the United States*, INTELLECTUAL PROPERTY: EASTERN EUROPE AND THE CIS (*forthcoming* 2010) [Muravina & Ayrapetova].

53. *See* Italian Copyright Act, arts. 44 & 45, respectively. Legge 22 aprile 1941 No. 633, Protezione del diritto d'autore e di altri diritti connessi al suo esercizio (G.U. No. 166 del 16 Iuglio 1941), text consolidated to Feb. 9, 2008, *available at* http://www.interlex.it/testi/l41_633.htm (last visited Apr. 28, 2010) [Italian Copyright Act]. An earlier version of the law is available in English translation in the WIPO Collection of Laws for Electronic Access. *See* Law No. 633 of Apr. 22, 1941, for the Protection of Copyright and Other Rights Connected with the Exercise Thereof (as amended up to Nov. 16, 1994), *available at* http://www.wipo.int/clea/en/text_html.jsp?lang=en&id=2475 (last visited Apr. 28, 2010).

54. Italian Copyright Act, *supra* note 53, art. 47; the first part states, "The producer shall have the right to make such modifications in works utilized in a cinematographic work as are necessary for their cinematographic adaption."

55. *Id.*, art. 47, states: "In the absence of agreement between the producer and one or more of the authors referred to in Article 44 of this Law, the question whether modifications effected or to be effected in a cinematographic work are necessary shall be decided by the Chairman of the Council of Ministers in accordance with the rules contained in the Regulations. The findings of the College shall be final."

This provision adds a nice touch of objectivity to the thorny question of disputes over cinematographic transformation.[56] The Italian terminology is evocative, because it draws attention to a curious fact: in a sense, a film is always an adaptation of the underlying work of the contributors. When a screenplay becomes a film, for example, the director is involved in retelling the story originally expressed in the medium of the screenplay through a completely different form of narration—the composite work, blending images and sound with words, that is the film. What works well in the screenplay may or may not be effective in the context of the film.

Film moral rights become even more interesting in the case of a film that is made out of a pre-existing work, such as a book. Not only are the moral rights of film coauthors involved, but the rights of the original author of the underlying work must also must be considered. Selling the rights to film a novel, for example, will not take away the novelist's moral rights.[57] The problem of maintaining the integrity of a literary work in the case of a film adaptation can be exceptionally difficult. The demands of the new medium may be very different from the conventions of the original form. What is perfection in one genre may be dysfunctional in another.

In an interview, director Alfred Hitchcock claimed that he would not film a great work of literature such as Dostoevsky's *Crime and Punishment*, because "in Dostoyevsky's novel there are many, many words and all of them have a function . . . . [T]o really convey that in cinematic terms, substituting the language of the camera for the written word, one would have to make a six- to ten-hour film." His interlocutor, François Truffaut adds, "Theoretically, a masterpiece is something that has already found . . . its definitive form."[58]

Italian law also provides explicitly that the authors shall enjoy a right of attribution that includes their names and details of their roles in the production. In contrast to German law, it also provides that a producer's failure either to finish production or, indeed, to show the work within a period of three years will release all participants from their contractual obligations, and render them free to do whatever they choose with their respective contributions.[59]

Russia is a post-Communist country with an important tradition of film-making. Its new Civil Code provisions, valid from January 1, 2008, include

---

56. Of course, it must be assumed that the government body charged with this determination makes an objective assessment, and is not unduly influenced by the power of the producer or vulnerable to corruption.

57. For an interesting Indian case on this issue, see *Mannu Bhandari*, *supra* note 11. The case involved the Bollywood adaptation of a literary Hindi novel and was a seminal moral rights precedent.

58. François Truffaut, with the collaboration of Helen G. Scott, Hitchcock 72 (rev. ed. Simon and Schuster 1984) [Truffaut, *Hitchcock*].

59. Italian Copyright Act, *supra* note 53, art. 50.

moral rights in film.[60] As in the civil law countries of Western Europe, Russian law considers the film to be an expression of coauthorship, and the authors of the film are the director-producer,[61] the author of the screenplay,[62] and the composer of original musical works, with or without words, used in the film. In Russian law, however, it is clear that two works exist at all times: moral rights subsist in the screenplay for the film, for example, and also, in the film as a finished product. As Elena Muravina and Karina Ayrapetova point out, Russian industry practice is to transfer rights in both the screenplay and the film from the screenwriter to the person exploiting the film, notably, the producer.[63] However, these kinds of licensing arrangements can only clarify the exploitation of economic rights: moral rights remain with the authors, and cannot be either transferred or waived under Russian law. Again, Muravina and Ayrapetova illustrate how Russian agreements work within the moral rights framework, by providing that the transfer of rights to a producer occurs "to the full extent now or hereafter permitted by applicable law."[64] Crucially, the moral rights available to the authors of the film are limited to rights of name and the inviolability of the work;[65] they do not benefit from a right of withdrawal either in relation to the underlying work or with respect to the film itself.[66] But Russian law, too, is unsatisfactory in failing to clarify the relationships among coauthors. In particular, the role of the director in finalizing the use of screenplay and music is not recognized; in the absence of clarification, it would appear that the moral rights of all three coauthors are treated on an equal basis. This model of filmmaking is apparently collaborative in nature; but how practical is it? Without any provision for the special, or supervisory, role of the director, the moral rights of the screenwriter or the film composer could interfere with the process of finalizing the film. Unlike French law, no reference is made in Russian law to the need for collaborative agreement among the authors in order establish the final version of the film.

On the question of film authorship, the example of India offers some insight. It is typical for India to represent, and somehow reconcile, apparent contradictions. This rule of Indian culture applies perfectly to film. India is a developing country that is also the world's largest producer of films.

---

60. The subject had been closely addressed in the Draft Civil Code provisions of 2001, which were largely, though not entirely, followed in the 2008 Russian Civil Code. *See* Sundara Rajan, *Copyright and Creative Freedom*, *supra* note 8, at 188–98.
61. The Russian term is *"regissër-postanovshchik."* *See* 2008 Russian Civil Code, *supra* note 23, art. 1263.2(1).
62. *"Avtor stsenariya." See id.*, art. 1263.2(2).
63. *See* Muravina & Ayrapetova, *supra* note 52.
64. *Id.*
65. 2008 Russian Civil Code, *supra* note 23, art. 1228(2).
66. *Id.*, art. 1269.

The garishness of its commercial film industry may be unparalleled; the delicacy of its art cinema is as exquisite as the petals of a rose.[67]

The divide between economic ownership and creative integrity plays itself out in the Indian film community with unique intensity. As in its copyright law overall, the Indian treatment of film reveals an interesting inner tension between a common law tradition and a developing country perspective. Under the Indian Copyright Act, there is no ambiguity about the authorship of a film: the producer is the author.[68] However, the extensive treatment of moral rights in the Indian Copyright Act makes no special provision for film. Instead, section 57 of the Indian Copyright Act identifies the "author" of the work as the beneficiary of a permanent right of attribution, and a right of integrity that lasts at least as long as the copyright in a work. Since moral rights are not excluded from "cinematographic works," two logical results follow. First, moral rights of attribution and integrity exist in Indian films. Secondly, those rights are enjoyed by the producer.

On this second issue, the Indian Copyright Act creates an anomalous situation. Producers, who are the economic forces behind the work, enjoy moral rights. But moral rights are normally held by the individuals who represent the creative forces engaged in a work. In addition, section 2 (l) (uu) of the Indian Copyright Act specifies only that the producer must be "a person who takes the initiative and responsibility for making the work." Nothing in the Indian Copyright Act specifies that the human person, alone, is entitled to moral rights.[69] By defining the producer as the "author" of a film, Indian law creates an unusual situation, where a corporation could hold moral rights in a film.[70]

---

67. The most famous of Indian art-film directors is certainly Satyajit Ray (1921–1992), whose Bengali films have acquired an international cult following.

68. *See* Indian Copyright Act, sec. 2(d)(v); a look at the pending amendment bill shows that this provision will remain the same. Indian Copyright Act 1957, Act 14 of 1957, sec. 57; the act is published online by the Government of India at http://copyright.gov.in/Documents/Copy-rightRules1957.pdf (last visited Apr. 28, 2010). [Indian Copyright Act]. The proposed Bill is available on the website of PRS Legislative Research at http://prsindia.org/uploads/media/Copyright%20Act/Copyright%20Bill%202010.pdf (last visited May 2, 2010) [2010 Indian Amendment Bill].

69. Nothing in the overall logic of the Indian moral rights scheme seems to exclude the possibility of corporate moral rights. *See* Mira T. Sundara Rajan, *Moral Rights in Developing Countries: The Example of India*, 8(5) & 8(6) J. INTELL. PROP. RIGHTS 357 & 449 (2003), *available at* http://nopr.niscair.res.in/bitstream/123456789/4907/1/JIP%208(5)%20357-374.pdf (last visited Apr. 28, 2010), and http://nopr.niscair.res.in/bitstream/123456789/4911/1/JIPR%208(6)%20449-461.pdf (last visited Apr. 28, 2010) [Sundara Rajan, *Moral Rights in Developing Countries, Parts I & II*].

70. The same consequence occurs in Japanese law, where the "author" holds moral rights, but "author" is not defined to exclude corporations. On the contrary, the Japanese law explicitly provides that a "legal person" may hold more moral rights. *See* Japanese Copyright Act, arts. 15(1) & (2), available in English translation on the website of the Copyright Research and Information Center at http://www.cric.or.jp/cric_e/clj/clj.html (last visited Apr. 28, 2010) [Japanese Copyright Act].

Indeed, the situation of economic rights in film is also far from clear-cut in Indian law. Problems arise because the layering of rights in a film is acknowledged, but the relationships that it leads to are not clarified. Soundtracks are a case in point. *Filmi* music is a gigantic industry in India. Regarding the soundtrack to a film, the Indian Copyright Act suggests that there is a separate copyright for a musical work used in the film, and that this copyright may itself be split into the rights of music composer and lyricist.[71] And yet, as pointed out by a paper produced for the Indian Ministry of Human Resource Development, the producer has a right to authorize the sale of a film soundtrack. The study states:

> Music is an integral part of any cinematographic work. In India, film soundtracks account for almost 80% of the total music market. Even if [the] film producer has the copyright in the film, the music included in the film is the outcome of efforts undertaken by a separate group of creative people such as the composer, lyricists etc.—each of which is a rightholder of its own right. Generally the producer sells this right to a music company who makes cassettes/CDs of such songs for sale in the market. The incidence of a large number of rights in a single work and the involvement of a variety of right holders make the copyright issue very complicated in cinematographic works.[72]

The internal contradictions in this statement are difficult to reconcile. In particular, if the copyright in the musical works used in the film rests with the composers of those works, the producer can only sell musical rights insofar as is permitted by the contractual arrangements between him and the artists. But in this case, it is not clear why the definition of "cinematographic work" in the Copyright Act includes the musical soundtrack.[73] This line of

---

71. Indian Copyright Act, *supra* note 68, sec. 2(p), defines a "musical work" as "a work consisting of music and [that] includes any graphical notation of such work *but does not include any words or any action intended to be sung, spoken or performed with the music.*" (emphasis added). The Act clearly attempts to separate musical, literary, and dramatic works, as nearly as possible, into watertight compartments—to the extent that a song which includes both music and words is essentially seen by the Act as a composite product containing two works, one musical, one literary.

72. *See* N. K. Nair, A. K. Barman, & Utpal Chattopadhyay, *Study on Copyright Piracy in India* (1999), Sponsored by Ministry of Human Resource Development, Government of India, *available at* http://copyright.gov.in/Documents/STUDY%20ON%20COPYRIGHT%20PIRACY%20IN%20INDIA.pdf (last visited Apr. 21, 2010).

73. But there is little doubt that it does. *See* Indian Copyright Act, *supra* note 68, sec. 2(f):

> (f) "cinematograph film" means any work of visual recording on any medium produced through a process from which a moving image may be produced by any means *and includes a sound recording accompanying such visual recording* and "cinematograph" shall be construed as including any work produced by any process analogous to cinematography including video films. (emphasis added; footnote omitted).

interpretation then raises the problem of competing moral rights among the different participants in the creation of a film. Will the film composer and the director see eye to eye on the use of the music in the film? And, if they do not, what right does an Indian director have to promote his own view? By a supreme irony, the copyright law of the country of Satyajit Ray never so much as mentions the word "director" in relation to a film.[74]

B. The Film as a Derivative Work: An Argument Against Moral Rights?

As these examples show, the composite nature of film has an important legal consequence: it implies an awkward situation of coexisting rights, belonging to different persons, in the same work. When considering moral rights in film, it is essential to resolve the issue of potentially competing rights. An approach that arises in the U.S. context is to consider a film as a "derivative work"—notably, a work derived from the screenplay.

Assessing the meaning of derivative work in American law is an important exercise, especially from a moral rights perspective. This is because the doctrine of unauthorized derivative works operates as one of the most powerful substitutes for formalized moral rights protection in the United States. The argument is a practical one, and it goes as follows. If the editing of a work is sufficiently interventionist, it can create a new work, deemed "derivative" by American courts. Copyright rules require, of course, that the making of any derivative work be authorized by the creator of the original work. Unauthorized editing can therefore lead to a finding of copyright infringement. When plaintiffs object to unauthorized editing because it distorts the original work, the argument becomes a practical substitute for the moral right of integrity. This argument led the Monty Python troupe of comedians to victory in their well-known lawsuit against America's ABC network, *Gilliam v. ABC*.[75] ABC broadcast edited versions of skits by the comedy troupe, apparently in order to protect viewers from material that they could find offensive. But the comedians felt that removing off-color references from their work deprived their humor of its original quality.[76]

---

74. Indian Copyright Act, *supra* note 68. The word director appears three times, in sec. 69, and is used in the Indian sense of head, or "director" of a company or firm.

75. Gilliam v. American Broadcasting Companies, 538 F.2d 14 (2d Cir. 1976) [*Gilliam*].

76. *Id.* The British case of *Frisby v. BBC* [1967] Ch. 932 (Ch) [*Frisby*] is similar: it involves the removal of single, "obscene" word from a radio play for broadcast by the BBC. These cases are interesting because they remind us of the rebellious and nonconformist aspects of creative expression, which can easily place artists at odds with social norms in the normal exercise of their professions.

As illustrated by *Gilliam*, American law shows a broad appreciation of what constitutes a derivative work. Yet, even in the American context, it does not seem entirely correct to adopt the terminology of "derivative" work for a film. There is some truth in the idea that a film is derived from an underlying screenplay and other component parts, such as music. However, a connotation of inferiority seems implicit in the term "derivative." It conveys the idea that there is something "secondary" about the work—that, like a performance in relation to a composition, film is a kind of work which depends fundamentally on another work for its existence. There is a definite hierarchy involved; the original work takes precedence over the "derivative" work.[77]

To modern eyes, it seems unsatisfactory to characterize a film in this way. When we do so, the hierarchy that is established places the director below the screenwriter. This view may have made sense at an earlier point in film history, when this form of creative expression was itself less developed. Pascal Kamina's observations about the initial approach to film copyright are interesting, although he seems to draw inadequate attention to the practical reasons why the director gradually grew into authorship. Kamina points out the role of aesthetic theories of filmmaking:

> Following the success of sound movies, in the 1930s and the 1940s, the director as creator became secondary to the writer. This conception of the director as a mere technician was clearly adopted in Europe in pre-war case law and legal literature. In this respect, it is interesting to observe that, under the list of co-authors set by the Italian Act of 1941 and the French Act of 1957, the director comes last, the first author mentioned being the scriptwriter. Then came the so-called *auteur* theory, initiated by French film critics.[78]

A consideration of the relationship between a film and its component parts may help to clarify this issue. For example, it is true that a film depends

---

77. *But see* Kamina, *supra* note 3, at 291–92, "Basic problems of moral rights protection in relation to films"; he suggests that this may be appropriate and comments that "audiovisual works are almost always derivative works, the production of which involves the use or adaptation of numerous pre-existing or underlying works (literary works, scripts, music, etc.). As a consequence, moral rights problems arise not only between film contributors and producers or users, but also between film authors and authors of adapted or included works. This creates potential conflicts of interests (too often, film directors are ready to claim, as creators, rights they refuse to authors of adapted works). Of course, when the law acknowledges the collaborative nature of audiovisual works, such conflicts can also exist between the co-authors of the film. In practice, producers and users are faced with an unprecedented number of potential moral rights claims, and with the difficulty of identifying their origins." It seems unnecessarily problematic to place collaborators and the director into the same relation as author of adapted work and director.

78. *Id.*, at 155–56 (footnotes omitted).

on performances, but there are several reasons why it would be inaccurate to characterize a film as a work "derived" from those performances. Notably, a performance can be provided by more than one actor. Countless examples of actor substitutions exist in Hollywood history. Even a film destined to become as famous as Alfred Hitchcock's *Vertigo* saw the director settling for his second choice of female lead, actress Kim Novak—she went on to deliver a classic performance.[79]

Indeed, it is difficult to say that the underlying performance truly qualifies as an *independent* copyright work at all, since the purpose of the performance is to be used in conjunction with the other elements of the film. A screenplay could be published as such, or re-written as a play; the musical score could be produced independently of the film. But this would certainly take these works out of the context in which their realization was first imagined; it might also require some adaptation of the works in question. It is not too fine a point of legal analysis to call these versions of a film's component parts new works—no more than saying that an edited version of Monty Python's television skits is a new, "derivative" work in its own right[80]—but the interdependence of the works makes the question difficult. Moreover, the interdependence between a film and its component parts reflects a new kind of hierarchy. The final version of the film is at the summit of this pyramid; it represents a higher-level work than any one component considered on its own terms.

This is not to attempt to devalue the importance of contributions to a film by the artists whose work makes it possible. Rather, the objective is to try to understand the creative process of filmmaking more accurately. As this discussion suggests, the process is clearly collaborative; but there is an undeniable element of hierarchy involved. Someone must be responsible for coordinating the countless elements that combine to make a film. And in that process, it is at least possible that the creative vision of that person, or persons, is engaged.

The principle of creative authorship in films has been recognized at least since the 1960s. The pioneering article, *A Certain Tendency in French Cinema*, by French film critic and, later, director, François Truffaut, is considered a manifesto of the "authorship" theory of filmmaking. With a nod to

---

79. *See* Truffaut, *Hitchcock, supra* note 58. The influential critics' poll by *Sight & Sound* magazine is conducted ever ten years; the 2002 edition saw *Vertigo* emerge as the number two film of all time (after Orson Welles' *Citizen Kane*). *See* the website of the British Film Institute at http://www.bfi.org.uk/sightandsound/topten/ (last visited Apr. 28, 2010).

80. *Gilliam, supra* note 75. Colin Tapper suggests that a useful test to determine whether a new "original" work has been created is to consider the issue of whether the derivative creation requires—or justifies—a new title (private communication, Jun. 16, 2010).

Truffaut and the directors of the French "New Wave,"[81] directors whose creative contribution is recognized are known as "*auteurs*." France has pioneered the recognition of a director's moral rights in its copyright law. The director's role in the creation of a film is one of practical leadership. To varying degrees, and according to the type of film, it may also be creative in its own right.

It is worth emphasizing this last point. Film is not just a technological creation; it is also a pure, classic example of creative expression. In contrast to computer programs or databases—other examples of works where the author confronts the dual task of assembling pre-existing components and generating a creative approach to those parts at a higher level—there is no need here for discussions about the nature of the contribution made by the filmmaker. The form may be new, but the essence is traditional. The end result is clearly an original creative work in the sense in which creativity has been recognized at least since the Romantic era. We do not need to ask whether the investment of labor should be sufficient to recognize moral rights. Moral rights, which seek to protect the creative expression of the author, are in natural sympathy with film.

Perhaps the director can be properly compared to the conductor of a symphony. The conductor plays no musical instrument himself, but he coordinates and guides the playing of the musicians in the orchestra. Indeed, without the conductor's overarching comprehension of the musical score and vision about how the different parts are meant to work together, it is questionable whether an orchestra of even the most renowned individual players could realize a symphony as it is meant to be heard. In this sense, the conductor's instrument is the orchestra as a whole. The conductor is in a position to see the larger picture; so, too, is the director of a film.

If we accept the "*auteur*" theory of filmmaking, even to a limited extent, it becomes difficult to justify the exclusion of moral rights from film. As a matter of principle, they should be protected. In practice, however, the striking complexity of the human relations embedded in a film may lead to intractable legal problems. Legal responses to these concerns must be extraordinarily well-conceived before they can hope to succeed.

C. Practical Challenges: Film Litigation in India and France

Given the complexity of this form of creative expression, it should come as no surprise that the protection of moral rights in film has proven to be a controversial issue for the international community. Two kinds of problems arise. The first

---

81. *Nouvelle Vague.*

involves the practical impact of moral rights on an expensive industry. Michael Handler characterizes film as "the product of an interdependent relationship between collaborative artistic creation and economic investment,"[82] and Schuyler M. Moore offers striking statistics to show that "[m]ost films lose money."[83]

The second is the potential for competing interests among those involved in the making of a film. Conflicts can arise in three ways: between the author of a film and the performers featured in it;[84] among the different "authors" of a film, themselves, such as conflicts between the director, screenwriter, or composer of original film music;[85] and, specifically, in the competing claims and interests dividing the director and the producer of a film.

This last relationship is perhaps the most difficult of all. In the common law countries, authorship of a film has traditionally been accorded to the producer. This continues to be the case, implicitly in the United States, and explicitly, in India.[86] However, better recognition for cinema as a creative art has led to an improved status for directors in the common law world. In the UK, current law reflects the need to harmonize the British tradition of recognizing producers with the Continental preference for directors. The result, however, creates some awkwardness: the producer is still considered the "author" of a film, but the British moral rights in the film are enjoyed by the director. Canada has no provisions clarifying who is to be the author of a "cinematographic work," leading to a situation of persistent ambiguity about moral rights in film.[87]

The resistance of America's film lobby to moral rights is well-known, and it is easy enough to understand the industry's fears about moral rights.[88] With so many creative elements coming together in the making of a film, moral

---

82. Michael Handler, Continuing Problems with Film Copyright (2008) University of New South Wales Faculty of Law Research Series 51 at 51 http://www.austlii.org/au/journals/ UNSWLRS/2008/51.html (last visited Aug. 17, 2010), originally published in 6 New DIRECTIONS IN COPYRIGHT LAW ch. 7 (Fiona Macmillan ed., Cheltenham, UK, and Northampton MA, USA: Edward Elgar 2007).

83. Schuyler M. Moore, *Financing Drama: The Challenges of Film Financing Can Produce as Much Drama as Takes Place on the Screen*, 24 LOS ANGELES LAW 2 (May 2008), *available at* http://www.stroock.com/SiteFiles/Pub610.pdf (last visited Apr. 21, 2010).

84. Of course, conflict can also arise with other contributors to a film who do not enjoy authorship status, notably, those responsible for the technical aspects of its creation.

85. *See* French CPI, *supra* note 21, art. L113-7 on the authorship of a film, which identifies not only these three persons as coauthors of the film, but also includes the possibility of an author of a spoken text, or the author of an adaptation, in this group.

86. *See* Indian Copyright Act, *supra* note 68, sec. 2(d)(v).

87. *See* Stephen Fraser, *Who Owns the Copyright in a Canadian Film? Answer: It Depends (And That's the Problem)* (2005), *available at* http://www.fraser-elaw.com/pdf/fraser_article_1.pdf (last visited Apr. 21, 2010) [Fraser, *Canadian Film*].

88. For an analysis of Hollywood's position, see Fraser, *Berne, CFTA, NAFTA and GATT, supra* note 7.

rights could translate into legal chaos, depriving films of their chance to reach the public. The economic consequences could be disastrous. Filmmaking requires a heavy financial commitment, and if moral rights led to the suppression of a film, the losses could make the industry unsustainable. Indeed, even the delay of a release date could translate into lost marketing opportunities.[89] For a medium based in the year-round paradise of Southern California's climate, Hollywood remains a seasonally driven industry.[90]

But there is nothing new about these concerns. In fact, many of the same issues could arise in relation to economic rights, as well. Competing economic rights and conflicts over the uses of works could present a serious challenge to the successful release of a film. Screenwriters and composers can certainly lay claim to copyright in their own work. Why do these same concerns militate against moral rights?

The answer to this question is partly practical, partly psychological. From the practical point of view, mechanisms exist to address the "layering" of economic rights in a film which are not available for moral rights. In particular, two possibilities should be noted. The first lies within copyright law itself—the "work-for-hire" doctrine, which allows the copyright in a work to be acquired by the purchaser. The doctrine is usual in the common law countries, but, in keeping with the tradition of protecting authors' rights, it does not operate in many civil law countries. Secondly, copyright contracts can address the ambiguities of film collaboration, clarifying the extent of rights and limitations when an underlying work becomes an integral component of the film.

The example of a screenplay provides a helpful illustration of how film contracts can work. Copyright in the screenplay may be transferred to the producer, or director, of the film; alternatively, the right to use the screenplay in the film may be licensed. No contract can be perfect, and copyright contracts are no exception. There is often room for dispute over the terms of a contractual relationship.[91] But a contract can hope to be reasonably comprehensive in defining the mutual obligations of the parties. Its success is ultimately measured by whether it is able to provide an effective working environment for the relationship. Beyond the terms of the contract, artists still have recourse against one another under tort law, and can sue, for example, for defamation. They may also find themselves in a position where the terms of the contract are considered unfair, and are corrected by judges who

---

89. *See* Dustin Putman, *Hollywood's Theories on Movie Release Dates* (Oct. 20, 2000), *available at* http://www.themovieboy.com/essays_releasedates.htm (last visited Apr. 21, 2010/ [Putman].

90. *Id.*

91. Examples include *Shostakovich v. Twentieth Century-Fox Film Corp.*, 80 N.Y.S.2d 575 (N.Y. Sup. Ct. 1948), *aff'd*, 87 N.Y.S.2d 430 (N.Y. App. Div. 1949) [*Shostakovich*], and *Huston, supra* note 6.

imply new terms into the contractual relationship.[92] Doctrines such as unconscionability, duress, and the outright claim of unequal bargaining power are at their disposal.[93]

The introduction of moral rights into a creative relationship would alter this situation in some ways, but how significant those changes would be is unclear. Two difficulties can occur. First, in an important contrast with economic rights, moral rights are not automatically conveyed to the buyer when economic rights are transferred. For example, the sale of a screenplay does not necessarily mean that its author will forego his moral rights. On the contrary, unless explicit provision is made for the moral rights, they will continue to rest with the author. If, as in the French scenario, the law provides that moral rights *cannot* be waived, this leads to what a common law lawyer might see as chronic imperfection in the assignment of copyright.[94] A contract cannot be used to waive moral rights. In theory, at the very least, the uncertainty generated by a continuing right of the author becomes a permanent part of the relationship. The screenwriter could revoke his permission to use the screenplay at any stage of the creative process, and the production would then be affected.

When attempting to assess the seriousness of these consequences, a consideration of the French example may be instructive. The French experience suggests how moral rights litigation works in practice—the practical solutions to disputes over film. The results seem reassuring. France's recognition of moral rights is extensive, and in relation to film, France recognizes at least three potential "authors" of the work: the director, the author of the screenplay, and the composer of the original musical works used in the film.[95] There have been a number of cases on film which involve conflicts between creative authors.[96] But the outcome of those cases has not been the suppression of a film. Rather, corrections are required before the film can be released. The goal is still to circulate the film to the public and to let it

---

92. *See, for example,* Schroeder Music Publishing Co. v. MaCaulay (Instone), [1974] 1 W.L.R. 1308.

93. The doctrine of unconscionability, in particular, is directly relevant to copyright contracts as it specifically embodies the problem of unequal bargaining power. As John D. McCamus points out, an allegation of unconscionability places the stronger party in the position of having to prove that the agreement is not unfair, unjust, or unreasonable. The doctrine is clearly explained in JOHN D. McCAMUS, THE LAW OF CONTRACTS 405 (Irwin Law 2005; digital ed. also available), and in EWAN McKENDRICK, CONTRACT LAW: TEXT, CASES AND MATERIALS ch. 20 (3d ed. Oxford Univ. Press 2008).

94. CPI, *supra* note 21, art. L121-1, provides that moral rights are "inalienable and non-transferable" ["*inaliénable et imprescriptible*"]. These important issues are examined in the notes to Article L121-1 in Sirinelli et al., *supra* note 25.

95. As noted above, the CPI, *supra* note 21, also makes provision for the adaptation of a film from another work. As the authors of a film, Article L113-7 includes the author of the screenplay; the author of the adaptation; the author of the spoken text; and the author of the musical compositions, with or without words, specially composed for the film; and the director.

96. *See* Sirinelli et al., *supra* note 25, at 119–21, for a selection of principles from cases.

achieve its audience potential. A moral rights claim is not likely to lead to the suppression of a film. Although French law provides for the moral right of withdrawal, it is difficult to see how the right could be exercised successfully by a single participant without the agreement of the others involved in the making of the film.[97]

There is no doubt that the world of French cinema is a different place from Hollywood. It is a smaller industry, perhaps with limited commercial potential in an English-dominated world. France may also represent a less litigious society than the United States, although it is not clear that French artists are especially hesitant to sue for their moral rights. But France also has relatively substantial experience with moral rights in film, and French patterns of litigation can certainly help to inform policies on film in other countries.

The power of the inalienability principle could also be mitigated by making it possible to waive moral rights in at least some circumstances. The special nature of film could justify a system of permitted waivers. In fact, the French provision that considers the moral right in a film to be limited to action against outsiders could be understood as a temporary suspension of disclosure and integrity rights, if not outright waiver of those rights, in favor of one's coauthors.

However, a system such as Canada's approach to moral rights, which allows moral rights to be waived comprehensively, does not seem ideal for film. It might encourage the standardized use of waivers in film contracts, which is what tends to occur in Canadian publishing,[98] and could invalidate the entire moral rights scheme.[99] It is also worth noting that the general availability of waivers may or may not protect a filmmaker from a lawsuit: judges might support a waiver as evidence of industry practice, but they might also strike it down as evidence of unequal bargaining power between the parties involved.[100] Judges should not interpret a contract against the explicit wording of the terms; but their position seems rather awkward. It is difficult

---

97. Note CPI, *supra* note 21, art. L121-6, which allows for the completion of a film in circumstances where one of the coauthors withdraws prematurely from the project.

98. *See, for example*, the website of the Guild of Canadian Film Composers, which, in its model contract, suggests that composers agree to a waiver of integrity, but require attribution to be maintain, http://www.gcfc.ca/Storage/18/1148_model_contract_e.pdf. The Writers' Union of Canada advises authors to "beware" or "stay away from" contractual clauses that require them to give up their moral rights, http://www.writersunion.ca/ht_clausecautions. asp (last visited Apr. 28, 2010). It would be interesting to learn how often Canadian authors who want to retain their moral rights are actually able to do so, as they are often in a position of greatly unequal bargaining power vis-à-vis publishers.

99. *See* Copyright Act, R.S.C. 1985, c. C-42, *available at* http://laws.justice.gc.ca/en/C-42/index. html (last visited Apr. 29, 2010) [Canadian Copyright Act], secs. 14(2)–(4); sec. 14(3) provides a mitigating consideration, that an assignment of copyright does not, by itself, imply waiver of moral rights.

100. The question of how judges see balance of power issues in copyright contracts deserves to be investigated in its own right.

to interpret the law when it seems self-contradictory. Standard-form contracts demand that moral rights be waived, while copyright legislation grants them general recognition. In the Canadian example, this point is an implicit critique of the current legislative framework for moral rights, which is unlikely to change when the Canadian government introduces copyright reforms in the coming year.[101] No challenge to standard-form waivers of moral rights has ever been brought before the Canadian courts.

In Canada, as noted earlier, the situation is complicated by the fact that Canadian legislation does not identify who is considered the author of a film and, therefore, would be entitled to hold the first copyright in it. Additionally, Canada's employment rule, in the film context, offers only a rough analogy to the American work-for-hire doctrine. As Stephen Fraser aptly notes, before copyright can be transferred from an author to an owner under Canadian law, an employment relationship must exist between the two.[102] Is the relationship between the producer of the film and its director such a relationship?—between the producer and the other creative collaborators on the film? It is conceivable that these relationships would be more akin to those between an employer and a consultant—a person hired to work in special circumstances on a given project. If this were the case, the individual would retain copyright in his work, even though it might be a component part in a film. From the perspective of moral rights, the failure to identify an author is, of course, profoundly troublesome, because it leads to a situation of potential conflict involving the moral rights of a number of people. The environment provided by the Canadian Copyright Act for filmmaking is clearly an uncertain universe.

India presents a fascinating comparison with both France and the United States. India's "Bollywood" is the Hindi-speaking cinema of North India; it caters to 300 million Hindi speakers in India, and to a large international market that includes parts of Africa.[103] What is less well-known is that India has an extraordinary tradition of intellectual cinema, though it is now largely eclipsed by Bollywood and its national counterparts, such as "Kollywood," the film industry of South India.[104] The idea of film as art—director as author—is certainly one that India shares with France. At the same time, the

---

101. *See* Bill C-32 tabled by the government on June 2, 2010 and available online, http://www2.parl.gc.ca/HousePublications/Publication.aspx?DocId=4580265&Language=e&Mode=1 (last visited Aug. 17, 2010).

102. Fraser, *Canadian Film*, *supra* note 87.

103. *See* the interesting comments in Jeffrey Larkin, *Bollywood Comes To Nigeria*, 8 SAMAR (Winter/Spring 1997), *available at* http://www.samarmagazine.org/archive/article.php?id=21 (last visited July 18, 2010).

104. The Bengali film industry is known as "Tollywood"; Nigeria's large, video-based industry is now known as "Nollywood."

reality of Indian film as mass-market powerhouse is closely aligned with the American experience.

1. India: Moral Rights in a Culture of Adaptation

In India, development in the entire field of moral rights litigation was initiated by film. The seminal case arose in 1986, not as a dispute among different film authors, but as a conflict over the adaptation of a novel into a film.[105]

a. Producer vs. Author: *Mannu Bhandari*

Mannu Bhandari is a well-known Indian novelist writing in Hindi. Rights to her novel, *Aap ka Bunty*, were purchased by Kala Vikas Pictures, a film production company interested in adapting her book into a film. In the agreement between Ms. Bhandari and the production company, the novelist agreed to allow the director and screenwriter of the film to make changes, in consultation with her, as "necessary" for the production of a "successful" film.[106] Ms. Bhandari would be credited as the author of the original novel.

As the project developed, Ms. Bhandari grew dissatisfied. The film's title was changed by the producers to "The Flow of Time." It was no longer offered as the story of "Bunty," the main character, as in the original title of the novel. The portrayal of the characters, the dialogue, and changes to the ending of the film were all objectionable in her view.[107] Ms. Bhandari finally brought a complaint against the production house, alleging that these modifications amounted to a violation of her moral right of integrity under section 57 of the Indian Copyright Act.

At trial, the judge considered the extent to which the recognition of moral rights is likely to interfere with the successful production and release of a film. The decision turned on an analysis of the contract between writer and producer. The fact that Ms. Bhandari had authorized changes that might be "necessary" to a film adaptation was subject to interpretation. In the court's view, the changes made by the producers fell within these terms.[108] Ms. Bhandari had effectively forfeited her right to object to modifications by the terms of her contract.

---

105. *Mannu Bhandari, supra* note 11.
106. *See* Dine, *supra* note 11, at 561: he quotes the clause in the contract as allowing "certain modifications in [her] novel for the film version, in discussion with [her,] to make it suitable for a successful film."
107. These grounds for the author's dissatisfaction with a film are identified by Dine, *supra* note 11, at 144, who also provides a detailed description of what these changes involved.
108. *See Mannu Bhandari, supra* note 11, para. 6 (quoting from para. 12 of the trial judgment). *See also Mannu Bhandari, supra* note 11, para. 12, disposing of the issue.

But the court then went on to make an apparent error of legal interpretation. At that time, India's moral rights provisions clearly stipulated that "any distortion, mutilation or modification" of a work would violate an author's right of integrity. A second clause provided that "any other action in relation to the said work which would be prejudicial to his honour or reputation" would also violate integrity . However, actions that were *prima facie* "modification[s]" objected to by the author did not require a demonstration that the author's honor or reputation would be affected by the mistreatment of the work. Section 57 has since been amended; but the language of the old provisions is unequivocal.[109] Any modification of the work could violate the right of integrity.

Not only did the court apply the standard of damage to honor or reputation to Ms. Bhandari's complaint, but it also did so in an eccentric manner. Jeffrey Dine calls it "an odd holding." As quoted by the Delhi High Court, the district court judge stated:

> In my view *prima facie* the plaintiff has not been able to establish on record that the defendants have changed the theme[,] distorted or mutilated the novel[,] or damaged the underlying idea thereof. The Plaintiff had *prima facie* authorized the defendants to make necessary changes in order to make a successful film based on the novel . . . . [T]the film is not at all going to harm the reputation of the plaintiff in any manner. The plaintiff's reputation can be harmed in the eyes of those only who have read her novel and seen the film also. Those who have read her novel and seen the film may change their views about the producer, [or] director of the film but not about the plaintiff.[110]

The lower court seemed to feel that the poor quality of the adaptation would make the producers, rather than the author, look deficient in the eyes of the public. But, as Jeffrey Dine suggests, there can be little doubt that the film effectively represents the work of the author to all those who see it.[111] If the film is successful, it may draw a readership to the author. But the issue is a delicate one. A poor adaptation may bring readers to an author who are in search of something that she cannot provide—a happy ending, a graphic sexual story, or, as in the present case, "vulgar dialogue"—or, for the same

---

109. For the pre-1994 sec. 57 provisions of the Indian Copyright Act, *supra* note 68, see website of the Commonwealth Legal Information Institute at http://www.commonlii.org/in/legis/num_act/ca1957133/ (last visited Apr. 28, 2010). The old sec. 57(1) provides that, "the author of a work shall have the right to claim the authorship of the work as well as the right to restrain, or claim damages in respect of—(a) any distortion, mutilation or other modification of the said work; or (b) any other action in relation to the said work which would be prejudicial to his honour or reputation."

110. *Mannu Bhandari, supra* note 11, para. 6. *See* Dine, *supra* note 11, at 561.

111. Dine, *supra* note 11.

reasons, it could drive potential readers away. A faithful adaptation may succeed in conveying the vision of the author, but lead to commercial (or critical)
failure. This situation could reduce the author's readership, or, if people
sense that the original work is good despite the flaws of the film version,
increase it. But it is difficult to imagine a situation where the adaptation of
the work would leave the author of the original work completely untainted.
The court's apparent skepticism about Bollywood movies might not be shared
by other Indians. Its assessment of reputation seems bizarre.[112]

Ms. Bhandari did not allow the issue to rest here: she pursued an appeal to
the High Court of Delhi. The parties then settled their dispute, with Kala
Vikas Pictures agreeing to remove all references to Ms. Bhandari and her
work from the film, and Ms. Bhandari relinquishing her right to claim "any
right or interest" in the film, or to object in any way to its release or distribution. But the parties nevertheless asked the High Court of Delhi to deliver its
legal opinion in order to establish a much-needed precedent on the making of
film adaptations. Ms. Bhandari "insisted that as a committed author she
would like the court to authoritatively resolve the question of the right of the
authors as the problem is repeatedly faced by the authors and there is no judicial decision."[113] Interestingly, the concerns of the defendants seem typical of
the concerns of filmmakers in common law countries about moral rights—

> The defendants' grievance, on the other hand, was that they had made a huge
> investment and have entered into contracts with the distribute choice. According
> to the defendants, the plaintiff has filed the suit with the ulterior motive of
> extracting more money than that paid under the contract.[114]

The request for a decision was a valuable one. Despite the best efforts of
Indian judges, it can take decades for a case to progress through the Indian
legal system. Few, indeed, are the litigants who can see a complaint through
to its ultimate end. For this very reason, judgments may fail to accomplish the
purpose of deterrence—however strongly the Indian courts protect the moral
rights of authors, the likelihood that an author or his heirs would have the
stamina for waiting out a lawsuit is rather slight. Justice, alas, is primarily
available for the wealthy; and, in India, the excellence of an artist does not
necessarily translate into wealth for his or her descendants. Indian cultural
traditions are partly to blame, as wealth and intellectual life are often not
seen as compatible. Colonialism, which outlawed the activities of many

---

112. The court also felt that Ms. Bhandari waited too long to bring her claim and made a finding
  of laches on her part. In particular, it felt that she should not have waited until the film was
  completed to make her complaints known, as appears to have happened in this case.
113. *Mannu Bhandari, supra* note 11, para. 16.
114. *Id.*, para. 3.

Indian authors over a significant period of time, must also bear a share of the responsibility.[115]

Given the extraordinary resources of time and money required to succeed in litigation, Indian legal practice has developed some interesting evolutionary modifications. Notably, an interim judgment in India can be surprisingly influential as a precedent. An interesting example of such a case arose in the moral rights litigation of *Amar Nath Sehgal v. Union of India*. A 1992 interim decision by the Delhi High Court led the Indian government to amend the provisions on moral rights in India's Copyright Act.[116]

In Ms. Bhandari's case, the writer found strong support in the High Court of Delhi.[117] By upholding her claim, the High Court established a pattern that it was to follow unerringly in future cases: the Court acted as an advocate for the individual artist against what it perceived as powerful and corrupt forces that threatened to demean her. For Mannu Bhandari, those forces were represented by the might of Bollywood; in the subsequent litigation of *Amar Nath Sehgal*, the Indian government, itself, was to blame.

The High Court of Delhi made three points that sought to clarify the terms on which film production and moral rights would coexist in the Indian context. First, it considered the role of moral rights in the interpretation of artists' contracts, with special attention to the question of whether and to what extent authors' moral rights may be waived under Indian law. Secondly,

---

115. *See* Mira T. Sundara Rajan, *Moral Rights in the Public Domain: Copyright Matters in the Works of Indian National Poet C. Subramania Bharati*, Singapore J. Legal Stud. 161 (2001) [Sundara Rajan, *Moral Rights in the Public Domain*].

116. Amar Nath Sehgal v. Union of India 2005 (30) PTC 253 (Delhi High Court) [*Sehgal*]; the previous hearing was (1992), Suit No. 2074 (Delhi HC), (1994) 19 Industrial Property Law Reports 160. When queried on this issue, Mr. Jagdish Sagar, who was responsible for drafting the amendments to India's moral rights scheme enacted in 1994, comments only that India was then concerned about implementing the provisions of the Berne Convention on moral rights successfully (statement by Jagdish Sagar, personal communication with the author, Feb. 2009). And, indeed, the 1994 language mirrors the language of Article 6*bis*. However, changes to the provisions would also make it difficult for an author to succeed on a claim for destruction of an artwork, and impossible to be able to proceed with a claim without showing damage to reputation. They respond directly to the circumstances of *Sehgal*.

117. *See* Dine, *supra* note 11: in fact, Ms. Bhandari was unsuccessful at trial, where the judge found that, "a bad film reflects poorly only on the filmmakers," and not on the original author of the work. Interestingly, the holding of the trial court in Ms. Bhandari's case was explicitly rejected by the High Court, which found that distortions in a work of adaptation can also offend the original author's moral rights: *Mannu Bhandari*, *supra* note 11, paras. 4–12. Clearly, the High Court viewed the nature of the relationship between an original work and an adaptation somewhat differently from the trial court, and saw the adaptation as being, in essence, a reproduction of the original work, rather than a new creative work in its own right. This perception was probably due to the Court's general interest in considering the case from the position of Ms. Bhandari and others like her, who might find themselves in relationships of unequal bargaining power.

it examined the meaning of the term "modifications" under section 57 of the Indian Copyright Act and considered its application to the film context. Finally, the Court discussed the social context which brings a special importance to authors' moral rights in India.

i. Moral Rights and Film Contracts

In the contract between producer and author for the making of the film, Mannu Bhandari had agreed to allow "certain modifications" to her novel, to be made upon "discussion with [the writer]," in the interest of creating a "successful" film adaptation.[118] In contrast to the trial judge, the High Court found that Ms. Bhandari's contractual consent to some modification of her work did not deprive her of the moral rights in section 57. "Certain modifications" were allowed; but others could still amount to violations of the integrity right.

Key to the Court's ruling was the notion that the terms of the contract for the assignment of copyright had to be read in conjunction with the provisions of section 57. Accordingly, modifications that were different from those agreed upon in the contract could violate the right of integrity; but so, too, could changes that were egregious in the eyes of the court. Interpretation of the contract on its own terms is not the central issue. Rather, the contract, itself, must fundamentally respect the terms of section 57. As a result, an author's moral rights in Indian law may override the provisions of the contract in much the same way that other kinds of public policy concerns predominate over contractual terms.[119] Justice Wad states:

> Reading the contract with Section 57 it is obvious that modifications which are permissible are such modifications which do not convert the film into an entirely new version from the original novel. The said "certain modifications" should also not distort or mutilate the original novel . . . . As a show business or as a box office collection, a film may be a success, but, it may do no credit to the reputation or the honour of the author. That is why Section 57 insists on the special protection to honour and reputation of the author.[120]

---

118. Clause (b) of the contract between the parties; the contract is reproduced by the Delhi High Court. See *Mannu Bhandari, supra* note 11, para. 8.

119. An interesting British analogy is the *Spycatcher* case, *A-G v. Guardian Newspapers Ltd. (No. 1)* [1987] All E.R. 316; *A-G v. Guardian Newspapers Ltd. (No. 2)* [1988] All E.R. 545; the publication of memoirs by a secret service agent who worked as a double agent during the Cold War led to the effective expropriation of the author's copyright by the British government. In its ruling, the House of Lords felt that it must offer a strong public policy decision to discourage such nefarious activities.

120. *Mannu Bhandari, supra* note 11, para. 11.

The Judge's position was, he felt, supported by the contract itself, which required that the author should be provided "proper publicity" for her contribution to the film. He comments:

> The contract requires that "proper" publicity should be given. The word "proper" has to be interpreted in contradistinction to "notoriety" or "bad name," causing harm to the honour and reputation of the author.[121]

This was an additional point; clearly, section 57 could have been invoked whether or not this terminology was incorporated into the contract itself.

The effect of the Court's position was to support the view that moral rights are generally inalienable under Indian law and, in definite contrast to the approach in other common law countries, cannot be waived in their entirety in a film contract.[122] As summarized by S. Ramaiah:

> [T]he author's special rights as provided in Section 57 of the *Copyright Act* may override the terms of [a] contract of assignment of copyright. To put it differently, the contract of assignment of copyright has to be read subject to the provisions of Section 57, and the terms of [the] contract cannot negate the special rights and remedies granted by Section 57.[123]

ii. "Certain Modifications"

But balance is at the heart of the High Court's approach. Within the terms of this contract, the author clearly did not have a right to object to any changes, but only to changes that went beyond "certain modifications" made to her work. The Court had a sympathetic understanding of the needs of adaptation, and commented:

> Filming a novel is quite different from literary re-production. There is a change in the medium. The theme of the novel is conveyed through audio-visual effects.[124]

---

121. *Mannu Bhandari, supra* note 11, para. 11.
122. Moral rights legislation in both Canada and the UK supports the availability of waiver as part of their moral rights schemes. *See* Canadian Copyright Act, *supra* note 99, secs. 14(2)–14(4). The UK provisions are discussed in David Vaver, *Moral Rights Yesterday, Today and Tomorrow,* 7(3) Int'l J. Tech. & L. 270, 274, 277–78 (1999).
123. S. Ramaiah, *India, in* Paul Edward Geller & Melville B. Nimmer, International Copyright Law and Practice (Matthew Bender 1998).
124. *Mannu Bhandari, supra* note 11, para. 4.

In fact, the Court felt that it would be ideal to have the benefit of expert evidence on the adaptation of a literary work into film. Justice Wad apparently made this suggestion to the parties, only to be refused—

> It is better to have [the] assistance of informal assessors . . . such as storywriter, directors and producers. I made this suggestion. But one party was not agreeable to have the assistance of [his] . . . peers.[125]

In attempting to define the scope of the "certain modifications" permissible under the contract, the High Court explored the meaning of the term "modifications" as it appeared in the Indian copyright legislation.[126] Could the legislative definition of this term help to set general limits on changes to a literary work during the process of adaptation, thereby establishing a fair and feasible equilibrium between the interests of author and producer?

The Court observed that the term, "modifications" should be read *"ejusdem generis* with the words 'distortion' and 'mutilation,'" which appear alongside it in section 57 of the Copyright Act.[127] Extrapolating from this contract, the Court establishes a useful rule for adaptations. The criterion is that the modifications should be "necessary for converting the novel into a film version."[128] In the process, however, they should not distort or mutilate the original work.[129]

But a "modification" need not be obviously or unquestionably "negative" to infringe the author's moral right. Rather, "necessary" modifications to an original work would be allowed under section 57.[130] As distinguished intellectual property lawyer, Pravin Anand, points out:

> Thus, in this case, even though the author had permitted the film producer under a written agreement to make modifications, the court held that there was a breach of section 57 as the extent of the modifications was more than

---

125. *Id.*, para. 4.

126. Indian Copyright Act, *supra* note 68, sec. 57(1)(a).

127. *Mannu Bhandari, supra* note 11, para. 11; *Anand Patwardhan v. Director General, Directorate General of Doordarshan and Others*, Suit No. 2259 of 2004 [*Anand Patwardhan*], 36.

128. *Mannu Bhandari, supra* note 11, para. 12. This contract had other implications, as well, discussed *infra*.

129. *Id.*, para. 12.

130. For a quick overview of the Indian scheme, see P. Narayanan, Law of Copyright and Industrial Designs, paras. 7.06–7.10, especially at para 7.07 (3d ed. Eastern Law House 2002). Narayanan gives much weight to the common law tradition surrounding quasi-moral rights actions in India and the UK, including the *Frisby* case. The court interpreted sec. 57(1)(a) to mean that an intellectual work is "inviolable."

necessary for converting the novel into a film version or for making the film a successful venture.[131]

It is well worth noting that "necessity" is open to interpretation.[132] The question of what is actually "necessary" arises repeatedly in the technological context, and it is rarely confined to purely technical manipulation.[133] In the case of a film adaptation of a novel, for example, it will be the rare example where dialogue can be lifted directly from the novel to the film.[134] Indeed, it is often the case that dialogue cannot be effectively transposed even from drama to film.

Finally, the Court's approach to the question of balancing the author's rights against the producer is important. It comments that "The basic question is how to balance [the] freedom (of expression) of the author with that of the director in th[is] . . . field of art."[135] For the High Court of Delhi, the author's right to fidelity in the transformation of her artistic vision from page to screen is fundamental—it is a feature of her own freedom of expression. Far from seeing the moral right as a part of the ownership interest bound up with intellectual property, the Court links moral rights with human rights. It does so while arriving at an eminently pragmatic test for the authenticity of adaptations.

iii. Remedies

In its search for an appropriate remedy, the Court considers the substance of the complaint, and assesses each point raised by the plaintiff to decide whether or not the objections of the writer should lead to changes in the film. If the case had been decided by the Court, it would have been possible, with these changes, to release the film. The changes were relatively minor ones which could probably have been accommodated in a minimum of editing sessions. Once again, the Court's approach is utterly practical. The producer would have secured the release of the film, and the writer would have achieved her reputation-saving measures. But there is something incongruous about a judge being called upon to decide what qualifies as a valid change for the

---

131. *Anand Patwardhan, supra* note 127, at 37. *See also* Dine, *supra* note 11, at 564: "The court appears to have made moral rights inalienable, while placing outside the prohibition on modifications such changes as are necessary to make the transition to a different medium."

132. As Shakespeare's King Lear comments: "O, reason not the need! Our basest beggars/Are in the poorest thing superfluous;/Allow not nature more than nature needs,/ Man's life is cheap as beast's." *King Lear,* The Arden Shakespeare (3d Series, Gen. Eds. Richard Proudfoot, Ann Thompson, David Scott Kastan), ed. R.A. Foakes II, ii, 453–56 (at 255).

133. *See, e.g.,* the discussion of "necessity" in the context of technological modifications to music that is used in ringtones, Chapter 6, notes 87–95 and accompanying text.

134. Colin Tapper (personal communication with the author, Jun. 10, 2010).

135. *Mannu Bhandari, supra* note 11, para. 5.

purpose of literary adaptation in a film. To Justice Wad's credit, he engaged in this exercise against his own will; and his comments on the issue suggest that expert evidence should be preferred in cases on moral rights in adaptations.

iv. Cultural Heritage

The opportunity presented by this litigation was an important one for India's judiciary. It was the first major case, not only on moral rights in film adaptations, but on the general concept of the moral right in Indian law. The Court understood that this was an opportunity on the grand scale, and commented:

> The hallmark of any culture is [the] excellence of [its] arts and literature . . . . Art needs [a] healthy environment and adequate protection. The protection which law offers is thus not the protection of the artist or author alone. [The] [e]nrichment of culture is of vital interest to . . . society. Law protects this social interest. Section 57 of the Copyright Act is one such example of legal protection. Section 57 lifts authors' status beyond the material gains of copyright and gives it a special status.[136]

The case of *Mannu Bhandari* has special resonance in the Indian context. In a sense, the Indian cultural scene is built on the art of adaptation. Adaptation is the foundation of everything. The example of India's ancient Sanskrit epics is illustrative. It is believed that the twin poems of the Ramayana and Mahabharata, both gripping stories of heroism, love, and war, began life as history and folk stories, until the traditional "warehouse" of cultural treasures, in the Renaissance sense of the term, was crystallized in these epic verses.

As Tamil poet, Pattanathar, comments, "[Life] becomes a lie, a legend, a dream, and softly fades away." But, in this case, the legend continues. Each one is many times the size of Leo Tolstoy's modern Russian "epic," *War and Peace*. In India, these poems gradually spread across the entire subcontinent, and touched the entire array of its cultures and languages. The Ramayana was translated into local languages in different parts of India—but what translations! It hardly seems fair to call them by this modest name. Local poets adapted the existing stories to the local environment, essentially creating new works that were completely innovative in language and imagery, yet bore the hallmark of spiritual fidelity to the original. Adaptations, like the Tamil version composed by twelfth-century poet Kamban, have become

---

136. *Id.*, para. 8, http://www.indiankanoon.org/doc/331111/ (last visited Aug. 20, 2010); these words are echoed in the interim ruling in the *Amar Nath Sehgal* decision. For an analysis that shaped the final ruling, see Mira T. Sundara Rajan, *Moral Rights and the Protection of Cultural Heritage:* Amar Nath Sehgal v. Union of India, 10(1) INT'L J. CULTURAL PROP. 79 (2001).

classics in their own right. Memorized by village *pandits*, the works were widely disseminated throughout India's social classes, and there is probably no individual alive in the Subcontinent today who does not know the personalities within them as well as members of his own family. In this way, cultural adaptation has been the foundation of Indian unity from very ancient times until the present. As a quintessentially Indian art, it reflects the shimmering interplay of authorial invention, scholarship, and poetic genius to create something authentically Indian.

For better or worse, film, too, has epic consequences in India. How else is it possible to explain the mass suicides that followed the death of M. G. Ramachandran, a Tamil film star of the 1930s?[137] Film has clearly inherited the capacity of the ancient epics to transcend social barriers, including the continuing obstacle of illiteracy. Against this background, it hardly seems surprising that Indian courts consider the moral rights of the author in a film adaptation to be an important cultural issue.[138]

By establishing a high threshold which must be met in the making of adaptations, the Court tries to support authors in a context where, as a group, they are relatively weak, both economically and socially. The Court recognized that there is an important connection between the integrity of an author's work and the maintenance of her reputation. In the case of popular film adaptations of creative works, there may be, *prima facie*, an implication that modifications to a work are likely to damage the author's reputation. The Court's approach suggests that, even where modifications are qualified by the requirement of prejudice, as in the case of the current section 57, Indian authors may have extensive moral rights protection in relation to film adaptations. Dine refers to these considerations as "the unique conditions of

---

137. *See* Radha Venkatesan, *Politics and Suicides*, THE HINDU (June 2, 2002), *available at* http://www. hinduonnet.com/2002/06/02/stories/2002060201871700.htm (last visited Apr. 28, 2010).

138. Interestingly, the tradition of cultural adaptation may also mean that Indian courts will be slow to recognize copyright infringement in the adaptation of stories. A lawsuit brought by Barbara Taylor Bradford for the apparent copying of her novel, *A Woman of Substance*, in an Indian television serial, was unsuccessful. Despite close similarities between the themes, Bradford was offered the rebuke that she did not have a monopoly on the story of a woman's rise from rags to riches. In another case, Warner's suit against a Bollywood production making a film entitled *Hari Puttar* was thrown out on the grounds that there was no likelihood of confusion among the relevant population, between "Hari Puttar" and Harry Potter. *See* Nyay Bhushan, *Warner Bros.' "Hari Puttar" Suit Thrown out: Film Will Be Released in India This Weekend*, HOLLYWOOD REPORTER (Sept. 22, 2008), *available at* http://www.hollywoodreporter.com/hr/content_display/film/news/e3i382d62ad1770e9ed1d42fc9e174bc653 (last visited July 18, 2010). For an interesting perspective, see Hariqbal Basi, Indianizing Hollywood: The Debate over Bollywood's Copyright Infringement (unpublished paper 2010), *available at* http://works.bepress.com/hariqbal_basi/2/ (last visited July 18, 2010). He refers to "Indianization" as a valid defense against charges of copyright infringement in the Bollywood context.

the Indian film business bearing upon . . . [the issue of] damage to the author's reputation."[139] The Court says:

> It is widely believed that there are investments and collections of crores of rupees in a successful Hindi movie and the heroes and heroines are paid fabulous amounts for their services. If the complaint of the author (of mutilation and distortion of the novel) is correct[,] the lay public and her admirers are likely to conclude that she has fallen prey to big money in the film world and has consented to such mutilation and distortions. The apprehension of the author cannot be dismissed as imaginary. It is reasonable. Her admirers are likely to doubt her sincerity and commitment and she is likely to be placed in the category of cheap screenplay writers of the common run [of] Bombay Hindi films.[140]

b. Digital Re-creation: *Anand Patwardhan*[141]

India's first moral rights case dealt with film; its latest case also involves movies. In a 2009 ruling, the Bombay High Court addressed the question of moral rights in the re-use of images from an existing film to make a new documentary. The film in question dealt with a sensitive national issue—the Bihar Movement, a student uprising which led to India's Declaration of Emergency in 1975.

The original film aired in 1977, but the new documentary, broadcast in 2003, presented the events in a completely new light. The new film is said to have "contained substantial footage from the suit film made in 1974–75," although the footage was apparently used with a different soundtrack. The perspective "differs radically and fundamentally" from the opinions offered by the original film. The director of the original film, who "follows a secular democratic ideology," alleged that the new film reflected political biases. It promoted the "Hindutva" ideology, a form of religious extremism based on controversial interpretations of Hinduism. For these reasons, could the new film be said to violate the copyright in the original work?

The makers of the new documentary claimed that they owned the copyright in the first film. They immediately confronted problems here, because

---

139. Dine, *supra* note 11, at 565. Not only is the Indian popular film industry the largest in the world; it also relies on formulaic filmmaking for its success, based on popular music, the exploitation of current trends in fashion, conventional values, and blatant appeal to viewers' sentiments. Critics, including the present author, will not hesitate to point out that Indian popular films and Indian art films come from different worlds. The meaning of quality, of course, is fundamentally different in each.

140. *Mannu Bhandari, supra* note 11, para. 17, *quoted in* Dine, *supra* note 11, at 565.

141. *Patwardhan, supra* note 127.

they could not demonstrate ownership in the form of a written agreement. In construing the contract between them, the judge found that only telecast rights had been assigned to the defendants. Accordingly, any use made of the images in the film was, to begin with, an infringement of copyright.

But the Court proceeded to a more interesting question: had the creator's right of integrity under Indian law been violated? The argument was made on two specific grounds—the association of the images in the film with new music, rather similar to the issue of associating music with an incompatible political ideology that arose in the U.S. case of *Shostakovich*;[142] and the use of the images to present political and religious view that were "completely contrary [to] and different" from the perspective of the original work.[143]

The Court found that it had. It draws a parallel with the *Amar Nath Sehgal* litigation, where damage and partial destruction of a work of sculpture were considered to violate the artist's right of integrity. "This case," says the Court,

> is much the same. The Plaintiff has by his own labour, skill, art and knowledge produced the suit film . . . . [T]he use of the part of the suit film, being contrary to the written agreement between the parties, would be tantamount to distortion and mutilation.[144]

The argument is tantalizing. Why is this case "the same" as the *Sehgal* litigation? In Sehgal's case, there was no question of a wrongful association on political or religious grounds, no issue of distortion by use in a derivative work. Is this the key to the ruling, that cutting and pasting images from the original film amounted to a violation of its integrity, and could be compared to damaging a work of art?

The Court does not offer an explicit consideration of whether the complaint meets the criteria for damage to the author's reputation, as is now required by the revised section 57 of the Indian Copyright Act. However, it does examine the question of whether the new film "defamed the Plaintiff" by "lower[ing] . . . his image [as] . . . a secular democratic person in the eyes of his relatives, friends and acquaintances." As an aside, the plaintiff apparently came to know of the existence of the new film when a cousin called him about it during the broadcast.[145] Interestingly, the Court defines the test for defamation as being able to show actual damage to reputation, and finds that

---

142. *Shostakovich, supra* note 91.

143. A similar point arose in the UK case of *Confetti Records*, which saw an allegation that the association of a song with gangsterism violated the composer's moral rights because of his ideological objections. The facts of the case led to a tongue-in-cheek treatment of the argument by the court: the original performance of the song had been carried out by a group filmed in gangster outfits. *See* Confetti Records v. Warner Music UK Ltd. [2003] EWHC (Ch) 1274.

144. *Anand Patwardhan, supra* note 127, para. 109.

145. *Id.*, para. 77.

the plaintiff has not succeeded in establishing it.[146] Under the moral rights provisions of the Indian Copyright Act, as well, the plaintiff would have had to establish damage to reputation; but whether the damage needs to be actual or constructive, concrete or reasonably to be expected, is not settled law.

In the final Order, damages for defamation are refused. Damages are awarded for copyright infringement, in the amount of 1 million rupees—approximately 25,000 dollars at current rates—and provision is also made that the "Defendants shall not screen or re-screen the impugned film . . . showing any stills/shots/images from the suit film." Has the Court effectively found a violation of the moral right of integrity without showing the required damage to reputation? The final ruling in the *Amar Nath Sehgal* case bypassed this requirement by relying on the status of Mr. Sehgal's work as an important part of India's cultural heritage, and invoking Indian membership in international cultural property conventions as a kind of higher-level norm which must inform the interpretation of moral rights under India's Copyright Act. In this case, too, the Court concludes with its assessment of the plaintiff as "a talented artist" and "a film maker of repute," and states that the film is unique:

> The production, editing, [and] photography of the suit film[,] aside from being a work of art[,] is seen to be the only such work of art on a historical topic which is both informative and educative[,] and reflecting character and constitutional ideology worth emulating in the Plaintiff's name rather than plagiarising . . .

It is a subtle link, but there can be no doubt that, in the Indian Court's mind, a film can be a work of art and an important part of a nation's heritage. Moral rights apply, and they should be interpreted with broad principles of public policy in mind.

2. Colorization: Producers vs. Directors in France

The debate surrounding the colorization of black and white films presents a sobering case study of moral rights in film. Colorization led to the first major discussion of moral rights in film at the national level in the United States. The experience laid bare the wound of a raw internal conflict within America's own film industry, and this is where its continued significance lies. The conflict between directors and producers was at least provisionally resolved on the producers' side—in favor of colorization. At the same time, international attention to the issue generated strong support for the plight of American directors in Europe, especially France.[147] This led to an embarrassing

---

146. *Id.*, paras. 120–121.
147. Represented by the *Huston* case, *supra* note 6; see discussion below.

situation, where American directors found greater sympathy for their opinions, and better protection for their rights, outside the borders of their own country. As Woody Allen comments, "American films are a landmark heritage that do our nation proud all over the world, and should be seen as they were intended to be."[148] Perhaps in France, but not in the United States.

The question of where artists can expect to enjoy their moral rights is worth a closer look. Since the United States joined the Berne Convention in 1989, the possibility of differential protection for the moral rights of Americans and non-Americans on U.S. soil has been raised as a possible solution to the problem of reconciling American law with the Berne Convention.[149] It is a troubling prospect. The logic of national treatment is that the regime of rights one grants to one's own citizens should also be available to foreign nationals. The goal is egalitarian—to avoid discrimination against foreigners. The protection of the law should be extended to everyone within the borders of one's own country. To offer protection to foreign nationals without granting it to one's own citizens would turn the very idea of national treatment on its head.

In copyright matters, the prospect of favoring foreigners is not a new idea. Once upon a time, the idea was considered by the Soviet Union in its first official foray into international copyright law— its application for membership in the Universal Copyright Convention (UCC), which it eventually joined in 1973. The Soviet move to join the UCC raised an outcry in both the international and Soviet literary communities. The fear was precisely this— that the protections of the UCC would be granted to non-Soviet authors within Soviet territory, while the rights of Soviet authors would continue to be "regulated," or eviscerated, by internal Soviet rules.[150]

In particular, Soviet copyright law of the time allowed the government to acquire works from writers on a "compulsory" basis. Once it did so, the decision to publish or not to publish them fell into the hands of the government.[151] Just as the Soviet government suppressed the publication of works by dissidents within the Soviet Union, its formal ownership of copyright in those works could empower it, through the UCC, to prevent their publication

---

148. Allen, *supra* note 1.
149. *See* the interesting article by Graeme Austin on the theme of U.S. Compliance with the Berne Convention after *Dastar*: Graeme W. Austin, *The Berne Convention as a Canon of Construction: Moral Rights after Dastar*, 61 N.Y.U. Ann. Surv. Am. L. 111 (2005).
150. As Mihály Ficsor points out: "There is the possibility of having also *provisions* which are not compatible with the conventions, but those can prevail only for *internal situations* (for the relations between national authors and users, where no international obligation is involved)." Mihály Ficsor, *The Past, Present and Future of Copyright in the European Socialist Countries*, 118 RIDA 33 (1983). See the quotation and related discussion in Sundara Rajan, *Copyright and Creative Freedom*, *supra* note 8, at 51–53.
151. In other words, by compulsory purchase of a writer's work, the Soviet government effectively acquired control of the author's moral right of disclosure.

outside the country. Other member countries of the UCC would be obliged to recognize Soviet copyright rules. This new development would have deprived repressed Soviet authors of one of their traditional outlets: publication abroad. In a statement whose authors are identified by the Times of London only as "a group of internationally-known Soviet dissident writers," the writers mourned:

> Our books will be stifled not only during the lives of their authors, but forever, until the end of publishing on earth. This situation did not exist even in Stalin's time for the books then ended by coming to the surface, at least posthumously.[152]

Even a commentator as knowledgeable as Michael Newcity wondered how seriously these claims should be taken, although his "depressing" conclusion that the Soviet Union had plentiful tools for the repression of writers without recourse to copyright law is hardly reassuring.[153] In fact, the subsequent comments of the Soviet government left little doubt about the intentions of the Soviet government. The Times of London of December 28, 1973, reported:

> In an interview, Mr. Boris Pankin [head of the new Russian copyright agency] denied accusations made last spring by six Soviet intellectuals, including Dr Andrei Sakharov, the nuclear physicist, that this was a prime reason behind the Soviet decision to join the Universal Copyright Convention on May 27.

However, he left no doubt that his agency from now on would prosecute foreign publishers of dissident works and Soviet citizens who supplied them.

> Mr. Pankin said his agency, set up in September, is now the sole legal Soviet body authorized to deal with foreign publishers on questions of copyright.[154]

Clearly, this is not the sort of memory that the United States wants to evoke in its own approach to membership in the Berne Union. It is true that American authors, unlike their Soviet counterparts, do not face routine

---

152. The letter is signed, "The Stifled *Samizdat.*" *See Soviet Dissidents Accuse UNESCO,* THE TIMES (LONDON), Mar. 27, 1973, at 8. The quote also appears in Sundara Rajan, *Copyright and Creative Freedom, supra* note 8, at 106, discussion at 100–07; and in Michael Newcity's study, COPYRIGHT LAW IN THE SOVIET UNION 152, n.12 (Praeger Special Studies, Praeger Publishers 1978).

153. See the discussion in Sundara Rajan, *Copyright and Creative Freedom, supra* note 8, at 100–07.

154. *Bar on publication abroad of Solzhenitsyn works,* THE TIMES OF LONDON at 6 (Dec. 28, 1973). The issue of Soviet membership in the Universal Copyright Convention received wide coverage in the Times of London of 1973–74. The period after 1973 was one of cultural stagnation in the Soviet Union, and it is difficult to assess the role of the UCC in it. Certainly, membership in the UCC did not help to open Soviet society to the West.

state persecution; but America is a passionately democratic country, and it should jealously guard the ideals of free speech. It is difficult to see how treating one's own nationals poorly can set a positive example —orindeed, how this approach can support America's international leadership on copyright issues. Reverse discrimination, too, can be a form of injustice.

The conflict over colorization arose in the early 1990s. It presented the spectacle of the first large-scale technological issue to affect the moral interests of filmmakers. The colorization experience was important for three reasons. First, colorization was widely protested by a number of prominent American filmmakers, from Martin Scorsese to Woody Allen. John Huston was deeply offended by the colorization of films that he had shot in black and white, including *The Maltese Falcon* and *The Asphalt Jungle*. His films became the subject of a seminal case on the issue in France, as discussed below.[155]

The debate over colorization pitted these directors against their own producers, who authorized the colorization of their works.[156] In this process, the identity of American filmmakers as independent artists and genuine creators hardened into a new mold. Fine fissures appeared in the image of an American cinema controlled by production values. The shift is captured by Woody Allen's commentary:

> Yet another question: "Why were directors not up in arms about cutting films for television or breaking them up for commercials, insulting them with any number of technical alterations to accommodate the television format?" The answer is that directors always hated these assaults on their work but were powerless to stop them . . . .
>
> Still, when the assaults come too often, there is a revolution. The outrage of seeing one's work transformed into color is so dramatically appalling . . . that . . . all the directors, writers and actors chose to fight.[157]

Secondly, the debate was an alarm bell that alerted the American film community to the possibilities of digital technology. Modifying film was going to be possible in a way that had never before been imagined. Through the miracle of digital intervention, the integrity of film was vulnerable, not only to alteration, but also, to what Woody Allen aptly called "assault." If a right of integrity for films was not necessary in the past, it might now make

---

155. *Huston, supra* note 6.
156. For example, Turner Entertainment had colorized *The Asphalt Jungle*; Turner had become part of Metro-Goldwyn-Mayer, the original producers of the film, by merger. *See Huston, supra* note 6. The decision has been translated into English in ENT. L. REP. 3 (Mar. 1995). A version is available on the website of Professor Andrew Chin of the University of North Carolina Law School at http://www.unclaw.com/chin/teaching/iip/turner.pdf (last visited Apr. 28, 2010) [Chin].
157. Allen, *supra* note 1.

eminent sense to recognize one. The integrity right would be a fitting response to the rise of new technological possibilities for manipulating film.

Finally, the colorization debate brought the issue of moral rights to the forefront of the American legal and cultural consciousness. This may or may not have been a good thing. Why should moral rights be examined on the testing-ground of the most treacherous copyright terrain that exists, the world of the audiovisual work? While the colorization debate brought the issue of film integrity before the American public, the principles that emerged from the controversy did not necessarily promote the cause of moral rights. The conflict ultimately reinforced Hollywood's resistance to the idea and, more generally, American caution about the Berne Convention.

In John Huston's case, protest against the colorization of his films came to a head when France's Channel 5 network, *La Cinq*, reached an agreement with Turner Entertainment to broadcast a colorized version of the film. The broadcast was scheduled for the evening of the 20th of June, 1988, at eight thirty. Huston was by then deceased; but a suit was filed by his children, including the actress Angelica Huston, with Ben Maddow, the screenwriter of *The Asphalt Jungle*. The plaintiffs argued that showing the film on television would amount to an affront on the director's moral rights. The judge at first instance agreed; he stated that the broadcast "could cause intolerable and irreparable damage to those who, defending the integrity of the work 'The Asphalt Jungle,' invoke respect for the will of John Huston."[158] The conclusion of the appeals tribunal was even stronger. It quoted Huston's own words about the film—"I filmed it in black and white, as a sculptor chooses to shape clay, to mold his work in bronze, to sculpt in marble."[159] The court then goes on to comment:

> It is not debated that his aesthetic sense, which was widely celebrated, rests on the play of black and white that allowed him to create an atmosphere in the context of which he directed the actors and chose the decor; that, in acting in a certain and direct manner on the sensibility of the viewer, colorization is likely to modify these impressions; thus, that the colorization of the film at issue, even in only some formats, against the will of the plaintiffs, amounts to an attack on their moral right; that, accordingly, they are entitled to demand that Channel 5 be prohibited from proceeding to the television broadcast of the film Asphalt Jungle in its colorized version.[160]

---

158. *Huston, supra* note 6: "pouvait entraîner un dommage intolérable et irréparable pour ceux qui, défendant l'intégrité de l'œuvre Asphalt Jungle, invoquent le respect et la volonté de John Huston."

159. *Huston, supra* note 6: "Je l'ai tourné en noir et blanc, comme un sculpteur choisit de façonner l'argile, de couleur [sic couler] son travail dans le bronze, de sculpter dans le marbre."

160. *Id.* "Qu'il n'est pas contesté que son esthétisme, qui lui a valu une grande notoriété, repose sur le jeu noir et blanc qui permettait de créer une atmosphère en fonction de laquelle il dirigeait

The *Huston* case established a number of important points of law concerning moral rights in the international community. First, as the case initially occurred before the United States had become a signatory to the Berne Convention, the French court affirmed that the enjoyment of moral rights did not depend on the nationality of the author.[161] Rather, under French law, moral rights would be generally available to creators belonging to any country. Secondly, the fact that moral rights were unavailable in the country of origin of the work, the United States, was irrelevant to the claim. Instead, what mattered was the fact that both France and the United States were members of the Universal Copyright Convention, which would allow Americans to enjoy the privilege of national treatment under French copyright law.[162] While the UCC did not make any mention of moral rights, the court ruled that it also did not impose any restrictions on the ability of member states to recognize moral rights. Thirdly, the aesthetic vision of the director was gleaned from the direct evidence of his work and his words. Through them, the director himself could lay claim to the status of individual artist, fully entitled to the protection of his moral rights.

As an epilogue to *Huston*, it should finally be noted that the practice of colorization, itself, has virtually died out. By the mid-1990s, Turner Broadcasting, which colorized two hundred-odd films from the "cream of the crop" of its film collection, had completely ceased to colorize films. Ironically, Turner Classic Movies now offers classic films, including silent movies, in their original formats.[163] There is no longer any fear that black and white has become obsolete. As James Danziger pointed out in a 1998 interview with the New York Times, "Young people won't watch black and white? . . . That's certainly been disproved by MTV. Many of the most interesting and avant-garde

---

l'acteur[s] et choisissait les décors; qu'en agissant de façon certaine et directe sur la sensibilité du téléspectateur, la colorisation est susceptible d'en modifi er les impressions; qu'ainsi, la colorisation du fi lm en cause, même sur certains supports seulement, contre le gré des demandeurs, constitue une atteinte à leur droit moral; qu'ils sont dès lors fondés à demander qu'il soit fait interdiction à La Cinq de procéder à la télédiff usion du film Asphalt Jungle dans sa version colorisée."

161. The Berne Convention entered into force in the United States on Mar. 1, 1989. *See* Berne Notification No. 1, Nov. 21, 17, 1988, WIPO website at http://www.wipo.int/treaties/en/html. jsp?file=/redocs/notdocs/en/berne/treaty_berne_121.html (last visited Apr. 29, 2010).

162. The *Cour de cassation* states: "In admitting the claim, this judgment referred in substance to the Universal Copyright Convention signed in GENEVA on 6th September 1952, ratified by the UNITED STATES, to deduce that this convention provides citizens of member States in FRANCE with the benefit of the Law of 11th March 1957, notably Section 6, which provides that the moral right is attached to the person and is perpetual, inalienable and imprescriptible." As translated in Chin, *supra* note 155.

163. *See* Rick Lyman, *Black and White Is Back: Color "Em Wrong,"* NEW YORK TIMES (Jan. 11, 1998), *available at* http://www.nytimes.com/1998/01/11/weekinreview/ideas-trends-black-and-white-is-back-color-em-wrong.html?pagewanted=1 (last visited Apr. 29, 2010).

videos have been done in black and white." But this trend was foreseen at the height of the colorization debate by Woody Allen, who commented:

> Probably false . . . is the claim that young people won't watch black and white. I would think they would, judging from the amount of stylish music videos and MTV ads that are done in black and white, undoubtedly after market research.[164]

D. Digital Technology: Film as a Technological Work

Where moral rights are concerned, the legal situation of film is difficult to grasp. The addition of a technological element into the process of filmmaking leads to scenarios that reach a new level of complexity. The future of filmmaking, like most other fields of human creativity, will increasingly feel the influence of digital technology. In particular, the blending of technological and human elements is likely to add a new layer of complexity to what is already the multilayered wedding cake of moral rights. The potential for digital intervention allows the editing of a film, re-using its parts in a new film or multimedia work, communicating the film via the Internet, and introducing radical new elements into the creation of a film, such as the "re-animation" of deceased actors through technology, allowing the appearance of their images, voices, and performances in current films. What are the implications of these film-making techniques for moral rights?

1. Editing, Creative Allusion, and Re-use: From Fan Films to Family Movies

In the digital environment, it seems, nothing is forever. Even a version of a film that has been agreed upon and finalized by all those involved in its creation— producer, director, writer, composer, actors, and technicians—can subsequently be altered by a viewer, or "user." This scenario is illustrated by the 2006 case of *Clean Flicks*.[165]

In the *Clean Flicks* case, films were edited with a specific purpose in mind— removing parts that could be considered "sensitive," making the film fit for viewing by families with children. In Continental and developing countries,

---

164. Allen, *supra* note 1.
165. *Clean Flicks of Colorado, LLC v. Soderbergh*, 433 F. Supp. 2d, 1236 (D. Colo. 2006) [*Clean Flicks*].

this kind of editing would clearly violate the author's moral right of integrity. Even in a country like India, which has faced many controversies over film censorship because of the objections—often violent—of militant social groups, a court has never found social objectionability to be a valid reason to curtail the author's moral right of integrity.[166] Indeed, the trial court in the *Bhandari* case actually commented that it is not the court's mandate to decide on the social acceptability of particular content when assessing the right of integrity.[167]

A different kind of problem arises in relation to fan films, a new genre of video creativity. In a fan film, an admirer of an existing film, television program, or video game will make a video based on the world of the original film—its characters and locales and, possibly, its storylines. As the name suggests, it is a form of homage to the original production. Fan films can be highly original in their own right, and some of them are made with the investment of substantial resources and talent.

Depending on its actual content, it is possible that a fan film could infringe copyright. A fan film could be considered a derivative work based on the original film, for which, the permission of the original author would be required. In contrast, however, moral rights are not obviously implicated in fan films. Where attribution is concerned, the idea of crediting the creators of the original work seems implicit in the very definition of a fan film. As for integrity, the fan film would usually not involve the use of footage from the original work, eliminating the likelihood of a violation of the right on the grounds that the work has suffered direct mistreatment.[168]

But one possible violation of the right of integrity should be considered: the use of characters from the original film in the new work. This situation resembles the *Hugo* case, in which a descendant of the writer attempted to prevent the publication of a "sequel" to Hugo's monumental *Les Misérables* that pursued the further adventures of its characters—including the resurrection of the deceased Inspector Javert.[169] In its ruling, the French *Cour de cassation* found that a decision in favor of the plaintiffs would amount to an excessive limitation on the new writer's right to free speech.[170] The judgment can be criticized on the grounds that the author and publisher clearly hoped

---

166. On film censorship in India, see the interesting comment by Shammi Nanda, *Censorship and Indian Cinema: The Case of War and Peace*, 38 Bright Lights Film J. (2002), *available at* http://www.brightlightsfilm.com/38/indiacensor.php (last visited Dec. 11, 2010).

167. *Mannu Bhandari*, *supra* note 11, para. 22.

168. *See, e.g., Shostakovich*, *supra* note 91: actual alteration of the work is required.

169. *Hugo c Societe Plon*, Arrêt n° 125 du 30 janvier 2007, Cass. Civ. 1re, *available at* http://www.courdecassation.fr/jurisprudence_2/premiere_chambre_civile_568/arret_no_9850.html (last visited Apr. 28, 2010).

170. For an interesting overview in English, see Kim Willsher, *Heir of Victor Hugo Fails to Stop Les Mis II*, Guardian (Jan. 31, 2007), *available at* http://www.guardian.co.uk/world/2007/jan/31/books.france (last visited Apr. 22, 2010).

to exploit Hugo's reputation for their own commercial benefit—the main reason leading Hugo's great-great-grandson to pursue legal action in the first place.[171] The fan film case seems much more sympathetic, as the films are traditionally not made for profit.

The film industry is increasingly supportive of fan films. In this sense, the industry seems to have learned something from the public relations mishaps that have dogged the music industry. However, situations do arise where fan films clash with copyright policy. A recent example is the case of the German fan film *Damnatus*, inspired by a British videogame called *Warhammer*.

Damnatus was directed and produced by Huan Vu over a period of four years. When it was completed, the release of the film was blocked by Games Workshop, the makers of the *Warhammer* game, because of concerns about the copyright implications of Huan Vu's work under German law. In particular, Games Workshop noted that German copyright law grants rights to authors that cannot be waived. The company had hoped to acquire all rights in *Damnatus* from Mr. Wu, but the structure of German law would prevent it from doing so. Games Workshop felt that Mr. Wu's copyright in *Damnatus* would imply that he also had rights of ownership over *Warhammer*. As reported by the BBC, a Games Workshop spokesman claimed that allowing Mr. Wu to release his film would mean that, "Games Workshop would essentially be giving up the title to the Warhammer 40,000 intellectual property."[172] Accordingly, in the words of Andy Jones, the head of Games Workshop's legal department:

> To lose control of Warhammer or Warhammer 40,000 is simply unthinkable. So we must be vigilant, and perhaps sometimes seemingly heartless in our decisions to safeguard the IP for the future success of the business and the hobby.[173]

The outcome of this dispute was devastating for Vu, who commented to the BBC, "It's really horrible for an artist not being able to show off their own work."

The ultimate irony of the situation is that Games Workshop's analysis of the legal differences between German and British copyright law is questionable. The main concerns appear to have been two-fold. First, the fact that German law would confer ownership of *Damnatus* on Mr. Vu, the "author" of the film, rather than Games Workshop as the "owner" of the copyright in the original work, seems to have presented a problem. German law does not

---

171. *Hugo, supra* note 168.

172. Mark Ward, *Copyright Law Scuppers Fan Film*, BBC NEWS (Nov. 6, 2007), *available at* http://news.bbc.co.uk/2/hi/technology/7010484.stm (last visited Apr. 22, 2010).

173. Quoted in *id.*

allow the outright transfer of copyright.[174] But it is difficult to see why Games Workshop could not simply license the use of *Damnatus* in connection with its video game, rather than seeking to acquire the copyright in *Damnatus*.

Secondly, the comment regarding concerns about rights that cannot be waived could also be a reference to Germany's protection of the moral rights of authors, far more extensive than their counterpart in British law.[175] As Fan Cinema Today comments,

> Under German copyright law, the filmmakers are given rights to their work that they can't give away, even if they want to—art is considered to be an extension of the creator him- or herself.[176]

But this interpretation of the law is puzzling. Once again, it seems that Games Workshop had little to fear. Huan Vu could not claim attribution or integrity rights in the products of Games Workshop; he could only enjoy those rights if, for example, the company created new products that were directly derived from his film. It is difficult to see how Games Workshop developed the notion that their own rights in their video game would be compromised by allowing Vu to retain his rights in an obviously derivative work. Wu would not own *Warhammer*; he would only own *Damnatus*.

If anything, an argument could be made that Vu's moral rights as an author were violated by Games Workshop. It initially authorized the making of his fan film, but then refused to allow him to disclose it on what were, essentially, unreasonable grounds. In the end, Vu effectively secured the release of his film by "leaking" it to the online community via the Pirate Bay. Ironically, the leaked version makes little mention of the origin of the film—no doubt, because of Mr. Vu's experience with Games Workshop. Fan Cinema Today says that the film appeared "with little indication of its relation to" the original game, jeopardizing the very interest that Games Workshop had wanted to protect: its association with its own work.

In the United States, which recognizes no right of integrity in films, the approach to editing movies is a difficult copyright problem. In this sense, editing presents a strong contrast to the question of re-using film images in a

---

174. *See* German Copyright Law, *supra* note 31, art. 29, on the "Transfer of Copyright": "Copyright may be transferred in execution of a testamentary disposition or to coheirs as part of the partition of an estate. Copyright shall not otherwise be transferable."

175. *See id.*, art. 39, on the "Alteration of [a] Work": "(1) The holder of an exploitation right may not alter the work, its title or the designation of author (Article 10(1)), unless otherwise agreed. (2) Alterations to the work and its title which the author cannot reasonably refuse shall be permissible."

176. *See Legendary Banned Warhammer 40,000 Fan Film Damnatus Leaked Online*, FAN CINEMA TODAY (Jan. 30, 2009), *available at* http://fancinematoday.com/2009/01/30/legendary-banned-warhammer-40000-fan-film-damnatus-leaked-online/ (last visited Dec. 17, 2010).

new context, as happened in the Indian case of *Anand Patwardhan*,[177] which is actually quite easy to resolve under the conventions of U.S. law. Unless it can be shown to be fair use, re-using substantial parts of a film without the owner's consent is a clear infringement of the owner's copyright. It amounts to the making of a derivative work without the owner's permission. As in the *Gilliam* case, the doctrine of derivative works can capture this moral rights problem in the United States.[178]

Film editing is a different issue. In *Clean Flicks*, the process by which family-friendly versions of films were distributed—sanitized or sterilized, according to one's perspective—infringed copyright. The process of "cleansing" films occurred as follows. First, a DVD of the original film was purchased, either by the consumer or by Clean Flicks itself. The company would then copy the film onto a computer hard drive and run the movie in a program that would allow the user to modify the areas of concern. Deletions and additions were both possible. The editing might be seamless, or the final version could include visible changes obscuring the unwanted scenes.[179] The edited version was then copied onto a DVD for sale to the consumer, or to a retailer of movies.

These facts beautifully illustrate the copyright paradox of ownership versus authorship. From the perspective of copyright ownership, there is little in these activities to trigger the response of U.S. copyright law.[180] Indeed, the activities of Clean Flicks almost certainly generated benefits to the copyright-owners, since many of the people who bought these films might not have purchased them otherwise. At no point were the owners of the films deprived of their royalties: Clean Flicks always carried out its work on a version of the film that was lawfully purchased, either by the company or by the consumer. Its money was made out of its services, and not from the film.

For the filmmakers, money may not be the essence of the matter. Rather, it is the misrepresentation of their work that generates discomfort. Interference with artistic control, possible damage to reputation, and confusion about the authenticity of the final work are all implicated in the "cleansing" process.

In fact, the United States has passed a federal law dealing with the issue of objectionable content in films—the Family Movie Act of 2005.[181] The Act was

---

177. *Supra* note 125.
178. *Gilliam, supra* note 75.
179. The editing process is described in detail by Suresh Pillai, *Mr. Soderbergh Goes to Washington: How Congress and the Clean Flicks Court Created Moral Rights for Filmmakers*, 17 DePaul-LCA J. Art & Ent. L. 339, 341–42 (2007).
180. *But see Gilliam, supra* note 75: filmmakers could argue that the edited versions were new derivative works, made without their consent.
181. Family Movie Act of 2005, Pub. L. No. 109-9, § 202(a), 119 Stat. 218, 223–24 (codified at 17 U.S.C. § 110 (2006)) [FMA]; Family Entertainment & Copyright Act of 2005, Pub. L. 109-9, 119 Stat. 218 [FECA].

passed as part of a larger piece of legislation, the Family Entertainment and Copyright Act, which is actually a piece of anti-piracy legislation targeting two activities: unauthorized recording of a movie while it is being shown in a theater, and the disclosure of a movie to the public prior to its official release date.[182] The rules on objectionable content are offered as an exception to copyright infringement under 17 U.S.C. § 110 (11).[183] "Skipping audio and video content," or the act of "making [material] imperceptible" through technology, in the words of the statute, is allowed for the purpose of rendering the film fit for "private home viewing."[184] The caveat comes in the concluding words: only if "no fixed copy of the altered version of the motion picture is created by such computer program or other technology" can the exemption to copyright infringement be claimed.[185]

Here, and only here, could the Clean Flicks defense fail: by copying the modified movies onto DVDs, it had made fixed copies of the works. On this ground, the Colorado court found that the filmmakers' copyright had been violated by Clean Flicks.

In effect, the wording of the statute was flawed. It was drafted with a certain kind of technology in mind. Since the case, new methods of "cleansing" films have continued to be available, such as DVD software that allows objectionable scenes to be blacked out while the film is playing. Some commentators have argued that the court's ruling effectively creates a moral right of integrity, and indeed, it has outlawed the creation of permanent records of the sanitized versions of films.[186] But this right is incomplete: public broadcast of the altered versions and the development of software that allows the films to be viewed or broadcast after purging, are still entirely permissible. The court has given a push to the development of "cleansing" technology in alternate directions.

Is the court's emphasis on fixation justified? From a moral rights perspective, it makes perfect sense. Fixation is a powerful method of establishing the authenticity of a given version of a creative work. In a digital environment, the concept of fixation is increasingly difficult to define. The court in *Clean*

---

182. *Id.*, § 102, also applies to computer software and music (*Id.*, § 103).

183. Section 202, amending FMA, 17 U.S.C. § 110, Exemption from Infringement for Skipping Audio and Video Content in Motion Pictures prohibits "the making imperceptible of limited portions of audio or video content of a motion picture, during a performance in or transmitted to that household for private home viewing, from an authorized copy of the motion picture, or the creation or provision of a computer program or other technology that enables such making imperceptible and that is designed and marketed to be used, at the direction of a member of a private household, for such making imperceptible, if no fixed copy of the altered version of the motion picture is created by such computer program or other technology."

184. *See* FMA, *supra* note 180, §§ 110(11).

185. In effect, this seems like a statutory exemption to the *Gilliam* scenario, *supra* note 75. FMA, *supra* note 175, 17 U.S.C. § 110(11).

186. *See, for example*, Pillai's perceptive remarks, *supra* note 178, at 363–68.

Flicks decided that fixation should remain the prerogative of the filmmaker, while post-film editing should not be granted an equivalent status by allowing the edited version to be fixed.

But in terms of policy, the court's decision is incomplete. The idea seems to be that no permanent damage to a work will occur if the modified versions of films are not fixed. They are ephemeral, perhaps the passing fad or fancy of a day, but the fixed version remains and is authentic. The court's position supports authenticity; but it does not address the possibility of damage to reputation, which can still occur if it is possible to view a modified version of the film. Under the ruling, it would be acceptable to broadcast edited versions of films, provided that no fixation occurred. When an edited film is viewed, could it not have a negative impact on the reputation of the filmmaker? The character of a motion picture could be changed fundamentally by obscuring or deleting scenes to make them "imperceptible," in the language of the Act.

This was the scenario in the *Huston* case: what mattered was the fact that the public would have been exposed to colorized versions of the director's films when they were broadcast on television. It was irrelevant to ask whether the colorized version was fixed. Rather, the issue was the "performance" of the film which reached the viewer in an altered—corrupted—form. In *Huston*, the court was concerned with the director's artistic reputation—not with the issue of preserving the integrity of the film. Until the question of reputation is clarified, the provisions of the Family Movie Act can be considered helpful for preserving authenticity, but they do not amount to a full-fledged moral right of integrity. Integrity, as it is currently understood, would need to include both authenticity and reputation interests within its scope.

In this sense, the *Clean Flicks* decision fits well with the general approach to film in the United States. A growing awareness of the importance of maintaining authenticity in films found expression in the National Film Preservation Act of 1988.[187] The Act makes provision for establishing a registry of films that are "culturally, historically, or aesthetically significant;" it is also an offense to distribute or exhibit to the public any film from the registry that has been "materially altered" or colorized. The Act has some limitations: the number of films that can be selected for inclusion on the registry is limited to 25 per year, and the film itself must be at least 10 years old.[188]

---

187. Public Law 100-446 (1988). The National Film Preservation Board, originally authorized by this Act, has most recently been renewed for a seven-year period from October 2009. For further information, see the National Film Preservation Board at http://www.loc.gov/film/filmabou.html (last visited Dec. 17, 2010).

188. Details of the Act can be found on the National Film Preservation Board website, *id.* The creation of the Registry is part of a larger project to preserve films that are of historical importance. In a fascinating paragraph, the National Film Preservation Board summarizes its mandate: "The Foundation's primary mission is to save orphan films, films without owners able to pay for their preservation. The films most at-risk are newsreels, silent films, experimental works, films out of copyright protection, significant amateur footage,

In these respects, the right conferred by the Act falls far short of what could be accomplished through a moral right of integrity, but it still represents an important achievement. Once a film is considered "significant," its status changes. It is no longer a mere commercial product; it is recognized as a culturally important work. The idea echoes the Indian approach to moral rights, as articulated in the *Amar Nath Sehgal* case, which affirms prerogatives for cultural treasures that transcend the usual limits of copyright law.[189]

For the proponents of economic rights in films, limiting the scope of integrity may be a good thing. As Suresh Pillai argues, imposing limits on moral rights would avoid the problem of a "chilling pall on the rights enjoyed by purchasers of protected material" that could flow from their recognition.[190] But Pillai goes on to suggest that a restrictive approach to moral rights should be promoted, not only for practical reasons, but also, because restricting moral rights would keep copyright law within the legal limits defined by the copyright clause in the U.S. Constitution.[191]

This point is conventional among U.S. copyright lawyers, but it deserves a closer look. It touches on a much larger issue: the relationship between copyright and freedom of speech in the United States.[192] The potential for conflict between moral rights and the U.S. Constitution is a debatable point, and an issue on which copyright scholars may be too quick to pronounce judgment. Moral rights certainly challenge free speech, but so, too, do the economic rights enjoyed by copyright-owners. In fact, proponents of moral rights could argue that they are less offensive to free speech than economic copyright, because they are based on a need to recognize the human rights of creators.[193] Indeed, a right to protect the work from intrusive editing could be

---

documentaries, and features made outside the commercial mainstream. Orphan films are the living record of the twentieth century. Hundreds of American museums, archives, libraries, universities, and historical societies care for 'orphaned' original film materials of cultural value. The Foundation will work with these film preservation organizations to preserve orphan films and make them accessible to 'present and future generations of Americans.'" *See* http://www.loc.gov/film/filmabou.html (last visited Dec. 17, 2010).

189. *See* discussion of the *Amar Nath Sehgal* case, Chapter 3, *supra*, "A Theory in Flux," notes 204–22 and accompanying text.

190. Pillai, *supra* note 178, at 368.

191. *Id.*, at 344–70.

192. This relationship is the theme of a multinational book of essays, Copyright and Free Speech: Comparative and International Analyses (Jonathan Griffiths & Uma Suthersanen eds., Oxford University Press 2005).

193. For a detailed discussion of the connections between moral rights and human rights, see Sundara Rajan, *Copyright and Creative Freedom*, *supra* note 8, Chapter IX, "Copyright and Human Rights: The Post-Soviet Experience and a New International Model." Other literature on this increasingly popular issue includes the seminal work of Peter Drahos, *Intellectual Property and Human Rights* 3 Intell. Prop. Q. 349 (1999). Of course, the economic rights of creators could also be seen as human rights and are noted as such in both the United Nations Declaration of Human Rights and the International Covenant on Civil and Political Rights.

seen as one aspect of the director's own right to free expression. The moral right is a kind of right to free creative speech.

As for the "chilling pall" that moral rights would impose on the rights of purchasers, the connotations of the expression are strongly negative, but the effect described is the very objective of the moral right. There is no escaping this conclusion. It was Ted Turner's nightmare—in response to the colorization controversy, Turner is said to have remarked, "Last time I checked, I owned those films."[194] Moral rights mean that one cannot do absolutely anything with a work that one owns; certain kinds of treatment are disallowed. Almost every case that has dealt with the right of integrity, whether in India, France, or Canada, is about setting limits on the right to use a work, *even if* one owns it. Film is a form of creative expression in which both authors and owners are engaged in the exploitation of the work, and it can be difficult to define the limits of ownership. As the colorization conflict shows, film can become a battleground that pits authors against owners, unless and until the terms of a lasting peace can be achieved.

2. Internet and the Communication of Films

Like music, films are increasingly available for downloading from the Internet. Moral rights are clearly implicated in this form of communication. However, film has enjoyed some distinct advantages over music. The communication of video is slower than sound, and this has meant that the Internet communication of films has not kept pace with peer-to-peer file-sharing in the music industry. The problems faced by the music industry have not developed as quickly in the film scenario, and, as a result, the film industry is in a position to benefit from the music experience.

In particular, the emergence of a legal framework for downloading films, such as Apple's iTunes, presents a likely solution to the vulnerability of film copyright. The extra-legal film counterpart to the iTunes model is YouTube, and here, as in the case of peer-to-peer music file-sharing, problems of copyright protection have arisen. When the YouTube service was first launched,

---

Article 27(2) of the Declaration states: "Everyone has the right to the protection of the moral and material interests resulting from any scientific, literary or artistic production of which he is the author"; sec. 15(c) of the ICESCR mirrors this language: "To benefit from the protection of the moral and material interests resulting from any scientific, literary or artistic production of which he is the author." Both instruments are available online at http://www.un.org/en/documents/udhr/ (last visited Apr. 28, 2010); http://www2.ohchr.org/english/law/cescr.htm (last visited Apr. 28, 2010). But the special connection between moral rights and human rights should probably be noted; commercial gain is not involved.

194. Russell Baker, *We Trashed Those Films Long Ago*, St. Petersburg Times at 25A (Nov. 28, 1986), *available at* http://news.google.com/newspapers?nid=888&dat=19861128&id=kDM MAAAAIBAJ&sjid=e2ADAAAAIBAJ&pg=3654,4099854 (last visited Apr. 22, 2010).

its purpose was ostensibly to allow users to post their original videos; but much of the material posted to YouTube was copied from television broadcasts of programs protected by copyright that viewers uploaded to the service. In 2007, entertainment giant Viacom filed a billion-dollar lawsuit for copyright infringement against YouTube, but the case has become mired in procedural tangles and shows little sign of moving towards a hearing.[195]

YouTube has responded by vaunting a newfound hair-trigger sensitivity to potential copyright infringement. Absurd claims of copyright infringement have prompted calls for affected users of YouTube to sue it, and its parent company, Google, for the removal of their videos.[196] YouTube has also adopted the more strategic approach of limiting the length of videos that can be posted on its site, in an effort to control the uploading of illegally copied videos.[197] In the meantime, other sites for sharing videos are developing. All of them will be closely vigilant when it comes to watching, not only the

---

195. For an update on the progress of the lawsuit, see the docket entries from the New York Southern District Court, Case No. 1:2007cv02103, *available at* http://news.justia.com/cases/featured/new-york/nysdce/1:2007cv02103/302164/. The case is usefully summarized by Liz Gannes, *No End in Sight for Critical Viacom-YouTube DMCA case,* NEWTEEVEE (Dec. 8, 2008), *available at* http://newteevee.com/2008/12/09/no-end-in-sight-for-critical-viacom-youtube-dmca-case/ (last visited Apr. 22, 2010). For a discussion of Google's alleged support for copyright infringement "as a business model," see Chloe Albanesius, *Viacom Releases Documents in YouTube Case,* (Apr. 16, 2010), *available at* http://news.yahoo.com/s/zd/20100416/tc_zd/250172 (last visited Apr. 28, 2010); *Copyright in the Age of YouTube: As User-Generated Sites Flourish, Copyright Law Struggles to Keep Up,* A.B.A. J. (Feb. 1, 2009), *available at* http://www.abajournal.com/magazine/article/copyright_in_the_age_of_youtube/ (last visited Apr. 28, 2010).

196. An interesting example was the case of Stephanie Lenz's video of her baby son dancing to the song, *Let's Go Crazy,* by Prince; when the video was removed from YouTube, Ms. Lenz sued Universal Music and obtained a judgment in her favor. Copyright-owners are now required to make a good-faith assessment of whether the video is a fair use of copyright-protected material before sending a take-down notice (under the DMCA). *See* Robert Plummer, *Lawyers Go Crazy at Baby Prince Fan,* BBC NEWS (Sept. 8, 2008), *available at* http://news.bbc.co.uk/2/hi/business/7599921.stm (last visited Apr. 22, 2010). On a similar story, see Marshall Kirkpatrick, *YouTube Copyright System Gone Mad, EFF Prepares to Sue,* READWRITEWEB (Feb. 3, 2009), *available at* http://www.readwriteweb.com/archives/youtube_copyright_system_eff_action.php (last visited Apr. 22, 2010).

197. YouTube's copyright compliance strategy is described by Glenn Brown, product counsel for Google, as summarized by Daniel B Wood, *Lawsuit over YouTube video: It's What Everyone's Watching,* CHRISTIAN SCIENCE MONITOR (Mar. 23, 2007), *available at* http://www.csmonitor.com/2007/0323/p02s02-usju.html?page=1 (last visited July 17, 2010). Wood comments, "Those additional measures include an automated takedown tool that can provide a quick search for copyrighted content, which YouTube offers to anyone who asks, he says. YouTube also has a 10-minute limit on videos, which limits abuse; a three-strikes provision that cancels the account of any three-time rule breaker; and a digital 'hashing" feature that records when a file has been taken down to help prevent re-uploading of the same or similar material . . . "

progress of the *Viacom* suit, but also, YouTube's "voluntary" strategies for copyright management.

The film industry has a chance to learn what the music industry took too long to discover—that viable alternatives to free Internet material should be offered in order to satisfy the "unmet demand" for access to entertainment via the Internet. At the same time, measures for dealing with potential copyright infringement should not be draconian. An overly strict approach leads to bad public relations, on the one hand, and to bad legal practice, on the other. Viacom's decision to sue YouTube instead of attempting to target individual users of the site reflects a lesson well learned from the music experience.

It seems unlikely that any legal developments will inhibit the growth of video file-sharing. As video technologies improve, the incentives to share videos will only increase. If the Viacom suit is successful, it may help to change the legal framework for video file-sharing in much the same way that the model of music file-sharing has been transformed over the past decade. As in the case of music, collective licensing or pay-per-use models are likely to be the way of the future for video downloads.

As in the case of music, downloading exposes the vulnerability of moral rights. The attribution and integrity of films can both be compromised by users in a YouTube scenario; in an iTunes-style model, moral rights are also likely to suffer neglect at the hands of the companies controlling downloads. Many of the same concerns affect music and film—maintaining the integrity and attribution of films is both a social issue surrounding the integrity of knowledge, and an issue of fairness affecting authors and artists. As in the case of music, the international legal dimension creates additional difficulties, because moral rights are not recognized in the United States, one of the world's largest producers—and consumers—of films.[198]

Issues of moral rights can also arise in user-made videos. For example, the posting of a private video that becomes a hit, as has happened a number of times on YouTube, can generate extensive re-use of the video, leading to a corresponding loss of control for its creator. In addition, the making of fan films can lead to concerns about the moral rights of the authors of the original work. Should a special exception along the lines of a parody exemption—primarily based on the intentions of the author—be created for these kinds of works?

---

198. It is well worth noting that under French law, the insertion of advertisements into a film without the authors' consent is a violation of moral rights. *See* Sirinelli et al., *supra* note 25, at 121, 3° *Modalités de la diffusion* (conditions of Broadcast), 11, "Coupures publicitaires" [Interruptions for advertising].

3. Fame Beyond the Grave: Reviving Deceased Actors

In Woody Allen's 1972 film, *Play it Again Sam*, the main character is fixated on Humphrey Bogart—his ideal of a man with a perfect understanding of women. In the film, Bogart coaches Allen's character towards a decision to do the right thing, in the process, re-creating the famous final scene of the 1942 classic *Casablanca*, starring Bogart and Ingrid Bergman, in an entirely new context.

In Allen's film, Bogart is played by actor Jerry Lacy. But computer technology now offers a new possibility. In a film like this, Bogart's own image could potentially be taken from his old films and re-used. The question of using the images of deceased actors in films presents a new kind of problem. The use of images, voices, or lines of dialogue associated with iconic characters—"Here's looking at you, kid!" "Frankly, my dear, I don't give a damn!"—leads to interesting questions about the association of a given actor's name and image with a new film. The film itself could be made for many kinds of purposes, from creative art—Allen's comedy—to advertising.

The use of a person's image after his or her death is a disconcerting prospect. The Digital Age is plagued with problems of identity—identity theft, misappropriation, or misleading association—and they are only likely to become more pronounced over time. At the same time, the law provides surprisingly little recourse to address these concerns. In common law countries, privacy issues are generally the province of personal torts which can only be invoked during a person's lifetime. Afterwards, except in those cases where special legislation might address the protection of a personality after his or her death, there is no obvious legal solution.

Moral rights are well adapted to these situations, for two reasons. First, they are fundamentally preoccupied with the protection of an artist's reputation. As such, they target precisely the kinds of issues that would be raised by the re-use of images of deceased actors in films. Similarly, moral rights can protect an artist's image after his death—possibly even in perpetuity. As such, they offer a viable method of protecting the integrity of a personality after the death of the individual concerned.

E. Recommendations

The art of film has developed throughout the twentieth century into an increasingly sophisticated medium of expression. It has proven its potential to convey the artistic vision of its creators. The history of film has been one of steady movement towards greater recognition for film-makers as creative artists. It therefore seems natural that a parallel legal development would see moral rights as appropriate for film. Moral rights should play an integral role in valuing the creativity of filmmakers. The challenge of recognizing moral rights in film is tremendous, but it is well worth the application of legal and creative ingenuity.

The traditional moral rights of disclosure, attribution, and integrity are all appropriate for film. However, each right should be tailored to the practical requirements of the medium. Disclosure cannot be the prerogative of all those involved in the creation of the film; but the concept of film disclosure can serve to represent, as in the French example, the agreement of the film-makers on the final product.[199] Attribution is already accommodated in films, in the form of film credits, and should be maintained by companies engaged in the distribution of movies via the Internet. Individuals should also be educated about the need to attribute videos properly when posting content to the Internet, a requirement that could indirectly support legitimate copyright interests on Internet video sites.

The moral right of integrity should be recognized in both its dimensions, authenticity—preserving the integrity of a film as envisioned by the direc-tor—and reputation—protecting the reputations of all of the creative contri-butions to a film. These would include directorial work, writing, music, and, by extension of the principles in the WIPO Performances and Phonograms Treaty to audiovisual works,[200] actors' performances in films. As moral rights come to be recognized in technical work, such as sound engineering and cin-ematography, provision for the protection of their reputations would also make sense.

Moral rights provisions should offer clarity in defining the relationships among the different parties involved in the making of a film. Once again, the French approach, which requires agreement on the final version among pro-ducers and coauthors, is a solid one. At the same time, it may make sense to craft specific provisions that allow the director's moral right to override the rights of other creative contributors after the final version of a film is estab-lished. This would avoid a situation where, for example, a bad review of an actor's performance triggered a moral rights suit against the director, based on the integrity principle.

Evidence from the countries where film moral rights are recognized sup-ports this approach. All the countries of Continental Europe, and countries with major traditions of filmmaking such as India and Russia, recognize the moral rights of the authors of a film. In the common law world, the example of India, which includes film comprehensively in its moral rights regime, is striking; but film moral rights are also recognized in the legislation of the UK,

---

199. CPI, *supra* note 21, art. L121-5.
200. WIPO Performances and Phonograms Treaty (adopted Dec. 20, 1996, entered into force May 20, 2002) (1997) 36 I.L.M. 76, *available at* http://www.wipo.int/treaties/en/ip/berne/trtdocs_wo001.html (last visited Apr. 28, 2010) [WPPT].

Canada, Australia, and New Zealand. The presence of moral rights does not appear to have "chilled" the film industry in any of these countries.[201] Indeed, India's is both the largest and the most flagrantly commercial film industry in the world.

The position of the United States is quite anomalous. Based on the experience of other countries with film moral rights, the fears of Hollywood appear difficult to justify; and Hollywood's neglect of moral rights translates into American disregard for America's own filmmakers. When other countries demonstrate their willingness to recognize the work of Americans, as has often happened in the history of film moral rights, the situation can generate national embarrassment.

There is also an international aspect to filmmaking, which should encourage Hollywood to rethink its strategy. In the global film arena, Hollywood may have something concrete to gain from moral rights. In particular, popular American films are increasingly noticed by India's Bollywood film industry. Many Bollywood films are simply remakes of Hollywood features—although it should be noted that Hollywood, too, is famous for its remakes of world cinema and television.[202] In cases such as Barbara Taylor Bradford's, *A Woman of Substance*, remade as the television program, *Karishma—The Miracles of Destiny*, or the Hindi film, *Hari Puttar*, playing on the popularity of *Harry Potter* films, Indian courts, usually pro-author, have been completely unwilling to support Hollywood interests against Indian producers.[203] From an Indian perspective, Bollywood may be continuing an age-old tradition of exuberant adaptation. But how are Hollywood films, themselves, faring in India? Is India a potential marketplace for them? Do the new, "derivative" adaptations of American stories produced by Bollywood support Hollywood interests by creating a taste with local viewers for the original; do they harm Hollywood by supplanting the American films; or, though it seems increasingly unlikely, are the film markets in the two countries insulated from one

---

201. Of the four countries, Canada is the only long-term example of a country with moral rights (from 1931); since it allows comprehensive waiver of moral rights, it is difficult to say what impact they have had on Canada's film industry. Moreover, it is probably fair to say that Canada's focus has generally been on the production of art and specialty films. For an interesting overview of the Canadian film landscape, see Fraser, *Canadian Film*, *supra* note 87. His earlier article, *supra* note 7, at 304–11, offers a more detailed treatment of Canadian film and cultural issues from an international trade perspective.

202. Of course, Hollywood, too, has had its share of remakes for cinema and television. To cite a couple of examples, the 1980s comedy program *Three's Company* was based on a British sitcom, *Man About the House*, and the 1987 Hollywood comedy, *Three Men and a Baby*, was based on the French film, *Trois Hommes et un couffin*.

203. For an overview of the Bradford case and other Indian cases involving Hollywood films, see Rachana Desai, *Copyright Infringement in the Indian Film Industry*, 7 VAND. J. ENT. L & PRAC. 259 (2005), and Ayan Roy Choudhury, *The Future of Copyright in India*, 3(2) J. INTELL. PROP. L. & PRAC. 102, 109–13 (2008).

another? Moral rights, already well supported by the Indian courts, could help to persuade Indian judges that certain limits should be imposed on Bollywood's gain, even when the films in question represent popular cultural "adaptations" in India.[204]

F. Conclusion

As the original art form of the twentieth century grows into maturity, the technological landscape of the twenty-first could help to rejuvenate film. New possibilities abound. A thoughtful approach to moral rights could help to recognize the contributions of film-makers to modern culture, and lend support to the preservation of film as a vital cultural artefact. The ideas of authenticity and integrity have captured the imagination of those involved with cinema throughout the world. Many countries have adopted useful and interesting provisions on film moral rights, and future decades should see the refinement of these provisions to reflect the sophistication of new technologies and their potential impact on film.

The United States, a world leader in movies and in copyright matters, should not be left behind. America has produced some of the world's great film artists. Production no longer occurs within a strict studio system, and legal support for greater equality of bargaining power between the producers and the authors of a film would reflect this practical reality. American directors, in particular, deserve to be recognized in their own country as they are already appreciated abroad. The introduction of moral rights would herald a cultural shift, but international experience suggests that there is little need for the American film industry to be fearful. On the contrary, moral rights can help to affirm pride of achievement in an industry that depends on human creativity. When stories fail, films fail. Money alone cannot rescue them; they are products of the imagination. What does America have to lose?

---

204. The pursuit of such an argument by an American filmmaker in India would be interesting but complicated. In particular, where film is concerned, Indian courts firmly adhere to the notion that there can be no copyright in ideas—the ground on which the *Bradford* case failed. *But see* T. S. Krishnamurti, *Copyright—Another View*, 15(3) BULL. COPYRIGHT SOC'Y USA 217 (1968), who suggests that the ancient Indian practice was to recognize "copyright in ideas." It seems likely that the recognition of ideas noted by had more to do with preserving the attribution interest than assuring any kind of financial benefit for the author.

CHAPTER
8

The Virtual Museum
Moral Rights in Art and Artefacts

The world was not the same . . . .

–Bill Reid, Haida sculptor, on his first view of
traditional Haida carving[1]

---

1. Quoted in Martine Reid, *Haida 1951–1967*, *in* THE RAVEN'S CALL, *available at* http://theraven-scall.ca/en/art/guided_journey/haida (last visited July 31, 2010); Martine Reid writes, "In 1954 [Reid] traveled to Haida Gwaii where he saw a pair of *deeply carved* bracelets engraved by his very talented great-great uncle, Charles Edenshaw. Those sculptural bracelets left a deep impression on him. In his own words, 'the world was not the same after that.'" *Id.*

The visual arts are different. Where moral rights are concerned, in contrast to every other sphere of creative expression, they seem to attract ready sympathy. In the world of the visual arts, moral rights receive at least two kinds of special treatment. First, they enjoy stronger protection than moral rights in other kinds of works. Secondly—and strikingly—they are even recognized where the general recognition of moral rights is in doubt.

Is the special treatment of moral rights in the visual arts appropriate for the world of technology? This question is important, not only in relation to individual works of art, but also, in terms of the collections of art galleries and museums as a whole. In fact, the world's galleries house an astonishing array of different kinds of artworks and cultural artefacts, drawn from all corners of the world. In a sense, digital technology and the Internet allow these objects to gain new life and new meaning. But is the digital reincarnation of objects compatible with their past lives?—Supportive of their future lives?

This chapter will explore the role of moral rights as art and artefacts from the world's museums increasingly find their way into virtual spaces. In particular, three questions arise. First, how do existing moral rights laws affect the virtual transformation of art and artefacts? Secondly, how should the approach to moral rights in the visual arts adapt to the needs of the virtual environment? And, finally, what can the treatment of moral rights in artworks teach us about the broader relationship between moral rights and cultural artefacts?

A. Special Rights and Privileges? Unique Moral Rights for Visual Art

If the visual arts are different from other forms of creative expression, it seems natural that they should give rise to different kinds of moral rights than those which are common to other art forms. A consideration of visual arts protection in various copyright laws reveals at least three aspects to the special treatment of the visual arts. The first, and in a sense most dramatic, is the presence of moral rights for visual art in legal systems that do not otherwise recognize moral rights. Secondly, the moral rights of visual artists often turn upon a special approach to the interpretation of the moral right of integrity in the visual context. Thirdly, the visual arts may attract other kinds of rights, such as the *droit de suite*, or artist's resale right, which is related to moral rights, but is not a moral right *per se*.[2]

---

2. A fascinating history of the *droit de suite* in France is provided by Paul Lewis in his interesting, but skeptical, study of the right. *See* Paul Lewis, *The Resale Royalty and Australian Visual Artists: Painting the Full Picture*, 8 MEDIA & ARTS L. REV. 306–07 (2003).

The United States is, of course, the classic illustration of the first case, offering moral rights protection only to visual artists. More than two decades after joining the Berne Convention, the United States has made little progress towards the general implementation of moral rights in its copyright law.[3] But moral rights in visual works were created soon after Berne membership, with the introduction of special legislation in 1990 known as the *Visual Artists Rights Act* (VARA).[4]

In many respects, VARA is a controversial law. It is true that VARA recognizes the basic moral rights of attribution and integrity, but it does so in unusual formulae. Attribution is framed in terms that are more specific than usual, but also, more restrictive. The VARA right explicitly includes two aspects of attribution—the right to claim authorship, and the problem of false attribution of another person's work to the author. In the context of the visual arts, the right against false attribution helps to address the problem of forgery.[5] In contrast, commenting on the Berne Convention, Silke von Lewinski argues that "moral rights only protect the relation of the author to her own work," leading to the general situation that "cases of false attribution are not covered by the right to claim authorship."[6] In this sense, VARA may surpass international standards.

Interestingly, attribution is also presented as a partial remedy to violations of the right of integrity which follows it. In the case of any detrimental treatment of the work that would damage the author's reputation, the author is entitled to prevent the association of his or her name with it as its original creator.[7] Presumably, this right is one that the author would have to assert; it should not be used to justify the removal of an artist's name from his work

---

3. *See* the detailed discussion of the approach to moral rights in the United States in Chapter 3, *supra* notes 69–122 and accompanying text.

4. Visual Artists Rights Act of 1990, Pub. L. No. 101-650, 104 Stat. 5128, 17 U.S.C. § 106A [VARA], available on the website of the U.S. Copyright Office at http://www.copyright.gov/title17/92chap1.html#106a (last visited July 28, 2010). William Patry provides a useful analysis of case law related to VARA, online at http://williampatry.blogspot.com/2006/06/no-vara-trophy.html (last visited July 26, 2010). In a second post, he provides an interesting look at the interpretation of VARA in relation to "site-specific art" and whether its removal can violate an artist's rights under the legislation. *See* http://williampatry.blogspot.com/2006/08/first-circuit-misses-boat-again.html (last visited July 26, 2010).

5. *See* VARA, *supra* note 4, § 106A (a)(1)(B)(2), providing that the author "shall have the right to prevent the use of his or her name as the author of the work of visual art in the event of a distortion, mutilation, or other modification of the work which would be prejudicial to his or her honor or reputation . . ." *See* Chapter 2, *supra* notes 4–5 and accompanying text.

6. Silke von Lewinski, International Copyright Law and Policy, para. 5.99 (Oxford Univ. Press 2008).

7. *See* VARA, *supra* note 4, §106A(a)(2), providing that the author "shall have the right to prevent the use of his or her name as the author of the work of visual art in the event of a distortion, mutilation, or other modification of the work which would be prejudicial to his or her honor or reputation . . . ."

without his consent.[8] It should also not preclude the artist from asserting his right of integrity.

The integrity right, at first glance, is framed more broadly than attribution. VARA goes so far as to prohibit the "intentional or grossly negligent destruction of a work of recognized stature," more than international law requires.[9] However, the integrity right in VARA is also subject to numerous qualifications, including the fact that mistreatment of the work must be "intentional" before the moral right of integrity be invoked.[10]

How significant is the limit imposed by intention? If the definition of intent encompasses negligence—which it may be possible to infer, more generally, from the language surrounding destruction—then the requirement does not really limit the right in any meaningful sense. In fact, it offers a convincing form of protection against potential abuses of the integrity right, or, indeed, the possibility of a purely subjective interpretation of integrity under American law that would give priority to the artist's own view of how his

---

8. *See* the interesting moral rights litigation under VARA initiated by David Ascalon, a well-known sculptor, in July, 2010. Ascalon's sculpture for a Holocaust memorial in Harrisburg, Pennsylvania was subject to restoration work that defaced the sculpture and effectively destroyed the artistic concept behind it. Among other forms of damage, the sculptor's name was ground off the work. Writing for the *1709 Blog*, Monika Bruss provides an interesting post on the case, *available at* http://the1709blog.blogspot.com/2010/08/it-is-fact-universal-ly-acknowledged-at.html (posted Aug. 16, 2010; last visited Aug. 24, 2010) [Ascalon post]. Bruss comments that, "by grinding off Mr Ascalon's name the Defendants successfully avoided violation of § 106A(a)(2)." But this interpretation seems mistaken. Rather, Ascalon's statement of claim identifies the removal of his name as part of the severe harm done to the work by the defendants, the Harrisburg Department of Parks and Recreation, and David Grindle, hired by the Department to restore the work. Ascalon's counsel writes: "The Federation's direction to Grindle, or alternatively its acceptance of Grindle's decision, to remove Ascalon's name from the Memorial amounts to grossly negligent and intentional destruction of the Memorial and prejudice to Ascalon's honor and reputation in violation of Ascalon's rights under 17 D.S.C.§106A(a)(3)(B)." It would seem that the right to remove the artist's name from his or her work, granted by VARA, is a choice that is supposed to remain with the artist. It may be a practical means of dealing with damage to a work that cannot be sufficiently corrected to restore the artist's reputation—or, at least, forestall further damage to it. The Statement of Claim in the Ascalon litigation is *available at* http://www.courthousenews.com/2010/07/28/Holocaust.pdf (last visited Aug. 24, 2010).

9. For an assessment of where destruction of an artwork stands in international copyright law, see SAM RICKETSON, THE BERNE CONVENTION FOR THE PROTECTION OF LITERARY AND ARTISTIC WORKS: 1886–1986, para. 8.109 (Centre for Commercial Law Studies, Queen Mary College, Kluwer 1987). *See also* the comments in VON LEWINSKI, *supra* note 6, para. 5.103. For a discussion of the debate surrounding the issue of whether or not destruction of a work is encompassed by the right of integrity, see Chapter 2, *supra* notes 35–43 and accompanying text.

10. *See* VARA, *supra* note 4. The curiously circular formula of § 106A(a)(3)(A) reads: "to prevent any intentional distortion, mutilation, or other modification of that work which would be prejudicial to his or her honor or reputation, and any intentional distortion, mutilation, or modification of that work is a violation of that right . . . ."

work has been treated. Henri Desbois' comments about the focus of French moral rights on the author's preferences come to mind.[11] A different mindset informs the American copyright system, which has the distinction of an explicit preoccupation with the public interest. Jane Ginsburg has noted that the divergences between French and American copyright principles tend to be exaggerated by commentators, but she, too, remarks:

> [T]he development of personalist doctrines, such as moral rights, by French copyright scholars and courts . . . did provoke theoretical and practical divergences between the French and U.S. copyright regimes.[12]

Significantly, American law, like the Canadian Copyright Act, allows moral rights to be waived, although the American provisions are more precise than the extremely general rule on the availability of waivers under Canadian law.[13]

The second case of special treatment for moral rights in works of visual art provides stronger protection than usual by adjusting the scope of the right of integrity. It is illustrated by the language of the Canadian Copyright Act.[14] In Canada, the moral right of integrity in a visual work is an unconditional right that can be invoked upon any unwanted change to an artist's work. The artist is under no obligation to prove that the alteration has damaged his reputation or honor.[15] This treatment amounts to a complete departure from the usual approach to integrity in Canadian law, which depends upon proof of harm,

---

11. HENRI DESBOIS, LE DROIT D'AUTEUR EN FRANCE, vii, 538–39, para. 449 (3d ed. Dalloz 1978). *See* the discussion in Chapter 2, *supra* note 40 and accompanying text.

12. Jane C. Ginsburg, *A Tale of Two Copyrights* 64(5) TUL. L. REV. 991–96 (1990). She goes on to make the important observation that "[t]he comparison of systems shows that their distinctions are neither original nor immutable. A copyright regime's initial instrumentalist formulation does not preclude later reception of more personalist notions of protection." This perspective is fundamentally supported by Carla Hesse's historical research on the origins of modern French copyright. *See* Carla Hesse, *Enlightenment Epistemology and the Law of Authorship in Revolutionary France, 1777–1793*, 30 REPRESENTATIONS 109 (1990).

13. VARA, *supra* note 4, § 106A(e)(1); Canadian law even provides that waivers can be extended to a third party who acquires rights from the person exploiting the copyright. *See* Canadian Copyright Act, R.S.C. 1985, c. C-42, *available at* http://laws.justice.gc.ca/en/C-42/index.html (last visited Jul. 26, 2010) [Canadian Copyright Act], sec. 14.1 (4). The pending Canadian copyright reform bill, enacted to bring Canadian law into conformity with the WIPO Performances and Phonograms Treaty, would extend an identical regime to performers' moral rights. *See* Bill C-32, Third Session, Fortieth Parliament, 59 Elizabeth II, 2010, secs. 17.1 and 17.2. The WIPO Performances and Phonograms Treaty provides for performers' moral rights in Article 5. WIPO Performances and Phonograms Treaty (adopted Dec. 20, 1996, entered into force May 20, 2002) (1997) 36 I.L.M. 76, *available at* http://www.wipo.int/export/sites/www/treaties/en/ip/wppt/pdf/trtdocs_wo034.pdf (last visited Jul. 26, 2010) [WPPT].

14. *Id.*

15. *Id.*, sec. 28.2(2) ("Where prejudice deemed").

and has been affirmed by recent commentary from the Supreme Court of Canada in the *Théberge* case.[16]

But the broader scope of the integrity right may also be qualified by certain specific limitations that apply to the visual arts. Once again, Canadian law provides a useful illustration. It explicitly states that attempts made in good faith to restore a work of art cannot lead to a violation of the integrity right.[17]

Canadian law also provides for a more controversial exception. To some extent, the conditions in which a work of art is displayed may not lead to a violation of the integrity right—in particular, "a change in the location of a work, the physical means by which a work is exposed or the physical structure containing a work."[18] In fact, the Indian Copyright Act provides a more detailed stipulation, with an "explanation" that integrity will not be violated by new conditions of display.[19] This principle poses some problems in the digital environment, and the implications for digital galleries are discussed in detail below.

Thirdly, where special kinds of rights arise in works of visual art, there are at least two categories: hybrid rights and true moral rights. The widely protected *droit de suite,* or visual artist's resale right, is often called a moral right, but it would be more precise to characterize it as a hybrid right. The *droit de suite* allows an artist to receive a commission for the sale of his or her work by new owners to new purchasers. The resale right has an important commonality with moral rights, in the sense that it continues to be vested in the artist even after he has sold his work and enjoys no more rights of ownership over it. Unlike moral rights, however, the *droit de suite* is a purely economic right. It reflects the realities of the art market, and the often slow growth of an artist's reputation. It does not really have anything to do with the special relationship between the artist and the work in the sense in which moral rights protect that relationship.

In terms of true moral rights, the American prohibition against destruction of an artwork is a striking example—a bold expansion of the integrity right to cover a circumstance that is still ambiguous in international law.

---

16. For the standard rule on integrity under Canadian law, see Canadian Copyright Act, *supra* note 13, sec. 28.2(1); *Théberge v. Galerie d'Art du Petit Champlain Inc.* [2002] 2 S.C.R. 336, 2002 SCC 34 [*Théberge*], *available at* http://csc.lexum.umontreal.ca/en/2002/2002scc34/2002scc34.pdf (last visited Jul. 26, 2010). Among the many intricacies of Théberge, the case involved damage to the reputation of a visual artist by the production of "copies" of his paintings on canvas backing that could, the artist apparently felt, lead buyers to confuse them with his originals.

17. Canadian Copyright Act, *supra* note 13, sec. 28.2(3)(b).

18. *Id.*, sec. 28.2(3)(a).

19. *See* Indian Copyright Act 1957, Act 14 of 1957, Explanation to sec. 57; the Act is published by the Government of India, http://copyright.gov.in/Documents/CopyrightRules1957.pdf [Indian Copyright Act] (last visited July 26, 2010).

In fact, the language framing the American provision parallels the approach adopted by the Delhi High Court in the *Amar Nath Sehgal* case. Destruction that is intentional or "grossly negligent," and that affects a work "of recognized stature," is prohibited by U.S. law. When it comes to artworks that are an important part of national cultural heritage, American and Indian law are closely aligned with one aother. But a similar legal result is achieved in the two jurisdictions by different means—legislative reform in the U.S. case, judicial precedent in India.

Prohibiting destruction leaves one difficult question open: what happens when an artist wants to destroy his own work? The point is neatly illustrated by Adolf Dietz, who offers the example of Munich's Olympic Stadium. Even the architect who designed the stadium was apparently willing to redesign it for new needs, but the decision to do so was opposed by the German authority for the protection of monuments, which also happened to represent public opinion in this case.[20]

The potential conflict between the public interest in protecting heritage and the artist's moral rights of integrity and withdrawal presents a harrowing choice. There may be many reasons why an artist wants a work of art destroyed. It is difficult to argue that the artist's desire to see his own work removed from his catalogue should be disregarded. At the same time, an artist may not be the best judge of the quality or importance of his or her own work.

There is also the traditional knowledge aspect of this question, as some works of traditional culture are meant to be destroyed—Tibetan sand mandalas, for example.[21] Is an outright prohibition on destruction the best way to deal with the potential conflict between private desires and public needs?

Works of art that are situated in public locales pose a unique challenge to moral rights doctrine, especially in view of its generous treatment of visual artists. The specter of conflict between artistic intent and the practical requirements of the public looms over moral rights in public art. The law is confusing. The United Kingdom explicitly provides that anyone can make a photograph or image of public art.[22] In the United States, this issue is not addressed explicitly by copyright law, but, depending on the nature of

---

20. *See* Adolf Dietz, The Importance of Moral Rights for Cultural Heritage and Diversity 51 (paper presented at the 2008 ALAI Conference) (on file with author).

21. See the interesting discussion of these creations on the website of the Drepung Loseling monstery at http://www.mysticalartsoftibet.org/index.cfm#top (last visited July 28, 2010).

22. *See* Copyright, Designs and Patents Act 1988 (ch. 48), Office of Public Sector Information, *available at* http://www.opsi.gov.uk/acts/acts1988/UKpga_19880048_en_1.htm (last visited July 26, 2010) [Copyright, Designs and Patents Act, CDPA], sec. 62.

the use, photography of public art may be restricted.[23] As far as moral rights are concerned, neither the UK Copyright, Designs and Patents Act of 1988 nor the U.S. *Visual Artists Rights Act* clarifies the status of moral rights in public artworks.

In Canada, the Copyright Act states that photographing a work of public art will not be an infringement of copyright. However, the provision is not quite as straightforward as it might seem at first glance. In fact, the advice on interpretation provided by the Act itself leaves open the possibility that this section may be intended to allow photography only for private and noncommercial purposes.[24] At least one Canadian municipality—the city of Duncan, situated on Vancouver Island and famous for its totem poles—has enacted a policy stating that any commercial use of photographs of these poles must first be approved by the City. The purpose of the policy is essentially to support the protection of Aboriginal cultural heritage in the city's public spaces by controlling the public spread of images. Where appropriate, the City hopes to secure some economic benefit for the creators of the poles and, in cases where it has acquired rights from the artists, for the City, itself.[25] The policy is also intended to support the artists' moral rights of attribution and integrity.[26]

---

23. Public art is not explicitly addressed in U.S. copyright legislation, but fair use provisions in 17 U.S.C. § 107 identify "the purpose and character of the use," with a focus on whether or not it is commercial, and the "nature of the copyrighted work" as relevant factors in making this determination. *See* the website of the U.S. Copyright Office, *available at* http://www.copyright.gov/title17/92chap1.html#107 (last visited July 28, 2010).

24. Canadian Copyright Act, *supra* note 13, sec. 32.2(1)(b)(ii), and sec. 32.3 on Interpretation.

25. *See* Shannon Moneo, *Do You Have a Permit to Take That Photo?*, NATIONAL PHOTOGRAPHERS ASSOCIATION OF CANADA (Oct. 4, 2007), *available at* http://npac.ca/?p=47 (last visited July 26, 2010). See the interesting article inspired by the issue, by David Spratley, *Copyright Law Offers Poor Protection for Aboriginal Cultural Property*, LAWYERS WEEKLY (Nov. 23, 2007), *available at* http://www.lawyersweekly.ca/index.php?section=article&articleid=578. The municipality of Duncan followed up on the issue by developing a policy to clarify the issue (unpublished Opinion on Duncan Totem Policy by Mira T. Sundara Rajan, prepared for the City of Duncan, Jan. 2008) [Totem Policy]. The focus of the Totem Policy was on implementing measures to provide for respectful treatment of these works of art: "The development of a policy should encourage photographers to treat the works with deference, and in particular, to think carefully about the suitability of proposed uses." (on file with author).

26. Totem Policy, *supra* note 25; see also *Duncan introduces totem toll*, Canada.com (Aug 15, 2007), *available at* http://www.canada.com/victoriatimescolonist/news/story.html?id=13cccad8-8159-4530-8c89-36a4fca94068&k=23116 (last visited Aug. 1, 2010). ("Anyone thinking about making a profit out of one of Duncan's totem poles, whether it's a picture used for postcards, calendars, or for that movie they're wanting to shoot, will have to go through Duncan City Council first, as they've just adopted a City of Duncan Totem Copyright Policy").

A recent Spanish case tested a similar issue. In Spain, the issue arose, not in relation to public artworks of a decorative nature, but specifically in relation to works of architecture. The case involved a bridge designed by celebrated architect, Santiago Calatrava, who is known for the flamboyance and elegance of his bridge designs. For the convenience of pedestrians, the city of Bilbao decided to add a footbridge to Calatrava's structure. Calatrava sued for the violation of his moral right of integrity. At first instance, the trial court disagreed with his claim, and came to the practical conclusion that the public interest in pedestrian access to the bridge outweighed the artist's prerogative. The addition of the footbridge could not qualify as a violation of the architect's right of integrity.[27]

The decision is entirely understandable from a practical point of view, yet it leaves a slightly bitter aftertaste . A bridge is a difficult thing to classify. It serves a practical purpose, but the greatest bridges often become iconic representations of the cities where they are built—Paris' Pont-Neuf, London's Tower Bridge, New York's Queensboro, San Francisco's Golden Gate, Vancouver's Lion's Gate—and how many more? As William Patry notes:

> To me the works of these designers and others were not only art, but great art. Calatrava's bridge at Bilbao is art by anyone's definition. In New York City, he designed the new Path transportation Station at the World Trade Center, and has designed a wild apartment building at 80 South Street consisting of stacked cubes. Despite his training as an engineer, Mr. Calatrava asserts that function follows form, and there can be no doubt that his works are sculptural.[28]

Alterations to a bridge may become necessary, and it seems fair to limit the availability of moral rights for works which have an essential practical function. The practical shortcomings of Calatrava's bridge are

27. The authors of *The IPKat* blog, which provides a wealth of online resources related to IP issues, comment that "The IPKat is glad that common sense has prevailed here. It would make life extremely difficult if architects could object to alterations to buildings which others have commissioned from them, and would enable them to control other people's 'real property.' More fundamentally, the IPKat questions the wisdom of granting a right of integrity over works of architecture in the first place. This wouldn't be such a problem in the UK since an architect's right of integrity only gives him the right to have his name removed from buildings which have been altered in a way which is derogatory to his reputation." *Right of Integrity over Bridge Fails*, THE IPKAT (Dec. 4, 2007), *available at* http://ipkitten.blogspot.com/2007/12/right-of-integrity-over-bridge-fails.html (last visited July 26, 2010).

28. William Patry, *Calatrava, Bridges, and Moral Rights*, THE PATRY COPYRIGHT BLOG (links omitted), *available at* http://williampatry.blogspot.com/2007/10/calatrava-bridges-and-moral-rights.html (last visited Aug. 1, 2010).

apparently significant. Elizabeth Nash, writing for the Independent newspaper, notes:

> Initially ridiculed for "leading from nowhere to nowhere," Calatrava's footbridge is beautiful, but not exactly user-friendly. Its limpid glass floor tiles, designed to reflect the grey-green waters of the river Nervion that flow beneath, are notoriously slippery when wet. For 10 years residents and visitors have complained of skidding and tumbling.[29]

But functional works which can lay claim to a certain aesthetic stature should also be treated with care. There can be little doubt that works of architecture constitute an important part of a nation's cultural heritage—Greece's Parthenon and India's Taj Mahal are but two examples. In this regard, moral rights can help to supplement laws for the protection of monuments by offering, in effect, a comparable level of protection to works that are still within the copyright term. In Calatrava's case, for example, a simple solution may have been to ask the architect himself to assist with the alteration plans, rather than making the unfriendly gesture of engaging a rival architect to undertake the work.[30] An architect may or may not agree to be involved in the alteration of his own work; and the law could limit the architect's rights by giving him or her a first right of refusal in cases such as these.

In his interesting analysis of the case, Spanish copyright lawyer, Juan José Marín López, notes:

> The judge criticized the actions of the city council, stating that it had been wrong not to have put Mr. Calatrava himself in charge of the extension to his bridge. But no penalty was imposed.[31]

The dilemma between art and function is neatly expressed by the court. As López translates its statement, the court comments:

> In addition to constituting a singular artistic creation suitable for protection, the work is [a] public one, offering a service to the citizens, and thus satisfies a public interest. If we weigh these interests, the public must prevail over the private.[32]

---

29. Elizabeth Nash, *Calatrava Sues for "Violation of Copyright" over Bridge Changes*, THE INDEPENDENT, *available at* http://www.independent.co.uk/news/world/europe/calatrava-sues-for-violation-of-copyright-over-bridge-changes-397965.html (last visited July 26, 2010).
30. In the recently filed Ascalon case, the sculptor offered to undertake restoration work on his sculpture himself. Monika Bruss observes, "Mr Ascalon offered to carry out any necessary restoration work, but was eventually not taken up on that offer." Instead, the work was carried out by another person. *See* Ascalon post, *supra* note 8.
31. Juan José Marín López, *In the Courts: Bridging Moral Rights and Public Utility*, WIPO MAGAZINE (Feb. 2008), *available at* http://www.wipo.int/wipo_magazine/en/2008/01/article_0004.html (last visited July 26, 2010).
32. *Id.*

In fact, the court expressed sympathy for the idea that Calatrava should have been asked to modify his own work. For José J. Izquierdo Peris, the judgment of the court provides useful guidance on upholding the architect's right to make any alterations to his own work that become necessary. However, the court's statement on this issue is not entirely authoritative, and Peris advises:

> Ultimately, one sees how difficult it is for an architect, who is commissioned to complete a functional work, to retain any possibility . . . [of] stop[ping] modifications done by [the] public authorities . . . On the positive side, in one way or another, the owner of the work is expected to contract changes to the author, not to a third party. But this expectation is far from being other than an obiter dictum. For . . . [this] reason, when receiving a contract from a public authority, designers and architects should perhaps negotiate an explicit provision, to help the author retain at least some contractual rights in case alteration is done under circumstances like those in this suit.[33]

On appeal, the perspective of the provincial court hearing Mr. Calatrava's complaint was entirely different. In contrast to the practical resolution of the case offered by the court at first instance, the higher court felt that Mr. Calatrava had already provided a public service by constructing the bridge. Further convenience for the public was not reason enough to overrule the architect's moral right of integrity. In particular, the decision to construct a footbridge was a matter of choice, and the authorities could have chosen other means of facilitating public access to the bridge without ruining Calatrava's design. The higher court's perspective is summarized by López:

> Mr. Calatrava's bridge, on its own, already served the public interest by providing a means to cross the river at a place where it was not previously possible. After crossing the bridge, pedestrians had to go down one flight of stairs and up another to reach the residential area. The footbridge added to Mr. Calatrava's bridge fulfilled a function of simple comfort, as it allowed a direct connection with the residential area, without the need to go up or down stairs. The Court considers that, in these circumstances, the footbridge does not represent a public interest that prevails over and above the author's moral right. Simple comfort is not then, at least in this case, a public interest prevailing over the moral right.[34]

---

33. José J. Izquierdo Peris, *A Bridge Too Far: Calatrava's Bridge is Copyright-Protected, But Not Enough*, 3(4) J. Intell. Prop. L. & Prac. 218–20 (2008) ("Current Intelligence").

34. Juan José Marín López, *Copyright in the Courts: Moral Right in Architecture (Part II)*, WIPO Magazine (June 2009), *available at* http://www.wipo.int/wipo_magazine/en/2009/03/article_0012.html (last visited July 26, 2010) [López II].

Crucially, the higher court noted that Calatrava's stature as an architect was relevant to its determination. The city should not have expected to hire an architect of his reputation and style, and then alter his work without his consent. As López notes:

> The Town Hall recruited a prestigious architect, such as Mr. Calatrava, not in order to plan the complete work provided for in the urban plan, but only to design and construct a bridge over the river. Some time later, once the bridge was complete, it decided to add the footbridge in order to connect the bridge to the residential area. According to the Court, the Town Hall could have made good on the provision made in the urban plan, by facilitating direct access to the residential area, in a manner that did not harm Mr. Calatrava's moral right. However, as it did not do so, it infringed the copyright.[35]

B. Sanctum Sanctorum: Originality and the Special Status of Art

Why are works of visual art treated differently? This question can probably be answered in a single word: originality. Originality is a concept of unrivaled significance in the art world, and this applies in both the material and moral senses of the word. As an issue of material originality, it generally happens that the artist only has one final copy of the finished work. If this work is damaged, it may be impossible to restore the status quo where the work, or the reputation of the artist, is concerned. At the same time, if copies of the work did exist, they may not be entitled to claim the same degree of authenticity as the initial work made by the artist's hand. Depending on the circumstances, even copies of a work made by the artist himself might not be considered as authentic as the original. For this reason, it may make intuitive sense to set higher standards for the treatment of artistic work. Accordingly, as the Canadian example illustrates, any alteration of the artwork that is of concern to the artist should attract the sanction of moral rights law.

This leads to the subtler moral issue posed by artistic originality. Works that are "original" can become immensely valuable because of their provenance directly from the artist's "master hand." Even a small sketch by a celebrated artist—a Gauguin or a Van Gogh—will be worth millions, to say nothing of a painting, sculpture, or other substantial work. But this definition of originality can only be comfortably applied to a relatively small subset of artistic works— those that are of known and uncontested authorship. Artists from the period

---

35. *Id.*

of the Renaissance, such as Leonardo da Vinci, often worked within a studio system where they trained junior artists, and a painting may be a product of the artist's *atelier*, rather than his own, "original" work. In fact, modern artists of such renown as Picasso and Rodin also operated large ateliers. In Rodin's case, the gifted Camille Claudel, his former student and lover, apparently felt that he had stolen her ideas.

The problem of understanding and recognizing artistic "originality" may also arise when works of art emerge from cultural traditions that have a different view of originality.

This situation is illustrated by the fascinating case of master sculptor Bill Reid, an artist of the Haida people of Canada's West Coast. By the time of his death in 1998, at age 78, Reid had reinvigorated the Haida tradition of sculpture. It is possible that Bill Reid belongs to that exceptionally rare class of artists who are, in a sense, Renaissance-makers. The Italian philosopher, Mazzini, writes about the conditions in which artistic genius may flourish, arguing that times of great prosperity and great despair, alike, may produce great men and women. Based on his theory, Subramania Bharati speculates that, at times of extreme oppression, "sages may be born to redeem [a] nation."[36] Bill Reid, like Bharati himself, may well be admired by his people as one of these.

But in the year following his death, Reid was the subject of a controversial article in Canada's *Maclean's* newsmagazine.[37] The article drew attention to the role of the artists working for Reid, exceptional craftsmen who were largely responsible for realizing the concrete details of Reid's artistic vision through their skill. The fact that Reid was suffering from Parkinson's disease throughout the 1990s shows how important, both practically and spiritually, their involvement must have been.

The article cited interviews with a number of the artists involved, and found mixed feelings—humiliation and disappointment for some, but for others, a sense of honor and privilege. None of these artists had been forced to work by Reid. On the other hand, all of them lived by their art and needed the work.

The problem is fundamentally one of moral rights.[38] It appears that the contribution of these artists was never recognized publicly by Reid.

---

36. Quoted in S. Vijaya Bharati, Subramania Bharati: Personality and Poetry (Munshiram Manoharlal 1975).

37. Jane O'Hara, *Reid Controversy*, Maclean's Magazine (Oct. 18, 1999), available on the website of the Canadian Encyclopedia at http://www.thecanadianencyclopedia.com/index.cfm?PgN m=TCE&Params=M1ARTM0012023 (last visited July 26, 2010) [*Reid Controversy*].

38. But this is not to say that financial considerations were not important. The article points out that many of the artists involved felt that they were poorly paid for their work and that Bill Reid's actions were partly driven by his own need for financial success.

According to the *Maclean's* piece, every formal context in which Reid was honored was one in which he, and he alone, received the credit for the work.

If we were to apply the logic of authors' moral rights to this story, what would we conclude? There can be little doubt that it was both wrong and illegal under existing Canadian law to deny attribution to these artists.[39] But how should they have been attributed? As coauthors alongside Reid? As his assistants? Or as unique creators of the works, or portions of the works, which were made with their own hands? It is now openly acknowledged that "Raven and the First Men" was not physically carved by Reid. And yet, as the *Maclean's* article notes, the sculpture was "[b]ased on an original eight-centimetre box-wood carving done by Reid in 1970." The artist was then at the height of his creative powers, physically as well as mentally. It seems that the concept behind the work was clearly, undeniably, Reid's.

Modern copyright law must frown upon such an assessment. The origin of the concept behind the work, from a copyright perspective, is of limited importance. Even on the most liberal interpretation, copyright law cannot protect ideas in the absence of a thinker's eventual involvement in the physical creation of the work.[40] And yet, without the concept, no work can exist. And it is rare, indeed, that artists are recognized primarily for their craftsmanship—although Bill Reid at first saw himself as the maker of the "well-made object."[41] An artist is undoubtedly known for his or her artistic vision: the greater the vision, the greater the artist. Vision is arguably what separates a true artist from the merely successful author of poem or painting.

A large part of the difficulty of Reid's case has to do with the Western society in which Haida culture operates, and the corresponding models of authorship and creativity to which Aboriginal art is subject. Western society idolizes the artist made in a certain mold—the individual, original, and independent genius who creates valuable works. To every work its artist. The Western model is based on the presence of individual and readily identifiable

---

39. *See* Canadian Copyright Act, *supra* note 13, sec. 14.1(1), defining the right of attribution. It is a peculiarity of Canadian law that attribution must be "reasonable in the circumstances."

40. The House of Lords case of *Designer Guild Ltd. v. Russell Williams (Textiles),* [2001] 1 All E.R. 700, *available at* http://www.publications.parliament.uk/pa/ld199900/ldjudgmt/jd001123/design-1.htm (last visited July 26, 2010), has come closer than any other common law ruling to claiming that ideas may be protected by copyright law. Lord Hoffman made the eminently sensible argument that idea and expression are united in any creative work; rather than viewing them as opposites, his discussion suggests a spectrum along which copyright protection moves from idea to expression. As the idea becomes increasingly detailed, copyright protection crystallizes. Alluding to Isaiah Berlin, Lord Hoffman points out that, "Copyright law protects foxes other than hedgehogs." The traditional artistic law of India is, apparently, an exception to the traditional rule, requiring the protection of ideas as well as expression. T. S. Krishnamurti, *Copyright—Another View*, 15(3) Bull. Copyright Soc'y USA 217–18 (1968).

41. Reid, quoted in *Reid Controversy, supra* note 37.

contributions to a work of art. As soon as the nature of the creative work becomes more complex, this model founders.

Work such as Reid's acquires its extraordinary power from the culture behind it. The work is a product of tradition; it seeks to give new life to that tradition. It embodies the relationship between artist and creation in an incredibly sophisticated way. The very fact that Reid's work was made as it was—through the collaborative efforts of several outstanding artists— suggests that there may not have been any other way to make it. Perhaps it was too massive, physically and spiritually, for any one person to control.

Of course, to the extent that the Maclean's reportage is based on facts, there can be no defense of Reid's behavior towards his fellow artists. And Allan Antliffe is absolutely right to point out that Reid missed an opportunity to fight the inequities and stereotypes of the art world.[42]

But it is also apparent that Reid was himself the victim of a system—a system that demands that artists should look a certain way, talk a certain way, and, of course, work in a certain way. As a society, we seem to have lost our sense of diffidence when confronted with genius. We think of it as something predictable and well defined, but a little observation would reveal the largely aleatory path along which nature strews her gifts (and society provides, or does not provide, for their development). Otherwise, artists and authors could never emerge from disadvantaged backgrounds. In many ways, Bill Reid resisted social stereotypes. In this particular regard—perhaps he was worn out after a lifetime of path-breaking—Reid was not quite strong enough to overcome society's expectations.

The modern stereotypes of artistic creation are also of questionable use to Western artists. If an artist is able to survive long enough, he or she may be able to use the system for his benefit, but the decision could come at a spiritual cost. There is something quite uncomfortable about the thought that an artist must conform to socially accepted notions of what an artist is. It limits creativity.

For artists who are not so clever, or so lucky, the situation becomes more troublesome. An artist may be a visionary who is, in some sense, ahead of his or her time. As a practical matter, this means that it will take some time for society to be able to recognize his or her worth. It often happens that an artist does not live long enough to enjoy the benefits of that recognition. Vincent van Gogh is the classic illustration of this paradox. The impoverished painter who sold but one painting in his entire lifetime is now the most expensive and elite name on the market for art.

---

42. *On Determining Authenticity and Authorship in Art*, FOLIO (Univ. of Alberta newspaper) (Oct. 29, 1999), *available at* http://www.folio.ualberta.ca/37/05/07.html (last visited July 26, 2010).

But the delayed recognition of an artist's value may also be due to another factor—the difficulty of perceiving the outstanding nature of those who live among us. The real explanation behind society's unwillingness to allow artists to break free of stereotypes may be simple ignorance. Whatever the reason, there can be little doubt that the stereotype of impoverished genius works against the artist, and indeed, may condemn him to a lifetime of misery.

C. Moral Rights and Traditional Art: The Legal Paradox of Living Traditions

As Bill Reid's case suggests, where traditional cultures are concerned, the underlying patterns of cultural development may collide directly with modern notions of authorship. This happened in the famous Australian case of *Yumbulul v. Reserve Bank of Australia.*[43] Decided in 1991, neither Australia nor any other jurisdiction has yet been able to address in its copyright law the concerns about the use of traditional images that this litigation raised.[44]

Yumbulul was an Aboriginal artist, initiated by his clan into the knowledge needed to make a ceremonial "morning star pole"—a mystical object which embodies Aboriginal knowledge of astronomy and reflects the spiritual world-view of the people who imagined it. Yumbulul was approached by the Australian government about the possibility of designing an image of a morning star pole to appear on a banknote. He agreed, but later attempted to withdraw his agreement. In fact, he was faced with the difficult prospect of displeasing his own community by allowing the Pole and the knowledge that it embodied—held as restricted and privileged by them—to be disseminated in this form. When the dispute between Yumbulul and the Australian government eventually went to court, the judge openly acknowledged the limits of copyright law, pointing out that "the question of statutory recognition of Aboriginal communal interests in the reproduction of sacred objects is a matter for consideration by law reformers and legislators."[45]

Once again, the models of creativity that support the Western copyright system fail to adapt to a different reality. From a copyright perspective,

---

43. (1991) 21 I.P.R. 481 (Aust.) [*Yumbulul*].
44. Australia toyed with the idea of an "Aboriginal communal moral right" in a 2001 bill, but the law was never passed. Had it succeeded, it would have left much to be desired in clarifying Aboriginal cultural rights. *See* Chapter 3, *supra* notes 123–52 and accompanying text.
45. *Yumbulul, supra* note 43, para. 20.

Yumbulul, the individual creator of the Pole, is the author. The Aboriginal community has no right to intervene in an author's decision about the disclosure of his own work. The community has no role in "creating" the work.

From the Aboriginal point of view, however, this meditation on authorship might be meaningless. The creator of the work has certain rights and privileges; so, too, does the community of which he or she is part. Certain rules define the parameters of this relationship, and those rules may not have much in common with the rules governing copyright transactions.

In fact, the attempt to apply copyright concepts to this kind of problem is of questionable value. Copyright cannot help to clarify the nature of the rights and obligations involved, nor does copyright language really help to translate Aboriginal cultural reality into Western concepts—a process which would ultimately benefit both. Rather, copyright superimposes Western relationships and concepts onto the underlying reality of Aboriginal thought. The results are often highly incongruous. In the *Yumbulul* scenario, neither Yumbulul nor his Aboriginal community can have been happy with the result. The trust in the relationship was broken. In every such instance, a process of healing and rehabilitation will surely be required.

The question of moral rights is slightly different. Here, too, as noted in relation to Bill Reid, the concept of authorship underlying moral rights may be irrelevant. But the interests protected by moral rights are clearly of some importance to Aboriginal cultures at the level of the community. In particular, an important aspect of the intellectual property concept for Aboriginal groups is probably the fact that it can empower outsiders to lay claim to Aboriginal cultural symbols, stories, and knowledge. The danger lies in the ease with which copyright can be acquired by outsiders. Even in a post- *Feist* context, a work with a minimal level of creativity will satisfy the originality requirements for copyright protection. At the same time, Aboriginal cultural knowledge is not associated with a single identifiable author, or with a group of joint authors in the copyright sense of the term. Moral rights in Aboriginal culture remain abstract until they can coalesce around an identifiable and unified entity, whether it is an individual or a group.

A possible solution to the dangers of cultural appropriation would be to create an Aboriginal moral right that would be vested in the community concerned. While the cultural work, knowledge, or tradition is in use within the community, the moral right would remain latent. In the situation where an appropriation of the work is attempted without the consent of the community, the moral right could be invoked in an action for infringement.

But there are always at least two layers of transactions in these kinds of dealings. The first layer, in which Aboriginal right and newcomer's attempt confront one another, is relatively easy to address through legal measures. The second layer, however, may be completely impenetrable by Western law. It is the problem of relationships within each Aboriginal community— between different groups associated with the same cultural tradition, among the different members of a group hailing from a particular cultural tradition, and between the givers and receivers of ceremonial knowledge.

The practical difficulty of applying an Aboriginal moral right led to controversy over the provisions of the Australian government's bill on the Aboriginal "communal moral right" proposed in 2002.[46] If the principle of cultural self-determination is to be upheld, Western law can have no moral basis for claiming to regulate relationships within Aboriginal communities. And yet, Aboriginal cultures, like every other human environment, can become spheres of injustice where unfair claims are made, and individuals are subject to mistreatment or exploitation. Tradition can be a two-edged sword. The fact that something has been done in a certain way "since time immemorial" does not necessarily justify the practice. To some extent, each generation reinvents tradition, and it can even be difficult to know with certainty what exactly is "traditional." Ideally, these conflicts would be resolved according to principles of fundamental justice. But who is entitled to decide on justice in cases such as these? Would it be appropriate to subject them to rulings by councils of elders or judges in Aboriginal communities? And would these councils be recognized as lawmakers by Western courts? This is one of many possible compromise solutions. If moral rights are ultimately seen as a valuable framework for cultural rights, compromise, in some form or another, will be unavoidable.

D. Artworks and Artefacts: Intellectual Property or Cultural Property?

These examples of traditional culture lead to another issue: the apparent distinction between the works of individual artists and the cultural heritage of a nation. From a strictly practical point of view, there is something anomalous about these categories. It is clear that they cannot be watertight compartments. To a very significant degree, the cultural heritage of every nation is composed of the work of individual artists, whether living or dead, known or unknown.

It is more than possible to theorize about the nature of individual authorship. Volumes have been written about authorship as a "social construct."[47]

---

46. Copyright Amendment (Indigenous Communal Moral Rights) Bill 2003 (Cth) (Austl.). Notably, the Aboriginal moral right could only be invoked in cases where the Aboriginal artist and his or her community had entered into an agreement about the work. This clumsy attempt to forestall conflicts within communities seems utterly impractical. *See* discussion *supra* Chapter 3, notes 123–52 and accompanying text.

47. Michel Foucault, *What Is an Author?*, *in* THE FOUCAULT READER (P. Rabinow ed., Pantheon Books 1984).

It is stridently argued that individuals are simply "products of their societies" or creatures of historical circumstance. But it remains a matter of *fact* that individual human beings, for whatever reasons and in whatever circumstances, have made a contribution to culture *as individuals*. Questions about how these artists are recognized, or what kind of contribution their communities have made to the creation of their work, are of secondary interest.

Nevertheless, legal dealings with art depend upon the rather artificial distinction between art and cultural heritage.[48] Where legal thought is concerned—and law is both a manifestation of social perceptions in this regard and a factor shaping them—it is essential to categorize an artwork as either a work of individual authorship or a manifestation of cultural heritage. Only by doing so can we have recourse to the law in order to clarify the social conditions of its existence—who has the right to own or acquire it, what it is "worth," and the conditions in which the work should be maintained.

1. Property or Heritage?

Accordingly, in modern legal terminology, a work of art can be classified as one of two things: intellectual property or cultural property. The distinction is significant, because two different kinds of legal frameworks apply to these two categories of culture. Intellectual property is almost entirely governed by national laws on copyright, and these, in their turn, are shaped by the requirements of international copyright agreements. Copyright law is an area of "private" law, having to do with the rights of private individuals and corporations, who either create works or purchase the right to exploit them.[49] In the case of intellectual property disputes, anyone can be a plaintiff—individuals, groups, or, as occasionally happens, governments of countries.[50] Intellectual property rights are modeled on rights in tangible property, among the most

---

48. The distinction in terminology between cultural property and cultural heritage should be duly noted, and has been greatly emphasized in the seminal scholarship of Prott & O'Keefe. *See* Lyndel Prott & Patrick J. O'keefe, 3 Law and the Cultural Heritage (Butterworths 1990). For an interesting review and overview of the work, see Charles Sparrow, *Review (Untitled)*, 40(1) Int'l & Comp. L.Q. 248 (1991). Invoking the power of property while attempting to recognize the special nature of heritage, the discussion in this chapter makes use of both expressions.

49. Although international copyright agreements represent both private and public frameworks, the "public" ones, regulated by the World Intellectual Property Organization of the United Nations, function on a largely "private" basis, and depend on domestic laws for their enforcement.

50. Bumper Development Corporation Ltd. v. Commissioner of Police for the Metropolis and Others [1991] 1 W.L.R. 1362 (CA) [*Bumper*]. The case is summarized in two useful notes: Sandy Ghandhi & Jennifer James, *The God that Won*, 1 Int'l J. Cult. Prop. 369–82 (1992), and, focusing on its Canadian angle, Robert K. Paterson, *The "Curse of the London Nataraja,"* 5(2) Int'l J. Cult. Prop. 330 (1996).

fundamental rights protected in modern democracies.[51] Once again, the analogy is far from perfect, but it is of the utmost legal significance. In order to claim intellectual property rights in a work, certain criteria must be met: the work must be artistic or intellectual in nature, original, and "fixed" in a tangible medium.[52] It must also have an identifiable author.[53]

In contrast, international conventions on cultural property reflect the framework of public international law at its most traditional: they formally empower states to act in favor of cultural heritage at the international level. Even this course of action is subject to some important limitations. Cultural property conventions set out rights of ownership associated, not with individuals, but with a country of origin. No specific "author," either individual or group, is implicated. The conventions affect relations between countries and, potentially, they will allow legal action to be brought to restore an object to its country of origin.

A suit for the return of cultural property must be brought by the government of a country. Typically, legal action will be brought in the country where the object has been seized, and the government bringing suit faces the disadvantages associated with a foreign legal claim. Since cultural property that is illegally exported from its country of origin is very often from developing countries, the cost of an attempted recovery can be prohibitive.[54] Indeed,

---

51. *See also* the African Charter on Human and Peoples' Rights (Banjul Charter) (Nairobi, Kenya, 1981), art. 14, which protects property as a human right, *available at* http://www. achpr.org/english/_info/charter_en.html (last visited July 26, 2010).

52. But traditionally, it has been extraordinarily easy to satisfy this requirement in common law countries, which have applied a labor standard to originality and defined it as virtually anything not copied. See the seminal British case of *Kenrick v. Lawrence* (1890) L.R. 25, Q.B.D. 99. This approach has now changed, with common law countries apparently moving to higher standards of originality that are closer to the position that was previously associated with civil law jurisdictions. The movement started with the U.S. case of *Feist Publications, Inc. v. Rural Telephone Service Co.*, 499 U.S. 340 (1991), which dealt with databases and demonstrates the increasing influence of civil law concepts of copyright in the digital environment. Higher standards of originality have also been supported in Canada, in the case of *CCH Canadian Ltd. v. Law Society of Upper Canada*, [2004] 1 S.C.R. 339, *available at* http://csc. lexum.umontreal.ca/en/2004/2004scc13/2004scc13.html (last visited July 28, 2010); and *CCH*, in turn, was followed in the Indian case of *Eastern Book Co. & Ors v. DP Modak & Anr.*, 2008 (36) PTC 1, 2008 (1) SCC 1.

53. It is worth noting that joint authors are often explicitly included in this scheme. *See, for example*, Canadian Copyright Act, *supra* note 13, sec. 9 (1). The case of works created under a pseudonym or anonymously is also addressed by many copyright laws, including Canada's.

54. Interestingly, greater prominence has been brought to this issue in recent years as museums and galleries face requests for the return of artworks confiscated from private owners by the Nazis. *See, for example, Return Nazi-Looted Art: Austrian Panel*, CBC NEWS ONLINE (July 12, 2010), *available at* http://www.cbc.ca/arts/artdesign/story/2010/07/12/austrian-panel-return-artworks-nazi.html (last visited July 28, 2010). See the note on British policy, which cites and reproduces Jasper Copping, *National Galleries to Hand Back Nazi Art*, DAILY TELE-GRAPH (Oct. 18, 2008), *available at* http://www.elginism.com/20081020/1446/ (last visited

even a successful suit can involve surprising costs: a third party who has purchased the object in the reasonable belief that it was legally available for sale
may be entitled to compensation.[55] Whatever their potential at the international level, it is clear that cultural property laws can do little to influence the
treatment of cultural heritage on the domestic stage. At most, it may be hoped
that countries will craft domestic laws on cultural heritage that are influenced
by the international conventions.

Clearly, these two different legal frameworks represent fundamentally different ways of thinking about cultural heritage. From a legal point of view, the
two categories do not overlap. Intellectual property law and cultural property
law are not connected with each other in any meaningful way.

But there is another way of looking at these two legal regimes. They do not
overlap; but it may still be possible to bridge the two categories, substantially refining the law and enhancing its potential to protect cultural heritage.
Moral rights may provide this bridge.

2. Moral Rights and the Life-Cycle of an Artwork[56]

The distinction between intellectual and cultural property could be understood as one of authorship status. If we think of it in these terms, it becomes
apparent that the natural life-cycle of most works of art involves a legal transformation—a movement from the category of intellectual property to classification as cultural heritage. In fact, from a legal point of view, it is possible to
identify three distinct stages in the life of an artwork: early life as intellectual
property, mid-life under copyright protection after the author's death, and a
final phase as cultural property.

Aug. 2, 2010). The Council for British Archeology notes that the Heritage Protection Bill has
since been dropped. *See* Dan Hull, *Heritage Bill Dropped Again!*, CBA INFORMATION (July 1,
2009), *available at* http://www.britarch.ac.uk/news/090701-heritageprotection (last visited
Aug. 2, 2010) *See also* Draft Heritage Protection Bill Presented to Parliament by the Secretary
of State for Culture, Media and Sport By Command of Her Majesty, April 2008, *available at*
http://www.official-documents.gov.uk/document/cm73/7349/7349.pdf (last visited Aug. 2,
2010).

55. *See* art. 7(b)(ii) of the UNESCO Convention on the Means of Prohibiting and Preventing
the Illicit Import, Export and Transfer of Ownership of Cultural Property (Nov. 14, 1970)
823 U.N.T.S. 231 [UNESCO Convention], *available at* http://portal.unesco.org/en/ev.
php-URL_ID=13039&URL_DO=DO_TOPIC&URL_SECTION=201.html (last visited July
27, 2010).

56. Note, once again, the distinction between "property" and "heritage." The term "objects" used
in this chapter is meant in both the material and metaphorical senses.

a. Phase 1: Intellectual Property

The artwork begins life as the creation of an author. Authorship of the work may take many forms. The work may be created by an individual or by joint authors; the author might be named or unnamed. But copyright law is capable of capturing most of these situations—even anonymous authorship—and it seems fair to say that the initial status of a work of art is that of a work of authorship protected by copyright law.

b. Phase 2: *Post Mortem Auctoris*

The death of the author initiates a period of transition. For a time, the work continues to be classified as intellectual property. The precise duration of that status is defined by national legislation, which, in its turn, operates according to certain minimum terms of copyright protection defined by international agreements.[57] The history of duration in copyright law has been one of progressive increase, and at present, most copyright works are protected for a period of seventy years after the author's death.[58]

Interestingly, some countries have found themselves becoming involved in discussions about copyright policy for works of art after the author's death, and whether an increased term of protection *post mortem auctoris* would be beneficial for cultural heritage. In India, the issue arose, not in the context of visual art, but in relation to literature. In 1992, India's Parliament voted to prolong the duration of copyright protection from fifty to sixty years after the author's death.[59] The explicit rationale behind this move was to extend protection for the works of India's Nobel Laureate in literature, Bengali poet Rabindranath Tagore (1861–1941), whose copyright would otherwise have expired at that time. Tagore's copyright was administered by Viswa Bharati University, in Shantiniketan, founded by the poet. It was thought that the

---

57. *See* the Berne Convention for the Protection of Literary and Artistic Works (adopted Sept. 9, 1886) 1161 U.N.T.S. 3, art. 7, *available at* http://www.wipo.int/export/sites/www/treaties/en/ip/berne/pdf/trtdocs_wo001.pdf (last visited July 27, 2010).

58. This term of protection currently applies in the European Union member countries, and other countries have attempted to harmonize their laws to this level. The extension of copyright term has always been contentious. In the United States, the extension of the term of protection to life of the author plus seventy years from the previous international standard of life plus fifty years led to a legal challenge on the grounds that the increase in the term of copyright protection was unconstitutional. The case was put forward by Creative Commons founder, Lawrence Lessig. Extension of term for performers has been a more recent controversy in the UK and Europe. *See* Chapter 6, *supra*.

59. *See* Copyright (Amendment) Bill, 1992, Bill C-35 (Mar. 17, 1992), *available at* http://parliamentofindia.nic.in/ls/bills/1992/1992-06.htm (last visited July 27, 2010) [Indian Copyright (Amendment) Bill].

extension of copyright term would help to protect his important literary legacy by prolonging the rights of Viswa Bharati—which, of course, would also benefit financially from this arrangement. The Indian Government affirmed:

> Gurudev Rabindranath Tagore died in the year 1941 and copyright in his pub-
> lished works, which stood vested in Visva Bharati was to expire on 31st
> December 1991. There had been numerous demands for according extended
> protection to his works in view of their national importance. While it was not
> considered feasible and appropriate to extend the term of copyright in respect
> of one author alone, the Government reviewed the whole question of what
> should be the appropriate term of copyright and decided to extend the term of
> copyright generally in all works protected by the Copyright Act . . .[60]

But an earlier series of similar discussions around the contribution of C. Subramania Bharati (1882–1921), the Indian National Poet who wrote in the Tamil language, led to the opposite conclusion. Bharati's copyright was nationalized in 1949. Soon afterwards, it was given to the people of India as a "gift." A copyright that "should" have expired in 1971, according to Indian copyright law of the time, was effectively surrendered from 1949.[61] This, too, was said to be done for the benefit of cultural heritage.

The Indian case is not unique—pre-Revolutionary Russia also amended its copyright term out of respect for a single author's work. A petition from Madame Pushkin saw the extension of copyright term for the sake of Pushkin's copyright. In the Russian case, the objective appears to have been practical rather than cultural—to ensure that Pushkin's wife continued to have means of subsistence from her husband's work.[62]

During the period of copyright's validity after an author's death, there is one obvious and crucial change in the status of the work: there is no living author to take care of it. Usually, copyright is inherited by the heirs of the

---

60. *See* the Statement of Objects and Reasons to the Amendment Act 13 of 1992, *reprinted in* Professional's THE COPYRIGHT ACT, 1957, BARE ACT WITH SHORT COMMENTS 4 (Professional Book Publishers 2006).

61. *See* the detailed discussion of these transactions in Mira T. Sundara Rajan, *Moral Rights in the Public Domain: Copyright Matters in the Works of Indian National Poet C. Subramania Bharati,* SINGAPORE J. LEGAL STUD 161 (2001) [Sundara Rajan, *Moral Rights in the Public Domain*]. The government of Tamil Nadu State continues to favor nationalization as an approach to literary heritage. Mira T. Sundara Rajan, *The Lessons of the Past: C. Subramania Bharati and the Nationalization of Copyright,* Editorial 6(2) SCRIPTed 201 (2009), *available at* http://www.law.ed.ac.uk/ahrc/SCRIPT-ed/vol6-2/rajan_editorial.pdf (last visited Aug. 2, 2010).

62. MIRA T. SUNDARA RAJAN, COPYRIGHT AND CREATIVE FREEDOM: A STUDY OF POST-SOCIALIST LAW REFORM (Routledge 2006) [Sundara Rajan, *Copyright and Creative Freedom*].

author. Depending on the circumstances of the author's family, the work may or may not be well cared for by the author's descendants. It might be widely publicized or greatly restricted. Of course, it is also possible for the author to bequeath the copyright deliberately to anyone of his or her choice.[63] The inheritor of the copyright then becomes its administrator. This approach, too, can have its positives and negatives in practice.

Once the term of copyright protection expires, the work falls into the public domain. Its connection with its creator has become relatively remote; on the other hand, its connection with country or community may be stronger than ever. At this point, a distinction arises between material works of art and intangible ones. Two points should be noted. First, the expiry of copyright in a work of visual art is less significant than it is in relation to other kinds of works. Copyright is generally of secondary importance where artworks are concerned, because material possession of the work is normal and supersedes any questions of copyright. Interestingly, in the 1741 case of *Pope v. Curll,* the separation of literary copyright from ownership of the work was considered in relation to letters written by the author; it was found that material ownership of the letters did not translate into a right to publish them, which remained vested in the author.[64] In the scenario of visual art, a vestige of copyright control can perhaps be said to remain with the author in the form of the artist's *droit de suite,* or resale right, which allows an artist to claim a percentage of proceeds from future sales of his works. The *droit de suite* may also be valid in the literary context. The Berne Convention provides that it is a legitimate right in relation to the sales of original manuscripts. India is among the few countries that recognize this right explicitly in their copyright legislation.[65]

The expiry of copyright in an artwork therefore signifies something different from the end of copyright term in other kinds of works. Most probably, it will not be the mechanism by which the work moves out of its owner's control. Perhaps it ends the owner's ability to control derivative uses of his works—pictures, photographs, and other reproductions.

---

63. Chellamma Bharati intended to bequeath the copyright in her husband's work to the public of India after death; since circumstances compelled her to part with it much earlier, she did not have the chance to do so. *See* the epigraph in Sundara Rajan, *Moral Rights in the Public Domain, supra* note 61.

64. Pope v. Curll, (1741) 2 Atk. 342, 26 Eng. Rep. 608.

65. *See* Indian Copyright Act, *supra* note 19, sec. 53A, Resale Share Right in Original Copies; the provision was adopted in the 1994 amendments to Indian copyright law. The principle is explicitly excluded by the European Directive on *droit de suite*, recital (19). *See* Directive 2001/84/EC of the European Parliament and of the Council of 27 September 2001 on the resale right for the benefit of the author of an original work of art, *available at* http://eur-lex.europa.eu/smartapi/cgi/sga_doc?smartapi!celexapi!prod!CELEXnumdoc&numdoc=32001L0084&model=guichett&lg=en (last visited Oct. 5, 2010).

c. Phase 3: Cultural Property and Moral Rights

Once copyright has expired, material works of art fall into the public domain. At that time, they may become "cultural property" in the legal sense of the term. The treatment of the work is no longer restricted by copyright laws; instead, the work may be freely used by the public. The use of the work must not contravene cultural property conventions; but, in practice, all this means is that works of cultural property must not be stolen, leave their countries of origin illegally, or be imported illegally.[66] The conventions on cultural property have little to say about how works should be treated by their lawful owners within borders; how disputes over their treatment should be resolved; or what practices the public should observe when dealing with art. On the other hand, intangible works are freely available for use once copyright in those works has expired.

But this explanation leaves one unresolved issue: moral rights. In those countries where moral rights expire with, or before, the expiry of copyright, the question of moral rights in the public domain is irrelevant. Even here, the moral rights idea experiences a new twist, as the possibility of moral rights in public domain works has sometimes received a more sympathetic consideration in case law than the moral rights of a living artist. The United States provides an interesting illustration of this point. To date, both the first and last U.S. cases on moral rights—*Shostakovich* in 1949 and *Dastar* in 2003— have assessed the possibility of moral rights in public domain works. The earlier judgment in *Shostakovich* might have brought moral rights for public domain works into U.S. law, but the attempt failed because of the ambiguity of the principle in the absence of legislative guidance. The *Dastar* case rejected moral rights in public domain works on the grounds that restricting the public domain would be contrary to American traditions of free use where the public domain is concerned.[67]

In countries where moral rights continue to exist even after the expiry of copyright, they provide a clear link between the worlds of intellectual

---

66. The two most significant international conventions are the UNESCO Convention, *supra* note 55, and the UNIDROIT Convention on Stolen or Illegally Exported Cultural Objects (June 24, 1995), 34 I.L.M. 1322, *available at* http://www.unidroit.org/english/conventions/1995cul turalproperty/1995culturalproperty-e.htm (last visited July 27, 2010). An extraordinarily useful online resource on cultural property is offered by Louise Tsang, *Features—Legal Protection of Cultural Property: A Selective Resource Guide*, LLRX (Apr. 24, 2007), *available at* http://www.llrx.com/features/culturalproperty.htm (last visited Aug. 1, 2010). A number of major art-market countries have joined the UNESCO Convention in the new millennium, including the UK (2002) and Switzerland (2003); the United States has been a member since 1983, and Canada joined in 1978. A list of member countries and their dates of joining is available on the UNESCO website at http://portal.unesco.org/la/convention. asp?KO=13039&language=E (last visited July 27, 2010).
67. See Chapter 3, *supra* notes 102–15 and accompanying text.

property and cultural property. With no legal basis for excluding them, principles of attribution and integrity continue to apply to works that are classified as cultural property. Moral rights could be an extraordinarily powerful tool for protecting the status of these works, thereby helping to maintain the integrity of cultural heritage.

The fundamental practical objection would seem to be the question of who should be empowered to act on behalf of cultural property. In the absence of specific legislative provisions governing moral rights in the public domain and identifying those who will have the capacity to assert them, the rights would be largely meaningless.[68] In relation to sensitive works, such as cultural property based on traditional knowledge, or works that document past historical eras, government may also not be the best agency to undertake the protection of moral rights.[69]

Where duration of moral rights is concerned, the case of India is an interesting one. Historically, India's provisions on moral rights were protected without the specification of a precise duration of protection. Given the language of Indian copyright law, it was reasonable to assume that the rights could be protected in perpetuity, leading to significant potential for the use of moral rights to protect cultural heritage that was no longer protected by other aspects of copyright law.[70]

In the Indian amendments of 1994, however, a new phrase on timing was introduced.[71] The integrity of the work would be protected against "any distortion, mutilation, modification or other act in relation to the said work which is done *before the expiration of the term of copyright* if such distortion,

---

68. The same problem is generally confronted in relation to the protection of folklore. *See* UNESCO Model Provisions for National Laws on the Protection of Expressions of Folklore Against Illicit Exploitation and other Prejudicial Actions (1985), art. 9 on Authorities, *available at* http://unesdoc.unesco.org/images/0006/000637/063799eb.pdf (last visited July 27, 2010). A major weakness of the scheme may be the idea that "borrowing expressions of folklore for creating an original work of an author or authors" requires no authorization— perhaps reflecting the fact that the model provisions pre-date the digital environment, where information is readily available and intellectual property, strongly valued.

69. *See* Mira T. Sundara Rajan, *Moral Rights in Developing Countries: The Example of India, Part I*, 8(5) J. Intell. Prop. Rights 357–68 (2003) [Sundara Rajan, *Moral Rights in Developing Countries*]. The article is available online, but has been printed with a number of errors by the JIPR: http://nopr.niscair.res.in/bitstream/123456789/4907/1/JIPR%208(5)%20357-374.pdf (last visited July 27, 2010). The old sec. 57 is still available on the website of the Commonwealth Legal Information Institute at http://www.commonlii.org/in/legis/num_act/ca1957133/ (last visited July 27, 2010).

70. Mira T. Sundara Rajan, *Moral Rights and the Protection of Cultural Heritage:* Amar Nath Sehgal v. Union of India, 10(1) Int'l J. Cultural Prop. 79 (2001) [Sundara Rajan, *Amar Nath Sehgal*].

71. Act 38 of 1994. *See* Sundara Rajan, *Moral Rights in Developing Countries, supra* note 69, at 368–71, and Sudhir Ahuja, *Latest Amendments to the Indian Copyright Act*, 44 Copyright World 38 (1994).

mutilation, modification or other act would be prejudicial to . . . [the author's] honour or reputation."[72] With this specification, the amended section does not quite say that moral rights will expire with the end of economic rights; but, in practice, it will lead to that result. The Indian integrity right provides that legal action for moral rights can only flow from acts that occur while the work is still within the term of copyright protection. However, there is no limitation period on suing for those violations. In theory, at least, damage that occurred in 1978, as in Amar Nath Sehgal's case,[73] could be brought before the courts for the first time in 2010—provided only that Sehgal's copyright was still in force in 1978.[74] But damage to the work after the expiry of Sehgal's copyright—calculated at sixty years from the author's death in December of 2007, Sehgal's copyright would expire in 2067—could not be subject to a moral rights suit.

i. Works in Copyright

But the *Amar Nath Sehgal* case has led to another, altogether extraordinary, possibility. In Indian law, where cultural heritage is concerned, the precise language of the statute may not matter. Instead, the doctrine of moral rights found in the Indian Copyright Act could be substantially enlarged by interpreting it in the light of international cultural property conventions signed by India. In Sehgal's case, duration was not a problem; he was still alive while the claim was in progress. However, the court offered its new interpretation in relation to another, equally important issue: the question of proof of damage to an author's reputation where a violation of the moral right of integrity is claimed.

On this crucial point, the court found that international conventions on cultural property take priority over national law. The work in question was considered a part of India's cultural heritage—a "national treasure." In this situation, the moral rights provisions should be read in the larger context of Indian membership in international conventions for the protection of cultural property. In order to honor these obligations at international law, India would have to intervene to protect damage and destruction affecting important cultural works.

---

72. Indian Copyright Act, *supra* note 19, sec. 57(1)(b) (emphasis added). The subsection goes on to state that "the author shall not have any right to restrain or claim damages in respect of any adaptation of a computer programme to which clause (aa) of sub-section (1) of section 52 applies." Sec. 52(1)(aa) provides for exceptions to copyright infringement of computer programs for fair dealing and for the purposes of regular use or making back-up copies.
73. Amar Nath Sehgal v. Union of India 2005 (30) PTC 253 (Delhi High Court); the case is discussed in detail in Chapter 3, *supra* notes 209–27 and accompanying text, and in overview, below.
74. See the detailed discussion of the evolution of India's moral rights in Chapter 3, *supra* notes 172–232 and accompanying text.

The reasoning of the Indian judge established two important principles where artworks are concerned. First, there can be no doubt that destroying a work of art affects the reputation of the artist. It does so by damaging his overall "creative corpus."[75] After this precedent, it seems clear that, whatever the international position, the destruction of artworks is prohibited in India by section 57 of India's Copyright Act.[76] Secondly, where an outstanding work of art is involved, there is an overriding obligation to protect its integrity.

The interpretation of Indian moral rights is, accordingly, dependent on the nature of the work. In the *Amar Nath Sehgal* case, the work had not yet entered the public domain. Nevertheless, the status of the sculpture and its creator were such that the work could be classified as a "national treasure"—an important contribution to Indian cultural patrimony. It is worth pointing out that the judge did not need to enter into an assessment of the quality of the work: the sculptor and the work, itself, were sufficiently well-known in India. The question could have been much more difficult to deal with if the artist were younger and less established—although, indeed, he or she would have grown old in the course of this litigation, which spread over nearly three decades from 1978 to 2005. If the artwork had been inherently controversial, the court might have found itself in difficulty. However, Indian judges have consistently adopted a deferential attitude towards artists who pursue legal complaints. Any significant work of visual art might meet the court's definition of valuable cultural property. Given the extraordinary delays and difficulties of litigation in India, the court's approach can easily be justified on practical grounds.

The case also raises the interesting problem of when a work of art becomes a "national treasure." In the case of Sehgal's sculpture, the work attained iconic status upon its completion.[77] Mr. Sehgal had many years left to live. In contrast, when Vincent van Gogh was alive, it seems doubtful that the Dutch government would have dreamed of calling any of his paintings "national treasures." The problem of recognition is an undercurrent running through all of these discussions about art. Nevertheless, moral rights that persist after an author's death, whether for the limited duration of the author's copyright or beyond, can clearly enrich the protection of cultural heritage. They can do so by harnessing the power of an intellectual property concept in the service of cultural property. As a legal matter, the moral right can protect cultural heritage from harm in a way that is far beyond what can be accomplished by international cultural property agreements.

---

75. Sundara Rajan, *Amar Nath Sehgal, supra* note 70, at 83; *Amar Nath Sehgal, supra* note 73, para. 31.
76. This does not, however, resolve the issue of what happens if an artist himself or herself wants to destroy his or her own work.
77. It is also worth noting that his work was well placed to do so by its association with Nehru and the Vigyan Bhavan. *See* Sundara Rajan, *Amar Nath Sehgal, supra* note 70.

It should be noted that visual art moves more easily into the category of national treasure than other kinds of works, and the treatment of these treasures is more straightforward. Avoiding damage to a work of art may be inherently simpler than assessing damage to music or poetry.

Nevertheless, if we separate moral rights from the merely legal idea of cultural heritage, which is largely focused on property, it is apparent that moral rights can also offer some protection to cultural heritage in its intangible forms—literature, music, and folk culture being some examples. The case of the Indian National Poet is representative in this regard—his writings are considered "national literature," and the copyright was acquired by the government, and then publicized, for this reason. What would have happened if the continued subsistence of moral rights in the poet's work had been publicly acknowledged by the government when it gave this gift? Indeed, the first independent Indian Copyright Act was adopted only in 1957, but it created moral rights; would Bharati's works be entitled to these? As a practical matter, there can be no doubt that much of what has occurred in the treatment of Bharati's works since 1949 would amount to violations of his moral rights of attribution and integrity.[78] The Indian government, itself, claimed to recognize the value of copyright for protecting intangible cultural heritage when it prolonged Tagore's rights in 1992.

At least where works of visual art are concerned—and possibly beyond—Indian moral rights may be much greater than they seem. They are not just what is stated by the rather conventional language of section 57. Through their relationship with cultural property conventions, they may take flight beyond the normal bounds of moral rights protection.

ii. The Public Domain: Shiva Nataraja's Rights of "Attribution" and "Integrity"

What happens to perpetual moral rights when the work has otherwise entered the public domain? In fact, there are two possible answers to this question. The first is that, where moral rights are concerned, the work never truly enters the public domain—at least, not in the sense in which the U.S. legal community would understand the public domain, as an area where all rights have expired. They have not; moral rights continue to exist. This fact leads to situations like the recent French case of *Hugo*, which saw the great-great-grandson of writer Victor Hugo bringing a lawsuit for the protection of *Les Misérables* in 2008—148 years after it was first published in 1862.

But let us say that we travel into the future by another two hundred years. By this time, the descendants of Hugo may or may not know of their ancestry, or be able to prove their connection to the great man. They will have merged

---

78. *See* Sundara Rajan, *Moral Rights in the Public Domain, supra* note 61.

with the general population. In these situations, if the work is still in publication, who will have the right to assert moral rights?

A further step forward in the analysis takes us directly into the world of folklore and traditional knowledge. Works of folklore may be culturally valuable and important, but their creators have become unknown. Moral rights may still have a role to play in protecting the integrity of these kinds of works. They can also support attribution, if not to an individual author, then to the group or country to which the work belongs. Indeed, the emphasis of cultural property laws on the "country of origin" seems tantamount to recognition of the attribution principle in a new guise. But who shall assert the rights? And on what legal basis can they do so?

These difficult questions on entitlement might have a Russian solution. Where moral rights are concerned, Russian law provides that "any interested person" may act on behalf of the work.[79] This approach, reflecting practical realities, is inclusive . If a person brings a legal action and can demonstrate his or her "interest" in the work, that person will be granted standing in the case. In an interesting example which occurred while the Russian Copyright Act of 1993 was still in force, the Tretyakov Gallery in Moscow sued for the right to assert moral rights in artworks that it owns, in order to prevent the use of pictures of them in literary books produced by a Moscow publishing house.[80] The museum had to bring its claim under old legislation that assigned the right to act to an "agency empowered by the state." No such agency had been created by the Russian government. The Gallery therefore made a creative, yet convincing, argument. In the absence of an identifiable state body, the Gallery itself should be considered legally equivalent to a state agency empowered to act by the legislation.

In the common law countries, as noted in the Indian example of Amar Nath Sehgal's case, solutions may also be found in case law. As illustrated by *Sehgal,* those solutions may be highly innovative. The *Sehgal* judgement emerged out of legislative provisions on moral rights; its conclusions are still defined by its connection to the Indian Copyright Act. But it is also possible for entirely novel doctrines to develop out of case law, bringing extraordinary and unforeseen elements to bear on the issue of moral rights in cultural heritage.

---

79. *See* Part IV of the Russian Civil Code on intellectual property: *Grazhdanski Kodeks Rossiiskoi Federatsi, Chast' Chetvërtaya* [Civil Code of the Russian Federation, Part IV], Federal Law No. 230-FZ of December 18, 2006, *Rossijskaja Gazeta* No. 289 (4255) of Dec. 22, 2006 = *Sobranie zakonodatel'stva RF* (SZ RF) No. 52 (Part I) of Dec. 25, 2006, Item 5496, at 14803 [2008 Civil Code], art. 1267 (2) on "the protection of authorship, name, and inviolability after the author's death"; *see also* art. 1266 (2) on the protection of inviolability.
80. Chapter VIII of Sundara Rajan, *Copyright and Creative Freedom,* 202-03.

The extraordinary British judgment in *Bumper Development Corporation v. Commissioner of Police for the Metropolis* is such a case.[81] Decided in 1991, this precedent remains valid, and no attempt has been made to discredit it in subsequent case law. Some American commentary has considered the decision "bizarre" and "exotic," though it probably would not seem either of those things to Indians.[82] It is a unique decision. The judgment is as much idea-driven as it is derived from legalities; yet its apparent sophistication where cultural differences are concerned makes it a difficult legal precedent to reject.[83]

The *Bumper* case centers on a bronze statue of the Indian deity Nataraja, traditionally portrayed as a dancer in ecstatic motion and known as the Lord of the Cosmic Dance. The image of the divine dancer is laden with symbolism and represents one of the great mystical traditions of India. The story of the Nataraja bronze in this case is quite typical of conflicts over cultural property that have arisen at various times and places, always across borders; but its legal resolution is unique.

The incident at the heart of this case began in 1976, with the unearthing of a bronze figure of Nataraja in the South Indian state of Tamil Nadu. Sacred images made in bronze have been the pride of Tamil craftsmanship for more than a millenium. Famous examples have been prized by art collectors all over the world. These bronze statues were made, not to adorn museums, but for active worship. Nevertheless, their antiquity and excellence has called for special preservation measures even in South India, where a display gallery of unparalleled beauty has been built for them at the Madras Museum.[84]

---

81. *Supra* note 51.
82. *See* J. H. Merryman, Book Review, *The Ethics of Collecting Cultural Property: Whose Culture? Whose Property?*, P. M. Messenger, ed. (1991) 85 Am. J. Int'l L. 737 at 739. Merryman not only assesses the *Bumper* decision as "bizarre," but he also goes on to refer to the Shivalingam, controversially, as, "a phallus-shaped stone emblem." The question of what the lingam represents is open to debate, and Merryman fails to express an understanding of the place the lingam would occupy in a Saivite Hindu temple, analogous to the *sanctum sanctorum* of a church. P. M. Bator, *An Essay on the International Trade in Art*, 34 Stan. L. Rev. 275, n.13 (1982), considers the naming of the deity as a claimant in the *Bumper* case and in the Norton Simon case to be "an exotic feature," and goes on to refer to the deity incorrectly as a "goddess." The terminology, "goddess," is also used with reference to the *Bumper* case by J. E. Bersin, *The Protection of Cultural Property and the Promotion of International Trade in Art*, 13 N.Y.L. Sch. J. Int'l & Comp. L. 125, n.67 at 151 (1992).
83. *Supra* note 50.
84. For a description, see the website of the museum at <http://www.chennaimuseum.org/draft/gallery/01/arch.htm> (last visited July 26, 2010). Mr. and Mrs. John D. Rockefeller the 3rd, well-known for their passion for Asian Art, owned at least one of these statutes in their collection. *See* the information on an exhibition of Chola bronzes from their collection, *available at* http://asiasociety.org/files/Chola%20Bronzes%20press%20release.pdf (last visited Aug. 24, 2010).

The bronze, known as the Pathur Nataraja for the town where it was discovered, was found by a poor laborer named Ramamoorthi.[85] Ramamoorthi lived in a hut that was adjacent to the site of a ruined temple. He was digging foundations to build a cow shed when he struck a metal object. The object which he discovered, buried alongside a number of other bronze figures, was the Nataraja statue.

Immediately aware that he had uncovered something of value, Ramamoorthi reburied the objects. He contacted a friend who put him in touch with a dealer in stolen art objects. The dealer purchased the Nataraja from Ramamoorthi and sold it to another dealer. The Nataraja eventually resurfaced in London, where a dealer named Sherrier sold the object to Bumper Corporation on the basis of a false certificate of origin. The irony of the transaction is that the buyer, Bumper Corporation's chairman Robert Borden, bought the bronze with good intentions—he wanted to add it to a collection of art for display in Canadian museums. Borden apparently held "deep concern for the understanding of cultures," and, as Richard H. Davis observes in his detailed study of the incident, a "conviction that exhibiting works of art can aid this understanding by demonstrating the quality and depth of other civilizations past and present."[86]

But the bronze had been concealed underground for centuries, and it was in a state of great deterioration. The Corporation decided against transporting it immediately to Canada.[87] Instead, it was taken to the staff of the British Museum for an appraisal and conservation work prior to travel. While the bronze was at the British Museum, it came to the attention of the Metropolitan Police, who seized it with a view to returning it to its rightful owner.

Bumper Corporation brought an action against the police, seeking the return of the statue with damages. The Corporation argued that it had purchased the bronze in good faith, based on the certificate of provenance that had been provided by the dealer. Its claim was opposed by the Indian government which hoped to secure the return of the bronze to India.

The dispute eventually led to the English Court of Appeal, which found itself confronting a difficult legal problem. The Indian government had brought the suit, but it had never "owned" the object. Fundamentally, this litigation was about a right to possess, and, in keeping with the norms of British property rules, the Indian government would have to be able to show a title that was superior to Bumper's. In the hope of meeting this test, a number of plaintiffs were added to the suit. They included some highly unusual characters—for

---

85. RICHARD H. DAVIS, LIVES OF INDIAN IMAGES ch. 7, *Loss and Recovery of Ritual Self* (Princeton Univ. Press 1997).

86. *Id.*, at 238 (quoting Borden from trial testimony, and then citing it for his information).

87. The bronze was believed to have been buried to protect it from destruction at the hands of Muslim invaders. *See* Ghandhi & James, *supra* note 50, at 370.

example, the ruined temple where the bronze had been discovered, which was represented by its custodian, Sadagopan. Ultimately, the God Shiva, Himself, was included. He was represented by a stone carving which had been discovered with the bronze, known as a Shivalingam.[88] The Shivalingam was also put forward as a claimant on the grounds that it represented the "pious intention" of the thirteenth-century notable who had endowed the temple.[89]

At trial, Justice Kennedy found in favor of the Indian claimants and awarded possession of the statue and compensation for the costs of the proceedings to India.[90] His decision was later upheld by the English Court of Appeal. The Corporation was said to have bought the image in good faith. Its role in the transactions seems extraordinarily naïve—how could Robert Borden not have known that the image was probably, almost certainly, removed illegally from India? In an earlier case involving a bronze Nataraja from Sivapuram acquired by the Norton Simon Foundation, Mr. Simon commented, "Hell, yes, it was smuggled . . . . I spent between $15 million and $16 million over the last year on Asian art, and most of it was smuggled."[91] Davis notes that Borden "consciously disregarded all questions of provenance when purchasing the Nataraja."[92] This sounds like negligence, and Justice Kennedy, while not questioning Borden's intentions, nevertheless issued an order for the complete reimbursement of the legal costs of the Indian plaintiffs, which exceeded £300,000.[93]

(a) Legal Issues Assessed by the Courts

The *Bumper* rulings are innovative in two respects. First, the case was unusual for its time in ordering the unconditional restoration of the disputed object to

---

88. *See* Davis, *supra* note 86, at 249. A Shivalingam is a stone sculpture which is a symbol of cosmic unity and, as such, represents the god, Shiva. In traditional Saivite temples, the lingam is the main focus of worship, and this is perhaps one of two reasons why the case focused on the claim of the Shivalingam rather than the Nataraja itself; a second reason might be the need to avoid the awkwardness of an object asserting "ownership" over itself! Since the case focused on "ownership," it perhaps makes sense to identify another object as the "owner" of the disputed one. At trial, Justice Kennedy studied Hindu law to reach the conclusion that, as Davis explains, "the pious aim of the founder continues to reside in the physical idol as representing and symbolizing that aim." Sadagopan, who claimed as the representative of the temple, also sued as a third claimant on his own behalf.

89. See *Bumper*, *supra* note 50, at 1367; *see also* Ghandhi & James, *supra* note 50, at 369–70.

90. The English Court of Appeal substantially followed the judgment of the Trial Court, delivered by Justice Ian Kennedy.

91. Quoted by Davis, *supra* note 86, at 241.

92. *Id.*, at 240. Davis quotes Borden as commenting, at trial, "I have bought enough objects to know that one simply doesn't ask those questions."

93. Davis, *supra* note 86, at 251. Paterson, *supra* note 50, at 333–35, argues that the approach of the courts has important implications for the legal regime regulating the international movement of cultural property.

the Indian claimants. Secondly, the line of reasoning which led to this result was unique.[94]

In particular, the courts made a valiant attempt to take into account the cultural perspective of the Indian claimants, which probably could not be more removed from a modern British context. For South Indians, Nataraja is an ecstatic figure, the visible embodiment of myth and magic on a cosmic scale, and the originator of an entire tradition of mysticism. His marvelous personality is celebrated with unparalleled splendor in the temple of Chidambaram that is dedicated to him.[95] In assessing the Indians' plea for the return of this bronze, British judges made a remarkable effort to bridge the gap in values between the concerns of the Indian claimants, whose arguments were based on the ancient traditions of a developing country, and Bumper Corporation, whose dealings with the bronze were standard market activities in a leading art-market country. The trial judge, Justice Kennedy, was able to achieve something almost impossible: translating an awareness of different cultural values into a viable legal framework within the traditions of the common law.[96]

Both at trial and in the subsequent consideration given to the case by a highly sympathetic Court of Appeal, it is apparent that the courts are driven by more than strictly legal considerations. Indeed, the appellate court asks bluntly, "What does justice demand in a case such as this?"[97] The discussion is framed in legal terms, but the approach to the dispute demonstrates the high priority given to the non-legal rationales underlying the positions of the parties.

(i) *Title*

The first and most important legal issue involved title to the object, which would then confer the right to sue on its owner. At trial, Justice Kennedy followed three routes leading to title for the Indian claimants. First, he determined that the ruined Hindu temple, suing through its rightful representative, had a title to the Nataraja that was superior to Bumper's. Secondly, Justice Kennedy found that the intentions of the notable who endowed the temple were represented in the Shivalingam which had been discovered with the statue, and that the title of the Shivalingam was therefore superior to that of Bumper. Finally, the trial judge noted that the Indian state of Tamil Nadu,

---

94. Paterson, *supra* note 50, at 330.

95. See the interesting analysis of Siva's dance on the Temple's website ("tillai," for the "milky mangrove" tree, common to the region, seems to have been the original name of the place), at http://www.tillai.com/natarajar/tandavam.aspx (last visited July 26, 2010).

96. The English Court of Appeal's findings were subsequently approved in Canada, by the Alberta Court of Queen's Bench. *See* India (Union) v. Bumper Development Corp. [1995] A.J. No. 380 (Q.B.) [Alberta Judgment].

97. *Bumper, supra* note 50, at 1373.

where the bronze was discovered, would have title to the Nataraja under Tamil Nadu cultural property statutes. In keeping with principles of international comity, a British court was bound to respect this right.[98]

In appealing the issue of title, Bumper specifically questioned the trial judge's attribution of legal personality to the temple, whether directly or through its representative, and to the Shivalingam. Bumper argued that none of the claimants had succeeded in showing that it had a title to the bronze which could be recognized in an English court.

(ii) *Legal Capacity under Local Law*

In order to determine whether the temple could be recognized in English law as a legal person, the trial judge first considered the issue of legal capacity under local law—the law of Tamil Nadu, where the bronze originated. In British law, determining the substance of foreign law is a matter of fact which must be established by expert evidence. However, Justice Kennedy not only relied upon the testimony of the experts presented to the court by the disputing parties, but he also undertook research of his own into the nature of legal personality under Indian law. While the Court of Appeal acknowledged certain restrictions on the ability of the trial judge to investigate factual matters beyond the testimony of the experts, it upheld the bases of his finding that the ruined temple would have legal personality under Indian law.[99]

(iii) *"Juristic Entity" in English Law*

Having determined that the temple could sue in an Indian court, the English Court of Appeal went on to consider the issue of whether the capacity of the temple to sue would be recognized under English law. The court adopted the phrase "juristic entity" to signify a "person, body of persons or object" which would be capable of holding title to an object and exercising the rights associated with its ownership in England.[100] In particular, could a foreign legal person which was not recognized as a legal person under English law sue in an English court?[101] In order to decide this issue, the court relied on three principles.

First, the Court of Appeal considered the extension of legal personality to entities other than individuals under English law. It pointed out that the assignment of legal personality in English law is usually restricted to

---

98. Details of these statutes are noted by Ghandhi & James, *supra* note 50, at 372.
99. The Court of Appeal pointed out that the trial judge must restrict his research to texts which have been referred to by the expert witnesses, since they have been introduced into evidence by the experts. *See Bumper, supra* note 50, at 1367–71; *see also* Ghandhi & James, *supra* note 50, at 375–76.
100. *Bumper, supra* note 50, at 1366.
101. *Id.*, at 1367.

corporations or other, similar "groups or series of individuals."[102] Under English law, legal personality has its basis in the "animate content" which the legal person represents.[103]

However, the Court of Appeal recognized that there is no reason of logic or policy to limit the recognition of legal persons in this way. It observed that restricting legal personality to groups of persons is a matter of "tradition and practice" in English law, and is not compelled by analytical or practical necessity.[104] As a result, the recognition of the ruined temple as a juristic entity could be considered comparable to the attribution of legal personality to corporations.

Secondly, the Court of Appeal went on to consider the recognition of legal personality in institutions by assessing the hypothetical case of a Catholic cathedral which was assigned personality by the legislation of its country. The court argued that the principle of "comity of nations" encouraged British courts to recognize the legal personality of the cathedral in order to show respect for the laws and customs of its country of origin.[105] In the modern context, it felt that a non-Christian institution would be equally entitled to claim legal personality in Britain.[106]

Finally, the Court of Appeal argued that the recognition of legal personality in a foreign institution under English law would promote English objectives of public policy. Quoting from English precedent, the court asked what it saw as the fundamental question in this case—"'What does justice demand in such a case as this?'"[107] The Court of Appeal pointed out that artificial procedural considerations should not prevent the recognition and enforcement of a legitimate legal right. With these arguments, it upheld the trial judge's finding that the Indian temple had a title to the Nataraja which was superior under English law to the title acquired by Bumper Corporation. In view of this finding, the court felt that it did not need to go on to consider whether the

---

102. *Id.*

103. *Id.*

104. *Id.*, at 1372.

105. This aspect of the court's reasoning is reminiscent of the case of *Autocephalous Greek Orthodox Church of Cyprus v. Goldberg*, 917 F.2d 278 (7th Cir. 1990) [hereinafter *Autocephalous*]. In *Autocephalous*, a Cypriot church sought to recover a series of elaborately decorated mosaics which had become an important symbol of the history of Greek Cypriot culture. A group of these mosaics was removed from the church in the 1970s and brought to the United States by an art dealer. In deciding to return the mosaics to the church, the court developed the idea of a due diligence requirement for purchasers. The court also considered the church to have ownership of the mosaics, through the Archbishopric of the Church of Cyprus. *See Autocephalous*, 917 F.2d at 289–90; *see also* Bersin, *supra* note 82, at 125–27.

106. *Bumper*, *supra* note 50, at 1372–73.

107. *Id.*, at 1373 (quoting Viscount Simonds in *National Bank of Greece & Athens S.A. v. Metliss* [1958] A.C. 509, 525).

Shivalingam would also be entitled to assert ownership of the statue in an English court.

(b) A Moral Rights Perspective

In addition to seeing the Nataraja dispute as a matter governed by cultural property conventions, it is interesting to explore its connections with moral rights. What is the scope of protection that moral rights could theoretically offer to cultural property such as this bronze masterwork?

For moral rights to be invoked, two criteria would have to be met. First, perpetual moral rights must be found to exist under the relevant legislation. Would English or Indian law apply? England did not recognize moral rights by any statutory means. The common law generally leaves open a degree of flexibility in English law, but the ancient rejection of a common law copyright in *Donaldson v. Beckett* has meant that English courts are constrained in their ability to develop a jurisprudential doctrine of moral rights. However, following the reasoning of the Court of Appeal in the *Bumper* case, and considering the later U.S. decision on the subsistence of copyright in the *Russian Kurier* case, it would clearly be more appropriate to apply the Indian Copyright Act to what is essentially a question about the subsistence of rights.[108] Until 1994, the Indian Act arguably did grant perpetual protection to moral rights.

Secondly, some provision must be made to clarify who is entitled to assert moral rights when the work is of great antiquity, placing it beyond the reach of authors and their heirs or appointed trustees. In India, at the time of this dispute, moral rights existed and were not limited in time, but no provision was made for their exercise once heirs could no longer be traced.

The concept of attribution is important for cultural property, touching upon so many aspects of its existence. Attribution represents provenance; attribution of "authorship," and possibly ownership, may both be appropriate to a situation like the Nataraja's. A focus on attribution could help to establish the legal status of cultural property, and make it more difficult to offer works of improper or unknown attribution for sale. At the same time, it would become more difficult for a buyer to claim ignorance of an object's status. In the most extreme cases, attribution could also provide a powerful rationale for the repatriation of an object—especially if, as in the case of the Nataraja bronze, the object has been removed from its country of origin in contravention of export regulations.[109]

The integrity principle is also of fundamental importance to cultural property. One of the major reasons why the illicit trade in art is so distressing is

---

108. Itar-Tass Russian News Agency v. Russian Kurier, Inc. 153 F.3d 82 (2d Cir. 1998).

109. *See* UNESCO Convention, *supra* note 55, art. 6. Essentially, every member country of the Convention undertakes to prohibit the export of valuable cultural property without appropriate documentation.

because it places cultural property in grave danger of damage, destruction, or loss. In the case of the Nataraja, the bronze was deliberately broken by the "dealers" who acquired it from Ramamurti; they wanted to see whether the statue was actually made of gold, in which case, as Davis observes, "presumably they would have reduced the image to its raw material."[110] But, once again, the principle of integrity does not necessarily offer an easy resolution to the question of repatriation. It is often argued that cultural objects from developing countries will be better preserved in developed countries, and that this may well justify their presence in the Western world as part of the heritage of "humanity"—an approach pioneered by the work of John Henry Merryman.[111] It is really our understanding of "integrity" that must be brought to bear upon this issue. If we take it at face value, as a question of physical preservation, then the argument might be persuasive. However, a cultural "object," no matter how splendid and alluring it might be as a work of art, often represents much more than its physical presence . The Nataraja bronze illustrates this point perfectly. Its *raison d'être* is to provide a focus for active worship in a temple, surrounded by clouds of incense and smoke from oil lamps, bathed regularly in ablutions of milk and *ghee,* adorned by profusions of roses and jasmine. It was not meant to sit in splendid isolation in a dust-free museum.

Nevertheless, even within India, it may not be practical to "use" these ancient objects in the traditional way, and attempts have been made to create suitable modern spaces for them such as the Government museum.[112] There is something important about leaving these choices in the hands of the people whose forefathers produced the works. If anyone is qualified to define what is really meant by the integrity of the work, it is probably them.

Against this example stands the situation of works such as the Buddha of Bamyan, destroyed by the modern warlords of the Taliban in the name of their religion. The Taliban have now left power in Afghanistan, and the Afghan people have begun to discuss the idea of restoring the Buddhas. Writing for the International Herald Tribune, Carlotta Gall notes:

> [S]imply preserving what remains is daunting. Once the niches, grottos and caves were covered with murals, but 80 percent were obliterated by the Taliban, [Japanese historian Kasaku] Maeda said. Art thieves also did damage, using ropes to climb into caves 30 meters up on the cliff face and hacking away

---

110. Davis, *supra* note 86, at 235.
111. Merryman argues that cultural property is perhaps best seen as "components of a common human culture." *See* John Henry Merryman, *Two Ways of Thinking about Cultural Property,* 80(4) Am. J. Int'l L. 831 (1986).
112. But Davis describes a sadder product of modern-age India, an Icon Centre built at Tiruvarur in Tamil Nadu state to protect statues in danger of theft, but housing them in utterly unsuitable conditions. *See* Davis, *supra* note 86, at 257–59.

priceless medallions depicting seated Buddhas. One of these made its way to Tokyo, where an art dealer, suspecting its illicit provenance, showed it to Maeda, who has managed to retrieve more than 40 stolen artefacts.

"One day I hope we will return them to Afghanistan," he said.[113]

It is possible to imagine a scenario in which the ritual destruction of a work might be important, or even necessary. But the decision to destroy substantial works in metal or in stone—ostensibly built to last—seems too extreme to justify. We live in an era when our environment is suffering rapid impoverishment, in both biological and cultural terms. Given the present state of the world, intentional destruction of cultural property is undoubtedly something that should be banned.

E. Moral Rights and Modern Art: The Transition to Virtual Galleries

In the digital world, technology complicates the circumstances of art and artefacts. Two crucial developments have occurred: the ability to reproduce images of artworks on a scale that was previously unknown, and the possibility of communicating those images with extraordinary ease via the Internet. Apart from the potential for copyright infringement, the moral rights implications of digital imagery are striking.

1. Digital Images: New Technology to Reach Old Masters

The circulation of an image such as a photograph of an artwork leads to new and interesting questions. An initial concern is whether moral rights are infringed when the photograph is circulated without attributing the artist who created the work, or in a manner that is likely to be derogatory. In the case of artworks created by living artists, or whose creators are still known, the problem is obvious. Provided that moral rights have not expired, failure to attribute and derogatory treatment will both constitute violations of the artist's moral rights.

When we explore the idea of a moral right in public domain works or cultural property, the question becomes more difficult to answer. The photograph

---

113. See the interesting update by Carlotta Gall, *Afghans Consider Rebuilding Bamiyan Buddhas—Asia-Pacific-International Herald Tribune*, New York Times (Nov. 5, 2006), *available at* http://www.nytimes.com/2006/12/05/world/asia/05iht-buddhas.3793036.html (last visited Aug. 2, 2010).

is a picture of an artefact or cultural object, and does not portray an artwork created by an identifiable artist. Once again, attribution could be interpreted in a number of ways to support the idea that, in such cases, the provenance of a work should be indicated. How far back in the pedigree of a work should such attribution extend? For example, in the case of the Nataraja bronze owned by the Rockefeller Foundation, should it be displayed with an indication that it belongs to the Rockefeller collection? That it is from India? Tamil Nadu? The town of origin? Concerns about the status of cultural property suggest that attribution should generally be as complete as possible.

Integrity is a subtler issue. Where the reproduction of an artwork is concerned, at least two distinct problems can arise. The first is the quality of the reproduction: does a poor-quality digital reproduction constitute a violation of the artist's right of integrity? The argument that it does has been made in relation to the reproduction of music for use as mobile ringtones in Germany. In that scenario, the German *Bundesgerichtshof* found that the conversion of music into files suitable for a ringtone implied a certain degree of alteration due to "digital . . . process[ing]."[114] In its assessment, the court may have been a bit behind the times—fidelity and quality are increasingly prized in ringtones[115]—but its analysis is directly applicable to reproductions of visual art. Is a degree of deterioration to be expected in a digital reproduction and, accordingly, to be tolerated? On the other hand, does it make more sense to argue that art galleries and museums are under an obligation to represent their collections in the most favorable light possible, and that deterioration in the quality of images is a serious affront to the right of integrity? The solution here involves striking the right balance between the standard of care expected of museums, which should be high, and a degree of reasonableness in applying it.

In relation to three-dimensional works, such as sculptures, reproducing them in two-dimensional photographs involves a fundamental change. A poor-quality photograph of a sculpture may misrepresent the work, and this could, indeed, be considered a violation of the sculptor's right of integrity. At the same time, the threshold for making such a determination should be quite high, as a change in quality is definitely implied by photography of a three-dimensional object. If the artist has given permission, it should be harder to establish that the act of photography has violated his or her moral rights.

Secondly, where painting is concerned, the question of authenticity is potentially disturbing. This is because of a degree of overlap between the nature of the original work and the form of the reproduction. For example, it is possible that a photographic image could be used to generate new "hard

---

114. *See* Chapter 6, "More Than Musicians: Moral Rights and Digital Issues in Music," notes 90–95 and accompanying text.
115. *See* Chapter 6, "More Than Musicians: Moral Rights and Digital Issues in Music," notes 90–95 and accompanying text.

copies" of the original work. To make matters more complicated, it may not be the fault of the author-photographer or owner-gallery that new hard copies surface. Unless the image files are somehow devised to make printing impossible, anyone who has access to them could print them.

The problem of potential confusion between an original artwork and unauthorized copies arose in the Canadian case of *Théberge*. In this case, the facts showed an interesting twist: the reproductions were not photographs. Instead, they were made by a process of lifting ink from postcards— which were, themselves, authorized reproductions of Théberge's original paintings—and superimposing the ink onto canvas.[116] The artist felt that these canvas-backed reproductions could create confusion in the mind of the public, which might mistake them for his original works. At the same time, Théberge was also concerned that these reproductions could ultimately degrade the saleability of his original work.[117]

The artist's moral rights of attribution and integrity were clearly implicated in this case. Nevertheless, the suit failed. But the failure was an extremely interesting one, and raised the fundamental question of how to decide on the characterization of a claim as moral or economic under the terms of Canadian copyright law. In fact, Théberge had not framed his claim as a moral rights complaint. His cautious counsel probably wanted to avoid making a legal claim based on moral rights because it is generally difficult to obtain a positive judgment in this area from Canadian courts. In particular, it has proven to be difficult to offer the courts persuasive evidence of damage to reputation. In Théberge's case, the decision to avoid moral rights was probably a strategic error, but his situation presents something of a "catch-22." Justice Binnie, writing for the majority of the Canadian Supreme Court, emphasized the different and higher standard of proof required to show a violation of moral rights, reflected in the requirement that an author must be able to prove damage to his reputation.[118] Théberge had made no attempt to satisfy it; if he had, it is hard to say whether he would have been successful.

To add to these ambiguities, the creation of a photograph can lead to new moral rights in the image, itself—the moral rights of the photographer. If a museum plans to use photographs, it needs to be aware of these overlapping rights. Appropriate steps should be taken to protect both the moral rights of the photographer as the creator of the image, and the moral rights of the underlying artist or cultural group.

---

116. *Théberge, supra* note 16.

117. *See Théberge, supra* note 16, para. 20. The artist commented, "Being a party to the distribution of these things means that they [clients and friends] assume that I hatched a plot in which I am a participant. I'm getting money, royalties or . . . that I make money off of it— otherwise, it's just not possible. How can you allow such a thing, Mr. Théberge?"

118. But note that s. 28.2 (2) infers damage to reputation if distortion of a painting is found to have occurred.

Finally, it is worth noting that displaying an image of an artwork changes the environment in which the artwork is perceived. In a sense, this is one of the most exciting aspects of the artistic experience. Linking apparently disparate works and artists through novel combinations of images can illuminate connections that we never knew were there—juxtaposing Picasso's paintings with traditional African art, or showing van Gogh's and Gauguin's paintings side by side.[119] When individuals can create their own collections of images, finding connections that might be quite original, the experience of viewing art is unexpectedly democratized.[120] Discovering the unity of apparently unrelated things is an essential part of creative expression. But could this approach to images lead to violations of the artist's moral right of integrity?

2. Building Virtual Galleries

The specific question of how museums and galleries use images of their own collections is worth a closer look. Museums are increasingly creative in their use of images, and many of them have undertaken to build true "virtual galleries." A virtual gallery is no mere collection of reproduced artworks or artefacts. More than replicating the real-world structure of the museum, a virtual gallery creates original pathways and experiences through the medium of the Internet. Its purpose is to show viewers how to appreciate a collection by guiding them through the experience of viewing.

Museum websites may even allow viewers to generate their own virtual galleries.[121] "Interactive" websites allow viewers to assemble their own collections of images from the museum's collection. The idea is a striking one, and seems marvelously exciting for the public profile of art museums. It is a

---

119. *See, e.g.,* the Van Gogh Museum's exhibition, "Van Gogh and Gauguin: The Studio of the South," *available at* http://www.vangoghgauguin.com/ (last visited July 26, 2010). Britain's National Gallery featured an exhibition entitled, "Picasso: Challenging the Past," in which paintings by Picasso were displayed alongside earlier classic works of the same types of subject-matter. *See* http://www.nationalgallery.org.uk/whats-on/past/picasso-challenging-the-past (last visited July 26, 2010).

120. Although, as Russell Smith of the Globe and Mail notes, expert curators may be skeptical about the value of interactive tools for cultivating artistic taste. See his interesting article, Russell Smith, *The cloud sees a milk jug, curators see Vermeer, available at* <http://www.theglobeandmail.com/news/arts/russell-smith/the-cloud-sees-a-milk-jug-curators-see-vermeer/article1624729/> (last visited July 27, 2010). The "cloud" refers to users of the Internet and the descriptive tags they associate with artworks.

121. *See, for example,* the Virtual Collections of the Pitt Rivers Museum, Oxford, *available at* http://www.prm.ox.ac.uk/vcollections.html (last visited July 27, 2010); the Digital Collection of the St. Petersburg Hermitage Museum, *available at* http://www.hermitagemuseum.org/fcgi-bin/db2www/browse.mac/category?selLang=English (last visited July 27, 2010); *see also* Pitt Rivers; Hermitage, and the Virtual Museum of Canada, *available at* http://www.museevirtuel-virtualmuseum.ca/index-eng.jsp (last visited July 27, 2010).

creative attempt at outreach by museums to their public, and encourages individuals to engage with art in an interesting way, through technology. The potential for public education about art seems virtually limitless. All of these opportunities offer the truly extraordinary possibility of being able to "visit" a museum in "virtual" form without having to travel to its physical location.

In these situations, more than ever, questions could surface about the circumstances in which a work is "virtually" displayed. Most likely, when an image of an artwork appears on the Internet, it is presented in a new context that may be fundamentally different from the conditions in which the work of art is usually viewed. For example, an image of Bill Reid's "Raven and the First Men" might be used to decorate a website having nothing to do with his work. Similarly, Shiva Nataraja's image appears in relation to countless enterprises that might not be spiritual in nature.

Generally speaking, it is not clear that the conditions in which an artwork is displayed can lead to a violation of the right of integrity. Nevertheless, the possibility seems to be at least implicitly recognized by the very presence of specific exemption clauses on this issue in various copyright laws. For example, in its "Explanation" of section 57 on the author's personal rights, the Indian Copyright Act states that the conditions of display will not violate the integrity of an artwork. The specification was probably introduced in order to address the *Amar Nath Sehgal* case, which involved, among other things, a situation where the artwork was said to be improperly displayed.[122]

The question becomes still more difficult when discussing contested artworks, or artefacts from vulnerable cultures. What happens in the case of works of Aboriginal art displayed in government museums? Even if the works are properly attributed, is their integrity maintained? In these situations, for reasons of culture and cost, it can happen that people whose ancestors created the works are no longer able to have access to them in any meaningful way. In at least some circumstances, what the Indian government calls a "failure to display a work properly" may indeed violate the moral rights of creators.

This problem is one that calls for the utmost sensitivity. The viewing experience in a virtual gallery is a precious gift. It allows viewers to experience art in a new way, with the kind of privacy and intimacy that was previously reserved to music. The experience may not be authentic in the same way as a musical experience—reproduction of an artwork is not the same thing as a musical recording—but it is still an important step that brings the public

---

122. Another example is sec. 28.2(3)(a) of the Canadian Copyright Act, *supra* note 13, which exempts "a change in the location of a work, the physical means by which a work is exposed or the physical structure containing a work" from the moral right of integrity in works of visual art. The exceptions in VARA, *supra* note 4, § 106A(c), include "public presentation, including lighting and placement, of the work," unless those conditions represent "gross negligence." This section seems to apply perfectly to the *Sehgal* scenario.

closer to art.[123] An appropriate legal solution may be to provide that any good-faith attempt to build a virtual gallery will not lead to integrity violations. At the same time, associations that offend human rights could be explicitly prohibited. But the dividing line between the permissible and the forbidden will always be a tenuous one. The creative mind of the viewer is likely to prove as unpredictable in its own way as the genius of the artist.

If these virtual "private collections" remain private, there should be no need to talk about moral rights. As in the case of copyright law as a whole, it makes sense to limit the relevance of moral rights to public uses of artworks. If, however, private collections become accessible to other visitors to the museum's website, the question of moral rights will arise. In this situation, the solution to the attribution problem is fairly simple: it is the responsibility of the museum to organize its visual files with attribution included. The question of integrity, once again, is more difficult. The specific goal of the museum may be to help the viewer to rearrange the images of artworks. How can it be expected to take responsibility if these new orderings violate an integrity right?

In addition, yet one more layer of rights and interests may arise in the form of the Internet site creator's moral rights of attribution and integrity. These moral rights could limit the ability of any museum to deal with those involved in the creation of virtual displays as employees only. But it could also restrict the ability of the museum to undertake new projects that build on its past constructions. Where moral rights arise, the explicit agreement of the individuals involved in the construction of the site will be required.

3. Artistic Innovation: From Collages to Parodies

There is nothing new about the collision between modern art and copyright law. The example of Andy Warhol, his Campbell's soup cans and his reproductions of Marilyn Monroe's photographs, suffices to illustrate the point.[124] It is pleasantly ironic, but in the natural order of things, that the Warhol Foundation is now vigilant against violations of Warhol's copyright in his own works.[125]

---

123. But it is well worth noting that authenticity in music, too, is increasingly difficult to define. For example, recording engineer Steve Epstein notes that the term "live recording" generally means only that a percentage of the recording is recorded live. Tthe portion that is live may also not have been captured in a single session. (Private interview, June 22, 2010, New York.)

124. An image of Warhol's soup cans can be viewed on the website of the Museum of Modern Art (MoMA), New York, at http://www.moma.org/collection/object.php?object_id=79809 (last visited July 28, 2010); *see also* the commentary on his "Gold Marilyn" http://www.moma.org/collection/object.php?object_id=79737 (last visited July 28, 2010).

125. *See, for example*, the discussion of licensing rights on the website of the Andy Warhol Foundation for the Visual Arts, http://www.warholfoundation.org/licensing/index.html (last visited Jul. 27, 2010).

The availability of digital images greatly enriches the potential for creative innovation in new artistic forms—from collages to parodies, from virtual galleries to commercial web pages. The artist who wants to use images for the creation of new works faces formidable legal and ethical challenges involving questions of copyright ownership as well as moral rights. The artist must respect the moral rights of attribution and integrity of all those who came before him or her, although the practicalities of doing so are not easy to contemplate. Similarly, galleries that wish to show the work of modern artists engaged in experimental work may find themselves facing difficulties because of the need to respect moral rights.

At first glance, any form of art that makes use of pre-existing images will face the problem of moral rights. In these situations, two questions arise. First, it is not clear that every use of a pre-existing image will lead to a moral rights violation. Rather, in keeping with the theory behind moral rights, the component of the work that is used must retain a real connection with the original author. An appropriate test is needed.

The general test for copyright infringement is one of substantiality: if the copied image represents a substantial part of the original work, it will constitute an infringement of copyright.[126] What is substantial depends on a number of factors, and both quantity and quality are relevant to this determination. In the case of moral rights, similar principles can be used to assess the strength of the link between a particular image and its creator. For example, merely copying a color may not be sufficient to establish a link with the author of the work. On the other hand, if the color is highly distinctive, or if it invokes the artist in the context in which it is used—Mark Rothko's or Matisse's Red, for example—it may be a violation of moral rights to copy it. This is not to suggest that any artist could, or should, restrict the use of a color. Rather, the idea is to prevent something unfair: the exploitation of the work of the original artist without identifying him or her. A useful connection can be made here between moral rights and trademark principles. Trademark law will only protect an image that invokes its brand *when its use raises this association in the mind of the viewer.* Nothing is protected, or restricted, in the abstract. This principle of association seems to be well suited to the context of digital art.

The second question has to do with the practical issue of how moral rights should be recognized. What constitutes adequate attribution? If a work is extremely well-known, is it fair to argue that the use of the work implies attribution to its original creator? This appears to be the principle behind parody,

---

126. Ladbroke v. William Hill [1964] 1 W.L.R. 263, *available at* http://wikijuris.net/cases/ladbroke_football_ltd_v_william_hill_football_ltd_1964_1_wlr_273 (last visited July 27, 2010); University of London v. University Tutorial Press [1916] 2 Ch. 601 (Ch.D.), available at http://wikijuris.net/cases/university_of_london_press_ltd_v_university_tutorial_press_ltd_1916_2_ch_601 (last visited July 27, 2010).

which can only operate as a defense to copyright infringement if the work and its author are well-known. Without this expectation of recognition from the public, the use of a little-known work, without giving credit to the author, cannot be justified as a parody.

The format of an artwork may not lend itself to easy attribution. Web pages can be broken up into component parts, and the presence of attribution in any part of the page may be sufficient. But what happens when the image can be printed or physically reproduced in some other way, and separated from the attribution information? What about the case of original works such as collages, which may be signed by the artist, but are not likely to include attribution to the artists whose earlier works are integrated into the collage? It is also worth noting that the U.S. doctrine that allows a transformative work—an original work made out of pre-existing components—to escape liability for copyright infringement may not help to resolve the questions of attribution and integrity raised by moral rights.[127]

F. Recommendations

Technology has helped to make the world of visual art accessible to the public in new ways. It seems poised to bring about democratization of a new kind, truly opening a new vista of aesthetic experience to the public. The tremendous potential of technology for visual art means that the regulation of new activities in this area should be approached with care. The objective of protecting cultural heritage must remain in focus; no lesser concern can justify the imposition of restrictions on the creative use of artistic images. At the same time, the potential of technology translates into new dangers of misappropriation, misrepresentation, and abuse. These injustices require an adequate response from the law.

The use of images clearly invokes a moral rights element, and the general principle of upholding artists' moral rights of attribution and integrity should undoubtedly apply to the digital environment. Indeed, moral rights can help to support the educational and aesthetic goals of projects like virtual galleries.

---

127. For a helpful examination of the interplay between derivative works, transformative uses, and fair use under U.S copyright law, see Mary W.S. Wong, *"Transformative" User-Generated Content in Copyright Law: Infringing Derivative Works or Fair Use?*, 11 (4) VAND. J. ENT. L. & TECH. 1075, 1104–37. She comments: "The fundamental idea seems to be that if the use will advance knowledge and enable progress (in the constitutionally mandated manner), it may be fair and thus permissible, subject to the other factors in the case; more specifically, such a use could be transformative in that it does more than 'supersede the objects' of the original work—it also generates new and socially desirable 'knowledge.'" [footnote omitted].

The layering of multiple moral rights and images means that novel techniques of attribution should be supported by the law. At the same time, integrity rights in works of art should be carefully framed. The traditional requirements stipulated by the Berne Convention, that alterations of a work must be shown to damage an author's honor or reputation, may not be appropriate for the visual arts. In contrast to other kinds of creative expression, damage to a visual work may be beyond correction or redemption. As such, the extra care which can be achieved by making any modification a *prima facie* violation of the integrity right, along the lines of Canadian and American legislation on moral rights in the visual arts, makes eminent sense. In relation to visual art, the moral right of integrity should address specific issues, including the protection of conservation efforts, the evaluation of the context in which an artwork is displayed, and prohibition of the outright destruction of a work of art.

Finally, consideration should be given to the important possibility that moral rights should be available for works of art in the public domain. As India's *Sehgal* case suggests, moral rights can make an important contribution to the protection of cultural heritage, supplementing relatively weak international agreements like the UNESCO and UNIDROIT conventions on cultural property with a powerful legal alternative.

G. Conclusion

The museum is no mere relic of the past. On the contrary, museums continue to be counted among the most important of our cultural institutions. In the coming century, their significance is only likely to increase. As people migrate throughout the world, interest in world cultures is growing in intensity. By a suitable irony, the combination of ancient collections with modern technology is extraordinarily powerful. Technology makes it possible to connect people with the images, ideas, and knowledge that represent the treasures of human civilization everywhere. Museums now have an opportunity to provide access to culture and education on a grand scale.

But they must also rise to this extraordinary challenge. The world of technology is a place of shifting values. As culture in all its forms becomes more available to the public, it may also face new vulnerabilities. The various controversies that have confronted museums in recent years are daunting—from the repatriation of human remains and the return of cultural objects, to the restoration of stolen or looted art. They demand the almost impossible mental feat of placing oneself outside the familiar dimensions of a dominant culture and attempting to think in new ways about other cultures, and about the past.

Moral rights, and the principles that they represent, can provide us with sophisticated tools. In particular, the ideas of attribution and integrity can make a contribution to the status of artworks and artefacts in the museums of the virtual world. They can help to preserve, not only the material shell of the past, but also, the spiritual essence of what our ancestors have left us.

Friends or Enemies? Moral Rights and Open Access

The writer as a writer has but one
heir—the public domain.
–Victor Hugo[1]

---

1. The quote has been widely attributed to Hugo in the context of the recent French case, *Hugo v. Editions Plon*, about the right of an author to write a sequel to *Les Misérables*. *See, for example*, Kim Willshire, *Heir of Victor Hugo Fails to Stop Les Mis II: France's Highest Appeal Court Allows Modern Sequel to 1860s Masterpiece*, GUARDIAN (Jan. 31, 2007), *available at* http:// www.guardian.co.uk/world/2007/jan/31/books.france. *See* the final ruling, *Hugo c Societe Plon*, Arrêt n° 125 du 30 janvier 2007, Cass. Civ. 1re, *available at* http://www.courdecassation. fr/jurisprudence_2/premiere_chambre_civile_568/arret_no_9850.html (last visited Apr. 29, 2010). In his speech at the International Literary Congress held in Paris in 1878, Hugo affirmed, "The book, as a book, belongs to the author, but the thought belongs—the term is not too vast—to the human race." (*"Le livre, comme livre, appartient à l'auteur, mais comme pensée, il appartient—le mot n'est pas trop vaste—au genre humain."*).

Copyright is a successful concept. It represents a well-established legal tradition that has evolved over the centuries, and proven its remarkable ability to adapt to social change. In common law countries, copyright law traces its pedigree back to the Statute of Anne, enacted three centuries ago, in 1710.[2] Civil law countries are not far behind, having settled comfortably on copyright principles by the latter part of the eighteenth century.[3] Developing countries have been conversant with Western copyright concepts at least since colonization—post-socialist jurisdictions, since the end of the twentieth century.[4]

But now, a dramatic change has occurred. The survival of copyright is under threat. Why is a legal concept of such longevity and widespread acceptance suddenly threatened with destruction?

At first glance, the obvious cause is technology. There can be little doubt that technological change has brought completely new pressures to bear upon the world of copyright. Through digital media, the publication, reproduction, and communication of knowledge take place with unprecedented ease and fluency. The crucial moment in the life of a work has become its debut in digital format. Once a work is digitized, it can be transformed into different media, transferred to an individual, broadcast to the public, or communicated across borders with virtually no restrictions. The digital environment has the unprecedented potential to loosen historic restrictions on the flow of knowledge. By implication, it renders middlemen unnecessary.

This is the primal fear of the copyright industries: redundancy. How can they face a new reality in which their role as disseminators of knowledge is no longer needed? In industry's response to this challenge, two possible strategies have been explored. The first is, as the expression goes, to fight fire with fire—in this case, technology with technology. The development of digital "locks" that make information inaccessible was initially favored by industry, but the technique has had limited success. No encryption technology is entirely secure, and code-breaking is a persistent threat.

---

2. Statute of Anne (1710) 8 Ann., c. 19.
3. France's first copyright law is usually considered to be the Revolutionary Decree of July 19, 1793, *Archives parlementaires*, July 19, 1793, at 186; *see* Carla Hesse, *Enlightenment Epistemology and the Law of Authorship in Revolutionary France, 1777–1793*, 30 REPRESENTATIONS 109, 125 (1990). But Hesse (at 126) draws attention to Le Chapelier's law of January 13, 1791, and the still earlier series of 6 decrees on the book trade, issued on August 30, 1777, granted legal recognition to authors for the first time in French law (Hesse, at 111). *See also* the discussion in Chapter 2, *supra*, "Moral Rights: History of an Idea," notes 61–81 and accompanying text.
4. But some post-socialist countries have a much older relationship with international copyright. For example, Bulgaria and Hungary joined the Berne Convention in 1921 and 1922, respectively. *See* Contracting Parties to the Berne Convention, *available at* http://www.wipo.int/treaties/en/ShowResults.jsp?lang=en&treaty_id=15 (last visited Aug. 23, 2010).

A second and subtler strategy has been to raise a more abstract fight—to resist the freedom of digital media by attempting to impose legal restrictions on the use of copyright works where technological limits either do not exist, or can be circumvented. But here, corporate strategy has not only attempted to hold on to existing rights. Rather, copyright industries have also attempted to expand their rights in the digital environment—lobbying governments to enact copyright reforms, and pursuing lawsuits against groups and individuals who could be held responsible for copyright infringement.[5] The approach of industry to new media has been all-inclusive. Every activity that involves the reproduction and communication of works in digital format should be restricted by copyright rules. In practice, this means that every digital use of a work would require the authorization of the copyright owner, and every digital transaction would generate a fee.

But this is not quite how copyright works. Historically, only some uses of a work fall within copyright rules. Notably, a bright line generally divides the exploitation of a work for commercial purposes from private use, which is outside the scope of copyright law. Much of what happens in the digital era involves activities that resemble what is usually thought of as the private use of works.

This was what led Professor Charles Nesson to argue, in Joel Tenenbaum's defense, that the university student had done nothing wrong by downloading music from file-sharing networks.[6] The defense was a classic interpretation of fair dealing theory; but it failed on the American tradition that an activity causing damage to the economic interests of the copyright-owner is, indeed, an infringement of copyright.[7] Where file-sharing is concerned, one person's use may not cause economic damage; when multiplied by millions, however,

---

5. Both Internet service providers (ISPs) and individuals have been targeted; well-known lawsuits against individuals include the *RIAA v. Tenenbaum* case, against a student, discussed in Ben Sheffner, *Oy Tenenbaum! RIAA Wins $675,000, or $22,500 Per Song*, ArsTechnica (July 31, 2009), *available at* http://arstechnica.com/tech-policy/news/2009/07/o-tenenbaum-riaa-wins-675000-or-22500-per-song.ars (last visited Apr. 25, 2010); and the *Jammie Thomas* case, against a Minnesotan single mother, discussed in Wired magazine: David Kravets, *RIAA Jury Finds Minnesota Woman Liable for Piracy, Awards $222,000*, Wired (Oct. 4, 2009), *available at* http://www.wired.com/threatlevel/2007/10/riaa-jury-finds/ (last visited Apr. 25, 2010) Tenenbaum was defended by famed Harvard law professor, Charles Nesson; *see* discussion below. Examples of ISP litigation, from Europe and Canada, include the *Promusicae* case and the *BMG v. John Doe* litigation. *BMG Canada Inc. v. John Doe*, 2005 FCA 193, [2005] 4 R.C.F. 81 [*BMG v. John Doe*], and *Productores de Música de España (Promusicae) v. Telefónica de España SAU (Telefónica)*, Judgment of the Court (Grand Chamber) of Jan. 29, 2008, Case C-275/06, *available at* http://eur-lex.europa.eu/LexUriServ/LexUriServ.do?uri=CELEX: 62006J0275:EN:HTML (last visited Apr. 25, 2010).

6. *See* the overview of Nesson's approach and the commentary it excited in John Schwartz, *Tilting at Internet Barrier, A Stalwart Is Upended*, New York Times (Aug. 10, 2009), *available at* http://www.nytimes.com/2009/08/11/us/11download.html (last visited Apr. 25, 2010).

7. Jonathan Band, *The Long and Winding Road to the Google Books Settlement*, John Marshall Rev. Intell. Prop. L. 227, nn.304–310 and accompanying text.

the private activity of an individual can lead to the destruction of an industry. In its landmark ruling in the *Grokster* case, the United States Supreme Court felt that there could be no doubt about it: file-sharing was causing grave distress to the music industry. Justice Souter comments:

> ... MGM's evidence gives reason to think that the vast majority of users' downloads are acts of infringement, and because well over 100 million copies of the software in question are known to have been downloaded, and billions of files are shared across the FastTrack and Gnutella networks each month, the probable scope of copyright infringement is staggering.[8]

Outside the United States, this perspective on the public-private divide is not universally shared. In an interesting difference of legal opinion, Canada's courts have been noncommittal about the illegality of music file-sharing. In the case of *BMG v John Doe*,[9] the Canadian Federal Court placed privacy concerns above copyright, and went on to suggest that the downloading of music clearly falls into the category of personal use that is exempt from copyright restrictions. The Court also commented that music file-sharing did not show the requisite element of "authorizing" illegal acts to qualify as an infringement of copyright under Canadian law.[10] On appeal, the trial court was reprimanded for making a premature statement on the legality of file-sharing, but the Federal Court of Appeal nevertheless stood firm on the lower court's determination to protect privacy.[11]

A similar position emerged in the *Promusicae* case at the European Court of Justice, but the European court had the luxury of passing "the hot potato" of its recommendations on the scope of liability for Internet service providers (ISPs) to the national governments of its member states.[12] Canada's music market is relatively small; Europe is a major market for music, and it is largely dominated by American music. Recent European cases dealing with

---

8. MGM Studios, Inc. v. Grokster, Ltd. 545 U.S. 913, 923 (2005) [*Grokster*].

9. BMG v. John Doe, *supra* note 5.

10. The trial court commented (at para. 25) that "downloading a song for personal use does not amount to infringement." The court went on to cite the *CCH* decision of the Supreme Court of Canada, to this effect: "the case of *CCH Canadian Ltd. v. Law Society of Upper Canada*, 2004 SCC 13 (CanLII) [2004] 1 S.C.R. 339 established that setting up the facilities that allow copying does not amount to authorizing infringement. I cannot see a real difference between a library that places a photocopy machine in a room full of copyrighted material and a computer user that places a personal copy on a shared directory linked to a P2P service. In either case the preconditions to copying and infringement are set up but the element of authorization is missing." *See* BMG v. John Doe, 2004 FC 488, [2004] 3 F.C.R. at para. 27 [*BMG v. John Doe, F.C.*] http://www.canlii.org/en/ca/fct/doc/2004/2004fc488/2004fc488.html (last visited Apr. 28, 2010); and CCH Canadian Ltd. v. Law Society of Upper Canada, 2004] 1 S.C.R. 339, 2004 SCC 13 [*CCH*].

11. BMG v. John Doe, *supra* note 5, paras. 46–53.

12. *See supra* note 5. *See also* Fanny Coudert & Evi Werkers, *in The Aftermath of the Promusicae Case: How to Strike the Balance?*, 18(1) Int'l J. L. Info. Tech. 50 (2010).

the issue of music downloads, such as the *Pirate Bay* ruling, suggest that an American perspective is likely to dominate the European Union, with file-sharing condemned as an illegal activity.[13] But European sensibilities could help to soften the American position, as concerns about privacy and human rights have been consistently articulated in European copyright cases.[14]

Europe has also been proactive about exploring alternate models of file-sharing. These include the idea of a "global licensing" model that would allow unlimited downloads on payment of a single fee—seriously considered in France, but now superseded by the new "three strikes" approach, which would penalize users by disconnecting Internet access after three warnings from the user's ISP—and the "bundling" of access to music with other services.[15] Britain's Digital Economy Act will involve the implementation of measures to disconnect individuals who are regularly involved in illegal file-sharing, though their exact shape is yet to be decided.[16] The Isle of Man continues to advocate for a global licensing model in its country; the "bundling" approach essentially seems quite similar, except that it would be controlled by corporations rather than government, and therefore, has greater commercial potential.[17]

---

13. *See Court Jails Pirate Bay Founders*, BBC NEWS (Apr. 17, 2009), *available at* http://news.bbc.co.uk/2/hi/technology/8003799.stm (last visited Apr. 24, 2010). *See* the interesting reaction at Greg McKenzie & Greg Cochrane, *Paul McCartney: Pirate Bay Verdict "Fair,"* BBC NEWS (Apr. 20, 2009), *available at* http://news.bbc.co.uk/newsbeat/hi/music/newsid_8007000/8007950.stm (last visited Apr. 24, 2010). Paul McCartney points out that preserving music royalties is the only way that bands can make money out of their work. Of course, McCartney is working with existing models of distribution. If there were methods for bands to distribute their work directly, without the intervention of publishers, then there is at least a theoretical possibility that they could make all the money out of their work, and not just royalties.

14. *See, for example, Promusicae, supra* note 5. It is worth noting that the entire field of international copyright jurisprudence at the ECJ was initiated by the *Phil Collins* complaint, which led to a finding that nondiscrimination, as defined by art. 10 of the European Charter of Human Rights, mandated the equal treatment of complainants in different member states of the EU. *See* Phil Collins v. Imtrat Handelsgesellschaft mbH; Patricia Im-und Export Verwaltungsgesellschaft mbH and Another v. EMI Electrola GmbH, Joined Cases C-92/92 and C-326/92, *available at* http://eur-lex.europa.eu/smartapi/cgi/sga_doc?smartapi!celexplus!prod CELEXnumdoc&lg=en&numdoc=61992J0092 (last visited Apr. 28, 2010).

15. *See* Eric Pfanner, *Isle of Man Plans Unlimited Music Downloads*, NEW YORK TIMES (Jan. 25, 2009), *available at* http://www.nytimes.com/2009/01/26/business/worldbusiness/26music.html (last visited July 20, 2010).

16. *See* The Digital Economy Act, 2010, c. 24, *available at* http://www.legislation.gov.uk/ukpga/2010/24/contents (last visited Aug. 23, 2010). Concerns about the Act include the invasiveness of its provisions allowing data on Internet use to be gathered. Its measures also require the co-operation of Internet service providers (ISPs), and have already led to a lawsuit brought by two ISPs against the government, based on the concern that consumers will prefer smaller ISPs which are not included in these anti-piracy provisions. *See BT and TalkTalk Challenges Digital Economy Act,* BBC NEWS (Jul. 8, 2010). *See also Q & A: The Digital Economy Bill,* BBC NEWS (Apr. 9, 2010), *available at* http://news.bbc.co.uk/2/hi/technology/8604602.stm. The BBC comments that "[m]easures could include sending letters to people identified as downloading illegal content and asking them to stop and pointing out legal alternatives."

17. Pfanner, *supra* note 15.

As these examples show, technology is only a partial explanation for the current vulnerability of copyright. There is a deeper underlying reason: social choice. In particular, actors in the copyright industries have made controversial choices about how to respond to new technology. In most cases, those choices have failed to address cultural transformation— of which, an inflexible copyright law is certain to become a casualty. Established relationships will change—authors and artists, publishers and record labels, readership and audience are all in new situations. The existing balance of power is altered. Current business models in the copyright industries *must* adapt.[18]

Change is inevitable, but none of it necessarily implies the death of the copyright concept. If the destruction of copyright is indeed at hand, the strategies of key players in the copyright industries are at least partly to blame. They have helped to generate the strongest anti-copyright sentiment in the history of the law.

To an extent, the position of the copyright industries is understandable. They are engaged in a struggle for survival, and the use of any weapon at their disposal is, from their perspective, fully justified. The reaction may be excessive—techniques such as pursuing individuals in copyright cases represent a terrible approach to public relations and undercut public sympathy for the real plight of entertainment companies. Indeed, the aggressiveness of their approach has generated a backlash. The reaction can be summed up in the word "free."

"Free" means different things to different people. In the context of music downloads, to most members of the public, "free" means available without payment. But advocates of "free" software and "free" culture claim something different. Richard Stallman, the founder of the Free Software Foundation, defines free software as—

> a matter of liberty, not price. To understand the concept, you should think of "free" as in "free speech," not as in "free beer."[19]

---

18. This point was made in an editorial by the author in Canada's *Globe and Mail* newspaper in August 2009, to encourage the Canadian government to adopt a responsible attitude towards copyright reform. Ironically, it generated tremendous ire in some parts of the Canadian business community, who felt that the call for "balance and clarity" in copyright law placed ownership interests under threat. *See* Mira T. Sundara Rajan, Opinion, *Copyright: Let's Take Ownership*, GLOBE AND MAIL (Aug. 4, 2009), *available at* http://www.theglobeandmail.com/news/opinions/copyright-lets-take-ownership/article1238407/. The article was cited as one of the day's six international editorials of interest by the Times Online Comment Central http://timesonline.typepad.com/comment/2009/08/tuesdays-comment-from-the-papers-in.html (last visited July 20, 2010), and it was picked up for comment on BBC News/Magazine Monitor/Web Monitor, http://www.bbc.co.uk/blogs/magazinemonitor/2009/08/web_monitor_54.shtml (last visited Apr. 28, 2010).

19. *See The Definition of Free Software*, GNU OPERATING SYSTEM, *available at* http://www.gnu.org/philosophy/free-sw.html (last visited July 20, 2010).

Creative Commons "guru," Professor Larry Lessig, acknowledges a profound debt to Richard Stallman in his own work, *Free Culture*, and describes the idea in similar terms:[20]

> [W]e come from a tradition of "free culture"—not "free" as in "free beer" (to borrow a phrase from the founder of the free-software movement), but "free" as in "free speech," "free markets," "free trade," "free enterprise," "free will," and "free elections." A free culture supports and protects creators and innovators. It does this directly by granting intellectual property rights. But it does so indirectly by limiting the reach of those rights, to guarantee that follow-on creators and innovators remain as free as possible from the control of the past. A free culture is not a culture without property, just as a free market is not a market in which everything is free. The opposite of a free culture is a "permission culture"—a culture in which creators get to create only with the permission of the powerful, or of creators from the past.[21]

The terms of the debate on copyright are strongly polarized, with industry in a largely successful push for maximum restrictions, on the one hand, and on the other, anti-copyright movements that argue for the removal of most, if not all, copyright restrictions on knowledge. The players in this drama are industry versus activists. The activists behind the Creative Commons movement are, in a sense, an unlikely group—law professors—while those behind open source, or free software, are programmers. The party who remains offstage is the author.

There is no real reason why the sympathies of the open access movement should tend against authors. In fact, the anger of open access movements is properly directed at the corporate owners of copyright works, who overwhelmingly enjoy the financial rewards of copyright control. Current practice in Western copyright industries gives short shrift to the author, who is typically entitled to royalties on sales of his work in the range of 1 to 15 percent of net receipts.[22] The situation in non-Western countries is perhaps

---

20. *See* Chapter 5, *supra* note 9. Lawrence Lessig, Free Culture: How Big Media Uses Technology and the Law to Lock Down Culture and Control Creativity (Penguin Press 2008) [*Free Culture*]. Appropriately, the book is also available for free download at http://www.free-culture.cc/freeculture.pdf (last visited Apr. 28, 2010).

21. *Free Culture*, *supra* note 20, at xiv.

22. The calculation of royalties is a contentious matter. There is significant variation in royalty rates depending on the type of book involved—a scholarly book might attract a royalty of 2.5%, while the rate for a trade book might be as high as 15%. Calculating the actual amount of the royalty may depend, not on the list price of the book, but on the amount that it was actually sold for. It is common for publishers to sell books at "deep discounts" to various buyers, including bookstores and libraries, book clubs, and other types of bulk orders and special sales. The American Authors' Guild advises writers to limit the ability of publishers to sell discounted books. *See* http://www.authorsguild.org/services/legal_services/books.html

even worse. In a country like India, the featured country at the London Book Fair of 2009, authors often pay to have their work published. The fact that Indian books are increasingly of international interest has done little to alter Indian publishing practices, solidly rooted in a cultural tradition that artists do not, and should not, care about money.

Ironically, socialist countries have perhaps been unique in daring to acknowledge the potential for conflict between authors and publishers. A 1938 commentary on the Russian copyright law noted:

> [It] is characteristic that, except for a small group of bourgeois authors, the author's right is the property, in bourgeois society, not of the author, but of the publisher, of a big capitalist, an industrialist.... . [T]he author's right in capitalist countries is made into a tool of the interests of the monopolist-publisher, a means of exploiting the author and retarding the cultural growth of the masses of the people....[23]

The structure of modern publishing puts the author in an awkward position. In order to enjoy any economic reward from his work, he depends on sales. However, the vast majority of the money made from sales accrues to the publisher; only a small, often tiny, proportion of those receipts finds its way into the hands of the author, in the form of royalties. Without those royalties, however, the author has nothing at all. The position of authors makes them at once dependent on their publishers and antagonistic to them—at once for and against free access. Not surprisingly, many authors are sympathetic to the goals of open access movements, but the problem of economic survival— to say nothing of the desire for financial success—may align them with publishers.

This point takes us back to the question of "freedom" and what it means in the Digital Age. Lessig's definition of "free" is an appealing one, as is his call for a balanced approach to copyright law. The easing of copyright restrictions makes eminent sense. But the difficult question becomes, where exactly should the line be drawn? Free access movements offer a powerful

---

(last visited Aug. 20, 2010). The Writers' Union of Canada offers an interesting brief on this issue, presented to the Canadian government's Standing Committee on Heritage, http://www.writersunion.ca/pdfs/brief200302.pdf#xml=http://writersunion.ca.master.com/texis/master/search/mysite.txt?q=royalties&order=r&id=58d022305000420b&cmd=xml (last visited Aug. 20, 2010). Some general information on royalty rates in the United States is also offered by royalty software company Kensai, http://www.royaltysoftware.net/Q_royalty_rates.html (last visited Aug. 20, 2010).

23. *See A Text Writer's Opinion,* GRAZHDANSKOE PRAVO (Civil Law), Part I, 254–55 (Moscow 1938); MATERIALS ON SOVIET LAW 35 (John N. Hazard, trans. Columbia Univ. 1947). *See* Mira T. Sundara Rajan, *Copyright and Creative Freedom: A Study of Post-Socialist Law Reform* 93–97 (Routledge 2006), for a detailed discussion of this perspective [Sundara Rajan, *Copyright and Creative Freedom*].

counterweight to corporate lobbying, and as such, their contribution to copyright discourse is immense. However, the apparent absence of the author from "copyleft" discussions is a crucial deficiency. In fact, the strong stand of open access movements against the corporate ownership of knowledge is, in its own way, equally extreme. Corporations want to be overpaid for copyright works; open access wants copyright works for nothing. The copyleft position is white to the corporations' black.

The entire debate is defined, not by authorship, but by ownership.[24] Corporate interests claim to own knowledge; for the copyleft thinker, the public owns it. This is an important point. Whether or not proponents of copyleft use the terminology of ownership, the effect of copyleft is to confer ownership on the public. This is because the point of copyleft is public access: to say that "no one" owns knowledge may not be quite enough to convey the practical thrust of the copyleft position. If no one *owns* knowledge, there may still be other reasons for restricting it—for example, in the case of sacred knowledge protected by cultural traditions.[25] But copyleft is fundamentally against restricting access to knowledge. For both sides, pro and anti, the terms of the argument are accordingly defined by the practical concept of ownership.

When copyleft writers talk about the "public interest," they are actually referring to something quite specific: the public interest in access to works. However, there is little reference to other aspects of the "public interest." Preserving the integrity of culture is surely a public interest issue; so, too, is the authenticity of knowledge. There is a public interest in encouraging artists, as Lessig notes, but in his view, that appears to be adequately recognized by providing some copyright protection.[26]

Yet—perhaps paradoxically—ideas of authorship have quietly crept into open access movements. Notably, they appear in the form of provisions recognizing the moral interests of authors in the license documents by which open source arrangements for the use of works can be made. This chapter will examine the implicit recognition of authors' moral rights in open access movements, with a view to answering three questions.

First, how significant is the presence of authors' moral interests in model agreements for open access licensing? Is it truly a form of recognition for

---

24. I am indebted to Colin Tapper for pointing out that the concept of ownership is, itself, potentially misleading when used in relation to knowledge (personal communication with the author, July 14, 2010). Nevertheless, the concept of "intellectual property" is definitely built upon the analogy between intangible knowledge and tangible property, however imperfect it may be. The purpose of the discussion here is to emphasize the contrast between the idea of "ownership" that informs intellectual property law, and the concept of "authorship" as it is refers to the creators of artistic and intellectual work.
25. Yumbulul v. Reserve Bank of Australia (1991) 21 I.P.R. 481 (Austl.).
26. *Free Culture, supra* note 20, at xiv.

moral rights? Secondly, what is the rationale behind the presence of moral rights in open access licenses? In particular, what are the philosophical reasons, as well as the legal explanations, for their presence? Thirdly, does the recognition of moral rights compensate for the reduction of economic rewards to the author in the open access model? Four case studies will be considered: Creative Commons; open source software; projects for the collective creation of works via the Internet, such as Wikipedia; and the creation of Internet libraries, including the Google Books project.

A. Creative Commons: Implicit Recognition of Moral Rights

In the usual scenario, acquiring the right to use a copyright-protected work involves two steps. First, one must obtain permission to use the work; and secondly, one is generally obliged to pay a fee for that use. Both factors can particularly inhibit the creative re-use of a work—citation or allusion in a new work, for example. While certain attempts to re-use a work may fall within the definition of "fair use" or "fair dealing," there is no bright line conveniently separating a fair use from an infringement of copyright. Rough guidelines are sometimes provided—in Canada, photocopying a book is restricted to 20 percent of the total content[27]—but copyright infringement is classically about the "quality" of copying, as much as the quantity.[28] In the case of works whose copyright owners are impossible to locate, often known

---

27. *See, for example*, the useful website of the University of Waterloo on copyright at http://www. lib.uwaterloo.ca/copyright/index.html#basics13. Similar information is provided by most Canadian universities. Much copyright in the educational context is regulated through Access Copyright, an organization whose approach to copyright is increasingly facing criticism as excessive and detrimental to education. *See, for example*, Rory McGreal, *New Copyright Fee Will See Students Pay More for Learning Materials*, EDMONTON J. (Apr. 14, 2010), *available at* http://www.edmontonjournal.com/business/copyright+will+students+more+le arning+materials/2904884/story.html (last visited Apr. 28, 2010). The same guidelines of showing 20% are observed by Google Books when it provides "snippets" of copyright-protected books for users to browse their content: *see* Google Book Settlement, *available at* http://www.googlebooksettlement.com/ (last visited Apr. 28, 2010). The fact that the "snippets" are machine-generated could potentially pose a problem for moral rights, as they might misrepresent a work: *see* Google Books Settlement and Moral Rights: What Role Have They Played? What Role Should They Play?, presentation given to the Eighteenth Annual Fordham Intellectual Property Law & Policy Conference, Fordham University Law School, New York, April 8–9, 2010 (transcript forthcoming).

28. *See, for example*, the judgment in *Ladbroke (Football) Ltd. v. William Hill (Football) Ltd.* [1964] 1 W.L.R. 273.

as "orphan" works, the new use of the work, in its turn, may have to be abandoned.[29]

The objective of the Creative Commons movement is to circumvent this system entirely. Creative Commons aims to promote the dissemination of works without the restrictions of copyright law. It provides an alternative to copyright protection by proposing that authors release their works under the terms of a license to the general public. The exact terms of the license vary according to a number of possible models provided by Creative Commons, and examples may be seen on the Creative Commons website.[30]

All Creative Commons licenses aim at the common goal of allowing any person to use a work without requiring the permission of the copyright owner or the payment of royalties. However, the Creative Commons use of a work is not entirely free of conditions. A closer examination of the Creative Commons licenses reveals the presence of the author in a new and interesting form.

1. Copyright Infringement and Creative Commons: License or Contract?

The general license to the public generated by Creative Commons operates very much like a contract between parties, which can override the terms of copyright law. For example, copyright law might state that, in a "work-for-hire" or employment relationship, the initial copyright in the work is owned by the employer.[31] But an individual's contract of employment may provide that he retains copyright in his own work, and this contractual arrangement will prevail over the copyright law. In the case of the Creative Commons licenses, should the new user of the work fail to respect the conditions of use specified in the license to the general public, he will become liable for infringing the copyright in the original work.

---

29. In some cases, arrangements can be made to use an orphan work if the user has made an attempt "in good faith" to locate the owner of the copyright. In Canada, the Copyright Board has issued a number of licenses to use orphan works; on June 4, 2008, the EU released a Memorandum of Understanding on the issue. *See* Memorandum of Understanding on Diligent Search Guidelines for Orphan Works, *available at* http://ec.europa.eu/information_society/activities/digital_libraries/doc/hleg/orphan/mou.pdf (last visited Apr. 28, 2010).
30. *See* http://creativecommons.org/about/licenses/ (last visited Apr. 28, 2010).
31. *See* the Canadian Copyright Act, R.S.C. 1985, c. C-42, *available at* http://laws.justice.gc.ca/en/C-42/index.html (last visited Apr. 28, 2010) [Canadian Copyright Act], sec. 13.3, Work Made in the Course of Employment, which states, in part, "Where the author of a work was in the employment of some other person under a contract of service or apprenticeship and the work was made in the course of his employment by that person, the person by whom the author was employed shall, *in the absence of any agreement to the contrary*, be the first owner of the copyright" (emphasis added).

Copyright infringement is a means of enforcing the Creative Commons license. While the terms of the license are respected, it is an action held in reserve. Once an improper use of the work is made—a use not allowed under the terms of the license—the license is invalidated, and copyright infringement can be invoked by the author of the original work.

The relationship between Creative Commons licenses and contracts receives an important treatment in the 2008 case of *Jacobsen v Katzer*.[32] The court interprets the terms of the license as equivalent to the "conditions" of a contract, and, therefore, binding upon those who make use of the work. Judge Jeffrey S. White comments:

> Thus, if the terms of the Artistic License allegedly violated are both covenants and conditions, they may serve to limit the scope of the license and are governed by copyright law. If they are merely covenants, by contrast, they are governed by contract law.[33]

The court goes on to offer a detailed analysis of the Creative Commons framework for software, explaining how the economic and moral elements of the license work together to accomplish important practical goals:

> The clear language of the Artistic License creates conditions to protect the economic rights at issue in the granting of a public license. These conditions govern the rights to modify and distribute the computer programs and files included in the downloadable software package. The attribution and modification transparency requirements directly serve to drive traffic to the open source incubation page and to inform downstream users of the project, which is a significant economic goal of the copyright holder that the law will enforce. Through this controlled spread of information, the copyright holder gains creative collaborators to the open source project; by requiring that changes made by downstream

---

32. Jacobsen v. Katzer, 535 F.3d 1373 (Fed. Cir. 2008), *remanded*, 609 F. Supp. 2d 925, 89 U.S.P.Q.2d 1441 (N.D. Cal. 2009), settled Feb. 16, 2010] [*Jacobsen*].

33. *Id.*, at 1380. The case was settled on Feb. 19, 2010, and drew the comment: "Th[e]... Terms [of the settlement] can include an affirmative obligation of a commercial developer to 'give back' its own changes to the code for the benefit of others. They invariably also include an obligation to acknowledge the authorship of those that had created the earlier code." *See* Andy Updegrove *A Big Victory for F/OSS: Jacobsen v. Katzer is Settled*, ConsortiumInfo (Feb. 19, 2010), *available at* http://www.consortiuminfo.org/standardsblog/article.php?story=201002190850472 (last visited Apr. 22, 2010). *See also* the Comment by Ashley West, *Little Victories: Promoting Artistic Progress Through the Enforcement of Creative Commons Attribution and Share-Alike Licenses*, 36(4) Fla. St. Univ. L. Rev. 903 (2009). West notes, at 913, that "After the Federal Circuit released the Jacobsen opinion, the technology blogosphere praised the decision, announcing that the judicial system had finally given a definitive answer that public licensing regimes are enforceable as a matter of law. Part of this enthusiasm likely stemmed from the simple fact that Jacobsen was the first case to specifically discuss the Creative Commons movement in a significant way." (footnotes omitted).

users be visible to the copyright holder and others, the copyright holder learns about the uses for his software and gains others' knowledge that can be used to advance future software releases.[34]

2. The Basic License: Attribution Affirmed

According to the terms of a Creative Commons license, a person wanting to use a work released under the license must meet one fundamental condition: the new user must credit the creator of the original work in his new creation.[35] The Creative Commons attribution license does not cancel the copyright in the original work, which remains as an underlying right of the author. Instead, the license suspends the operation of copyright.

Under the attribution license, if someone were to use the work without attributing it to the original creator, the user could be sued for copyright infringement. Copyright becomes a fall-back position—it serves, implicitly, to enforce the terms of the Creative Commons license.

A closer look at the attribution license reveals something interesting: the license represents a total rejection of copyright restrictions. Any use can be made of a work released under this license, including commercial uses. So, for example, a photograph released under the attribution license could be used in a commercially released documentary or feature film. But the profit from the film would go exclusively to its producers; the person making the photograph would have no claim on any earnings from the project. This would be the case, regardless of how significant the image was—even if it were central to the successful marketing of the film, for example, appearing on publicity posters. But the condition of attribution remains, and attribution must be done according to the terms required by the original author.[36]

Attribution is the foundation of moral rights, and as such, the attribution license could be called a "moral rights" license for the use of the work. It is a license that protects the author's right of attribution without imposing any financial obligations on the user, or providing in any way for economic rewards to the author. The attribution license does leave open the question of integrity, but the explanation of the license by Creative Commons states that "the author's moral rights" are "[i]n no way... affected by the license."[37] In other words, and with particular reference to countries where the author enjoys moral rights under the copyright statute, the attribution license explicitly operates *in addition to* the existing legal framework for the protection of

---

34. *Jacobsen, supra* note 32, at 1382.
35. *See* http://creativecommons.org/about/licenses (last visited Apr. 28, 2010).
36. *See* the explanation at the Creative Commons website, *available at* http://creativecommons.org/licenses/by/3.0/ (last visited July 21, 2010).
37. *See* http://creativecommons.org/licenses/by/3.0/ (last visited Apr. 28, 2010).

authors' moral rights. If the copyright law of a country offers extensive protection for moral rights, the attribution license is merely reinforcing the law. But, in the case of a country where moral rights are not well-protected, the Creative Commons license may offer moral rights protection that is not otherwise available in this form—for example, in the United States.

This situation presents a contrast to the author's economic entitlement under copyright law, which he effectively "contracts out of" by the attribution license.

3. The Creation of Derivative Works: Integrity or Attribution?

Creative Commons licenses build upon each another in consecutive steps, each group more restrictive than the last. Based on the attribution concept, the second level of license provides, first, for a "share alike" principle. Should an author create a new work out of his creative re-use of an existing work, he will be required to release it under the same type of Creative Commons license as the original work. At the same level, a second, "attribution non-commercial" license prevents anyone re-using the work from doing so for commercial purposes. This license is noteworthy because of its considerable restrictiveness: any subsequent use of the work which leads to commercial gain, whether intentionally or accidentally, would invalidate the license, placing the user of the work in a situation of potential copyright infringement.

From the perspective of the moral right of integrity, the third license in this group, which adds a "no derivatives" principle to the attribution license, is noteworthy. It provides that no person should make a derivative work based on the original work; as the Creative Commons group explains,

> This license allows for redistribution, commercial and non-commercial, as long as it is passed along unchanged and in whole, with credit to you.[38]

At the next level, two types of licenses can be found. The first combines attribution with the principles of noncommercial use and the need to "share alike"—to allow the use of the new work only on the same terms as the original work. Secondly, a more restrictive version of the "no derivatives" license includes this rule alongside noncommercial use. This license is said to provide "free advertising" for the creator of the original work, as it allows the work to circulate freely in noncommercial contexts, provided that attribution of the author is maintained and the work itself is not altered.

---

38. *Attribution No Derivatives*, Creative Commons, *available at* http://creativecommons.org/about/licenses (last visited July 20, 2010).

The principle of restricting the creation of derivative works includes within it the integrity right, which would prohibit alterations to the original work. But the no-derivatives principle is both larger and more general than the integrity right. It completely prohibits the making of derivative works, even where the derivative creation might not violate the integrity of the original work. At the same time, it cannot protect a work from intervention that will not result in the outright creation of a new, ostensibly "derivative," work. Only in special cases, where the alteration of the work is so egregious as, in effect, to create a new work—the Monty Python scenario[39]—would the integrity right and the non-derivation principle be truly equivalent.

As in the case of the attribution right, any statutory moral rights apparently continue to exist alongside the no-derivatives principle. Once again, given the international use of Creative Commons licenses, the persistence of statutory moral rights is important. Even if the user of the work did something less dramatic than the creation of a derivative work, but altered the original work—for example, if he shared a piece of music from which, one of the stanzas of a song had been removed—this could certainly qualify as a violation of the moral right of integrity. The integrity of the work would be violated even though a derivative work would not necessarily have been created.

The close relationship between derivative works and the integrity principle is important in American law, and there is every reason to interpret Creative Commons licenses with this legal culture in mind. However, the "no derivatives" idea is a distorted reflection of the moral right of integrity. In fact, the real clue to the significance of the restriction on making derivative works lies in the consideration that derivative works must traditionally be authorized by the copyright-holder. In Creative Commons, the "no derivatives" idea is not just a species of integrity right; it can also be seen as a manifestation of the attribution right. Its purpose is to allow the author to control what is done with his work.

This realization leads to the insight that reputation is the true heart of the Creative Commons system. In the Digital Age, reputations can be promoted exponentially by the freedom to communicate information. The practice of new popular music groups posting videos of themselves on YouTube to create a reputation, quite literally out of thin air, is just one example of how technology works to promote reputations. The emphasis on disseminating information through Creative Commons makes sense in the light of a broader preoccupation with reputation. Ironically, copyright law can actually interfere with the growth of a reputation, by impeding, and possibly preventing, the dissemination of works through new technologies—a fact that the founders of Creative Commons have thoroughly understood.

---

39. Gilliam v. American Broadcasting Companies, 538 F.2d 14 (2d Cir. 1976) [*Gilliam*].

4. Reputation: The Heart of Open Access

The presence of attribution and "no-derivatives" requirements in the Creative Commons model amounts to a form of recognition for moral rights. The attribution principle occupies a central role in Creative Commons licenses. As for the principle of "no-derivatives," it could be considered an extremely narrow form of the integrity right, but it should also be recognized as a manifestation of the attribution principle. In addition, Creative Commons licenses specifically allow moral rights, as defined by law, to coexist with the terms of the licenses. This stands in stark contrast to the author's economic rights at law, from which he essentially chooses to "opt out" by releasing his work under the license.

Why does Creative Commons build its licensing system around these moral rights principles? It is apparent that, at some level, and in spite of its populist rhetoric, Creative Commons is preoccupied with authorial control. An overall consideration of the components of Creative Commons licenses suggests that, seen in context, the requirement of attribution, like the "share alike" and "no-derivatives" principles, aims to promote the individuals behind the creation of works. In particular, all three principles accomplish the same goal: they affirm the author's right to control his or her own work.

The formulation of the attribution right in the Creative Commons attribution license offers an interesting illustration of this principle. Not only is the author's attribution protected, but the author also chooses the method by which he wants to be attributed. No moral rights statute in the world appears to provide for the author to control the method of attribution, yet it is a basic right recognized by Creative Commons.

But the type of author imagined by Creative Commons is a specific kind of individual. Entrepreneurial and tech-savvy, the Creative Commons author is, above all, an amateur. Notwithstanding Lessig's idealistic definition of "free," embracing the goal of "Free Culture" in practice means forfeiting the opportunity to be paid for one's work. None of the Creative Commons licenses provide for payment for the uses of a work. Reputation is everything; money is nothing. Creative Commons cannot, therefore, be a comprehensive solution to the problems of excessive copyright control. It is a solution for those who do not need, or do not want, to earn money for their creative work.

What happens to creative life in a world where the choice lies between corporate control of culture and the free distribution of works? The obvious answer is academia. It is the ideal Creative Commons career. One earns a salary, independent of earnings from publications or other public manifestations of one's work, and thereby enjoys the luxury of being able to afford to distribute one's work to the public free of charge.

5. The Dark Side of Open Access: Art as a Profession in Decline

What happens when intellectuals and artists cannot expect to be paid for their work? Given the multiple connotations of "free" access to culture, this question deserves a closer look. In fact, two consequences follow. First, artists will, of course, cease to be professionals. Being unable to earn a living from creative work means that the artist must earn his or her living by some other means. The lucky ones might come from independently wealthy families. For others, the ubiquitous "day job" can guarantee a double life to look forward to—the tension of a lifetime spent in struggle to find the time to do what the artist wants to do, and, perhaps, what he or she does best.

But making intellectual creation "free" does something even larger: it negates society's principal method of recognizing value. Money is the means by which society acknowledges value, whether that value arises in things, labor, or information. No doubt, it is a flawed system for assigning value. How flawed is it?

The classic example of how money valuation is misdirected in the cultural arena is to point out that a work of mass culture will generate more money than a work of art. But in fact, it is probably more accurate to say that the life-cycles of these two kinds of works are different. A popular work generates its returns in the initial period of its publication, but a work of art generates its revenues over the long term. As Ernest Hemingway commented, "Good books always make money eventually."[40] Van Gogh's paintings were worthless during his lifetime, but he is now the highest-grossing artist of all time.[41] F. Scott Fitzgerald's novel, *The Great Gatsby*, did not sell out its original print run; it is now considered one of the greatest works in English of the twentieth century, and is currently in print in new editions. The fact remains: money is the principal method by which society recognizes value. It is not the only one, and, when it comes to culture, there are other ways of showing appreciation—for example, creating a new work, in homage or in parody, or helping to publicize work that deserves an audience. But it is not clear that any alternative can provide a totally adequate substitute for money. To remove money valuation altogether from creative works is to create an instant bias against the recognition of their value by society.

---

40. Ernest Hemingway, Green Hills of Africa 23 (Scribners 1935).
41. *See, for example, The Art Gems that Broke the Bank*, BBC News (June 19, 2006), *available at* http://news.bbc.co.uk/2/hi/entertainment/4883296.stm (last visited July 20, 2010); the issue is discussed in Chapter 1, *supra*, "Introduction: Moral Rights in the Virtual Age," note 55 and accompanying text.

And why should the person who is capable of intellectual creation be deprived of money because he happens to have the misfortune of an intellectual gift in lieu of business capital? George Bernard Shaw claimed that a true artist could never be happy doing anything for a living but creating.[42] However, throughout most of human history, this is exactly what artists have had to do. Turning the clock backwards, and finding ourselves in any European capital some two hundred years ago, we could have witnessed this story playing itself out in the lives of artists who have since become famous—musicians like Mozart and Beethoven, writers like Jane Austen or Voltaire. Franz Schubert was famously torn between his living as a schoolteacher and his work as a composer. Society can take some comfort in the psychological theory that inner conflict such as his produces great art. But how does that justify painful conditions of life?

Indeed, prior to the Romantic era, the means of sustenance for artists were few. Those who were successful sometimes came from aristocratic families; more often, their talents won favor for them from a wealthy patron, a king or a duke who was willing to support them, if only for a time. Independence was a luxury that few artists could afford.

Patronage provided a poor infrastructure for intellectual life. With the expansion of mass culture in the nineteenth century, many intellectuals were understandably eager to entrust themselves to the public for their livelihood.[43] Experiences could be bitter—Friedrich Schiller's faith in the public led to disappointment and bankruptcy[44]—but the alternatives were equally unsatisfactory in their own ways.

Looking further afield, in both space and time, we can consider the history of India. The birthplace of a number of the world's great intellectual and artistic traditions, Indian culture developed a highly formal relationship between intellectual and material wealth. Intellectuals and artists earned a livelihood from their work, but they did so largely by indirect means.

---

42. In MAN AND SUPERMAN (Brentano 1903), Shaw writes: "The true artist will let his wife starve, his children go barefoot, his mother drudge for a living at seventy, sooner than work at anything but his art." The play is available online, through Project Gutenberg at http://www.gutenberg.org/files/3328/3328-h/3328-h.htm (last visited Apr. 28, 2010).

43. In India, the experience was felt into the twentieth century: Tamil Renaissance poet, C. Surbramania Bharati, satirized his experiences at the court of the Ettayapuram Maharaja (and the Majaraja himself), in the delightful short novel, CHINNA SHANKARAN KATHAI [The Story of Little Shankaran]. The work is pending availability in English translation (S. Vijaya Bharati & Mira T. Sundara Rajan), though it is occasionally referenced in other works: *see, e.g.,* see A. R. VENKATACHALAPATHY, IN THOSE DAYS, THERE WAS NO COFFEE: WRITINGS IN CULTURAL HISTORY 167 (Yoda Press 2006), on the growth of biographical fiction in South Indian literature. Coffee-drinking, as immortalized in R. K. Narayan's humorous tales, is the endemic social passion of South Indians.

44. *See* CALVIN THOMAS, THE LIFE AND WORKS OF FRIEDRICH SCHILLER 71 (Kessinger Publishing 2004) (1901), who describes the experience as Schiller's attempt to live as a "literary free-lance who served no prince, but only the public."

Tradition compelled the wealthy and worldly castes to provide financially for their educators and learned men.

By separating intellectual work from money, Creative Commons is therefore not proposing anything truly new. Without providing an alternate system for the support of creative individuals, however, the movement leaves a fundamental question unanswered. How does society intend to support the creation of culture? If the marketplace will not support artists, who will? Is it time for a new system of patronage, perhaps in the form of state support? After all, if society can go so far as to claim "coauthorship" of creative works, as at least one commentator has suggested, does society not have a corresponding obligation to provide financial support?[45] And if so, should the support not be generous, to free an artist for intellectual life, in every sense, from all extraneous demands? In the absence of market opportunities to sell his work, what would be the use of a pension that allows an artist less than what he needs to survive, and, in this new scenario where works would be available free of charge, would deprive him of any chance at financial stability?

The question of artistic livelihood leads to another, troubling consideration: how can an artist or intellectual build material stability for himself if society prevents him from doing so? In contrast to a person who is able to amass material property, the profit from an artist's creation is taken away from him by society, apparently for the general benefit. No one takes away the property of a landowner, or the assets of a businessman. In the worst case, it is taxed, but the bulk of it remains, supporting the entrepreneur throughout his life and, for some period afterwards, his descendants. This is not considered to be detrimental to society. Rather, the accumulation of capital is seen as a positive achievement in most modern democracies—one that benefits society by "creating wealth" and "creating jobs."

On the other hand, the value that could be generated out of an artist's work does not evoke a comparable response. Art, it is said, belongs to society; sooner or later, it enters the public domain. Yet the effect of rendering artists' works into the public domain means that they are deprived of their own livelihood—their own "assets." And, certainly, they have no chance of leaving anything for their families in the form of an inheritance. An artist's family is condemned to eternal poverty—unless at least some of his descendants learn how to do other things.[46] Each generation has to begin over again and cannot

45. *See* Roberta Rosenthal Kwall, *The Author as Steward "For Limited Times,"* 88 B.U. L. Rev. 685 (2008), review of Lior Zemer, The Idea of Authorship in Copyright (Ashgate 2007).

46. Pierre Hugo, a great-great-grandson of Victor Hugo, who brought suit against Francois Cérésa for his sequels to *Les Miserables*, is apparently a goldsmith by trade. *See* Kim Willsher, *Heir of Victor Hugo Fails to Stop Les Mis II: France's Highest Appeal Court Allows Modern Sequel to 1860s Masterpiece*, The Guardian (Jan, 31, 2007), *available at* http://www.guardian.co.uk/world/2007/jan/31/books.france (last visited Apr. 28, 2010).

build on the achievements of its ancestor—they are deemed to be public property. But the heirs of businessman are generally considered to be "entitled" to their wealth and the social advantages that it secures.

It is easy to forget that a person with intellectual capabilities may have *nothing else* of equal value to contribute to society. Yet society considers itself the rightful owner, and the rightful beneficiary, of what he or she creates. What is the fundamental difference between property and creative work? The capacity to exclude—society *can* take away the product of an artist's mind, so it does. It cannot do the same to an entrepreneur, a businessman who makes money. It is difficult to remove property, to confiscate money without the owner's consent. And if conflicts escalate, the owner has the resources to compel the law to his side—to launch suits, to propagate his point of view through the use of his material resources, to advertise and generate publicity on his side. An artist, who lacks material resources, cannot command the same things from society. This is the dark side of "open access"— the dispossession of human beings.

B. Open Access: A Practical Need for Moral Rights

The history of copyright law is a curiously poetic one. Poetry lies in the means, if not in the end: copyright is built on the development of analogies.[47] Each form of copyright protection is accepted because it is somehow akin to previously known forms—film grows out of photographs, music, like literature, is also a form of written expression.[48] The protection of computer software, widely debated in its early history, was no exception to this rule. Software eventually became subsumed under one of copyright's metaphors—after all, computer programs are written forms of intellectual expression, "like" literary works.

But there is nothing inevitable about copyright protection for software. Through the early 1990s, a number of alternative approaches to software were

---

47. The history of copyright readily invokes the idea of a "deep structure," which is embedded in the narrative structures of the law.
48. Canadian history on this issue is instructive. A 1968 case found that a musical broadcast did not infringe copyright because the true copyright work was not the music, but was the written score of the music. Canada's copyright law was subsequently amended to include a definition of music that accepted both the written score and the music itself as subject to copyright protection. *See* CAPAC v. CTV Television Network, [1968] S.C.R. 676, 68 D.L.R. (2d) 98, *available at* http://csc.lexum.umontreal.ca/en/1968/1968scr0-676/1968scr0-676.html (last visited Apr. 28, 2010).

debated.[49] Software might be patentable as a scientific invention, or it might be entitled to a new form of protection, a system of *sui generis* rights, reflecting its own novelty.[50] An important possibility remained the option of no "protection" at all—free and unrestricted access to software. When copyright won out, it represented a victory for major players in this burgeoning industry, such as Microsoft Corporation, who would enjoy the benefits of automatic and extended protection for their works. Established software designers stood to benefit; for new companies and would-be innovators, copyright protection introduced new restrictiveness to what had previously been an open playing field.

When copyright protection for software was accepted, it seems natural that alternative regimes for rights in software should have died a natural death. In fact, this did not happen. The persistence of other approaches probably reflects the dissatisfaction generated by a premature attempt to resolve the software conundrum. Alternative approaches to the recognition of software as a new form of intellectual creation remain. If anything, they have gained strength with the passage of time. They coexist alongside copyright protection, raising interesting questions about the nature and extent of intellectual rights in software, and the consequences of restricting growth in this crucially important field.

Alternatives to copyright protection share the common intuition of a poor fit between software as a new form of intellectual creation and the conventional precepts of copyright law. Patents in software respond to this concern by introducing protection that is both more specialized and more limited than copyright. They can protect the specific aspects of software associated with the functions of programs, without crippling further development.[51] In contrast, copyright could impose large-scale protection on computer programs, restricting features that should be generally available for the development of the technology. In the landmark ruling of *State Street Bank*, an American court found that software could be patented as a "business model" under U.S. law, unleashing a spate of new precedents granting patents in software.[52] At the same time, patent protection is subject to the

---

49. In fact, Colin Tapper points out that "the argument about whether copyright or patent was most appropriate for software was at its height in the 1960s." He observes that "the debate was closer then because it pre-dated the personal computer, and the software in issue was system software (normally in machine code)." (personal communication with the author, July 14, 2010.)

50. *But see* Jane C. Ginsburg, *Four Reasons and a Paradox: The Manifest Superiority of Copyright over Sui Generis Protection of Computer Software*, 94 Colum. L. Rev. 2559 (1994); Ginsburg is skeptical about the possibility.

51. In addition, Colin Tapper notes that "the main advantage of patent as a means of protecting software is that it allows the idea (or aim) of the software to be protected given that software is so versatile that the same effects can be created by any number of different sequences of instructions in any number of different software systems." (personal communication with the author, July 14, 2010.)

52. State Street Bank & Trust Co. v. Signature Financial Group, Inc., 149 F.3d 1368 (Fed. Cir. 1998).

rigors of registration and review before it can be granted, and the duration of protection never exceeds twenty years, as compared to copyright's seventy.[53]

However, the possibility of patent protection for software has met with an interesting obstacle—the formalization of copyright protection for software in international regulation. In particular, the TRIPs Agreement provides that computer programs must be recognized as copyright works by the member countries of the World Trade Organization (WTO). In an important phrase, TRIPs specifies that they should be protected "as literary works."[54] No distinction is made between computer programs and other types of literary works. The implication is that any and all rights enjoyed by literary works will be available for computer programs, as well. In most of the member countries of the WTO, with the notable exception of the United States, this classification implies that the moral rights of authors must be recognized in computer programs, as in all other literary works.

In terms of patent rights, the significance of TRIPs is immense. If computer programs must be protected as literary works under copyright law, how can software patents be recognized? Will they exist as an additional form of protection for a program, alongside copyright in the work? There is no prohibition in intellectual property law or theory against the coexistence of different types of intellectual property rights in a single work; but this option always raises the possibility of excessive protection for a given type of intellectual creation.[55] Indeed, concerns about excessive restrictions on software led to the rejection, in 2005, of a proposal for the recognition of software patents in the European Union.[56]

---

53. Copyright term for software in the United States is currently seventy years from the date of making. The term of copyright protection was extended in 2002, and a constitutional challenge, arguing that the extended term contravened the limits on copyright in the U.S. Constitution, failed in 2003. *See* Eldred v. Ashcroft, 239 F.3d 372 (3d Cir. 2001), *aff'd*, 537 U.S. 186 (2003); *see* Legal Information Institute, Cornell University Law School, http://www.law.cornell.edu/supct/html/01-618.ZS.html (last visited Apr. 28, 2010). The U.S. Constitution, art. I, § 8, cl. 8, states: "The Congress shall have power . . . to promote the progress of science and useful arts, by securing for limited times to authors and inventors the exclusive right to their respective writings and discoveries," http://topics.law.cornell.edu/constitution/articlei#section1 (last visited Apr. 28, 2010).

54. Agreement on Trade-Related Aspects of Intellectual Property Rights (opened for signature Apr. 15, 1994, entered into force Jan. 1, 1995) (1994) 33 I.L.M. 1197 [TRIPs Agreement], Article 10.1.

55. For example, the Canadian Supreme Court addressed the question of overlapping trademark and copyright protection in what is widely known as the case of the chocolate bar wrappers. *See* Euro-Excellence Inc. v. Kraft Canada Inc. [2007] 3 S.C.R. 20, 2007 SCC 37.

56. For an interesting summary of the positions surrounding the proposed European Software Patents Directive, see *Software Patents Bill Thrown Out*, BBC NEWS (July 6, 2005), *available at* http://news.bbc.co.uk/2/hi/technology/4655955.stm (last visited Apr. 24, 2010). An analysis of the problems from an open source perspective is provided by Heather J. Meeker,

The open access alternative is in direct opposition to intellectual property rights in software, and its continued importance reflects the unresolved controversy surrounding the copyright model of protection. But open access movements share something interesting with copyright: a moral dimension to their views. In the case of open access, the moral argument can mean two things. The first is a moral perspective in the largest sense of the term: many proponents of open access believe that it is morally wrong to restrict access to a technology of such importance to society. Richard Stallman, the founder of the Free Software Foundation, is the leading advocate for the moral imperative of access to software.[57] His comments on the different connotations of copyright for books and software are instructive:

> The copyright system was created expressly for the purpose of encouraging authorship. In the domain for which it was invented—books, which could be copied economically only on a printing press—it did little harm, and did not obstruct most of the individuals who read the books... .
>
> The case of programs today is very different from that of books a hundred years ago. The fact that the easiest way to copy a program is from one neighbor to another, the fact that a program has both source code and object code which are distinct, and the fact that a program is used rather than read and enjoyed, combine to create a situation in which a person who enforces a copyright is harming society as a whole both materially and spiritually; in which a person should not do so regardless of whether the law enables him to.[58]

But, secondly, open access also recognizes certain interests that resemble, at least superficially, the moral rights of authors in the literary and artistic context. The interests of attribution and integrity are present in the terms of open access software, both in the Free Software Foundation's GNU license and beyond. No doubt, this assertion would be rather unpopular with Stallman himself, who includes a rebuttal of the natural rights basis of "ownership" in his essay, *Why Software Should not have Owners*:

> Authors often claim a special connection with programs they have written, and go on to assert that, as a result, their desires and interests concerning the program simply outweigh those of anyone else—or even those of the whole rest of

---

The Fuzzy Software Patent Debate Rages On, Linux Insider (Feb. 23, 2005), *available at* http://www.linuxinsider.com/story/40676.html (last visited Apr. 24, 2010).

57. *See* http://www.fsf.org (last visited Apr. 28, 2010).

58. Richard Stallman, *The GNU Manifesto*, The GNU Operating System, *available at* http://www.gnu.org/gnu/manifesto.html (last visited July 20, 2010).

the world. (Typically companies, not authors, hold the copyrights on software, but we are expected to ignore this discrepancy.)[59]

In his critique of natural rights theories of copyright ownership, Stallman approaches the issue with a blunt tool rather than a finely tuned instrument. Stallman's analysis of natural rights raises three major issues. First, the analogy between a work and material objects is, indeed, overstretched, as natural rights theory would argue that the damage resulting from mistreatment of one's work is fundamentally different from material harm. The concept of moral harm is not well-developed in common law countries, but it is a foundation of civil law systems.[60] Secondly, the point that authors are not the main beneficiaries of copyright ownership is noted by him, but the fact that authors' natural rights provide a counterweight to the interests of the copyright-owner is not discussed. Finally, the analysis is quite United States-centric. What about the role of natural rights theories in other copyright systems of the world, which are author-focused in a way that U.S. law is not? Do natural rights of authorship lead to unethical situations, in Stallman's terms, in those cultural contexts?

---

59. Stallman goes on to comment:

> To those who propose this as an ethical axiom—the author is more important than you—I can only say that I, a notable software author myself, call it bunk.
> But people in general are only likely to feel any sympathy with the natural rights claims for two reasons.
> One reason is an overstretched analogy with material objects. When I cook spaghetti, I do object if someone else eats it, because then I cannot eat it. His action hurts me exactly as much as it benefits him; only one of us can eat the spaghetti, so the question is, which one? The smallest distinction between us is enough to tip the ethical balance.
> But whether you run or change a program I wrote affects you directly and me only indirectly. Whether you give a copy to your friend affects you and your friend much more than it affects me. I shouldn't have the power to tell you not to do these things. No one should.
> The second reason is that people have been told that natural rights for authors is the accepted and unquestioned tradition of our society.
> As a matter of history, the opposite is true. The idea of natural rights of authors was proposed and decisively rejected when the US Constitution was drawn up. That's why the Constitution only permits a system of copyright and does not require one; that's why it says that copyright must be temporary. It also states that the purpose of copyright is to promote progress—not to reward authors. Copyright does reward authors somewhat, and publishers more, but that is intended as a means of modifying their behavior.
> The real established tradition of our society is that copyright cuts into the natural rights of the public—and that this can only be justified for the public's sake.

See http://www.gnu.org/philosophy/why-free.html (last visited July 21, 2010).
60. *See* P. R. Handford, *Moral Damages in Germany*, 27(4) Int'l Comp. L.Q. 849 (1978), who remarks that "The civil law offers a refreshing contrast to the common law, not only because of its wholehearted acceptance of claims for injury to feelings and other non-pecuniary loss, but also because of its orderly appearance in comparison to the patchwork quilt of the common law." Handford at 851.

In fact, the Free Software movement recognizes attribution, integrity, and disclosure; but it recognizes them in precise and narrow forms. Attribution of the author of software may help to protect the integrity of source code. Knowing who has made given modifications can help to identify and correct problems. Stallman confirms:

> It is also acceptable for the license to require that, if you have distributed a modified version and a previous developer asks for a copy of it, you must send one, or that you identify yourself on your modifications.[61]

This right of attribution is not focused on the author *per se*. Rather, its objective is to protect the "work"—in this case, software—for the good of the community that uses and enjoys it, works with it, and, very possibly, attempts to improve it.[62] It is akin to a right to protect the integrity of a work of art for the sake of cultural heritage—the rationale of the Indian court in the *Amar Nath Sehgal* case.[63]

The person working with software also has the right to choose whether or not he will release those changes publicly—a classic statement of the right of disclosure.[64] There is an interesting contrast here between the apparent rejection of authorship as it confers any special privileges on the individual programmer, and the right to maintain control over your own modifications. "Freedom" apparently does not include the right to have access to other people's modifications of software. Stallman also makes another concession to authorship in his comments on the "motivations" behind free software: professional reputation and the admiration of one's fellows are recognized motives behind the making of free software.[65] These are exactly the same human drives underlying the moral rights of attribution and integrity.

In relation to software, Stallman's concept of "free" essentially has to do with the fact that the software is nonproprietary in nature. In describing the

61. Richard Stallman, *The Free Software Definition*, THE GNU OPERATING SYSTEM, *available at* http://www.gnu.org/philosophy/free-sw.html (last visited July 20, 2010) [Stallman, *The Free Software Definition*].
62. Although, in keeping with the principle of "freedom," any modification is allowed, even if it may not amount to an "improvement" in the next person's opinion. *See id.*
63. Amar Nath Sehgal v. Union of India 2005 (30) PTC 253 (Delhi High Court).
64. *See* Stallman, *The Free Software Definition, supra* note 61: "You should also have the freedom to make modifications and use them privately in your own work or play, without even mentioning that they exist. If you do publish your changes, you should not be required to notify anyone in particular, or in any particular way."
65. "To be admired. If you write a successful, useful free program, the users will admire you. That feels very good. Professional reputation. If you write a successful, useful free program, that will suffice to show you are a good programmer." *See* Richard Stallman, *Motives for Writing Free Software*, THE GNU OPERATING SYSTEM, *available at* http://www.gnu.org/philosophy/fs-motives.html (last visited Apr. 25, 2010).

fundamental differences between free software and open source, Stallman comments:

> For the free software movement, free software is an ethical imperative, because only free software respects the users' freedom. By contrast, the philosophy of open source considers issues in terms of how to make software "better"—in a practical sense only. It says that nonfree software is an inferior solution to the practical problem at hand. For the free software movement, however, nonfree software is a social problem, and the solution is to stop using it and move to free software.[66]

On the other hand, commercial uses of free software are accepted, and even encouraged, as long as the software that is sold continues to be "free"— amenable to modification and distribution at the will of the user. Many models of open access, or open source, software exist, and one approach is to restrict the right of a user to use the software for commercial purposes.

From a "free software" perspective, this issue is not important, as it is the right to use software freely that is really at the heart of this movement. Indeed, the preference for publishing software through "copyleft" models of licensing over simply releasing software into the public domain is due to the desire to prevent software from becoming anyone's property. In the "copyleft" scenario, anyone who attempts to convert the software into intellectual property will be legally liable for two things: breaking the terms of the software license, which he accepted when he acquired the software, and, potentially, violating the "author's" copyright in the software.

> Copyleft says that anyone who redistributes the software, with or without changes, must pass along the freedom to further copy and change it. Copyleft guarantees that every user has freedom.
>
> Copyleft also provides an *incentive* for other programmers to add to free software. Important free programs such as the GNU C++ compiler exist only because of this.

This reliance on the copyleft model again makes the attribution and integrity interests important. Attribution is needed because of copyright's dependence on an author to sue; integrity is needed in order to examine what kind of unauthorized use has occurred, and whether it would qualify as an infringement of copyright in the work. In particular, it would be important to show unauthorized appropriation, use, or the creation of an "unauthorized"

---

66. *See* Richard Stallman, *Why Open Source Misses the Point of Free Software*, THE GNU OPER-ATING SYSTEM, *available at* http://www.gnu.org/philosophy/open-source-misses-the-point.html (last visited Apr. 25, 2010).

derivative work. The threshold will be low; practically any evidence of modification will do, but some evidence must be offered.

The appearance of moral rights in alternative models of software regulation comes as a surprise. However, the practical relevance of moral rights to the needs of software is immediately apparent. A right of attribution can preserve accountability and access to help when problems arise; it can also protect useful knowledge and build community by drawing attention to the accomplishments of highly skilled and creative programmers. The integrity principle also has something to contribute to software. Preserving the integrity of code helps to develop knowledge, while protecting subsequent users from problems such as flaws, errors, or sabotage.

Moral rights also reflect certain philosophical parallels with the free and open software movements. The integrity principle can offer practical support to the goals of these movements. In the case of free software, it could prevent proprietary treatments of code; and, in effect, Stallman's concept that the conversion of free software into property would violate its moral integrity, in the larger sense of the term, finds ready sympathy in the moral right of integrity recognized in much of the world. Once again, this approach to integrity finds parallels in a right for the protection of cultural heritage. It is not so much an author-focused right as a work-focused principle.

Nevertheless, the author, too, makes an appearance in free and open software movements. Reputation matters. The needs of programmers may be different from those of artists, but that does not make the claims of artists unreasonable. Rather, as Stallman himself notes, the nature of their work is different. In the creation of software, attribution can support the needs of authorship; but the nature of the medium demands a willingness to change and be changed. Without the ability to change what comes before, to build upon it in freedom and without fear of limitation, a meaningful software community might cease to exist. The drive towards further development is a reality of all forms of human knowledge, but the degree of flexibility required, and the intensity of the intervention, will vary according to the nature of the work. If the need to intervene creatively in a work of classic literature could be colored a soft pearl grey, the software environment presents the case of a brilliant fuchsia. Where software is concerned, intervention is the key to innovation.

C. Collective Creation: Moral Rights and Web 2.0

Collective creation is one of the fascinating opportunities for human cooperation created by the Internet. In the Web environment, cooperation assumes totally new proportions, uniting people across vast distances who may never have been able to work together in the absence of technology.

The work might be undertaken anonymously or in explicit partnership—by a small group of collaborators or an indefinite worldwide community.

Wikipedia is perhaps the best-known collaborative phenomenon. The ubiquitous Web-wide encyclopedia is built almost entirely on the contributions of the general public, who initiate the coverage of new topics, or modify existing entries with a view to correcting and improving their content.[67] The founders of Wikipedia hope that this phenomenon will ultimately expand into new languages other than English.[68]

The possibilities of Web-based collaboration have only begun to be explored. They could include many activities, built on different approaches to gathering, developing, and disseminating knowledge. Music offers some interesting examples. Through Web-based interactions, South Indian classical music is now taught in the United States by teachers in India who have never flown in a plane.[69] The use of special instruments has transformed music in many traditions. Musicians from Western and non-Western traditions build artistic collaborations through technology, exploring and developing new forms of musical expression.[70] These creative possibilities have barely begun to develop, and they hint at a world of unimagined potential for the development of culture through technology.

To return to the example of Wikipedia, what is the legal status of contributors? Technically speaking, they are authors. They write the texts that form the basis of Wikipedia entries, and, according to universally recognized principles of copyright law, the level of originality required of a text writer can

---

67. *But see* Alex Krotoski, Liberty, Wikipedia and a Voice for All, BBC, *the Virtual Revolution: How 20 Years of the Web Has Reshaped Our Lives*, (July 21, 2009), *available at* http://www.bbc.co.uk/blogs/digitalrevolution/2009/07/liberty-wikipedia-and-a-voice.shtml (last visited July 20, 2010).

68. *See* Emma Barnett, *Jimmy Wales Interview: Wikipedia Is Focusing on Accuracy*, TELEGRAPH (Nov. 17, 2009), *available at* http://www.telegraph.co.uk/technology/wikipedia/6589487/Jimmy-Wales-interview-Wikipedia-is-focusing-on-accuracy.html (last visited Apr. 25, 2010).

69. The South Indian school of classical music is called "Carnatic" music, while the North Indian branch is known as "Hindustani." Both schools represent a common system of music with different styles, scales, and instruments. Teaching of Carnatic music in the United States is done via Skype—the free online software that allows Internet users to call each other from their computers by audio only, or by video and audio transmission. The U.S. connections made by Carnatic artists are widely publicized in India.

70. *See, for example*, the interesting discussion of cross-cultural musical conversations in Gary Giddins, *A Passage to India: Rudresh Mahanthappa Chooses a Heritage*, THE NEW YORKER (Mar. 2, 2009), *available at* http://www.newyorker.com/arts/critics/musical/2009/03/02/090302crmu_music_giddins#ixzz0m8WHdDnp (last visited Apr. 25, 2010). The article is among the first publications outside India to draw attention to the remarkable talent of South Indian saxophonist Kadri Gopalnath and his brilliant group, including leading violinist, Kanyakumari.

almost certainly be met by a contributor to Wikipedia.[71] Small modifications to existing text may not qualify for copyright protection; but larger changes and, of course, new contributions can. However, the contributions are made in the foreknowledge that they will be subject to editing. The integrity of the original contribution cannot be maintained—that was never intended to be the case. The very purpose of the contribution is to make something available to others for modification.

These circumstances could place Wikipedia in a situation of legal difficulty in countries where moral rights of attribution and integrity are recognized— something that Wikipedia should note as it attempts to expand globally. In particular, if there are restrictions on an author's ability to waive moral rights, as in France and Germany, the potential problem of an author wanting to assert rights of attribution and integrity could fundamentally threaten the existence of this resource.

The persistence of moral rights in a technological context whose very objective is to transcend the limits of individual authorship seems like a strange anomaly. If countries with strong moral rights protection are interested in encouraging technology-based collaboration on the Wikipedia model, they should consider special modifications to the legal limits on waivers. For example, a three-step test could be established. If the criteria of anonymity, the expectation of unlimited modification, and the goal of general public access are met by a given technology, it could be appropriate to say that the author agrees to suspend his or her moral rights in relation to a given project.[72]

The terminology of suspending one's moral rights seems to be a more accurate reflection of what should happen in the Wikipedia context than a "waiver" of rights. Waiver suggests that rights exist, but are set aside, In the Wikipedia context, however, it seems that one's involvement is entirely outside the scope of moral rights. To put it another way, you, as the contributor of text to Wikipedia, are not the author. Instead, the author is a collective entity, made up of the efforts of individual contributors, but a being which is greater than the sum of its parts.

Notwithstanding these arguments, it is also apparent that the concepts of attribution and integrity may have some relevance to Wikipedia. Attribution of contributors could help to establish that a particular piece of knowledge is

---

71. It seems likely that this would be the case whether the jurisdiction in question recognized the "sweat of the brow," labor-oriented standard of creativity in classic cases like e.g., *University of London Press v. University Tutorial Press* (1916) 2 Ch. 601 and *Ladbroke (Football) v. William Hill (Football)* 1964 1 All E.R. 465 (HL); the higher requirement of "skill and judgement," *in CCH, supra* note 10, and *Eastern Book Co. & Ors v. DP Modak & Anr.,* 2008 (36) PTC 1, 2008 (1) SCC 1 [*Eastern Book Co.*]; or the "modicum of creativity" in *Feist Publications, Inc. v. Rural Telephone Service Co.,* 499 U.S. 340 (1991) [*Feist*].

72. Wikipedia editors can be those who contribute anonymously, or regular editors who are identified through the system. For a discussion of the editing process and ongoing changes to it, see Barnett, *supra* note 68.

authoritative—for example, a person with specialist or insider knowledge of a given subject may be in a position to make a valuable contribution to a Wikipedia entry. At the same time, attribution for special contributors would probably go against the ethos of Wikipedia, which is democratic in the purest sense of the term. Wikipedia relies upon the contributions of the general public, and its audience is the general public, which seeks out information or knowledge on a particular subject.

One approach to the attribution problem might be to adopt a simple, cosmetic solution. Individual authors could be attributed by Wikipedia—for example, in a list of contributors to a particular page, to which any person modifying the page could add his or her name—while the possibility of removing or modifying another person's name could be excluded. What would be the value of such an attribution practice?

This leads to a second point—the importance of maintaining the integrity of an information resource like Wikipedia. Here, too, the problem presents a fundamental challenge to the philosophy underlying this public encyclopedia. It is possible for incorrect information to develop, and the global and popular reach of Wikipedia means that this resource could become a significant factor behind public misinformation.

A third point should also be noted. Moral rights are not limited to the contributors to Wikipedia; they are also enjoyed by many of the people who become subjects of Wikipedia entries. Moral rights are important where those individuals are themselves engaged in creative work. Wrongful information about a person or his work could damage his reputation—or, perhaps more precisely, his "honor." This archaic term in the Berne Convention carries a connotation of personal harm, and a strong argument can be made that harming a person's professional or personal reputation through a Wikipedia entry could violate that person's honor. Inappropriate comments about a person's work or personal life could amount to violations of the subject's moral rights of integrity or reputation.[73]

---

73. This is a fine legal point. As noted by the court in the U.S. case of *Shostakovich v. Twentieth Century-Fox Film Corp.*, 80 N.Y.S.2d 575 (N.Y. Sup. Ct. 1948), *aff'd*, 87 N.Y.S.2d 430 (N.Y. App. Div. 1949), modification of the work is usually a precondition to a finding that integrity has been violated. False information or reviews of a work could arguably qualify as a form of direct "modification"; perhaps for this reason, the French law recognizes a specific right against excessive criticism, although it is now a part of French personal law rather than the Intellectual Property Code. *See* GEORGES MICHAÉLIDÈS-NOUAROS, LE DROIT MORAL DE L'AUTEUR: ÉTUDE DE DROIT FRANÇAIS, DE DROIT COMPARÉ ET DE DROIT INTERNATIONAL, paras. 168–70 (Librairie Arthur Rousseau 1935); LAW AND THE GORBACHEV ERA: ESSAYS IN HONOR OF DIETRICH ANDRÉ LOEBER 287–89 (Donald D. Barry ed., Kluwer 1988). Comments about one's personal life do not violate the integrity of the work, but they may affect one's personal reputation; a moral right of reputation would be violated, but not the moral right of integrity. In relation to Wikipedia misinformation, a notorious incident in 2005 involved the falsification of journalist John Siegenthaler's biography, discovered by him four months after it was first posted. *See* the comment by Charles Cooper, *Perspective: Wikipedia*

From a moral rights perspective, collective creation along the lines of Wikipedia presents a fundamental challenge. Collective works are a dramatic demonstration of creativity whose essential purpose is to receive and modify texts provided by others. Wikipedia offers an infinitely more open model of knowledge than even free software. In the case of software, the nature of the medium demands the freedom to modify pre-existing works, and all models of nonproprietary software—free or open, commercial or nonprofit, pure or hybrid—rely on open access to at least some part of the code embedded in the software.[74] But in the case of Wikipedia, the text cannot exist without the freedom to modify. The underlying philosophy is that collective efforts will gather enough knowledge, expertise, and commitment to arrive at largely correct information—a phenomenon also known as "crowdsourcing."[75] In a sense, the principle of preserving the integrity of knowledge becomes self-executing through the law of averages.

If that is the hope, there is also widespread skepticism about the value of crowdsourcing. Modern media are totally nondiscriminatory. They offer the opportunity to project an opinion to anyone and everyone, and they build consensus among large and disparate groups of people. Depending on the circumstances, either feature of new media could have a positive or negative impact.

In a recent book, Jaron Lanier warns that Internet collectivism suppresses individuality and encourages the development of a mob-rule mentality.[76] Reviewing the book for the New York Times, Michiko Kakutani writes:

> Mr. Lanier sensibly notes that the "wisdom of crowds" is a tool that should be used selectively, not glorified for its own sake. Of Wikipedia he writes that "it's great that we now enjoy a cooperative pop culture concordance" but argues that the site's ethos ratifies the notion that the individual voice—even the voice of an expert—is eminently dispensable, and "the idea that the collective is closer to the truth." He complains that Wikipedia suppresses the sound of individual voices, and similarly contends that the rigid format of Facebook turns individuals into "multiple-choice identities."

---

and the Nature of Truth, CNET NEWS (Dec. 2, 2005), *available at* http://news.cnet.com/Wikipedia-and-the-nature-of-truth/2010-1025_3-5979331.html (last visited Apr. 25, 2010).

74. Colin Tapper notes that "modification can be accomplished either by access to source code or object code (the route from the former to the latter is no more than the application of another program, a compiler)," and he observes that "the more skilled the programmer the more he will choose to modify object code so as to achieve precisely the result that is sought." Personal communication with the author, July 14, 2010).

75. Julia Angwin & Geoffrey J. Fowler, *Volunteers Logoff as Wikipedia Ages*, WALL STREET JOURNAL (Nov. 23, 2009), *available at* http://online.wsj.com/article/SB125893981183759969.html?mod=rss_Today's_Most_Popular (last visited Apr. 25, 2010) [Angwin & Fowler].

76. *See* JARON LANIER, YOU ARE NOT A GADGET: A MANIFESTO (Alfred A. Knopf 2010).

Mr. Lanier's is not an isolated voice. An earlier and controversial book by Andrew Keen complained of the Internet's creation of a "cult of the amateur," where quality of knowledge and skill have ceased to be valued. The book touched a nerve in the open access community; among other reactions, it received a bitter response on Lawrence Lessig's website.[77] For all its flaws—among other things, Mr. Keen is not as clear as he should be about the meaning of "amateur"—the book may have sparked an important discussion about the future of culture. The strident reaction of the "blogosphere" almost seems to support his theory. Mr. Keen might be wrong; but why not consider the points that he raises? If the wisdom of the crowd is truly better, why not let it prove itself in action?

In fact, it is a truism that few technologies in the world are inherently good or evil. Rather, the use that is made of technology tends to give it its moral flavor. New technology offers tremendous hope for improving the conditions of life in many parts of the world—imagine the excitement of bringing information and education to a place like rural India, and helping to empower the lives of poor people. Technology has the potential to promote democracy on a global scale. What will we decide to use it for?

It is currently rumored that Wikipedia is moving towards a more hierarchical structure, with increased editorial supervision of its pages. One of the apparent reasons for this shift is concern for the integrity of Wikipedia's presentations in the wake of recent embarrassments.[78] The popularity of the Wikipedia project appears to be declining among users, who complain of overzealous editing that leads to the deletion of time-consuming and hard-won contributions.[79] The general vulnerability of Wikipedia to virtual "vandals" who deliberately post misinformation or advertising is also a growing concern.[80] Julia Angwin and Geoffrey J. Fowler note that the culture of Wikipedia is in the midst of a transition:

> Wikipedia contributors have been debating widely what is behind the decline in volunteers. One factor is that many topics already have been written about. Another is the plethora of rules Wikipedia has adopted to bring order to its

---

77. *See* http://www.lessig.org/blog/2007/05/keens_the_cult_of_the_amateur.html (last visited Apr. 28, 2010).

78. A premature declaration of U.S. Senator Ted Kennedy's death is one example. *See* Angwin & Fowler, *supra* note 75. A study by Dr. Felipe Ortega found that 49,000 people had stopped editing Wikipedia pages in the early part of 2009, as compared to about 4900 in a parallel period in 2008. Wikipedia disputes the statistics for various reasons. *See* *Wikipedia denies mass exodus of editors*, BBC NEWS (Nov. 27, 2009), *available at* http://news.bbc.co.uk/2/hi/technology/8382477.stm (last visited Apr. 25, 2010).

79. These editors are known as "deletionists," and the rate at which new contributions are now deleted is one out of four, as compared to one out of ten in 2005. Angwin & Fowler, *supra* note 75.

80. *See* Angwin & Fowler, *supra* note 75.

unruly universe—particularly to reduce infighting among contributors about write-ups of controversial subjects and polarizing figures.[81]

If these rumors prove to be true, they will signify the failure of the Wikipedia ethos—or at least, the watering-down of its pure-democracy vision. Every modern idealist should save one sigh for Wikipedia.

D. Ownership of Open Source? Google Books and the Alternatives

The prospect of digital libraries is among the most exciting developments of the Digital Age. From a practical point of view, digitization responds to the age-old problem of access to knowledge with marvelous directness. The constraints of geographical location and the need for library privileges could easily be overcome if digital archives were available.

To fulfil its purpose, however, a digital archive must meet certain criteria. First, the archive must be stable, in terms of both space and time. It should be available consistently across time zones and geographical regions, while its long-term existence and accessibility must be assured. Secondly, the information in the archive must be reliable. A third criteria exists, but it is legal rather than practical: any digital library project must adopt a successful approach to copyright rules.

On all three counts, the Google Books project has generated significant malaise. Google ultimately hopes to scan and create digitized versions of every existing book. At first glance, Google's initiative is very exciting, because it would permanently throw open the doors of knowledge to anyone who has access to the most basic technology. But the project has been mired in controversy almost from the beginning. Interestingly, the objections voiced by the various groups that have sued Google largely have to do with Google's treatment of copyright issues.[82]

---

81. Angwin & Fowler, *supra* note 75.
82. *See* the website of the Google book settlement at http://www.googlebooksettlement.com (last visited Apr. 25, 2010). The history of legal actions against Google since the books project was launched in 2004 is summarized by Hector L. MacQueen. Hector L. MacQueen, *The Google Book Settlement*, 40(3) INT'L REV. INTELL. PROP. COMPETITION L. 247 (2009) [MacQueen]. The issue of whether such an important initiative should be entrusted to a private corporation has also been prominent, particularly in Europe. It reflects concerns about reliability, but in a political sense rather than a practical one. *See, for example, Google Book Scanning: Cultural Theft or Freedom of Information?*, CNN (Feb. 8, 2010), *available at* http://edition. cnn.com/2010/WORLD/europe/02/08/google.livres.france/index.html (last visited Apr. 25, 2010); Scott Sayare, *France: More Publishers Sue Google (World Briefing: Europe)*, NEW YORK TIMES (Mar. 31, 2010), *available at* http://www.nytimes.com/2010/04/01/world/ europe/01briefs-Francebrief.html (last visited Apr. 25, 2010); more complete coverage may

Copyright law requires the authorization of the person who owns the copyright in a book before it can be copied. The only exception to this rule is where the purpose of copying is a "fair use" or "fair dealing" with the work that is not subject to copyright protection—private enjoyment, use of a small portion, or citation of the work would be common examples. Where books in print are concerned—works that are, in the language of the Google Books Settlement, "commercially available"—the authorization of the copyright-owner must be secured before the book will be made available through the online search facility.[83] It should be noted that, under the Settlement, Google would not be prevented from scanning books without authorization—only from making them available online.[84]

In relation to out-of-print books, Google's approach becomes more interesting. Sergey Brin, a cofounder of Google, identifies the objective of making out-of-print books available to the public as a fundamental goal of the project.[85] He also points out that the profit from "orphan" books is what makes the project financially viable:

> [A]ttorneys for Google and the book publishers and authors told [Judge] Chin that the settlement isn't perfect but is fair. Google's attorney told the court that the company is indeed interested in getting its hands on rights to so-called "orphan works," the term used to describe titles where the author isn't known or can't be found.
>
> The question of properly paying someone who is entitled to compensation under Google's plan but may not be aware of it has been a hot issue. *Google said that the money earned from orphan works is what will make the digital library a feasible business. Google's attorney said that others, such as Microsoft, who attempted to digitize books in the past couldn't monetize their efforts this way and that's why they failed.*[86]

---

be found at James Kantner & Eric Pfanner, *Google Tackles Fears on Rights in Book Deal*, NEW YORK TIMES (Sept. 7, 2009), *available at* http://www.nytimes.com/2009/09/08/technology/internet/08books.html (last visited Apr. 25, 2010).

83. The current version of the settlement was filed on November 9, 2009; the approximately170-page document is available online at http://www.googlebooksettlement.com/r/view_settlement_agreement (last visited Apr. 25, 2010).

84. *See* MacQueen, *supra* note 82, at 248. This is a curious aspect of the agreement. Regardless, how could Google's activities be monitored or controlled by outsiders? The project would have to be shut down on allegations of copyright infringement; it seems that in practice, there would not be any other way to prevent Google from scanning books.

85. Sergey Brin, *A Library to Last Forever*, NEW YORK TIMES (Oct. 8, 2010), *available at* http://www.nytimes.com/2009/10/09/opinion/09brin.html (last visited Apr. 25, 2010).

86. Greg Sandoval, *Google Book Settlement Draws Fire in Court*, CNETET NEWS (Feb. 18, 2010) (emphasis added), *available at* http://news.cnet.com/8301-31001_3-10456382-261.html (last visited Apr. 25, 2010).

Indeed, there is every reason to applaud the idea of digitizing out-of-print books. Books may go out of print for various reasons, including publishers' arbitrariness, conflicts between authors and publishers, and the inadequate marketing of valuable books. Digitizing them could provide a valuable second chance at life. In the case of "orphan" works, the holders of the copyright in these books cannot be located. Unclaimed by authors or publishers, orphan works are estimated to represent a large proportion of the overall collections of the world's libraries. Clearly, out-of-print and orphan works could represent a vast storehouse of human knowledge.

In dealing with out-of-print books, Google wants to dispense with the need to request "authorization" of copying that is usually imposed by copyright law. Instead, if an author or publisher who owns the rights in an out-of-print book decides that it should not be made available online by Google, he must object to the inclusion of the book in Google's project. Google advocates this "opt-out" approach for ostensibly practical reasons.

From a legal point of view, however, the "opt-out" provisions could not be more radical. Google is effectively reversing the normal operation of copyright rules. No authorization is required for scanning or online access; instead, the failure to object will lead to a presumption of consent. What is perhaps most significant about these arrangements is the fact that Google will be under no obligation whatsoever to attempt to locate the owner of copyright in the work.

The latest version of the Google Books Settlement introduces some moderation into this proposal by requiring an independent body to oversee the digitization of orphan works. Royalties from the dissemination of orphan works will be held for ten years. After that time, the monies earned are to be redirected into public nonprofit schemes in support of culture.[87] But these provisions would lead to permanent arrangements. If the owner of an orphan work were to come forward after ten years, he would have forfeited his rights and his royalties.

Once again, this is a fundamental rethinking of copyright norms. Ordinarily, the owner of the copyright in a work is under little obligation to show that he maintains an active interest in the work. Whether or not he is vigilant in protecting the copyright, he generally retains the right to sue for unauthorized use of the work throughout the lifetime of the copyright.[88] The Google scheme seems to require something like the vigilance of a

---

87. *See* http://www.googlebooksettlement.com/ (last visited Apr. 28, 2010).
88. This situation presents an interesting contrast with trademark law. *But see* ZYX Music v. King [1995] 3 All ER 1; on appeal [1997] 2 All ER 129 (CA). It is possible that a copyright-owner's conduct can be judged to amount to a form of acquiescence to the allegedly infringing activity. Such a provision tacitly seems to underlie the Google scenario; after ten years, an owner of copyright should reasonably be expected to know that his book is available via Google.

trademark-owner by the holder of the copyright in an orphan work. But copyright is not normally subject to "dilution" in the same sense as a trademark, which demands the practical vigilance of the trademark owner against exploitation by others.[89] Copyright depends, rather, on the act of creation. The author decides who should exploit the work on his behalf, and how.

The treatment of orphan works is the most controversial aspect of the Google Books project. Google plans to create a Book Rights Registry, which will also be empowered to license books to users other than Google; but further licensing will depend on the agreement of the copyright-holders in those books. In the case of orphan books, which Google will acquire without the permission of the copyright-holders, further licensing to anyone new will not be possible. In effect, Google would acquire exclusive ownership of these works. As Miguel Helft, writing for the New York Times, notes:

> While the registry's agreement with Google is not exclusive, the registry will be allowed to license to others only the books whose authors and publishers have explicitly authorized it. Since no such authorization is possible for orphan works, only Google would have access to them, so only Google could assemble a truly comprehensive book database.[90]

Other concerns about Google's plans involve broad social issues, such as privacy. Privacy has often been a thorny problem for Google, and the uses to which Google could put its vast store of digitized information extend into various kinds of information services that could violate both the privacy of users and the exclusivity of authors and publishers.

Underlying everything is a sense of Google's breathtaking audacity. Whether it is appropriate for a private corporation to undertake a project of such immense public significance is a persistent murmur surrounding much of the debate. On this point, the approach of the Internet Archive presents an interesting alternative: this American nonprofit organization aims, among other things, to create a Web page for every book ever published.[91] An organization like the Internet Archive could be entrusted with the scanning of out-of-copyright books. Funded by public sources, the digital archive could be made freely available, and the digital resource would then belong to the public.

---

89. This is the process by which a trademark registration can be forfeited or, in the worst case, become "generic."

90. *See* Miguel Helft, *Google's Plan for Out-of-Print Books Is Challenged*, NEW YORK TIMES (Apr. 3, 2009), *available at* http://www.nytimes.com/2009/04/04/technology/internet/04books.html?pagewanted=1&emc=eta1 (last visited Apr. 25, 2010).

91. The fundamental aim of the Internet Archive is the preservation of the Web itself as a stable resource through time. The Internet Archive is active on numerous preservation projects; for details, see http://www.archive.org/about/about.php (last visited Apr. 25, 2010).

In Europe, France's Minister of Culture has recently expressed his support for a state-funded initiative to match Google's archive. In his comments, Minister Frédéric Mittérand was careful not to raise the specter of French anti-Americanism. He argued:

> For my part, there isn't any anti-Americanism. Nevertheless, I believe [that] America isn't a monolith, and different opinions must be expressed. That's why I don't want the State to surrender before the markets... .
>
> It's not up to this or that private group to decide policy on an issue as important as the digitization of our global heritage. I'm not going to leave this decision up to simple laissez-faire.[92]

Moral rights have hardly been discussed at all in the context of Google Books, but they present an important problem.[93] Much of the debate on Google has focused on the issue of profit. Google's plan will allow the company to generate profit at the expense of copyright-holders. It will do so by securing profit out of making orphan works available, and by establishing a virtually assured monopoly in the possession of a truly comprehensive digital library.

But Google's project should be of intense public interest in another sense. There can be little doubt that Google's digital library will revolutionize our sense of cultural identity. In essence, if Google achieves its aims, an immense body of human knowledge will be transformed into a kind of giant Google document—subject to searching, copying, cutting, re-using, perhaps replacing. The burden of addressing this issue falls to authors—not to copyright-owners. The concerns of authors should extend beyond the question of royalties, to the issue of how Google intends to treat their works.

Will Google be required to maintain attribution of the works in its library? Will it preserve the integrity of these works, and will users be required to respect the integrity of works obtained from Google when redistributing them? Will the uses made of the books conform to moral rights requirements? For example, Google Books currently shows "snippets" of up to 20 percent of a book that is in copyright as a sample to potential buyers. Do those snippets

---

92. Quoted in *French Minister Wants Europe to Take on Google*, REUTERS (Nov. 27, 2009) (reporting by Sophie Hardach, editing by Charles Dick), *available at* http://www.reuters.com/article/technologyNews/idUSTRE5AQ4IJ20091127 (last visited Apr. 25, 2010). This discussion is reminiscent of the debate surrounding the human genome—and the private versus public undertakings to sequence it. See the note, *In Human Genome Race, Competition Spurred Better Science*, HARVARD SCIENCE (Feb. 23, 2001), *available at* http://harvardscience.harvard.edu/medicine-health/articles/human-genome-race-competition-spurred-better-science (last visited Apr. 25, 2010).

93. MacQueen's overview of the settlement is an exception; he believes that "moral rights of attribution and integrity can be the bulwark of other authorial interests." MacQueen, *supra* note 82, at 249.

accurately reflect the content of the books, or do they misrepresent the works, causing damage to the authors' reputations? In fact, the issue of "snippets" has already been litigated and found to violate the moral right of integrity in France.[94] In relation to orphan works, if nothing else, Google's approach clearly undermines the author's right to decide whether or not his work should be part of the Google Books archive—the moral right of disclosure.

Given Google's international reach, concerns about moral rights are particularly important. The current Google Book Settlement has now been scaled back to extend the proposed arrangements only to certain English-speaking countries—Canada, Australia, and the United Kingdom, as well as the United States. But, barring the United States, all of these common law countries protect the moral rights of their authors; and the Australian scheme, in many respects, is a powerful moral rights regime equivalent to Continental European norms. How can the tension between the need to recognize moral rights abroad and their absence from U.S. law be reconciled? There is every likelihood that Google may eventually want to extend its activities to Europe and Asia, as well. If the political climate supports this trend, Google will become actively engaged in countries that are strongly protective of moral rights.

In fact, the issue of maintaining the archive's quality should militate in favor of diligent protection for moral rights. Google's objective is to build a virtual Library of Alexandria.[95] If so, then the digital archive that it creates will represent the world's most important repository of written knowledge. At the same time, this repository will be preserved in a form that makes it vulnerable to manipulation. Indeed, from Google's perspective, the very purpose of creating the archive is to manipulate its contents. By providing "snippets" of books, making the text available for searching, offering links to retailers, and including "discrete advertising," in Robert Darnton's phrase, Google's purpose is to manipulate the archive and generate revenues.[96] Google is a corporation. It wants to make money, and, in order to do so from the Books project, the manipulation of the archive is a must.

---

94. *See* Band, *supra* note 7, at notes 304–10 and accompanying text: publisher La Martinière succeeded in obtaining 300,000 Euros in damages relying, in tandem with its claim for economic rights infringement that could not be excused as a "citation" for informative and non-commercial purposes, upon the integrity claim. A lawyer for the Société des Gens de Lettres drew attention to the fact that, "the extracts are unreadable, the quality execrable, the text decimated" ["*les extraits sont illisibles, la qualité exécrable, le texte tronçonné*"]. *Numérisation indécente? Google Books contre La Martinière* http://www.fluctuat.net/6914-Google-Books-contre-La-Martiniere (last visited Apr. 25, 2010); and "La Martinière: la condamnation de Google doit pousser à trouver un accord" (Dec. 21, 2009) http://www.google.com/hosted-news/afp/article/ALeqM5jsLS4Fi8q23mV9lOOySOa5V6Zlow (last visited Oct. 4, 2010).

95. *See* Brin, *supra* note 85.

96. *See* Robert Darnton, *Google and the Future of Books*, New York Review of Books (Feb. 12, 2009), *available at* http://www.nybooks.com/articles/22281 (last visited Oct. 4, 2010).

As a counterweight to this underlying reality, the rights of attribution and integrity should be emphasized. Indeed, in order to preserve authenticity—in relation to new and old works, owned and orphaned works—a digital archive would need to be governed by general principles of attribution and integrity that would be built into the archive, itself. A digital archive represents one of those rare cases where moral interests are so overwhelmingly important that their protection should not be left in the hands of authors and their descendants, whose ability to act is limited. Attribution and integrity should be protected in perpetuity in an archive.

Once again, the significance of disclosure in a digital environment stands out. An author should be able to exercise his or her moral right of disclosure to decide whether it would be desirable to participate in the Google Books project. From a moral rights perspective, it should be noted that the publisher's permission would not be enough; the author's permission must also be obtained. In an undertaking of such magnitude, one which will permanently transform the nature of a work, it seems entirely fitting to require permission for both economic exploitation and moral protection.

Professor Hector MacQueen is one of the few writers on Google Books to note the importance of moral rights. He remarks:

> Copying is unavoidable in the digital world…; so perhaps, at least in this context (which may increasingly be the only context that really matters), copyright as a right to prevent copying should be abandoned. Privacy and confidentiality rights may serve better to protect the work which the author does not intend for publication of any kind, while moral rights of attribution and integrity can be the bulwark of other authorial interests, offset by appropriately framed exceptions for education, research, news reporting, public libraries and parody.[97]

E. Freedom to Create: The Price and Promise of Copyleft Movements

The "copyleft" movements have been quick to grasp certain fundamental truths about the digital revolution. They are based on economic and moral realizations that can be summarized in two propositions. First, in the digital environment, it is not practical to restrict every act of copying with a view to monetizing each transformation of a work. The example of the music

---

97. MacQueen, *supra* note 82, at 249. The moral right of disclosure is also a means of protecting the work from publication against the author's will.

industry proves how difficult and acrimonious it would be to pursue such a strategy. Music is headed towards a compromise, where some acts of transformation will be restricted and subject to payment, and others will not. If the collective licensing approach to file-sharing ultimately predominates, then only two acts will attract payment: the act of publishing, in the traditional sense, and the act of making available in the general sense of releasing one's work to the Internet, via file-sharing sites or other media, for download. Individual acts of downloading will no longer be subject to payments, or penalties.

Secondly, it is not right to restrict access to works. Access to knowledge has been a painful battleground throughout much of human history, and restricting knowledge has been a universal tactic of oppression. The digital era signifies nothing less than an opportunity to break fundamentally with our past. Ignorance may be the single root cause of human conflict. But the power of technology can spread knowledge to disadvantaged groups in every society, and to virtually every corner of the world. Realizing the interdependent reality of human existence is no longer the esoteric dream of *yogis* seeking spiritual enlightenment; in some sense, it is now available for every person to grasp, at least intellectually if not experientially. The importance of spreading education through technology can hardly be overstated. It may be the key to our survival as a species.

But the goal of technology should be to connect human beings—not to replace human relationships with the relationship between man and machine, deepening our growing alienation from our physical and spiritual environment.[98] Information can be spread through technology; but education depends on the ability of human beings to communicate with each other about the significance of that information and its place in our lives. Behind every piece of knowledge, culture, or entertainment is at least one human being. The emphasis on "free" culture in the open access movements seems to negate the existence of that person and his or her efforts.

In fact, culture can almost never be "free" in the sense that it is free of cost. A cultural work represents the effort of a human being—whatever may have

---

98. The parallels between the degradation of the environment and the global degradation of culture are well worth exploring. For example, the loss of biodiversity is strikingly matched by the loss of linguistic diversity. In the words of researcher, Anthony Aristar, "When a language dies, it's just the same as when a species dies. You lose a part of the network of life, and you lose everything it could impart." *See* Alison Cross, *Loss of Global Languages Threatens Culture, History: Language Expert*, Ottawa Citizen (Nov. 3, 2009), *available at* http://www.ottawacitizen.com/life/Loss+global+languages+threatens+culture+history+Language+expert/2180283/story.html (last visited Apr. 25, 2010). The issue receives an interesting analysis in Anthony Löwstedt, *Loss of Language, Loss of Soul*, The Vienna Review (Mar. 1, 2009), *available at* http://www.viennareview.net/story/loss-language-loss-soul (last visited Apr. 25, 2010).

been the influences on that person, or the role of social or historical forces in shaping his work, the human person is essential to the act of creation. Medieval thought considered the author a "vessel" for inspiration, and modern criticism seems to see the author as a "channel" of social forces. But the author is still present, and it is his or her life that must be invested in the creation of the work. Without the author, there is nothing.

Concern for the humanity of the author is something more than copyright law in the ordinary sense. Copyright is a limited right, an economic right; in the American tradition, it is an artificial privilege instituted by the state in order to further the public policy of providing an incentive to create works of value, in the economic sense of that term. But when the image of the author rises before our eyes, it is no longer appropriate to talk only of state policies and economic priorities. We must turn to language that can express human priorities. The survival of the author—full-time or part-time, but above all, as a creative being—is an issue of human rights.

From a legal perspective, there is nothing particularly radical about the idea of an author's human right. It falls within the classical definition of human rights: individual rights arising from human characteristics that are universally shared, including, in this case, the potential for intellectual and creative activity. In the digital era, human beings are subject to new kinds of treatment. Through the mediation of technology, our position in the world is different. Human identities are affected by the collection and communication of personal data and information; human personalities are implicated in the development of digital media; human creative expression is influenced by new instruments for the creation and communication of our work. The digital world created by human beings is an ever-growing spider's web of amazing complexity. The spider at the center remains, spinning its web, but it is becoming increasingly difficult to see.

In the world of new technology, the fragility of the human personality brings a new urgency to the protection of human rights. The digitization of an author's work initiates a vast pool of ripple effects involving the transformation and re-transformation of the work for new digital media. Without the work, technology has nothing to work upon; once a work enters into the technological circuit, however, the link between the work and its human creator becomes increasingly remote. The author becomes a mere "content-provider," and the value of his work is limited to what technological re-mixing can achieve with it. The intrinsic value of the work is of secondary interest: its "value" is determined by what technology can make of it, and whether society will buy it. The utter degradation of the human creator in this scenario is something that should be universally rejected, in part, with the help of the law.

The digital era is already generating new human rights. The European Commission has been exploring the possibility of elevating the right of access to the Internet to the status of a human right. The recognition of this new human right would require a fundamentally new approach to copyright enforcement in the European Union member states. In particular, the proliferation of "three strikes" laws, which would allow users who are suspected of downloading infringing material to be disconnected from the Internet after two warnings, will need to be re-examined.[99] The right to Internet access has been proposed as part of a new Telecoms Package. As summarized by David Meyer,

> The new article states that any measures taken by member states to limit internet access or use must "respect the fundamental rights and freedoms of natural persons, as guaranteed by the European Convention for the Protection of Human Rights and Fundamental Freedoms and general principles of Community law."
>
> It also says any access or use limitations must be "appropriate, proportionate and necessary within a democratic society," and their implementation must include "effective judicial review and due process."[100]

The human right of the author, a perfect example of "respect [for] the fundamental rights and freedoms of natural persons," seems like a prime candidate to follow upon this European initiative. If access to technology is a human right, the possibility of human rights on the side of the creator should also be examined. Public policy on the creation and dissemination of information in a digital context will need to be comprehensive, and a policy on access without a corresponding policy on creation is only a partial solution to the problem.

A creator's human right could be framed as a right to create work with the intention of forming and maintaining a human connection to the world. By this formula, works that are primarily generated by technology could be distinguished from work that includes a significant component of human creativity, helping to avoid the expansion of what should be a precise and well-defined right. The moral rights of the author are an established form of legal recognition for the relationship between an author and his own work. As such, rights of attribution, integrity, and, as appropriate to the digital environment, disclosure could provide the basis for defining a digital human right

---

99. Ironically, the three strikes analogy is drawn from the quintessentially American game of baseball. After three "strikes," or failures to hit a fairly pitched ball, a player is taken "out" of play.

100. *See* David Meyer, *European "Internet Freedom" Law Agreed*, ZDNet UK (Nov. 5, 2009), *available at* http://news.zdnet.co.uk/communications/0,1000000085,39860587,00.htm?tag=mncol;txt (last visited July 20, 2010). Meyer quotes extensively from the comments of the European Commissioner for Information Society & Media, Viviane Reding. Critics of the provision feel that it makes a promising beginning but does not yet go far enough in "preserving a fundamental right of access to the net," in the words of Jérémie Zimmermann, cofounder of consumer rights group, La Quadrature du Net (La Quad) (as quoted by Meyer).

of creativity.[101] The purpose of the right would be to protect the integrity of the human personality behind every work—a new need in the technological context.

A human rights approach could help to elevate the problems of authorship to a new level of seriousness. At the same time, it is important to note that the conceptual appeal of human rights has some profound practical disadvantages. International human rights law suffers from vagueness and subjectivity. Human rights norms can be notoriously difficult to enforce. Attempting to define moral rights at a higher degree of abstraction, as required by human rights instruments, could ultimately harm, rather than help, the interests involved. As Colin Tapper suggests, moral rights might "then [be] regarded as suitable for analogous detailed treatment to that afforded to other… [rights] falling within the same broad generalization without sufficient further thought about the differences between them."[102] Keeping these difficulties in mind, it may still be useful to employ human rights language to talk about moral rights without necessarily removing them from a copyright framework. Invoking the terminology of human rights could help to characterize the problems of creative authorship as issues of human integrity, and infuse discussion about them with humanitarian ideals.

F. Recommendations

Open access movements generally recognize the importance of moral interests. These movements are ideologically diverse, but in all of them, moral rights seem to emerge out of practical concerns about maintaining the integrity of the open source environment. The language of natural rights of authorship is explicitly—perhaps disingenuously—rejected by the free software community, but the copyleft community has a soft-hearted sympathy for creative individuals.

An examination of the approach to moral issues in open access movements leads to a striking conclusion. Not only should moral rights be recognized in a digital environment, but their recognition should also be expanded in two important ways. First, as access to knowledge comes to be recognized as a human right, a corresponding human right of creators should be established. Moral rights can provide the foundational principles of such a right— disclosure, attribution, and integrity. Moral rights can also provide the proper

---

101. The right is analogous to the "right to create," or *droit de créer*, which has occasionally been recognized as a part of the moral rights package. Strömholm is skeptical, but a case for the right as a way of recognizing an author's right to free speech is made by Sundara Rajan, *Copyright and Creative Freedom, supra* note 23, at 218–24, 228–31.
102. Colin Tapper (personal communication with the author, July 14, 2010).

practical framework: the doctrine behind moral rights firmly excludes the possibility of corporate ownership or possession. They are personal rights of an author, dependent on a human being to invest them with meaning, and to exercise them. The recognition of a human creative right is important, not only to protect authors and their works, but also, to shield society as a whole from the consequences of losing contact with its own humanity. Intellectual life is an intrinsic part of human existence. Technology cannot replace culture; machine cannot replace man or woman.

The second area of growth for moral rights may, surprisingly, carry them into the area of economic rights. Much of the attitude of open access movements is based on the idea of "free" access. While the free software movement and Creative Commons both emphasize the importance of freedom in an ideological sense, in practice, the Creative Commons licensing system often implies freedom from payment.[103] In this sense, the model of "free" use has its appeal and its purposes. But it does not respond to the problem of how to maintain artistic professions or, in a more fundamental sense, how to establish value for intellectual creation.

Historically, intellectuals have often been an impoverished group. Given this reality, the denial of economic benefits to authors seems like nothing other than a new form of social oppression. It is cultural oppression, and it perpetuates stereotypes—the impoverished artist at work in his attic studio, caring little for the pleasures of the world—that can implicitly justify oppression.[104]

In a more just society, some economic value would be guaranteed to an author who made a work of quality. It would last for his lifetime and, in order to provide capital for future generations, for at least the lifetime of his children. At this point, it would make sense to release the work to the public for free use. In an ideal society, both intangible wealth and material capital should probably be released into the public domain for the benefit of society; but this change, however worthy, would be much more difficult to bring about than some mere alterations in the law of copyright!

Both the substance and the language of copyright should evolve to meet these new concerns. Copyright law should be meticulous in distinguishing between the author of a work and the owner of rights in it—once again, a clarification favored by the moral rights tradition. In the digital context, it is also clear that the right of disclosure, in both its moral and economic

---

103. Or the connection is presumed. The distinction between the two meanings of "free" is easily noted in French, through the use of two separate words to signify these separate ideas— "*gratuit*," for free of charge, and "*libre*" for the larger idea of freedom. The distinction is appreciated by Stallman, who offers a list of translations of the expression, "free software," into an amazing array of languages. Stallman makes use of these terms on his website at http://www.gnu.org/philosophy/fs-translations.html.

104. No doubt there are artists who fit this model. The argument here is that it should not be imposed on all artists.

dimensions, has acquired a new importance. The one right that can be definitely controlled by the author is the initial publication of his or her work. This initial release in digital form should perhaps generate the bulk of the author's earnings from the work. The problem of works appreciating in value over time could then be dealt with as in the artist's resale right, or *droit de suite*—by levying an author's royalty as a small percentage of the sale price on subsequent transactions. An author's royalty could easily be processed through collective licensing schemes for the use of creative work.

As for the Google Books scheme, Google should be prevailed upon to recognize authors' moral rights in all its dealings with works. Not only should attribution and integrity be recognized, but disclosure should also be respected. The implication of the moral right of disclosure for Google's plans is, of course, that the "opt-out" approach to books will not work. Authors' consent must be secured. In the case of orphan works, Google should institute a process to demonstrate good faith in its search for authors. If a work is truly "orphaned," Google should benefit from a waiver of the right of disclosure. The ten-year period in which authors could still come forward to claim orphan works would then be reasonable.

Finally, Google's book rights registry should be made publicly available, and the registry should rigorously protect the moral rights of works that it includes. Why should Google become sole owners of the digitized copies of orphan works? In such a case, Google's monopoly over information would dwarf any monopoly over knowledge previously known—including the very strongest examples of copyright protection. Given that the hard copies of books are likely to fall into obsolescence over time, Google's power over knowledge would be unimaginable. This is particularly the case where works from developing countries, or historical materials, which are vulnerable to physical deterioration, are concerned.[105] The well-known adage that "Absolute power corrupts absolutely" comes to mind. It would probably be best to spare Google so extreme a test of its motivations.[106]

---

105. Google has undertaken at least two interesting projects involving the digitsation of ancient books and works from developing countries, in Mysore, India, and in Florence and Rome. *See Google to Digitise 800,000 Books at Mysore Varsity*, Hindustan Times (May 20, 2007), *available at* http://www.hindustantimes.com/StoryPage/Print.aspx?Id=4e4d6d35-ef7f-4-e42-808c-589ea4540202 (last visited Apr. 25, 2010), and *Google to Scan One Million Books from Rome and Florence Libraries*, Telegraph (Mar. 10, 2010), *available at* http://www.telegraph.co.uk/technology/google/7415306/Google-to-scan-one-million-books-from-Rome-and-Florence-libraries.html (last visited Apr. 25, 2010).

106. But Colin Tapper notes that, "[w]hile . . . such a monopoly would be highly undesirable, I am dubious whether it would ever be achieved considering the ease and incidence of multiple copying of virtually anything once put into digital form." (Personal communication with the author, July 14, 2010.)

G. Conclusion

In many ways, open access movements and moral rights are likely to find themselves in sympathy with one another. Both represent fundamentally anti-corporate approaches to creative work. Each focuses on individual rights in its own way—for open access movements, the right of the public, for moral rights, the right of the author. The two ideals also share common concerns about the cultural sphere. Moral rights hope to protect culture by maintaining the connection between the human personality and creative work. Copyleft hopes to promote it by encouraging people to use and re-use culture to create new culture.

Both models have value, but the culture that emerges from each will be different. Even copyleft recognizes that there are limits to "creative destruction:" with no sense of preservation at all, even the "free" culture of copyleft cannot exist. This probably explains the migration of moral rights ideas into copyleft, which recognizes attribution and integrity as important principles in the digital environment.

An examination of alternatives to copyright supports the theory that moral rights will have a place, not only in the cultural landscape of the future, but also, within the cultural communities that are most determined to reject copyright law. But the theory of moral rights has much to learn from anti-copyright movements. Like them, its growth should develop as a grassroots phenomenon. The successful enforcement of moral rights will depend largely on the public—on its awareness of moral rights, and on its willingness to support authors. Moral rights without public support would be hollow laws, ironically devoid of moral credibility.

In the digital context, public education means democratic education. Technology can be said to have brought democracy to culture by placing the tools for its creation and development within the reach of the public. But the ability of the public to make use of these tools depends largely on the initiative of individuals— their interest, their engagement with culture, and their determination to educate themselves. The relationship of hierarchy between author and public has been altered fundamentally; in the digital environment, it more closely resembles a circular relationship of mutual communication and exchange among relative equals. At different times, individuals may find themselves at different points in the cycle of creativity, sometimes using, sometimes shaping, sometimes creating new work. The author is no longer an outsider; he is within each one of us. When the user of copyright works finally sees himself or herself reflected in the author, society will indeed be poised on the verge of an exciting transformation.

CHAPTER

10

Conclusion

Moral Rights and the Future of Copyright Law

An exploration of moral rights in the world's legal systems reveals a robust doctrine. Although moral rights are formally included under the rubric of copyright law, their situation offers a marked contrast to the economic aspects of copyright. The struggle to preserve copyright rules, and to maintain the commercial picture that they generate for business and industry, has led to a widespread backlash against the copyright concept. Copyright reforms are poorly received in many countries, and, despite the concerted efforts of law-makers and industry officials, few effective means of overcoming copyright "piracy" seem to exist. Copyright may now be one of the most unpopular legal concepts in the world. It is also a highly polarized aspect of the law. The logic of compromise and common interest has largely disappeared from the copyright scene.

And yet, where moral rights are concerned, none of this holds true. Moral rights are widely accepted in countries representing diverse traditions—common law and civil law, developing and post-socialist jurisdictions. It is a striking development that, as the twenty-first century begins, it may no longer be accurate to talk about a "common law" approach to moral rights. The common law treatment of moral rights now represents a range of approaches, from limited recognition in the United States to comprehensive protection in Australia. Ongoing law reform in Canada and India, and the reassessment of moral rights in the United Kingdom—and, possibly, the United States—will ultimately bring further complexity to the common law landscape.

The trajectory of moral rights has been one of spectacular growth. Countries that are highly technological have promoted the extension of "moral rights to new technologies, from computer programs to collaborative works, such as film. Those that are rich in traditional culture have explored the extension of moral rights to aboriginal traditions and folklore. The moral rights idea has been treated as an aspect of freedom of speech and thought in countries emerging from political oppression. Not all of these experiments have led to successful law reform, but there can be little doubt that the world-wide trend is towards greater acceptance of moral rights principles. It seems very likely that ideas such as moral rights in folklore will eventually find acceptance among interested countries, and on the global stage.

The expansion of moral rights has invariably been accompanied by introspection, and the doctrine often resurfaces in new forms. While the general principles of attribution, integrity, and disclosure seem to apply universally to creative expression, the precise legal forms in which they are recognized vary according to cultural context. The moral right of a computer programmer may be different from the moral right of an artist. The rights of a performer will be different from those of a composer, but also, from those of a *Tonmeister*, or sound engineer.

The development of moral rights has taken place during the continuous eruption of the digital revolution. The culture has changed. Finding information, once a treasured achievement, has now become one of the easiest things in the world to accomplish. The world is awash in information. Projects like Google Books, whatever the outcome of the class action lawsuit, promise to make it more widely available, in more forms than ever before. Much of the discussion about the Google case seems to overlook the fundamental reality that Google has already scanned millions of books, and continues to do so as the case evolves. The Settlement may provide for what Google can do with the scans; but the digitized works are there, available for Google's use, whether in the public arena of the Google search, or behind closed doors. The culture has moved with Google. Its focus is on digital and online access, free access—as far as possible—and the possibility of "re-mixing" what is available to make something "new."

Restrictions on knowledge fundamentally go against this culture. Why have moral rights expanded in this environment?

An initial reaction to this question might be to note that copyright law, too, has expanded in the environment of new technology. But the story of its expansion is a different one. Copyright has grown and spread because of the lobby power of the industries involved. In many ways, the expansion of copyright law represents an attempt to hold on to established business models in these industries. At the same time, the intrusion of copyright principles into the digital realm is supported by a new, global infrastructure for copyright law—the World Trade Organization and the WIPO Internet Treaties. The two regimes should also be distinguished from one another: the WTO system relies on the availability of international trade dispute settlement to enforce copyright, while the WIPO Treaties are enforced informally. This is not to say that the WIPO system is without power; rather, the system is driven by other kinds of enforcement mechanisms, such as pressure exerted by the United States on a bilateral basis through its Special 301 Report against countries that fail to respect the WIPO norms.

The growth of moral rights has occurred in a different way. Practically speaking, moral rights are excluded from the operation of the WTO dispute-settlement system. The WIPO Performances and Phonograms Treaty requires a moral right for performers—though not in the audiovisual context—but, like Article 6*bis* of the Berne Convention, the implementation of this promise depends on the political will of national governments. No doubt, there is a connection between the expansion of copyright and moral rights, as corporations probably see any form of restriction on the circulation of knowledge as another device promoting the commercial viability of intellectual products. But the connection is an accidental one.

Moral rights are also different from copyright in another sense. While copyright restrictions are rejected by the open source community, moral rights principles are welcomed. Indeed, moral rights ideas guide the development of open source practices. Attribution is central to all open-access movements. To varying degrees, an awareness of integrity is also present in some open-access scenarios.

The reasons behind these patterns are probably much deeper than the conventional explanations. As the first blush of the re-mix culture fades, there is a growing sense that culture needs protection. This intuition may help to explain why the moral rights idea has remained alive, and why it is likely to grow in the public imagination as the re-mix culture matures.

The argument to be made for moral rights is that they are needed, as never before, in an environment of cultural flux. Moral rights support two invaluable causes. The first is to protect knowledge in an environment where it is vulnerable to harm—distortion, destruction, misappropriation, abuse. The second is to turn social attention to the human side of culture—to help to maintain the connection between human beings and their creative work, whether it takes the form of art or software, and to encourage the use of technology as a means of connecting human beings with one another. Moral rights support human rights, and human values, in a technological society.

The challenges of shaping moral rights for this environment are tremendous. Each aspect of human creativity must be considered anew, as the appropriate level and kind of protection for moral rights will be different in each context. At the same time, moral rights will always need to be balanced against freedom of expression. In fact, the problem is one of balancing mutual rights and freedoms. Both the freedom of expression of the creator of a work and the expressive freedom of the public who seek access to it must gain adequate recognition.

Ultimately, the key to this dilemma may lie in the recognition that the relationship between creator and public has been transformed. Through technology, the public is in a position to take a more active role in the enjoyment of culture. The author is, in turn, heavily reliant upon the public to respect his work. This new and closer relationship could represent a new world of education and opportunity. It all depends on how the culture evolves—on how we choose to use technology. Do we have the ability to put ourselves spiritually in the place of the author, just as technology allows us, practically, to take the author's place? The moral rights of the author are a way of recognizing and honoring creators—not only the authors of creative works, but also, the creator within ourselves.

Index